western theatre

WESTERN THEATRE
Revolution and Revival

Patti P. Gillespie University of Maryland, College Park   **Kenneth M. Cameron**

Macmillan Publishing Company *New York*   Collier Macmillan Publishers *London*

Macmillan Publishing Company
866 Third Avenue, New York, New York 10022

Collier Macmillan Canada, Inc.

Library of Congress Cataloging in Publication Data

Gillespie, Patti P.
  Western theatre.

  Includes bibliographies and index.
  1. Theater—History. I. Cameron, Kenneth M.,
Date. II. Title.
PN2101.G53 1984   792'.09   83-5410
ISBN 0-02-343050-8

Printing: 1 2 3 4 5 6 7 8   Year: 4 5 6 7 8 9 0 1 2

ISBN   0-02-343050-8

pReface

We believe very strongly that there is a binding connection between a culture and the theatre that is a part of it, and we believe that when the culture's perception changes, so does the theatre's.

In his book *The Structure of Scientific Revolution* (1970), Thomas S. Kuhn postulated a theory of the history of science in which the field has moved forward by revolutionary lunges as well as by orderly and regular evolution. Each lunge has been occasioned by a change in what he called *paradigm*—the perception of the nature of nature.

We believe that the theatre has shared that same historical pattern: that is, its history is marked not only by progression, but also by abrupt changes in the way in which the theatrical event is organized and the way in which its audience perceives it. We have taken Kuhn's concept of the paradigm and used it to examine the very arrangement and structure of the stage itself.

We find three major "paradigms" in the Western theatre's history: the facade stage of Greece and Rome; the simultaneous and emblematic stage of the Middle Ages; and the illusionistic stage of the Renaissance and its heirs into the twentieth century. In addition, we have suggested the existence of a modern period of irresolution that we have called a *theatre in search of a paradigm*—our own age, in fact.

Unquestionably, change has occurred within each of these major perceptual models, but those changes have not, we suggest, altered the basic paradigm of each. Changes have redefined it, but always within the limits of the model—until a cultural revolution has occurred, and with it a profound shift in the theatre.

This is a book of theatre history, but it is also a book about theatre history. Therefore, we have made historiography itself part of the structure of the book; we have distinguished between what the historian Kitson Clark calls the "framework of fact," and history itself. As much as possible, we have put the framework of fact into lists, charts, maps, and time lines, and we have put the theatre's history into the prose. The book has, therefore, many lists, charts, and time lines that will be useful as study aids because they put facts into accessible form. Of equal importance, however, the prose is thus freed of often cumbersome details that are better displayed as lists.

We do not think that the distinction between interpretive history and framework is either a casual or a shallow one. Students and seasoned historians both need facts; they also both need history. Each supports and enriches the other, and neither can stand without the other.

Theatre history is a complex subject. It is a challenge for any student to assimilate it in a course of two semesters or even less. We hope that the structure of this book will make assimilation and real understanding easier.

P.P.G.
K.M.C.

acknowledgments

We should like to acknowledge the help of the following people, whose time, work, and knowledge were generously given and very gratefully received: Mr. Bernard Weisberger; Professor Rinda Lundstrom; Professor Patrick Schmitt; Professor George B. Bryan; Professor Attilio Favorini; Ms. Mary Huth of the University of Rochester Libraries; Professor Briant Hamor Lee; and the staffs of the special collections of the libraries of the University of Rochester; the University of South Carolina; Bowling Green State University; the Bodleian Library; and the Fitzwilliam Museum.

contents

List of Sources of Illustrations

Appelbaum, Stanley. *Advertising Woodcuts from the Nineteenth Century Stage: 268 Copy-right-free Illustrations for Artists and Designers.* New York: Dover Publications, 1977.

Appleton's Journal.

Bapst, Germain. *Essai sur l'Histoire du Théâtre: la Mise en Scène, le Décor, le Costume, l'Architecture, l'Eclairage, l'Hygiene.* Paris, 1893.

Barre, Louis. *Herculaneum et Pompei: Récueil Générale des Peintures, Bronzes, Mosaiques, etc.* Paris: Firmin Didot fils et cie., 1839.

Baumeister, August. *Denkmaler des Klassichen Altertums zur Erlauterung des lebens der Griechen und Romer in religion, Kunst, und sitte.* Munich and Leipzig: R. Olden-bourg, 1889.

Besant, Walter. *London in the Time of the Stewarts.* London: A. C. Black, 1903.

————. *London in the Time of the Tudors.* London: A. C. Black, 1904.

Bourgeois, Emile. *Le Grand Siècle: Louis XIV, Les Arts, Les Idées.* Paris: Librairie Ha-chette et cie., 1896.

The Century: Illustrated Monthly Magazine. (Formerly *Scribners*)

Carter, Huntley. *The New Spirit in the European Theatre, 1914–1924.* London: E. Benn, Ltd., 1925.

Cobden, John C. *The White Slaves of England: Compiled from Official Documents.* Auburn and Buffalo: Miller Orton and Mulligan, 1854.

Collignon, Maxime. *L'Archéologie Grecque.* Paris: A. Picard, 1885.

Combe, William. *The Tour of Doctor Syntax, in search of the picturesque.* Illus. T. Row-landson. Philadelphia: T. E. Bell, 1865.

Current Literature.

Diderot, Denis. *Encyclopédie, ou Dictionnaire Raisonné des Sciences, des Arts, et des Mé-tiers, par une Société de gens de Lettres.* 7 vols. Paris: Briasson, 1751–65.

Dolby's British Theatre series.

The Dome.

Dorpfeld, Wilhelm, and Reisch, Emil. *Das Griechische Theater: beiträge zur geschichte des Dionysos-theaters in Athen und anderer griechischer Theater.* Athen: Barth and von Hirst, 1896.

The Drama Review.

The English Illustrated Magazine.

Farmer, James Eugene. *Versailles and the Court Under Louis XIV.* New York: Century, 1905.

Fiechter, Ernst Robert. *Das Dionysos-Theater in Athen,* vol. III. Stuttgart: Kohlhammer, 1935–50.

Fischel, Oskar. *Das Moderne Bühnenbild.* Berlin: Verlag Ernst Wasmuth A-G., 1923.

Fitzgerald, Percy. *Romance of the English Stage.* London: R. Bentley, 1874.

Die Gartenlaube.

Ginisty, Paul. *La Vie d'un Théâtre.* Paris: C. Reinwald, 1898.

Graevius, Joannes Georgius. *Thesaurus Antiquitatum Romanarum, in quo continentur lectissimi quique scriptores, qui superiori aut nostro seculo Romanae reipublicae rationem, disciplinam, leges, instituta, sacra, Artesque togatas ac segatas explicarunt & illustrarunt.* 1694–1699. Vol. 9.

Hammond, N. G. L. "The Conditions of Dramatic Production to the Death of Aeschylus." *Greek, Roman, and Byzantium Studies*, 13, 4(Winter 1974): 387–450.

Hill, G. F. *Illustrations of School Classics.* London: Macmillan, 1903.

Hotson, Leslie. *Shakespeare's Wooden O.* New York: Macmillan Co., 1960.

Hutton, Laurence. *Curiosities of the American Stage.* New York: Harper and Brothers, 1890.

Jerome, Jerome K. *Stageland.* London: Chatto and Windus, 1889.

Lacroix, Paul. *Les Arts au Moyen Age et a l'époque de la Renaissance.* 2nd ed. Paris: Librairie de Firmin, 1869.

————. *Moeurs, Usages, et Costumes au Moyen Age. . . .* Paris: Firmin Didot Frères, Fils et cie., 1873.

Lanciani, Rodolfo. *The Ruins and Excavations of Ancient Rome.* New York: Houghton Mifflin Co., 1897.

Laumann, E. M. *La Machinerie au Théâtre Depuis les Grecs Jusqu'à Nos Jours.* Paris: Firmin Didot et cie., 1897.

Leacroft, Richard. Photographs by Richard Leacroft of models prepared by students of the School of Architecture, Leicester Polytechnic, England.

Loliée, Frederic. *La Comédie-française, histoire de la maison de Molière de 1650 à 1907.* Paris: L. Laveur, 1907.

Lubke, Wilhelm. *Outlines of the History of Art.* Rev. ed. 2 vols. London: Smith, Elder, and Co., 1904.

Magazine of Art, The.

Markov, P. A. *The Soviet Theatre.* New York: G.P. Putnam's Sons, 1935.

Matthews, Brander. *The Theatres of Paris.* New York: Scribners, 1880.

Mirror, The.

Pemberton, T. Edgar. *The Kendals.* New York: Dodd, Mead, 1900.

Petit de Julleville, Louis, ed. *Histoire de la Langue et de la Littérature française des Origines à 1900.* Paris: A. Colin, 1896–99.

Picture Magazine, The.

Pougin, Arthur. *Dictionnaire historique et pittoresque du Théâtre et des arts qui s'y rattachent.* Paris: Firmin Didot et cie., 1885.

Rigal, Eugène. *Le Théâtre Français avant la Periode Classique.* Paris: Librairie Hachette, 1901.

Robert, Carl. *Die Masken der Neueren Attischen Komoedie.* Halle: Max Niemeyer, 1911.

Saturday Magazine, The. (London)

Sayler, Oliver, ed. *The Moscow Art Theatre Series of Russian Plays.* New York: Brentanos, 1923.

Scientific American.

Scientific American Supplement.

Sharp, Thomas. *A Dissertation on the Pageants or, Dramatic Mysteries Anciently Performed at Coventry. . . .* Coventry: Merridew and Son, 1825.

Siddons, Henry. *Practical Illustrations of Rhetorical Gesture and Action, Applied to the English Drama.* From a work on the same subject by M. Engel. London: R. Phillips, 1807.

Smith, Edmund. *The New English Theatre.* Multiple volumes. London: 1776–1977.

Streit, A. *Das Theater: untersuchunge uber das Theater-Bauwerk Bei den Klassischen und modernen volkern*. Wien: Verlag von Lehmann und Wentzel, 1903.

Theatre Arts.

Le Théâtre.

Theater, The. (London)

Theatre, The. (New York)

Theatre Notebook.

Theatre Survey.

Thornbury, George Walter. *Old and New London: A Narrative of its History, its People, and its Places*. London: Cassell, Petter and Galpin, 1872–1878.

Trusler, Rev. John. *The Works of William Hogarth in a Series of Engravings and A Comment on Their Moral Tendency*. London: Jones and Co., 1833.

Vasari, Giorgio. *Lives of Seventy of the Most Eminent Painters, Sculptors, and Architects*. Edited and Annotated by E. H. and E. W. Blashfield and A. A. Hopkins. New York: C. Scribner's Son, 1897.

Voltaire, *The Works of Voltaire*, ed. John Morley. Akron, Ohio: The Werner Company, 1905.

Walker, Joseph Cooper. *Historical Memoir on Italian Tragedy*. . . . London: E. Harding, 1799.

Webster, Benjamin. *A Collection of Early Nineteenth Century Drama*. Multiple Volumes. Nottingham: National Acting Drama Office. Various Dates.

Weddigen, Otto. *Geschichte der Theater Deutschlands: in hundret abhandlungen dargestellt nebst einem einleitenden ruckblick zur geschichte der dramatischen dictkunst und achauspielkunst*. Berlin: Ernst Frensdorrf, n.d.

Wieseler, Friedrich Julius. *Theatergebaude und Denkmaler des buhnenwesens bei den Griechen und Romern*. Gottingen, 1851.

Willemin, Nicolas Xavier. *Monuments français inédits pour servir à l'histoire des arts*. . . . Paris: Mlle Willemin, 1839.

Winckelmann, Johann Joachim. *Monumenti antichi inediti spiegati ed illustrati da Giovanni Winckelmann*. Rome: C. Mordacchini, 1821.

Yellow Book, The.

part one

History and
Historical Methods

PART ONE

Mrs. Cibber in *The Orphan* (ca. 1775), J. B. Booth as Sir Giles Overreach (ca. 1800), and Joseph Jefferson in *The Octoroon* are said to be actors of three different styles: the neoclassical, the romantic, and the realistic. Can useful distinctions be inferred from the pictures? [From the authors' collection and *Century*.]

1

Viewpoints of History: Assumptions and Consequences

According to Henry Ford, history "is more or less bunk"; according to frustrated students, it is just "one damn thing after another"; according to Cicero, "History is the witness that testifies to the passing of time; it illumines reality, vitalizes memory, provides guidance in daily life, and brings us tidings of antiquity."

What Is History?

Like other apparently simple questions, the question about history has no short, unequivocal answer. The word *history* is used regularly to mean at least three different things: the past, a record of the past, and a method of inquiry aimed at comprehending the past.

Even within each of these uses of the word lurk differences of opinion. For example, among people who use *history* to mean merely "what happened," some argue that its use should be restricted to only the important things that happen. Daily life, because it is so often trivial, is excluded from any real history. Others urge that events in the recent past are not history; for them a field called *contemporary history* is a contradiction in terms. Although each of these views has merit, each introduces problems: If trivial events that occurred in the past are not a part of history, of what are they a part? If what happened yesterday—or five minutes ago—is not history, what is it? In this book, any past event, however trivial or recent, is considered a part of history.

History seen as a record of the past likewise harbors certain assumptions and certain dangers. First, people expect a historical record to tell the truth: to say what did, in fact, happen, insofar as that can be determined. As well, most historians agree that a list of random events drawn from many centuries and several countries and placed willy-nilly in a line would not be a history of anything. Some kind of pattern and coherence in the account of past events is required before the record qualifies as history. Histories therefore generally try to tell not only what happened but also why and how it happened, and how this particular happening fits in with other happenings. Clearly, then, the writing of the record called *history* requires the selection of relevant and the discarding of irrelevant information, and so history depends on human judgment exercised on available evidence. Written history is therefore fallible, because people are fallible; and history changes, for people change. These problems are considered in greater detail later. For now, let us simply agree that the word *history* may mean a record of past events when the record tries to tell the truth and when it gives some pattern and coherence to the events that it describes.

Finally, history is often viewed as a special method of inquiry, a distinct kind of study. As a kind of study, history has been compared with science, with detective work, and with literary art.

3

Historical study strives to be as accurate and precise as any science. Historians search out and collect information that bears on a question that they wish to answer, and they ascertain whether the information they use is both authentic and reliable. After studying and assessing the available data, historians, as scientists, organize them into a single, rational, systematic account that is congruent with the information. Because historians try to uncover information about what happened in the past, they cannot rely on all of the methods commonly used by laboratory scientists. Historians cannot, for example, create an event in order to study it, duplicate an event a number of times in order to shift variables, or even establish a series of controls in order to manipulate a single variable. Indeed, historians usually cannot even directly observe the events that they study.

Because historians can seldom see or hear the events themselves, they must work indirectly. Like detectives, historians seek clues about what happened from various remnants out of the past. Such remnants, known collectively as *evidence*, provide the basis for a series of inferences that in turn serve as the basis for some general conclusions about the nature and meaning of the events under consideration. In his book *The Historian as Detective*, Robin W. Winks extended the comparison:

> Much of the historian's work, then, like that of the insurance investigator, the fingerprint man, or the coroner, may to the outsider seem to consist of deadening routine. Many miles of intellectual shoe leather will be used, for many metaphorical laundry lists, uninformative diaries, blank checkbooks, old telephone directories, and other trivia will stand between the researcher and his answer. Yet the routine must be pursued or the clue may be missed.[1]

Once the historian–scientist and the historian–detective have figured out what happened (and perhaps why), the historian-writer must communicate an account of the events to others who want to know about them. During the writing phase, historians are often compared with literary artists, for both write stories (narratives) in language that strives to be at once clear and interesting. Obviously, historians differ from novelists in that their stories must rest firmly on evidence rather than on imaginative fabrication, but like novelists, historians are expected to convey their understanding through ordinary language rather than through special vocabularies (jargon) or esoteric sign systems. Good historians, then, strive to write with the precision of a scientist but with the verve of an artist; their accounts aim to be as unambiguous and factual as a scientific report but at the same time as compelling and engaging as a good detective story. Scientist, detective, and artist are all important roles for historians whenever history is conceived of as a method of inquiry.

Because this book is a history of theatre, we need next to consider the meaning of the word *theatre*.

What Is Theatre?

Theoreticians through the ages have proposed many different answers to the question, What is theatre? For our purposes, however, it will suffice merely to distinguish theatre from drama, from related arts, and from the "theatrical" as it appears in daily life.

When we speak of theatre, we mean performances by living actors that take place in the presence of living audiences. When we mean the play script or text of such performance, we use the word *drama*. It is tempting, of course, to define theatre as "the play in performance," but as we shall see, theatre in some periods has not depended on plays in any sense that we would recognize.

By our definition of theatre, we are also excluding film and the electronic media (radio and television), for they do not depend on an interaction between live performer and audience. In order to distinguish theatre from opera, ballet, circus, or even football, we need to define the word *performance* very carefully, limiting it to events that depend more heavily on language than on music and movement and on impersonation rather than on games and rules. The aesthetic issues raised here are exceedingly complex and must be left to another study. We hope that the gross differences between theatre and the other arts and pastimes are clear enough to permit us to understand one another, and so we will not labor here over these very thorny problems.

One final clarification may be needed, however. When we talk of theatre in this book,

FIGURE 1.1

At the end of the last century, theatre was changing its visual conventions from a painted to a three-dimensional reality. *A Bird of Passage* (top) from Webster's, and Émile Zola's *L'assommoir* from *Le Théâtre*. [Courtesy, Rare Books Room, University of South Carolina.]

we mean only the institution of theatre. We do not include the many events, people, and circumstances that occur in real life that are called dramatic or theatrical. That is, we exclude the theatrical elements that appear in a religious ritual, a surgical procedure, or a dazzling gown. When we discuss acting, we limit ourselves to that art and craft as it is consciously practiced by people during performances. That is, we do not deal in the make-believe world of children, the ecstatic transports of shamans, or the prevarications of devious adults. And when we talk of setting, costume, or lighting, we refer only to these elements as they appear in the theatre; we do not include their use in Burkean pentads, high-fashion clothing, or rock concert strobes.

The word *theatre,* as used in this book, then, has a fairly restricted meaning: it is an institution aware of itself as an institution; it is a performing art different from other performing arts, although related to them; and it depends on live actors performing in the presence of live audiences.

What Is Theatre History?

We may say, then, that theatre history is anything that relates to the past of the institution of theatre. Theatre history is also a patterned, coherent, and (we hope) truthful account of that past. As well, theatre history is a particular method of inquiry.

Regrettably, as a record of the past and a method of inquiry, theatre history has too often been what J. H. Hexter called a "tunnel history," a field of inquiry "continuous from the remote past to the present, but practically self-contained at every point and sealed off from contact with or contamination by anything that was going on in any of the other tunnels."[2] Thus, students of theatre history have all too often studied about theatre buildings, artists, plays, and practices of the past without a due regard for the society of which they were a part. Although such parochialism is seldom desir-

able, it is particularly undesirable when the subject is theatre history because theatre, of all the arts, is the most people-centered. Its subject is "the actions of men;" its mode of presentation involves living actors in contact with living audiences. A meaningful study of its past, therefore, necessarily involves to an uncommon degree the study of the people surrounding it, their social organizations, religious beliefs, philosophical assumptions, aesthetic preferences, and so on. Obviously, theatre is only one of many human activities, and to understand its past requires some understanding of the society in which it has found itself and of the people who have been both its producers and its consumers.

Why Study History?

History educates us in subtle ways. It makes us increasingly aware of the myriad alternatives that are available to us at a given moment. It educates us by exposing the complexity of the events that make up our past, our heritage. It educates us by broadening our horizons beyond those that we can see during our short lifetime from our limited geographic and temporal setting. A knowledge of the past and a study of its records teach us to be uncertain, to ask appropriate questions, to be skeptical of easy answers, to tolerate and embrace ambiguity, and to appreciate our heritage for what it can (and cannot) give us. Morris Cohen summarized its value well when he said that "History is necessary to control the exaggerated idea of our own originality and of the uniqueness of our own age and problems. To live from day to day without a wider vista is to fail to see all that is involved in the issues of the day."[3]

Why Study Theatre History?

Individual answers to this question tend to cluster around three general goals: humanistic, practical, and professional. Although in practice the goals overlap, they can be usefully separated for purposes of discussion.

Humanistic

Some people study theatre history with the simple and laudable goal of becoming better educated. They see in theatre's plays and practices an opportunity to learn more about the human condition. They find in its scenery and costumes important links with the visual arts and fashion and in its buildings and machinery helpful parallels with architecture and engineering. They value biographies of its actors and playgoers for the insights offered into social customs and aesthetic preferences, and they pour over inventories and financial records to become familiar with contemporary business practices and economic changes. In short, such people want to understand more about the past, and they correctly perceive that theatre is an important and telling part of that past.

Practical

Probably more people study theatre history because they want to prepare themselves to be theatre practitioners—actors, directors, designers, playwrights. They believe (or their advisers believe) that they can contribute better to the theatre of the present and the future if they know something about the theatre of the past. They learn how Greek tragedies were originally financed, how medieval pageants were costumed, and how romantic melodramas were acted in order to gain some perspective on contemporary practice and, at the same time, to discover creative alternatives to it.

Theatre has always depended on an interaction between performers and audiences; therefore dramatic texts and their theatrical presentation have always rested on the presumed existence of some sort of common ground where audiences and performers could meet in understanding, if not accord. Theatre artists must therefore discover what their audiences will accept: What do audiences believe (or what will they be willing to accept) about the human condition? About the nature of time? Of space? Probably the artists' personal observations and reflections are their best source of information for the age in which they live.

When artists want to revive a play from another age, however, they have a more complex problem. They must discover, insofar as possible, the nature of the relationship that existed between the original performance and its audience and then attempt to recapture that relationship. That is, artists wishing to revive a play from another time must attempt to *reconstruct the relationship—not the original performance*—by means of creative decisions about acting, costuming, lighting, scenery, properties, and so on. For discovering the nature of the original relationship between performers and their audiences, an understanding of theatre history is invaluable.

It should be stressed that no revival can be an exact replica of the original performance, nor should it be. Even if each element of the staging could be reproduced exactly (probably an impossible task), the original audience could not be retrieved, and so the nature of the interaction between performers and audiences would be changed. It is for this reason, of course, that theatre artists are always more than mere copyists. A costume designer, for example, does not trace historical fashions and then build costumes from them but rather captures the spirit of the period and the play *as it can be understood by a contemporary audience*. Theatre artists who know only "the facts" of a given historical period are doomed always to resort to their lackluster and mechanical manipulation; those who know history, on the other hand, are able to transfer the sense of the age and the play into their own art and their own time.

Theatre practitioners, then, will want to understand the prevailing views not only of the age in which they live but also of the major ages of the drama, for they will be called on to con-

FIGURE 1.2

Each actor represents a Greek hero. Each costume, however, reflects its own age: the one, Mr. Lewis as Hippolytus (ca. 1775 in England); the other, Mounet-Sully in *Andromaque* (ca. 1875 in France). [From Smith, E. and Matthews.]

sider both as they strive to reach contemporary audiences with new plays and to capture for them the excitement of old ones. Clearly, those who know something about the past and who know how to learn more have two valuable tools with which to approach the particular artistic problems posed by dramatic revivals. As a bonus, they gain a vocabulary and a perspective that facilitate communication with their educated colleagues.

Professional

Some people find in the study of theatre history an intellectual thrill that comes from the discovery of new facts and previously unseen relationships. Such people are driven by their desire for an ever more profound and lasting understanding of the art and craft of theatre, and they actually derive pleasure from systematic research into the past and from the triple roles of the historian: scientist, detective, and literary artist. These people are apt to become professional historians of the theatre and, as such, to teach in universities and write for scholarly publications. Although in any college class their number is usually relatively small, they are a fervent bunch whose contributions often belie their small numbers.

What Are Major Problems in Historical Study?

The Nature of Fact

The word *fact* is properly used to designate anything whose reality can be demonstrated through more-or-less objective means. Generally, such objective verification requires, among other things, the presence of several corroborating pieces of evidence. That President Kennedy was assassinated in Dallas during 1963 is a fact: a number of people who are still living saw the event and agree *that* it happened (although they do not agree *how* it happened); numerous daily newspapers, radio stations, and television channels stated publicly that it happened; a great many contemporary public records say that it happened; and at a public funeral attended by a large number of people who knew Kennedy well, a body was interred and honored as that of the late President. With such overwhelming agreement across such a wide range of sources, any historian today or any in the year 2180 can agree that the *fact* of President Kennedy's assassination has been clearly established. In general, events that have been recorded in several official documents and corroborated by personal accounts and public records can be accepted as fact. (True, some philosophers argue that there are *no* facts because life is only an illusion; such questions, although interesting, are irrelevant to our purpose and will not be further pursued.)

Inferences are sometimes mistakenly taken for facts, but there are important distinctions between a fact and an inference. To infer is to draw a conclusion from a fact or a premise. For example, a historian who discovers a series of ocean maps may infer that the culture used them for purposes of navigation. The *fact* is that the maps exist; the *inference* concerns their use.

Clearly, a good deal of history is written on the basis of inferences drawn from the available evidence. Whenever inference rather than fact is the basis of a historical report, prudent readers will try to discover both the *reasonableness of the inference* (Was sound reasoning used in moving from the fact to the inference?) and the *sufficiency of the inference* (Are other equally reasonable explanations possible?). Failure to differentiate between facts and inferences underlies many misunderstandings about past events and about the written records surrounding them.

Insufficiency of "Mere Fact"

Frederic Harrison alerted us nearly a century ago to a problem that even then was becoming acute: "Facts are infinite, and it is not a millionth part of them that is worth knowing. . . . A statement may be true, and yet be wholly worthless."[4] As he suggested, many pitfalls of historical study can be traced to the failure to distinguish between "mere facts" and history, a distinction that G. Kitson Clark highlighted when he differentiated history from its "framework of fact." He explained that a fact "is only the framework on which history rests, it is not history. History to mean anything must be more than rehearsal of facts, it must include an interpretation of facts."[5] Indeed, much of the aversion that students often have to the study of history can be explained by their failure (and perhaps that of their teachers) to distinguish between mere facts and history. This failure has caused them to see history as simply "one damn thing after another."

Accessibility of Facts

The problems of historical study are complicated by the nature of the factual framework on which history rests. The number of available facts varies enormously from century to century and from country to country. In general, the density of information declines as one moves back through time. For example, the number of available facts about America between 1970 and 1980 is staggering; the number of known facts about America between 1470 and 1480 is meager. For this reason, the problems facing historians of modern or contemporary events are often associated with sifting through myriad details and with selecting and ordering them so as to guard against what computer technicians call *information overload.* The reverse challenge usually confronts historians of the distant past. They must search a variety of sources (manuscripts, archaeological remains, works of art, and so on) in order to uncover a very few "facts," many of which cannot then be proved for lack of corroboration.

The accessibility of facts also affects their use. When facts are abundant, they can be checked against one another and compared for the possible patterns or trends that they reveal. When facts are scarce, on the other hand, each one known takes on an enormous, perhaps unwarranted, significance as a historian tries to construct a coherent story of "what happened."

In general, after the advent of printing (in the fifteenth century), records became both more accessible and more reliable. Before presses were able to produce multiple copies of a document at a reasonable cost and within a reasonable length of time, all written records (including pictures) had to be copied by hand. The time required for a single person (or even a small group of people working together) to reproduce a book was great indeed, and in such a "scribal culture" relatively few copies of any one document existed anywhere, and seldom more than one at a single location. A person wishing to "do research" had to travel from place to place,

consulting the available documents wherever they might be housed. Such "traveling scholars" were unable to compare different versions of manuscripts or different accounts of the same event except in the very largest libraries, where many such manuscripts were housed—and even these holdings were far from complete. Also, reading handwritten accounts was laborious, time-consuming, and occasionally impossible. These conditions help to explain why preprint documents regularly underwent change and corruption as they were copied over and over and were transferred from library to library and from generation to generation. In general, later "editions" tended to be *less* accurate than earlier ones.

But just as serious as the progressive corruption of manuscripts was the likelihood of their being lost. Fires, wars, and simple carelessness resulted in many manuscripts' being destroyed or misplaced, some never to be found again. When the relative number of accounts was slight, the destruction of even one or two manuscripts might well mean the obliteration of the only accounts of a certain event or of all the known facts about a given person. Too often these facts and accounts could not later be recovered.

With the arrival of presses, multiple copies at reasonable costs helped to assure that fewer records would disappear. Also, because such records could be widely disseminated, many scholars could have access to several different accounts simultaneously and could identify discrepancies, make comparisons, exercise judgments, and raise pertinent questions. At the same time, when they found errors in the account or in the printed text, they could tell the original scholar or the printer of the error so that new editions would be improved, eventually becoming more-or-less error-free. Through printing, then, records could be transmitted more easily and more regularly than before, and their later editions were likely to become better rather than worse.[6]

Clearly, the framework of fact tends to get

denser and more reliable the closer it comes to the present; it tends to get progressively (if erratically) sparser and less reliable as it moves back through time. These tendencies have important implications for the student of theatre history, as a single example can illustrate. The only comic playwright from the fifth century B.C. in Greece from whom we have complete extant plays is Aristophanes. Our understanding and discussions of "Greek Old Comedy," therefore, necessarily depend primarily on his eleven extant plays. What if, in the year 2180, the only comedies of this century still in existence were those of Neil Simon? Of George Kaufman? Of Douglas Turner Ward? Of Maria Irene Fornes? Clearly, our picture of "the comic drama of the twentieth century" would be vastly different.

Transmission of Facts

Facts seldom come down through the ages as a result of sheer accident or mere serendipity. Instead, facts tend to come down to later generations because someone thought they were worth recording and saving. Obviously, different people—or, more often, different institutions—have rather different views of what constitutes an important fact. In the ninth century, the Church maintained relatively extensive records. It can be safely assumed that they selected what they wanted to save and cast away whatever seemed trivial or unworthy. Obviously, a band of robbers might have built and kept another sort of record, a military officer yet another sort, a blacksmiths' guild another, and so on. Evidently, then, the accounts of history that have come to us are based to a degree on the people who have kept and transmitted the records.

Elaboration on Facts

There is a related problem: "A reliable framework has never covered the whole of life. Things have always been done which have left no record at all. . . . Even when there is some record the evidence it may present may well be equiv-

ocal and uncorroborated."[7] In such instances, people have tried to fill in that part of the "framework of fact" that is empty. And each person has provided the filler in keeping with his or her own assumptions about the nature of people and the patterns of history.

For example, relatively little is known about the emergence (or the rediscovery) of theatre during the Middle Ages. Consequently, historians have theorized about it, with spectacularly different results. Medieval theatre has been accounted for, on the one hand, through demonstrations of its presumed connection with the Catholic Mass (itself a "drama") and, on the other hand, as a continuation of Roman theatre by some as yet unexplained process.

The Word and the Fact

Because histories, whether oral or written, depend on words, yet another problem surfaces. Words may change their meanings from age to age and from country to country. And certain words take on strong values at certain times and places. The simple word *black*, for example, has long been associated with ignorance and evil, as when *enlightment* refers to a movement from ignorance (dark) to knowledge (light) and *black-hearted* refers to unrelieved villainy. In our own time, however, *black* has added connotations that are related to beauty and strength, as in the expressions "Black is Beautiful" and "Black Power." The U.S. Constitution promised that all men were created equal, but *men* here clearly did not include black men or red men, nor did it include women, as it presumably does when general humanity is meant.

Today the word *orchestra* probably brings to mind a large musical group that plays symphonies or supports the performances of operas, ballets, or musical comedies; for some, it may further suggest the section of the theatre on the first floor in front of the stage ("the best seats in the house"). In former days in Greece, however, the word referred to a circular flat space where performances of songs and plays

FIGURE 1.3

Changing cultural attitudes were reflected in changing theatrical practice. In the nineteenth century, white audiences watched comic portrayals of blacks by white men in blackface; by the late twentieth century, mixed audiences were applauding black actors portraying serious and significant black characters. [Rice as Jim Crow, from Hutton. Production of *Streamers*, directed by James A. Patterson, University of South Carolina.]

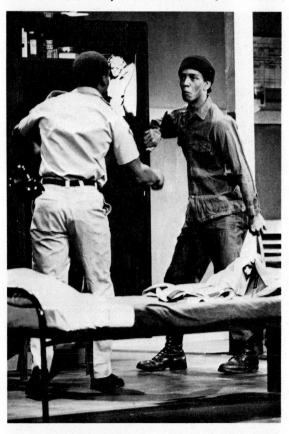

took place. Clearly, in attempting to reconstruct a coherent account of the past, a reader must take care to understand the way in which words were used at the time, and writers must take care to select the most precise and accurate word to convey the idea they intend.

How Does Bias Affect the Writing of History?

To acknowledge bias is to suggest neither dishonesty or mental rigidity; rather, it is to ac-

knowledge the nature of history. Because history is more than "mere fact," many inferences and conclusions are an inevitable and proper part of it. Inferences and conclusions obviously invite bias because they depend on human judgment, and judgments vary.

"All historical writing is shaped to a degree by the historian who produces it, and each historian is in turn shaped to a degree by his own experiences."[8] As the quotation suggests, there can be no such thing as a completely objective historian. All writers of history are biased to some degree, and as they are the ones who select, arrange, and interpret the words and facts of history, all historical accounts are, to that degree, biased. Careful students of history will try to identify the assumptions and biases of the historians whose accounts have intervened between them and the events they study.

Just as students of history often fail to see the historian's bias in what they read, they are also unaware of how their own biases affect their understanding of history. Just as historians are influenced by their experiences, so too are readers. In general, for example, readers will more readily accept as "true" or "probable" those historical accounts that are most congruent with their own personal biases, and they will most readily reject those historical accounts that fly in the face of their own assumptions and predispositions. Merely knowing this tendency does much to make readers less naive in their study of history.

In history, then, the biases of both the historian and the readers should be taken into account. Although there are as many kinds of bias as there are individuals to hold them, some patterns of belief tend to be repeated and can be identified. The particular patterns cited next are intended to be suggestive and provocative rather than exhaustive.

The Nature of History

Some people believe that "history repeats itself," that existence flows in a pattern like the one described by the ancient Egyptians who saw birth, development, maturity, decay, death, and rebirth as an inevitable cycle. Other people see history as a long march toward a particular goal; for example, many Christians believe that events are moving inexorably toward some cataclysmic end associated with the Second Coming of Christ and the Last Judgment of this world. Still other people see history as essentially static, as a group of more-or-less random occurrences that tend to repeat again and again, without much change and without much significance. Clearly, three persons holding these three sets of as-

sumptions would write rather different accounts of the "same" event.

The Nature of Truth

Some historians believe that truth is absolute and unchangeable; others regard truth as relative, dependent on its context and its perceiver. The former would be expected to draw rather different conclusions from the latter when confronted by the "same" event.

The Nature of Change

Historians who see change as an evolutionary event are likely to select, arrange, and interpret facts differently from those who believe that change is the result of revolution. Those people who see in earthly happenings the demonstration of a divine plan will write different accounts from those who are convinced that history depends on the actions of a few extraordinary people. Both of these historians will differ from one who thinks that people are battered about by disinterested and amoral forces that lie outside their conscious control, forces like heredity, physical environment, economic class, or subsconscious urgings.

In sum, because no historian and no student of history can ever be entirely free of certain preconceptions or assumptive bases or biases (as they are variously called), prudent men and women will strive to identify the particular form that these inevitable biases assume in themselves and in others.

How Does Bias Affect the Writing of Theatre History?

Theatre history as a method of inquiry is a relatively new field. True, Aristotle writing in the fourth century B.C., offered an abbreviated (and now suspect) history of tragedy and comedy in Greece from their origins to his own time, but such occasional forays into the past do not constitute a field of inquiry. It was not until the end

The
Stage Heroine.

The
Comic Lovers.

The
Stage
Comic Man.

The
Stage Villain.

14

of the nineteenth century that theatre history's first major scholars emerged and produced those early works that are now considered standards in the field. That theatre history began in the late nineteenth century is significant, for it helps to explain the direction in which the field moved.

As theatre history was coming into its own, a number of quite spectacular advances in the physical and biological sciences were causing many traditional disciplines to take stock of their basic assumptions and procedures. For example, the clear progress of subjects like chemistry, bacteriology, and physics led scholars to observe that scientific knowledge was incremental; that is, one fact built on another so that the body of knowledge systematically grew, and the field became increasingly sophisticated. Not mere change but progress resulted. When anyone asked if chemistry or physics or medicine was better in 1890 than it had been in 1850, the answer was clear and unequivocal: yes. The same question posed about academic fields like English, history, or music produced no such clear answer; rather, the question was likely to cause discomfort, even embarrassment.

In attempting to account for the progressive nature of scientific knowledge, some scholars turned to examining the method of inquiry used by scientists. A scientist, they found, typically posed a specific question, gathered data related to that question, analyzed and evaluated the data objectively, and finally proposed a solution to the problem based on that evaluation. Because the so-called scientific method seemed to produce results, some scholars recommended using it for research in all academic disciplines. At about the same time, Charles Darwin's theory of evolution was gaining adherents. The theory seemed to suggest, among other things, that progress (as opposed to mere change) was the natural order. The simplest living things apparently, in time, evolved into complex organisms, and these complex organisms survived because they were more fit than simpler ones. Biological progress became well accepted, and its acceptance encouraged the view that all areas of existence (social and academic as well as biological) had to progress in order to survive.

The field of history (as a method of inquiry) moved to become "more scientific." For this reason, historians of the late nineteenth and the early twentieth centuries tended to place a premium on the accumulation of facts, the quantification of data, and the apparent objectivity of the historian. They wanted to uncover "all the facts" and then stand aside and let the facts "speak for themselves." Massive compilations of data (preferably including figures as well as words) were highly prized as *quantification* and *objectivity* become bywords in historical study. Again modeling themselves after scientists, some historians attempted to uncover basic laws of history, that is, general patterns by which all events might be conveniently explained. Evolutionary theory appeared to be an appealing possibility in this regard, as did (somewhat later) the economic theory proposed by Karl Marx. In general, the earlier view that good history was no more than a clear and compelling narrative of what had happened (and perhaps why it happened) fell into disfavor; such history was often contemptuously dismissed as mere "story history."

The reevaluations taking place in the mainstream of historical study exerted a profound influence on the fledgling field of theatre history. Its early historians, writing in the last two decades of the nineteenth and the first two de-

FIGURE 1.4

With changing times, stage characters once considered true and believable may come to seem improbable and therefore seem suitable materials for caricature. [From Jerome.]

cades of the twentieth centuries, displayed consistent biases in favor of accumulating data and presenting them objectively. As well, most adopted some version of the view that history was progressive and evolutionary, that it moved from simple events to more complex ones, the latter being superior to the former. Thus, when E. K. Chambers was writing his massive work *The Medieval Stage* (1895–1903), he set out to reproduce as many documents as he could find and to suggest how the medieval stage prepared the way for the (superior) Shakespearean theatre. He explained that he "wanted to collect, once and for all, as many facts . . . as possible" (I, vii) in order to "state and explain the preexisting conditions which, by the latter half of the sixteenth century, made the great Shakespearean stage possible" (I, v–vi). The documents themselves, as it turned out, did not tell a simple tale when ordered chronologically: some of the most complex ones bore early dates, and some of the simplest ones bore late dates. Chambers concluded that the most likely explanation for this apparent anomaly was that many documents had disappeared, creating a lapse that obscured a clear, evolutionary pattern. He therefore organized the play texts in a sequence based roughly on relative complexity in order to clarify the "probable" line of development: "disregarding . . . the dates of the manuscripts, it is easy so to classify the available versions [of the *Quem Quaeritis*] as to mark the course of a development" (II, 28). What Chambers did for the study of medieval theatre and drama, others did for the study of Greek and Roman theatre, and most tended to display many of the same strengths and weaknesses.

In part because they were the first serious attempts to treat many aspects of theatre's past, but also in part because they were excellent studies of their kind, these early works of theatre history have continued to exert enormous influence on the field. For example, when Karl Young published his two-volume study, *The Drama of the Medieval Church*, in 1933 he acknowledged his debt to Chambers's earlier work

and adopted many of its procedures and most of its assumptions. In fact, the underlying biases of Chambers's supposedly objective study were not seriously attacked until 1965, when O. B. Hardison (*Christian Rite and Christian Drama in the Middle Ages*) urged careful reappraisal of those assumptions. The point here is certainly not to disparage Chambers or to elevate Hardison. Rather, it is to underscore the inevitability of bias and to suggest that the biases of one era are only gradually replaced by those of another. Students of theatre history should therefore note well the dates of the historical accounts that they consult, for the periods that produce the historians often shed considerable light on the kind of history that they write.[9]

Why Is History Continually Rewritten?

"History must always be rewritten because we can only approximate to absolute truth, never hope to attain it."[10] Reevaluation and rewriting are continuing attempts to lessen the distortion that inevitably accompanies accounts of "what happened." Clear factual errors made in early accounts need to be corrected by later ones. As new information is uncovered and a new point of view is brought to bear, deeper insights can often be reached and alternate explanations offered. Because the passage of time provides new perspectives and supplants the biases of one age with those of another, the facts of the past need to be periodically reinterpreted.

To reduce distortion requires, of course, that historians be alert to its most likely causes. Because more people read history than write it, an even more important goal may be for *readers* to understand historical distortion in order to guard against becoming trapped by it. Since the advent of print, distortion can most often be traced to bias, to abbreviation, to carelessness, and, less often, to fraud. Because distortion based on bias has already been discussed, only the remaining three sources of distortion are considered here.

Distortion Through Fraud

Although instances of deliberate falsification in scholarly fields are rare, they have occurred. During the last two centuries, for example, there was a highly publicized unearthing of a skeleton that was hailed as the long-sought "missing link" between humans and the great apes; the skeleton was later exposed as a fraud, the result of an imaginative pastiche of bones drawn from several different sources. Not all willful distortion is malicious. The tale of George Washington and the cherry tree, for example, apparently flourished after a historian, thinking it was a good story and one likely to inculcate desirable attitudes in the young, included it in a second edition of his work on George Washington.

Distortion Through Carelessness

Carelessness in the duplicating of manuscripts is one source of distortion. Generally, such errors are easily detected and cause little difficulty, as when a letter is omitted from a word or two letters are transposed in a name. In instances where symbols and numbers predominate, however, addition, substitution, transposition, or omission can go undetected and may gain general acceptance for long periods. Once transmitted, incorrect tables and charts can provide easily accessible misinformation to large numbers of people, with the potential for unhappy consequences.

As well, misinformation can result from careless research or imprecise writing. Carelessness in attending to the dates of various Greek and Roman artifacts, for example, gave rise to mistaken views about the appearance of theatrical masks and about the physical layout of early theatres in the two countries for many years.

Distortion Through Abbreviation

The most usual cause of distortion, however, is abbreviation. Clark described this particular distorting process well:

> Anyone who has taken the trouble to compare a textbook with the historical work it epitomizes can realize how devastating the results of abbreviation can be—how stark and meaningless a fact can be without the background which should explain it, how peremptory and dogmatic a statement becomes without the argument by which the author originally justified it. . . . But most depressing of all is the gradual degradation of an historical theory as it becomes detached from its originator's carefully considered and guarded words and reappears, first in a popularized version, then in notes dictated in class and then comes to rest at last, in dreadful caricature, in the answer to a question in a school examination paper.[11]

Among the most seductive techniques of abbreviation is a resort to what Clark calls "generic statements":[12] "Germans believe . . ."; "the nineteenth century view is . . ."; "Asian geography is . . ."; "lower classes customarily . . ."; and so on. Because it is manifestly impossible to deal with every event and every individual in detail, historians, in order to organize their data, necessarily group and classify people and events. Such a procedure is wholly proper and absolutely essential. Readers must understand, however, that all such classifications are suggestive rather than "true." Indeed, anyone who pauses to think realizes at once that not all Asians or all lower classes or all nineteenth-century people could be identical—any more than all students or all Americans or all theatres are identical. Generic statements must be accepted for what they are (useful conceptualizations) and for what they are *not* (truthful descriptions of particular events).

When Greek tragedy is discussed, for example, the reader must understand that no

two Greek tragedies are exactly alike and that there is no such thing as the typical Greek tragedy. Rather, the generic term *Greek tragedy* is a conceptual construction by which the historian hopes to suggest distinctions between these plays and the tragedies of, say, Shakespeare or Racine. Similarly, when *romanticism* is used to designate a style of theatrical production, the reader must recognize that the word is being used to call up a group of associations, not all of which necessarily apply to a *particular* case.

Difficult as generic statements are to make and to assess, they are essential to the writing of history. Their use is inevitable, and their

FIGURE 1.5

Mr. King as Rimeni (ca. 1770), Mr. Kean as Hamlet (ca. 1820), and Mr. Mayo as Davy Crockett (ca. 1875) offer three contrasting views of the ''hero.'' [From the authors' collection and Hutton.]

misuse can generally be controlled by frequent references to their evidentiary base and by constant recollection of their conceptual nature. Certainly, no one should believe that any century, any age, any race, any nation, or any social class can be completely and accurately described by a label or contained in a pigeon hole. Each student of history must understand that generic statements are an imperfect human effort to deal with the complexity of history and to render it intelligible through introducing order and coherence into the account of it.

History must be rewritten, then, because it changes as people change. One age's truth is another's distortion; one person's irrelevant gossip is another's relevant opinion. Only through periodic, careful reexamination of evidence can the lessons of history be learned, the very special lessons having to do with inquisitiveness, skepticism, tolerance, and humility.

ENDNOTES

1. Robin W. Winks, *The Historian as Detective* (New York: Harper & Row, 1968), p. xvii.
2. J. H. Hexter, *Reappraisals in History,* 2nd ed. (Chicago: University of Chicago Press, 1979), p. 258.
3. Morris Cohen, *The Meaning of Human History,* 2nd ed. (La Salle, Ill.: Open Court Publishing, 1961), p. 277, as cited by Lester D. Stephens, *Probing the Past: A Guide to the Study and Teaching of History* (Boston: Allyn and Bacon, 1974), p. 124.
4. Frederic Harrison, *The Meaning of History* (New York: Macmillan, 1902), pp. 10–11, as cited by Stephens, p. 123.
5. G. Kitson Clark, *The Critical Historian* (New York: Basic Books, 1967), p. 42.
6. For an excellent treatment of the most complex and interesting relationship between the coming of print and the study of history, see Elizabeth L. Eisenstein, *The Printing Press as an Agent of Change,* 2 vols. (Cambridge: Cambridge University Press, 1979).
7. Clark, p. 46.
8. Stephens, p. 41.
9. Full citations for all works cited in this discussion of medieval historiography can be found in our Bibliography, Part III.
10. Lucy Maynard Salmon, *Why Is History Rewritten?* (New York: Oxford University Press, 1929), p. 30, as cited in Stephens, p. 63.
11. Clark, p. 36.
12. Clark, p. 129.

2

Evidence: Sources, Uses, and Evaluations

Between the construction of a framework of fact and the act of interpretation lies much of the historian's work. It is not enough to collect data and interpret them; there are questions to be posed, hypotheses to be tested, and further materials to be collected, organized, and analyzed.

What Is a Historical Question?

"Dr. Pell [in the seventeenth century] was wont to say in the Solution of Questions, the Maine Matter was the well stating of them; wch requires mother-witt, and Logick . . . : for let the question be but well-stated, it will worke almost of itselfe." George Edward Moore echoed this view in about 1900 when he remarked that scholarly disagreements "are mainly due to a very simple cause: namely to the attempt to answer questions, without first discovering precisely *what* question it is which you desire to answer."

The point is, of course, that answers are intimately related to questions. Answers cannot be found until questions are posed. Not all answers are useful because not all questions are worth asking. The way to discover a consequential answer is, of course, to begin with a significant rather than a trivial question. Significant questions generally go beyond "What happened?"—whose answer provides the necessary framework of fact—and on to questions like "What were the antecedents and conse-

quences?" "What is the significance of what happened?" "What is the relationship of what happened to other phenomena?" When historians pose good questions, their studies—as Dr. Pell said—will work almost of themselves.

Framing good questions is one of the historian's most vexing challenges, and indeed, some historians never learn to pose questions that are at once stimulating, relevant, and answerable. Perhaps no one can teach the techniques of discovering fruitful questions, for this act of discovery is at base a creative one that depends on insight and imagination. Although courses in research methods generally address the issue in detail, for our purpose it is sufficient to know that *good historical study rests on the decision to answer certain questions* rather than to read generally on a given subject; therefore, it is only after relevant questions have been formulated that the collection of evidence begins in earnest.

What Is Evidence?

In a legal sense, evidence is any information (e.g., personal testimony, documents, and objects) that can establish the fact or the point in question. In historical sleuthing, evidence is somewhat more loosely conceived: it is any grounding for a belief, any testimony or facts that tend to prove or disprove a conclusion, or anything from which inferences may be responsibly drawn. The limits of the word as used in historical study will become clear as we consider the kinds, sources, and tests of evidence.

How Does a Historian Deal with Evidence?

Evidence is central to every historical study, for every written history rests on its framework of fact, and *every framework of fact rests on the evidence used to build it.* Regardless of the particular area of their study, historians ask roughly the same five questions about their evidence:

1. What kinds of evidence are available for answering the question?
2. Where can such evidence be found?
3. Is the evidence authentic?
4. Is the evidence reliable?
5. What reasonable interpretations can be given to the evidence?

What Kinds of Evidence Are Available for Answering the Question?

Various schemes exist for classifying evidence because no single scheme is entirely satisfactory. In order to make some preliminary judgments about availability and reliability, however, it may be helpful initially to think of evidence in these ways: as direct or indirect; as written or unwritten; as primary or secondary; and as intended or unintended.

In some fields of inquiry, *direct* observation provides the answers to most research questions. For example, medical researchers may test new drugs by administering them to laboratory animals and then observing their effects. Although such direct observation carries with it a presumption of greater accuracy than does reliance on *indirect* methods, historians typically must reach their answers indirectly, for their own personal (direct) observation of past events is usually not possible. Answers must therefore be constructed from the collection and the assessment of remnants from the past.

Many of the remnants are *written* (e.g., government records, church documents, diaries, and letters); but many are *unwritten* (e.g., buildings, coins, household items, and paintings). *The availability of written materials exerts a profound influence on the nature of the historical record.* Invented in several cultures between 4000 and 1000 B.C., writing brought enormous changes to historical study. Before writing, only artifacts and oral accounts could be passed from generation to generation. Essentially mute, artifacts grasp and transmit relatively little specific information, whereas oral accounts are subject both to the limits of human memory and to the vagaries of personal retelling. With writing, it was possible for the first time to provide detailed descriptions and explanations that could be checked. Also, information discovered later could be added to a first account, and so to a degree never before possible, one generation could learn from another. Writing gave the culture "a greatly expanded memory" through "the transmission of masses of data and ideas."[1] A second major shift in the nature of historical study came about when printing replaced handwriting, because (as we have seen) written materials then became both more accessible and progressively more accurate: the accuracy of handwritten accounts tends to decrease through successive duplications, whereas that of printed materials tends to increase; handwritten manuscripts tend to be protected and thus preserved by restriction of their use (by being chained to a table in a library, for example), whereas printed documents tend to be widely distributed, their preservation being trusted in part to their large numbers and extensive dissemination. Some historians now caution about the use of written materials, however, reminding us that they were produced by a relatively small, educated group and reflected the prejudices of that group rather than recorded the situation of their more numerous but less lettered compatriots.

In recent times, written materials have come to constitute the majority of historical evidence,

FIGURE 2.1

The pegs at the feet of this ivory statuette, now believed to be a Roman tragic actor of about the second century A.D., were once used as evidence of the use of thick-soled boots by Greek actors several hundred years earlier. Historians obviously had difficulty authenticating this statuette. [From Baumeister.]

but *nonwritten materials* remain exceedingly valuable for certain purposes. Nonwritten materials are most often collected and assigned meaning by specialists in fields other than history; the historians then make use of the conclusions reached by these other specialists. For example, human bones may provide information for anthropologists, old coins for numismatists, and so on. From nonwritten materials, specialists are often able to assess a society's technological triumphs, aesthetic sensibilities, religious beliefs, and trading practices: stone tools, pyramids, metal jewelry, and photographs describe vastly different sorts of cultures to those who know how to read them. Nonwritten materials have two major advantages in addition to their usual durability: they are generally unbiased, in that they were seldom intended to persuade anyone of anything (ballads, myths, and tall tales represent the major exceptions to this generalization); and they tend to reflect to a great degree the cultural and aesthetic preferences of the age that produced them. Their major drawback is, of course, that they do not often provide detailed and systematic information of the sort provided by written records, and so they must nearly always be interpreted along with other materials that can explain or corroborate their mute testimony.

Some of the most useful bits of evidence, written or nonwritten, are those that existed at the same time as the events being studied; such materials are call *primary*. But other helpful information may be found in accounts appearing many years after the event, accounts often written by persons who themselves drew from primary sources. Material removed in time from the event itself is called *secondary*. Whenever possible, historians rely more heavily on primary than on secondary evidence because, as a general rule, firsthand accounts are more reliable than second-or third-hand accounts. Often, however, historians have virtually no primary sources from which to draw. Their only accounts are the second- or third-hand reports of people who lived long after the events they have described. In such instances, historians have no choice but to try to build a coherent and probable account from secondary materials.

Finally, some evidence has been consciously transmitted; that is, it was *intended* to serve as a record. Other materials have survived almost accidentally; that is, they were *not intended* as records or evidence. The distinction is useful because it is generally assumed that consciously transmitted materials are more likely to harbor bias than those unconsciously passed along. Consciously transmitted materials include diaries, memoirs, autobiographies, genealogies, recorded interviews, and works of art. Unconsciously transmitted materials include bones, tools, weapons, jewelry, and customs. Among consciously transmitted materials, memoirs, diaries, and autobiographies are particularly suspect because they are so apt to be self-serving and to record events in a way that bolsters the reputation of the author at the expense of rivals or enemies.

Where Can Evidence Be Found?

In our time, public and university libraries are generally the most complete repositories of written evidence from the past. At any medium or large library, rare primary materials are customarily available in various special collections and in rare-book rooms. Microfilm and microfiche collections now make available books that have long been out of print and that were previously available only at major research centers; they also make accessible certain kinds of unpublished materials, like doctoral dissertations. Serial publications, government documents, and reference books provide a wide range of research materials, and most libraries can secure additional items through a system of interlibrary loan. Although libraries now have larger holdings than ever before, historians still sometimes travel to distant libraries in order to obtain the evidence that they need for a study.

Because library holdings (even those in relatively small institutions) are so substantial, the

intelligent and efficient use of libraries has become at once more important and more difficult than ever before. Bibliographies (often computerized), indexes, reference guides, and shelf lists permit the systematic and timely collection of evidence on any topic. Several excellent books on research methods exist to help the historian–detective. Finally, however, sheer doggedness in the search for evidence will often uncover sources overlooked by others.

Despite the extreme richness of libraries, they are not the only repositories of historical evidence. Government buildings often contain materials unavailable elsewhere (e.g., tax rolls and property deeds). Museums have artifacts generally not found in libraries (e.g., furniture, jewelry, painting, and sculpture). Personal interviews or popular songs may offer insights unavailable elsewhere. Old buildings may themselves serve as evidence, as may cemeteries, archaeological digs, curio shops—the list is endless.

Is the Evidence Authentic?

In assessing evidence, historians must first decide if the evidence is what it purports to be. The possibility of forgery, for example, must be considered, but more honest error rather than fraud may render a piece of evidence inauthentic. Portraits may have been "improved"; furniture may have been restored; buildings may have been remodeled several times. Documents, especially early ones, may bear incorrect dates, or they may have been severely corrupted during the process of transmission. Because a historian's conclusions are never better than the evidence on which they are based, the authentication of all evidence is an important step in the process of historical research. But to authenticate evidence often requires a number of special skills, many of which a historian may not possess. Therefore, the process of authentication often depends on various auxiliary sciences: *archaeology*, the study of primitive civilizations through an examination of their remains; *chronology,* the study of calendars and other means of assessing them; *diplomatics,* the study of official documents; and *epigraphy,* the study of inscriptions found on metal, stone, clay, and so on. In many cases, historians must finally rely on the judgment of others (including librarians) for the authentication of evidence. As a practical matter, items housed in the research collections of major libraries can usually be assumed to be authentic (some may not be). Common sense dictates that a single historian cannot personally verify every document used: "It is not possible to check everything; it is only possible to remember that ideally everything ought to be checked."[2]

Is the Evidence Reliable?

A document can, of course, be wholly authentic and still tell appalling lies. Former President Nixon's early accounts of the Watergate break-in were without question *his accounts* (that is, they were authentic). Later evidence, however, suggested that his early accounts were not entirely truthful (that is, they were not reliable). Once historians determine that a document is what it seems to be, therefore, they must still move to discover if the information it provides is likely to be accurate—that is, if the document is reliable. In attempting to assess reliability, historians need to determine if the source of the information was both able and willing to tell the truth. If the source could not know the truth or had some reason to hide it, the reliability of the account is in doubt.

The situation is seldom so simple as it may first appear. Documents are usually reliable *to some degree;* that is, most often, questions of reliability cannot be answered with a simple yes or no.

If a diary describes a traffic accident and the diarist was definitely an eyewitness to the event, the account may be highly reliable. If, on the other hand, the diarist was not present at the event and was only passing along a friend's report, the account is probably less reliable. (In fact, secondhand reports are merely hearsay, and hearsay, because of its general unreliability, is inadmissible as evidence in a court of law. Unlike lawyers, historians may rely on hearsay, but only cautiously and in full awareness of its limitations as reliable evidence.) In the first case, the diarist was able, in general, to know what happened; in the second case, the diarist's ability to tell what happened was dependent on the accuracy and completeness of a friend's report.

Even if the diarist saw the event and was able to tell the truth, however, he may have been either anxious—or unwilling—to do so. For example, if the diarist actually witnessed the accident and wanted to help the police, he may have tried to report exactly what he saw; if, on the other hand, he witnessed the accident and was trying to protect a friend whose recklessness caused it, he may have shaded the truth to help the friend. The reliability of the two eyewitnesses is quite different even though their ability to tell the truth is roughly the same.

Ability and willingness to tell the truth are not merely matters of honesty. Individual differences in seeing and hearing limit the ability to tell the truth about events experienced through these senses. As well, some people have no interest in literal "truth." A poet's purpose, for example, is to make a good poem, not to tell the literal "truth." The point is that *even authentic documents vary widely in their ability and their desire to tell the truth,* and so historians must be alert to both factors in assessing the *reliability* of evidence.

What Reasonable Interpretations Can Be Given to the Available Evidence?

After documents have been probed for authenticity and reliability, they must be interpreted. The facts must be examined for the relationships that they suggest and for the explanations that they offer for the events. Gordon Leff wrote that good interpretations meet three tests: (1) they agree with the evidence on which they are based; (2) they show relationships among several events or between a single event and its context; and (3) they avoid "unlikely, implausible, or unacceptable assumptions."[3]

Interpretation is the historian's most important and creative act, for through it he or she gives meaning to the many facts and, in this way, builds history from their framework. Interpretation requires imagination, but imag-

FIGURE 2.2

Mr. Edwin Booth, an American actor, in *Othello* (top); M. Vertepré, a French *vaudeville* actor, in *Agnès Sorel* (left); and Mr. Benson, an Englishman, in Voltaire's *Orphan of China*. Why do all of these actors have a plumed hat as part of their costume? [Authors' collection.]

ination that is firmly grounded in the evidence at hand. The goal of the interpretation is, of course, to provide the best possible description and explanation of what happened in light of all the available evidence. In moving from the facts to their interpretation, historians (and their readers) must persistently ask if the reasoning that bridges the gap is sound and, if it is sound, whether equally sound alternative explanations could be inferred from the same evidence.

Because interpretation is a personal and creative act, it puts the historian's judgment and intellect to their severest test, and it is for this act that the historian has been called "a prophet in reverse."

What Particular Problems of Evidence Face the Historian of Theatre?

Like other historians, those of the theatre must discover, assess, and interpret evidence. The nature of theatre art, however, presents some special challenges that are worth noting.

First, because theatre is a complex art that involves playwrights, actors, directors, designers, and (often) musicians, dancers, and choreographers, the scope of historical investigation in theatre is potentially very broad indeed. Moreover, to uncover and describe the dramatic, visual, technical, and musical dimensions of the art often requires different sets of skills. Theatre historians, for example, may need to understand architecture in order to discover the nature of the envelope that enclosed a given production or to discover the relationship between theatre architecture and civic architecture of a particular period. Theatre historians may need to investigate the history of drama in order to uncover changes in its structure and content. They may focus on the practices of costumers or directors, or on styles of acting. They may produce biographical studies of artists or economic analyses of companies. The danger of

producing a series of tunnel histories is great, but the extreme complexity of the art requires analytical work on each of its components. The evidence suitable for each sort of study is different, and its accessibility varies widely.

Second, the task of theatre historians is made difficult by the ephemeral nature of the art. Like life itself, a theatrical performance, once completed, can be neither recaptured nor exactly reproduced. Theatre historians, therefore, can study only various artifacts and residues that surround the art; they cannot study the living art itself. Whereas other art historians may line up a series of paintings or a number of statues to study and compare (and to test conclusions against), a theatre historian must be content to study only the inert things that surrounded the living event, things like written descriptions of performances, paintings done of the leading actors, and (more recently) photographs or videotapes of the event. In no case can the theatre historian, like the art historian, retrieve the actual work of art and study it directly.

Third, the study of theatre history is complicated by the unusually intricate relationship that exists between theatre and society. Live performers in contact with live audiences, besides rendering the art ephemeral, also make it *social* in a way that literature or painting or television is not. Theatre depends on audiences. These audiences vary in size, but they almost always consist of a *group of people* brought together at a particular place and a particular time. The expectations and attitudes of this group are important to the art—and to an understanding of its history. During any age, a desire to please audiences—or at least to avoid offending them—influences (to varying degrees) the content of plays, the personal lives of performers, the scenic conventions of designers, and the very shape and size of the theatre building. Evidence relating to the actual and potential audiences of an age, therefore, is relevant to a study of the theatre of that age. But such evidence—particularly evidence of the attitudes, behavior, and influence of the audience—is particularly difficult to unearth and validate, and thus it represents a major challenge for historians of theatre.

Also, the precise relationship between the theatre and the society of the time is not well understood. Some scholars believe that theatre is a mirror of the society of which it is a part, that it accurately reflects the life of its age. Others believe that theatre leads the society of its time, promoting new attitudes, altering behavior, and manipulating public opinion. Still others believe that theatre lags behind its society, perpetuating conservative positions and validating outworn stereotypes. No doubt, it does all three of these things—to some degree and under certain conditions; unfortunately, it is very difficult to determine to what degree and under which conditions.

Finally, because theatre is inextricably bound to its society, the study of its history is intertwined with the social, political, and economic practices of the day. Disentangling theatre's history from the general social history of each age becomes a major challenge for the historian, for deciding which aspects of society influenced theatrical practices, in what ways, and to what degrees is an exceedingly tricky business. Yet the theatre historian must strive to discover the relevant factors and to dismiss the irrelevant ones in order to render the theatre's history intelligible: too little social history, and theatre's history becomes disengaged from the world at large, its study trivialized because it is artificially restricted; too much social history, and theatre's history becomes submerged under the myriad details of everyday life.

Where Do Theatre Historians Locate Resources?

The major theatre collection in the United States today is probably the New York Public Library at Lincoln Center, where a wide range of theatrical books, journals, microfilms, and memorabilia is housed. As well, excellent collections of theatrical materials exist in this country at universities like Harvard, Yale, Indiana, Ohio State, and Texas. Works like *Performing Arts Collections: An International Handbook,* as well as the footnotes and bibliographies of major works in the field, can indicate the depth and the variety of holdings at various libraries.

Because many resources needed to investigate theatre's past are not traditionally housed in general libraries (e.g., photographs, programs, and promptbooks), no standard method of cataloging or indexing the materials exists from collection to collection. This situation complicates the search for materials. For example, a single piece of evidence might be useful to several different historians, but the library's cataloging system may render it inaccessible to some of them. A single photograph might be taken (1) by Martha Swope (2) of George C. Scott (3) playing the role of Willy Loman (4) in Arthur Miller's (5) *Death of a Salesman* (6) in a production at Circle in the Square. A given collection may provide access to the photograph through only one entry, for example, the title of the play. A person researching theatrical photography by Swope, or illustrations of Scott, or photographs of plays by Arthur Miller, or of productions at Circle in the Square would stumble on this photograph only indirectly—or the researcher might miss it altogether unless he or she understood the cataloging procedures of the library. Thus, because libraries house and catalog theatrical memorabilia in eccentric ways, theatre historians face uncommon problems in unearthing useful evidence.

What Kinds of Evidence Are Generally Used by Theatre Historians, and What Are Their Salient Characteristics?

In addition to classifying evidence as direct or indirect, primary or secondary, written or unwritten, and intended or unintended, theatre historians often adopt other schemes.

One scheme commonly used by theatre historians categorizes evidence according to its form: *verbal, iconographic, artifactual,* and *architectural.* Words, either written or spoken, form the basis of verbal evidence, and images and pictures form iconographic evidence. Artifactual evidence consists of the things themselves rather than verbal or pictorial descriptions of them, and architectural evidence is artifactual on a grand scale, for it includes buildings and monuments (or their remains). Members of each class tend to share certain traits. For example, as a class, iconographic evidence is seldom as explicit as verbal evidence but is often richer in details; architectural evidence tends to be more durable than artifacts like hand properties but seldom reflects the subtle shifts and trends of style that occurred within any period.

Another useful scheme for classifying theatrical evidence depends on its source. Evidence can be grouped roughly according to its relationship to theatrical production: (1) that from a production; (2) that related generally to the theatre of the age; (3) that with a tangential relation to the theatre of the time: and (4) that

FIGURE 2.3

These three photocopies, all examples of iconographic evidence, reproduce examples of iconographic (a sketch), architectural (remains), and artifactual (a gem) evidence. [Properties for C. Kean's production of *The Winter's Tale,* from *Magazine of Art*; photograph of Epidaurus courtesy of Briant Hamor Lee; and gem from Winckleman.]

which studies past productions, practices, and context.

Evidence from Productions

A single production typically generates a large number of items. Some of the items are written, for example, the play's text, the promptbook, the actors' sides, the musical score, the choreographic notations, the advertisements, the programs, the tickets, the reviews, the contracts, the attendance figures, and the financial reports. Some are not written, for example, the designers' sketches and renderings, the construction drawings, photographs, masks, costumes, properties, and scenic pieces. Because the presumed purpose of all such items is to communicate something about the production to those who will see it or participate in it, all such materials carry the presumption of a high degree of reliability. They must be viewed, however, with a heavy infusion of common sense. Advertisements, for example, are sure to present the best face of the performance, for their goal is to bring audiences into the theatre. Reviews inevitably reflect the biases of the reviewer and may, as well, be shaped by current love affairs, personal animosities, public policies, or even bribes. Photographs are often posed rather than candid and are routinely improved during processing.

Although most evidence that comes directly from performance is relatively reliable and easily assessed, the play text itself poses special problems for the historian, and so its use deserves further discussion.

From certain periods, written scripts represent the best evidence of dramatic and theatrical practices of the time. Our understanding of classical Greek, Republican Roman, and Shakespearean practices would be greatly impoverished were it not for the texts that have come down to us. Their usefulness, however, does not alter the fact that play texts, unlike promptbooks, do not contain specific information about a specific production. For this reason, some theatre historians consider texts sec-

ondary rather than primary evidence. The classification is unimportant as long as it is clearly understood that a text is only a set of cues for a production and that the actual performance may have existed at a considerable distance from its text.

A single script often provides some fairly specific, if very limited, information about staging; several scripts when taken together may suggest patterns of theatrical production. For example, we learn from scattered references in classical Greek tragedy that different colors of costumes were used and that the colors could signify certain things; we learn, too, that various properties were used in the theatre; and we learn that some machines existed for revealing dead bodies and others for flying the actors. We can also infer certain things about styles of acting and about assignments of parts from these texts. Information of this sort derives from techniques called *external criticism* and usually depends merely on careful reading, simple calculation, and common sense.

Play texts are also examined for *internal* evidence that can be used as the basis of inferences about the age in which they were written and the philosophy of the playwrights authoring them. For example, the view that extraordinary people determine the course of history is readily apparent in plays like *Prometheus* and *Henry V*. A world operating in accord with some divine plan is easily visible in *Everyman* or *Abraham and Isaac*. A picture of a world ruled by other-than-divine forces surfaces in plays like *The Weavers* and *The Bad Seed*. An historian can study changing "assumptive bases" or operative "world views" by comparing different dramatic treatments of the same story: Aeschylus' *Oresteia* and O'Neill's *Mourning Becomes Electra*, Sophocles' *Antigone* and Anouilh's *Antigone*, Euripides' *Hippolytus* and Racine's *Phèdre*. Such studies are fascinating and provocative, but conclusions drawn from them must not be generalized beyond what can be supported through a judicious use of corroborating evidence. Although popular in programs of comparative literature and the history of ideas, such studies should be undertaken and reported with extreme caution.

Because drama has its own intellectual content, which is expressed in ordinary language (rather than musical or mathematical symbols, for example) and in gestures by characters who are impersonated by living actors, some critics and historians have been seduced into accepting the action of a play as a literal representation of the actions of its age, and its characters as literal representations of real people. Such direct translations from art to life are very misleading. H. D. F. Kitto explored the confusion that too often results between drama and life when he compared our reactions to a piece of sculpture and to a piece of drama:

> We know, without being told, that a certain man, the sculptor, set to work with lumps of stone, his tools, his skill, and with a certain idea or subject in his head. We know that these are solely responsible for everything that we can see in the pediment . . . [and so] if on looking at the pediment we noticed that one warrior had no spear, we would not think of asking where he had dropped it, or whether he had forgotten it; we would at once ask ourselves why the sculptor had represented him spearless. . . . we do not find it so easy to remember that the *Antigone* began as a pile of clean paper on Sophocles' table.[4]

Historians may use the intellectual content of drama to draw conclusions about the age, then, but they must do so with full awareness that *drama is a work of art*, whose major goal is probably *not* a literal presentation of the life of the time.

Evidence from Theatre in General

Any age generates a large amount of material that is related to the theatre but that has little to do with specific productions. Some material relates to the institution, such as government or church records of annual festivals; regulations governing who can perform when, where, and under what circumstances; copyrights and patents; licenses; censorship records; correspondence among producing groups; and correspondence between producing groups and outside agencies. Some of the materials relate to theatre buildings, such as rental agreements; property deeds; building contracts; zoning laws; architectural drawings; and physical remains. Some relate to personnel, such as contracts; records of payment; guild memberships; autobiographies; interviews; memoirs; diaries; letters; and portraits, photographs, and sculptures. Some relate to supporters, such as subscription lists; foundation reports; and grant applications and reports. Some are theoretical essays that treat the theatre of the day, such as studies in aesthetics, architecture, audiences, acting, directing, design, and machinery.

Evidence about the theatre in general is invaluable because it provides the background against which specific productions can be better understood. Also, historians attempting to reconstruct a specific production use such information to fill in the many aspects of production for which no clear records exist.

Tangential Evidence

In any age, some items relate to theatre only incidentally. For example, novelists may feature a fictional theatre artist as the hero of a novel and so treat the institution of theatre in great detail, or novelists may skillfully interweave fact and fancy in producing a fictionalized biography of a real artist. A painter may elect to depict theatrical scenes on canvas, and a poet may eulogize an actor or author. Engravings, vase paintings, bas-reliefs, frescoes, sculptures, line drawings, and so on may take some aspect of theatre as their subject. All such materials may be useful, of course, but they must be used carefully, for they present several special problems.

First, artists choosing a theatrical subject may or may not know of it firsthand. For example, the famous eighteenth-century painter and engraver William Hogarth produced a se-

FIGURE 2.4

A theatre company's history is often suggested by its property room. A comic view of an imaginary theatre's past productions is shown in this nineteenth-century engraving of a theatrical auction sale. [Authors' collection.]

ries called *Mariage à la Mode*, which depicts the perils of adultery. An earlier play by Dryden with the same name dealt with the same subject. No one knows if Hogarth knew the play or if he intended his prints to relate to it in any way. Indeed, the similarity in title may have been wholly coincidental. On the other hand, it is possible that Hogarth saw the play and that his prints represent aspects of a real production. We cannot know unless further information is uncovered.

Second, even assuming that the artist knows the subject firsthand, his or her intention is to make a distinct work of art, not to tell the truth about a subject. Some details may be heightened to achieve excitement, others omitted in order to gain focus. The result, although artistically pleasing, may be far removed from any similar play or scene or artist in the real theatre of the period.

Third, each art has its own materials, which exert control over the artist's rendering of the subject. For example, a theatrical scene painted on a vase involves taking a three-dimensional, living art and rendering it as a two-dimensional, static one. Further, the size of the vase places clear restrictions on the amount of detail that can be included; and the colors available to the artist are prescribed by the soil and the firing process used for the work. Clearly, even if a vase painter set out to tell the literal truth (an unlikely prospect), he or she would probably be unable to do so because of the particular restrictions imposed by the artistic medium.

Fourth, each age and each artist have their own style. Because style affects the general appearance of a work, it manipulates the truth that the work tells. For example, styles of drama are often defined by their degree of correspondence with literal reality; thus, naturalism is "extreme realism"; impressionism is "selective realism"; and absurdism is "non-(or even anti-)realism." In painting, the Renaissance artists' fascination with perspective was not shared by medieval illustrators, and Claude Monet's landscapes differ markedly from Vincent Van Gogh's.

FIGURE 2.5

Stage sailors were important characters on the nineteenth-century stage, but the photograph of the Kendals in a version of Jerrold's *Black Eyed Susan* [from Pemberton] is rather more detailed than the artist's sketch of Lydia Thompson as Sindbad [from Hutton] and the character type depicted by Jerome. Do these stylistic differences reflect changes in theatre, in art, or in both?

In addition to evidence that relates to theatre incidentally, every age offers considerable evidence that does not treat theatre at all but that remains useful to theatre historians nonetheless. Information about contemporary fashion, music, dance, visual arts, morals, economic conditions, and so on may form an important part of any study because all of these are parts of the vital context of the theatre of the age.

Later Studies

Many excellent studies are now available for historians of the theatre. Since the late nineteenth century, the amount of information has fairly exploded as scholar after scholar has added to the store of facts and interpretations. Some researchers have compiled calendars and cast lists of productions and organized them by company, city, and country; others have contributed biographies of the theatre's major artists. Some have concentrated on pivotal events, like the great Astor Place Riot; others have traced movements, like the rise of independent theatres. Some have specialized in individual theatres, like the Red Bull during Shakespeare's age; others have examined entire periods, like the early medieval theatre. Critics, too, have arisen to evaluate both theatre artists and previous historians. General histories of the theatre have appeared that examine world theatre from its origins to the present; specialized histories have conveyed more detailed information about more restricted topics. And finally, textbooks have emerged to offer distilled but encyclopedic coverage of the theatre's past. The best of all these studies are very good indeed, and almost all can be useful to some degree as long as they are approached with knowledge and skepticism.

Much current scholarship properly and necessarily rests on these secondary studies for, as Clark so wisely observed, "it is not possible for scholars to reconsider and check all the evidence used by other scholars. If they felt called upon to do so, the wheels of scholarship would grind to a halt."[5] In general, historians can comfortably rely more heavily on secondary materials at the periphery of their own research questions; they must insist on a greater proportion of primary sources the closer they come to the core of their own study. Certainly, general histories—of society and the other arts, as well as of theatre—are an important source of background information for anyone launching a research venture. Secondary materials, then, should be used along with other kinds of evidence: materials taken from productions themselves, from the theatre in general, and from the society surrounding that theatre.

After Evidence, What?

Few theatre historians ever believe that they have enough evidence to answer their questions with complete confidence. "The more we study, the less we know" is a complaint common in the ranks. And indeed, a tension always exists between the desire to keep looking for more evidence and the need to draw conclusions based on what has already been collected. Of course, the evaluation and the interpretation of evidence proceed throughout any investigation, but at some point, this process must stop so that the director can begin rehearsals, so that the actor can undertake the role, the designer produce the renderings, the scholar write the article or publish the book. Although no clear rule governs when the search should end (at least as it relates to the project in hand), each historian probably needs to continue to look for evidence as long as pertinent facts are regularly unearthed. When new information begins to dribble in only occasionally or when the new information is merely a constant reiteration of the old, the historian considers ending this phase of the research process. In the last analysis, each researcher must simply decide when the evidence at hand is sufficient to the needs of the problem that has been set; and his or her judgment in this regard is one index of competence in the field.

Jacques Barzun summed up well what the historian faces:

> History, like a vast river, propels logs, vegetation, rafts, and debris; it is full of live and dead things, some destined for resurrection; it mingles many waters and holds in solution invisible substances stolen from distant soils. Anything may become a part of it.[6]

ENDNOTES

1. Robert Jones Shafer, *A Guide to Historical Method,* rev. ed. (Homewood, Ill.: Dorsey, 1974), p. 70.
2. G. Kitson Clark, *The Critical Historian* (New York: Basic Books, 1967), p. 121.
3. Gordon Leff, *History and Social History* (University: University of Alabama Press, 1969), p. 126.
4. H. D. F. Kitto, *Poeisis* (Berkeley: University of California Press, 1966), pp. 14–15.
5. Clark, p. 119.
6. Jacques Barzun, *Clio and the Doctors* (Chicago: University of Chicago Press, 1974), p. 95.

3

Interpretations: The Origins of Drama, a Case Study

In the first two chapters we have explored the nature of history and historical writing, and we have examined some of the problems that historians face in their search for "what happened." We have suggested that, even today, history abounds in unresolved questions, disputed facts, and alternative explanations. The history of the theatre is no exception. Thus, although the issues raised in the first two chapters could be illustrated by any one of several controversies within our field, we have chosen one—the origins of Western drama—for study. Its selection, although to a degree arbitrary, is warranted by the vital importance of the question, the persistence of the controversy, the improbability of its speedy resolution, and the wide disparity among the explanations offered.

Because Western drama first appeared in the distant past (probably in the sixth century B.C.), evidence about it is scant and facts are few. Oral accounts of it (only later written down) and written accounts transmitted by hand have introduced problems of authenticity; moreover, because none of the accounts was written at the time of the event it describes, reliability is also a question. In the absence of an adequate framework of fact, therefore, historians have fleshed out the existing framework by interpreting and elaborating the few facts in order to create the semblance of a coherent account of what happened. Not surprisingly, their explanations are radically different, reflecting not only different interpretations of the available facts but also the different assumptions of these historians about how history operates.

Not all the discrepancies have been caused by the manipulation of facts, however. The various scholars seem to have posed rather different questions about the origin of drama, and so they have drawn on markedly different sorts of evidence to answer their questions. It will be instructive, therefore, to compare four accounts of the origin of drama and to pay particular attention to these questions:

1. What problem did the historian set for himself?
2. What evidence did he bring to bear on it?
3. How well does the explanation agree with the evidence?
4. How well does the explanation account for the events?
5. Are the assumptions undergirding the account plausible?

Of the many available theories of the origin of Greek drama, we have chosen four that are sufficiently esteemed to be worth our study and sufficiently diverse to suggest the wide range of explanations offered. The theories to be considered are those of Aristotle, Gilbert Murray, William Ridgeway, and Gerald Else.

Aristotle's Account: History or Theory?

With admirable directness, Aristotle opened the *Poetics* by stating his subject: "I propose to treat of Poetry in itself and of its various kinds, not-

FIGURE 3.1

Two interpretations of Shakespeare's Globe Theatre. Streit, a German scholar, in 1903 imagined that it resembled a proscenium theatre with illusionistic scenery; Hotson, an English scholar, in 1960 imagined that it partook strongly of medieval elements like scaffolds. [Hotson reprinted with permission of The Macmillan Co., from *Shakespeare's Wooden O* by Leslie Hotson. Courtesy also of Rupert Hart-Davis, London.]

 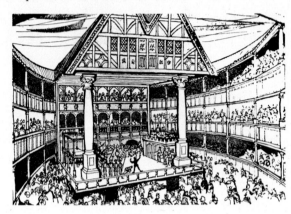

ing the essential quality of each; to inquire into the structure of the plot as requisite to a good poem; into the number and nature of the parts of which a poem is composed; and similarly into whatever else falls within the same inquiry."[1] His guiding research questions can be inferred: What is poetry? What are its various species, and how do they differ? What is plot, and how is it structured? What are the number and parts of a poem? The questions point clearly to a work whose major focus is theoretical rather than historical. Nevertheless, as a part of his investigation of poetry, and in particular of tragedy, Aristotle set forth a brief statement concerning the origins and early development of drama.

The core of this account is found in Book IV of the *Poetics,* the salient part of which is reproduced here. Bracketed materials are our addition:

> Tragedy—as also Comedy—was at first mere improvisation. The one originated with the leaders of the Dithyramb, the other with those of the phallic songs, which are still in use in many of our cities. Tragedy advanced by slow degrees; each new element that showed itself was in turn developed. Having passed through many changes, it found its natural form, and there it stopped.
>
> Aeschylus first introduced the second actor; he diminished the importance of the Chorus, and assigned the leading part to the dialogue. Sophocles raised the number of actors to three, and added scene painting. Moreover, it was not till late that the short plot was discarded for one of greater compass, and the grotesque diction of the earlier satyric form for the stately manner of Tragedy. The iambic measure then replaced the trochaic tetrameter, which was originally employed when the poetry was of the satyric order, and had greater affinities with dancing. Once dialogue had come in, Nature herself discovered the appropriate measure [the iambic]. (p. 19)

Somewhat earlier, in Book III, Aristotle aired claims about the place where drama emerged. Because that passage is also relevant to the issue at hand, it too is quoted:

some say, the name of "drama" is given to such poems [plays], as representing action. For the same reason the Dorians claim the invention both of Tragedy and Comedy. The claim to Comedy is put forward by the Megarians—not only by those of Greece proper, who allege that it originated under their democracy, but also by the Megarians of Sicily, for the poet Epicharmus, who is much earlier than Chionides and Magnes, belonged to that country. Tragedy too is claimed by certain Dorians of the Peloponnese. In each case they appeal to the evidence of language. Villages, they say, are by them called κῶμαι [komai], by the Athenians δῆμοι [demoi]: and they assume that Comedians were so named not from κωμάζειν [komazein] "to revel," but because they wandered from village to village (κατὰ κώμας), being excluded contemptuously from the city. They add also that the Dorian word for "doing" is δρᾶν, [dran] and the Athenian πρττειν [prattein]. (pp. 13, 15)

These two passages, the heart of the matter, are supplemented by only three other relevant references. Aristotle suggested, also in Book IV, that both the desire to imitate and the delight taken in imitation are innate traits of human beings, as is the instinct for "harmony" and "rhythm." Building on these traits, he said, people developed their gifts and moved from mere improvisation to poetry. Aristotle next explained that Homer was the fount of both the serious subjects of tragedy (from his *Iliad* and *Odyssey*) and the ludicrous subjects of comedy (from his *Margites*) but that thereafter poets, including dramatists, tended to specialize in one or the other, either the tragic or the comic. And finally, in Book V, he reported that tragedy had passed through a series of changes that were well known but that comedy's past was obscure because at first people paid little attention to it.

Of the *Poetics'* twenty-six books, parts of only three address the origins and development of drama. Of the twenty-four pages of text given the *Poetics* in one modern translation, fewer than two treat the subject even peripherally.

Is the *Poetics* Authentic?

Do we in fact have Aristotle's *Poetics?* The best answer is a qualified yes; the major qualifications are three:

First, it is well to remember that Aristotle did not write, "For the same reason the Dorians claim the invention of both Tragedy and Comedy." Rather, he wrote something that looked like this: διό καί ἱ αντιποιουνται της τε τραγῳδίας καί της κωμῳδίας οι Δωριεις. Obviously, most of us study the *Poetics* as translated, and translation inevitably produces distortion. Seldom can exact equivalents for words be found even in the translation of contemporary materials from other languages. The problem is greatly complicated when exact equivalents are sought from ancient Greek to modern tongues, for many Greek customs, practices, and even concepts (so familiar to them) were rendered by a single word or phrase. These same customs, practices, and concepts (so foreign to us) are accessible only through a careful study of Athenian history; the Greek words used to describe them can be understood only through a careful comparison of these words as they were used in various contemporary documents. No single English word or phrase can "translate" the Greek associations that cling to their words. For a simple example, we need go no further than the Greek word πολις (*polis*); which is customarily translated into English as "city state." In fact, however, there is no modern equivalent of a Greek *polis*, with its unique form of participatory democracy and civic responsibility. Unless we understand what in fact a *polis* was, we are misled rather than enlightened by the English rendering of *polis* as "city state."

Second, the usual problems of translations from the Greek are compounded by the extremely terse—even elliptical—prose of the original. Its abbreviated, staccato quality has led some scholars to argue that the text itself was only the outline for a book that was to be written, or the notes for lectures that Aristotle pre-

pared for his own oral presentation. Far from fluid sentences like "I propose to treat of Poetry in itself and of its various kinds, noting the essential quality of each," and so on, the original rather lurches forward in a manner familiar to students accustomed to taking class notes: "Poetry: kind, quality of each; best structure of plot; number and nature;" and so on. Any translation of the *Poetics*, therefore, is an interpretation of the *Poetics*, for each translator must decide how to fill out the outlines provided by the original.

FIGURE 3.2

Two interpretations of a medieval theatre: one by a German artist who conceived the theatre on three levels, representing heaven, earth, and hell (a view rejected by modern scholars); the other in a modern production of the "N-Town Plays" in Grantham, England, which uses temporary scaffolding of various levels. [English photograph courtesy of Chris Windows. Drawing from Weddigen.]

Third, each translator must decide which version of Aristotle's *Poetics* he or she will translate. We do not have the *Poetics* in Aristotle's own hand. Rather, we have various copies of it that have come down from antiquity. Curiously, some of the earliest versions to reach western Europe were not in Greek at all but in Arabic, translations of the original that were themselves then translated into Latin and other languages. Not all of the versions agree; in fact, discrepancies are common. For many passages in the *Poetics*, there is general agreement about both meaning and authenticity; for many, however, there is little or no agreement. Regrettably, as we shall see, one section that deals with the origins of tragedy has been declared genuine and significant by some scholars, spurious and wholly irrelevant by others.

Is the *Poetics* Reliable?

Probably no book has exerted so much influence on dramatic theory as Aristotle's *Poetics*. Written about 335 B.C., it is the earliest theoretical study of drama (in particular, tragedy), and as such, it has served as a source for most later accounts. Of all the extant evidence that purports to treat of the origin of drama, the *Poetics* is the closest in time to the event that it strives to describe. In part because of its date, then, the *Poetics* has served as a starting point for almost all later attempts to construct a theory of origin. Although Aristotle cited no sources for his claims, scholars have assumed that he consulted records that stretched back into the sixth century B.C., the century during which tragedy was first officially recognized in Athens.

The date of the work alone, however, probably cannot explain its profound influence. That it has been so long studied is also explained in part by the reputation of its author, Aristotle, who was a respected scholar in his own day, after being a student and colleague of Plato for about twenty years. After the death of his teacher, Aristotle became the tutor of Alexander of Macedon (later, Alexander the Great) and then

a teacher at the Lyceum in Athens. His intellect was prodigious, and with it, he attacked problems in rhetoric, metaphysics, ethics, and biology, as well as in poetics. Respected during his own day, Aristotle was revered during much of the late Middle Ages and the Renaissance, when many of his works (as translated and interpreted) were considered unimpeachable sources of information on a variety of subjects.

Finally, the *Poetics* itself is an astute theoretical inquiry into the best form of tragedy. Neither a rule book for critics nor a do-it-yourself manual for playwrights, the *Poetics* is, rather, a philosophical treatise that probes through logic the thing called *tragedy* and strives to offer an encompassing description and definition of it. The ideas expressed in the *Poetics* are tantalizing, provocative, and challenging. Scholars from the sixteenth century down to our own day have argued both its meaning and its contemporary worth. The excellence of the work itself, then, accounts in part for its lasting influence and for its continued acceptance by many scholars. Because the whole work is excellent, each of its parts gains a presumption of reliability.

Still, there are a number of reasons for questioning the reliability of the *Poetics* when it speaks of the origin and the early history of drama. In the first place, Aristotle clearly did not set out to write a history. Information about the origins and the early development of drama is included for the insights it can provide into the nature of tragedy (his major subject). If he considered the material peripheral to the major line of his argument, he may simply have recorded currently accepted views and moved on to what were (to him) more important matters.

Second, although Aristotle's account is the oldest to have survived, and although he lived closer to the origins and the early development of drama than did any other commentator whose works have come down to us, still he was writing over one hundred years after the events that he studied. The first official recognition of drama in Athens came about 534 B.C.; it probably originated even earlier. Sophocles and Euripides, the last great tragic authors, died ca. 406 B.C., and tragedy declined shortly thereafter. Yet Aristotle was not born until 384 B.C., 150 years after the first official recognition, 22 years after the deaths of Sophocles and Euripides. Because Aristotle was not living during the great age of tragedy, he must have depended on the records and accounts of others in constructing Books III, IV, and V of the *Poetics*. Who were these others? He does not tell us. Were they able and willing to tell the truth? We do not know. We do know that Aristotle lived long before the age of printing when, as we have seen, the transmission of records invited progressive corruption rather than increasing accuracy.

It is well to keep these two points in mind when turning to the passages themselves, for they contain some statements that invite skepticism and others whose ambiguity cannot yet be resolved.

What Reasonable Interpretations Can Be Given to the Account Found in the *Poetics?*

In considering the account, let us agree to pause only over areas where legitimate controversy exists, and let us begin with the more general assertions and move later to particular issues.

When Aristotle speaks of imitation as innate, he seems to be on theoretical rather than historical ground; that is, he appears to ask and answer the question: *Why* does drama arise? rather than When, where, and through what *agency* did drama arise? In answering his question, he connects the coming of drama with human instincts for imitation, harmony, and rhythm and their subsequent development in such a way that simple improvisations were transformed into poetry (including drama). On this subject, Aristotle said no more, and so scholars have felt free to speculate. Some have supposed that he described an inevitable process, but to assume such inevitability requires us to believe that all peoples will, in time, im-

provise and evolve dramatic poetry. Clearly, however, no such inevitable progression can be shown, for several societies as sophisticated as the Athenian never developed drama. And if sophisticated societies have existed that did not give rise to drama, can imitation, harmony, and rhythm be innate? The issue is important for two reasons. First, the account underscores Aristotle's reliance on Athenian art and culture for his evidence. He did not have any tragedy to study except that produced in Athens, and he had relatively little knowledge of cultures beyond his immediate area. Second, if not all societies develop drama, then not all societies develop in the same way, and so the emergence of drama cannot be considered a part of any natural and inevitable process common to all societies.

In the same book, Aristotle attributed the invention of tragedy to the "leaders of the Dithyramb." (Because tragedy was officially recognized in Athens earlier than comedy, its origins may be equated with those of drama, and so our discussion treats only tragedy.) In attributing the invention of tragedy to the "leaders of the Dithyramb," however, Aristotle selected a word for leader that is not one normally used either for the leader of the dithyrambic chorus (κοβρυφαῖος *coryphaeus*) or for its poet–author (διδάσκαλος, *didaskalos*). What leader was meant then? The word he used (εξαρχος *exarchôn*) generally refers to "the leader of the whole performance," but to our knowledge, the dithyramb of the fifth and fourth centuries B.C. had no such leader (it had instead a *chorus* leader), although an *exarchôn* had been in existence much earlier, when the dithyramb was a revel song.[2]

The selection of the word *exarchôn* to mean "leader" in the passage has caused confusion about the sense in which Aristotle was using the word *dithyramb*. The dithyramb is traditionally associated with Dionysus, the god of wine and fertility (among other things). Aristotle, however, did not mention Dionysus in connection with these dithyrambs, and in Ar-

FIGURE 3.3

Directors regularly interpret scripts, often producing quite different productions from the "same" text, as a comparison of Maurice Maeterlinck's *Blue Bird* in London (1909, top) and Paris (1911) handily show. [From *Le Théâtre.*]

istotle's own day, the dithyramb had abandoned its Dionysiac heritage: by then, the word *dithyramb* could be used to mean nothing more than "a lyric presentation of heroic subjects."[3] Perhaps by his choice of word for "leader," Aristotle wanted to suggest that he meant the early (pre-fifth-century) dithyramb; perhaps by his omission of Dionysus, on the other hand, he meant that he was using the word in the (to him) modern sense of "lyric on a heroic subject." Scholars understandably disagree on the meaning of the word *dithyramb* as used in the passage. Some insist that it means the traditional, Dionysiac, cyclic dithyramb; others argue that it means simply heroic lyrics; and some even argue for a primitive protodithyramb out of which both tragedy and true dithyrambs developed.

In connection with the third interpretation, we run afoul of another set of disagreements, those that surround the lines "and the grotesque *diction of the earlier satyric form [was discarded] for the stately manner of Tragedy. . . .* when the poetry was of the satyric order, and had greater affinities with dancing" p. 19, (the italics are ours). The italicized portion of the quotation can be equally well translated "through its ceasing to be satyric drama."[4] Some scholars argue, therefore, that Aristotle said, in effect, that tragedy arose from a dithyramb in which the chorus were dressed as satyrs; others prefer the translation that implies only a change in language. Gerald Else has insisted that the passage is not Aristotle's at all but a later emendation: "The words are spurious, being incoherent in themselves and inconsistent both with the surrounding context and with Aristotle's thought as a whole."[5]

If the words are Aristotle's, they pose very real problems in interpretation, for they seem to connect tragedy with satyrs, satyr choruses, and satyr plays. Satyrs, however, were a far cry from any characters found in Greek tragedy as we know it. In Greek legend, satyrs were rude, cowardly, and lecherous half-beasts–half-men; satyr dramas were short, often licentious, and

robustly comic pieces. If tragedy was derived from satyr choruses or from satyr drama, it would have had to undergo an extraordinary shift between its inception and its appearance in the fifth century B.C.

Those who favor the view that tragedy derived from satyric elements usually cite as evidence some combination of the following: (1) dithyrambs were originally hymns to Dionysus, and in legend, Dionysus was raised by satyrs; (2) abundant visual evidence attests to the presence of satyrs in legend, and ample visual evidence shows satyr choruses and satyr dramas beginning in the sixth century B.C.; (3) the word *tragedy* came from *tragôidia*, itself derived from *tragôn ôidê*, or "song of goats," and satyrs were often dressed as goats; and (4) Aristotle said so, and he was a reliable source writing near the event.

Those who oppose the view that tragedy derived from satyric elements generally counter with these arguments: (1) no example of a satyric dithyramb has ever been found; (2) the extant tragedies show absolutely no satyric elements in their characters, language, content, or tone; (3) the word *tragôidia* cannot be properly derived from *tragôn ôidê* at all, and anyway, satyrs were usually shown as horses, not as goats;[6] and (4) Aristotle was the only early commentator who linked satyr plays with tragedy, and so either (a) the passage is not his, or (b) Aristotle was not recording history from evidence at all but was proposing only a theory of the origins of tragedy.

In Aristotle's treatment of origins and early development, there are other areas of minor disagreement: Did Aristotle endorse the Dorians' claims as the inventors of both tragedy and comedy, or did he merely report them? Did Aristotle mean that the origin and the early history of tragedy were well known and that evidence pointed to no lacunae in the account, or did he refer only to certain shifts in practice (masks, number of actors, and so on) that were well known? None of these minor disagreements need detain us.

Before leaving Aristotle, however, we should note some remarkable omissions from his account, remarkable because he is so often cited as the source of some of the following beliefs. First, Aristotle did *not* ascribe tragedy to any part of Dionysiac worship. Indeed, Aristotle did not mention Dionysus at all. Second, Aristotle did *not* credit Thespis with being the inventor of tragedy. In fact, he did not mention him, even though he wrote of the contributions of both Aeschylus and Sophocles. Third, Aristotle did *not* suggest that tragedy depended on a chorus that was originally a protagonist in the tragic drama. On the contrary, he spoke of tragedy as depending on an individual set against the chorus. The point here is not to disparage these beliefs, but to reiterate, with the text before us, that Aristotle is not legitimate evidence for them.

Ritual Theories of the Origin of Drama

"Perhaps no book has had so decisive an effect upon modern literature as Frazer's."[7] The book to which Lionel Trilling referred is *The Golden Bough*, its author Sir James G. Frazer. Certainly in the field of drama, Frazer's massive work exerted untold influence, both by promoting new theories of the origins of drama and by offering new interpretations of familiar plays.

Published first in England in 1896, the two volumes of *The Golden Bough* (expanded to twelve by 1915) marshalled evidence from societies past and present around the globe. Frazer seemed delighted by modern historians' ability to trace the development not merely of a single race or nation but "of all mankind, and . . . to follow the long march, the slow and toilsome ascent, of humanity from savagery to civilization."[8]

This march, according to Frazer, consists of three historical stages: a society first depends on hunting, then on grazing, and finally on growing its food. It consists as well of three stages of belief: ages of magic, of religion, and finally of science. During the age of religion, Frazer observed, various fertility and vegetative cults feature dying and reviving year spirits (like Osiris, Dionysus, and Christ). The myths surrounding such gods are, in fact, only remnants of rites earlier performed in their honor, and so myths can provide information about prehistoric customs and practices—or so Frazer set out to demonstrate.

The Golden Bough captured the imagination of its reading public almost immediately, and it continues to exert some influence even now. Its popularity can no doubt be explained in part by the enormous quantity of anthropological and archaeological fact and theory that it sifted and organized; it can be explained in part, as well, by the compelling prose style of Frazer. But at least some of its popularity must be attributed to its successful synthesis of many diverse (and, indeed, often competing) intellectual strains of the late nineteenth and early twentieth centuries.

For example, *The Golden Bough* exploited an interest, then current, in the relationships among cult, ritual, myth, and religion. The successful deciphering of cuneiform in the 1830s led to a new understanding and to new histories of Greece, Israel, and the Near East. It led as well to a new spurt of biblical scholarship, some of which strove to untangle the Bible's presentation of history from that of myth (the so-called Higher Criticism). When Friedrich Nietzsche published *The Birth of Tragedy* in 1871, he capitalized on a blossoming interest in myth and catapulted the names of Dionysus and Apollo into popular prominence. Thus was the mythic ground made fertile for the ideas presented in *The Golden Bough*.

Frazer's work also siezed on a contemporary interest in both the methods and matters of history and an interest embodied in two relative newcomers: comparative cultural anthropology and the "scientific" method of historical study. By means of its clear and compelling narrative, the book placed historical matters that

FIGURE 3.4

Two very different interpretations of *Oedipus Rex*. The production of the Missouri Repertory Theatre used no masks, whereas that of Canada's Stratford Shakespearean Festival, Stratford, Canada, used highly stylized masks in a production designed by Tanya Moiseiwitsch, directed by Tyrone Guthrie, with a cast that included Douglas Campbell, Eleanor Stuart, and Robert Goodier. [Photographs courtesy of the producing companies.]

had previously been available only to specialists within the grasp of all educated adults, fascinating them and goading them into new ways of thinking about contemporary issues.

In identifying the progressive stages of human society, *The Golden Bough* echoed beliefs both in the efficacy of science as an agent for improving the lot of humankind and in the inevitability of social progress toward stages that are more humane because more scientific. In the same way, the book unconsciously capitalized on the age's fascination with Charles Darwin's theory of evolution (*Origin of Species* had first been published in 1859), converting Darwin's principles of biological evolution to notions of an inexorable cultural development that led from a primitive (magical) beginning to a mature (scientific) present.

Through his massive accumulation of anthropological data, then, Frazer incorporated the period's "passion for the resonant concreteness of the observed object";[9] through his imaginative writing, he revitalized the age's badly battered optimism by reaffirming the improvement of society through the agency of its maturing citizenry; and through his cultural comparisons, he asserted a pervasive unity underlying existence and giving it meaning. "It is in this attempt to *construe* the data in universal terms, just as much as in its unparalleled coverage of them, that the distinctive significance of *The Golden Bough* really lies; and this it is that has earned for it the status of a classic."[10]

The impact of *The Golden Bough* on the field of anthropology was immediate, that on classical studies and literature almost so. By 1915, no fewer than six new theories of the origins of drama had found their way into print in English, and the influence of Frazer's book was clear in all of them. Although they differed in many details, all found the origin of drama in a primitive religious ritual of some kind. Thus, the myths and heroes of classical Greek drama were seen as muted replays of earlier ceremonies. Of these several ritual theories, the best known and most widely accepted among English-speaking people is that of Gilbert Murray.

Gilbert Murray's Theory of the Origin of Tragedy

Murray and Frazer, along with Jane Harrison and F. M. Cornford, were the leading members of what admirers called the Cambridge School of Anthropology and what detractors dubbed the Armchair, or Covent Garden, School of Anthropology (the latter being a jab at the group's failure to conduct primary field research). It was in Harrison's book *Themis* (1912) that Murray first published his theory, in an essay entitled "Excursus on the Ritual Forms Preserved in Greek Tragedy." In the essay, revised and republished in 1927, Murray began by setting forth his basic assumptions:

> The following note presupposes certain general views about the origin and essential nature of Greek Tragedy. It assumes that Tragedy is in origin a Ritual Dance, a *Sacer Ludus*. . . . Further, it assumes, in accord with the overwhelming weight of ancient tradition, that the Dance in question is originally or centrally that of Dionysus; and it regards Dionysus, in this connection, as an . . . "Eniautos-Daimon," or vegetation god, like Adonis, Osiris, etc., who represents the cyclic death and rebirth of the Earth and the World. . . . It seems clear, further, that Comedy and Tragedy represent different stages in the life of the Year Spirit; Comedy leads to his Marriage Feast, his κῶμος and γάμος, Tragedy to his death and θρῆνος. See Mr. Cornford's *Origin of Attic Comedy*. [11]

After a brief review of other recent theories of the origins of tragedy and references to those ancient commentators who seemed to bolster his assumptions, Murray moved to show how anthropology and drama could be synthesized through the agency of myth:

If we examine the kind of myth which seems to underlie the various "Eniautos" celebrations we shall find:

1. An *Agon* or Contest, the Year against its enemy, Light against Darkness, Summer against Winter.
2. A *Pathos* of the Year-Daimon, generally a ritual or sacrificial death in which Adonis or Attis is slain by the tabu animal, the Pharmakos stoned, Osiris, Dionysus, Pentheus, Orpheus, Hippolytus torn to pieces (σπαραγμός).
3. A *Messenger*. For this Pathos seems seldom or never to be actually performed under the eyes of the audiences. . . . It is announced by a messenger. "The news comes" that Pan the Great . . . is dead, and the dead body is often brought in on a bier. This leads to
4. A *Threnos* or Lamentation. Specially characteristic, however, is a clash of contrary emotions, the death of the old being also the triumph of the new. . . .
5. and 6. An *Anagnorisis*—discovery or recognition—of the slain and mutilated Daimon, followed by his Resurrection or Apotheosis or, in some sense, his Epiphany in glory. This I shall call by the general name *Theophany*. It naturally goes with a *Peripeteia* or extreme change of feeling from grief to joy.

Observe the sequence in which these should normally occur: *Agon, Pathos, Messenger, Threnos, Theophany*, or we might say, *Anagnorisis* and *Theophany*. [12]

After this initial publication, Murray reaffirmed his theory repeatedly in essays and books like "Greek and English Tragedy: A Contrast" (1912), *Aeschylus* (1940), and "Preface to the Third Edition," *The Literature of Ancient Greece* (1956).

Meanwhile, Cornford, in his *Origin of Attic Comedy* (1914), traced the structure and content of ancient Greek comedies and discovered that "the ritual drama lying behind Comedy proves to be essentially of the same type as that in which Professor Gilbert Murray has sought the origin of Tragedy."[13] And in 1914, Murray took the next logical step, a step that assured him and his theory a lasting place in dramatic history. He applied his theory to a non-Greek tragedy, *Hamlet;* he was followed in 1916 by Harrison, who found that John the Baptist was in fact an "Eniautos-Daimon." Soon thereafter, others were detecting this same ritual form in places as diverse as a European mummers' play and a Punch-and-Judy show. This shift in subject from Greece to literature at large was one reason that Murray's theory has remained so appealing, so pervasive, and so tenacious. Theodore Gaster's words proved prophetic:

> "Frazer's reconstruction of the primitive ritual patterns may in fact be epoch-making for literature as well as anthropology; for if that pattern can indeed be detected behind the conventions of certain literary genres, the way is open for an appreciation of literary forms not merely as the product of artistic creativity or individual inventiveness but also—at least, in certain aspects—as an expression of religion, running parallel to cult.[14]

Gilbert Murray led the way in 1914; in 1957, Northrop Frye published his *Anatomy of Criticism*, in which he proposed a "metacriticism" for literature, one based on (presumed) mythic patterns among diverse literary genres.

Although the theory continues to gain wide acceptance, it is by no means without flaw.

First, the work of Frazer, on which Murray's theory depended, has been largely abandoned as a reliable account of primitive societies (although it is still revered as a landmark in historical thought). Frazer's insistence on cultural growth from a primitive "magical" system of belief to a religious one, for example, has been rejected as simply another instance of the late nineteenth century's penchant for applying evolutionary, biological principles to other, often irrelevant, fields. Frazer's account of dying and reviving gods, the year-spirits so crucial to Murray's theory, has been largely superseded; his Osiris myth, for example, is now thought to

have dealt with a succession of human kings rather than with a change of seasons. Most reappraisals of Frazer have concluded that his procedures were faulty in three ways: (1) His sources were often unreliable, because he accepted the accounts of untrained observers who often recorded what they saw only in terms of what they expected to see; (2) His evidence was drawn willy-nilly from everywhere and from every period; and (3) He assumed (and interpreted evidence in keeping with the assumption) that customs and practices are always remnants of a (hidden) recurrent pattern from the past. Thus, he often rejected an (accurate) historical explanation in favor of an obtuse mythical one. This collapse of Frazer as a credible source obviously undercut, perhaps fatally, the supposed framework of fact on which Murray constructed his theory of the origin of drama.

Second, there is absolutely no evidence in Greece of the sort of ritual described by Murray. No known dithyramb took his form of *Agon*, *Pathos*, Messenger, and so on; and no other Dionysiac ritual found in Greece took such a form. Indeed, death and rebirth in a single ritual would be most surprising, for, in Greece, the two would normally have taken place at different times of the year (representing winter and spring, respectively).

Murray himself recognized problems and alerted readers to them in his essay. For example, he noted that theophanies are often absent from individual tragedies; he explained the omission by supposing that the joyful satyr play, which customarily concluded each series of three tragedies, served as their theophany. The absent or ill-positioned *anagnorisis* (recognition) and *peripeteia* (reversal) in several plays were likewise dismissed in favor of the concluding satyr plays. Theophanies in which a hero dies "onstage" while a god flies off in glory were attributed to the "doubling of the hero into himself and his enemy" or to the year-spirit's assuming multiple forms that are only later reunited. In analyzing the plays of Sophocles, Murray resorted to phrases like "faded Theo-

FIGURE 3.5

Two interpretations of the witches scene from *Macbeth*: one an engraving by J. R. Cruikshank for a frontispiece, the other purporting to show an actual production at the Princess' Theatre. [Authors' collection.]

phany" (*Oedipus at Colonus*) and "much atrophied Messenger" (*Ajax*) and to apologies that the *Philoctetes* "is rather far from any type." Clearly, even Murray's imaginative manipulations were no match for Sophocles' plays, and so he finally conceded that "Sophocles is influenced more by the Ionic Epic and less by the Attic Sacer Ludus than are the other two tragedians."

Another problem not directly addressed by Murray is a problem, nonetheless. We know, as certainly as we know anything about Greek drama, that early tragedies (from ca. 534–ca. 500 B.C.) had only one actor. With whom did that actor have his *agon?* Contests normally require two people. Assuming for a moment that the *agon* could have been between the chorus and the actor (a bit of a stretch), what of the remaining ritual pattern? The single actor must leave the performance area in order to be "killed" out of sight of the audience (*pathos*). He returns as the messenger to announce his own death, whereupon the chorus begins its lament (*threnos*). He must leave the performance area again to reassume the identity of the hero, now slain, so that the chorus may somehow discover his body (*anagnorisis*), after which he is resurrected while the chorus's lamentations shift to

songs of joy. Murray's ritual pattern seems most difficult to apply to one-actor tragedy (the earliest form of tragedy).

And if tragedy was based on rituals of the god Dionysus, why does the god appear in so few of the tragedies, and then so peripherally?

The conclusion is inevitable: Murray's formula, when strictly applied, does not fit the largest proportion of extant Greek tragedies.

When the ritual pattern is only loosely defined and applied, however, it will fit almost anything, as William Ridgeway showed in such a devastating manner:

> On a garden lawn is a happy family, two old sparrows feeding their young; enter the lady's favourite cat; she pounces on a baby sparrow (*Peripeteia*); a short struggle (*Agon*), speedy death (*Pathos*), and the cat retires rending her victim (*Sparagmos*). All under the eyes of little Tommy, who (*Messenger*) runs to tell his mother what the naughty cat has done; meantime the parent sparrows are expressing their grief (*Threnos*) in unmistakable terms; the lady comes forth and discovers (*Anagnorisis*) the cat (*Theophany*) returning (possibly with an eye to another of the brood), her former victim lodged comfortably inside, the two now in the process of forming one body, if not one personality.[15]

Pickard-Cambridge examined these and other flaws in Murray's theory before 1930.[16] Why, then, does the theory continue to collect adherents? What are the strengths of the theory that explain its tenacity? The question is not an easy one, and in the absence of evidence, we can only speculate.

The initial reception of Murray's theory was quite enthusiastic, and thus, its early acceptance among students and scholars was immediate and widespread. The first popularity can no doubt be explained in part by the excellent reputation and pervasive influence of Frazer's *The Golden Bough*. Through the clever combination of these new anthropological discoveries with elements drawn from familiar Greek tragedies, Murray was able to capture the imagination of many theatre people as well as of classical scholars. Both groups were captivated by the theory because it provided a new prism through which to see plays, and its use promised fresh insights.

Murray's theory was a particularly inviting one, for it held out the promise of revealing an underlying unity for a vast array of previously isolated items. Like Frazer, Murray set about "to *construe* the data in universal terms." By analyzing a single play for its ritual form, a critic could compare it handily with other plays and eventually discover in them all those recurring patterns that pointed to a shared past. The neatness and elegance of the theory were almost irresistible. It offered a model against which plays could be measured—not only Greek plays, but *all* plays. And the model came equipped with its own (impressive) vocabulary. That is, the theory came with a complete set of jargon, and jargon is a powerful stimulant, for it permits users to talk among themselves in a controlled language that sets them apart. And Murray's model had yet another advantage: for those who preferred to approach plays without much thought, it offered a way of seeming to say a great deal while saying, in fact, relatively little. For example, the model could be first explained (two or three pages), then the play could be put through its paces according to the model (six or eight pages), and conclusions could be drawn about the degree to which the play did or did not closely parallel its ritual forebears (two or three pages)—just the right length for a publishable article or a term paper. Because the entire enterprise could be couched in erudite language, it would seem to have worth and significance and so to bestow worth and significance on the critic. The point is perhaps too strongly made, but it should be clear.

Once a theory's popularity is firmly established, its rejection is often very slow in coming, particularly within an academic community. Regrettably, teachers often teach what they have been taught; and writers often merely reproduce the currently accepted views. Students hear the teachers and read the texts and may, in fact, learn that Murray's theory explains the origin of tragedy. Many of these students never learn otherwise, for they never take another course in drama. For them, therefore, Murray's theory *is* the origin of Greek tragedy. Other students attend college and take classes from teaching assistants who merely teach what they were taught. And so, fifty years after Pickard-Cambridge exposed the inconsistencies in Murray's theory, many people who are teaching are still unacquainted with Pickard-Cambridge; and students continue to be taught that Greek tragedy developed out of religious rituals originally dedicated to the year-spirit Dionysus.

We would propose, then, that the theory's own appeal combines with scholarly laziness to assure its continuing popularity even in the face of demonstrated weaknesses.

William Ridgeway's Theory of the Origin of Tragedy

As early as 1904, William Ridgeway offered his theory of the origin of drama because, as he said, he had long been dissatisfied with the theories generally held. He did not agree that tragedy was the invention of the Dorians, and he ar-

FIGURE 3.6

Although the styles seem quite different, both scenes from *Julius Caesar* were designed by Lucien Jusseaume for a production in Paris in 1911. [From *Le Théâtre*.]

gued that Aristotle had never said that it was. He did not agree that tragedy developed entirely from Dionysiac worship either, and he insisted that the weight of ancient opinion supported him in his view. He did not agree that satyric drama arose in Dorian lands and developed there alongside tragedy. He attributed these erroneous beliefs to the unfortunate tendency of scholars to approach their investigation of the origins of drama "from the *a priori* standpoint of pure Aesthetics" rather than "by a rigid application of the historical and inductive method." [17]

In order to discover the real origins of drama, Ridgeway determined to solve the problem by "approaching it from the anthropological standpoint." [18] His examination of the evidence led him to suppose that the origin of tragedy could be found in rituals for the dead. Although other scholars held similar views, Ridgeway was the most persuasive advocate in English of what came to be called the *tomb theory* or the *hero-cult theory*. Although the first publication of his theory had preceded Murray's first essay by eight years, Ridgeway's theory was never so widely accepted, despite his passionate defense of it in many articles and in two books, *The Origin of Tragedy* (1910) and *The*

Dramas and Dramatic Dances of Non-European Races (1915).

Ridgeway succinctly summarized his theory in the introduction to his second book:

The present writer was led in 1904 to the conclusions that (1) Tragedy proper did not arise in the worship of the Thracian god Dionysus; but (2) that it sprang out of the indigenous worship of the dead . . . ; (3) that the cult of Dionysus was not indigenous in Sicyon but had been introduced there . . . and had been superimposed upon the cult of the old king; (4) that even if it were true that Tragedy proper arose out of the worship of Dionysus, it would no less have originated in the worship of the dead since Dionysus was regarded by the Greeks as *a hero* [1] (i.e., a man turned into a saint) as well as a god.

(His footnote cites Plutarch.) (pp. 5–6)

It should be noted that Ridgeway differed from the leading German proponent of the "hero-cult theory" in his suggestion that the original rituals for the dead were later joined by Dionysiac ceremonies. His evidence for this innovation was a single account by Herodotus (fifth century B.C. Greek historian) who related how the tyrant Cleisthenes found choruses at

Sicyon depicting the sufferings of Adrastus, a former hero, and how the tyrant introduced elements of Dionysiac worship into these ceremonies for political reasons. From this account, Ridgeway hypothesized that a similar pattern was followed throughout Attica so that the worship of local heroes was fused with that of Dionysus everywhere. By proposing a fusion between two cults, Ridgeway effected two results: he brought his theory more closely into line with the traditional views of the origin of drama (as connected with Dionysiac revels), and he provided an explanation of the two altars that seem to have existed simultaneously in several Greek theatres.

Crucial to the acceptance of Ridgeway's theory was a demonstration that rituals were regularly performed in honor of the dead. Ridgeway, therefore, presented an impressive array of data to demonstrate the existence of funeral rituals and to identify features common among them. In Greece proper, Ridgeway found one ritual for the dead at Sicyon in honor of Adrastus and another on the third day of the Anthesteria, "a very ancient festival of the dead."[19] Outside of Greece, however, he discovered and cited even more examples, from Rome at the funeral games in ancient days to the Cathedral of Seville, Spain, in 1909. Indeed, more than three hundred of the four hundred or so pages in *Dramas and Dramatic Dances* were devoted to cataloging instances of ritual dances performed (either currently or originally) in honor of the dead. The examples were taken from various periods and from the entire world, as the book's section headings suggest: Western Asia, Ancient Egypt, Hindustan, Java, Burma, Malay, Cambodia, China, Japan, the Pacific Islands, Australia, Africa, and America. Among the many festivals for the dead, Ridgeway found some recurrent ceremonies. Honoring the dead, for example, regularly involved pouring drink offerings into the tomb, often through a hole adjacent to it. Occasionally, appeasement of the dead heroes (or gods) required a sacrifice of an animal or a human, as when a military man's

horse was slain at his tomb or, less happily, when his wife was killed so that she could accompany him on his last journey. As well, at their death, heroes were often honored by various games and contests, which could take place at tombside.

In further support of his theory, Ridgeway reviewed information about Thespis, whom tradition credited with originating tragedy, and interpreted some of the accounts in terms of his theory. For example, Thespis presumably painted his face white (or used a white mask). Whereas such a mask would be wholly inappropriate for Dionysiac worship, according to Ridgeway, it would be most suitable for representing ghosts. Also, the lawmaker Solon's angry outburst at Thespis, Ridgeway explained, came about because Thespis had impiously removed the dramatic ceremonies from a shrine where they had been performed for the dead, thereby changing their purpose from religion to mere entertainment.

Finally, Ridgeway moved on to test his theory against the Greek tragedies themselves, laying particular emphasis on those of Aeschylus, the earliest writer from whom we now have plays. He searched for instances of heroes' tombs, offerings at such tombs, and lamentations for the dead, reasoning that if such scenes occurred frequently, they were remnants of early tombside rituals. In one early, one middle, and one late play by Aeschylus, Ridgeway found actions taking place at the tombs of heroes, complete with offerings and lamentations, and he discovered a similar pattern in the three Sophoclean and three Euripidean tragedies that he analyzed.[20] Figuring that ghosts would reasonably form a part of celebrations of the dead, he examined the plays for ghosts and found that they appeared with confirming regularity in the plays of all three authors. The emphasis given to sanctuary in several extant tragedies also supported his theory, Ridgeway asserted, because dead heroes remained interested in the fate of their friends and family and would intervene to aid and protect them if necessary, or so the primitive people believed, and so began the practice of seeking refuge at tombs that pursuers would fear to violate.

The tomb theory displays certain clear strengths. The subject matter of Greek tragedies, for example, is well accounted for by this theory, for the plays do depict mighty heroes deciding and acting in immutably serious ways that could well echo tombside reenactments of their lives and deeds. The overall tone of the plays, too, can be more easily connected with lamentations for the dead than with joyful revels of the sort commonly associated with the worship of Dionysus, god of wine and fertility. As well, the frequent presence of tombs, libations, and lamentations in the plays lends support. In fact, the tomb theory corresponds better with the evidence provided by the plays than does the theory proposed by Gilbert Murray, for the impersonations in tragedy are of epic heroes rather than gods, and the language is temperate and rational rather than frenetic and possessed.

The theory's major weakness is that, with the possible exception of Adrastus at Sicyon, no evidence can be found of dramatic performances at the tombs of any Greek heroes, although nondramatic funeral rites were not rare. Moreover, materials drawn from around the world are of limited, if any, value in establishing practices in Athens in the fifth or sixth century B.C., however interesting they may be in their own right.

In addition to its major flaw, however, Ridgeway's theory is rendered suspect by its reliance on several unlikely—perhaps even erroneous—renderings of original Greek texts and more than a few unwarranted conclusions. For example, the white masks of Thespis may not have been white; in any case, they must surely have been used to impersonate living as well as dead characters: nowhere is there evidence that rites for the dead were peopled only by ghosts. Also, Solon said that he was angry because Thespis was telling lies in public (acting plays?), not because he had moved performances away

FIGURE 3.7

William D. Roberts' rendering and the completed setting for Molière's *The Miser* can be compared as an aid to visualizing what the production at Charles Playhouse, Boston, in 1965, looked like. [Courtesy of Mrs. William D. Roberts.]

from a sacred shrine. And the Anthesteria may not have been a festival for the dead at all and may not have included any public *threnos*.

Despite some clear strengths, then, Ridgeway's theory remains unproved and largely unaccepted by the scholarly community.

Gerald Else's Theory of the Origin of Tragedy

The most radical modern theory of the origin of tragedy is that of Gerald Else, who has rejected the commonly held view that tragedy developed gradually out of dithyrambs (or anything else) and has insisted instead that Greek tragedy was "the product of two successive *creative acts* by two men of genius,"[21] Thespis and Aeschylus. Else does not find the tragic spirit a universal one but considers it rather a peculiarly Athenian impulse. In this respect, he differs markedly from Murray and Ridgeway, and consequently he chooses rather different sorts of evidence to support his theory.

After a few preliminary remarks, Else sets forth the basic assumptions on which he has built his theory:

1. Whatever may have happened elsewhere, in Polynesia or Peloponnese, it is Athens alone that counts.
2. The origin of tragedy was not so much a gradual, "organic," development as a sequence of two creative leaps by Thespis and Aeschylus, with certain conditioning facts precedent to each.
3. Although the two leaps were separated from each other by a considerable space of time, the second followed in direct line from the first. There is no room between them for a reversal of tragedy from gay to solemn.
4. There is no solid evidence for tragedy ever having been Dionysiac in any sense except that it was originally and regularly presented at the City Dionysia in Athens.
5. There is no reason to believe that tragedy

grew out of any kind of possession or ecstasy (*Ergriffenheit*), Dionysiac or otherwise.[22]

The research question with which Else apparently began, then, was something like "What were the factors in the societies of Thespis and Aeschylus that might have encouraged the creation of a new poetic genre?" In casting about the sixth century (the century of Thespis), Else settled on two men whose careers might explain Thespis' invention. The two were Solon and Pisastratus.

Solon was a major political leader of the early sixth century and, except for Thespis, its only literary figure. The society that he led was badly divided, in large part because of an uneven distribution of wealth and power: the nobles of Athens lived very well indeed and wielded power so that their continued good life was assured; the poor lived in wretched contrast and lacked the legal recourse that might have provided relief. Solon was elected to reconcile the angry differences between the two groups. His solution was to try to establish justice for all under the law, rather than to attempt a redistribution of wealth. An eminently practical man, Solon molded a system of government that achieved a precarious balance between freedom and responsibility, between the rights of the individual and those of society. His religious beliefs were evidently of the same hard and practical bent. His poetry spoke of a man who believed that there is order and meaning in human endeavor and that there is no need to resort to revelation or frenzy in order to comprehend the mystery and grandeur of life. As a mediator between competing factions and as a rational man in the midst of religious enthusiasms, Solon often found himself denounced by groups on all sides of a question. He was, according to Else, very close to being a solitary tragic hero of the sort later depicted in Greek tragedies.

Solon was also Athens' greatest literary figure of the century. His early poems, written in elegaic couplets, were primarily public exhortations and civic instructions; they tended to be impersonal, in keeping with the meters and traditions of elegy. Late in his career, Solon adopted both the iambic and the trochaic meters (generally associated in Greece with poems of personal revelation) to present his exhortations to the citizens, but these later works placed greater focus on the writer, for in them Solon increasingly depicted himself in relation to others of the society. The poetry was, then, at once public and personal: public, because Solon continued to treat issues of general concern and to present himself as a public figure; and personal, because he presented *himself* striving to understand competing factions, differing motivations, and conflicting claims within his social order. Else has found these later poetic utterances important for two reasons. First, a dual point of view also characterizes Greek tragedy, in that the hero is presented both as he sees himself and as the chorus sees him. Second, Solon, the century's only poet, adopted the iambic and trochaic meters, the same meters later used in Greek tragedy.

Solon likewise provided an early and clear example of public impersonation. When the Athenians passed a law that was repugnant to him, Solon donned the garb and adopted the attitude of a madman. He went into the public square and recited an original poem in which he lashed out against the law. The incident was instrumental in establishing his reputation among his countrymen. Else considered the incident significant, as well, because it showed that Solon recognized poetry as a means of airing public issues and impersonation as a vehicle for presenting such poetry.

Finally, Solon may have been instrumental in popularizing Homeric myths in Athens. Attica had relatively few local myths and legends; in this regard, it differed from other areas of Greece. About the middle of the sixth century, Solon (or perhaps a son of Pisastratus) instituted in Athens a contest for rhapsodes in which the contestants were required to recite an as-signed portion of the *Iliad* or the *Odyssesy*, each contestant reading aloud in turn. Else viewed the contest as significant for several reasons. It allowed the entire population of Athens to become familiar with the Homeric myths, and the myths then served to instruct a generation of Athenians in heroic behavior. As well, the contest changed the nature of epic art from a dependence primarily on oral composition and delivery to a dependence on the delivery of a fixed text. Also, as the texts selected for delivery were those of Homer, they became by implication the "best," the models against which other mythic accounts were to be measured. The result was, according to Else, that "Attica suddenly became *the* repository of the Homeric heritage" in Greece. With Homer as the city's "core curriculum," the citizenry became both more educated and more united than ever before.[23]

The contributions of Pisastratus were of a rather different order. Whereas Solon provided intellectual, literary, and legal leadership, Pisastratus was primarily an organizer and administrator. It was he who consolidated many of the gains that Solon had precariously established. Pisastratus helped make Athens the center of Greece through careful foreign alliances, domestic programs, and religious reforms. Through his aggressive patronage, he caused public buildings to be erected and minor arts, like vase painting, to flourish. He strove to develop Athens and, as a part of that process, to develop Athenian art and artists. To this end, he embellished the festival that contained the rhapsodes' contest and established another major festival, the Great (or City) Dionysia, in honor of the popular god Dionysus. From the outset, tragedy was a central feature of this festival; only later did dithyrambs, satyr plays, and comedies become a part of it. In light of this evidence, Else has posed a provocative question: "Is it too much to suggest that if tragedy was not created for the Dionysia, the Dionysia was created for it; that Pisastratus established his new festival as a frame for a new kind

FIGURE 3.8

From sketches made by Mahelot in the early seventeenth century, Professor Lawrenson has tried to reconstruct the setting for the original production of *Pyrame*. [Drawing from Petit de Julleville; production photograph by Ivor Dykes courtesy of Lawrenson and *Theatre Survey*, in which it appeared.]

of poetry which he thought deserved such a setting?"[24]

The society of Solon and Pisastratus was also the society of Thespis, first winner of the tragic contest at the City Dionysia. His great creative act, according to Else, was the bringing together of three elements: an epic hero, impersonation, and iambic verse. The result was *tragôidia*, a form distinguishable from tragic drama (Aeschylus' contribution) by its distinctly undramatic nature. It was a form that allowed little conflict and little change in an initial situation. *Tragôidia* consisted of a prologue and set speech (delivered by an actor) and a choral presentation. On this point, there is general scholarly agreement.

But Else has further asserted that Thespis invented both the role of the actor and that of the chorus; that is, Thespis did not merely adjust an earlier choral form and make it into *tragôidia*. On this point, Else has departed radically from earlier views, and so his argument needs to be reviewed.

First, Else appealed to the evidence of language in two instances. He showed that the usual derivation of *tragôidia* from the Greek for "goat song" would be inconsistent with the derivation of similar words in Greek. In order to be consistent with other derivations, *tragôidia* must have been derived from an intermediate form, *tragôidos*, or "goat singer" ("goat bard"). The point is significant, for it means that the word for the first poet–actor preceded the word for the form itself, a fact that, if true, would imply the early primacy of actor over chorus. As well, Else argued that the word *hypocrites* ("answerer") was adopted only after the second and third actor were added to Greek tragedy and that it applied only to them, the word *tragôidos* being used to refer to the first actor–poet. Only after the poet ceased to act in his own works was the word *hypocrites* applied to the protagonist (the leading or first actor) as well as to the deuteragonist (second actor) and the tritagonist (third actor). The interpretation is important because, if true, the word *hypocrites* might signal that the two lesser actors answered the protagonist rather than that the protagonist answered the chorus, as in the traditional view.

Second, Else noted that from the outset the actor, but not the chorus, received a prize for the best performance in tragedy, suggesting again that the actor–author rather than the chorus was the central feature of the new form.

Third, Else discovered little or no conflict and change in early Aeschylean tragedy and so concluded that *tragôidia* was not really a tragic drama but was rather a form in which the actor and the chorus worked in tandem, with the actor's set speeches leading and directing the responses of the chorus. That the actor led the choral responses in Aeschylean tragedy suggests that the same was true in *tragôidia*; if true, the actor was at least as important as the chorus from the outset, and so Thespis, in creating *tragôidia*, did not merely alter in a minor way a former choral presentation (like dithyramb).

Fourth, Else concluded that the subject of *tragôidia* was from the beginning the solitary (epic) hero; it was his *pathos* (his failure and suffering) that was depicted. Traditional notions that the chorus was primary came from two mistaken interpretations of evidence, according to Else: first, that tragedy developed out of dithyrambs; and second, that Aeschylus' play *The Suppliants* was a throwback, an example of an earlier, primitive, Thespian tragedy (the play was once thought to be our earliest surviving tragedy). In fact, except for *The Suppliants*, all Aeschylean tragedies focus on the hero (his discoveries, decisions, and actions) rather than on the chorus. Because *The Suppliants* is now known to be a later play, its form (with the central chorus) no longer offers compelling evidence for the early centrality of the chorus in Greek tragedy. From these two facts, Else concluded that heroes (not choruses) were the central subjects of *tragôidia*.

And finally, Else proposed that Thespis' very name may have derived from *thespis aoidê* or *thespis aoidos,* an expression found twice in the *Odyssey* and translated as "divine song" or "divine singer." If the derivation is correct, a strong connection is established between Thespis and the art of epic, a connection that would strengthen the view that he would have made the epic hero rather than the chorus the central feature of his *tragôidia*, and that the epic rather than the dithyramb was an important precursor of tragedy.

Although the hero's *pathos* was the primary focus of *tragôidia*, the role that Thespis created for the chorus was nonetheless important, Else argued. Through the chorus, the audience received its second view of the hero. Through the chorus, too, the audience was linked to the hero in a very special way. Because the chorus usually represented either citizens or followers of the hero, it represented the view of the common people; that is, it represented the view of the audience. Else has suggested that Thespis, like Solon, consciously sought a means of unifying Athens: "Tragedy represented, in effect, the beginning of a new spiritual unification of Attica."[25] It was the power and the purpose of the new poetic form *tragôidia* that caused Pisastratus to provide it with a home: "He established it as the center and crown of his new festival for all Athenians, the Dionysia."[26]

For the first thirty years, from the time of Thespis until the coming of Aeschylus, *tragôidia* was the presentation of a single hero's situation as seen both through the eyes of the hero and through the eyes of the chorus. Because neither change nor conflict was easily accommodated in this form, Thespis's *tragôidia* was not, strictly speaking, tragic drama. This second creative leap belonged to Aeschylus, according to Else.

Aeschylean Athens differed from that of Thespis, Solon, and Pisastratus in several ways. Athens had become a democracy and had risen to a position of leadership among the Greek city states. Athens had survived—and indeed had risen to glory as a result of—the Persian Wars, during which its entire citizenry had behaved with such courage and valor at Marathon and Salamis that it had become an inspiration to the other Greek states. At the City Dionysia, contests for tragedy had been joined by those for dithyrambic choruses, and satyr plays were now given alongside each group of three tragedies, perhaps in response to complaints from the populace that the City Dionysia had "nothing to do with Dionysus." Aeschylus, then, found the society changed, but *tragôidia* was essentially unchanged since Thespis: it was still, according to Else, the presentation of the hero's *pathos* and a choral lamentation arising from it.

Aeschylus initiated a number of changes, but the decisive one was to introduce change into the hero's situation by providing a series of episodes leading up to and away from his decision and resulting *pathos*. In envisioning a causal universe for his tragedies, Aeschylus required (and so added) a second actor, an innovation that also opened the way for increasing conflict and contrast within the plays. *Tragôidia* thus became tragic drama of the sort that we would recognize, according to Else.

To accommodate his increasingly complex vision, Aeschylus experimented with writing connected trilogies, three plays on a related subject to be performed on the same day. In adopting the trilogic form, Aeschylus broadened the action of the play to include several generations and to unfold in several places. His trilogies as well often involved rather radical reinterpretations of Homeric myths so that their ultimate conclusion was cautiously optimistic. As the conception increased in complexity, so did the sureness and boldness of the staging that Aeschylus adopted: he introduced new kinds of dances for the chorus and a new manner of scenic painting. Else has suggested that Aeschylus' shift from tragic situation to tragic action was in keeping with the Athenian view, seen earlier in Solon, that a person's decisions and actions have consequences: the world operates according to cause and effect, even when the pattern remains hidden to the human intellect.

In seeking a cultural stimulus for this shift from tragic situation to tragic action in Aeschylus, Else settled on the Persian Wars. Aeschylus was impelled to introduce his insight into tragedy because of experiences that he and his countrymen had shared. The Persian Wars began as a national catastrophe and ended as a national triumph because of decisions that the citizens of Athens made and because of actions that they took in keeping with those decisions. The heroic behavior of even the common peo-

ple might be attributed, according to Else, to their familiarity with the vision of epic heroes granted them through regular public instruction by the rhapsodes. In the war they found a stimulus sufficient to revitalize the heroic impulse of the whole people. Because the Athenians as a people had chosen to fight and because they won, they emerged as the moral leaders of Greece. Their leadership gave to Aeschylus a deep conviction of the rightness of a universe marked by suffering. He, like Solon before him, saw "the connection between men's choices and their fates; for as they chose, so they fared."[27] And indeed, as Else suggested, the wars seem to have exerted a remarkable influence on Aeschylus, for when he wrote his own epitaph, he said nothing at all about his role as poet and teacher of his people. He spoke instead of his role in the war: "Aeschylus, Euphorion's son, Athenian, lies in this tomb, perished in wheat-bearing Gela. Of his valor and fair fame the sacred grove of Marathon can tell, and the long-haired Persian who learned to know it there."[28] And with this epitaph, Else closed *The Origin and Early Form of Greek Tragedy*.

Else's theory eliminates a number of problems encountered in the proposals of Murray, Ridgeway, and even Aristotle. In Else's account, tragedy did not arise out of some presumed ritual forebear, of which no trace has thus far been found in Greece. The theory avoids the difficulty posed by a Dionysiac origin that supposes an abrupt shift in tone from revelry to solemnity. It does not depend on any presumed evolutionary development of an art form, evolution being clearly demonstrable in biological systems but being absolutely without an evidentiary base in art. And it does not suggest some underlying pattern for tragedies that (on analysis) the extant tragedies fail to display.

In addition to avoiding certain problems of prior theories, Else's offers appealing features of its own. It accounts well for both the tone and the subject matter of the extant tragedies. It offers a plausible reason for the centrality of the tragic hero rather than the chorus in the over-

FIGURE 3.9

Both illustrations show artists' version of Junius Brutus Booth as Richard III. Does the costume appear to be the same? Is it reasonable to assume that Booth wore different costumes for this role? [From *Century*.]

whelming majority of extant tragedies. It suggests why tragedy developed where and when it did—in Athens of the fifth century B.C. rather than in Egypt or Sparta earlier or later. Finally, for persons who prefer that view of history that stresses the importance of individual decision and action, Else's theory makes human agency the cause of tragedy.

However, the theory is not without problems. It is, for example, a marked departure from any view of origins that has come down to us from antiquity, including that of Aristotle (on which most later accounts doubtless depend), and it is radically different from the dominant

views of other nineteenth- and twentieth-century scholars. Moreover, the theory's applicability is highly restricted. Unlike Murray's and Ridgeway's, for example, it offers no guidance about how drama might have arisen in other cultures (China, Japan, Europe during the Middle Ages, and so on), and it offers no ready formula through which to read and understand tragedies.

Finally, it fails to *explain* much of anything. At base, it is reducible to the fact that tragedy is an art that depends on a genius for its creation. Doubtless, a careful study of virtually any society could reveal elements that might induce an art to flower. The crucial test is whether the art *did* flower. If it did, according to this view, a genius was at work. The theory, then, leaves us either attempting to account for human genius or being satisfied to stop short of an explanation of the origins of tragedy.

Conclusions

The four theories offer rather different versions of what happened. Part of the difference in the accounts can be attributed to the questions that the scholars posed for themselves. Although each asked, in a general way, "What is the origin of drama (or tragedy)?" each formulated his precise question rather differently. Aristotle, to the degree that he was interested in origins at all, seemed concerned primarily with which features in human nature led to art and which Greeks should receive credit for inventing the forms later called comedy and tragedy. Murray and Ridgeway seemed to ask, "What is the origin of tragedy *as it appears whenever and wherever it appears?*" Unlike Aristotle, these scholars knew that plays called tragedies existed outside of the fifth century B.C. and in countries far distant from Greece. They apparently sought an explanation of origins broad enough to encompass all dramas that they knew. Both Englishmen, as well, seemed to embrace an unstated assumption that human societies develop in recognizable ways and that they pass through discernible stages. Else's assumptions, and therefore his questions, were markedly different. His major question might be phrased, "What was the origin of *Athenian tragedy* in the sixth century B.C.?" Unlike Aristotle, Else knew more than Greek dramas, but unlike Murray and Ridgeway, he considered Athenian tragedy unique.

With such different research questions, the scholars understandably relied on different kinds of evidence to arrive at their answers. Because Murray and Ridgeway conceived of tragedy in universal terms, they felt free to gather evidence from various times and places, and because they believed that societies went through discernible stages, they felt free to combine data from different places and periods, as long as the stages of social development appeared roughly comparable. Else, on the other hand, considered Athenian tragedy unique, and so he admitted only such evidence as came from Athens at the time of its first dramas.

The degree of correspondence between evidence and explanation also varies among the four theories. Murray lacked a crucial piece of evidence needed to support his explanation—the ancient ritual out of which tragedy presumably grew and took its form; moreover, his theory fails to account well for the subject matter and tone of the extant Greek tragedies. Ridgeway's theory accounts fairly well for the subject and tone of the tragedies but is dependent on funeral rituals, evidence of which in Athens is almost entirely lacking. Both theorists marshalled impressive evidence that rituals of various kinds existed in Greece (and throughout the world); neither, however, was able to present the ritual that became drama or to identify the crucial step that turned a ritual (a religious ceremony) into a drama (a self-conscious piece of art). Else lacked any ancient corroboration for his views of origin and indeed had to jettison even Aristotle's account if his own theory was to be accepted. To undercut Aristotle is particularly troubling because of his early date and his acceptance by other ancient writers. (Many later writers probably drew from Aristotle in formulating their own accounts.) If so reputable and widely accepted a source as Aristotle is erroneous in this instance, on what source can theories of origin be confidently built? The implications of this question are necessarily unsettling.

Just as the questions posed and the evidence used in constructing the four theories differ, so too do the assumptions that apparently guided the studies. These assumptions, not surprisingly, seem to reflect the historical circumstances of the theorists themselves. The Englishmen Murray and Ridgeway wrote at the beginning of this century, when Darwin's theory of biological evolution had been diluted, adapted, and extended to fields as diverse as sociology and art, and when Frazer's massive work was at the height of its popularity. At the time, societies were thought by many to evolve from the simple to the complex, even as art was presumed to evolve from ritual to drama. Else, writing in the 1960s in Chicago, subscribed to views then popular among the Neo-Aristotelians, views that emphasized the importance of form and structure, of wholeness, of thingness, and of individuality.

The once-popular assumptions of Frazer, Murray, and Ridgeway have been largely discredited; the assumptions of Else were never so popular and, perhaps for this reason, have endured largely unchallenged. Nonetheless, many theatre scholars continue to prefer the theories of the ritualists (some versions of which continued to be published in the 1960s and 1970s), perhaps because they seem to explain more, unifying a wide range of plays and binding drama firmly to universal human needs as expressed in religious experiences of various kinds.

Despite flaws and gaps in the theories themselves, the theorists (Aristotle excluded, and rather different principles may be operating there) have usually been careful to expose their assumptions, to present their evidence for inspection, and to point to areas of controversy or inconsistency. Regrettably, as the theories have become assimilated by others and altered and reproduced in various essays and textbooks, the careful explanations and accompanying scholarly apparatus have too often disappeared. Too many accounts of the origins of drama printed since 1960 fail to suggest that they are offering the reader *theory* rather than *fact*. Somewhere, the important distinction between what is known and what is surmised has been lost, and the carefully formulated ideas of the original scholars have come to rest in "dreadful

caricature," to borrow again the expression of Clark. For example, an account first offered in the 1920s but reprinted as late as 1963 says that "Dionysus . . . is father of full-fledged tragedy and comedy as well as the more directly appropriate Satyr-play." A textbook published in 1962 analyzes a play and finds that it "contains all the elements of the basic ritual which produced the drama in Greece." A German textbook that was translated into English for distribution in the United States in 1972 proclaims that one of the two sources of tragedy was "the fertility rites of dancing satyrs" and "Dionysus, the incarnation of drunkeness and frenzy . . . the wild spirit of contrast . . . the ecstatic contradiction of bliss and horror . . . [whose] double nature . . . found elementary expression in Greek tragedy." And a scholarly book of essays published the same year begins:

> To survey the history of the theatre from that early moment when the choric dithyramb became part of the City Dionysia at Athens in the sixth century B.C., down to the last quarter of the twentieth century in what is still loosely thought of as the Christian era . . . is to see basically a straight line of development.[29]

On what evidence, finally, are such declarations based? Where is the qualifier in the first account that will alert the reader to the possibility that Dionysus was *not* the father of tragedy? What is the "basic ritual" referred to in the second account, and where in Greece has such a ritual been discovered? Do we in fact *know* that tragedy arose from dancing satyrs, as the third account asserts? And what is elementary about the expression of Greek tragedy, an art whose maturity has dazzled critics through the ages? In the fourth account, is this choric dithyramb the one that was introduced at the City Dionysia some thirty years *after* tragedy appeared? If not, which dithyramb is meant? And what straight line of development can be drawn from Greek tragedy to *Everyman* and thence to *Endgame*?

Readers and writers have an obligation to

FIGURE 3.10

Interpretations often depart considerably from the truth in order to make polemic points. Compare the portrait of the Catholic Mme. de Maintenon and a Protestant caricature of her in the late seventeenth century. [From Bourgeois.]

confront historical accounts with care and skepticism. Remembering the nature of history and the role of the historian, both should read and study with several questions firmly in mind. In constructing history from its framework of facts, have the authors taken care in their selection and use of evidence? Have they assessed it for authenticity and reliability, for the exact meaning of the words included in it, and for the preferences and purposes of those transmitting it? Does the resulting account depend primarily on facts or inferences, and if inferences, are they reasonable? Are they sufficient? Are the biases of the author discoverable, and have these biases intruded into the use of evidence or the drawing of inference? Is the account carefully written so as to avoid distortion through thoughtlessness or abbreviation?

To acknowledge the existence of conflict and uncertainty is to move toward maturity as a thinker and a scholar. While we examine the history of Western theatre as an artistic and social institution, let us remain alert to its complexities and ambiguities, its richness and diversity, and let us remain alert as well to the scholarly controversies (like those surrounding origins) that may be raised and examined throughout the history of our art.

ENDNOTES

1. All translations of Aristotle, unless otherwise attributed, are those of S. H. Butcher, *Aristotle's* *Theory of Poetry and Fine Art,* 4th ed. (London: Macmillan, 1923). This quotation is from p. 7.

2. For this analysis we are heavily indebted to A. W. Pickard-Cambridge, *Dithyramb, Tragedy, and Comedy* (Oxford: Clarendon Press, 1927), pp. 122–125.

3. Gerald F. Else, *The Origin and Early Form of Greek Tragedy* (Cambridge, Mass.: Harvard University Press, 1965), p. 13.

4. Pickard-Cambridge, p. 124.

5. Else, p. 16.

6. Else, pp. 25–26, 17–18.

7. Lionel Trilling, *Beyond Culture* (New York: Viking Press, 1965), p. 14.

8. James G. Frazer, *The Golden Bough*, 3rd ed. (London: Macmillan, 1911), Vol. 1, p. xxv.

9. John B. Vickery, *The Literary Impact of The Golden Bough* (Princeton, N.J.: Princeton University Press, 1973), p. 36. We are indebted to Vickery for many of the ideas presented in this section.

10. Theodor H. Gaster, "Editor's Foreword," *The New Golden Bough* (Garden City, N.Y.: Doubleday, 1961), p. xvi.

11. Gilbert Murray, "Excursus on the Ritual Forms Preserved in Greek Tragedy," in Jane Ellen Harrison, *Themis*, 2nd ed. (New York: World Publishing, 1927), p. 341. See Bibliography, Part II, for full citation on Cornford.

12. Murray, pp. 343–344.

13. As cited by William Ridgeway, *The Dramas and Dramatic Dances of Non-European Races* (Cambridge: Cambridge University Press, 1915; reprinted, New York: Benjamin Blom, 1964), p. 63.

14. Gaster, "Additional Notes," *The New Golden Bough*, p. 222.

15. Ridgeway, pp. 60–61.

16. Pickard-Cambridge, pp. 185–208, provided many of the ideas that appear in our discussion.

17. Ridgeway, p. 1.

18. William Ridgeway, *The Origin of Tragedy* (Cambridge: Cambridge University Press, 1910; reprinted, New York: Benjamin Blom, 1966), p. vii.

19. Ridgeway, *Dramas*, p. 10.

20. Erroneously, Ridgeway considered *The Suppliants* the earliest extant play. A papyrus unearthed about mid-century dates it after 467 B.C., making *The Persians* (472 B.C.) the earliest extant tragedy.

21. Else, p. 2.

22. Else, p. 7.

23. Else, p. 47.

24. Else, p. 49.

25. Else, p. 76.

26. Else, p. 77.

27. Else, p. 102.

28. Epitaph as translated and cited by Else, p. 102. Aeschylus' authorship has not been established with certainty.

29. In order, these quotations can be found in Sheldon Cheney, *The Theatre: Three Thousand Years of Drama, Acting, and Stagecraft*, rev. ed. (New York: David McKay, 1929; reprinted 1963), p. 33; E. J. Burton *The Student's Guide to World Theatre* (London: Herbert Jenkins, 1962), p. 44; Margaret Berthold, *A History of World Theatre*, trans. Edith Simmons (New York: Frederick Ungar, 1972), p. 128; and R. G. Collins, "Introduction," *From an Ancient to a Modern Theatre* (Winnipeg: University of Manitoba Press, 1972), p. vii.

BIBLIOGRAPHY
Part One

Barzun, Jacques. *Clio and the Doctors.* Chicago: University of Chicago Press, 1974.

———, and Graff, Henry F. *The Modern Researcher,* 3rd ed. New York: Harcourt Brace Jovanovich, 1977.

Brockett, Oscar G. "Research in Theatre History." *Educational Theatre Journal* 19 (June 1967): 267–275.

Brown, Ivor John Carnegie. *The First Player: The Origin of Drama.* New York: William Morrow, 1928.

Butcher, S. H. *Aristotle's Theory of Poetry and Fine Art,* 3rd ed. London: Macmillan, 1902.

Clark, G. Kitson. *The Critical Historian.* New York: Basic Books, 1967.

Eisenstein, Elizabeth L. *The Printing Press as an Agent of Change,* 2 vols. Cambridge: Cambridge University Press, 1979.

Else, Gerald F. *The Origin and Early Form of Greek Tragedy.* Cambridge, Mass.: Harvard University Press, 1965.

Frazer, Sir James G. *The Golden Bough,* 3rd ed. London: Macmillan, 1911.

Gaster, Theodor Herzl. *Thespis: Ritual, Myth and Drama in the Ancient Near East.* New York: Schuman, 1950.

Hexter, J. H. *Doing History.* Bloomington: Indiana University Press, 1971.

———. *The History Primer.* London: Penguin, 1972.

———. *Reappraisals in History,* 2nd ed. Chicago: University of Chicago Press, 1979.

Huizinga, Johan. *Homo Ludens: A Study of the Play Element in Culture.* Boston: Beacon Press, 1955.

Hunningher, Ben. *The Origin of the Theatre: An Essay.* New York: Hill and Wang, 1961.

Kirby, E. T. *Ur-Drama: The Origins of Theatre.* New York: New York University Press, 1975.

Leff, Gordon. *History and Social Theory.* University: University of Alabama Press, 1969.

Levi-Strauss, Claude. *The Savage Mind.* Chicago: University of Chicago Press, 1966.

———. *Myth and Meaning.* New York: Schocken, 1979.

Murray, Gilbert. "Excursus on the Ritual Forms Preserved in Greek Tragedy," in *Themis,* by Jane Ellen Harrison. New York: World Publishing, 1912.

Pickard-Cambridge, Arthur W. *Dithyramb, Tragedy, and Comedy.* Oxford: Clarendon Press, 1927.

Ridgeway, William. *The Dramas and Dramatic Dances of Non-European Races.* 1915; rpt. New York: Benjamin Blom, 1964.

———. *The Origin of Tragedy.* 1910; rpt. New York: Benjamin Blom, 1966.

Shafer, Robert Jones. *A Guide to Historical Method,* rev. ed. Homewood, Ill.: Dorsey, 1974.

Stephens, Lester D. *Probing the Past: A Guide to the Study and Teaching of History.* Boston: Allyn and Bacon, 1974.

Trilling, Lionel. *Beyond Culture.* New York: Viking Press, 1965.

Vickery, John B. *The Literary Impact of The Golden Bough.* Princeton, N.J.: Princeton University Press, 1973.

Winks, Robin W. *The Historian as Detective.* New York: Harper & Row, 1968.

part two

The Classical Facade Stage

PART TWO

Figures in front of a neutral background are shared by sculpted figures on a pediment, top (Temple of Zeus, from Colignon); painted figures on a vase, middle (from Colignon); and comic actors on a facade stage, bottom (Phlyakes vase, from Weiseler.)

4

Greek Theatre, 534 B.C.–ca. A.D. 476

The birthplace of Western drama was Athens,

which, within two centuries and a half, gave birth to Solon, Pisastratus, Themistocles, Aristeides and Pericles among statesmen, to Aeschylus, Sophocles, Euripides, Aristophanes and Menander among dramatists, to Thucydides, the most impressive of all historians, and to Demosthenes, the most impressive of orators, to Mnesicles and Ictinus, architects of the Acropolis, and to Phidias and Praxiteles the sculptors, to Phormio, one of the most brilliant naval commanders, to Socrates and to Plato. . . . During the same period she beat off Persia, with the sole aid of 1,000 Plataeans, at Marathon; did more than the rest of Greece together to win the still more critical victory at Salamis; and built up the only truly Greek empire that ever existed. For a considerable part of this period the exquisitely designed and painted Athenian vases were sought and prized all over the Mediterranean and in Central Europe, and—perhaps the most remarkable thing of all—the popular entertainment, that which corresponds to our cinema, was the loftiest and most uncompromising drama which has ever existed.[1]

Where and what was this Athens that gave so much to Western civilization? In the southeastern section of what is now called Greece lies the peninsula of Attica, whose land size (approximately a thousand square miles) makes it a bit smaller than the state of Rhode Island. Attica, like other regions in Greece, offered great variety—deep valleys and craggy mountains,

fertile plains and wooded slopes—but Attica was more fortunate than most, for it had an unusually mild climate, an easy access to the sea, and a source of wealth: a silver mine at Laurium (see Figure 4.1).

Tradition has it that Theseus, finding Attica's twelve towns weakened by internal strife, persuaded them to form a single political unit with offices at Athens—the *polis*. Although the role played by the legendary Theseus in organizing Attica is unclear, it is certain that, by the time recorded history began, Athens was Attica's political and cultural center as well as its largest town, with a population of about 100,000; and all people who lived in Attica were henceforth called Athenians. Its benign climate permitted large civic events to be held out of doors throughout most of the year and offered an easier life for its people than did the rugged mountain areas to the north. With its own port (Peiraeus), Athens was an early leader in sea travel and trading, olives and pottery being primary exports. Its silver mine provided unexpected wealth, out of which public works and military expenditions could be financed (see Figure 4.2).

Across the Aegean sea from Attica (see Figure 4.3) was Ionia, a land perhaps settled originally by Athenians fleeing from invasion. The Athenians and the Ionians shared a common language, and the ties between the two peoples were strong and lasting.

Rivaling Athens and her allies were the Greeks of the Peloponnese—the Dorians—whose major *polis* was Sparta. As a result of re-

FIGURE 4.1
Map of Attica.

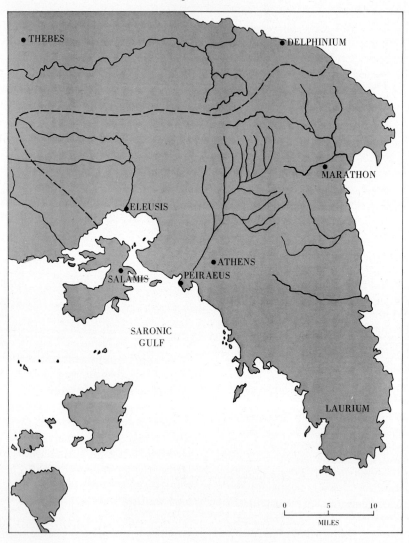

forms attributed to Lycurgus, Sparta early became the leader among Greek *poleis*, perhaps because of its rigidly organized society, which stressed self-discipline, military preparedness, and service to the society. Its citizens were trained to be soldiers, and citizens formed an elite minority within their own *polis*, the majority of whose residents were women, minors, or serfs to the Spartan community at large. In the sixth century B.C., while Athens was still only a second- or third-rate *polis*, Sparta was already an acknowledged leader: her artistic competitions attracted poets from overseas; her choric dances (and accompanying music in the "Doric mode") were famous for their "manliness"; the Olympic games that she administered created the first Panhellenic center; and her Spartan alliance served as a model for coalitions among other Greek *poleis*.

In addition to Athens and Sparta, there

FIGURE 4.2
Map of Athens and Peiraeus.

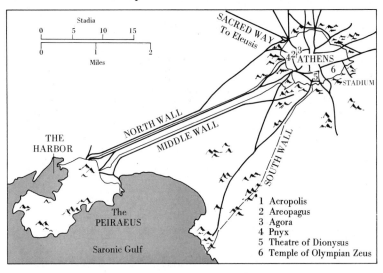

1 Acropolis
2 Areopagus
3 Agora
4 Pnyx
5 Theatre of Dionysus
6 Temple of Olympian Zeus

FIGURE 4.3
Map of the Greek world.

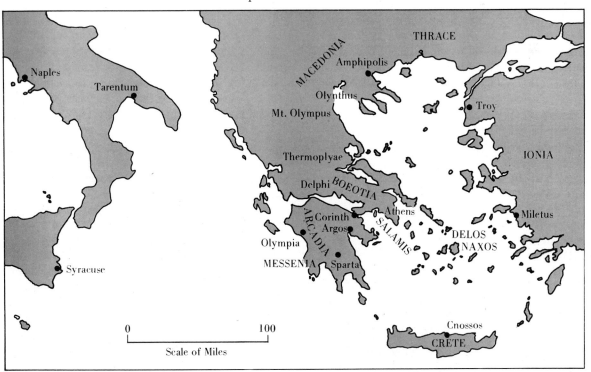

FIGURE 4.4

Time line: Major periods of Greek theatre.

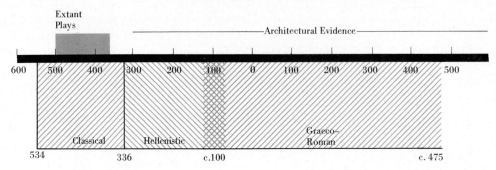

were in Greece a number of other important and independent cities, like Thebes (the leading center of Boeotia, to the north of Athens), Delphi (home of the famous and influential oracle, north of Thebes), and Corinth (a commercial center about midway between Athens and Sparta). So long as the several *poleis* were small and independent, so long as they did not need to encroach on one another's territories because of population expansion or commercial requirements, they were able to coexist peacefully.

Until the start of the sixth century, several Greek *poleis* overshadowed Athens; by the start of the fifth century, in part because of the reforms of Solon and Pisastratus, Athens was their equal, a power to be reckoned with. As Athens flourished, so did that peculiarly Athenian institution, the drama. When Athens changed politically, so did many of its institutions, including drama and theatre. Thus, it has been customary to divide Greek theatre and drama into the same three major periods as its political and social history: the Classical (534 B.C.–336 B.C.), the Hellenistic (336 B.C.–ca. 150 B.C.), and the Graeco-Roman (ca. 150 B.C.–ca. A.D. 476).

Each of the periods will be treated in turn, but it is well to note at the outset that Greek theatre and drama existed for over a thousand years; no generalizations could possibly cover such a span. Also, the Classical period was only half as long as the Graeco-Roman, yet most histories (for perfectly good reasons) emphasize the

Classical Period and exclude, or treat summarily, the Graeco-Roman period. Finally, all but one of our extant plays comes from a brief period *within* the Classical (ca. 472–388), yet almost all of our architectural evidence comes from the *later* two periods (see Figure 4.4).

The Classical Period (534 B.C.–336 B.C.)

By the time the fifth century began in Athens, the social reforms made by Solon and Pisastratus had been carried yet another step in the direction of democracy. The power of ancient noble families had been further reduced when old political units (based on family and clan) were replaced with new ones contrived to ensure that a cross section of Attica's population would be represented in each *tribe*, as the new units were called. This reorganization promoted a sense of unity within Attica by two means: first, it discouraged rivalries between urban and rural interests, because both interests were represented in each of the ten tribes; and second, because the citizens now voted by tribe, fought by tribe, and competed by tribe, loyalty to the old family and clan was undermined and finally replaced by loyalty to the tribe—which included citizens from throughout Attica. Also, the reorganization increased the importance of Athens within Attica, for in this city all discussion, debate, and voting took place; obviously, only citizens living in or near the city could easily participate in the democratic process through which decisions were made.

As earlier restrictions relating to birth and wealth were relaxed, more men became eligible to participate in government. (Women, youths, and slaves were not citizens.) An elected Council of Five Hundred (fifty from each of the ten tribes) was the final administrative authority; it negotiated with other *poleis,* managed finances, and proposed legislation. All major decisions, however, were reserved for the Assembly, membership in which was open to all citizens. Only the Assembly, for example, could declare war or pass laws. Thus, every Athenian citizen could vote on all matters of policy and could elect those he wished to administer the policies for him.

The citizens were the government; their opinions and decisions were translated quickly and directly into action. If they decided to go to war, for example, they were the soldiers, for Athens had no standing army and no permanent generals. Athens had no special class of lawyers. If a citizen had a complaint, he argued his own case in court; if a complaint was brought against him, he defended himself in court; he was called regularly to judge the pleas of others. When choral contests were scheduled, some citizens formed the choruses, others formed the audience, and still others were the judges, for Athens had no separate class of actors or dancers or critics. When money was needed, citizens provided it, according to their capacities and under clear and published safeguards. In short, the existence of the Athenian *polis* depended on the active participation of interested and competent citizens, who were amateurs rather than specialists in their many activities.

Because of the importance of participation in government and the extremely public nature of a citizen's life, speaking and listening skills were greatly prized by the society. Votes depended on the persuasive oral presentation of ideas. Decisions of war and peace resulted from open discussion and debate of the issues. The protection of the law depended on oral attacks and oral defenses. Education rested more on things heard and discussed than on things read. Although writing was known and records were kept (often on stone), books were rare, for each one had to be handwritten. The culture of Athens was an oral, not a print, culture.

Because communication depended primarily on people talking face to face, the transmission and dissemination of ideas were both relatively restricted and relatively slow: restricted to persons within hearing distance, and slow because time was needed for people to travel and tell others about new ideas. Change was slow. Most citizens clung to traditional values and views long after questions were raised by a few. The old ways thrived among most people even after alternative, often better, ways were discovered by a few.

Conservativism was also encouraged by the fact that Athens was still, at the beginning of the fifth century, more rural than urban: its population, modest by modern standards, lived more in the countryside than in the city. Wealth was still measured in terms of land rather than coin (although coin was used). Most citizens were still farmers, growing not only food for themselves, but olives and grapes for export. The farmer's home and family were generally self-sustaining, with clothing and tools being manufactured on the farm where they were needed. Although in the city some specialized craftsmen were at work (e.g., the potter, the smith, and the cobbler), in the country the single family and farm prospered according to the talent and the hard work of the people who lived there.

Although a careful chronicling of this two-hundred-year period is outside the scope of this book, a summary of the major events will be helpful in grounding the theatre and drama in the period.

The rivalry between Athens and Sparta that had marred much of the sixth century was temporarily interrupted when the threat of a Persian invasion united most Greek *poleis* under Spartan leadership. Athens challenged Sparta for leadership, however, when, at the battles of Marathon (490) and Salamis (480), Athenian courage and wit brought victories against unlikely odds. With the Persian threat contained, the *poleis* lost their reason for unity, and the hostile camps formed again: Athens (a sea power) central to one, Sparta (a land power) central to the other.

At about mid-century, a leader of rare power and vision arose in Athens—Pericles (fl. 469–429)—under whose guidance Athens increased her strength at sea and moved to form a vast empire. Athens soon became a city of international importance, a city of trade and learning to which all members of the empire came in order to pay tribute. Athens constructed new public buildings and statuary and painted them brightly, a declaration of civic pride. However, the expanding influence and growing arrogance of Athens soon produced dissatisfaction among the empire's member states, which sought and found support for their disaffection among the Spartans. In two Peloponnesian Wars (460–446 and 431–404), the Athenian Empire was crushed, Attica sacked, and Athens' fortifications dismantled. The city became subject to the rule of Sparta.

But Sparta as well as Athens had been weakened and corrupted by the long struggle; therefore, the Greek *poleis* (including Athens) were soon jockeying again for positions of power. Self-interest and cynicism marked the foreign policies of them all. Although Athens briefly prospered again as the head of an alliance (377–ca. 357), internal discord and external pressures finally combined to destroy both her alliance and her sea power. At a crucial moment, neither Athens nor Sparta could exert the leadership needed to resist encroachments into Greek territories from Macedonia. And so, when Philip of Macedon died and Alexander (later, the Great) acceded to power, his descent into Greece (336) resulted in his election as "General of the Greeks." The Classical Age was at an end; the Hellenistic Age had begun (see Figure 4.5).

Athens at the end of the Classical period was a very different society from the one at its opening. From a small *polis*, it had grown to a giant empire. Its rural population had become urban, and its agricultural base had been transformed into a commercial one with coin, rather than land, as its measure of wealth. The influence of the upper classes continued to wane as that of the middle and lower classes grew. Proportionately fewer people gave support to the *polis* as more received support from it. Self-sufficiency of farm and *polis* had given way to in-

FIGURE 4.5

Time line: Major periods of Greek theatre related to political events.

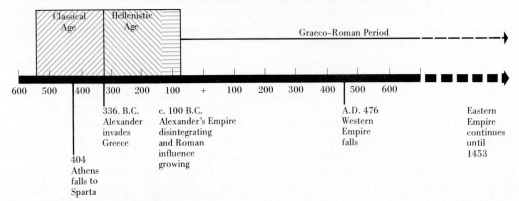

terdependence, and so the specialist replaced the amateur in the workplace and the government: Athens by the end of the Classical Age had a standing army, a professional navy, professional musicians, and professional speech writers. Conservative values and traditional beliefs were questioned and attacked, with the personal search for truth becoming more important than the citizen's responsibility to his *polis*. As traditional values tottered, the society fragmented: the old were often pitted against the young, the religious against the skeptical, aristocrats against democrats, men against women, the farm against the city, the land against the sea.

The artistic achievements of Athens during the Classical Age, then, occurred in spite of political and social conditions that can be described only as tumultuous. Between 534 and 336, this small *polis* underwent three major constitutional reforms and two civil wars; its countryside was invaded nine times, and its city was once blockaded into submission. Plague ravaged the city while it was crammed with refugees from its invaded countryside, and its population plummeted. Athenian expeditions to Egypt and Sicily were disastrous during the same period that Athens first formed and then lost Greece's only empire. Seemingly undaunted, she built a new (much weaker) confederacy and then lost that as well. In sum, drama and theatre were flourishing in a *polis* that was enduring constant upheaval.

Why drama became a major art during the period must remain a mystery. Perhaps, as Else suggested, drama came simply from the creativity of two geniuses. Perhaps it was the inevitable expression of a proud and self-conscious culture. Perhaps it was a new society's attempt to grapple with the problem of individual rights within social bondings. Perhaps it was an attempt to teach a citizenry about its past in order that it might be better prepared to cope with its present and future. Perhaps it was a means of allowing ordinary citizens to consider profound philosophical problems together. Perhaps Ath-

enian drama was all of these, or none of them, but it was unquestionably one of the great artistic triumphs of all times and all places.

Its importance remains undiminished to our own time. Its profundity and timelessness let it speak to all ages and all sorts of people. At the time of Christ, a Roman playwright was still adapting its stories. In the sixteenth century, an attempt to recapture its grandeur led to the development of modern opera. When in the nineteenth century Freudian psychologists sought names to describe universal psychological traits, they seized on the names of characters in Greek tragedy, so truly had these characters been depicted. When in the 1960s a radical theatre group wanted to shake contemporary audiences out of their complacency and into a new understanding of the human condition, they produced *Dionysus in '69*. The dramas of Athens have been consistently translated, revived, and rewritten from the time of its own Golden Age to the present. Although very much a product of its own culture, Greek drama, as few others, has transcended it and become an expression for all times and all places.

The Festivals

From their outset, drama and theatre were closely tied to the *polis*—the people and the government of Athens. Among the major activities of the *polis* were a large number of outdoor festivals, many of which honored Greek gods and heroes.[2] Drama was performed at three of these public festivals throughout the classical age and was administered jointly by public officials and private citizens. The most important of the festivals to feature dramatic contests was the City (or Great) Dionysia, where Pisastratus had established the first contest for tragedy in 534 B.C. (see pp. 53–54).

Tradition holds that Thespis won the first prize ever awarded, but little else is known about the contests until the end of the sixth century, when, perhaps as a part of constitutional reform, a new contest was added for dithyram-

FIGURE 4.6

Two recent productions of *Prometheus Bound,* revealing very different interpretations of the text. Above, a production at Indiana University, directed and designed by Richard L. Scammon; below, a production at the University of Northern Iowa, directed by Michael Robertson. [Photographs courtesy of the universities.]

bic choruses (see pp. 40–42) and the rules for the tragic competitions were codified.

After about 509, then, each tribe competed with a dithyrambic chorus of fifty members: five tribes brought choruses of men; the other five, choruses of boys. All members of the choruses had to be both tribal members and citizens by birth. The chorus members were, it is believed, exempt from military service during their time of training and performance (a period of perhaps eleven months), during which all members received both vocal and physical training—and possibly dietary instructions. Perhaps the institution of these dithyrambic contests was an effort to increase loyalty to the newly formed tribes at the expense of the old family ties, but proof of this motive is lacking.

Shortly thereafter (possibly around 501), rules for the tragic competitions were set down. Every year, three poets competed, each offering three tragedies and one satyr play; thus, at the City Dionysia, each year there were nine tragedies and three satyr plays. Perhaps, as Else suggested (see pp. 55–56), the introduction of the dithyrambs and satyr plays were a response to a public demand for "more of Dionysus" in the festival bearing his name; evidence is too scant to permit certainty, however.

Supervision of the dramatic contests rested with a high civic official, the *archon eponymos*. One of his duties was to appoint wealthy citizens (called *choregoi*) who would pay for the expenses of a chorus (their training, costumes, and so on). The financial burden on the *choregoi* could be substantial. For example, a dithyrambic chorus was said to have cost 50 *minae* and a tragic chorus 30 *minae* in 409 and 410, respectively. Although correct translations of Greek currency are probably not possible, contemporary records suggest that an Athenian construction worker of the day would have worked for about four and one-half years to pay for the dithyrambic (and about two years to pay for the tragic) chorus; an American economist has proposed tentatively that 50 *minae* was equal to

about $15,000 and 30 *minae* to about $9,000 in 1970 U.S. dollars.[3]

Given the heavy financial burden, why did the *choregoi* participate? Several factors seem to have been operating. First, all Athenian citizens were expected to contribute regularly to the public good, and wealthy citizens were expected to provide financial support—by funding a chorus; by building, equipping, and commanding a warship for a year; by providing a public dinner for the town; and so on. The expenses for a chorus were not more burdensome than other such civic obligations. Second, an effort was made to distribute the financial burdens fairly, and mechanisms were provided for lessening the burden on those unable to execute their responsibility. For example, once during the Peloponnesian War, when money was scarce, *two choregoi* were appointed to share the expense of each chorus. Also, if a *choregos* believed himself unable to fulfill his duty, he could ask to be excused; should he be challenged, however, he was required to exchange fortunes with the challenger, who would then serve as *choregos* for the event. Third, and probably most importantly of all, a *choregos* could earn the esteem of his fellow citizens by performing his duty well. If his chorus won, his name was listed on public documents alongside those of the *archon* and the poet. That serving as the *choregos* for a dramatic contest was viewed as roughly equivalent to outfitting and commanding a warship argues forcefully for the importance of drama in the life of the *polis* and, consequently, for the importance of the *choregos* in the eyes of its citizenry. The sense of civic duty and pride may well explain why our records speak more often of generous and willing *choregoi* than of stingy and grumpy ones.

Sharing with the *choregoi* in the expenses of production was the public treasury, which provided the theatre, the prizes, and all the needs of the actors.

Civic officials and citizens also shared the responsibility of judging the contests. The council first selected a number of possible judges from each tribe. Their names were placed in ten urns that were sealed and kept in the Acropolis until the contests, when they were brought to the theatre. To tamper with these urns was a capital offense. Before the contests, the archon drew one name from each urn and swore in these ten men as judges. At the end of the competition, each judge wrote down his verdict and placed it in an urn. The archon then drew five votes at random. These five votes decided the winner, who was then proclaimed by a herald and crowned with ivy by the *archon*.

At the conclusion of each festival, the assembly met to examine the work of the archon and the other public officials and to hear any complaints of misconduct during the festival.

At no time was the City Dionysia more central to the life of the *polis* than during the rule of Pericles. At that time, the Dionysia was the major international festival, one at which Athens' allies paid their annual tributes (some of which were displayed in the theatre) and foreign dignitaries converged to conduct business. It was a time when those rendering conspicuous service to Athens were publicly thanked and when orphans of fallen Athenian soldiers were blessed by the assembled Athenian citizens. Holding the City Dionysia in March, after the winter seas were again safe, doubtless encouraged its status as an international event.

The Dionysia was, however, a religious as well as a civic festival. Dedicated to the god Dionysus, the festival was preceded by a reenactment of Dionysus' initial entry into Athens, and it opened with a formal and lavish processional that featured choral dances at various altars and ended at the sacred precinct of Dionysus with sacrifices. A statue of the god was present in the theatre during the dramatic contests, and from the time of our records, the priest of Dionysus had a seat of honor in the theatre. A day-by-day schedule of events can show the meshing of the Dionysia's several elements:

1. Day of preparation: the reenactment and a *proagon* (at which each dramatic poet described the play he would present).
2. Festival opens: the procession; the dithyrambic contests; a revel song (?).
3. Dramatic contests: three days for tragedies (one for each poet); one day (after ca. 486) for comedies; order uncertain.
4. Another Athenian festival, the Pandia.
5. Meeting of the assembly.

During the fifth century, at least two new contests were added: a contest for comic poets (ca. 486) and a competition for tragic actors (ca. 449). The contest for comic poets allowed five poets to compete; each offered a single play, and all were performed on the same day, either immediately before or immediately after the three days of tragedies. During the Peloponnesian Wars, probably in an effort to save time and money (both of which were desperately needed for the building of warships), the rules were altered so that only three poets competed and one comedy was performed at the end of each day of tragedies. The second new contest, that for tragic actors, limited competition to the three leading actors (the protagonists). Under the rules, a protagonist could win the prize for acting even though the tragedies in which he appeared were not awarded a prize.

The increase in the number of contests during the fifth century may signal several important changes: a growing interest in drama generally; a new acceptance of comedy as a legitimate form of drama; an increasing specialization among theatre artists; and a changing sense of the importance of actors vis-à-vis poets. Whatever may have led to the establishment of the new contests, the result was to increase still further the amount of time devoted to theatre within the City Dionysia, Athens' major public festival. And the prominence accorded theatre in this festival argues convincingly for its centrality in the life of the *polis*.

Although the City Dionysia was the most

important Athenian festival to feature contests in theatre and drama, it was not the only one. Two older Dionysian festivals, the Lenaia and the Rural Dionysia, included such contests before the end of the fifth century. (The other Athenian festival for the god Dionysus, the Anthesteria, did not regularly include drama.)

The Lenaia, held in January, was a local festival: foreigners seldom attended, probably because the rough winter seas made travel difficult. Although established before the City Dionysia, the Lenaia offered contests in theatre only later: ca. 442 saw the first contests for comic poets and comic actors; ca. 432 the first contests for tragic poets and tragic protagonists. As the dates may suggest, comedy was more important at this festival than tragedy. Neither satyr plays nor dithyrambs were part of the Lenaia. As at the City Dionysia, each comic poet offered one play, and five playwrights competed annually (except during the Peloponnesian Wars). Only two tragic poets competed each year, each offering only two plays. The great *tragic* poets did not compete often at the Lenaia. Although major *comic* poets competed there regularly, even they seemed to prefer a victory at the Dionysia. That the Lenaia lacked the prestige of the City Dionysia may explain why noncitizens could sing in the choruses and serve as *choregoi* at the Lenaia.

About the Rural Dionysia, little is known. Held in December, these festivals were organized in various towns throughout Attica, probably on different days and under different regulations. The rural festivals at Peiraeus, Salamis, and Eleusis were the best known (see Figure 4.1). Common to all such festivals was a phallic procession, a version of which was dramatized by the comic poet Aristophanes in his *Acharnians*. Although dramas may have been offered at certain of the rural festivals even before the mid-fifth century, not until the fourth century do enough records exist to suggest a possible pattern; that is, plays from the City Dionysia were revived at the Rural Dionysia by

actors of limited talent. (This large number of records extant from the fourth century may be significant: it may suggest the great popularity of drama at the end of the classical age, and it may account, at least in part, for the presumed familiarity of the Athenian people with the great tragedies of the fifth century.)

In sum, during the Classical Age, theatre and drama were an important part of three public festivals held in Athens in honor of the god Dionysus. Support for the contests came from both public and private funds, and interest in the contests seems to have grown throughout the two-hundred-year period.

The Theatres

Scholars agree that the word *theatre* comes from the Greek *theatron*, a place where people gathered to watch a *thea*, or spectacle.

About little else do scholars agree:

> In modern times the great theatre of fifth-century Athens, the theatre of Dionysos, the scene of the productions of Aeschylus and Sophokles, Euripides, and Aristophanes, has almost vanished from before our eyes. At one time its form seemed sufficiently clear and substantial, though architecturally simple. Now, after repeated down-dating of the scanty remains, only faint outlines or vestiges are left, seeming to mock the earnest student of this most vital time and place in theatrical history.[4]

The earliest theatre for the dramatic contests of the City Dionysia and perhaps the Lenaia was probably located "downtown" in the Agora, or marketplace (see Figure 4.2). Certainly there was a circular performance space there, although its precise location is disputed, and certainly wooden seats were erected there from time to time. Probably in the early years of the fifth century, the theatre was moved from the Agora, perhaps because of overcrowding in the downtown area or perhaps because of the collapse of the wooden seats. Little else is known about this theatre in the Agora.

Of far more importance to historians is the theatre located on the southeastern slope of the Acropolis in the sacred precinct of Dionysus, adjacent to his ancient temple (see Figure 4.7). It is believed that this theatre, the Theatre of Dionysus, at first consisted of two major parts: the performance space (*orchestra*), located on a terrace specially built to hold it; and an area for spectators (*theatron*), the hillside at the base of the Acropolis. Within the *orchestra* may have been an altar to Dionysus. Leading into the *orchestra* was one, or perhaps two, pathways (*eisodoi* or *parodoi*) through which the performers entered. There was, as well, a large rock outcropping, approximately five meters square that impinged on the *orchestra*; this outcropping may have been used in staging some fifth-century plays, for early ones, like *The Persians* (472),

The Suppliants (ca. 463), and the *Prometheus* (date unknown, but probably before 450), call for rocks and mounds. On the other hand, the outcropping may never have been used in staging; it was removed before the end of the fifth century, perhaps because it was a nuisance[5] (see Figure 4.8).

Increasingly after 458, the extant plays are set in front of palaces and temples. This fact has caused virtually all scholars to agree that after 458 a scene house (*skene*) was added. (The word *skene*, meaning "tent," also meant "booth" and was used to refer to the flimsy booths used by merchants in the Agora.) This *skene* (if it existed) was made of wood and must have been quite temporary, for no solid foundations from this period have been found. In the absence of architectural evidence, the appearance of this temporary skene cannot be known, but certain features of it can be inferred from the extant

FIGURE 4.7

A reconstruction of the early Theatre of Dionysus, showing audience area, *orchestra*, rock outcropping, and temple. Compare with Figure 4.8.

FIGURE 4.8

A reconstructed ground plan of the early Theatre of Dionysus. [Adapted from Hammond.] Compare with Figure 4.7. A. Circle of 26m. diameter as drawn by Dörpfeld; B. Circle of 24m. diameter as drawn by Dörpfeld; C. Altar; D. Piece of retaining wall of western *eisodos*; E. Piece of supporting wall of original *orchestra* (found under sockethole of Periclean theatre); F. Piece of supporting wall of original *orchestra* (found 1.80m. below level of Periclean theatre); F–G. Eastern *eisodos* as shown by Dörpfeld; H. Rock outcrop, removed at some time before building of Periclean theatre.

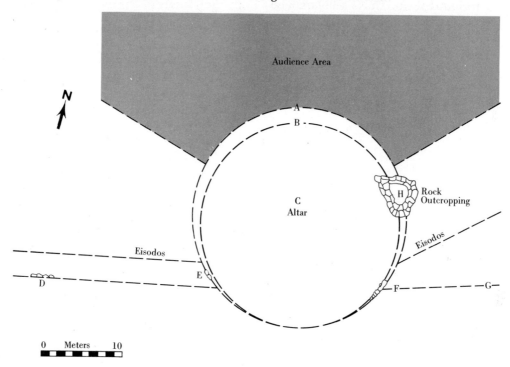

plays (all but one of which date from this period):

1. The building probably had a roof, for references in several plays refer to people standing or sitting on top of a house.

2. The building must have had at least one door. No extant play requires more than one door, although several could benefit from having two. On the other hand, later stone buildings most often had three doors, and perhaps they merely preserved in stone what was already traditional in the temporary wooden structure. The *skene*, then, probably had one, two, or three doors.

3. The door (or one of the doors) was probably large enough to accommodate a wheeled platform (*ekkyklema*) on which several people could stand or lie. Several extant plays require "dead bodies" or other tableaux to be moved into the view of the audience (see Figure 4.9).

4. At the front of the building may have been a raised platform, a stage. If present, it was probably low and easily accessible from the *orchestra*. Few controversies about the ancient theatre have caused more agitation than this one. Those scholars who believe that there was a raised stage point out that (a) the plays refer to going up and down and to characters' talking

"above" the chorus; (b) ancient commentators all talk as if there were a raised stage; (c) no ancient commentator announces the introduction of such a stage, and so it must have been there from the beginning of the theatre; and (d) all later theatres had such stages, and they were presumably conforming to traditional practices when they included them. Those scholars who believe that there was not a raised stage counter that (a) not only do the plays not require a stage, they encourage instead the unimpeded mingling of all performers; (b) the ancient commentators were writing many years after the period of the extant plays and were therefore probably writing about only the theatres that they knew; (c) the scarcity of our records easily explains our

FIGURE 4.9

Conjectural reconstruction of *mechane, ekkyklema,* and *periaktoi.*

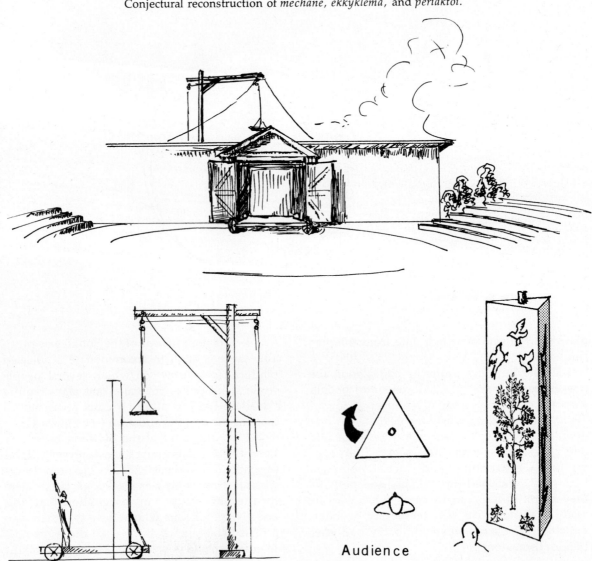

having no account of the introduction of a stage; and (d) the practices of later theatres are no proper guide to the practices of earlier ones. Only one thing is certain. If there was a raised stage, it was of wood and it was much lower than those found in the later Hellenistic theatres.

5. Connected with the *skene* in some way was a machine (*mechane*) capable of lifting and lowering at least two performers at a time. Extant plays talk unambiguously of performers' being flown in and out of the performance area. It is usually assumed that the rigging required for the operation of the machine was housed in, on, or behind the *skene* (see Figure 4.9).

In light of the plays and recent archaeological evidence, then, the Theatre of Dionysus during the period of the extant plays depended rather more on a clever use of natural space than on elaborate buildings. The natural slope of the hill provided the seats with good sight lines, and the Acropolis sheltered the patrons from brisk March winds, even while it provided acceptable acoustics. The scene house served primarily to focus the attention of the audience and to facilitate the action of the plays (hiding costume changes and housing machinery). It was both temporary and simple, a wooden structure in a land whose timber was both scarce and costly. Between the time when the Theatre of Dionysus opened and the time that the *skene* became a more-or-less permanent feature of it, two hundred years may have elapsed. Probably the appearance of the *skene* changed many times, reflecting the needs of particular plays and the preferences of particular people. In any event, the elaborate *skene* of later stone theatres apparently stands in stark contrast to these early wooden structures that were easily erected and just as easily dismantled (see Figure 4.10).

Exactly how the performance space was used is unclear. Evidence about scenic practices is limited to that deducible from the extant plays and to scattered references in later commentaries, many of which were clearly describing much later practices.

Some properties were almost certainly used, but their appearance is disputed: Were they "real" or were they "abstract"? Extant tragedies very often allude to an altar or altars within the view of the audience; many require, as well, statues of various gods. Less often, horse-drawn carriages, funeral biers, carpets, canopies, torches, and couches appear. In comedy, furniture and household items (chopping boards, pots, pans, cheese graters, scales, and so on) were probably used. But what these items looked like and how they fit in with the rest of the scenery are matters that continue to be hotly disputed. In general, the controversy is between those who view classical theatre as being much like modern (illusionistic) theatre and those who believe that it was, rather, suggestive and highly conventionalized. Although today no scholar advocates either extreme, a consideration of the extremes may help to clarify the issues being debated.

Those scholars who favor an illusionistic theatre argue that the Greek audience saw a more-or-less real-life version of what the play described. Thus, for *The Persians*, a literal canopy and tomb were needed; for *Prometheus*, a real rock and an earthquake. They argue that, after its introduction, the *skene* was painted or otherwise decorated to resemble the place described in the play, and that changes of place within a trilogy or play were accompanied by changes of scenery: "It is indubitable that the Greeks strove for illusion, and tried to achieve this through scenic illusion."[6] Scholars holding this view have argued for the use of the rock outcropping in early Aeschylean plays, the painting of realistic scenes on *pinakes* (the Greek equivalents of modern-day flats), and the use of *periaktoi* to "change scenery." (*Periaktoi* are three-sided prisms that can be rotated to reveal a different face and therefore a different scene to the audience. No clear case can be made for the existence of *periaktoi* in the fifth century; although *pinakes* almost certainly existed, their nature and use are not entirely clear; see Figure 4.9).

FIGURE 4.10

Ground plan showing *skene* in the Theatre of Dionysus at the time of the *Oresteia*. [Adapted from Hammond.] See also Figures 4.7 and 4.8. *A.* Circle of 26m. diameter as drawn by Dörpfeld; *B.* Circle of 24m. diameter as drawn by Dörpfeld; *C.* Shallow step?; *D.* Stage?; *E.* Doors?; *F.* Backstage areas.

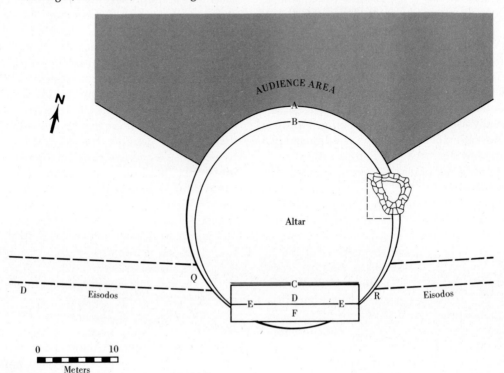

Those scholars who favor a nonillusionistic theatre argue that Greek drama was "a kind of Rezitationsdrama in which actors did little more than stand and deliver their lines, leaving all visualization of the play to the imagination of the audience."[7] For such scholars, the *skene*, when present, was merely a neutral background for the action and could, unadorned, serve equally well as a palace, a temple, a military tent, or a cave. Changes of place could be accomplished through choric dance and song, the actors' dialogue, and the audience's imagination. Properties, if used at all, were important only insofar as they facilitated the action of the play, not as they produced an environment or suggested a historical moment or a specific location.

The controversy, although important, cannot be resolved, because we do not understand the conventions of Greek staging; and our scant evidence is ambiguous. For example, the use of masks argues for a nonillusionistic theatre, but masks of the period were natural rather than exaggerated or stylized. The use of choral song and dance argues for a nonillusionistic theatre, but the use of a machine to permit supernatural creatures to fly into sight argues for a theatre interested in literal representation.[8]

Doubtless the conventions of staging rested somewhere between extreme illusionism and extreme abstraction, but precisely where between them cannot yet be determined.

Toward the end of the classical age, a major renovation of the theatre took place. This renovation was, until recently, attributed to Pericles, but new archaeological evidence (unearthed pottery and types of building materials) puts the remodeling about one hundred years later, near the middle of the fourth century. As a part of this renovation, a new temple to Dionysus was built, the position of the *orchestra* was shifted slightly, and changes were made in the seating. At that time as well, a new solid stone foundation was erected. It carried a heavy wall that, on one side, marked off the precinct of Dionysus and, on the other, served as a retaining wall for the *orchestra* and as a support for certain wooden structures: a series of slots cut into the stone were clearly intended to hold timbers, either for a *skene* or for a stage or for both. Toward the center of this wall and jutting forward toward the *orchestra* was another stone foundation that may have provided additional support for a *skene* and/or an additional platform; or it may have had a purpose wholly unrelated to the theatre but related instead to certain civic activities that continued to take place in this theatre (see Figure 4.11). Although the appearance of the *skene* (and the stage, if there was one) in this theatre is no more certain than before, its *structure* was most certainly less flimsy, less temporary, and less flexible than the earlier one. The presence of the stone foundation argues for a substantial wooden structure that was intended to last for several years. Various scholars have offered conjectural reconstructions of this *skene* with the stone foundation (although they have misdated it), but none of the reconstructions can be adopted on the basis of the available evidence (see Figure 4.12).

It should be noted that none of our extant plays was written for this theatre: most date from the earlier, more temporary theatre, and

FIGURE 4.11

Ground plan of the Theatre of Dionysus following remodelings. Note especially *F*, which may be a platform for civic events. *A*. Old retaining wall; *B*. New retaining wall; *C*. New orchestra; *D*. Old orchestra; *E*. Old temple; *F*. Other stone foundation.

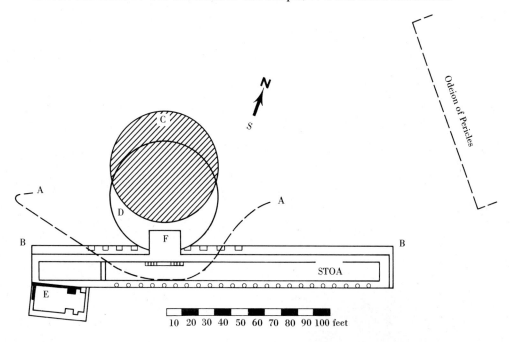

FIGURE 4.12

Several imaginative reconstructions showing an elaborate wooden *skene*, now attributed to the fourth century, although once thought to be from the fifth. [From Fiechter and reproduced with permission of the estate.]

one dates from a later, still more permanent theatre. Nevertheless, at the time that this theatre was in use, drama was a very popular entertainment.[9]

The Audience

Although the size of the Athenian audience is not known, all indications are that it was remarkably large. The capacity of the theatre has been estimated at fourteen thousand, and some relationship between capacity and anticipated audience can probably be assumed. Also, a number of contemporary records speak of people jostling for seats, thereby suggesting that seats were in great demand. If the population of Athens has been correctly estimated at about 100,000, then the theatre could hold more than 10 per cent of the population of the city at any performance. The percentage, if anywhere near correct, is astonishing. *All* of the theatres in New York can accommodate less than 0.3 per cent of that city's population, for example.

How can such a high rate of attendance be explained? Doubtless making theatre a part of the public festivals encouraged attendance, for during major festivals "the whole city kept holiday. . . . Business was abandoned; the law courts were cleared; . . . even prisoners were released from gaol to enable them to share in the common festivities."[10] Also, because the festivals were annual affairs, the opportunity for seeing theatre was concentrated into a few days, probably increasing the sense that theatre was a very special event. And organizing theatre into contests probably heightened interest by promoting rivalries among various tribes and cliques. Clearly, however, attendance was great also because the Athenians believed that theatre formed an important part of their civic life. So important was it during the fifth century that a public fund was established to buy tickets for citizens who could not otherwise afford them; and (for a time) any proposal to divert these funds to other purposes was an offense punishable by death.

Admission to the theatre was by ticket, and by the late fourth century tickets cost two obols (roughly one third of an average day's wage). Tickets probably guaranteed access to a particular section rather than to a specific seat. Sections seem to have been designated for members of the council, members of each tribe, slaves, courtesans, and other women. In addition to this general ("two-obol") seating, there were a number of special reserved seats located close to the *orchestra*. These seats were set aside for civic and religious officials, foreign dignitaries, public benefactors, and, perhaps, the orphaned sons of Athenian veterans. Although the theatre was clearly open to all classes of society, citizens seemed to outnumber women, slaves, and youths, and Athenians far outnumbered foreigners even at the City Dionysia. (At the Lenaia, the number of foreigners was negligible.)

Evidence about the behavior of Athenian audiences is ambiguous. Certainly, extant tragedies argue for audiences that were intelligent, demanding, and serious, and several extant comedies assume a knowledge of the tragedies as well as an interest in current political, economic, and military matters. The language of the plays, including intricate patterns of versification and elegant figures of speech, likewise seems aimed at literate and sophisticated patrons. And some ancient authors (including Aristophanes) commended the taste of Athenian audiences. On the other hand, certain public officials were charged with keeping order in the theatre, and several anecdotes tell of unhappy patrons hissing, pelting actors with various missiles, and kicking their heels against the seats. Also, a law was passed making violence in the theatre punishable by death, a law that might suggest that violence was either a threat or an actuality. Probably, the behavior of audiences during the fifth and fourth centuries was as diverse as the audiences themselves. Patrons came to the theatre at dawn and stayed until dusk, and so probably, there was much roaming about inside the theatre. For most of that period, general seating was on backless benches that were no doubt uncomfortable despite the pillows and blankets that many patrons brought with them. Also, the very size of the group made noise and misbehavior (at least among some of the patrons) very likely. In general, however, we must conclude that disruptions were few and that attention to the performances was high.

The Performers

In the Greek theatre, there were two sorts of performers: actors and chorus members.

According to tradition, from the time of Thespis to Aeschylus, the poet was himself the only actor, but then Aeschylus added a second actor, and Sophocles a third. No more actors were added thereafter. In fact, there may have been a rule that only three actors could be used. Such a rule seems less odd when we recall that contests generally prescribe the number of contestants in order to avoid unevenly matched teams and that Athenian classical theatre was cast in the form of contests. Whether or not there was a rule, it is a fact that all the extant tragedies can be performed by three actors, occasionally supported by one or two mute persons. Some extant comedies absolutely require five speaking actors, however, suggesting either that the "rule" did not apply to comedy or (more probably) that it was less rigidly interpreted.

To perform a play with only three actors meant that one actor often played several roles. Such doubling was made easier both by the large theatre (which distanced performers from the audience) and by the masks worn by the actors. As well, the structure of the plays facilitated doubling, for generally the episodes (in which dialogue among the actors predominated) were separated by choral odes (in which the chorus sang and danced). During choral odes, there was ample time for an actor to change costume and mask before reentering the performance as a different character. Although leading actors (protagonists) might play only one role, second and third actors (deuteragonists and tritagonists) typically played three or four. By charting the speaking actors in each episode, scholars have been able to determine how the roles were distributed among the three actors in most plays. The inevitable conclusion is that Greek actors could embrace a large range of roles within a single play. Such a range argues for exceedingly skillful performers, although with skills rather different from those expected of modern actors.

Because Greek actors were masked, their tools of expression were limited to voice and gesture. Of these, the voice was the more highly prized. The actor's delivery was a mixture of song, recitative, and speech; and each mode of delivery had its own distinctive metrical patterns. For example, speech unaccompanied by music was generally written in iambic trimeters (-|-|-|), a verse form akin to normal speech. Recitative shifted to various dimeters and tetrameters (-|-|-|-|, most often) and added musical accompaniment. Songs employed still other meters and might use any one of several musical modes and keys (about which we know almost nothing). Both the songs and the recitative were accompanied by a flute (or, for special effects, a lyre), whose notes were probably pitched somewhat higher than those of the actor. Until late in the fifth century, the music, although important, was clearly subordinate to the words of the text; during the fourth century, however, music became increasingly ornate and eventually rivalled the words for the attention of audiences. This shift probably has implications for the vocal delivery of the actors, but its precise effect is not known.

All Greek actors evidently needed a voice trained for song and recitative, perhaps like that of a modern opera performer. They also needed great interpretive skill to recite the various poetic meters and at the same time make the words and meaning of the text comprehensible to a large audience. Although vocal power was important because of the size of the theatre, quality of tone, clarity, and correctness of pronunciation, as well as adaptation of the voice to the particular demands of the role, were more highly regarded by the audiences.

The flexibility asked of the voice was also required of the actor's body. The extant plays demand that the actor run, kneel, struggle, lie prostrate, and crawl on all fours. Clearly, any notion that Greek acting was static or statuesque should be dismissed, as should any assumption that it resembled modern acting.

We do not know precisely what classical acting was like, but we do know that Athenian audiences demanded competence. Records tell of crowds that hissed at actors who merely "roared" their words, that mocked actors for mispronouncing words, and that called one actor "monkey" because he used gestures inappropriately. Perhaps because of the high expectations of the audiences, the actors in Greece dieted, fasted, and engaged in vocal warm-ups regularly in preparation for public performances.

During the Classical Age, two related trends appeared: acting became an activity for specialists, and the art of acting became officially recognized and highly regarded. Specialization began with Aeschylus' introduction of the second actor and then accelerated. As soon as a second actor was introduced, acting became an activity separate from composition; that is, an actor other than the poet was needed. Although Aeschylus continued to act in his plays, Sophocles did not; with Sophocles, the separation of actor and poet was complete. The protagonist, who had at first been the poet, was now chosen by the poet. Contests for actors, distinct from those for poets and plays, gave legitimacy to the new art, and additional contests recognized comic acting as distinct from tragic acting. When acting became important in its own right, each poet was assigned his protagonist by lot from among those available. Before the end of the classical period, each protagonist acted in one play by each poet, presumably to assure each poet equally competent performers (see Figure 4.13). By the end of the Classical Age, three-man acting troupes, each with a flute player, were touring the rural festivals. Acting was by then a separate profession, and actors were, according to Aristotle, more highly prized than poets.

Chorus members were the other performers in Greek drama. This group of men spoke, chanted, and sang (most often in unison) while

FIGURE 4.13

Time line: Contests and rules for the City Dionysia and the Lenaia.

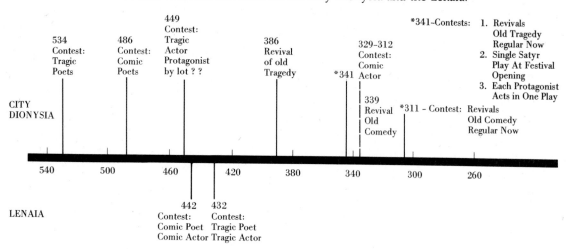

they marched, gestured, and moved according to the metrical demands of the text. Shifts in meter within the plays, then, had visual as well as aural effects, a point too often overlooked in attempts to imagine what Athenian performances looked like.

The Athenian chorus, led by a flute player, typically entered the *orchestra* through the western *eisodos*. In tragedy, they entered most often to meters that were like march steps, even like a military drill; in comedy, the entrance was less formal and might include a variety of meters, some of which were quite free and lively. Once in the *orchestra,* the chorus arranged itself into ranks and files, forming a rectangle rather than the circle associated with dithyrambic dance.

The extant plays make clear that the chorus danced (in the Greek sense of "moved rhythmically"). Because very little is known about either Greek music or Greek dance, however, the exact contribution of the chorus to the performance is difficult to imagine. We do know that hand gestures performed an important part of Greek dance and that storytelling through gestures was common. It is therefore possible to

offer tentative conclusions about choral performance in the plays.

Major dances were performed during the choral odes, but some dance probably accompanied the actors' lines, as well. Probably, too, the chorus reacted to the actions of the play. All choral dances were probably suited to the words and ideas of the drama (the metrical patterns in the plays usually shift as the ideas of the drama shift), and the importance of hand gestures and choreographed storytelling suggests that the choral performances might have shared traits with modern mime. Considerable evidence attests to differences between the tragic and comic choruses: the tragic choruses tended to be stately and formal, the comic choruses to be livelier, less rigidly structured, and occasionally quite lewd. When the dramatic action required, however, tragic choruses could appear excited or disordered, as in *Seven Against Thebes* and *The Eumenides,* and comic choruses could be sublime, as in the *parodos* to *The Frogs.* Very little is known about satyric dance.

As the importance of actors increased late in the fifth century, that of the chorus declined. Early, in the plays of Aeschylus for example, the chorus performed a major role. In both *The Suppliants* and *The Eumenides,* the chorus is a major participant in the drama, having half of the lines or more. In the later dramas of Sophocles and Euripides, on the other hand, the choral lines usually account for less than a quarter of the play; and in several plays by Euripides, the chorus is more an onlooker than a participant in the action. Indeed, by the end of the fourth century, the chorus seldom figured directly in the dramatic action; it had become a mere interlude, with the result that choral odes were occasionally interchanged among different plays.

Whatever its relation to dramatic action, the chorus was necessarily an element of dramatic spectacle because of its size. Although the evidence is slight, scholars agree that comic choruses consisted of twenty-four and satyr choruses of twelve throughout the classical period. About the size of the tragic chorus, there has been less widespread agreement. Most scholars now think that Aeschylus' chorus numbered twelve and that, with Sophocles, the number rose to fifteen, where it remained throughout the Classical Age. Most scholars now reject the idea that the tragic chorus ever numbered fifty. This old error had two sources: the (probably mistaken) notion that tragic choruses evolved from dithyrambic choruses; and the faulty dating of *The Suppliants* (see p. 55), combined with the assumption that the size of the chorus in *The Suppliants* was dictated by the myth. (In the myth, there were fifty suppliants.)

Twelve to twenty-four people, masked and costumed, speaking and singing and dancing in unison made a striking visual statement. And in several plays (e.g., *The Suppliants* and *The Eumenides*), there was probably more than one chorus, thus multiplying the impact of the spectacle on the audience.

Masks and Costumes

The appearance of actors and chorus members during the Classical Age has long interested scholars, but areas of agreement are few.[11] Information about masks and costumes comes from three kinds of evidence: the surviving plays and fragments; iconographic materials (mostly vase and wall paintings, as well as terracotta and stone statues and masks); and late commentaries (most written five hundred to fifteen hundred years after the events described). Within the extant plays, difficulties of interpretation abound. For example, if a character mentions a costume item in the dialogue, is it because the item was worn (and visible to the audience, so that the dialogue confirmed what the audience saw) or because the item was *not* worn (and not visible to the audience, so that the dialogue directed the audience to imagine it)? This most important question cannot be answered with certainty because we do not understand the conventions of Greek staging. Also, the usefulness of iconographic evidence is difficult to assess, for it comes from many different places and periods and treats nondramatic as well as dramatic events. All conclusions about the performers' appearance, then, must be considered tenetative; nonetheless, some attempt at a visualization must be made.

Masks

Tradition holds that Thespis at first painted his face and later used a mask. From then on, all performers, except the flute player, wore masks that covered the head and carried hairstyles, beards, and decorations on them. The masks were made of cork, linen, and wood, and the mask makers were apparently highly skilled, for references describe comic masks that ranged from fanciful animals to recognizable caricatures of contemporary Athenians. Presumably, within any play, the choral masks were similar (to emphasize the group) and the actors' masks were individualized (to heighten the contrast among characters). The eyes, mouths, and hairstyles of masks of the classical period were not exaggerated; exaggerated masks belonged to a later period. Variety among masks was great;

FIGURE 4.14

Mask from the Classical Age. Notice that the eyes, mouth, and hair do not appear exaggerated. [Photographs courtesy of American School of Classical Studies at Athens: Agora Excavations, and reproduced with their permission.]

standard (or stock) masks, like exaggerated ones, belonged only to a later period (see Figure 4.14).

Costumes

Variety existed in the costumes as well as the masks. Plays and fragments most often allude to street wear (e.g., *chiton, himation,* and *peplos;* see Figure 4.15). Probably, then, most actors and choruses who were impersonating ordinary people wore something akin to daily dress, although it may have been made more elegant for tragedy and somewhat less elegant for comedy. On the other hand, unusual characters and occasions called forth distinctive costume items. References to special veils, wreaths, crowns, brooches, belts, cloaks, animal skins, armor, and rags attest that many actors wore not ordinary street clothes but distinctive costumes that were developed in terms of the character being impersonated. Choral dress also varied from play to play. Most choruses represented ordinary

people and so probably dressed in ordinary ways. But some assumed unusual identities (sailors, sea nymphs, birds, wasps, furies, and so on), and their costumes were probably appropriately spectacular. As with the masks, the costumes for chorus members were probably similar in order to emphasize the group, whereas those of the actors were probably different in order to stress the differences among the characters.

Although there probably was no standard costume for either tragedy or comedy, some conventions seem to have operated. Color apparently carried meaning; for example, black garments were often worn by characters in mourning (e.g., in *Alcestis* and *Helen*), and yellow garments were worn by effeminate males and young girls (as in *The Frogs* and *Lysistrata*). Style and decoration may have marked nationality, for entering characters were occasionally described as "dressed like a foreigner" or

FIGURE 4.15

Common Greek garments, some version of which probably formed the basis for both comic and tragic costumes.

Chiton   Peplos   Himation

"dressed like a Greek." In comedies, large artificial *phalloi* were worn by at least some of the actors (not the chorus) during at least some of the plays (see Figure 4.16). That a *phallos* was a stock item for all actors in comedy must be doubted, however, because some actors impersonated women and sympathetic old men, for whom such an item would have appeared inappropriate. The view that a standard costume existed for tragedy and one for comedy cannot be sustained by the evidence and should therefore be abandoned. Also, exaggerated footwear for tragedy (the *cothornos*), once attributed to this period, clearly belonged to another, later period.

The only plays of the Classical Age for which standardized masks and costumes were probably used were the satyr dramas. One line in *Cyclops* (our only extant satyr play) and several vases argue for chorus members dressed in tights and goat skins and wearing horns, tails, and *phalloi* (see Figure 4.17).

In sum, as with the physical theatre during the Classical Age, we know less than we once thought we knew about masks and costumes. During that period of about two hundred years, considerable experimentation doubtless went on, and so costumes and masks may have looked different from play to play and year to year. Evidence suggests that some version of daily dress formed a basis for many costumes, but variety and bold innovation were clearly required for many others. Masks, too, varied from the natural to the fanciful. Except in the case of satyr plays, stock costumes and masks were probably not used until the Hellenistic and Graeco-Roman periods, when the exaggerated footwear, headdresses, and masks also dominated.

From the scant information available, some conclusions about style of performance suggest themselves. Performance style was clearly *not* like that of modern realism; there was no attempt to make the audience forget that it was in the theatre. The audience could see itself as well as it could see the actors because of the daylight

FIGURE 4.16

A character from Old Comedy, seemingly barefooted and with a large artificial *phallos* for comic effect. [From Robert.]

ances now so familiar through cinematic close-ups.

Playwrights and Plays

Well over three thousand plays were written and performed during the classical period. Of these, only forty-five plays and some fragments remain. Although commentaries on Greek classical drama are necessarily based on these plays and fragments, it is well to remember that our conclusions are based on only about 1 per cent of the written dramas and thus may well be mistaken. Also, most of our plays come from only four authors (Aeschylus, Sophocles, Euripides, and Aristophanes), and we do not know how representative these four playwrights are.

Aeschylus (525–456) lived and wrote during the first half of the fifth century, when the Greek states were united against the Persian threat and Athens was wresting leadership from Sparta. He won his last dramatic victory soon after Pericles seized power and before Athens launched its empire and came into conflict with its Greek neighbors. He was, then, writing while Athens was in its ascendancy.

Aeschylus wrote more than eighty plays, of which six (or seven) remain. All were written late in his career and probably represent his work as a mature artist. Attributed to Aeschylus are *The Persians* (472); *The Suppliants* (ca. 468); *Seven Against Thebes* (467); and *Agamemnon, The Libation Bearers*, and *The Eumenides* (all 458 and, taken together, called the *Oresteia*). The *Oresteia* is of particular interest because it is our only extant trilogy and because it is the earliest production that seems to require a *skene*. *Prometheus* (468–440?), once attributed to Aeschylus, is now thought to be the work of another, unknown poet; scholarly opinion remains divided on this point, however.[12]

Aeschylus was clearly a man of the theatre. At first, he not only wrote but also acted in his own plays. As well, he choreographed the choral dances and taught the chorus. Ancient commentators credit him with devising new kinds

of the outdoor theatre; and the audience saw the dramatic action not through a frame (as in proscenium theatre, movies, or television), but against a background (or statuelike, within space). Men played women's roles, and actors played several roles during a performance. Both actors and chorus were masked. The dialogue was metrical, a mixture of song, recitative, and speech, and the chorus was present throughout most of the play, speaking, singing, and dancing. The theatre of the classical period, then, emphasized those pleasures that come from music, dance, and spectacle perhaps more than those subtle, intimate, and psychological nu-

FIGURE 4.17

Section of a vase painting thought to show actors in a satyr play. Note masks, ears, tails, *phalloi,* and nude figures. What artistic liberties may the artist have taken? [From Wieseler.]

of dance and with introducing new techniques of costuming and scene painting, although the nature of these presumed innovations is unknown. His addition of the second actor revolutionized the art of playwriting (see pp. 55–56); and his use of the third actor (introduced between 468 and 458, probably by Sophocles) was as sure as it was startling (see, for example, Cassandra in *Agamemnon*). In his plays, the chorus matched the actors as a focus of attention. As a protagonist in *Seven Against Thebes* and an antagonist in *The Eumenides*, the Aeschylean chorus often delivered one half or more of the lines of the play. Aeschylus' bold use of visual effects made him the most spectacular of the ancient poets. Multiple choruses in *The Suppliants*, the funeral procession in *Seven Against Thebes*, the prophetic and vengeful ghosts in *The Persians* and *The Eumenides*, and the carriage and carpet in *Agamemnon* provided a visual equivalent of the mighty verse and momentous subjects of his tragedies.

Unlike Sophocles and Euripides, Aeschylus often wrote trilogies, presumably because his tragic vision required greater scope for its expression than was possible in a single play. His subject was nothing less than the nature of universal order; exploring the nature of this order, Aeschylus probed the relationship between the human and the divine. Perhaps because his interest was in the order of things, Aeschylus dealt with the effects of human decision and action on succeeding generations rather than on a single individual. Thus, in the

Oresteia, the nature of justice was explored (an old order gave way to a new, old gods were transformed, impersonal law replaced personal vengeance) even as the god-inspired actions of Agamemnon, Clytemnestra, and Orestes were traced. The form of the trilogy was well suited to such a vast tragic conception.

The tragedies of Aeschylus were revered in their own day. Indeed, the Athenian citizens honored Aeschylus as they did no other playwright: they decreed after his death that anyone wishing to produce his plays should be awarded a chorus and allowed to be one of the three competitors at the Great Dionysia.

Like Aeschylus, Sophocles participated actively in the life of the *polis,* but unlike Aeschylus', Sophocles' life (496–406) spanned Athens' most glorious period in history. As a youth of

FIGURE 4.18

Three actors play Sophocles' Oedipus: Mr. Sheridan in the eighteenth century [from Fitzgerald], Mounet-Sulley in the nineteenth [from Loliée], and an American college production of the 1880s. [From *Century*.]

great talent and beauty, Sophocles led the chorus of thanksgiving after the victory in the battle of Salamis; as an adult, he was elected general and fought in the field with Pericles; and when he was over eighty, again responding to a call from the *polis,* he helped restore Athens after the crisis precipitated by the disastrous Syracusan defeat. He died only two years before Athens fell to Sparta. Sophocles was known in his own time as a citizen, a statesman, a general, and a poet.

Sophocles began competing in dramatic contests in 468, when he won first prize. During his long career, he wrote more than 120 plays, of which 7 tragedies remain, all dating from the second half of the century: *Ajax* (450–440?), *Antigone* (441?), *Oedipus Rex* (430–425?), *Electra* (418–410?), *Trachiniae* (413?), *Philoctetes* (409), and *Oedipus at Colonus* (406). Of these plays, *Oedipus Rex* is the acknowledged masterpiece. Chosen by Aristotle as a model against which other tragedies could be judged, it is still considered by many critics the greatest tragedy ever written.

More than Aeschylus, Sophocles focused on *human* tragedy. Given a universal order, how does humankind fit into the scheme? Again and again, the fact of an ordered universe is affirmed through the fulfillment of prophecies; over and over, human beings are shown struggling to understand and obey that order. Deviations from the order produce catastrophe; traditional values are therefore upheld.

With his different tragic vision, Sophocles adopted dramatic techniques different from those of Aeschylus. He introduced a third actor and used him to provide new points of view from which to examine the tragic protagonist. He increased the chorus to fifteen members and assigned it a role in further illuminating the central character, but he reduced the number of lines it delivered, thus giving the actors greater focus. He reduced the ceremonial and spectacular elements of production and replaced them with scenes of human suffering, discovery, and decision. He abandoned the trilogy in favor of a single, self-contained play in which the protagonist commits a tragic error and suffers the consequences of his or her own actions. (Although *Antigone, Oedipus Rex,* and *Oedipus at Colonus* are on the same subject, they were not intended for production on the same day and therefore do not form a trilogy.)

Sophocles was the most successful of the three tragic poets. After he defeated Aeschylus for first prize in 468, he went on to another twenty-three victories, and he never placed lower than second in any competition.

Euripides (ca. 480–407), a younger contemporary of Sophocles, was a spokesman for new and liberal ideas that were flowing into Athens, especially from Ionia. Euripides reached maturity in the Athens of expansion and commerce, the Periclean Athens that was in almost constant rivalry with other Greek *poleis.* Pericles and his mistress, Aspasia, were at the center of an intellectual circle that included leading Ionian and Athenian thinkers who called into question traditional beliefs about the nature of the universe, the place of the gods, and the proper behavior of humans. These new ideas found a receptive audience among the advanced thinkers in Athens, a city now teeming with foreigners, sailors, and merchants. Among those disenchanted with old solutions and traditional answers to new and pressing problems of commercial Athens was Euripides, who is said to have studied with Anaxagoras and Protagoras (members of Pericles' circle) and with Socrates, the age's leading phiosopher.

Perhaps because his liberal views were at odds with those of the majority of Athenians, Euripides was personally unpopular, a near recluse. His plays incorporated some of his advanced views, and they, too, were unpopular among Athenians during Euripides' lifetime. In some plays, for example, Euripides seems to have advocated a kind of situational ethics. Although Euripides wrote about ninety plays, he was awarded only five victories, and one of these posthumously. He often finished third among the three competitors.

Seventeen tragedies and one satyr play by Euripides remain: *Alcestis* (438), *Medea* (431), *Hippolytus* (428), *The Children of Heracles* (427?) *Andromache* (426?), *Hecuba* (425?), *Cyclops* (a satyr play, 423?), *Heracles* (422?), *The Suppliants* (421?), *Ion* (417?), *The Trojan Women* (415?), *Electra* (413?), *Iphigenia in Tauris* (414–412?), *Helen* (412), *The Phoenician Women* (409?), *Orestes* (408), *The Bacchae* (405?), and *Iphigenia at Aulis* (405?). Although Euripides wrote a play named *Rhesus*, scholars are now agreed that the ill-written *Rhesus* that has come down to us was not by Euripides but was the work of an unknown poet of the fourth century. That so many of his plays have survived attests to the esteem in which they were held by later audiences and scholars.

Many of Euripides' techniques, although condemned in his own day, were revered and adopted by playwrights of the fourth century and later. For example, Euripides' characters are neither so noble nor so statuesque as those of Aeschylus and Sophocles. Rather, Euripides drew characters in more social and human situations, dressed them in less elegant costumes, and caused them to speak more conversationally and colloquially. He reduced further the centrality of the chorus: it is often merely an observer of the action and often seems mostly to separate acting episodes, serving as interlude entertainment. The actors are clearly central. At the same time, he experimented with musical forms that increased the intricacies of melody and rhythm at the expense of words and meaning. He experimented, as well, with dramatic elements that later came to be called *melodramatic:* rapid reversals of fortune, last-minute reprieves from almost certain destruction, and sentimental episodes of love and family life (the reunion of long-lost family members, for example). He wrote prologues that were omniscient: a character (often a god) began by summarizing the story that was to follow, perhaps to reduce the importance of the dramatic action and to increase the importance of the ideas of the play. His endings, too, are obviously contrived and often feature a god flown in to set matters right (the so-called *deus ex machina*). Obviously, Aristophanes in *The Frogs* satirized both the dramatic and the thematic innovations of Euripides, comparing them unfavorably with the traditional values and techniques of Aeschylus and Sophocles.

Aristophanes (ca. 448–ca. 380) was an arch conservative in politics and in drama. Before the comic poet reached the age of twenty, Pericles was dead and Athenian glory was in decline. By the time he was thirty, Aristophanes saw that Athens had adopted a cynical foreign policy, abandoning former friends, forging alliances with former enemies, and electing to positions of leadership citizens whom he considered flashy rather than substantial. Aristophanes saw the invasion of Attica, the seige of Athens, and the final defeat of the empire. In the climate of a disintegrating *polis*, Aristophanes urged, through his comedies, a return to past glories, which he believed depended on traditional values in life and art.

Of the forty or so plays written by Aristophanes, eleven remain: *The Acharnians* (425), *The Knights* (424), *The Clouds* (423), *The Wasps* (422), *Peace* (421), *The Birds* (414), *Lysistrata* (411), *The Thesmophoriazusae* (411), *The Frogs* (405), *The Ecclesiazusae* (392?), and *Plutus* (388). The plays written before 404 are our only examples of so-called Old Comedy; the two plays written after 404 are our only examples of Middle Comedy. Old Comedy is distinguishable from Middle Comedy both by its highly formal structure and by its treatment of contemporary social and political events. Middle Comedy is considered merely a transitional phase between Old and New Comedy (popular during the Hellenistic Age). The assumption is that Old Comedy was censored out of existence when Sparta took control of Athens and that Middle Comedy was the result of comic authors' seeking new subjects and new structures for their art.

Although no two of Aristophanes' Old Comedies are exactly alike, and although the works of no other author survive, scholars have nonetheless offered a "model" for Greek Old Comedy:

Part One, or Attic Portion: presentation and acceptance of the Happy Idea that will be the basis of the play's action
   Prologos: scene prior to the entrance of the chorus
   Parodos: choral entrance
   Agon: debate
Parabasis: highly formal choral presentation, often involving direct address to the audience on political, social, or artistic issues of the day
Part Two, or Doric Portion: demonstrations of the results of putting the Happy Idea into effect
   Alternating episodes and songs
   Exodos: processional exit

Within this model, Aristophanes made pointed attacks on war and warmongers (*The Acharnians*, *Peace*, and *Lysistrata*), the "new" morality and art (*The Thesmophorizusae*, *The Clouds*, and *The Frogs*), and other contemporary issues. He also made personal and often quite vicious attacks on contemporary leaders who he believed were corrupting the country and leading it to ruin. He included lyrical sections of great beauty and juxtaposed them to visual and verbal gags that were often so obscene that translators feared to render them honestly. Not since Old Comedy has such a disparate cluster of elements been housed within a single dramatic structure. Old Comedy, at least as written by Aristophanes, is unique in dramatic history.

In Middle Comedy, the subjects became more generalized and less topical. Often burlesques of mythology or stories of domestic bliss and intrigue form the basis of the action. Structurally, the plays resemble the tragedies of Euripides (episodes separated by choral odes) rather than the works of Old Comedy.

How typical are Aristophanes' plays of other Old and Middle Comedies? The question is difficult to answer. Comic competitions were held for sixty years before Aristophanes' first extant play, and doubtless comedy had changed considerably in the interim. Also, Aristophanes was not generally a successful competitor: he evidently won only four first and three second prizes, yet we have no idea why his rivals' works were deemed superior. As our only extant examples of comedies from the period, however, Aristophanes' plays are necessarily the evidence on which we build our conclusions about Old and Middle Comedy. As the latest group of extant plays, they also serve to signal changes in Athenian society during the last quarter of the Classical Age and to suggest new directions for comedies in the Age of Alexander that was to follow. We must remember, however, that the plays may be atypical and our conclusions badly skewed.

The Hellenistic Period
(336 B.C.–ca. 150 B.C.)

Macedon was only a semicivilized area at the northern reaches of the Greek lands when Philip connived to become the leader of all Greece. He aspired to unite the *poleis* and lead them to victory against the great Persian Empire. Through both warcraft and statecraft, Philip moved toward his goal—until his assassination in 336.

Alexander (356–323) shared his father's aspiration, and when he succeeded Philip in 336, he marched into southern Greece. Sacking Thebes and courting Athens, Alexander brought all of Greece under his leadership through a combination of coercion, terrorism, and hope. In fewer than fifteen years, he built an empire that united Greeks, Persians, and Macedonians and that stretched to Russia, Egypt, and India (see Figure 4.19). He was worshipped by some as a god and called, by many, the Great.

His unexpected death at the age of thirty-three left the empire without a leader. Confusion and civil war reigned briefly, and soon Alexander's empire split into several smaller monarchies, each of which recognized (at least

FIGURE 4.19

Map of Alexander's empire at its height.

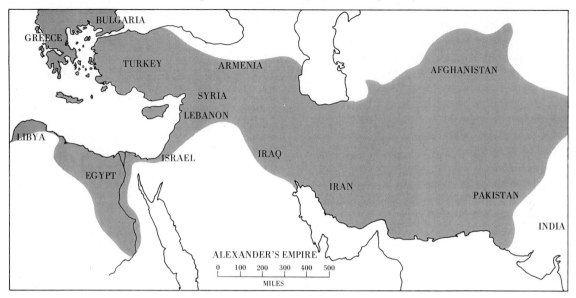

sporadically) the legitimacy of the others. Although never entirely stable, the arrangement lasted until the end of the Hellenistic Age, another 175 years. The Hellenistic monarchies gradually folded and were absorbed by a new, aggressive land and sea power, Rome. Historians agree that after about 150 B.C., the Hellenistic Age ended, for thereafter Roman influence shaped the direction of Greek life and art.

The Hellenistic Age saw the collapse of the *polis* as a form of government. For one thing, the ideal of a citizen as a man capable of participating in all aspects of civic life had eroded after Pericles until, by the time of Alexander, it had ceased to exist. Only specialists could serve the needs of the large, urban commercial centers that cities like Athens and Corinth had become. Also, the autonomy and diversity of the *poleis* were weakened as Alexander and later monarchs forged large governing units. Government was thus separated from the people and, because distanced, lost its former cohesive force. At the same time, the traditional gods of the *polis* were gradually delocalized; they became in-

stead protectors of larger groups, for example, protectors of all Greeks instead of merely Athenians. Also, among some, the worship of living kings as gods became fashionable, and these god–kings (like Alexander and the Ptolemies in Egypt) required allegiance beyond a single *polis*. Among the popular philosophies of the period, only Stoicism advocated active participation in civic life; the Skeptics, the Cynics, and the Epicureans urged withdrawal.

Accompanying the weakening of the individual *polis* was the increasing sense of unity among all Greek *poleis*. In part, the new solidarity was encouraged by an increased awareness of their common heritage, a heritage quite different from that of the foreigners among whom the Greeks increasingly found themselves following Alexander's conquests. The practical needs of commerce likewise contributed to unity. Imperial coinage (based on the Attic standard) facilitated trade by eliminating the need for money changers at every turn. A universal Greek language (a modification of Attic Greek) gradually supplanted local dialects and served not only businessmen in the market-place but also the writers of a growing Hellenistic literature. Communication among cities was eased as harbors were improved and manuals of seacraft devised. Indeed, the Greek cities seemed anxious to cultivate friendly relations among themselves and so negotiated pacts of friendship, provided financial support in times of crisis, and even conferred citizenship on members of friendly *poleis.* During the Hellenistic Age, then, *Greece* came into being; Athens was an important part of Greece, but only a part nonetheless.

Perhaps most important of all, the Hellenistic Age was marked by enormous shifts in population. Overcrowded cities in the homeland found relief as its people flooded foreign lands; about 275 such Hellenistic colonies are now known by name. As Greeks pushed into these territories, they took their civilization with them.

During the Hellenistic Age, Greek art was exported to an unprecedented degree. The construction of new towns and the reconstruction of old ones popularized Greek architecture throughout the Mediterranean lands and beyond. At cities like Delos, Pergamum, Priene, Antioch, and Alexandria, construction proceeded according to plans that had developed in Greece; the plans called for streets, temples, palaces, theatres, libraries, and gymnasia, all built according to Greek ideas of usefulness, appropriateness, and beauty. At Alexandria, for example, the new library became a center of learning that rivalled the Athenian academies for intellectual leadership. At Ephesus, the theatre could seat twenty-three thousand, more than could be accommodated at the Theatre of Dionysus. Because civic and military leaders were customarily honored by commemorative statues, Greek sculpture spread throughout the civilized world as thousands of statues were commissioned, completed, erected, and viewed. Painted vases found their way into Italy, India, and Russia, and jewelry made by Greek artists from Alexander's plundered gold and silver found markets throughout the commercial world. The well-to-do throughout the empire looked to Athens for cultural leadership, and so knowledge of Athens and its arts became the mark of an educated person. By the second century, educated Romans could speak Greek as well as Latin, and Greek intellectuals were sought after in Roman circles. In sum, as Athenians and other Greeks lived and traded throughout Alexander's vast empire, they took their way of life—buildings, sculptures, religion, literature, and drama—with them. Athenian art had become Greek art, and Greek art had become the art of the Western civilized world.

Festivals

As Greek art spread, so did the festivals and, with them, theatrical contests. Such contests were then included at festivals for gods other than Dionysus and at festivals given to honor political and military leaders as well as gods. For example, after Alexander captured Thebes in 335, he held a nine-day festival devoted primarily to dramatic contests, and, at Sicyon, a festival was established to honor a hero who died there in 213. This increased dramatic activity became a part of the increasingly cooperative spirit of many Greek cities, which now regularly exchanged invitations to festivals. And some time after about 275, artists from throughout the Greek world gathered regularly at Delphi for a major arts festival.

As both the number of cities and the kinds of festivals that included theatre increased, the rules governing festivals probably diversified to meet local interests and needs. At the City Dionysia, for example, revivals of old tragedies and old comedies became a regular part of each festival, whereas only one satyr play was given, and it at the beginning of the days devoted to drama.

Producing arrangements also changed. The *choregoi* were replaced (between 317 and 307) by an elected civic official (*agonothetes*) who managed the dramatic contests and used public funds set aside for that purpose. All artists connected with the festival theatres (poets, performers, musicians, costumers, and chorus trainers) organized into a union sometime before 275, and, thereafter, the *agonothetes* drew contracts for performances through the union. The union provided everything required for the production. Its members traveled widely; for example, one monument dating from the early third century commemorated the victories of one actor at Athens, Thebes, Argos, Dodona, and elsewhere (often in plays by Euripides, evidence of that poet's rising popularity after the fifth century). Three actors and a flute player were still used, but the number of chorus members seems to have declined in both tragedy and comedy (to seven and then four?), perhaps as a consequence of cost. Guild records alluding to members wrote of both solo and ensemble musicians, chorus trainers, and costumers, suggesting that the trend toward increased specialization in theatrical production was continued throughout the Hellenistic Age.

Called Artists of Dionysus, the union had three major branches: the Athenian, the Isthmaian, and the Ionian, each with several subdivisions that enjoyed a measure of independence. Its members almost certainly had a privileged status, for they traveled unimpeded throughout the empire and occasionally served as accredited diplomats among political leaders. At least some were exempt from military service, from arrest, and (by 146) from taxes and public service. On the other hand, members of the guild could be severely fined if they failed to meet their contractual obligations.

Theatres and Staging

The Hellenistic Age witnessed the building of an unprecedented number of theatres and, at the same time, the remodeling of many older theatres in order to bring them into accord with Hellenistic ideals. In Attica alone, during the Hellenistic Age, there were at least twelve theatres, including the Theatre of Dionysus. Outside of Attica, theatres were built in the Greek homeland, Asia Minor, Africa, and Italy, in towns like Delos, Ephesus, Epidaurus, Oropus, Priene, and Sicyon (see Figure 4.20).

Like the cities built in Alexander's empire, the Hellenistic theatres seem to have been constructed in accordance with a model, for, despite regional variations, they shared a number of common features. The theatres consisted of a circular or nearly circular *orchestra*, a two-storied *skene*, and an audience area situated on a hillside. They differed from earlier theatres mainly in their *skene*, which was built of stone and included a stage (*logeion*) that was high (ca. 8–12 feet), narrow (ca. 6½–14 feet), and long (ca. 45–140 feet). At the rear of the stage was the *skene* wall (*episkenion*) pierced by either one to three doors or one to seven larger openings called *thyromata*. Supporting the stage at its front edge was the *proskenion*, which may have provided a background for performances in the *orchestra* in some theatres. Access to the stage was often by means of ramps or steps that led from the end of the stage into the *eisodoi*; in other theatres, however, access was perhaps through the *skene* only, for no ramps or steps have been unearthed.

In some theatres, the stage and the *proskenion* cut into the *orchestra* circle slightly, reducing the circle somewhat but not yet cutting it to a semicircle. Hillside seating, sectioned by vertical and horizontal aisles, consisted of backless stone benches, except for the thronelike chairs near the *orchestra* that were used as seats of honor. The capacities of the theatres varied widely: 3,000 at Oropus and about 23,000 at Ephesus (see Figure 4.21).

The use of stone rather than wood and the inclusion of a high, raised stage obviously had implications for staging, but their effects are unclear. Because stone buildings are more permanent than wooden structures, less experimentation can perhaps be assumed. Also, the presence of a high, raised stage suggests that the performances unfolded there. This view, however, is not without problems. If the per-

FIGURE 4.20
Map showing known sites of Hellenistic theatres.

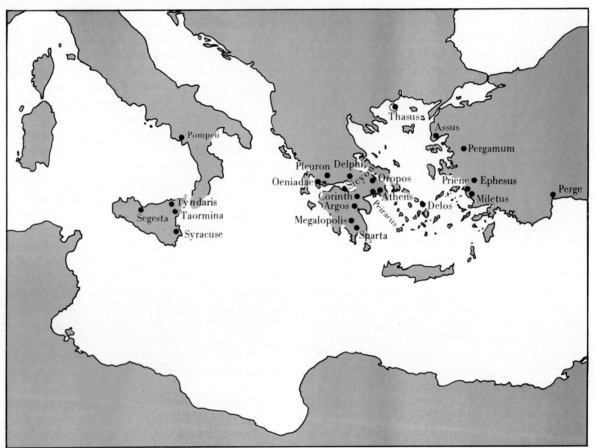

formers were on the stage, where did the chorus dance? If the chorus no longer danced (and so could fit on the stage), how were they kept out of the way of the actors? Even reduced in number, choruses were large, given the narrow stages (seven feet deep) of many Hellenistic theatres. Or if still dancing and necessarily in the *orchestra*, how did the chorus interact with the onstage performers? Twelve vertical feet is a sizable distance for the convenient exchange of dialogue, and the ramps at the ends of the stage (where present at all) do not suggest easy communication. Or were the actors also in the *orchestra*? But if everyone was in the *orchestra*,

why was there a stage? If everyone was in the *orchestra*, then the *proskenion* must have served as a background for the action. In some Hellenistic theatres, however, the *proskenion* was so low that doors in it would have been too low for actors wearing the built-up footwear and masks of the period.

Where, then, was the performance? Were all of the performers onstage? In the *orchestra*? Were the actors onstage and the chorus in the *orchestra*? Were revivals of old plays (in which the choruses were large and well integrated into the action) given in the *orchestra*, and performances of new plays (with small and largely in-

FIGURE 4.21

The Theatre at Epidaurus, the most perfectly preserved of all Greek theatres, is a model of a Hellenistic theatre. [Photograph courtesy of Briant Hamor Lee.]

cidental choruses) produced on the stage? Did the practices vary from theatre to theatre, depending on the repertory offered and on local architectural peculiarities? This important possibility deserves more study. Epidaurus (built ca. 350, at the end of the classical period) may well have been an innovator in the use of the raised stage, others adopting it soon thereafter in their new buildings. The Theatre of Dionysus, on the other hand, seems to have been conservative both in its repertory and in its building program (its Hellenistic *skene* was not completed until near the end of the Hellenistic Age). Answers are not yet available to such important questions, however.

Other unanswered questions raise again the issue of Greek staging: Was it illusionistic or conventionalized? Some scholars have imagined that the *thyromata* were adopted in order to increase the depth of the stage and to provide "rear stages" on which scenes could be played,

thyromata thus functioning like miniature proscenium arches. Apart from the difficulties with sight lines that such a practice would introduce, its suggestion of acting behind a frame (in the manner of post-Renaissance stages) implies a degree of illusionism not common on facade stages. At the *proskenion*, some scholars have imagined that *pinakes* or *periaktoi*, painted with representational scenes, were placed between the columns. Indeed, in some theatres, the columns are notched, as if to hold panels of some sort. *Periaktoi* could, of course, be turned to reveal a new face to the audience and thus change the play's setting quickly (see Figure 4.9). Other scholars, although accepting the presence of *pinakes* and *periaktoi*, argue that they were painted with highly conventionalized, perhaps geometric, designs (see Figure 4.22).

Certain of the theatres had underground passageways ("Charon's steps") that connected the interior of the *skene* with the middle of the *orchestra*. Were these used for miraculous appearances and disappearances, or did they serve less spectacular needs? And were the thunder and lightning machines (*bronteion* and *keraunoskopeion*, respectively) described by Pollux nearly three hundred years later really used in Hellenistic theatres? Although considerable archaeological evidence remains, the dearth of plays from the Hellenistic Age prevents our answering such important questions about the staging practices of this two-hundred-year period.

Performers and Their Costumes

Trends noted in the declining years of the Classical Age apparently continued into this period, although the evidence (one play, assorted fragments, ambiguous iconographic pieces, and a few commentaries) does not permit certain conclusions.

The role of the chorus probably declined further; it often performed only incidental music between episodes. As music became increasingly ornate and sometimes overpowered

FIGURE 4.22

Conjectural reconstruction of a typical Hellenistic theatre showing *thyromata* and *pinakes*. Reconstruction may be utterly false, for no one knows how the *episkenion* and *proskenion* looked. [Adapted and redrawn from Dörpfeld.]

the words, professional singers were hired to perform in the choruses of both tragedies and comedies. The size of the chorus was reduced, perhaps to seven or four, at least in performances of some new plays in certain theatres.

Actors, on the other hand, increased in importance. At the beginning of the Hellenistic Age, Aristotle complained that actors were already more important than poets: probably the popularity of revivals helped shift the emphasis away from poets and toward actors. Also, acting contests were numerous and were often more interesting then the contests among poets; for example, in 254 at the City Dionysia, there were contests for the best actor in an old tragedy, an old comedy, and an old satyr play. The visual emphasis on the actor also increased. Tragic actors by the end of the period wore platformed boots (*cothornoi*) and a high headress (*onkos*), both of which increased their stature. Comic actors, although dressed in ordinary street clothes of the sort popular among Athens' middle class, often wore highly exaggerated masks, as did the tragic actors. If both sorts of actors performed on a raised stage (as seems likely), they gained still more emphasis.

Some scholars rely on a Greek lexicographer, Pollux, for additional data on costumes; he reported that the characters and the costumes in both tragedy and comedy had become somewhat conventionalized. He listed about thirty-five types of tragic masks and forty-five types of comic masks (and, by implication, of characters). As well, he indicated that certain colors had come to be associated with certain characters; for example, young women wore white, and comic slaves had red hair. But Pollux was writing in the second century A.D., about three hundred years after the Hellenistic Age. Because his aim was to define certain words rather than to write a history of theatrical practice, he may have considered chronology unimportant. He may have described the theatre of his own day and may therefore be a wholly unreliable source of accurate information about practices in the Hellenistic period.

Plays, Playwrights, and Critics

Although considerable archaeological evidence exists to aid in the reconstruction of Hellenistic theatres, very little remains to offer information about its plays. Of the several thousand plays and several hundred poets from this period, only a single complete play has survived, alongside assorted titles, fragments, and poets' names. This scant information allows us to surmise that the popularity of New Comedy and mime increased while that of tragedy and satyr plays declined.

The single extant play is a New Comedy entitled *Dyskolos* (*The Grumbler*, 316) by the poet Menander (ca. 342–291). This recently discovered (1959) play, a series of Menanderian fragments unearthed in Egypt in 1905, scattered references in antiquity, and the plays of the *Roman* authors Plautus and Terence (fl. 200–160), who presumably copied Greek originals, form the basis for scholars' conclusions about New Comedy.

New Comedy abandoned the topical satire and personal allusions of Old Comedy and took as its subjects the romantic and domestic intrigue of upper-middle-class Athenians. Typically, the plays' action unfolded on a street (the stage?) in front of several houses (the doors, or *thyromata?*). A married couple in love, separated through a series of misunderstandings, might be reunited; or a young man might win his heart's desire over the objections of an interfering father, when (with the help of a slave) money was found or stolen to buy the girl or when she was discovered to be of good family and the father's objections were withdrawn. The violation of maidens, the abandonment of babies, and the reconciliation of long-separated families figured prominently in many plots, and these recurrent situations gave rise, in turn, to recurring types of characters: husbands, wives, young men, young women, slaves, and fathers, all supplemented by soldiers, slave dealers, courtesans, parasites, and cooks.

New Comedy abandoned, as well, the highly formal structure of Old Comedy (*prologos, parados, agon, parabasis*, etc.). Instead, an expository prologue introduced a series of episodes (often five) separated by choral interludes. The use of an expository prologue, which gave the audience information withheld from the characters, increased opportunities for irony. Indeed, the technique of the prologue, the relaxed structure, and the sentimental and melodramatic incidents have caused some scholars to suppose that Euripides was a major influence on the development of Greek New Comedy.

Although modern critics have found fault with Menander and New Comedy because of its limited range of characters and situations, ancient scholars and audiences apparently admired both. The plays of Menander were often revived, and in antiquity Menander's fame was eclipsed only by that of Homer and Vergil (author of Rome's major epic, the *Aeneid*). One Alexandrian critic ranked Menander second only to Homer among all Greek writers, apparently because of his ability to capture life in his art: "O Menander, O Life, which of you imitated the other?"[13]

As the popularity of New Comedy increased, so did that of the mime, a form different from New Comedy—but how different, we do not know. Perhaps as an antidote to the standardized plots and characters of New Comedy, mimes were extraordinarily diverse. Some works called mimes were written; some were improvised. Some were performed; others were read. Some were for solo performers; others needed several actors. Some were in song, others in speech. Some were in verse, others in prose. Some were travesties of myths, others parodies of tragedies, and still others sketches of daily life (in which adultery often figured prominently). Some were crude; others were polished. Some obscene, some not. All were short. The term *mime*, then, may not have described a kind of play (like *comedy*) so much as a length of work (like *one-act play*) or a recognizable system of delivery (like *television*).

The history of mime, too, is difficult to reconstruct. Occasional references to mime date from the fifth and fourth centuries in Athens, the Peloponnese, and Magna Graecia (as the Greek colonies in Italy were called). In the Doric colony of Syracuse, for example, Epicharmus was writing plays between 485 and 467. Some scholars insist that he wrote mimes; others believe that his plays merely foreshadowed later, Doric mimes. (It is, of course, on Epicharmus that the Dorians based their claim as the originators of comedy; see pp. 36–37. And Doric mime was thought by many to have influenced the second portion of Old Comedy; see p. 94.) In Athens in the fourth century, the philosopher Plato admired certain prose mimes of his day and even described a mime performance in his *Symposium*.

References to mime increased markedly during the Hellenistic period. At the beginning of the third century, Rhinthon in Syracuse was writing *hilarotragoidia* (tragic parodies probably based on Euripides), and within fifty years, Herodas in Alexandria was writing *Mimiambi* for solo reading only. In Athens, at about the same period, a terra-cotta lamp showing three actors

and bearing the Greek inscription: "Mimologoi. Hypothesis: The Mother-in-law" confirmed that mime performances were continuing there as well.

Some scholars have imagined that Greek mimes in Magna Graecia (where they were called *phlyakes*; see Figure 4.23) were the source of the Roman mime, but no definite link has yet been established.

Performers in the mimes (the plays) were also called mimes. These performers are of interest to theatre historians for several reasons. First, mime troupes were probably the first to include women performers, a fact that may account for the low esteem in which mime performers were held. Mimes were never, for example, permitted to join the Artists of Dionysus, and until Hellenistic times they seldom per-

FIGURE 4.23

A detail of a vase. Notice again the use of comic nudity. Whether the scene is theatrical or mythical is unclear. [From Winckelman. Courtesy of the Rare Books Room, University of South Carolina.]

formed at the great civic festivals. Second, mimes were almost certainly the first professional actors, and as a part of their profession they traveled widely in order to survive. Finally, some mimes performed without masks (and perhaps without shoes), a clear departure from the practices of the respected festival actors. As mime increased in popularity and began to be performed at festivals during the Hellenistic Age, the connection between masks and theatrical performances weakened (and by late in the Roman Empire, it almost disappeared).

The popularity of both satyr plays and tragedies declined during the Hellenistic Age. Little is known of the satyr plays, but Hellenistic tragedies apparently continued in directions taken at the time of Euripides. For example, the incidental role of the chorus and the preference for obscure myths marked Hellenistic, as well as Euripidean, tragedy. Revivals of Euripides' works were common throughout the period, and newly written plays also featured romantic, sentimental, melodramatic, and spectacular episodes of the sort first popularized by Euripides.

The Hellenistic Age produced as well a number of important critics of the drama. The first and by far the most important was Aristotle (384–322), a philosopher, scientist, and scholar so respected in his own day that Philip of Macedon chose him as the tutor for Alexander. After Alexander's accession to power, Aristotle returned to Athens to open his own school, where he wrote widely in biology, logic, metaphysics, philosophy, physics, politics, rhetoric, and poetry. Of his major works on the drama (including a compilation of festival records from the fifth and fourth centuries, the *didascalia*), only the *Poetics* has survived. Its influence on subsequent dramatic theory and criticism has been incalculable.

After a brief history of the origin of drama (see pp. 35–37), Aristotle in the *Poetics* examined the six parts of a play (plot, character, thought, diction, music, and spectacle); the means of achieving unity (and thus beauty); the nature of probability; the parts of a plot (suffering, discovery, and reversal; complication and denouement); the kinds of plot (simple and complex); the nature of the tragic hero; and so on. Because of the complexity of the ideas being treated and the cryptic prose of the original, the *Poetics* has been variously interpreted. Even now, the work remains controversial as scholars seek to understand it better, and almost all contemporary work in dramatic theory acknowledges a debt to the work, if only finally to disagree with its conclusions.

But Aristotle was not the only critic and theorist. By the middle of the third century, important critical activity had begun in earnest at Alexandria. Original editions of Greek dramas had been transferred from the archives at Athens to the library at Alexandria, which had already purchased Aristotle's collection of books after his death. At Alexandria, then, a large number of critics worked to arrange, criticize, and annotate Greek texts, explaining allusions whose references might be unclear to later generations.

Some modern scholars have proposed that this shift from the production of original dramas to the criticism of those dramas serves as an appropriate metaphor for the shift from a free, independent, and creative *polis* to the censored, bureaucratized, and scientific spirit of Alexander's *cosmopolis*, or world society.

The importance of the Hellenistic Age is often unappreciated by those who are dazzled by the drama of the Classical Age. The Hellenistic Age is the one that spread Greek arts and culture to distant lands and established them as models to be emulated by civilized Western countries. As M. Cary noted some time ago, "Rome was the pupil of Greece . . . and Hellenistic, not Classical Greece, was her teacher."[14]

The Graeco-Roman Period (ca. 150 B.C.–ca. A.D. 476)

As Roman commerce throve, Rome gradually but relentlessly encroached on territories once held by Alexander. Although her inroads were uneven and erratic, Rome eventually gained political dominance over former Greek lands. In many instances, she adopted Greek art and culture, and in others, she replaced them with her own. Often, however, Roman and Greek customs merged to form a new, Graeco-Roman practice. For example, although new (Roman) theatres were built throughout the Roman empire (including in Greek lands), Hellenistic Greek theatres were also remodeled so as to be brought into accord with Roman ideals of usefulness and beauty. In general, these remodeled, Graeco-Roman, theatres had an ornate *skene* that included side wings jutting out at each end (*paraskenia*). The stage was lowered to about five feet and was deepened (usually by cutting into the *orchestra*, reducing it to a semicircle; see Figure 4.24).

After the second century B.C., very little in Greece remained untouched by Rome; Greek customs, politics, and art became Romanized, and the Graeco-Roman Age was under way. Although Greek life and art continued, the world was no longer defined in terms of Greece. Instead, the influence, and therefore the interest,

FIGURE 4.24

Remains of the Theatre of Dionysus in its final, Graeco-Roman form. [Photograph courtesy of Briant Hamor Lee.]

had shifted to Rome, the Eternal City, where they would remain for the next seven hundred years.

ENDNOTES

1. H. D. F. Kitto, *The Greeks* rev. ed. (Baltimore: Penguin Books, 1957), pp. 95–96.
2. The standard work on Athenian festivals is A. W. Pickard-Cambridge, *The Dramatic Festivals at Athens* (Oxford: Clarendon Press, 1953), from which we have drawn heavily in our discussion.
3. William J. Baumol, "Economics of Athenian Drama," *Quarterly Journal of Economics* 85 (August 1971): 369, 372.
4. R. E. Wycherley, *The Stones of Athens* (Princeton, N.J.: Princeton University Press, 1978), p. 203.
5. Discussion of this outcropping and its possible use in staging can be found first in N. G. L. Hammond, "Dramatic Production to the Death of Aeschylus," *Greek, Roman, and Byzantine Studies* 13 (1972): 387–450.
6. A. Muller (1886), as cited by Oliver Taplin, *The Stagecraft of Aeschylus* (Oxford: Clarendon Press, 1977), p. 31.
7. As summarized by Taplin, p. 33.
8. Points suggested by Taplin, pp. 34–36.
9. Discussions of new archaeological discoveries and their importance for theatre can be found in Hammond, Wycherley, and Taplin. The earlier views were best set forth by A. W. Pickard-Cambridge, *The Theatre of Dionysus in Athens* (Oxford: Clarendon Press, 1946).
10. A. E. Haigh, *The Attic Theatre*, 3rd rev. ed and partially rewritten by A. W. Pickard-Cambridge (London, 1898; reprinted, New York: Haskell House, 1968), p. 1.
11. A review of the evidence and its interpretations are in Thomas Harvey Van Brunt, "A Reevaluation of the Evidence Used to Reconstruct Athen-

ian Theatrical Costume of the Classical Age" (Ph.D. diss. Indiana University, 1978), to whom we are indebted for much of the following discussion.

12. Mark Griffith, *The Authenticity of "Prometheus Bound"* (Cambridge: Cambridge University Press, 1977).

13. Aristophanes of Byzantium, as quoted by George E. Duckworth, *The Nature of Roman Comedy* (Princeton, N.J.: Princeton University Press, 1952), p. 31.

14. M. Cary, *A History of the Greek World from 323 to 146 B.C.*, 2nd ed. (New York: Barnes and Noble, 1951), p. 375.

Greek Theatre, 534 B.C.–ca. A.D. 476

105

5

Roman Theatre, 240 B.C.–ca. A.D. 476

Roman civilization lasted over one thousand years. Although its public entertainments regularly played to audiences numbering in the tens of thousands, theatre was only one of these entertainments and was never so popular as, say, horse racing. Moreover, Roman theatre, although popular, was never central to the life of the city or its people. From the outset, theatre and drama in Rome were conceived of primarily as entertainments and were treated accordingly. Theatre was a commercial, professional enterprise rather than a civic, communal celebration. Rome imported and adapted plays from Greece. She borrowed, however, not the great classical tragedies of Aeschylus or Sophocles nor the Old Comedies of Aristophanes but contemporary, Hellenistic tragedies and Greek New Comedies. Such transplanted plays failed to take root, and once their novelty had worn off, legitimate drama in Rome died.

Under these circumstances, it is ironic that Rome more than Greece (or perhaps more accurately, Greece as interpreted through Rome) shaped the direction of later theatre and drama in western Europe. When Renaissance authors searched their past for literary models, they read the Roman authors Terence, Plautus, and Seneca. When they sought rules for the formation of plays, they turned to the Roman theorist Horace. And when they inquired after architectural principles for the building of theatres and scenery, they discovered the writings of the Roman architect Vitruvius.[1]

The importance of Roman theatre and drama, then, rests less with itself than with its very considerable influence on the later culture of western Europe, and so the study of Roman theatre and drama is, in one sense, the study of a pipeline. Hellenistic drama and theatre fed into the line at one end. At the other end came out those Romanized Greek plays and practices that were to exert such a profound influence on the writers and thinkers of the Renaissance.

Some of the most obvious changes that Rome made in the Greek models can be attributed to the influence of another theatrical tradition in Rome: a theatre packed with subliterary entertainments that predated the arrival of legitimate Greek drama and flourished long after its disappearance. This popular theatre tempered the Greek practices it received, shaping them to Roman tastes. But this popular theatre is important for two additional reasons. First, some scholars have seen in it the sources of the medieval farces, the commedia dell'arte, and even the professional actors of the Middle Ages. Second, it was this popular theatre—especially the mime—that earned the enmity of the Christian Church and began that antipathy between Church and theatre that exists to this day.

Because both the literary (Greek-inspired) and popular traditions were influenced by Rome's political fortunes, we often refer here to Rome's two major political periods: the Republic (ca. 500 B.C.–27 B.C.) and the Empire (27 B.C.–A.D. 476 in the West and to 1453 in the East). But because changes in Rome's theatrical prac-

107

Roman Theatre, 240 B.C.–ca. A.D. 476

tices did not coincide with these political periods, we will study her theatre in four major periods: (1) the origins of the popular tradition (ca. seventh century B.C.–240 B.C.); (2) the literary tradition (240 B.C.–ca. 100 B.C.); (3) the writers and scholars and the triumph of the popular tradition (c. 100 B.C.–A.D. 476 or 1453); and (4) the move east (A.D. 330–A.D. 1453). A careful study of Figure 5.1 can provide a solid grounding for the remainder of the chapter. Obviously, as in Greece, we are dealing with over a thousand years of theatre, and so generalizations, although necessary, are apt to be misleading. Also as in Greece, our evidence is sparse and what we have is not continuous. Most of what we know about the drama dates from the Republic (from which we have plays intended for the theatre), but most of what we know about the physical theatre dates from the Empire (from which we have architectural remains).

The Origins of the Popular Tradition (Seventh Century B.C.–240 B.C.)

Rome's beginnings were modest and did not foretell her future position as a world leader. Probably founded in the eighth century B.C.,

Rome nestled on the banks of the Tiber River in an area called Latium, sandwiched between rival cultures more powerful than she. To the north were the Etruscans, civilized traders whose contacts with the Greeks (both in Italy and on the mainland) were well established. To the south was Magna Graecia, whose major cities, like Syracuse in Sicily and Tarentum on Italy's heel, were centers of trade and culture. Across the Mediterranean lay the powerful maritime city of Carthage, whose sphere of influence already included Spain, North Africa, Sicily, and Sardinia. To the west of Rome and running the length of the Italian peninsula lay the Apennine mountains, discouraging expansion in that direction. Backed up against the mountains, Rome found herself facing civilizations whose commerce and culture were already advanced (see Figure 5.2).

At the beginning of the fifth century, when Pisastratus' reforms were launching Athens into her greatest age, Rome was still under Etruscan domination and struggling to oust the foreign kings who ruled her. She finally established herself as an independent republic sometime between 500 and 450 B.C. At the beginning of the fourth century, when Sparta's defeat of Athens had tarnished the Athenian Golden Age, the young Roman Republic was threatened with extinction, as fierce tribes from northern Europe (the Gauls) overran the city of Rome. Not until Alexander subdued Athens and

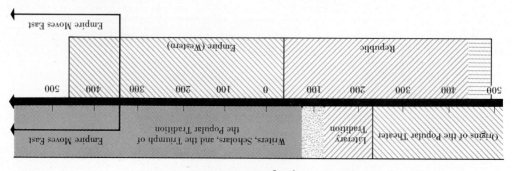

FIGURE 5.1
Time line: Major periods of Roman drama.

Greece entered its Hellenistic Age did Rome's fortunes begin to improve. She first overcame other cities in Latium to become that region's acknowledged leader (338). Almost immediately, she fought and defeated another Italian people, the Samnites (Oscans) to become ruler of central Italy (290). Her war with the Samnites, in turn, brought her into direct contact with the Greek cities to the south, and within seventy-five years, they too were bound to Rome (275). By 264 b.c., Roman supremacy extended to every part of the Italian peninsula.

During this stage of its growth, the Republic was a solidly rural culture. The family, its basic social unit, was ruled by the eldest male member, who held absolute, life-and-death control over his wife, his children, and his slaves. The state religion discouraged exotic or emotional practices in favor of a no-nonsense appreciation of solid Roman virtues: agriculture, family, and country. Rome's wars were fought by a citizen army, and her policies were set by the Roman Senate, a group of elder statesmen who, like the soldiers, were mostly self-sufficient landholders. Triumphal processions featured military heroes who displayed their war spoils in formal parades through the central city. Funeral processions included masked men who impersonated the heroes and events of the recent and distant past, reviewing the illustrious deeds of the newly dead and cataloging those of his most famous ancestors.

This Rome had no literature and no drama. But it had other arts and entertainments, which, like its culture, were highly derivative, the result of Rome's collisions with more advanced cultures. Adopting whatever was congenial and rejecting whatever was not, Rome typically adapted new ways to her own tastes, creating in the process a unique amalgam of different elements that then became "Roman."

Etruscan Influences

Rome's first cultural collision was with Etruria, which dominated Rome during the seventh and sixth centuries b.c. Etruria had long-established contacts with Greek and other Eastern cultures and had a highly developed civilization that already included a wide variety of public entertainments: drinking, dining, dancing, gaming, gladiatorial combats, horse rac-

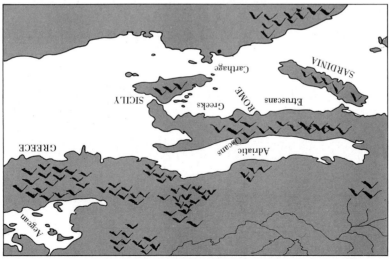
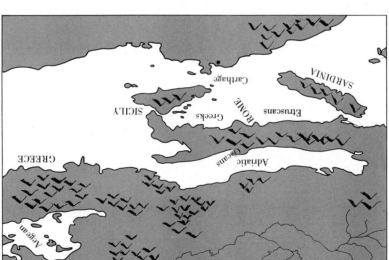

FIGURE 5.2
Perspective map of Italy and neighbors.

ing, boxing, wrestling, and animal shows. Her public activities were filled with music, and variety was their hallmark. Etruscan wall paintings confirm the popularity of such entertainments, for they show audiences in movable seating, on stadium-style benches, and even in elevated, private, curtained boxes. Such entertainments found their way, piecemeal, to Rome. The last Etruscan kings of Rome brought in triumphal processions and instituted the first public festivals, or games, the *ludi Romani*. With the first festival, they introduced circuses, or horse racing. In 364, Etruscan dancers were brought to Rome to appease the gods and thus end a plague that was threatening the city. In 264, the first gladiators appeared in Rome.

Etruria, too, probably gave to Rome the short, improvised, and often obscene dramatic sketches called *Fescennine Verses* (from the town of Fescennium in Etruria?). Typically performed at harvests, wine festivals, weddings, and (later) triumphal processions throughout north and central Italy, these rustic pieces originally featured masked clowns who sang and spoke in varied meters and alternating verses.

Hundreds of years before Rome imported her first Greek play, then, she had already instituted festivals, like those in Etruria, where a variety of incidental entertainments mingled and throve. She had adapted, as well, a kind of subliterary farce whose origins were most likely Etruscan.

Oscan Influences

During the fourth century B.C., the Etruscan influence on Rome was replaced by Oscan influences. Originally a mountain people, the Oscans were driven by overpopulation to spill out of the mountains and into the lowlands, taking over some cities (like Cumae) that had originally been Greek. Oscan expansion into the areas around modern Naples thus brought her into contact (and conflict) with both Rome to the north and Magna Graecia to the south.

From Oscan lands came a type of short, im-provised farce that Roman writers took care to distinguish from mime (which it resembled). Called *Atellan farce* (after the Oscan town Atella?), this improvised comedy depended on stock costumes and masks as well as stock characters. There were four or five coarse, greedy characters that were repeated from skit to skit: Maccus, Bucco, Pappus, Dossenus, and (perhaps) Mandacus. Probably Mandacus was a chewer, a monster with great jaws, and Pappus was a foolish old man. Both Maccus and Bucco were fools, the former perhaps a stupid guzzler and the latter a boastful buffoon. Some scholars have suggested that Dossenus was a hunchback and, by extension, a wise fool, but others believe him to be identical with Mandacus. The actors in Atellan farce were probably given only the barest outlines of a plot, from which they were expected to improvise their performances. They apparently sought laughter through physical (often obscene) gags as well as from riddles, patter songs, and abundant topical allusions. As in mime, the stories of Atellan farces often featured an intrigue that was facilitated by the disguise of one or more characters.

This popular farce was well developed in Oscan lands by the time the Romans encroached there. Although some farces continued to be given in Oscan lands and language, increasing numbers appeared in Rome in Latin. Thus transplanted, the farce was originally performed by amateurs but was soon taken over by professionals. It assumed a literary form briefly during the early first century B.C., when Pomponius and Novius wrote short *Atellanae* (three hundred to four hundred verses) to serve as afterpieces (*exodia*) for regular plays. After another brief spurt of popularity during the reign of the emperor Hadrian (A.D. 117–138), the Atellan farce virtually disappeared from existing records.

The significance of this Atellan farce is twofold. First, some of the characters' names suggest that the form may have derived from—or been early influenced by—Greek sources. Should such a link exist, then the argument for a continuous tradition from Greece to Rome *in the popular as well as the literary theatre* is strengthened. Second, the Atellan farces' stock characters and improvised plots have suggested to many scholars that it is the source of *commedia dell'arte*, the Italian popular comedy of the Renaissance. Again, if true, the argument for the existence of an uninterrupted tradition (from Rome through the Middle Ages to the Renaissance) is strengthened. Although both conditions are possible, neither can be proved on the basis of the available evidence. The Atellan farce thus remains one of theatre history's most tantalizing puzzles.

FIGURE 5.3
Political map of Italy.

Western Greek Influences

Theatre was flourishing in sections of Magna Graecia as early as the fifth century B.C. Epicharmus was writing farces at Syracuse before Aristophanes first appeared in Athens. Aeschylus was said to have retired to, and to have produced at least one play at, Syracuse. Athenian prisoners of war allegedly earned their freedom in Syracuse by reciting verses from Euripidean tragedies. By the fourth century, Dorian farces and *phlyakes* mimes were known in the Greek city states of Sicily and southern Italy, especially in Tarentum and Paestum and less often in Cumae and other Oscan territories. By the early third century, Rhinthon of Tarentum was writing his *hilarotragoidia,* and theatres at Tarentum, Segesta, and Taormina had joined the one at Syracuse. Within a single generation of Rhinthon, Livius Andronicus of Tarentum wrote and acted in the first play produced at a Roman festival. The play, performed in 240 B.C., was a Latin translation of a Greek original. Its performace marked the official beginning of Roman drama—and indeed of all Roman literature.

Despite such clear and consistent theatrical activities in Magna Graecia from the fifth century, no definite connection with Roman practices can be proved prior to 240. The possibility of such influence remains too strong to dismiss, however. Both the Etruscans and the Oscans were in close contact with Western Greeks from early times, and both influenced Roman theatrical practices. Early in the third century, the Romans were themselves in increasing contact with Syracuse and Tarentum. Indeed, success in war allowed the Romans to ship Tarentine prisoners to Rome in large numbers during the early part of the century. In the absence of proof, we can only speculate, but it would seem odd under the circumstances if no Western Greek influence—Greek mime, for example—seeped into Roman practices (either directly or indirectly) prior to Livius Andronicus.

The Literary Tradition (240 B.C.–ca. 100 B.C.)

From the time of Livius Andronicus, the dominant cultural influences on Rome were from Greece (see Figure 5.4). In the two major Punic Wars (264–241 and 218–201), Rome clashed with Carthage and entered the world of international (Mediterranean) politics. By the end of the third century, Rome was the unopposed leader of the western Mediterranean, where she abutted to her east the remnants of Alexander's old empire. These Hellenistic kingdoms were poised in a precarious balance of power. As alliances shifted and exposed the weaknesses among them, Rome was repeatedly urged to intervene and restore the balance. She soon found herself embroiled in a series of wars with first one and

FIGURE 5.4

Time line: Relationship between Greek and Roman theatre.

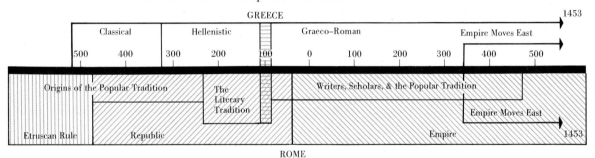

then another of the deteriorating monarchies. Probably without premeditation or intent, Rome gained control of Greece, Macedonia, Syria, Egypt, and Pergamum. By the end of the second century, the Mediterranean had become the "Roman lake," with Rome dominating both its eastern and its western shores (see Figure 5.4).

The interpenetration of Greek and Roman civilizations had begun in earnest. Greek slaves, because well educated, were favored domestic servants, and they functioned as clerks, teachers, physicians, and cooks, as well as housekeepers. In this way, Greek traditions influenced the family life of affluent Romans. Greek culture spread as well into Rome's public life, where new buildings used Greek marble and Greek architectural principles. Greek sculptures adorned Roman streets and parks. Greek authors (like Menander) served as models for Roman writers. Soon thereafter, educated Romans read and spoke Greek as well as Latin.

Not all the consequences of Rome's conquests were so benign. Family farms gave way to large estates that were worked by foreign slaves—prisoners of Rome's many wars or kidnapped men sold to the Romans by Mediterranean pirates. Returning veterans and displaced landowners poured into the city, where overcrowding and unemployment posed staggering problems. Rome's population grew from about 100,000 to nearly 1,000,000. The gap between rich and poor increased. Moneylending became rampant, with interest rates hovering between 24 and 48 per cent. A few millionaires lived lavishly, but the urban poor survived in multileveled, rickety, fire-prone tenements without light, water, or sewage systems. Politicians cynically manipulated public opinion through gifts of free grain and ever more opulent and frequent public games. Thus, the restless urban mass became a major force in Roman politics. Through its overwhelming numbers, the Roman populace could shift the balance of power among rival politicians, and so the fickle urban poor gained power at the expense of the conservative Roman Senate.

The last seventy-five years of the Republic were chaotic. Wars and slave revolts within Italy gave Rome's already powerful military an unhealthy grip on the affairs of state, because successful generals soon became the popular heroes of the poor. It was an ominous feature of Republican government that these generals held the absolute allegiance of their soldiers, for the generals rather than the Republic paid the salaries of the soldiers. As the power of the Senate weakened and the power of popular military men grew, a series of military strong men were catapulted into positions of civic leadership, and as they jockeyed for position against their rivals, Rome was plunged into almost continous civil wars: Marius (fl. 107–86) gave way to Sulla (fl. 88–78). Pompey (fl. 70–50) was outflanked by Julius Caesar (fl. 50–44). Caesar's assassination raised Mark Antony to power briefly (44–31), but his unwise alliance with Cleopatra led to his downfall and the elevation of Octavian. The political turmoil of the century finally subsided after Octavian, under the name of Augustus (63 B.C.–A.D. 14) and the pretense of "restoring the Republic," established the Roman Empire, which would rule most of the known world for the next several hundred years.

During the final years of the Republic, Rome ceased to be a student and became rather a partner—or even a teacher—of other cultures. As the center of influence had once shifted from Athens to Alexandria, it now shifted to Rome. Roman architects experimented with new materials and new forms and developed a kind of auditorium that could be supported by vaults rather than being cut from a hillside. Latin joined Greek as a universal language of the marketplace and the arts. Although Roman drama declined, other forms of Roman literature flourished, and so Roman youths studied Latin as well as Greek authors. Historians (both Greek and Roman) now wrote Roman as well as Greek history. For the next several centuries, the Greek and Roman civilizations mingled, with influences flowing freely in both directions. Thus, Roman theatre and drama, although prepared by the Estruscans and the Oscans, was finally shaped and defined by Hellenistic Greece.

The Festivals

Arrangements for producing plays in Rome roughly paralleled those of the Hellenistic lands (see pp. 96–97). Plays were given as a part of large, public, outdoor festivals or games (*ludi*). Some games were held in conjunction with particular occasions—a nobleman's funeral, a military victory, the dedication of a new public building—but most were annual celebrations honoring a god. Although occasional festivals were financed by wealthy citizens (often for political gain), most were financed with state funds designated for the purpose. Civic officials (*aediles* and *praetores*) were charged with overseeing the festivals, and they regularly supplemented state appropriations with their own money in order to assure the success of the games and bolster their own political fortunes.

For those festivals that included plays, the civic officials contacted the head of each acting troupe that was to appear. Because several troupes might perform at a festival, the civic official often conferred with four or five different people. Once the civic official had completed the contracts, the major responsibilities for the dramatic performances shifted to these heads of troupes, most of whom both managed and acted in their companies. Each actor–manager then secured a script, rehearsed the actors, provided the musicians, and oversaw the costumes and properties; that is, he supervised all aspects of the dramatic portions of the festival.

Until 220, the only public festival in Rome was the daylong *ludi Romani*, at which horse racing and, after 240, drama were the major entertainments. Thereafter, both the number of festivals and the days set aside for dramatic performances steadily increased. By 190, between seven and eighteen days were scheduled for plays, and by the time of Augustus, at least forty-three days were so designated (see Figure 5.5).

The number of days actually devoted to theatrical performance, however, probably averaged an additional six or seven days each year because of *instauratio*, the Roman practice of repeating any festival that contained a blemish likely to offend the gods. *Instauratio* accounted for the repetition of the *ludi Romani* in eleven of the fifteen years between 214 and 200; and the *ludi plebei* were repeated seven times for the single year 205. It has been suggested, in light of the frequency of *instauratio*, that blemishes were contrived in order to provide an excuse for repeating popular plays and festivals—a sop to the urban populace.

FIGURE 5.5

Summary of Roman festivals having dramatic entertainments

Title	In Honor of	Instituted	Made Scenic	Approximate Dates
Romani	Jupiter	6th cent. B.C.(?)	364 B.C. 240 B.C.	Sept. 4–19
Florales	Flora	238 (made annual 173)	?	Apr. 28–May 3
Plebei	Jupiter	220(?)	By 200	Nov. 4–17
Apollinares	Apollo	212	By 169	July 6–13
Megalensia	Great Mother	204	By 194	Apr. 4–10

Adapted from Beare, *The Roman Stage*; p. 162.

The Theatres

Because Rome had no permanent theatre until the final years of the Republic, performances took place in temporary wooden structures, the locations of which varied with the festival and the year. Locations for dramatic performances during the Republic probably included the Circus, the Forum, in front of Apollo's temple, and in front of the Great Mother's temple. Perhaps because of the religious nature of the public festivals, temporary theatres were (always?) erected close enough to a temple to permit the statue of the honored god to oversee the performance.[2]

Although several stone theatres were begun in Rome during the Republic (179, 174, 154), not until 55 B.C., during its last years, was one completed. Some scholars have explained this tardiness as a growing antipathy to Greek influences on Roman civilization. Others have credited the Romans' fear of offending a god by building a theatre so far away from the temple that the god could not see the proceedings that were dedicated to him or her. Still others cited the suspicion with which Roman government officials regarded the theatre. Whatever the reason, the reliance on wooden theatres during the Republic has made it necessary for historians to reconstruct their appearance from the extant plays, scattered contemporary references, various paintings, and later commentaries.

From the extant plays, scholars have reconstructed the essential features of the wooden theatres of the second century B.C. The theatre had a roofed scene house (*scaena*) whose front wall (*scaena frons*) was pierced by three (perhaps recessed) doorways, each outfitted with sturdy and practicable doors. These doors opened onto a stage (*pulpitum*) that was enclosed at each end by wings (*versurae*), each of which had a single entrance. No front curtain was used until after the period of the extant plays (introduced about 133?). In at least some theatres, steps led from the stage into the semicircular *orchestra*, which in the Roman theatre

was seldom used for performances. Some important people might sit in the *orchestra*, but most patrons were on temporary wooden seating in the area set aside for the audience (*cavea*) (see Figure 5.6).

Although scholars generally agree on these functional parts of the early theatres, they disagree strongly about the appearance of the parts. Some imagine that the theatres were quite flimsy, like the stages shown in Figure 5.7.[3] Others think of them as wooden versions of the later elaborate stone theatres, illustrated in Figure 5.17. Both views, or neither, may be correct. During the two hundred years of Republican performances, hundreds of theatres could have been built, all different. Probably, the early wooden theatres were simpler than the later ones, for by the first century, quite elaborate wooden structures apparently existed. One supposedly had a stage house three stories high and a seating capacity of eighty thousand; another was said to consist of two theatres built back to back and capable of being rotated to form a single large amphitheatre—while the spectators remained in their seats.[4] Although highly improbable, the accounts nonetheless point to the presence of elaborate—even though temporary—theatres. The latest reference to a temporary theatre built in Rome was in 17 B.C., but wooden theatres continued to be erected in the provinces well into the period of the Empire.

The staging conventions of early Rome resembled those of Hellenistic Greece in many details. In comedy, the stage most often represented a city street (*via* or *platea*), with the doors of the scene house becoming entrances to private homes, but the stage might represent a country road or even a seashore, with the doors adjusted accordingly. The side entrances usually represented paths to the harbor and foreign ports, on one side, and the town, market, or forum, on the other. This pattern, too, was flexible enough to permit the side entrances to represent any distant places. Each play made clear

FIGURE 5.6

Conjectural reconstruction of Roman stage at the time of Plautus and Terence.

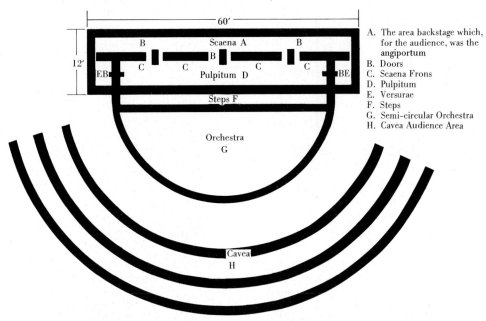

A. The area backstage which, for the audience, was the angiportum
B. Doors
C. Scaena Frons
D. Pulpitum
E. Versurae
F. Steps
G. Semi-circular Orchestra
H. Cavea Audience Area

FIGURE 5.7

Stage structure drawn on a wall in the "Room of the Masks," house of Livia, Rome, and a model constructed from it by Professor Richard J. Beacham. [Both photographs are courtesy of Professor Beacham, whose source was Gabinetto Fotografico Nazionale, Rome.]

its own location through the prologue and the lines of the play, but the meaning of each side entrance may have been clarified as well through the use of *periaktoi* on which were painted identifying scenes. An altar figured prominently in the action of many of the extant comedies and so probably was a permanent feature of the stage. Other properties (most often domestic furniture, dishes, and farm tools) were probably carried on and off by the actors as needed.

The absence of a front curtain and the nature of facade staging led to several conventions quite unlike those of a modern proscenium theatre. First, all scenes were almost certainly staged out-of-doors, even those depicting such indoor activities as cooking, eating, and napping. Second, as a way of facilitating eavesdropping and the interruption of secret plans, the characters in the plays apparently saw and heard only what the play required; that is, when a slave needed to eavesdrop, the characters simply did not see him, and when a developing plan needed interruption, the characters conveniently heard a door squeak, announcing the arrival of an interloper. Third, the *angiportum*, an imaginary street conceived of as running behind the houses and connecting them, was a convention that explained the arrival of a character who had exited through one door or wing only to reenter shortly through another.

About the staging of tragedy less is known, for no extant plays remain. Probably, as in Greece, the stage represented an area in front of a temple, a palace, or other public building, with the *scaena frons* being the front of that building and the doors the entrances to it.

Questions about the use of scenery abound. Was it used? If so, what did it look like? Was it changed between plays? Within a single play? What sorts of scenes were painted on the *periaktoi*? Generally, scholars have answered such questions in light of their assumptions about the degree to which the Roman theatre was illusionistic or conventionalized. Some argue for a high degree of illusion; others argue for a very

simple and highly formal theatre (see pp. 79–80 and 97–99). As in the case of the Greek theatre, the questions cannot be answered with certainty given the evidence now available, but probably the Roman theatre, like the Greek, was more conventionalized than illusionistic.

The Audience

All classes of Romans went to the theatre, and the audiences probably numbered in the tens of thousands. Attendance was free, and the seating was first come, first served, with men and women seated separately. Front seats were prized, for patrons in the rear often found it difficult to hear. After 197 B.C., those seats closest to the stage (in the *orchestra* and the first fourteen rows) were reserved for civic leaders, a decision that caused considerable rancor among the less privileged. Ushers stood ready to help patrons find seating (even after the play had begun) and, less often, to keep order. Although performances were continuous throughout the day, no provisions seem to have been made for securing refreshments inside the theatre.

Roman audiences, on the whole, were probably more unruly than Greek audiences. Playwrights and politicans apparently considered them fickle and undiscriminating. For example, the prologues to several plays appeal for quiet in the audience and beg for attention to the performance; and the politically astute Cicero (106 B.C.–43 B.C.) complained that the increasing lavishness of the games was nothing more than a demagogic appeal to women, children, and unthinking men. Because enthusiastic approval of a performance could result in substantial bonuses to the favored troupe or actor, selected spectators were often paid to respond appropriately and noisily to the performance, and public officials were bribed to notice such responses.

The size of the audience gave it considerable political clout. In addition to courting its favor through increasingly opulent games, politicans regularly used its behavior as a barometer of their own political fortunes and those of their rivals. According to Cicero, theatrical applause guaranteed immortality, and hisses signaled political death for any Roman official.

Although the audiences regularly interpreted the dramatic lines in terms of contemporary issues, such issues were not treated openly in plays, probably because of the government's prosecution of an early playwright: for unseemly references to a ruling family, the playwright Naevius (ca. 270–ca. 201) was imprisoned and ultimately banished from Rome. Subsequent dramatists, fearing the same or worse treatment, either avoided political references altogether or veiled them so completely that they were harmless. Nevertheless, civic officials occasionally insisted on seeing a play before its public presentation, perhaps as a further check on potentially seditious or inflammatory materials. Clearly, because Roman drama could not air controversial civic issues, it could assume neither the educational significance nor the political centrality of Athenian drama of the Classical Age.

The Performers

Roman actors were organized into a troupe (*grex*) headed by an experienced actor–manager (*dominus*). The size of an average troupe is unknown, but any of the extant comedies could be performed with five actors, if they doubled some roles. Early in the Republic, when the acting profession was young, a single actor performed in both comedies and tragedies; by late in the Republic, however, actors tended to specialize. All festival actors were male, although women appeared in mime (as in Greece).

The social status of Roman actors was generally below that of their Greek counterparts. Most were of humble origin. Many were slaves, brought to Rome and trained to act in order to turn a profit for their owners. Many others were aliens or freed slaves. Indeed, the very words *grex* (also applied to a flock of sheep) and *dominus* ("master") suggest a position of inferiority,

FIGURE 5.8

Professional entertainers were often of low social standing. Two views of a bronze figurine depicting a (probably slave) musician. Notice the odd hat (hairstyle?) and the ring through the penis. [From Winckelmann. Courtesy Rare Books Room, University of South Carolina.]

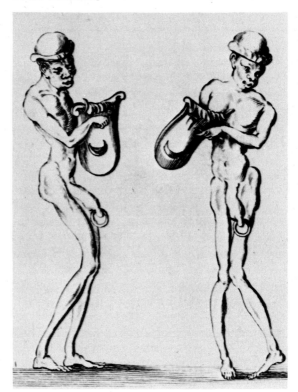

a position underscored by the Plautine jest that an actor "who has made a mistake will be beaten; he who hasn't will receive a drink."[5] Respectable Romans considered most actors disreputable and held them in contempt. When Mark Antony's enemies wished to discredit him, for example, they accused him of consorting with actors, "the agents of his lust and crime."[6]

On the other hand, some actors were clearly respected. Some belonged to organizations like the Collegium Poetarum, whose members held civil rights. A few actors held or attained the

rank of knight, an official class in Rome, corresponding roughly to our upper middle class.
And at least one actor was a member of the
prestigious government Commission of Seven.

Probably, then, the social class of actors
varied in keeping with several factors like family heritage, income, and acting specialty.
Mimes were held in lower esteem than festival
actors, and professional actors in lower esteem
than amateurs, for example.

Part of the disdain in which upper-class
Romans held the acting profession may have
stemmed from their general contempt for people engaged in gainful employment. Acting—
and, indeed, theatre—in Rome was a strictly
commercial enterprise. Late in the Republic, a
young and promising actor–slave was valued at
200,000 sesterces (a soldier of the time earned
between 500 and 900 sesterces a year). Roscius,
the age's leading comic actor, earned about
250,000 sesterces a year; and Aesop, the leading
tragic actor, left an estate of 20,000,000 sesterces. Obviously, popular actors could become
quite wealthy, for they could supplement their
regular earnings by teaching young actors and
by winning prize money for themselves and
their troupes. Probably minor actors could not
earn enough at festivals to live comfortably for
the year, however, because during the Republic, the number of days set aside for theatrical
performances never exceeded forty. Minor actors probably worked elsewhere, possibly touring the provinces, performing in the homes of
wealthy patrons, or even serving in nonacting
capacities as employees or slaves.

About acting style, little can be said. As in
Greece (see pp. 83–84), actors were masked, and
men played women's roles. The actors' major
tools were voice and gesture, voice probably
being the more important. Cicero reported, for
example, that the audience hissed Aesop for
being a little hoarse because they sought only
the "pleasure of the ear."[7] Vocal power and resonance were prized, but so, too, was the ability
to render the music and verse accurately. A flaw
in rhythms—the addition or deletion of a sylla-

ble—or an incorrect pitch could result in the actor's being hissed off the stage. This insistence
on good vocal technique is more understandable when we realize that the majority of most
Roman plays was accompanied by music, a fact
that explains why Roman actors were called
cantores ("singers") as well as *histriones* (from
the Etruscan *ister*, meaning "player").

Musical accompaniment, usually provided
by a double-piped flute, influenced the actor's
movement as well as his voice. Early in the Republic, dramatic music was plain and regular,
even severe, but later it became so elaborate that
the actors tended to adopt unnatural and ornate
gestures. Because their gestures needed to be
both lively and precise, the actors were urged
to train in gymnastics and dance.

As in Greece, then, Roman acting apparently made its impact on the audience through
skills other than those associated with psychological realism.

Masks and Costumes

At one time, scholars believed that masks were
not used in festival plays until near the end of
the Republic. That view is now rejected, and
most agree that masks were used from the beginning of the Roman theatre. As in Greece,
masks helped to distinguish characters, to facilitate doubling, and to enable men to play wom-
en's roles. Masks for regular comedies and tragedies were appropriate to the character being
impersonated; that is, old men tended to be
balding or graying, women to have long hair,
and slaves to be redheaded. There were many
exceptions, however, to the general patterns (see
Figure 5.9). Probably, the only actor of regular
drama who appeared maskless was the speaker
of a prologue when he spoke as himself rather
than in character. Standardized masks were used
for the Atellan farces. Only mimes regularly appeared maskless.

Roman theatrical costumes (*ornamenta*)
varied with the kind of play. All of our extant
plays from the Republic are comedies based on

FIGURE 5.9

Masks reproduced in a twelfth-century manuscript of Terence's plays, itself probably a copy of a ninth-century manuscript. [Photographs courtesy of the Bodleian Library (MS. Auct. F. 2. 13, folio 3r), Oxford, England, and reproduced with permission.]

Greek New Comedies. From the evidence of these plays, it appears that the actors wore a version of everyday Greek dress that included *chiton, pallium,* and sandals or slippers (*socci*). The color and cut of the costumes were appropriate to the age, sex, and traits of the characters; that is, old men tended to wear white or subdued colors, young men bright colors; women tended to wear long, flowing garments; and so on. As well, some characters provided clues to their occupations by what they wore or carried: a purse (slave dealer), a hat (traveller), a sword (soldier), a cook's knife, a fishing net, a rake, and so on. Again, such practices were tendencies rather than rules. Beyond details such as these, the costumes seem to have been relatively indistinguishable except during episodes requiring disguise, when outlandish costume details might be added. (Because the character *was* the mask, the actor did not change masks during his disguise.)

For Roman tragedies based on Greek originals, the costumes were probably, as in Greece, a more elegant version of everyday Athenian wear. *Cothurni* (thick-sole boots) were used, at least late in the Republic.

Plays that depicted Roman life, whether seriously or comically, were probably costumed in native dress: *toga,* tunic, and shoes. Plays that featured Roman heroes used the special toga worn by Roman magistrates, the *praetexta,* a white toga with a purple border. Mimes often played barefooted, and some wore a special hood (*racinium*) to facilitate disguise. Inasmuch as the Atellan farces had a rural quality, their costumes may have included various rustic details, but nothing certain is known of their appearance except that the recurring characters almost certainly were dressed in garments that included recurring, identifying details.

In general, then, Roman festival practices in mask and costume paralleled those of Hellenistic Greece; that is, masked actors wore some version of daily wear, adapted as needed to the theatrical demands for clarity or comedy. As we shall see, costumes formed the basis for classifying Roman dramas.

Playwrights and Plays

Roman drama—indeed all Roman literature—is said to have begun in 240 B.C., when Livius Andronicus, a Greek, offered Latin translations of Greek plays at the *ludi Romani.* Unlike the short, improvised dramatic sketches long familiar to Romans in Fescennine verses and Atellan farces, Andronicus' plays had a connected plot and so were called *fabulae. Fabulae* have been classified on the basis of the items worn by the characters appearing in them. Regrettably, neither ancient nor modern scholars agree on the meaning of all terms, but the most usual interpretations are summarized in Figure 5.10.

FIGURE 5.10

Classifications of *Fabulae*

Name	Derived from	Classification	Dealt with
fabula palliata	*himation* (Gr.) or *pallium* (Lat.): Greek mantle of everyday wear	Play (usually comedy) translated or adapted from Greek	Greek middle class
f. togata	*toga*: native dress of Romans	Early, any play not translated from Greek; later, such comedies	Italian peasants, outside of Rome
f. crepidata	*crepida*: a Greek open shoe or sandal, for everyday wear	Play, translated or adapted from Greek; not necessarily tragedy; often used interchangeably with *f. palliata*	Greek upper class; mythological heroes
f. praetexta	*praetexta*: purple-bordered toga worn by Roman magistrates	Historical play on Rome's recent or distant past	Roman heroes, past or present
f. raciniata	*racinium*: hood	Mime	Wide range of subjects
f. saltica	*salto*: to dance	Pantomime	Wide range of subjects; usually serious; single dancer

Between 240 and about 100 B.C., Roman drama flourished. We know the names of over twenty playwrights and by title or reputation about four hundred plays. Only twenty-seven plays from the period survive, however, all written by Plautus and Terence and all based on Greek New Comedies.

Early Drama

Livius Andronicus wrote at least eleven plays, all based on Greek originals. Although Cicero carped that the plays were not worth a second reading, his judgment may have been too harsh, for Andronicus' success enticed several others to write plays for profit. By 235, the Oscan Gnaeus Naevius began writing. Apparently more prolific than Andronicus (forty titles remain), Naevius not only translated Greek plays but also developed a new kind of native drama, the Roman history play. His interest in contemporary affairs spilled over into his comedies, where his frequent allusions to contemporary Roman events eventually landed him in jail. Perhaps the fear of punishment or perhaps rather an inability to construct original plots

prevented later Roman authors from producing history plays. For whatever reason, the Roman history play virtually disappeared after Naevius.

Tragedy

After Andronicus and Naevius, dramatists specialized in either comedy or tragedy, rarely writing both. The names of only three authors of tragedy are known: Ennius (239–169), Pacuvius (ca. 220–ca. 130), and Accius (170–ca. 6 B.C.). All translated or adapted Greek originals, favoring those elements associated with Hellenistic rather than Classical tragedies, that is, sudden twists of plot, rhetorical flourishes, horror, romance, sentimentality, and so on (see pp. 93; 103). Although modern critics tend to scoff at these plays, Roman audiences at first admired them, in part because of their novelty and in part because of their capacity to display virtuoso acting (an art whose popularity grew during the Republic). Interest in Roman tragedy for the stage, however, was short-lived. After the death of Accius, the form was moribund. It existed almost exclusively in revivals (and per-

FIGURE 5.11

Time line: Roman comic authors related to Menander.

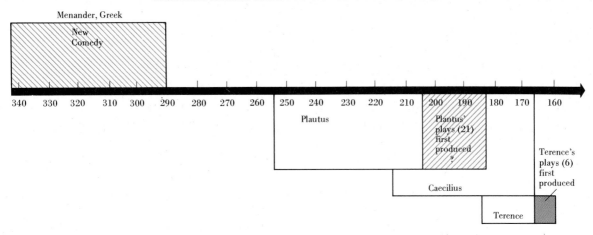

haps suffered, therefore, from productions that were self-consciously exotic and artificial) or in works written by a literary elite for private readings or recitations. Some tragedies continued to be well known through the closing decades of the Republic, however, for on one occasion when an actor missed his cue, "the whole theatre" supplied the line.[8]

Comedy

Roman comedy was both more popular and more lucrative than tragedy. Although based on Greek New Comedy, the Roman comedies did not use a chorus. Of the fifteen comic playwrights known to us by name, three were especially important: Plautus (254–184), Caecilius (ca. 219–168), and Terence (ca. 185–160). (see Figure 5.11).

Andronicus and Naevius were probably still active when Titus Maccus Plautus produced his first play. His popularity was phenomenal, and revivals of his works were frequent, both during his lifetime and after his death. So great was his popularity, in fact, that other playwrights and managers evidently affixed his name to others' plays in order to gain a more favorable hearing. Eventually some 130 plays were attributed to Plautus, many of the attributions

being almost certainly spurious. In an attempt to correct errors of authorship, the literary scholar Varro (116 B.C.–27 B.C.) examined all of the works and placed each in one of three groups: those that were unquestionably by Plautus, those that were probably by Plautus, and those that were probably the work of another. In the first group, Varro placed twenty-one plays, all of which have survived (see Figure 5.12). Although the individual dates of production are not known, most were probably offered first between 205 and 184.

FIGURE 5.12

Extant Roman comedies

By Plautus

Amphitryon, Bacchides, The Braggart Warrior, The Captives, The Carthaginian, Casina, The Casket, The Churl, The Comedy of Asses, Curculio, Epidicus, The Haunted House, The Menaechmi, The Merchant, The Persian, A Pot of Gold, Pseudolus, The Rope, Stichus, Trinummus, and *Vidularia*

By Terence

Andria (166), *The Mother-in-law* (165), *The Self-tormentor* (163), *The Eunuch* (161), *Phormio* (161), and *The Brothers* (160)

Plautus' plays were all adapted from Greek New Comedy, but all were amply spiced with allusions to Roman life and customs and were written with a keen sense of what the Roman audience would hear, see, and applaud. Like other Roman entertainments, Plautus' plays capitalized on the delights offered by variety. The plays varied in length, some being twice as long as others. The major actions were often interrupted to allow extended visual gags or outrageous verbal displays. Music figured prominently, with more than two thirds of the lines intended for accompaniment. For these lines, Plautus selected and manipulated an astonishing variety of meters. Although farcical elements dominated most of the plays, sensitive human relationships were portrayed in some. Thus, Plautus Romanized his Greek models, making them racier and more robust in the process. The plays were eminently actable, with idiomatic and fast-paced dialogue and abundant opportunities for visual gags. It has been proposed that the plays' theatricality resulted from Plautus' own experiences as an actor—perhaps in Atellan farce, as his name Maccus suggests.

About the plays of Plautus' successor, Caecilius Statius, less is known, for only forty-two titles and a few hundred lines remain. The plays seem to represent a transition between Plautine comedy and comedy as written by Rome's last major comic poet, Terence.

Like most other Roman dramatists, Publius Terentius Afer was not a native of Rome. He was probably brought from Carthage as a slave. His youth and physical beauty earned him the attention of an elite literary circle in Rome, the members of which encouraged his early efforts in playwriting. His efforts brought financial rewards. He once received 8,000 sesterces for a play, roughly ten times the annual wage of a soldier. The sum was considered extravagant at the time, suggesting that he (and perhaps others) customarily received less.

Terence met an untimely death in (or on the way back from) Athens. That fatal trip to Greece,

some said, was a search for new manuscripts from which to make Roman plays; others said that he went to Greece to escape slander or to console himself after being used and discarded by the Roman aristocrats who had earlier flattered and promoted him. Before his death, Terence wrote only six plays, all of which survive (see Figure 5.12).

Controversy surrounded Terence. An older poet, probably jealous of the young and favored rival, attacked Terence viciously, alleging that he stole from old Latin plays, that he spoiled the Greek originals from which he drew, and that he had failed to prepare himself adequately for a career in playwriting. Terence responded to the accusations in the prologues of his plays, arguing that his combinations of elements from several Greek plays (*contaminatio*) resulted in plays better than those of his rivals.

Indeed, Terence's plays did differ in several respects from those of Plautus. In his six plays, Terence stressed the humanity rather than the foibles of his characters. It is significant that he more often chose to adapt plays by Menander, the most sentimental writer among the authors of Greek New Comedy. Terence decreased the number of farcical episodes in favor of tightly constructed actions, and he refined his language, making it less varied, more restrained, and more polished than that of Plautus. He replaced monologues with dialogues, increasing further the seeming naturalness of his plays. Because his prologues were neither expository nor omniscient, his plots necessarily were self-contained, and so he introduced new techniques of surprise, suspense, and preparation. Finally, by eliminating all topical allusions, Terence generalized and universalized his plays, making them suitable for production outside Rome. Still, the plays are profoundly of their own times. They are optimistic and confident; they depict a social order in which people can affect their own destinies. They suggest that the Roman Republic possessed dignity, serenity, and stability.

The decreased theatricality and increased

sentimentality of the plays were not immediately popular with Roman audiences (audiences walked out once to watch a ropedancer and another time to find a gladiatorial show). Nevertheless, Terence's plays were read after his death and throughout the Middle Ages, probably because of the gracefulness of his Latin, the morality of his characters, and the dignity that he gave to daily life.

Contemporaneously with Terence arose a new kind of Roman comedy, plays depicting life in rural Italy. Like Roman history plays, however, these native comedies quickly declined in popularity, so that by 100 B.C., new ones ceased to be written except by dilettantes aiming at a reading or listening (rather than a theatre) public. Even old ones were seldom revived.

The Decline of the Drama

By about 100 B.C., the writing of both comedy and tragedy had ceased. Although a small literary elite continued to write for private readings well into the Empire, almost no new dramas were written for the public stage. Legitimate drama existed for a time in revivals—and then not at all.

Although the decline of legitimate drama doubtless rested on a combination of causes, the financial arrangements in Rome certainly encouraged revivals rather than original plays. Typically, an author sold his play outright to an acting troupe or an actor–manager. Such a lump-sum payment meant, of course, that the playwright took no risks: he lost nothing should the play fail, but he received no additional money should its success warrant frequent revivals. Such an arrangement also meant that actor–managers could cut both costs and risks by reviving a successful play that they already owned. Revivals were therefore both cheaper and safer than original plays, and for a time revivals kept legitimate drama on the Roman stage. Early in the Empire, however, even revivals disappeared. The era of the Greek-inspired Roman drama was at an end.

Writers, Scholars, and the Triumph of the Popular Tradition (ca. 100 B.C.– A.D. 476 in the West; 1453 in the East)

Trends visible in the declining days of the Republic continued into the Empire. Authority became increasingly centralized in the person of the emperor, who was soon considered a god. Political support increasingly depended on the restless urban populations, who were more interested in getting than in giving civic works. The boundaries of the Empire erratically but relentlessly expanded, until linking and governing the distant lands posed almost insurmountable problems. As the Empire grew, non-Romans constituted an increasing percentage of its population and its swollen bureaucracies. A youthful Christianity competed with a variety of rival cults, first for acceptance and then for dominance. Once dominant, the Christians organized to purge the Empire of all non-Christians and to purify Christendom of dissenting interpretations of the faith.

By the early fourth century A.D., efficiency required that the Empire be divided so that it could be more easily governed. Thus came into being the Eastern and the Western branches of the Roman Empire. In 330, the first Christian emperor, Constantine, moved the capital of his empire out of Rome and into Constantinople, a new city that he had built near the old town of Byzantium, close to modern-day Istanbul. Thereafter, both the emperor and his government became evermore Eastern (Greek, Persian, Oriental), opulent, and bureaucratic. The emperor and the East became gradually separated from the people of Rome and the West. The political schism found a parallel in the growing split within Christianity. Believers who lived in Eastern lands departed considerably in matters and practices of faith from believers residing in the West. The city of Rome, after losing its position of prominence, quickly declined. It withstood a series of incursions from northern tribes but finally fell to invaders in 476. As power had once shifted from Athens to Alexandria to Rome, it now shifted East again, from Rome to Constantinople.

During the Empire, Roman architecture and engineering flourished, for it was an era of building: towns, roads, waterways, temples, bathhouses, athletic fields, and theatres. Early in the Empire, the architect–engineer Vitruvius compiled accounts of the major Hellenistic and Roman building practices. Although the age of drama had passed away with the Republic, the most fruitful period of Roman literature coincided roughly with the rule of Rome's first emperor, Augustus (27 B.C.–A.D. 14). During his reign, the poets Ovid and Vergil, the historian Livy, and the theorist Horace were at work. Soon thereafter, the politician and poet Seneca emerged. And for the next several centuries, the popular—subliterary—entertainments of Rome throve.

Writers and Scholars

Horace

By the first century B.C., Rome was developing its own literary scholars. By far the most influential for Renaissance theorists was Horace (65 B.C.–8 B.C.), whose *Ars Poetica* was known throughout the Middle Ages. Written about 19 B.C., perhaps at the request of a friend who intended to write a play, Horace's somewhat informal and disjointed work faintly resembles Aristotle's *Poetics*. (Horace had studied at Athens.) The Roman work, however, is both more superficial and more prescriptive than Aristotle's and is, finally, more a practical manual for playwrights than a philosophical inquiry into the nature of drama.

Its prescriptions were taken very seriously by Renaissance scholars, and so its major points should be noted. The purpose of drama, said Horace, was to edify and delight, goals best achieved by appealing to the feelings of the audience. Plays should have unity, and unity depends on harmony and proportion. Each play should have five acts, defined by choral odes that are appropriate to the play's action. The incidents of a play should be shown rather than told, except when they are revolting or incredible, in which case they should be narrated. Horace advised poets to select meters that are appropriate to the play's action and to realize that comic and tragic meters are seldom compatible. Finally, because acceptable writing depends on both wisdom and goodness, Horace believed, poets should be both moral and well educated.

Because the work was in Latin and because it was never lost during the Middle Ages, the *Ars Poetica* formed the basis of many dramatic theories devised during the Renaissance. For a time, its tenets were more influential than those of Aristotle. Thus was Rome's influence transferred to the drama and dramatic theory of the modern Western world.

Seneca

During the closing years of the Republic and the early years of the Empire, closet drama (drama read rather than staged) as well as literary criticism was popular. Several notable Romans wrote such dramas, for no stigma attached to them as to plays intended for the public stage. Ten such tragedies survive, nine of which were written by Seneca (ca. 5 B.C.–A.D. 65). The tenth play, *Octavia,* was long attributed to Seneca but is now believed to be the work of another. A history play that includes Nero's wife among its characters, *Octavia* is our only example of the form developed by Accius.

Lucius Annaeus Seneca was born in Spain, the son of a famous rhetorician. He was exceed-

FIGURE 5.13
Extant Senecan tragedies

Mad Hercules, Trojan Women, Phoenician Women, Medea, Phaedra, Oedipus, Thyestes, Agamemnon, Hercules on Oeta.

FIGURE 5.14

An illustration from a fifteenth- or sixteenth-century manuscript of Seneca's *Medea*. [Photograph courtesy of the Bodleian Library (MS. Can. Class. Lat 86, folio 102), Oxford, England, and reproduced with permission.]

ingly well educated, in preparation for assuming a position of leadership in the Roman government. Although his political fortunes sagged under the emperor Caligula (fl. A.D. 37–41), they revived when Seneca was appointed tutor to the future emperor Nero (fl. A.D. 54–68). For a time, Seneca was one of the most powerful men in the Empire, serving as one of Nero's major advisers; but he quickly fell from favor and was forced to commit suicide.

Seneca wrote on many subjects and in many modes, his plays constituting only a minor part of his total literary work. His tragedies are important because of their influence on Renais-sance authors rather than because of any intrinsic merit. They are generally more rhetorical than dramatic. Debates between characters are common, and the dialogue tends to be carefully balanced and well phrased. Lengthy descriptions and catalogs often interrupt the plays' action, and *sententiae* (pithy remarks about the human condition) are sprinkled liberally through them. Although a chorus is used, its odes are not integrated with the action and therefore serve merely to separate the episodes. Because there are often four odes, the plays often have five parts. The characters tend toward superhuman qualities and are often depicted in the grip of some overriding passion—love or revenge—before which they are helpless. The characters reveal their innermost thoughts by means of asides, soliloquies, and confidants, and they engage in actions replete with spectacle and horror, murder and torture being particularly common. Most of the plays unfold in a single place and within a limited time. Such qualities can also be found in many of the tragedies of early Renaissance writers who consulted Seneca as a guide for their own developing craft.

The Popular Tradition

As legitimate drama receded into a literary form intended for private readings, the public theatre became the haven of mime and assorted speciality acts.

Mime

By far the most popular dramatic entertainment of the imperial period was the mime. For a time in the first century B.C., a literary mime had developed in Rome and enjoyed a modest following, but most Roman mime, like the Greek, was subliterary. Like Greek mimes, those of Rome offered astonishing variety, the more so because Roman mimes sprinkled various specialty acts like tumbling and juggling among their dramatic skits (see pp. 101–103). Mimicry was the mainstay of the mime, although either story or character could be its binding force. Though some mimes were based on mythological travesty, most apparently depicted scenes of daily life, in which adultery often figured prominently. Typically, in such pieces, the wife and her lover conspired to trick her foolish husband and perhaps to murder him, often with poison.

The mime's distinguishing features were its inclusion of women and its maskless players. Both features help account for the importance of personal appearance among mime performers. The most successful ones were either remarkably pretty (handsome) or comically ugly, perhaps even deformed. Starring performers often dressed at the height of current fashion in order to emphasize their beauty; others used costume to underscore their physical peculiarities. By the time of the Empire, the leading mimes had developed large and faithful followings, for whom they set fashion and influenced behavior. Obviously, as the prevalence of mime increased throughout the Empire, the presence of masks in the theatre declined. Acting style was doubtless affected by this shift, but the nature of the changes is unknown.

The notion that all Roman mimes were obscene and violent is most certainly false. Probably the outrageous reputation of mime can be traced to three conditions. First and most important, most of our information about mime was transmitted by Christian writers who hated and feared it because it regularly ridiculed Christian beliefs and sacraments. Second, it was the extreme, rather than the typical, practices of mime that were preserved, precisely because they were unusual and therefore notable. And third, mimes were regularly denigrated by aristocratic Romans as merely the popular entertainments of the masses, a vulgar display for the lower classes. Despite its unhappy reputation in later years, Roman mime was probably more often banal than evil.

On the other hand, some mimes were clearly quite lurid. Some women performers specialized in striptease and eventually appeared nude onstage, at least occasionally in connection with trained animals. One emperor apparently required that all scenes of sexual intimacy be actually performed by the actors. Late in the Empire, violence as well as sex increasingly figured in some mimes. For example, at least one mime involved an actual crucifixion, and condemned prisoners were substituted for professional actors for the final *coup de théâtre.* Most enraging to the Christian community, however, was the sport that mimes regularly made of their religion. Indeed, these outrageous and irreligious jests against the faith, combined with the explicit sex and violence of *some* mimes, led to an unrelenting attack on *all* mimes—plays and players—by Christian writers like Tertullian. Attacks on mime, the major theatrical form of the Empire, were then expanded to become attacks on theatre in general—both its drama and its performers. Despite such wholesale condemnation of theatre by certain members of the early Church, however, theatre flourished in Rome until that city's collapse, and it throve in Constantinople for centuries thereafter.

Other Popular Entertainments
Competing with theatre for the support of imperial audiences were several other forms of public entertainment: pantomime, racing, gladiatorial combats, wild beast hunts, and mock naval battles.

Pantomime was a kind of dramatic dance. To the accompaniment of flutes, pipes, and cymbals, a small chorus declaimed, or sang, a story that a solo performer interpreted by means of gesture and movement. Although early pantomimes were occasionally comic, most were serious stories taken from history or myth. For them, the solo dancer wore a long tunic, a cloak, and a mask with a closed mouth. In order to interpret the several characters of the story, the dancer probably changed masks often. Introduced to Rome in 22 B.C. by Pylades and Bathyllus, pantomime for a time seemed to fill the void created by tragedy's retreat to the salon. After the second century A.D., however, it, too,

FIGURE 5.15

Imaginative Renaissance reconstruction of Rome's Circus Maximus. [From Graevius. Courtesy Rare Books Room, University of South Carolina.]

was swept from the public stage by the growing popularity of mime.

Other public entertainments were considerably less benign. Indeed, some scholars have argued that the increasing violence and licentiousness of mime were due to certain of the entertainments with which it had to compete. Chariot racing (see Figure 5.15) had always enjoyed enormous popularity, but its appeal increased during the Empire after the leading stables organized themselves into factions whose members wore distinctive livery. Public support of rival factions grew quite frenzied and often took on political overtones.

Gladiatorial combats, at first presented under private sponsorship, were big business by the time of the Empire, when gladiatorial schools could train thousands of fighters at a time. The obvious political danger of trained fighters in the employ of ambitious politicians was clear, and so the emperors took control of all gladiators and retained a virtual monopoly on that sport. Early in the Empire, Augustus set 320 pairs of fighters before an enthusiastic crowd, but Trajan (fl. A.D. 98–117) easily topped this display when he offered up 10,000 gladiators during a single festival. Although the first Christian emperor tried to outlaw gladiatorial combats in A.D. 325, their popularity kept them alive for several decades more.

Similar to gladiatorial combats were the wild beast hunts (*venationes*), for which exotic animals were brought to Rome from throughout the Empire. For the opening of the vast am-

FIGURE 5.16

Renaissance depiction of a Roman *venatio*. [From Graevius. Courtesy Rare Books Room, University of South Carolina.]

VENATIO

L · REGVLVS

III·

phitheatre called the Colosseum, more than nine thousand animals were killed. When Trajan produced 123 days of public games for his Romans, more than eleven thousand beasts were slaughtered. (See Figure 5.16.) Far less frequent, but apparently even bloodier, were the great sea fights (*naumachia*). Begun late in the Republic (46 B.C.), these mock sea battles took place on lakes or in flooded amphitheatres, where warships filled with gladiators, sailors, or prisoners confronted one another in deadly combat. Some of the battles were reenactments of Roman naval victories from the past; others were fights to the death among rival ships and crews. All were deadly. On one occasion, for example, the emperor Claudius assembled almost twenty thousand condemned men from throughout Italy for a naval battle to celebrate the opening of a new waterway (see Figure 5.17).

Many of the gladiatorial fights, wild beast hunts, and great naval battles used costumes, scenery, and elaborate special effects. Indeed, many feats of stagecraft and engineering described in connection with these quasi-theatrical entertainments would tax the ingenuity of modern producers.

For city dwellers of the Empire, then, public entertainments exploded in number, lavishness, and variety. The famous Colosseum, completed during the first century A.D., could accommodate fifty thousand Romans, about 5 per cent of the city's population. By then, approximately 150 days were devoted to public games, twice the number set aside late in the Republic. But even this number was raised to 176 by the middle of the fourth century.

Augumenting the entertainments offered at great public festivals were the daily pleasures afforded by the heated baths, which offered separate areas for exercise, swimming, and bathing, all arranged for the maximum comfort of the patrons. So popular had the baths become by the second century that one emperor limited their hours in order to permit the work of Rome to proceed. Perhaps a single piece of graffiti scrawled on a city wall outside Rome summed it up: "Hunting, bathing, gaming, that's living!"

For the hunting and gaming and for the gladiatorial combats, Romans went to the amphitheatres, the largest of which was the Colosseum. For the races, they went to the great circuses, and for bathing to the public baths. For theatrical entertainments, they went to theatres. Versions of all such buildings appeared in cities and towns throughout the empire, although in Greek lands (where Rome's bloodier entertainments were never very popular), few amphitheatres were built. There, when the occasion required, a theatre might be temporarily converted. For example, its *orchestra* might be flooded for a water ballet or a modest *naumachia* or its walls heightened for a wild beast hunt.

Permanent Theatres

Although wooden theatres had been available for hundreds of years, Pompey completed

FIGURE 5.17

Renaissance illustration of a Roman *naumachia*. [From Graevius. Courtesy Rare Books Room, University of South Carolina.]

Rome's first stone theatre in 55 B.C. Others appeared almost immediately. Thereafter, the presence of one or two stone theatres became a hallmark of Roman towns and cities throughout the Empire. Although Roman theatres were occasionally built in former Greek lands, the more usual practice there was to remodel existing Hellenistic theatres, bringing them into closer accord with Roman ideals of beauty and function (see p. 104).

Roman theatres differed from Greek Theatres in two major ways. First, they were usually erected on level ground so that the audience area was built up, stadium-style, rather than cut from a hillside. This innovation was possible because of Roman advances in building materials and methods, specifically the development of concrete, the arch, and the vault. Second, in Roman theatres, the scene house and the audience area were usually connected at their roofs, forming a single, compact, unified, freestanding structure instead of the terraced hillsides and detached *skenes* that were so typically Greek. Roman theatres differed as well in several minor details. The Roman *orchestra* was a half circle rather than a circle, and its stage was enclosed at each end by *versurae*. The stage, about 5 feet high, up to 40 feet deep, and perhaps as

FIGURE 5.18

A conjectural reconstruction of the Roman theatre at Orange. [From Baumeister.]

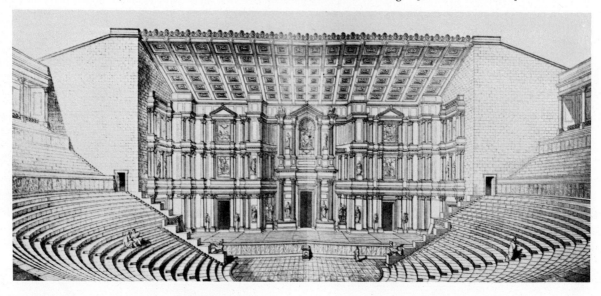

long as 300 feet, extended from an exceedingly ornate facade that was punctuated with porticoes, niches, columns, and statuary. By the third century, some such facades included deeply recessed sections whose curved lines cut well into the scene house itself (see Figure 5.18).

The comfort of imperial audiences was carefully provided for by numerous aisles that facilitated movement within the theatre and abundant entrances (*vomitoria*) that allowed the theatre to fill and empty quickly. In some theatres, giant awnings (*vela*) protected the viewers from sun or rain, and primitive air-conditioning systems (fans blowing across snow that was brought in from nearby mountains) provided relief from the summer heat. The front rows, the *orchestra*, and the boxes over the vomitories nearest the stage offered seating for important persons, and free tickets were distributed to others in an attempt to reduce the jostling for seats.

Little is known about staging in these permanent theatres, for we have no plays written to be performed there. Two sorts of curtains were in use: a front curtain (*auleum*) and a back curtain (*siparium*). The front curtain was perhaps first lowered into slots at the front of the stage, but later it seems to have been opened or raised as in a modern theater. (Architectural remains show slots located at the front of the stages of permanent theatres built before ca. 100 A.D.) The back curtain probably entered the theatres with the mimes, who had first used such a curtain as a simple background for their performances. Why mimes continued to use this back curtain is uncertain, for even enlarged, its painted surface could have covered only a fraction of the massive *scaena frons*. Perhaps they found the curtain a more suitable background for their improvised performances than the increasingly elaborate *scaena frons*.

Vitruvius

Probably more influential in the Renaissance than the stone theatres themselves, however, was the tantalizing description of them that survived in the massive ten-volume work by the architect Vitruvius. After serving as a military engineer under Julius Caesar and Augustus, Vitruvius wrote *De Architectura* (ca. 15 B.C.), a compilation of architectural practices in town planning, building, and civil engineering. Its fifth book was devoted to a detailed consideration of such public buildings as forums, basilicas, baths, and theatres. Along with some general information about the erection of theatres, Vitruvius described aspects of the scenery. He wrote:

The "scaena" itself displays the following scheme. In the center are double doors decorated like those of a royal palace. At the right and left are the doors of the guest chambers. Beyond are the spaces provided for the decoration—places that the Greeks call periaktoi [on which were painted] three kinds of scenes, one called the tragic, second, the comic, third, the satyric. Tragic scenes are delineated with columns and pediments, statues, and other objects suited to kings; comic scenes exhibit private dwellings, with balconies and views representing rows of windows, after the manner of ordinary dwellings; satyric scenes are decorated with trees, caverns, mountains, and other rustic objects delineated in landscape style.

Because Vitruvius' was the only treatise on architecture to survive the Middle Ages, its influence on Renaissance architects, designers, and theorists was enormous. Regrettably, however, Vitruvius did not provide illustrations of all he described, and so later designers freely embroidered his words with their own imaginations to produce decidedly unlikely—but nonetheless influential—reconstructions of Roman theatres and scenic practices. Thus did Rome's influence penetrate theatrical design in Renaissance Italy and, thereafter, in western Europe (see Figure 5.19).

The Empire Moves East (A.D. 330–1453)

Although the Western Empire did not "fall" until A.D. 476, the city of Rome lost its imperial preeminence shortly after 330, when Constantine and a retinue of about eighty thousand moved to the new capital of the Empire, Constantinople. This transplanted Roman city quickly grew to a quarter of a million inhabitants, all of whom considered themselves Roman, called themselves Romans, and spoke a language that they called Romaic (although it was a version of Greek). Constantine's successors likewise considered themselves emperors of the whole Roman Empire and periodically tried to recapture the West from the barbarians. For example, during the sixth century, Justinian (ruled 527–566) retook Italy and restored the Empire to a recognizable approximation of its former self. He also codified existing Roman law

FIGURE 5.19

Time line: Roman drama and Roman politics.

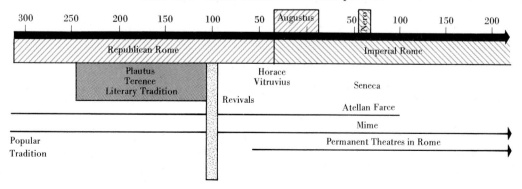

in Latin, still the official language of the Empire, but he included new laws not in Latin but in Romaic, recognizing that it was the spoken language of most of his citizens. Although literature and the arts in the West were in decline, those in the East were flourishing. These Roman entertainments that had been transported to Constantinople continued to be popular. Indeed, so intense did the rivalries between racing factions become there that a riot between them resulted in the burning of half the city and the death of about forty thousand people in the Hippodrome, Constantinople's equivalent of the Roman Colosseum.

By the middle of the eighth century, the gap between East and West was unmistakable. The West was in disarray; the East was at the height of prosperity. The Eastern emperor was the ruler of both State and Church, and Christianity was the Empire's official religion. The imperial court had grown in a luxury and pomp that were reminiscent of Oriental or Persian, but not Roman, governments. The bureaucracy was bloated with civil servants drawn from Greece, Persia, and the Orient. The citizens of the East enjoyed unprecedented wealth, and some boasted that two thirds of all the world's riches lay within their capital city. The city itself had lavish public buildings, including the Hippodrome, which seated close to eighty thousand people. The city was the repository of the religious treasures of Christendom, brought there when most of Italy had again fallen before invaders (751) and the Arabs had threatened to overrun the Holy Land. Monasticism, emerging early in Egypt, had become institutionalized in

FIGURE 5.20

Map of the Byzantine Empire about 1050 A.D.

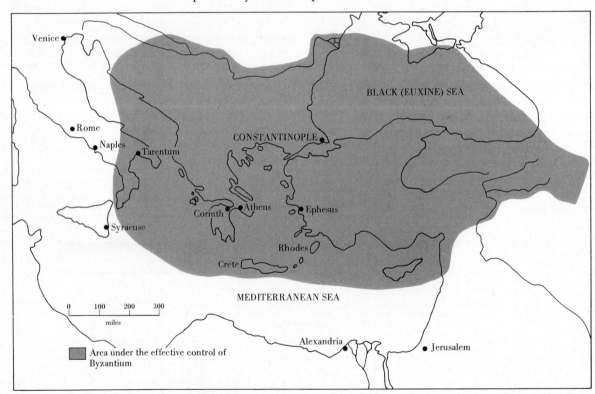

the East by the fourth century and by the eighth was actively engaged in public works, including education. Teaching and learning flourished, and classical scholars studied and copied Greek masterpieces of the Classical Age.

As travel west became increasingly difficult, Constantinople turned to the East for products and cultural inspiration. And because doctrinal differences separated Eastern from Western Christians, religion served to divide further rather than to unite the old Roman Empire. Roman Christians of the East believed that their wealth and stability, which lasted to the eleventh century, was God's reward for the correctness of their faith; they saw in the shambles of the Western Empire, God's punishment for the errant Western beliefs (see Figure 5.20).

By the thirteenth century, however, the Eastern Empire was also in decline. Her population had fallen drastically as the result of wars and plague. Weak emperors had allowed a grasping aristocracy to gain control of the Empire's dwindling resources. The fourth of six crusades, launched by Western Christians in 1204, presumably to oust infidels from the Holy Land, turned instead to plundering the treasures of Constantinople, raping its women, stealing its gold, and killing many of its people. The city never recovered, either physically or psychologically, from this onslaught by members of its own former Empire. Constantinople, thus weakened, fell before the advancing Turks in 1453. As citizens of the Eastern Empire fled west, many took precious manuscripts with them. Suddenly western Europe was flooded with artifacts of Eastern (especially Greek) life and learning. Where for almost a thousand years the cultural exchange had been a modest, if steady, trickle, suddenly products from the advanced civilizations of the East burst on the West.

Scholars of theatre and drama have long been intrigued by the influence of Byzantine culture on later developments in Western theatre and drama. Some influence is clear. It was Eastern scholars who preserved and transmit-

ted many of our extant classical documents relating to theatres—plays and treatises from Greece, for example. Other influences, although possible, are in dispute. It is agreed that mime flourished in Byzantine lands. Indeed, the mime Theodora married the emperor Justinian and shared his rule (see Figure 5.21). But did Byzantine mimes travel west, bringing theatrical performances to sections of the former West-

FIGURE 5.21

An ivory diptych from Byzantium, showing Justinian and Theodora watching charioteers. [Photograph courtesy of Photographie Giraudon.]

ern Empire during the period once called the Dark Ages? Some scholars argue that they did and that there was thus a continuous theatrical tradition from Rome through Constantinople into western Europe. Others insist that they did not and that Roman theatre in the West died with the fall of Rome. It is also agreed that the Eastern Church had a number of dramatic rites—the Mass, certain sermons, antiphonal songs—and even several religious plays (of uncertain dates, with estimates ranging from the fourth through the fourteenth centuries). But did the Eastern Church transmit its plays (if they existed early) to the West by means of their traveling clerics? If so, was the Eastern Church the source of the drama that appeared in the Western Church during the tenth century? Some scholars argue for such a continuous tradition, but others vehemently deny it. Because the evidence is insufficient to resolve these problems, they will continue to be debated by theatre historians.

ENDNOTES

1. The reasons for Roman, more than Greek, influence on the Renaissance are many and complex, but two can be mentioned here. More people in the West read and wrote Latin than Greek, and so Roman works tended to be more accessible by virtue of their language. Also, literary works from Rome were closer to the Italian Renaissance in both time and space than were those from Greece. Roman works, therefore, tended to be more readily available for study.

2. A position argued persuasively by J. A. Hanson, *Roman Theatre Temples* (Princeton, N.J.: Princeton University Press, 1959).

3. A recent treatment of this issue is Richard Beacham, "The Development of the Roman Stage: A Missing Link Restored," *Theatre Research International* 5,1 (Winter 1979–1980): 37–45.

4. Pliny the Elder (A.D. 23–79) in the same account, described a style of scene painting so realistic that it fooled birds into trying to nest on the painted surfaces.

5. *The Casket*, line 785.

6. Cicero's brother Quintus, as cited by F. Warren Wright, *Cicero and the Theatre* (Northampton, Mass.: Smith College Classical Studies, No. 11, 1931), p. 25.

7. Quoted by Wright, p. 11.

8. W. Beare, *The Roman Stage*, 3rd ed. rev. (London: Methuen, 1964), p. 81, who cites Cicero.

6

Facades in Revival

Introduction

Together, the Greek and Roman theatres in the West lasted for about one thousand years. These two national theatres differed from one another in many details, and each changed markedly throughout its own history. Nonetheless, the two theatres bore marked similarities when grouped and compared with other, later theatres—the medieval or the Renaissance theatres, for example. It may therefore be useful to consider the elements shared by the Greek and Roman theatres, ignoring for a time their myriad differences and focusing instead on important, recurring, shared features.

Artists

In order to discover the defining elements of this classical theatre (as Greek and Roman theatre taken together are often called), we can survey briefly some of the major choices open to theatrical artists of any age. Obviously, other artistic choices could be profitably discussed, but these we believe are especially important. Obviously too, the choices discussed here separately are often intimately related; we separate them for clarity even as we freely acknowledge the importance of their interconnections. Finally, although each artist makes choices based on her or his own needs, artists tend to repeat successful techniques; and so during certain historical periods, some patterns of treatment seem preferred over others.

First, artists can manipulate space and time. To this end, two issues are usually germane. The first is to separate the time and space of the art from that of the real world. For example, painters may choose a space that is self-limiting (they may paint on a vase); or they might instead choose to frame a space, thus limiting the relevant artistic area (in effect, declaring the space outside the frame irrelevant); or they might solve the problem in other ways. Similarly, time within an artwork can be made congruent with that outside; or it can be made to move either faster or slower than "real" time; or it can be made to bear no apparent relationship to worldly time.

Once having set off artistic time and space from their surroundings, the artist must still organize both elements inside the work. For example, space may be organized for viewing from a single point or from multiple points; the outline of an object against its background can be sharp or blurred; and the artwork may depict a single place, several places at once, or no place at all. Time may be very important, or not important; its passage can be marked by music or lights or relative position; or its passage can be altogether ignored. Space and time may be treated as fixed or elastic, as limited or limitless.

Second, artists can manipulate details: their amount, kind, and mode of expression. Artists can include almost no detail; they can bombard the senses with many; or they can choose the wide range of possibilities that lie between these two extremes. Not only can *amount of detail* be manipulated; so, too, can the *kind of detail*. Some artists elect to include only details that are beautiful in themselves; others prefer the sordid or ugly; and many mix the two. Amount and kind of detail do not necessarily interact; that is, an artist can choose one or many beautiful details *or* one or many ugly details. Details may be variously rendered. The details of a play's setting, for example, might be described by the words of an actor, or they might be painted on some flat surface, or they might be constructed out of several different kinds of materials. Again, *method of rendering* is independent of both kind and amount of detail; thus, a single beautiful flower might be described, painted, or constructed—and so might a cluttered, lower-class barroom.

Third, artists can manipulate the degree of correspondence between material reality and art. Some artists seem to seek a very close correspondence, others no correspondence. Some achieve an almost exact reproduction of external, surface reality, as in a photograph; some seem determined to wrench their art from any recognizable likeness of the external world, as in modern abstract art; others seem indifferent rather than hostile to such correspondence, as in Byzantine mosaics. For example, in theatre, Henrik Ibsen at the end of the nineteenth century achieved a high degree of correspondence between the world of middle-class Scandinavians and the world that he created on the stage. On the other hand, several so-called expressionists of the early twentieth century seem to have been determined to create a world on the stage at great variance from the observable world outside, and so they consciously distorted scenery, properties, speech patterns—even the human form of the actors—in order to separate the worlds of art and life.

Society

In making these and other decisions, theatre artists are doubtless influenced to some degree by the world in which they live and the audiences that they believe will see their work. Whenever possible, therefore, we should seek to discover the role of time, space, detail, and "reality" in the world *outside* the artwork as well as within it. For example, the clock's invention perhaps made time more important in human affairs than ever before. Perhaps, too, the view of space changes when one believes that the sun rather than the earth is the center of the universe or that the earth is round rather than flat.

Probably, objects considered beautiful by some are not so to others; and certainly, the amount of domestic detail considered desirable to one age is not always desirable to the next. Probably, too, a world that explains humanity's origins by references to Genesis partakes of a reality different from a world that responds with references to DNA molecules and Mendelian ratios.

Only by studying both the world of the artwork and the world of the audience can we approach an understanding of their critical conjunction. The rest of this chapter attempts to relate the classical theatre to the world that surrounded it. We shall begin by identifying the essential shared characteristics of that theatre. We shall then look for similar characteristics in other arts, and we shall finally seek correspondences for these qualities in the culture at large. Again, the emphasis will be on similarities, not differences, and on typical practices rather than exceptions. The danger of distortion through reduction is great (see pp. 17–19). Nonetheless, we hope that by posing good questions, we will direct attention to important issues even when our answers must remain uncertain, tentative, and perhaps even wrong.

The Theatre and Other Arts

As we have seen, most organized theatre in Greece and Rome took place on the occasion of great public festivals dedicated to gods or civic heroes. Theatrical performances unfolded out-of-doors, usually in places set aside for such events. The theatre building consisted of a permanent architectural facade pierced by doors or other openings. The actors played in front of the facade, usually on a raised platform. At first, a circular space between the facade and the audience offered a (second?) performance area, but this space declined in use and size well before the end of the period. The audience could watch the performance from three sides, and most members looked *down* on the performance, because the arced rows of benches where they sat rose steeply. Tragedies performed in these theatres depicted public leaders engaged in affairs of civic importance. Although early comedies also portrayed public affairs, comedies by the fourth century B.C. regularly focused on domestic rather than civic matters.

Question: How Were Theatrical Space and Time Defined in the Classical Age?

Both spaces and times were public rather than private. Theatre buildings were public rather than private buildings, and they were located in public places rather than on private lands. Tickets were regularly provided through public funds. The serious plays dealt with important civic issues that were usually a part of the culture's shared past (history or myth); they did not, like the plays of our own day, explore the internal, private concerns of ordinary folk. Performances were held outside, and the plays were themselves set out-of-doors. Actors and audiences shared the same light and formed an open, acknowledged, and public community.

Theatrical spaces and times were set aside from the ordinary pursuits of daily life. Theatrical activity usually took place in buildings especially constructed and reserved for the purpose. These buildings were located in special places, adjacent to sacred precincts or in view of gods' shrines. Rather than daily or weekly, performances were given only on special occasions as part of annual festivals or as one-time celebrations of great civic events. Thus, theatre probably seemed both *formal* and *special* (by virtue of being set apart from the activities of daily life) and *significant* (by being public rather

than private). (An interesting question suggests itself: As the number of occasions on which theatre was performed increased, did the specialness of the theatre decline?).

Daytime, outdoor performances made actors and audiences equally visible. In both Greece and Rome, the audiences' attention was focused on the performances by the establishment of a background in front of which the actors played. This background defined the artistic space by offering an area against which the actors could be better seen. Still greater focus resulted when the actors played on a raised platform, the condition for most, if not all, of the period. The actors, then, were not contained within a frame (as in a modern proscenium theatre) but were highlighted against a background (as in a sculpted frieze) (see Figure 6.1).

In permanent theatres, the background was the facade of a building that abutted the stage. In the serious plays, the facade generally represented the front of a single, public building; its doors represented the various entrances to that building, and the stage (and sometimes the *orchestra*) a public space in front of the building. In the comic plays, the conventions were considerably more varied, but often after the fourth century B.C., the facade represented the front of several houses, the doors the entrances to them, and the stage a street in front of them.

The subject of the plays, too, was at first the public actions of public characters. Thus, Aeschylus' *Oresteia* dealt with the reordering of a system of justice, and Aristophanes' *The Clouds* dealt with methods of educating the young. By the Hellenistic period, however, a slight turn toward private concerns can be seen in the plays: tragedies, although still treating of public issues, now included scenes of romance and sentiment, and New Comedy presented the domestic tribulations of families. Influenced by Hellenistic Greek practices, the Romans regularly incorporated domestic details into their plays, especially into their comedies.

Certainly, after the theatres were built in

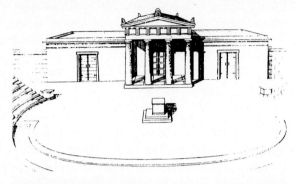

FIGURE 6.1

Ancient theatres (top) shared a facade, an *orchestra*, and an audience area, open to the weather, that, stadium-like, looked down on a performance. By contrast medieval theatres (lower left) tended to depict several places simultaneously, using emblematic scenery, and Renaissance (and later) theatres typically featured a proscenium arch with illusionistic scenery. [From Dörpfeld, Rigal, and Combe, respectively.]

stone (and probably long before), the same stage and facade represented very different places from play to play. During a single play, the place represented by facade and stage (and *orchestra*) usually did not change, but on those occasions when it did, the words and actions of the performers seemed to effect the change: elaborate scenic shifts were not required to illustrate it. True, occasional references point to some changes in visual background, but the size of the facade made its visual transformation exceedingly unlikely. Probably, then, the purpose of "scenery" was to signify rather than to illustrate a location. If this assumption is correct, then audiences may have been willing to transform the facade through their imagination into various public buildings and houses and to accept that the facade, stage, and *orchestra* (where relevant) represented now one place, now another; or they may have simply ignored the background altogether, finding it irrelevant to the human action played before it.

Similarly, the plays' action tended to unfold within a limited period of time. On rare occasions, however, months or even years passed during a single play. Again, the words and actions of the performers seem to have been enough to cause the audience to accept a radical ordering of artistic time.

Perhaps the audiences' acceptance of unillustrated shifts of time and place was encouraged by the plays' relative lack of interest in either. Because even artistic events *must* occur somewhere and sometime, a location of some sort is inevitable, but during the Classical Age, few details of time or place were included in the texts. The result was that *the particular* place and time of the action received little emphasis. *When particularity and specificity are relatively unimportant, the literal illustration of place and time may be equally unimportant.*

A brief look at the most significant visual arts of the period (architecture, sculpture, and vase painting) shows similar tendencies.

Until rather late in the period, all major architectural efforts were aimed at great public buildings rather than at private dwellings. The Greeks, for example, were especially noted for the perfection of their temples. Indeed, so strong was their tendency that a maxim developed: Greek citizens, it was said, "keep their bodies in hovels but their souls in the Acropolis." And it is true that many wealthy Athenians lived in small and often uncomfortable homes, while atop the Acropolis the Parthenon proclaimed the grandeur of the city to all who approached it. Built for the glorification of the goddess Athena, the goddess of wisdom and the patron of Athens, the Parthenon was shaped and colored to be seen from miles around, and it was to be viewed from outside rather than from within, a fact made very clear by the smallness of its internal spaces.

Like the Greeks, the Romans emphasized public buildings, but they shifted attention away from temples and toward spaces designed to accommodate large numbers of people gathered for various kinds of pleasures: public baths, arenas, amphitheatres, and theatres. Also, Roman engineers stressed the importance of roads and bridges for moving people and armies and of triumphal or ceremonial arches for providing a patriotic focus on wars and heroes. When private dwellings became of interest to Roman architects, they, too, were lavishly designed, with large spaces for gathering: a central open court, elaborate rooms for dining and entertaining, and large public gardens, with ample walks and pools.

Like architecture, most sculpture in Greece and Rome aimed at the glorification of gods and public figures of high distinction—statesmen, athletes, scholars, and military heroes. In Greece, the statutary was almost always displayed in public spaces, and although much of it existed as independent art (freestanding and complete in itself), some was incorporated into the design of public buildings. In the Parthenon, for example, sculpture was a major element of a continuous low-relief frieze, and of

ninety-two panels, and of two large triangular spaces in the pediments. The Romans both imported and copied Hellenistic (and later) Greek sculpture; and like the Greeks, the Romans tended to display it in major public buildings—baths, theatres, arenas, and so on. Unlike the Greeks, however, they regularly incorporated sculpture into private homes and tombs, and it is perhaps for this reason that the Romans rather than the Greeks developed portrait sculpture, work that aimed at a close likeness of a real person.

Of all the major Greek arts, only vases and vase paintings were closely associated with private and domestic spaces. By the nature of their use—drinking, cooking, and storing—these pieces were home-bound, but the scenes depicted on them were often of gods and heroes in action. In these scenes, a few figures dominate a neutral background. On some Greek vases, the figures are red and the background black; on others, the background is red and the figures black; but on both, the background serves as a neutral space against which the figures are to be viewed.

Perhaps it does not stretch the point too far to think of actors against a facade and figures sculpted in relief on a frieze and designs drawn on red or black vases as visual relatives. They all seem to suggest a way of seeing art that does not require an accurately detailed background (see illustrations opening Part Two).

Question: How Were Details Handled in the Classical Theatre?

The question is devilishly difficult to answer because our primary evidence is necessarily the play texts, and yet the practices of setting and costume, could we know them, are usually more revealing with respect to details. Still, the plays suggest a minimal use of detail.

As we have already seen, the playwrights

offered relatively little specific information about time and place. The number and details of character are similarly sparse: in *Oedipus Rex*, we have only eight speaking characters (and a chorus), and we know almost nothing about the tragic hero Oedipus beyond what is absolutely required by the play's action. Such terseness is in stark contrast to most—say, Shakespearean—dramas. In *Romeo and Juliet*, for example, there are twenty-six characters and a host of supernumeraries, and for most of them, we are given many details of appearance, behavior, and motivation. The number and details of the incidents within Greek plays are likewise slight when compared with those of Shakeapeare. Again using *Oedipus Rex* as an example, we note a single action developed through fewer than ten scenes, whereas in Shakespeare's plays we regularly have several lines of action and often as many as thirty scenes. Even within the classical period, both the amount and the kind of detail changed. Apparently, by the fourth century B.C., more details were included, for Aristophanes complained that Euripides unnecessarily embellished the music of his tragedies, expanded the kinds of subjects and characters treated in tragedy, and introduced new details of language and costume. Supporting evidence like vase paintings and statuary does not contradict the impression offered by the play texts; and so even with our meager evidence, it is probably safe to conclude that *exclusiveness rather than comprehensiveness was the principle that governed the use of detail and that details increased after the fifth century.*

The details selected for inclusion seem to have been mostly of two sorts: those that facilitated the play's action and those that signified. Thus, in several Greek tragedies, details of color and cut told of the nationality or the emotional state of the characters wearing them, and in Plautus' *Menaechmi*, several details of costume were added and explained so that audiences could tell which twin was which. Indeed, in general, comedies seemed to have included a greater amount of detail than tragedies, and

some details in comedy seem to have served little purpose beyond comic effect—as when Dionysus changes outfits several times in *The Frogs* simply to provoke a laugh.

The point is an interesting one. Details of dress and items of setting were added to fulfill a clear function: to facilitate action, to underscore meaning, and to provoke laughter. Gratuitous details—those that did not contribute directly to the play's action—were few in comedy, fewer still in tragedy. Conspicuously absent was any suggestion of details that were added merely to decorate the stage or to authenticate the location of the action. Because the details were few, those that were included probably gained greater significance, perhaps more readily serving as signs for the audience. Such economy of detail may also have had the effect of generalizing the action and of promoting the particular characters and events to the status of representatives of something beyond themselves.

As we look at the other arts, we note that they, too, were very exclusive in their use of detail, at least during the periods for which we have extant plays.

Greek architecture took mathematics and function as its governing principles. The basic post-and-lintel construction (vertical columns supporting a horizontal beam) in combination with the available building materials assured a strong, low, horizontal line atop closely spaced, regular columns. Each part of the construction was in a careful and measurable relationship with every other part and with the whole (the Parthenon, for example, followed a formula of $n:2n + 1$). Plato (in *Philebus*) summarized: "Art has no end but its own perfection. . . . If arithmetic, mensuration, and the weighing of things be taken away from any art, that which remains will not be much." Such attention to mathematical proportion obviously limited and shaped the use of detail. During the Hellenistic period in Greece, interest in detail grew. After Roman engineers introduced arches and the vaults that grew from them, greater visual variety appeared in buildings—as the straight lines of the post and lintel were joined by the curves of arches and vaults. By the late Empire, the Romans were regularly indulging their taste for increased ornament and embellishment.

Apparently, changing tastes and newly developed techniques led to increased detail in architectural construction late in the period. For example, the progression taken by the Greek orders, as the styles of Greek columns are called, shows an increasing interest in embellishment over time. The Doric order was dominant during the fifth century B.C., the Ionic during the fourth. Neither includes much detail. The Corinthian order (popular in the fourth century and after) was considerably more ornate. Although the Romans knew all three orders, they almost always chose to copy the Corinthian. The facades of theatre buildings offer another example. Among the stone theatres, those of the Romans seem to display the more florid and ornate faces. It is perhaps significant, however, that the added details of the facade apparently did not signify anything within artistic time and space; that is, *as facade,* it was more detailed, but *as background,* it was still perceived as a generalized, neutral space.

In Greece at the time of Aeschylus and Sophocles, sculpture had only one subject: the human body; but the artists were not interested in individual people so much as in the structure of the human form. Gods were represented as perfectly formed men; men were depicted as well-developed athletes. Balance and proportion reigned; reason rather than observation controlled the way that the sculptor worked his materials. Again, Plato: "The qualities of measure and proportion . . . invariably constitute beauty and excellence." The idea was to discover a unity underlying the confusion of sensory impressions and then to present that unity to the viewer. The stone images, therefore, presented generalized bodies modeled after an ideal, rather than a real, man.

With the coming of the Hellenistic Age, the style of sculpture changed: the nude female fig-

ure joined the nude male as a popular subject; bodies in action replaced those in repose; portraiture became popular; and the detailed decoration of various objects became common. Because Roman artists tended to copy the later rather than the earlier Greek works, their sculptures tended to include a greater number of particularizing details. One later Roman emperor, for example, commissioned a bronze copy of himself that included "every wrinkle, rib, and whisker"[1] (see Figure 6.2).

Although vase painting in Greece probably developed in combination with mural and easel art, few examples of the latter survive, and these are from the Hellenistic period and later. Art historians have surmised (on little evidence) that painting in Greece followed the same general trends as sculpture. Roman painters (who presumably copied Hellenistic Greek art) specialized in what we would today call interior decoration. By about the time of Christ, Roman painting had apparently become merely decorative, merely an indulgence of gracious living.

Question: How Similar to External, Material, Reality Were Productions in the Classical Theatre?

For those in the twentieth century, it might seem most logical that the Greeks and Romans would have sought an illusion of surface reality in their theatres. Accustomed as we are to seeing domestic interiors faithfully reproduced onstage and to watching actors pose as ordinary people, we may find it momentarily strange that the Greeks and Romans were generally guided by other principles. The art of their theatre was easily distinguishable from the life outside it, and little or no attempt was made to produce a faithful picture of everyday reality—either visually or verbally. On the contrary, from the outset, the theatre artists in Greece and Rome

FIGURE 6.2

An Apollo of fifth-century B.C. Greece is depicted as an idealized and beautiful young man, with relatively few particularizing details. The statue of a shepherdess from Rome in about the fourth century A.D. (?) seems less ideal: she is an old, tired woman, with a number of particularizing details. [From Collignon and Lanciani, respectively.]

removed their art from any close resemblance to material reality. They seem to have been determined that their actors not look like "real" people (masks) and not sound like "real" people (verse, music, song, and chant). Audiences seem to have been unconcerned that the same facade, with little or no alteration, represented the front of a single public building one day and a series of private homes the next, and they seem not to have minded that men played women's parts.

It is true, of course, that comedy was a little less remote from daily life than was tragedy— perhaps because of the subjects treated, or perhaps because of the increased use of detail, or perhaps for other reasons. It is also true that the degree of correspondence between the world onstage and the one offstage changed during the thousand years. As early as the fourth century B.C. in Greece, for example, the importance of the chorus (a highly formal element) began to decline, and soon thereafter so did its numbers; in Roman comedy, it had disappeared altogether. Was the elimination of the chorus a conscious aesthetic choice in the direction of a greater correspondence with surface reality? Or was it an expedient decision aimed at cutting the costs of production? Whatever the intention, the result was almost certainly to increase the degree of correspondence. Again, although mime was never allowed in Greek festivals, it came to dominate those of imperial Rome. The effect of having unmasked performers in gender-appropriate roles was to move the world of the stage a step closer to the world outside. Did this increased correspondence help account for the rising popularity of mime, or were other factors more important in its domination of the imperial theatre? Also, during the days of imperial Rome, vast scenic displays became both lavish and popular. Did this late development signal an interest in spectacle for its own sake, or was it a desire to reproduce onstage the myriad details of the world offstage? Classical audiences obviously appreciated their theatre, as evidenced by their high percentage of attendance. Even late in the period, however, they apparently did not seek in it a mirror in which they could see a literal image of themselves or their lives.

As we have seen, early architecture and sculpture in Greece were idealized, governed by principles of mathematics rather than by those of illusion. Neither architecture nor sculpture featured many details, and each seemed complete without any literal reference to the external, material world. On the Parthenon, for example, were segments showing the labors of Hercules and battle scenes involving centaurs; famous freestanding sculptures took as their subjects Zeus, Poseidon, and idealized men. All were obviously products of the mind rather than of direct observation. These invented figures were shaped as perfect, without blemish and without particularizing details. The emphasis was on the beautiful face, the well-formed body, the balanced and harmonious form of the whole. "When you copy types of beauty," Xenophon remarked in his *Memorabilia*, "it is so difficult to find a perfect model that you combine the most beautiful details of several, and thus contrive to make the whole figure beautiful;" and Aristotle added, "Art has no regard for the individual case" (*Rhetoric I*).

In early painting, too, the urge was not toward a photographic likeness of any real scene. An ideal design rather than an accurate picture marked the early years. Encircling borders stressed the roundnes of the vase, and the center of the picture conformed to the vase's architectonic form. Although recognizable figures were as common as geometric patterns, both served the ends of decoration rather than of illustration.

With the Hellenistic Age, however, a trend toward illusion began. We have already noted that the art of portraiture became popular then. As the period wore on, the portraits abandoned an idealized view of their subjects in favor of more accurate representations. Roman sculpture was soon praised for portraits that were faithful to life, although the praise should not be understood too literally, for it was a common practice in Rome to mass-produce torsos to which a carefully sculptured likeness of a person's head could later be attached; thus, although the faces were presumably accurate copies of the subject, the bodies manifestly were not. Perhaps as a part of the trend toward illusionism, as well, the Romans developed an interest in telling stories in stone—stories of military exploits and political victories, where the emphasis was clearly on the subject rather than on architectural or sculptural elements.

One art historian summarized the trend this way: "From the fourth century onward sculptors became increasingly interested in realism. Subjects drawn from everyday life won new popularity; emotional and storytelling themes were exploited, and the desire for exact reproduction of tactile values led to astonishing technical dexterity."[2]

In painting, the move toward illusion—toward a connection with surface reality—was very pronounced indeed. The elder Pliny (first century A.D.) told of a fourth-century Greek painter whose pictures of grapes were so true to nature that birds flew up to them and about a contemporaneous Roman portrait painter whose works were so accurate that physiognomists could tell the age and the life expectancy of the subjects. Although doubtless exaggerated, such accounts do point to a painting style that placed a premium on the faithful reproduction of external, material reality—on surface appearances (see Figure 6.3).

In sum, during the age of the great Greek playwrights, theatre and drama were public and communal activities whose occasional nature gave them added significance. Usually, a limited space and time were depicted in performances, but so little emphasis was given to either that audiences easily tolerated departures from this norm. The sparseness of details and the lack of correspondence with surface

FIGURE 6.3

Although interest in abstract patterns continued, as in this mosaic from Pompeii [from Barré], some wall paintings of the time became quite illusionistic, with many recognizable details of the world. [From Hill.]

reality distanced the world of the stage. These features, together with the public nature of the characters and the action in the plays, tended to make performances an imitation of an ideal (generalized) rather than an individualized (specific) action. After the Golden Age in Greece, but approximately coincident with the worlds of Plautus and Terence in Rome, the nature of both theatre and drama began a slow change. The theatrical arts became somewhat more private and more professionalized, and the occasions for theatrical performances multiplied. Interest in detail increased, as did interest in domestic issues.

Long after the time of written drama in Rome and Greece, a highly detailed visual art developed, an art interested in achieving a close correspondence between the work of art and the external, material world. This period of visual illusionism paralleled the period when mime and scenic spectacles filled the theatres—and sea and animal battles filled the amphitheatres. Already underneath this world (by the third and fourth centuries A.D.), however, had begun to grow up yet another society and another visual art, a nonillusionistic, emblematic, Christian art on the walls of vast catacombs.

Art and Society

If we assume that art always bears some relationship to the society out of which it springs, then it should be possible to identify the social elements that could have promoted a public, nondetailed, nonillusionistic art during the fifth century B.C. in Greece. It should be possible to show, as well, shifts in that social order that might help to explain the turn toward detail and illusion with the coming of the Hellenistic period, and its culmination in the highly detailed and illusionistic art of the later Roman Empire.

We are struck at once by the importance of Man in fifth-century Greek Art: his actions form the subject of plays, his human form is the subject of sculpture, and his activities are the sub-

jects of vase painting. We are struck as well by the beauty and grandeur of his representation. Artistic attention focused on leaders rather than followers, winners rather than losers, the young and perfect rather than the old and blemished. Indeed, for the Greek philosopher Protagoras, "Man is the measure of all things."

A celebration of humanness, including a confidence in man's ability to govern himself, was indeed a dominant feature of Greek life during the fifth and fourth centuries. Every Greek citizen participated in the decisions that ruled his life. The size of Athens allowed that participation to be direct: citizens were expected to be able to outfit a warship and a chorus, to play an *aulos* and run a footrace, to fight a battle and deliver a speech.

Man's relationship with the gods was both close and clear. As Protagoras explained it, man was "the only creature to believe in gods because of his kinship with the godhead." Indeed, some men, like Hercules, could even become gods. Also, gods and men concentrated on the events of this earthly life rather than on the mysteries of death, suffering, and afterlife. Notably absent from Greek art are depictions of the torments of death or the promise of resurrection and afterlife. Instead, funeral art captured and memorialized events in the person's life, depicting the dead person as he might have existed in the beauty of his youth.

Men formed a perfect combination of body and mind; the two were not in conflict. Indeed, a perfect body accompanied—and was a sign of—a perfect mind. Thus, the study of anatomy and logic were complementary, for an understanding of both increased an appreciation of what it meant to be human.

The universe that man inhabited was capable of being understood by him, for it operated according to principles of reason and logic, not according to the blind will of mysterious and distant gods. Confident that the world was understandable, men set about to understand it, seeking always to discover the patterns (usually mathematical) that could explain the everyday experiences of the senses. Having discovered that music rested on describable mathematical ratios and that beautiful statues and buildings resulted from the application of formulas, the Greeks found their belief in the importance of human intellect and rational activity confirmed. And so their poets expressed supreme confidence in man's greatness:

> *Many amazing things exist, and the most amaz-*
> *ing is man.*
> *He's the one, when the gale-force winds*
> *Blow and the big waves*
> *Tower and topple on every side,*
> *Cruises over the deep on the gray tide.*
>
> *He's the one that to and fro*
> *Over the clods year after year*
> *Wends with his horses and ploughing gear,*
> *Works to his will the untiring Earth, the greatest*
> *of gods.*
>
> *He traps the nitwit birds, and the wild*
> *Beasts in their lairs. The ocean's myriad clan*
> *In woven nets he catches,—ingenious man.*
>
> *He has devised himself shelter against*
> *The rigors of frost and the pelting weather.*
> *Speech and science he's taught himself,*
> *And the city's political arts for living together.*
>
> *For incurable diseases he has found a cure;*
> *By his inventiveness defying*
> *Every eventuality there can be,—except dying.*

Sophocles, *Antigone*

Such was the celebration of a culture in which man was the measure of all things.

With the breakdown of the *polis* and the centralization of power under Alexander, citizens had less direct impact on the decisions of government. When cities became large and governments remote, the sense of community deteriorated, and life itself became less integrated. No longer was a single citizen expected to participate directly in all activities of life; henceforth, acting was left to actors, flute playing to musicians, and fighting to soldiers. As the world moved in the direction of specialists and professionals, interest in individuals—as they differed from one another—grew, and interest in the rights of the individual (as distinct from those of the city state) emerged. At the same time, interest grew in matters over which people still exerted some control: themselves as individuals, their homes, and the details of their daily life.

The Romans invaded this Hellenistic world and took its art back as war booty. They were themselves just emerging from the rather self-contained, small, rural, and republican city of Rome; and so the idealized human figures in sculpture and the domestic themes of Greek New Comedy seemed compatible at first. But when Rome abandoned republican forms of government, at about the time of Christ, in favor of large, highly centralized, rich, imperial ones, the social fabric changed—and with it the arts. Roman trumpets and drums replaced Greek lyres; amphitheatres and baths were more highly prized than temples and theatres. Concrete arches and vaults permitted the enclosure of vast spaces suitable for entertaining and pacifying the city's burgeoning poor. The aristocrats sought sanctury in their homes, which presented unadorned and unwindowed faces to the street, but which inside displayed beautifully decorated spaces with central heat and running water, where wealthy Romans could entertain friends in luxury, away from the hurly-burly of the city.

When the city and the Empire grew too large for even the systems of roads, laws, and entertainments devised by the emperor and his bureaucrats, interest in common sense and utility collapsed. Literary drama disappeared from the public theatre, its place taken by mime, pantomine, and spectacles of various sorts. Older religions based on service to the state and rational behavior fell before mystery religions and belief in miracles, perhaps the only hope in a world filled with despair, where individual human action seemed meaningless. By the fourth century A.D., the highly detailed and "naturalistic" visual art of the late Empire was existing side by side with the emblematic art of the most lasting of these mystery cults, Christianity.

FIGURE 6.4

Booth stages at a French fair of the eighteenth century and used by a small traveling troupe from South Carolina, Anstie's Limit. [From Bapst and the authors' collection.]

Revivals

There continue to be revivals of classical plays in our own century, particularly at universities and regional repertory theatres committed to preserving the masterpieces of Western drama. Some of these revivals strive to recapture the style of the original production; others alter the style, presumably to make the plays more accessible to contemporary audiences. Almost none, however, attempts to recapture the initial playing spaces—an *orchestra* and a stage in front of a facade.

In Italy, at the time of the Renaissance, however, attempts were made to copy both classical plays and classical theatre spaces. Thus, some Italian literary men translated Greek and Roman dramas, and others tried to write similar plays in Latin or Italian. At the same time, Italian architects and builders erected facade stages (with orchestras) inside large halls. As the Renaissance spread to other countries, so, too, did the interest and attempts at revival. That the revivals departed considerably from the originals should not be surprising, for Renaissance culture differed profoundly from that of the classical era. After the Renaissance, serious efforts to revive facade stages ceased, but Greek and Roman drama continued to be performed.

There is one afterimage of the classical facade stage, however, that has appeared regularly throughout the theatre's history. Its revival has probably been quite unconscious, the result of expediency rather than aesthetics. We refer, of course, to the ubiquitous "booth stage," the companion of itinerant players of every age.

The English word *booth*, like the Greek word *skene*, initially referred to temporary structures like tents or stalls or huts and often described the small houses used by merchants in the marketplace. A *booth stage*, then, is simply an impermanent (usually curtained) stall or hut at the back of a (usually raised) platform. All the elements necessary for a theatrical performance are provided by the arrangement. The front of the booth serves as a facade, a neutral background against which the actors are highlighted. The entrances and exits are masked by the booth itself, and inside it, the actors can dress and await cues. The raised platform (often quite temporary) lifts the actors above the heads of their audience, improving sight lines and focus. Large audiences are well accommodated, for they can crowd together and watch performances from three sides. In short, few theatrical arrangements are more efficient or more expedient than a booth stage.

Doubtless, it is this efficiency that has led to the almost universal use of the booth stage by those lacking a permanent theatre building. From visual evidence, we know that it was used, for example, in Germany during the Middle Ages, in France during the seventeenth century, and in America during the twentieth century (see Figure 6.4).

A careful look at some permanent theatres suggests that they, too, may be adaptations of earlier, booth stages. The public theatre of Shakespeare's England for example, seems a close relative, with its tiring house, thrust stage, and stand-up pit. At about the same time in Paris, the Hôtel de Bourgogne varied only slightly from the usual patterns of a booth stage. Indeed, except for the *orchestra*, the stone theatres of Greece and Rome seem merely permanent, enlarged, and embellished versions of a booth stage. Although it is tempting to believe that the classical theatre merely placed in wood and stone a theatre already well accepted by earlier traveling players, evidence to argue the point is weak.

ENDNOTES

1. Sheldon Cheney, *A New History of World Art* (New York: Henry Holt, 1959), p. 157.

2. Aline B. Louchheim, *5000 Years of Art in Western Civilization* (New York: Howell, Soskin, 1946), p. 28.

BIBLIOGRAPHY
Part Two

Allen, James T. *Greek Acting in the Fifth Century*. Berkeley: University of Cal. Press, 1916.

———. *Stage Antiquities of the Greeks and Romans and their Influence*. New York: Longmans, Green, 1927.

———. *The Greek Theatre of the Fifth Century before Christ*. 1920; rpt. New York: Haskell Press, 1966.

Anderson, M. J., ed. *Classical Drama and its Influence*. New York: Barnes and Noble, 1965.

Arnott, Peter D. *Greek Scenic Conventions of the Fifth Century B.C.* Oxford: The Clarendon Press, 1962.

———. *The Romans and Their World*. New York: St. Martin's Press, 1970.

———. *The Ancient Greek and Roman Theatre*. New York: Random House, 1971.

Bacon, Helen H. *Barbarians in Greek Tragedy*. New Haven, Conn.: Yale University Press, 1961.

Bain, David. *Actors and Audience: A Study of Asides and Related Conventions in Greek Drama*. Oxford: Oxford University Press, 1977.

Baldry, H. C. *The Greek Tragic Theatre*. New York: W. W. Norton, 1971.

Barnett, Lionel C. *The Greek Drama*. London: J. M. Dent, 1900.

Baumol, William J. "Economics of Athenian Drama." *Quarterly Journal of Economics* 85 (August 1971): 365–376.

Baynes, N. H., and Moss, H., eds. *Byzantium: An Introduction to East Roman Civilization*. Oxford: Clarendon Press, 1948.

Beacham, Richard. "The Development of the Roman Stage: A Missing Link Restored." *Theatre Research International* 5, 1 (Winter 1979–1980): 37–45.

Beare, William. *The Roman Stage: A Short History of Latin Drama in the Time of the Republic*, 3rd ed. London: Methuen, 1964.

Bieber, Margarete. *The History of the Greek and Roman Theatre*, 2nd ed. Princeton, N.J.: Princeton University Press, 1971.

Burn, A. R. *Alexander the Great and the Hellenistic Empire*. New York: Macmillan, 1948.

Bury, J. B., and Meiggs, Russell. *A History of Greece*, 4th ed. New York: St. Martin's Press, 1975.

Butler, James H. *Theatre and Drama of Greece and Rome*. San Francisco: Chandler Publishing, 1972.

Byron, Robert. *The Byzantine Achievement: An Historical Perspective, 330–1453*, 1929; rpt. New York: Russell and Russell, 1964.

Cary, M. *A History of the Greek World from 323–146, B.C.*, 2nd ed. New York: Barnes and Noble, 1951.

———, and Scullard, H. H. *A History of Rome Down to the Reign of Constantine*, 3rd ed. New York: St. Martin's Press, 1975.

Casson, Lionel. *Daily Life in Ancient Rome*. New York: American Heritage, 1975.

Cornford, Francis M. *The Origin of Attic Comedy*. Cambridge: Cambridge University Press, 1914.

Diehl, Charles. *Theodora: Empress of Byzantium*, trans. Samuel R. Rosenbaum. New York: Frederick Ungar, 1972.

Duckworth, George E. *The Nature of Roman Comedy: A Study in Popular Entertainment*. Princeton, N.J.: Princeton University Press, 1952.

Flickinger, Roy C. *The Greek Theatre and Its Drama*, 4th ed. Chicago: University of Chicago Press, 1936.

Fornara, Charles W., trans. and ed. *Translated Documents of Greece and Rome, Vol. 1, Archaic Times to the End of the Peloponnesian War.* Baltimore: Johns Hopkins University Press, 1977.

Forte, Bettie Lucille. "Greek Sentiment Toward Rome and the Romans: A Study in Greco-Roman Relations." (Ph.D. diss., Bryn Mawr College, 1962).

Fowler, W. Warde. *The Roman Festivals of the Period of the Republic.* London: Macmillan, 1916.

Friedlander, Ludwig. *Roman Life and Manners Under the Early Empire*, 7th rev. and enlarged ed. New York: E. P. Dutton, 1928.

Geanakoplos, Deno John. *Interaction of the "Sibling" Byzantine and Western Cultures in the Middle Ages and the Italian Renaissance (330–1600).* New Haven, Conn.: Yale University Press, 1976.

Griffith, Mark. *The Authenticity of "Prometheus Bound."* London: Cambridge University Press, 1977.

Haigh, Arthur Elam. *The Attic Theatre: A Description of the Stage and Theatre of the Athenians, and of the Dramatic Performances at Athens,* 3rd ed. rev. by A. W. Pickard-Cambridge. 1907; rpt. New York: Haskell House, 1968.

Hammond, N. G. L. "The Conditions of Dramatic Production to the Death of Aeschylus." *Greek, Roman, and Byzantine Studies* 13, 4 (Winter 1972): 387–450.

———. *The Classical Age of Greece.* New York; Barnes and Noble, 1975.

———, and Moon, Warren G. "Illustrations of Early Tragedy at Athens." *American Journal of Archaeology* 82 (Summer 1978): 371–383.

Hansen, Mogens Herman. "How Many Athenians Attended the Ecclesia?" *Greek, Roman, and Byzantine Studies* 17 (Summer 1976): 115–134.

Hanson, John Arthur. *Roman Theatre Temples.* Princeton, N.J.: Princeton University Press, 1959.

Harsh, Philip Whaley. *A Handbook of Classical Drama.* Stanford, Calif.: Stanford University Press, 1944.

Kaegi, Walter Emil, Jr. *Byzantium and the Decline of Rome.* Princeton, N.J.: Princeton University Press, 1968.

Kehoe, Patrick Edward. "Studies in Roman Mime." (Ph.D. diss., University of Cincinnati, 1969).

Kernodle, George R. "The Fifth Century Skene: A New Model." *Educational Theatre Journal* 20, 4 (December 1968): 502–505.

Kitto, H. D. F. *Greek Tragedy*, 2nd ed. New York: Barnes and Noble, 1950.

———. *The Greeks.* London: Penguin, 1951.

———. *Sophocles: Dramatist and Philosopher.* London: Oxford University Press, 1958.

LaPiana, G. "The Byzantine Theatre." *Speculum* 11 (1936): 171–211.

Lawler, Lillian B. *The Dance of the Ancient Greek Theatre.* Iowa City: University of Iowa Press, 1964.

Leffingwell, Georgia Williams. *Social and Private Life at Rome in the Time of Plautus and Terence.* 1918; rpt. New York: AMS Press, 1968.

Lesky, Albin. *A History of Greek Literature*, trans. James Willis and Cornelis de Heer. New York: Thomas Y. Crowell, 1966.

Lever, Katherine. *The Art of Greek Comedy.* London: Methuen, 1956.

Lucas, Frank L. *Seneca and Elizabethan Tragedy.* Cambridge: Cambridge University Press, 1922.

McDonald, A. H. *Ancient People and Places: Republican Rome.* New York: Frederick A. Praeger, 1966.

Murray, Gilbert. *Euripides and His Age*, rev. ed. New York: Oxford University Press, 1965.

Nicoll, Allardyce. *Masks, Mimes, and Miracles*. 1931; rpt. New York: Cooper Square Publishing, 1963.

Norwood, Gilbert. *Greek Comedy*. New York: Hill and Wang, 1963.

———. *Plautus and Terence*. 1932; rpt. New York: Cooper Square Publishing, 1963.

O'Connor, John B. *Chapters in the History of Actors and Acting in Ancient Greece*. Chicago: University of Chicago Press, 1908.

Pallottini, Massimo. *The Etruscans*, rev. and enlarged ed. Bloomington: Indiana University Press, 1975.

Pickard-Cambridge, A. W. *The Theatre of Dionysus in Athens*. Oxford: Clarendon Press, 1946.

———. *Dithyramb, Tragedy, and Comedy*, 2nd ed. rev. by T. B. L. Webster. Oxford: Clarendon Press, 1962.

———. *The Dramatic Festivals of Athens*, 2nd ed. rev. by John Gould and D. M. Lewis. Oxford: Clarendon Press, 1968.

Rees, Kelley. *The Rule of Three Actors in the Classical Greek Drama*. Chicago: University of Chicago Press, 1908.

Sanderson, Dennis Carl. "A Conjectural Reconstruction from the Ruins of the Ancient Greek Theatre at Morgantina, Sicily." (Ph.D. diss., Michigan State University, 1973).

Segal, Erich. *Roman Laughter: The Comedy of Plautus*. Cambridge, Mass.: Harvard University Press, 1968.

Sifakis, G. M. *Studies in the History of Hellenic Drama*. London: Athlone Press, 1967.

———. *Parabasis and Animal Chorus*. London: Athlone Press, 1971.

Sommerstein, A. H. "Aristophanes and the Events of 411." *Journal of Hellenic Studies* 97 (1977): 112–126.

Stambusky, Alan A. "Roman Comedy on Trial in the Republic: The Case of Censorship Against Gnaeus Naevius the Playwright." *Educational Theatre Journal* 29 (March 1977): 29–36.

Taplin, Oliver. *The Stagecraft of Aeschylus: The Dramatic Uses of Exits and Entrances in Greek Tragedy*. Oxford: Clarendon Press, 1977.

———. *Greek Tragedy in Action*. Berkeley: University of California Press, 1978.

Travlos, John. *Pictorial Dictionary of Ancient Athens*. New York: Praeger Publishing, 1971.

Van Brunt, Thomas. "A Reevaluation of the Evidence Used to Reconstruct Athenian Theatrical Costume of the Classical Age." (Ph.D. diss., Indiana University, 1978).

Vitruvius. *Ten Books of Architecture*, trans. by Morris H. Morgan. Cambridge, Mass.: Harvard University Press, 1914.

Walbank, F. W. *The Awful Revolution: The Decline of the Roman Empire in the West*. Toronto: University of Toronto Press, 1969.

Walton, Michael. "Financial Arrangements of the Athenian Dramatic Festivals." *Theatre Research International* 2 (February 1977): 79–86.

Wardman, Alan. *Rome's Debt to Greece*. New York: St. Martin's Press, 1976.

Webster, T. B. L. *The Birth of Modern Comedy*. n.p.: Austrian Humanities Research Council, 1959.

———. *An Introduction to Sophocles*, 2nd ed. London: Methuen, 1969.

———. *The Greek Chorus*. London: Methuen, 1970.

———. *Greek Theatre Production*, 2nd ed. London: Methuen, 1970.

West, M. L. "The Prometheus Trilogy." *The Journal of Hellenic Studies* 99 (1979): 130–148.

White, K. D. *Country Life in Classical Times*. Ithaca, N.Y.: Cornell University Press, 1977.

Whitting, Philip, ed. *Byzantium: An Introduction*. New York: New York University Press, 1971.

Wright, F. Warren. *Cicero and the Theatre*. Smith College Classical Studies, No. 11. Northampton, Mass.: March 1931.

Wycherley, R. E. *The Stones of Athens*. Princeton, N.J.: Princeton University Press, 1978.

PART THREE

The Theatre
of Simultaneous Emblem

PART THREE

Dancers in fools' costumes, thought by some scholars to have a very ancient origin. Facsimile of a thirteenth-century manuscript. [From Lacroix.] Devils' costumes were among the most detailed and imaginative in medieval theatre. [From Sharpe.] The Elizabethan stage clown and musician, Richard Tarleton. [From Thornbury.]

7

The Theatre of Latin
Music-Drama, 965–1250

It would be futile now to try to do without the term *Middle Ages* to describe the period between the collapse of Roman power and the beginning of the Renaissance; the term has proved useful to too many people and it has been in use too long. It has the disadvantage, however, of expressing a prejudice of which we are hardly aware. *Middle* was used by historians who saw the period as inferior to Rome and the Renaissance; the Latinate *medieval* had the same connotation. In using the term *Middle Ages,* therefore, we must try to rid ourselves of this sense of the in-between, the second-rate, for the period was as rich and is as rewarding of study and as exciting—both in the theatre and in general history—as the ages before and after it.

An older term that *has* fallen out of use is *Dark Ages,* to describe the early part of the period. Again, to historians for whom Rome's was an elevated civilization and the end of Rome, therefore, a fall, the age that followed seemed very dark indeed; however, as one scholar has noted, "These centuries, from the fourth to the eleventh, constitute a long period during which new and distinctively medieval elements appeared and developed. There must therefore have been vitality and novelty as well as decline, barbarism and darkness in the early medieval period."[1]

The Middle Ages, then, were an extended period in which a new order came into being—and a new theatre. We will concern ourselves in this chapter with the years from about 330 to about the thirteenth century, lumping this whole, complex, shifting era under a single title: *the early middle ages.*

The Early Middle Ages

The Rise of Localism

It must be remembered that what we now call Europe was not *Christian* Europe until well into the period: the Synod of Whitby in 664 marked the Christianization of England, for example. Rome was Christian; Byzantium was Christian; northern Europe was only partly so. Thus, the Church did not—could not—move immediately to fill the void left by the collapse of Roman law and Roman ethics. An interim condition came into being, one marked by a mixture of Roman institutions and local innovations. Thus, if a single pattern marks the period, it is *localism,* that is, the independent solving of social problems as the embracing force of Rome disappeared.

Norman Kantor has described these changes as they took place in France: "The new [seventh century] French society was marked by a very large group of dependent serfs . . . perhaps as much as sixty per cent of the entire population. . . .

The serf was probably better off than the [Roman] slave . . . : he may often have had less to eat, but he had much greater personal freedom. . . . [T]otal misery was replaced by partial misery."[2] As well, as Kantor noted, power shifted from public (Roman) hands to private ones, with most wealth and power held by "no more than 2 per cent of the population," and the middle class and the urban centers declined until, in 600, "not more than 3 per cent of the French population" lived in towns. Thus, by the seventh century, overarching Rome had been replaced by local and private power; and the institutions of a highly organized state had given way to highly varied local ones. Finally, the majority of the population lived at a subsistence level.

Medieval Institutions

This seventh-century situation was not a static one, however. What the withdrawal of Rome left was not vacuum but flux. New and important developments included the following.

Feudalism

Definitions of this peculiarly medieval institution vary. One historian sees it as "a type of government in which political power was treated as a private possession and was divided among a large number of lords."[3] Such government had an important basis in warfare, however: in the eighth century, Charles Martel of France tried to require each man of means to take the field as a mounted warrior. Many historians see that requirement as a defining factor in medieval feudalism; certainly, it explains some of feudalism's unique qualities: the reliance on land (for pasturage and food); the development of *vassalage*, the willing subordination of one man to another in return for protection, so that a chain of vassalage bound the society, link by link, from king down to lowest freeman; the creation of the *fief*, the estate, often of vast size, over which the lord ruled.

The mature feudal society was agrarian, aristocratic, and hierarchical. In its ideal form (which was rarely achieved) it had the potential of great stability; in actuality, feudal society had the weaknesses of oversimplicity and inflexibility. It had no place for cities, for example. It coped, with increasing difficulty, with the conflict between the divided duties to temporal lord and divine Lord. It had constant problems with the contradictions built into its own system: individuals found themselves caught between opposing responsibilities (a man with several pieces of land could be vassal to several lords who might go to war against each other); and more and more, lords who based their power on land found that land alone sometimes could not produce the wealth they needed.

The Church

A popular view of the Middle Ages would populate it with jolly, wine-bibbing monks and would endow the minds of all men and women with a remarkable and naive piety. The facts, however, suggest that before the tenth century, the Church saw some very hard times, and conflicts between *ecclesia* (the medieval term for the world of the spirit, particularly the world of the Church) and *mundus* (the world of the lords temporal) were severe. Nominally centered at Rome, the Church suffered from localism just as other institutions did; by the beginning of the seventh century, for example, Ireland had a church that was on the verge of separating from Rome, while powerful bishops in Spain, France, and elsewhere saw more benefit in allying themselves with nearby lords than with faraway Rome. In addition, the Roman emperor in Byzantium—and it must be remembered that there was a Roman imperial power in Byzantium until 1453—believed himself superior to the papacy for at least part of the period.

The history of the Church is not the same as the history of the papacy, but the two were closely linked. The more effectively the papacy could exercise power beyond Rome and Italy, the more it could exercise control over the early medieval church. If it could extend its control throughout Europe, it could become identical with the Church. Thus, much of the history of the Christian Church from about 600 to 1100 is the history of the papacy's fluctuating affair with power. Shortly after 600, Pope Gregory sent Augustine to convert the English; so successful

FIGURE 7.1

Agricultural serfs of the late twelfth century. [From Willemin.]

was the mission that by 664, Roman Christianity became dominant in Britain and the threatened separation of the Irish branch of the Church was averted. A century later, Pope Gregory II expanded his authority—although at some cost—by crowning Pepin king of the Franks; in return, Pepin accepted and dignified the authority of the Bishop of Rome. In 800, Pope Leo slapped a crown on Charlemagne's head—supposedly against Charlemagne's will—and proclaimed him emperor of the Romans, thus asserting a papal authority to take that title away from the Roman emperor in Byzantium and hand it out in Europe. Charlemagne used the title or a variation of it, but—significantly for the cultural future of Europe—it appears that Charlemagne really wanted to be ruler of a more northern empire, as if he saw even then that a natural division would persist between Latin and northern Christianity—between the world of the Mediterranean and the world of the north.

Feudalism was able to tolerate a powerful Church alongside powerful lords; in fact, the Church itself, and many churchmen as individuals, were temporal lords and vassals. Because an individual's vassalage went with the land to which he belonged, the Church—owner of many lands—had many temporal vassals; for the same reason, church men, including bishops, were both vassals and lords. Thus, the interpenetration of *ecclesia* and *mundus* was an early characteristic of feudal society. Theology accepted this "identification of the *ecclesia* and *mundus*. . . . [T]he church was one, indivisible, universal Body of Christ encompassing the whole world . . . . 'The church' and 'the world' were treated as identical and synonymous terms, and hence empires and kingdoms had to be regarded as entities not outside the church but rather within its universal bounds."[4]

Monasticism

Monasticism (life under a common set of rules of devotion and asceticism) and its predecessor, eremitism (solitary self-denial and devotion) came early into Christianity. Hermits were numerous in North Africa in the first centuries after Christ; early monastic houses grew up in Byzantium. In the West, the great organizer was Saint Benedict, who founded his monastic house at Monte Cassino (in Italy) in the sixth century. It became a model, and Monte Cassino itself grew to be one of the greatest of European houses.

Benedict wisely saw the strength of an institution dedicated to piety and labor. Piety most frequently took the form of prayer and devotion, and the lives of many of the monks were centered in what a modern observer might see as constant ceremony. Their other labors, when not devoted to necessities (e.g., farming, cleaning, cooking, and administering) were often aimed at the continuation of knowledge—the copying of the written word. As Benedictine monasteries multiplied, some of them became great storehouses of knowledge.

The rule of Benedict suffered erosion over the centuries, however. Survival in the feudal system meant membership in the world of vassalage, ownership, and duty. Donors gave land and buildings to the monasteries; they wanted fealty in return. Kings and lords saw the monasteries as producers of wealth because they often created excellent farms; they also wanted the power to appoint the heads of monastic houses (abbots) from among their own people. Abbots themselves were sometimes greedy. By the tenth century, the rule of Benedict had spread across Europe, but there was a crescendo of demands for reform.

The so-called Cluniac Reform began with the establishment of a new Benedictine house at Cluny (France) in 910. Its abbot was independent of secular control and renounced all secular claims. The activities of the monks of Cluny were to be devoted more and more to prayer, so that "service in the choir came to dominate the days and nights of the monks almost to the exclusion of other duties."[5]

Partly from this same reformist thrust came other new monastic orders: the Carthusians in the late eleventh century; the Cistercians in the very early twelfth century; and the Premonstratensians shortly after. These new orders grew quickly; with the Cluniac example, they escaped the local control of temporal lords or ecclesiastical powers and put themselves under the direct control of Rome. In this way, they became part of that "Body of Christ" that was the truly universal and nonlocal element of medieval society before the thirteenth century.

Knowledge and Education

Rome had prided itself on its intellect. The newcomers from the north were "barbarians" because they did not have Roman learning. As the invaders swept down through Europe in what must have seemed endless waves, men of education were trying to salvage and preserve the knowledge that had been Rome's. One of the most famous of them was the sixth-century bibliophile Cassiodorus, who founded a short-lived monastic house in southern Italy. He saved many works and he encouraged their copying by scribes (the only way, it must be remembered, that written works could be reproduced).

Efforts like those of Cassiodorus were rare. Neglect of the manuscripts was far more common. Ruination followed: parchment rotted; manuscripts were fed to fires, were used to wrap packages, and were allowed to blow away. Perhaps most cruel of all was the making of "palimpsests," pages from which the original work had been scraped so that a new one could be written down. "Many texts which had escaped destruction in the crumbling empire of the West perished within the walls of the monastery. . . . [T]he toll of classical authors was very heavy: amongst those palimpsested we find Plautus and Terence, Cicero and Livy, the Elder and the Younger Pliny, Sallust and Seneca, Vergil and Ovid, Lucan, Juvenal and Persius, Gellius and Fronto."[6] While these authors were being washed and scraped away, few were being copied in their place: "from the sixth century we have scraps of two Juvenal manuscripts, remnants of one of the Elder and one of the Yonger Pliny . . . : from the seventh century we have a fragment of Lucan; from the early eighth century nothing."[7]

Given this situation, then, what did a person of the period 600–1100 know? Of bookish things, if he was a peasant, nothing; if he was a lay brother or a priest, little more, for many of them were illiterate. If a woman, the situation was usually worse; only after the twelfth century were women, and then only in the north, book-trained. To be sure, a genuine scholar would have known much; he would have read and written Latin and at least one vernacular (but rarely Greek); he might have been able to do simple arithmetic, but not multiplication or long division. He would have known theology and canon law and perhaps secular law, as well; he would have known liturgy and the Bible; he might have known some classics, but mostly by accident.

And therein lay much of the problem: knowledge was accidental. Many people wanted and sought knowledge, but much of it was very hard to find. What one monastic library might hold, another might lack; what one scribe might labor to copy, another might scrape away. As a result, no one could be expected to have systematic or thorough knowledge. Individual knowledge was restricted, uneven, and unreliable, for it came from written sources that were restricted, uneven, and unreliable.

This is not to say that there was no effort to disseminate existing work. Especially after the ninth century, scribal centers called *scriptoria* made new copies of existing works. The Romans had often used slaves for the task; the medieval Europeans used monastic scribes. No matter how hard the copyists worked, however, and no matter how many *scriptoria* the monasteries set up, the problems of scribal culture remained.

Not the least of the effects of the highly selective and unreliable knowledge was the medieval person's sense of his or her world. Indeed, the sense of the spiritual world was probably more precise than the sense of the physical world, for the spiritual world was the subject of a number of forms of public discourse: the sermon, the picture, and later the drama. The physical world, however, was a very

FIGURE 7.2

Time line: 500–1600.

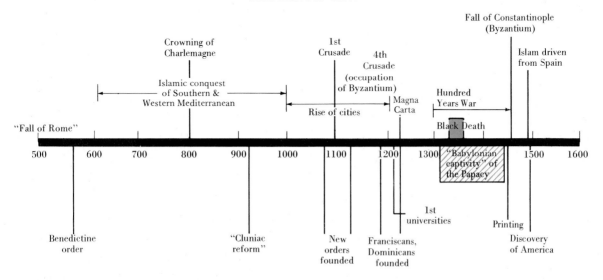

large blank sheet with a few details inked in very small. At the center, as it were, was the person and his or her immediate surroundings: room, house, village, and manor. Beyond that, in the case of the peasant, there was almost nothing— a blank, hazily smudged here and there with the stuff of superstition and with inaccuracies labeled *Rome* and *Germany* and *Jerusalem*. For the early merchant or soldier, there would be other, clearer pictures—places where he had actually been, as hard-edged as photographs when he had actually seen them. The overall picture was unclear, however, and toward the end of the medieval period, the vernacular dramatist John Rastell wrote a play, *The Four Elements*, that spent considerable time simply explaining a detailed map of the world.

The first reforms in education were not made to correct this spatial and geographical ignorance, however; indeed, this ignorance was so much in the grain of early medieval life that it went mostly unnoticed. Rather, the important pressure for the improvement of education came because of concern about a literacy rate so low that religion itself was threatened. The scholar Alcuin was brought to the court of Charlemagne in the eighth century to reform the palace schools. Education at the time was without consistency; where they could, monasteries and episcopal houses ran schools, the latter often for boys of cathedral choirs. In our sense, however, there was no "higher education." There was lower education, and little enough of that.

Cities and City Dwellers

It was said by a contemporary that there were only three classes in early medieval society: warriors, churchmen, and laborers. There were no city dwellers included in these classes, for cities were small and scattered and powerless. Feudal society had no place for them, therefore. When cities began to grow in the tenth century, they appeared as social nonentities.

The cities of the Roman Empire had shrunk or vanished. Some cities remained in Italy, to be sure—indeed, the rather different course of Italian history can be ascribed in part to the persistence of these cities—and Milan was always large. So was Rome, although it "consisted of scattered live sections in the midst of a ghost town."[8] Early medieval population figures are inexact, but the estimates are not impressive for the tenth century: Paris, 1,000 or so people; Milan, 14,000. Yet, three centuries later, Milan would have 200,000 people and Paris half that number.[9] The expansion between the tenth and thirteenth centuries was phenomenal and unprecedented, and the medieval structure did not easily accommodate it.

An important factor in this growth was trade. Improved travel, increased population, better agricultural methods and their surplus of goods, and contact with other cultures encouraged this growth. Much of the trade was conducted through *fairs*, where merchants gathered to function as middlemen—the first true internationalists, more traveled than even the wandering scholars. Still, as a class, the merchants had no place in society. Vassalage had no function for them. Communication and social contact were their goals, not the protection and ownership of land. Thus, they gathered into common quarters. Until their appearance, towns had existed as mostly ecclesiastical centers, and *civitas* or ("city") was simply the word for the seat of a bishop. After a certain critical mass of merchants was reached, however, *city* took on a different meaning, and new cities sprang up where there were no ecclesiastical centers.

Small lords sold land for cities outright in some cases; other locations "citified" themselves, on land that was useless for crops or grazing. Some cities grew up in symbiotic relations with the new universities. Wherever they were, they had, in a sense, to invent themselves as they went along. As a result, they were different from the rest of feudal institutions, and their relationship with feudal power was often an adversary one; city dwellers bought their identity at a price (often, quite literally, with money). The cities at the end of the early medieval period were the most modern elements in an uncertain structure—often fiercely independent and often hospitable to others who were at odds with the feudal establishment.

With the city-dwelling merchant came the shift from an economy based on goods and labor to one based on money. With him, too, came a decline in localism as trades and markets that had originally been established to serve local products sold surpluses. And with him came the *guilds* of the new cities (brotherhoods of men with common occupations or common interests). From the hierarchy of the merchant class came a new ruling class, often exercising power through the guilds as well as through civic politics. More than one historian has pointed out that medieval cities, for all their seemingly democratic selection of aldermen, mayors, and so on, were actually oligarchies, ruled by members of a relatively small merchant class.

Within the walls of the city, narrow streets twisted along the routes of old footpaths. There were parish churches everywhere, for men and women of the city were as pious as their fellows outside the walls. From a distance, the cityscape was dominated by the spires of the churches and by the bulks of the mother church or cathedral and the guildhall. The street names showed the gathering together of common trades: Goldsmiths Street, Mercers Street, Wool Lane, The Shambles (i.e., slaughterhouses). A man's trade was his secular identification; his collective life was the life of his trade guild. Each guild had its patron saint and its church, and the rivalry among guilds was also a rivalry among saints, parishes, and neighborhoods.

Outside the city walls, there was a sometimes hostile world. In time, however, the cities learned to join that world, hiring mercenaries to fight for them, endowing schools to educate their citizens in the world's knowledge, and standing against bishops and even popes who threatened their existence. By the middle of the thirteenth century, the cities had strength and identity, and they were on the verge of an explosive expansion.

Islam, Byzantium, and the Crusades

With the appearance of the Islamic prophet Muhammad (c. 570–632) and the rapid acceptance of his teachings, a new factor was introduced into Mediterranean politics. By the eighth century, huge areas of Christendom and of the old Roman Empire were Islamic—as if, at a stroke, two stable ties with the past had been slashed. Islam swept Egypt, North Africa, and most of Spain into its sphere of influence; some of the oldest of Christian communities in those areas were converted. Muslim armies almost swept into France. Sicily and Crete fell. Sea routes were cut or threatened.

By the tenth century, divisions within Islam combined with recovery in Europe to shift the balance again. In 1016, Genoa and Pisa drove a Muslim fleet out of Sardinia; in 1091, Viking–Norman invaders captured Sicily and southern Italy. A good part of the Mediterranean was European and Christian again. Trade could proceed. Spain, however, would not see the last of Islamic occupation until the time of Columbus.

The impact of Islam was incalculable. Perhaps most important, its conquests hastened the death of the idea of Rome. The Byzantine remnant of Rome was put on the defensive, and much of Christian Rome was converted. These changes gave early medieval Christians a feared, almost mythical enemy. Christianity was no longer struggling against barbaric, older religions; it was pitted against a new and readily identifiable religious force—a bogey man. When Christianity wanted to flex its muscles, Islam was waiting as an ideal enemy.

The encounter took place at the end of the eleventh century. Militant Christianity made a strike, since called the First Crusade. Like its successors, it had the nominal and estimable goal (from a Christian point of view) of recapturing Jerusalem from "the Saracens." Indeed, Jerusalem was recaptured (and later lost again), but the Crusades, almost from their inception, were such a typically medieval mixture of the noble and the base, the spiritual and the temporal, the romantic and the mundane, that their stated goals were far less important than their actuality. Historians still differ over the real significance of the Crusades—whether, for example, the cynicism of them drastically altered medieval self-perception, or whether the penetration into the Arab world opened Europe to a wealth of Arab knowledge. Certainly, the Crusades had and have symbolic significance as a reaching out by early medieval Christianity. That the gesture was both idealistic and self-seeking does not reduce that significance.

Militant Christian Europe and militant Islam represented two factors in the Mediterranean struggle; the third, enigmatic and fascinating, was Byzantium. As we have seen in Chapter 5, it was Greek in language soon after Constantine's movement to his new capital. It was hospitable to Eastern influence, and it incorporated Eastern elements into both its social and its religious life. The prostrating of subjects before the emperor and the wearing of costly court garments were Asiatic; in church ceremony, they became the basis for some of the ritual and some of the vestments of the Western as well as the Eastern rites.

Until the eleventh century, Byzantium expanded and contracted as it reacted to invasions, although Islam caused a permanent contraction in the East. Despite outer changes, the great city on the Bosporus flourished: a great university was created there; classics were preserved; libraries flourished; and theological studies went forward. Yet, there was a sterility in much of Byzantine intellectual life that finally ran opposite to the unlettered but increasingly vigorous mind of the West. When a Bishop Liudprand made an embassy to Byzantium in the tenth century, he was the representative of a lesser culture to a higher one; three hundred years later, the situation was reversed.

There were many contacts between Byzantium and Europe. Despite the religious split that took place in the eleventh century (the Eastern and Western churches excommunicated each other's leaders), contacts continued. In Italy, Byzantium had virtual colonies at Venice and Ravenna. Scholars and ecclesiastics of each culture were welcome in the other. Byzantine mosaic was a model for Italian painting; Byzantine music was one of the bases of Gregorian chant.

With the Crusades, however, this relationship was threatened. Perhaps it had not been so much stable as untested; once tested, it proved vulnerable. Jerusalem was the nominal goal of the Crusades, but Byzantium became the prize; in 1204, Crusaders turned their attentions directly to the city, sacking it and occupying it for half a century. When the Byzantines recaptured the city in 1261, they and Europe

FIGURE 7.3

Byzantium influenced western Europe in its ceremony, its symbolism, and the way it saw the human image. [From *The Magazine of Art.*]

were forever changed; it was a "trauma" from which they "never really recovered."[10] The rape of the Eastern capital of the Roman Empire marked the end of a great era—the end of the fiction of a living Rome.

Technology

The early Middle Ages were not without machines, although their power sources were unsophisticated. Many technological innovations were made, even in the early medieval period: for example, the water mill, the pulley and many of its systems, uses of the lever, a sail that allowed ships to sail against the wind, and the metal stirrup.[11] A society with an enormous population of landbound serfs has no great impetus to technological development, however.

Early Medieval Theatre and Its Drama

The centuries immediately after the withdrawal of Roman power were not hospitable to activities like the theatre. The theatre needs a sense of community in its audience and a certain size of audience; it needs, too, a commonality of signs and symbols. These things were lacking around 600. In fact, we have no records of theatre to speak of until the tenth century, and it would appear that the lack of data is the result of something other than a loss of documents.

So slight are the indications of continuity from Rome, in fact, that many scholars have given attention to the question of a "rebirth" of drama and theatre. It is as if the theories of the origin of theatre have to be run through all over again, as in Chapter Three. However, it is essential that we not forget that the conditions of this early medieval period were radically different from those of classical Greece—and not least because written records of Roman drama and theatre existed, however accidentally. Medieval scholars could form an idea of both plays and theatres from reading in medieval libraries, and

that idea could have had an enormous impact on any medieval "rebirth."

The Reemergence of Theatre and Drama

Theories of the reappearance of theatre include the following.

Continuity from Rome

Some scholars believe that there never was a break. Roman mimes remained popular until the end of the Western Empire, it is argued. These scholars cite the persistence into medieval Latin of such words as *mimi, histriones,* and *joculatores;* they cite such (rare) accounts as that of a mime, Vitalis, at the court of Charlemagne; and they point to the words of his contemporary, Alcuin: "Better to please God than actors" and "Better to feed paupers at your table than actors." Other historians, however, cite the distaste of the Germanic invaders for theatre; they argue that references scattered over several centuries do not suggest a tradition; and they point out that mentions of secular *mimi* do not seem directly relevant to literary drama, to theatre buildings, or to a drama of the Church, where drama next appeared.

The Example of Latin Drama

Although the knowledge of Latin works was spotty and accidental, some early medieval men and women are known to have read Terence, at least. As well, a later tradition of how Terence was staged also suggests continuity. More significantly, we know with certainty that a woman of the tenth century wrote "plays" in imitation of Terence: the six "comedies" of Hroswitha of Gandersheim are clearly dependent on the Roman playwright. We do not know that they were staged, however; there is even some question as to whether they were meant to be staged or are even stageable. Hroswitha may well have been both nontheatrical and unique, then.

Pagan Rituals and Mimetic Impulses

Certain ancient ceremonies show that "one important aspect of the medieval stage involved forms which had at their base rites of pagan provenance."[12] This line of argument has its beginnings in the work of the turn-of-the-century ritualists, particularly E. K. Chambers. In *The English Folk Play*, Chambers examined such "folk" events as Mummers' plays, Christmas plays, and sword dances as evidence of ritual survivals common to both popular social events and medieval theatre. He could find no direct link, and, indeed, no evidence for the folk "plays" themselves, much before the late sixteenth century; nonetheless, he argued that "a . . . silence which meets us in the Middle Ages is not necessarily conclusive against a primitive origin." This "primitive origin" was, of course, that seasonal ritual common to "the mental habits of men in various stages of civilization and in all parts of the world"[13] that was examined in Chapter 3. Other historians have argued that seasonal ritual has common ties to the Christian Mass and the first Christian dramas, but what they all seem to have in common is probably no more significant than what they lack. It seems as reasonable, and far simpler, to explain the appearance of medieval drama by what Grace Frank has called (in a slightly different context) "the perpetuity of the dramatic instinct."[14]

The Example and Influence of Byzantium

It has been thought for some time that Byzantium, as heir to Rome, must have had a theatre, even though little evidence of one survives. Byzantine theatre has not received the intensive scholarly scrutiny that Western theatre has, and so we do not yet have a very satisfactory understanding of it. Records were lost after the fall of Constantinople, and what survives is in a language that most Western theatre historians do not read; the evidence is scattered on both sides of the Iron Curtain; and recent scholarship is of variable quality. What emerges is mostly speculative: that Byzantium had a quasi-dramatic form, the "the dramatic homily," in the early medieval period; that Byzantium left us one play, the *Christos Paschon*, composed of lines from Greek tragedy and variously dated from the fourth to the eleventh century; that Byzantine hymnology had dramatic elements; and that scattered references to mimes and spectacles provide tantalizing hints but no facts. To be sure, there was plenty of contact between Byzantium and the West, but we have no evidence that any dramatic or theatrical influence passed because of it—or in which direction such influence, if any, flowed. It does appear that certain nondramatic elements that were a part of the material of early Church drama did come from Byzantium: elements of liturgy, liturgical music, and ecclesiastical vestments.

The Great Man—or Great Men

Scholars who would find an individual genius point at certain brilliant, educated products of the Carolingian renaissance, probably associated with the Cluniac Reform, not necessarily familiar with Terence and Roman drama but gifted with extraordinary insight and capable of seeing that Christian ceremony could be enriched with *enacted* liturgical song. Certainly, the Cluniac Reform enlisted brilliant men; certainly, when an early liturgical music–drama did appear, it accomplished precisely what such reformers might have wanted. In opposition, scholars argue that there is no evidence of any such one, great individual.

Christian Rite as Early Drama

The Christian Mass is itself "dramatic," it has been said. One need not be a ritualist to understand the statement:

"Some modern writers, taking a lead from medieval allegorists, would see the Mass itself as a drama of Christ's Passion, played by the celebrant in the theatre of the Church."[15]

"Its singing was antiphonal; its readings of the Gospel narrative frequently introduced voice-changes to indicate changes of speaker; its vestments, music and decorations shifted from solemn to festive with the seasons; it was performed by special groups before an audience to the accompaniment of chanting, genuflexions, and other gestures; its symbolism and emotional effect were cumulative and climactic."[16]

Opponents of this hypothesis point out that the Mass could be drama-*like* without being drama; that the Mass shared attributes with other ceremonies that were not dramas; that the presence of audience and speaker characterizes a number of rhetorical situations that are not theatrical; and that we have no evidence that the people of the time made an essential connection of the Mass with drama and then made a leap from that connection to early plays.

It is impossible to say what the origin or origins of early medieval drama and theatre were. A combination of causes, or different causes in different places, would be the somewhat waffling solution to the dilemma.

Latin Music–Drama in the Church

It cannot be said too often or too strongly that the first drama of the early medieval church was *sung* drama. Its artistic ancestry appears to have been musical, not literary, and it is as productively studied as a musical form as a dramatic one.

The responsive chant and choral song of the Carolingian renascence were the framework for this drama. Its language was Latin, not one of the European vernaculars. Its appearance was preceded by a very similar form called the *trope*, an expansion of the church liturgy.

Tropes
The three "speeches" that comprise the sung dialogue of the earliest forms are

Quem quaeritis in sepulchro, Christicolae?
(Whom do you seek in the sepulcher, people of Christ?)
Iesum Nazarenum, crucifixum, o caelicolae.

(Jesus of Nazareth who is crucified, o heavenly one.)
Non est hic, surrexit sicut praedixerat. Ite, nuntiate quia surrexit de sepulchro.
(He is not here; he is risen as was foretold. Go, tell that he is risen from the sepulcher.)

These lines appear in manuscripts of the musical embellishments called *tropes,* often gathered into books called *tropers.* Tropes were additions to the liturgy and its music, "commentaries upon the liturgical text," in Grace Frank's words. Although tropes were "not yet dramatic" in the words of Karl Young, the great early investigator of this field,[17] they provided both the words and the conditions of performance—choir, music, and church environment—for the use that would be accepted as dramatic.

There is scholarly controversy over the origin and early purpose of these sung lines. However, the consensus seems to be that "sometime in the ninth century a monk wrote [the *Quem quaeritis*] text and set it to music."[18] Whether these words and music then became part of the Mass, of an office called *matins* ("morning ceremony"), or of a pre-Mass procession, we do not know; what we do know is that they appeared almost simultaneously over much of Europe. They were copied and recopied, so that the dating of the first appearance in many places is impossible. *And they continued to appear as if for the first time in some places through the fifteenth century.* Localism and the medieval allowance for variety made it possible for *Quem quaeritis* to exist simultaneously in both its simplest and its most complex forms.

The *Visitatio Sepulchri*
Karl Young called the earliest liturgical play the *Visitatio Sepulchri* (the "Easter visit to the sepulchre"). The words are often identical to those of the *Quem quaeritis* trope; however, the addition of elements of theatrical presentation—and, probably the use of this "play" in some ceremony other than the Mass—made it, for Young,

the first medieval drama. Most scholars follow him.

Our earliest *Visitatio Sepulchri* is found in the *Regularis Concordia,* a book of rules and advice for English Benedictines set down in the middle of the tenth century by Ethelwold, Bishop of Winchester, England. Nothing about this *Visitatio Sepulchri* proves that it was the first one—or even that it came after or depended on a *Quem quaeritis* trope. David A. Bjork has suggested that the Winchester *Visitatio* "should probably be taken as representative of a practice widespread on the continent—at least in the

FIGURE 7.4

The Maries at the Tomb, the subject of the *Visitatio Sepulchri* (ca. 1020, from Germany). It is interesting as an example of medieval art—the plain background, the Byzantine eyes, the rather weightless bodies—but also for its resemblance to the theatrical scene. Note the thurible carried by one of the Maries. [Courtesy of the Bodleian Library (MS. Canon. Liturg. 319, folio 95ᵛ), Oxford University, and reproduced with permission.]

North—for half a century or more."[19] Such pieces "were in use for more than five hundred years" (Young) and can be found in records from much of Europe. Thus, the *Visitatio* was a short, sung drama in Latin that continued or reappeared erratically for five or more centuries.

What are the theatrical characteristics that make this piece a play? First, it was performed at matins, where it could be a separate entity and not an elaboration. Second, it specified performers: three male members of the choir who were to sing the words of the three Maries at the tomb of Christ, and a fourth those of an angel. Third, according to Ethelwold's instructions, the performers were to be dressed for the task, costuming themselves while the rest of the choir sang the third lesson. We might not recognize their clothes as costumes, for they were simply a form of ecclesiastical garment (alb and copes), but it is important that the garments were different from those of the rest of the choir. Fourth, there was a concept of representation: the singer presenting the angel was to enter so that he would be unseen until the moment when the drama calls for him, while those presenting the three women were to approach the sepulcher "in the manner of" the women, "slowly . . . looking around as if seeking something." When the angel told them that Christ was risen and that they should spread this news, they were to turn to "the people" (the rest of the choir? the congregation?) and sing, "He is risen."

At Winchester, the *Visitatio* concluded with a powerful link to other Easter ceremonies: "[T]he Marys laid the grave clothes on the altar, the prior initiated the *Te Deum Laudamus* [song in praise of God], and all the bells pealed. At this point sight of the performers is lost."[20]

To Karl Young's evolutionary eye, this *Visitatio* was the "first stage" of the drama's development. A second stage in his system included the new characters of the disciples Peter and John, and a third, Christ himself—more characters and more complex actions as evolution took the drama from the simple to the complex: the

FIGURE 7.5
Early Latin Trope and Music–Drama

Title	Type	Subject	Example*	Date of Example† (century)
Quem quaeritis	Trope	Easter visit	Winchester, England	early 10th
			St. Gall, Switzerland	early 10th or late 9th
			Brescia, Italy	15th
Visitatio Sepulchri	Drama	Easter visit	Winchester, England	mid-10th
			Clermont-Ferrand, France	14th
			Arras, France	11th
			Strasbourg, France	13th
Visitatio Sepulchri	Drama	Easter visit with *Hortolanus* and/or *Nolo me tangere*	Rouen, France	13th
			Prague, eastern Germany	13th
Ludus Paschalis	Drama	Easter cluster	Origny-Ste. Benoit, France	13th–14th
Peregrinus	Drama	Journey to Emmaus	Beauvais, France	13th
			Saintes, France	14th
Ascension	Drama	Christ's ascent into Heaven	Moosberg, Germany	14th
Pentecost	Drama	The inspiration of the Apostles	Halle, Germany	16th
Pastores	Drama	Christmas shepherds	Limoges, France	11th
			Rouen, France	14th
Magi, Stella, and/or *Herod*	Drama	Christmas star and the three kings	Compiègne, France	12th
			Sicily (Norman)	12th
Prophetae	Drama or procession	Prophecy of Christ's birth	Laon, France	13th

*Examples are highly selective; in most cases, there are *many* examples of the type.
†Dates are approximate; most data are from Young, *Drama of the Medieval Church.*

Hortolanus (Christ as the gardener) and the *Nolo Me Tangere* ("Do not touch me"). There is no hard proof of such development, however; rather, these forms often existed simultaneously or out of order in the mosaic of medieval history.

Other Liturgical Easter Dramas

Young and other scholars have cited a cluster of similar Easter liturgical plays. Young called the category *Ludus Paschalis* ("Easter Play"). (However, *ludus* was a word used for "play" only after the eleventh century. Many scholars find such Latin terms significant—especially *ordo* ("order"), *officium* ("office"), and *processus* ("procession")—because they were used for ceremonies that became dramas only when a later consciousness—that of the twelfth century and its "increased awareness of the terms of Roman drama"[21]—saw them as such. Thus, Young's term *Ludus Paschalis* may be too loaded.)

These analogues to the *Visitatio* include the *Peregrinus* (the pilgrimage to Emmaus), the *Ascension*, and the *Pentecost*. They share the same conditions of performance with the *Visitatio*. Their geography and chronology are erratic and the argument for their evolutionary development is far from proven.

Non-Easter Liturgical Music–Dramas

There are early dramas associated with holy days other than Easter—particularly Christmas. These include plays of the shepherds who were told of

Christ's birth by the angel, the *Pastores*; the *Magi* (the three kings), *Stella* ("star"), and *Herodes* (King Herod), three overlapping or intertwined stories; and plays of those who foretold the birth of Christ, the *Prophetae*.

There are clear similarities to the Easter texts: they were sung, not spoken; they were in Latin; they were performed in connection with offices, usually matins; they were closely identified with annual occasions like Epiphany and Christmas; and it appears that they were equally abstract in their use of space, properties, and costuming.

Again, there is no proof of evolutionary development. Still, one cannot overlook the argument made so cogently by Young and taken up by Grace Frank and others. There is variety of chronology: Does this mean that there was chronological order? There was a rough association with the Benedictine monasteries: Does this mean that there was a Benedictine system of communications that concerned itself with drama? There is a noticeable difference between simple and complex texts, with the complex ones often occurring later than the simple ones: Does this imply development from one to the other?

It is likely that evolutionists overstate the matter. However, to go to the opposite extreme and suggest that these plays came about through case after case of spontaneous generation would be witless.

The Theatre of the Early Latin Music–Drama

What was the "theatre" of these plays like? We know, from the *Regularis Concordia* and other documents, that:

1. *The performances were at unlikely hours* for theatre; matins, for example, was celebrated as early as 4 A.M.

2. *The theatre spaces were in churches*, but often churches of a special kind—monastic churches. The audience would rarely have been a lay one, therefore; George Bryan has argued that it would have been made up, instead, of clergy, novices, monks, and schoolboys, and that the drama was probably "not presented for the edification of the laity."[22]

3. *The language of the plays (Latin) was unintelligible to the general population.*

4. *No theatre, in the modern sense, was constructed.* The sepulcher of the *Visitatio* was often a real object; in some churches, tombs were used; and in some cases, temporary sepulchers were set up for the Easter season. The "acting space" had to be close enough to the main altar

FIGURE 7.6

Plan of Lincoln Cathedral, England. Note the Choir (O), separated from the more public nave and transept by a choir screen. It was in the choir that plays of the *Visitatio* type were probably staged, often at predawn hours. [From *Century*.]

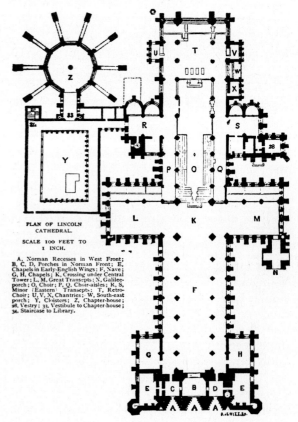

PLAN OF LINCOLN CATHEDRAL.

SCALE 100 FEET TO 1 INCH.

A, Norman Recesses in West Front; B, C, D, Porches in Norman Front; E, Chapels in Early-English Wings; F, Nave; G, H, Chapels; K, Crossing under Central Tower; L, M, Great Transepts; N, Galilee-porch; O, Choir; P, Q, Choir-aisles; R, S, Minor (Eastern) Transepts; T, Retro-Choir; U, V, X, Chantries; W, South-east porch; Y, Cloisters; Z, Chapter-house; 28, Vestry; 33, Vestibule to Chapter-house; 34, Staircase to Library.

so that the cloth and the cross could be included. It is clear that processional spaces were also used, not only in the *Visitatio* but also in most of the Easter and Christmas dramas. However, the actors were members of the choir, and the acting area was probably in that part of the monastic church reserved for the choir—a fairly large area behind a screen that separated it from the rest of the church. Thus, it would appear that the theatrical space of these early plays was rather unfocused, was cut off from the congregation, and was probably in and around the choir space.

5. *The distinction between actor and audience was unclear.* Monastic brothers of the choir played the Maries and the angel; at the end of the performance, they faced their brothers of the choir for "He is risen" and then joined them. Acting space and audience space seem to have flowed into each other, and the roles of actor and audience member overlapped, too.

6. *The costuming and properties were emblematic and not illusionistic.* The "actors" were distinguished by special ecclesiastical garments, not by "angel costumes" or "Mary costumes." A suggestion that "realism is increased when the angels are provided with wings"[23] is without basis in the evidence and is much influenced by modern taste. The Maries of the *Regularis Concordia* were to carry thuribles ("censers"), not the ointment pots of the Gospels. (Real ointment pots would not have carried the religious significance of the thuribles.) The historian Glynn Wickham has called this opposition of medieval meaning-bearing and the imitation of reality the opposition of the "emblem" and the "image." The emblem is a sign or a complex of signs; the image is a precise copy of something in life. Thus, the emblem is general in its reference, the image particular; the emblem tends toward idea and ideal, the image toward the concrete. Early medieval theatre was a theatre of emblems.

7. *The events may have been participatory ceremonies and not theatre in any modern sense.* The Mass, and all the ceremonies that surround it, were loaded with signs and symbols: events, gestures, and emblems whose understanding required participation. Many such medieval ceremonies were both symbolic *and* experiential: for example, when the paschal candle was brought to the church at Easter, the priest knocked on the church door, which had been previously shut against him; he was knocking for entry, but he was also symbolically announcing the return of God's grace.

We must ask, then, if a drama like the *Visitatio* functioned as a theatre for observers or as a participatory ceremony: Was the audience (probably a monastic choir) to watch and understand, or was it to become the crowd of the faithful and the disciples, waiting eagerly for the Maries' "He is risen"? We do not know.

More Latin Music–Drama in the Church

A shift in the terms that were used for the dramas—from *ordo*, *officium*, and *processus*, to *ludus* and *representatio*—occurred in or shortly after the twelfth century. Because it coincided with other changes—a greatly increased differentiation between audience and actor, musical complexity, a shift toward spectacle, and much longer plays—we take the shift of language to be at least symptomatic of a shift in the early medieval theatre.

Although there were performances outside the churches in this period, it is hardly possible to say that the dramas as a group moved outside—to "the church steps," as was once believed. As we have already said, in some places the *Visitatio* and the other early dramas remained vital in-church events right through the sixteenth century.

However, the plays of the twelfth century and after—as compared with the *Visitatio* and the other early texts—are ones that moderns would recognize as dramas. They are theatrical art of a high order—still music-drama in Latin, but sophisticated in their language, their music, and their theatricality.

FIGURE 7.7

Geographical distribution of the *Quem quaeritis* and the *Visitatio Sepulchri* in the tenth to sixteenth centuries.

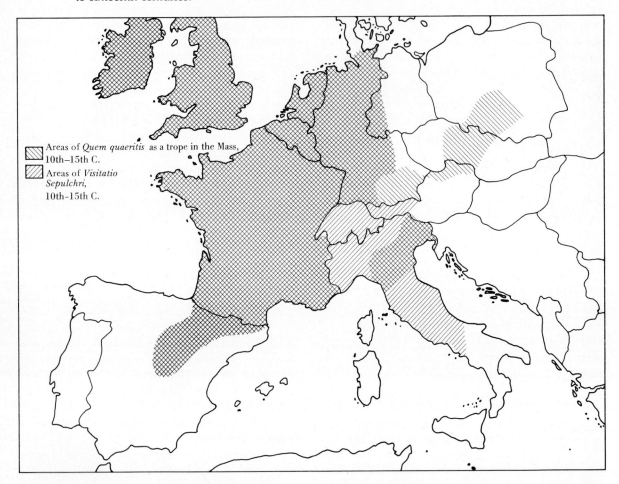

Plays of the Fleury Play-Book

In the French city of Orléans, Manuscript 201 of the Bibliothèque de la Ville contained about sixty pages that comprise what is now known as the *Fleury Play-Book*, thirteenth-century scribal copies of plays from the Benedictine monastery of St.-Benoit-sur-Loire at Fleury, France. There are ten liturgical plays in all. In the order in which they are bound, they are a group of four Saint Nicholas plays, the *Tres Fili* ("Three Daughters"), *Tres Clerici* ("Three Scholars"),

Iconia Sanctus Nicholaus ("Image of Saint Nicholas"), and *Filius Getronius* ("Getron's Son"); a *Herod*; an *Ordo Rachelis* (the lament of Rachel after the Slaughter of the Innocents); a *Conversion of Saint Paul*; and a *Raising of Lazarus*. Except for the last two plays, all have identifiable connections with the liturgical calendar, and most of the plays have instructions that connect them with a holy day and an office (usually matins).

These are sophisticated musical plays.

Modern musicologists have made the music accessible, and modern productions have delighted audiences. Because of detailed stage directions, we know that their costuming and staging were different from those of the *Visitatio* and that the separation between actors and audience was much clearer.

The Fleury *Herod*, like other dramas from the Fleury Play-Book, is a pastiche—even a "hodge-podge," to use David Bjork's word for the *Visitatio* plays—both in structure and in words. Three shorter plays can be identified in it: a *Pastores*, a *Magi*, and a *Stella*, neatly connected at their junctures. The text includes verses used in other plays of the same type elsewhere in France. The memorable character of the play is Herod, who dominates with a bold musical line and often violent action. Attendants greet him with the words, "Live forever, O King"—proof of his arrogance and impiety. He occasionally refers to the Roman poet Vergil. He is surrounded by scribes, attendants, and soldiers. He is a good example of a stage type that would persist to the end of the Middle Ages, the tyrant.

The *Ordo Rachelis* is a music play of impressive theatricality. Two groups of characters carry on musical actions simultaneously: while a large number of choristers process, dressed in white to symbolize the innocence of the children soon to be slaughtered, the Holy Family are in their manger scene near one of the church doors, and Herod is on his *sedes*, or throne, elsewhere in the church. One of the processing choristers carries an emblem of the Lamb of God—Christ as victim. As he does so, Herod takes up his own emblem—the sword. When the Holy Family escape into Egypt to avoid him, Herod sends out his soldiers, who chase the innocents (the white-robed choristers) and kill them; then their mothers, in the person of Rachel, lament. Herod dies (in pantomime, or "dumb show") and is replaced by his son; the Holy Family return, safe.

This play almost certainly used a large part

of a monastic church. There is musical cross-reference between the processing Innocents and the court of Herod and a potent interplay of emblems: the white-robed choristers are the children, but they *prefigure* the innocents who are to be saved at Doomsday; Rachel is the mother of a slain child, but she prefigures the lamenting Mary of the Crucifixion; the chorister who carries the emblem of the Lamb of God contrasts boldly with the sword-bearing Herod; and Christ is presented as both a helpless baby and the spiritual leader of the Innocents.

It is important to note here the use of *figuring* or *prefiguring,* a medieval device for using one person or one event to remind the audience of another. The device derives from the medieval view of history, in which events themselves were figures (also *types*). The medieval sensibility lived in a universe of emblems and symbols; time was relatively unimportant, and history was a divine pattern of figure and event, constantly reflecting back and forth on each other.

Of the other Fleury plays, the Saint Nicholas group deserves special mention. Of them, the *Filius Getronius* is particularly noteworthy. A dramatization of a legend from the life of the saint, it includes a Herod-like tyrant, Marmorinus, who sends out soldiers to capture victims, which include a Christian boy named Adeodatus ("Given of God"), the son of Getron of Excoranda. Marmorinus boasts and swears by Apollo; when the boy sighs for his home after a year of captivity, Marmorinus snarls that he will never be freed. Saint Nicholas appears, rescues the boy, and spirits him back to Excoranda and his parents. Again, this is a far cry from the *Visitatio Sepulchri*. It includes such spectacles as the siege of Excoranda and Saint Nicholas's transporting the boy to his home, probably by flying.

We can note the following on the basis of the Fleury plays:

1. *Multiple locations with emblematic set pieces.* Both the city of Excoranda and the throne of Marmorinus are shown, as well as a church

of Saint Nicholas. In *Herod,* the manger and Herod's throne, as well as the procession, are needed. In the *Conversion of Saint Paul,* the cities of Jerusalem and Damascus, thrones for a priest and Saul, and a bed are required.

2. *A generalized playing space among the set pieces.* Armies march; Innocents progress and are slaughtered; the Holy Family flees; the Magi meet and follow the star. The word *plateam* is used for this space.

3. *Spectacular effects.* The siege of a city was probably done by a few actors in armor, using ladders, weapons, and so on. In the *Conversion of Saint Paul,* the saint is lowered from the walls of Jerusalem in a basket. Saint Nicholas probably needed a machine to fly with the boy. *Herod* requires a movable star for the Magi. The star was a very common early property, and there are records of the use of machinery and lighting effects for it.

4. *Dumb show or pantomime.* Certain actions are presented without covering words, for example, the siege and Herod's death.

5. *Textual accretion.* In an age that had no idea of literary ownership, the use of materials from other sources was common. "Originality" was without value and was often suspect.

6. *Emblematic costumes and properties.* Scribes carry books to announce their profession, soldiers wear armor, and kings wear crowns. The armor of Herod's soldiers signifies both character and task; that is, the soldiers are nothing but soldiers. Herod's sword, on the other hand, conveys meaning about the kind of king he is: a military tyrant, a worldly power seeker, and an enemy of Christ.

7. *Generalized character.* Fidelity to the Gospels is very strong. Characterization beyond the Gospels is very rare. Herod and Marmorinus have great energy, but it is the energy of tyranny, not a specific, individual trait. Among groups like the Innocents, the Shepherds, and the Magi, individuals are hardly differentiated.

The plays of the Fleury Play-Book are of the same tradition as the *Visitatio Sepulchri* in their close association with liturgy and the church calendar, in their monastic associations, and in their frequent lack of audience definition. They are quite different in important respects, however, not the least of which is their exploitation of spectacle and of the theatrical potential of the church interior.

Other Liturgical Music–Dramas

Other outstanding examples include a *Daniel* play from Beauvais. Like the Fleury *Herod,* it has become well-known in a modern production and is available in modern recordings. Although the manuscript is from the thirteenth century, the play is believed to be from the mid-twelfth century and is probably the work of someone at the Beauvais cathedral school. (A *Visitatio* and a *Peregrinus* are known from the same source.) This is a play of stunning spectacle that includes several processions, a moving hand that writes on the wall, the glittering courts of Darius and Belshazzar, and the scene of Daniel in the lions' den. Its music is complex and stirring; although not scored for instruments, it is meant to be accompanied in places by at least harp and percussion, as the text indicates. Karl Young cited a description of a costume from the Beauvais treasury list that may have been for this play, "a black silk for a man made all about of silver."[24]

Often mentioned with the Beauvais *Daniel* are three plays of the twelfth century, probably by a "wandering scholar" named Hilarius: a *Daniel,* an *Icon of Saint Nicholas,* and a *Raising of Lazarus.* These plays also appear to have been written for a choir and for in-church production. Hilarius intermittently used vernacular French. Such embellishment and the very fact of his identity by name make Hilarius noteworthy.

Probably of slightly later date (the thirteenth century) are the plays of the so-called *Carmina Burana,* associated with the monastery at Benediktbeuern (Bavaria). Two plays of the Passion of Christ are included, a subject rare in drama at this date; there are long passages from

FIGURE 7.8
Major Latin Music–Drama of the Twelfth Century*

Usual Title	Textual Source	Place of Origin	Author	Plays Included
Fleury Play-Book	Orléans, Bibliothèque de la Ville, MS 201	Benedictine monastery of St.-Benoit-sur-Loire, France	Anon.	*Tres Fili, Tres Clerici, Iconia Sanctus Nicholaus, Filius Getronius, Herod, Ordo Rachelis, Conversion of Saint Paul, Raising of Lazarus, Peregrinus, Visitatio Sepulchri*
Beauvais *Daniel*	British Museum, Egerton MS 2615	Cathedral School, Beauvais, France	Anon.	*Daniel*
Plays of Hilarius	Paris, Bibliothèque National, MS lat 11331	unknown	Hilarius	*Daniel, Icon of Saint Nicholas, Raising of Lazarus*
Tegernesee *Antichristus*	Munich, MS lat 19411	Benedictine monastery, Tegernsee, Germany	Anon.	*Antichrist*
Ordo Virtutum		Nunnery, Bingen, Germany	Hildegard	*Ordo Virtutum*
Monte Cassino *Passion*		Benedictine monastery, Monte Cassino, Italy	Anon.	*The Passion of Christ*

*It must be remembered that the *Visitatio* and its many analogues continued throughout the period.

other plays; and there are a number of clearly allegorical characters: Archysynagogus in the Nativity play and Antichrist in a fragment. Like the plays of Hilarius, these of the *Carmina Burana* are ascribed to "wandering scholars," and, indeed, there is sophistication and education evident in them. Like the Beauvais *Daniel,* they use much spectacle, both glorious and grotesque: Herod's death includes his being devoured by worms. Most probably, these plays were the product of both chronological and geographical accretion, for they include direct borrowings from dramas of other times and other places.

In addition to these plays, there are others that show the same characteristics and a few that are clear exceptions. There is evidence of performance by women, for example, in a monastic house of women. There are several plays that appear to be single examples of types: a play of *Antichrist* from Germany that was topical and

allegorical; an *Ordo Virtutum* associated with the name of Hildegard of Bingen; and a Passion play from Monte Cassino (Italy). The *Antichrist* and the *Ordo Virtutum* are allegories: the *Antichrist* is a struggle for the world among titanic kings, the messiah and the false messiah, and characters called Hypocrisy and Heresy; the *Ordo Virtutum* offers Animus ("the soul"), sixteen Virtues, and the Devil in a cosmic struggle. Richard Axton has noted the "symbolic staging and iconographic costume" of the *Ordo Virtutum,*[25] and the words could apply equally well to the *Antichrist.*

The Monte Cassino play was discovered only recently (1936) and radically changed the view that the Passion was not a subject for Latin music–drama until very late. It remains a solitary example, although there are references to other Passions at Siena (Italy) in about 1200 (although the reference is dubious); Padua (Italy) in 1244; and Cividale (Italy) in 1298 and 1303.

We have already mentioned the *Carmina Burana* Passion plays.

The Monte Cassino play is thus the earliest of the type. Efforts have been made to associate it with Byzantium because of contacts between Byzantium and Monte Cassino in the period, but nothing can be proved. Other than its subject matter, the important point about the Monte Cassino play is its place of origin: Italy. The great bulk of other early music–drama is from Frankish (northern), rather than from Roman, Europe. The extensive Monte Cassino library may have been a factor.[26]

Conclusion

We have examined a relatively short period—overall, from about 600 to 1250, but in drama from about 900 to 1250—and, even more narrowly, from about 965 to the early thirteenth century, with the date so late only because of the *Carmina Burana* plays. And the longer and more complex music–dramas of the Fleury and Beauvais type can almost all be dated in the twelfth century.

We know that these plays, in their later and more spectacular forms, were staged with great pageantry. Still, they remained within the calendar and the ceremonial offices of the Church and were performed (as far as we know) inside churches, usually monastic churches. Their performers were almost always male, and the sexes were not, we think, mixed. Solo parts of considerable length and difficulty were written, but the choir remained the wellspring of the music, with unison and antiphonal singing much used. Character was typical or emblematic, and occasionally allegorical; the costumes bore out these same qualities while contributing to the spectacle. Properties contributed to the spectacle: arms, crowns, the gifts of the three kings, the banners of the Persian courts.

In most cases, we do not know what part or parts of the monastic church were used. Plays of the *Visitatio* sort appear to have been done in the choir; other and later plays almost certainly used other areas. Procession was as important to the plays as it was to Church ceremony and would have had more effect if done in the nave instead of the choir; however, it is important to remember that many Church processions took place at times of the day (or night) when it is unlikely that any congregation was present. Much action was vigorous and large-scale, although some of it was pantomimed. Theatrical effects using machinery became common.

The distinction between performers and audience was clarified whenever the playing space itself was made distinct. *Antichrist* called for seven *sedes* around a playing space that was open on one side. Some of the Fleury plays called for multiple locations with space among them for traveling and for playing. Thus, in many cases, the simultaneous existence of locations in view of the audience was normal, and simultaneous action in such locations was possible *but was very rare.*

It is difficult, and perhaps impossible, to speak authoritatively of the acting. We have to assume that such acting was as much a religious duty as was choral singing, and at least in the earliest plays it seems not to have been aimed at either the satisfaction of the audience or the satisfaction of the actor, but at the satisfaction of God. We assume that the acting, like the costumes and properties, was emblematic; that it showed only large, generalized matters; that it did not seek to individualize character; and that it drew from the common fund of recognized signs and gestures. Highly developed vocal technique was required. If iconographic evidence of the period is at all analogous, then the acting relied on such readily identifiable activities as swooning, pointing to Heaven, and weeping. Characters like Herod and Marmorinus may have been almost hectically active, but characters like the Magi, the Virtues, and Saint Nicholas were probably stately. Just as the acting space had no direct connection with real distance, the acting did not seek a direct connection with real behaviors.

FIGURE 7.9

Schematic: Examples of in-church simultaneous settings.

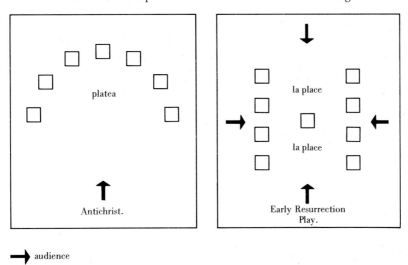

The Latin music–drama of the early medieval church was not without its opponents within the Church itself. The most often quoted one was Gerhoh of Reichersberg, who, in the mid-twelfth century, blasted clerical participation in plays that included wearing armor and playing the roles of devils and sinners. Such criticism must not be taken as the cause of the changes that were to come to this theatre, however. Rather, the changes in the theatre reflected changes in the medieval world after the Latin music–drama's high period in the twelfth century.

ENDNOTES

1. Robert S. Hoyt, ed., *Life and Thought in the Early Middle Ages* (Minneapolis: University of Minnesota Press, 1967), Hoyt's introduction, p. 5.
2. Norman F. Cantor, *Medieval History*, 3rd ed. (New York: Macmillan, 1976), p. 152.
3. Joseph R. Strayer, "The Two Levels of Feudalism," in Hoyt, pp. 51–52.
4. Cantor, pp. 252–253.
5. N. P. Zacour, *An Introduction to Medieval Institutions*, 2nd ed. (New York: St. Martin's Press, 1976), p. 163.
6. L. D. Reynolds and N. G. Wilson, *Scribes and Scholars* (London: Oxford University Press, 1968), p. 76.
7. Ibid.
8. Robert S. Lopez, "Of Towns and Trade," in Hoyt, p. 37.
9. Ibid.
10. D. J. Geanakoplos, *The Interaction of the "Sibling" Byzantine and Western Cultures. . . .* (New Haven, Conn.: Yale University Press, 1976), p. 11.
11. Lynn White, Jr., "The Life of the Silent Majority," in Hoyt, pp. 88 ff.
12. William Tydeman, *The Theatre in the Middle Ages* (Cambridge and New York: Cambridge University Press, 1978), p. 14.
13. E. K. Chambers, *The English Folk-Play* (Oxford: Clarendon Press, 1933), p. 12.
14. Grace Frank, *The Medieval French Drama* (Oxford: Clarendon Press, 1954), p. 5.
15. Richard Axton, *European Drama of the Early Middle Ages* (London: Hutchinson, 1974), p. 15.

16. Frank, p. 18.
17. Karl Young, *The Drama of the Medieval Church*, 2 vols. (Oxford: Clarendon Press, 1933).
18. David A. Bjork, "On the Dissemination of *Quem quaeritis* and the *Visitatio sepulchri* and the Chronology of Their Early Sources," *Comparative Drama* (1980):47–64.
19. Ibid.
20. George Bryan, *Ethelwold and Medieval Music-Drama at Winchester: The Easter Play, Its Author,* *and Its Milieu* (Berne: Verlag Peter Lang, 1981), p. 116.
21. Axton, p. 64.
22. Bryan, p. 124.
23. Young, Vol. 2, p. 402.
24. Young, Vol. 2, p. 486.
25. Axton, p. 99.
26. Robert Edwards, *The Montecassino Passion and the Poetics of Medieval Drama* (Berkeley: University of California Press, 1977).

8

Vernacular Religious Theatre of the Middle Ages, ca. 1250–1600

The Middle Ages after the thirteenth century were a period of accelerating change. Sometimes, the changes pulled institutions in opposite directions. We must tolerate these seeming contradictions, remembering the extreme localism of the Middle Ages, which made a crazy quilt of practices. The Latin *Visitatio* persisted in one place while, thirty miles away, a play of Plautus was being revived in the vernacular.

The Later Middle Ages

The Transformation of Medieval Institutions

The trends described in the previous chapter continued; however, their interaction produced new forces that radically altered the medieval structure. The seemingly stable world of the earlier centuries was in part a triumph of negligence: localism, rudimentary economy, and geographical isolation kept many potential conflicts from erupting. However, it was inevitable that a balance that included a feudal aristocracy, growing cities, and an expanding money economy would prove unstable. The metaphor of critical mass can be used: these forces, like fissionable materials, were safe until their critical mass was reached. Once it was reached, radical (although not always explosive) changes were inevitable.

Feudalism

As early as the thirteenth century, feudalism was weakening. When the English barons forced King John to accept the terms of the Magna Charta (1215), it could be said that feudal nobility was asserting its power. Thereafter, however, power ebbed and flowed between barons and monarchy, between primitive parliaments and kingship. By the sixteenth century, the nature of political power and those who wielded it had changed, and power was no longer a "private possession . . . divided among a large number of lords," but a flow toward the center, with the lords taking part by sometimes reluctant consent.

The liquidity of money gradually replaced the stability of land; the productivity of mercantilism and crude manufacture replaced, or greatly supplemented, the productivity of agriculture; the military preeminence of the knight on horseback waned. Landed gentry and landed aristocracy persisted, but the essential reason for the knight's power was undermined by new tactics and new weapons: massed footmen (peasants) with long pikes could withstand mounted knights; gunpowder, guns and cannon, and the longbow changed military tactics; and the availability of mercenaries made the chain of vassalage irrelevant. "Free companies" of unlanded knights and men-at-arms were available after the Crusades and were used widely by the city states of Italy and the north.

FIGURE 8.1

Craft guildsmen of the fourteenth century, each with the emblematic tools of his craft. [Facsimile, from Lacroix.]

By the fifteenth century, the German *landsknechts* were available in bands, companies, and even armies.

The Church

From the thirteenth through the seventeenth centuries, the Church suffered some of its bitterest struggles. None was more damaging than the subjugation of the papacy by secular power, climaxing in the so-called Babylonian Captivity of 1305–ca. 1420 and the Great Western Schism (1378–1418), when two men claimed to be pope. As well, there was wave after wave of "heresy," sparked by sincere men of powerful intellect, often in association with the new universities and sometimes supported by secular monarchs. These included Duns Scotus and William of Occam at Oxford; Marsilio at Padua; and Jan Huss at Prague.

In the centuries from the thirteenth onward, the Church was divided and the papacy lost much of its temporal power to monarchies: *mundus* triumphed. Repeated assertions of papal absolutism were met by both intellectual challenge, including the Oxford–Paris contention that the Body of Christ did not need a pope for its head, and the open violence of physical assaults on popes. After 1520, the Reformation slashed the ties that bound many Christians to Rome.

Monasticism

With the appearance of the Franciscan and Dominican orders as the twelfth century turned into the thirteenth, monasticism took a new direction. These were preaching, not devotional, orders. Their members were often associated with the new universities and the new cities, and they were often in the midst of the new theological controversies. Monasticism had ceased, in their case, to be an institution of withdrawal; it had become an institution of outreach. *Ecclesia,* in the form of preaching monks, was entering *mundus,* sometimes offending both Church and aristocracy by preaching doctrines that were thought to foment rebellion.

The new monastic orders played a large part in the settlement of Europe, especially eastern Germany, making them a factor in population growth and increased productivity. At first, they prepared lands for agriculture; when the lands were settled and populated, their preaching brought new ideas directly to the people. There is evidence that, especially in the case of the Franciscans and the Dominicans, theatre was one of the media of such ideas.

Knowledge and Education

The creation of prototypical universities came at the turn of the twelfth and thirteenth centuries. At Bologna, students eager to become lawyers in an expanding society "hired" lecturers and became for a time the university. The situation was unstable, however, and the granting of degrees and the selection of the faculty passed into other (usually ecclesiastical) hands. There was some secular control, however; from the beginning, the medieval university existed partly outside the Church.

FIGURE 8.2

A Ship of Fools for a sixteenth-century *Schembart* festival. [Courtesy of the Fitzwilliam Museum, Cambridge.]

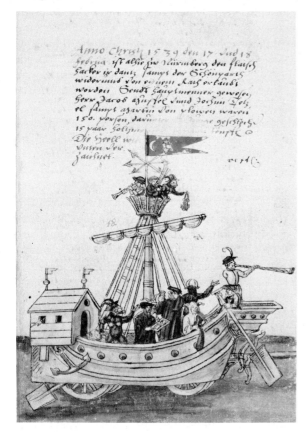

In Paris, a university evolved from a collective of lecturers, its subject theology. After a struggle, this faculty gained control of the admission of new masters to its own ranks—control over the granting of degrees—and became the arbiter of intellectual quality in much of Europe. It was paralleled by the rise of the universities at Oxford and Cambridge. Although none of them offered strictly secular education, some of the subjects (law and medicine) were secular, and the intense rationalism of Paris was a potential enemy of revealed religion.

Although it is hard to form an idea of literacy in these centuries, it is sure that the direc-tion was toward greater literacy in the upper classes and in the cities. By 1500, education in the upper classes was common. In the ninth century, Charlemagne had hardly been able to write his name; Henry VIII of England (d. 1537) penned sonnets.

The Rise of the Vernacular

One of the most important shifts of the period was that toward vernacular languages. Again, the tendency was irregular, and we find mixtures of Latin and vernacular words in the writing of a single scribe, as well as the coining of new amalgamations of vernacular and Latin. Accounts referring to theatrical activities in England, for example, mix *play* and *game* with *ludus*, and the Latin *platea* and the English *place* can be found describing the same thing.

Movement to the vernacular was a matter of politics as well as of language. "The growth of language implies the growth of nations," one scholar has written, finding the vernacular literature of the end of the thirteenth century "jubilant" in comparison with that in Latin, as well as "anti-idealistic, anti-feudal and anti-clerical."[1] Not all aspects of early vernaculars were so *anti*, but they were vigorous and they were, more often than not, of the world of humans rather than the world of theology. Chaucer in England, Dante in Italy, and Jean de Meung in France were masters of their vernaculars—identifiable individuals who asserted their own literary achievements. The age of anonymity was ending, and certain kinds of assertion—of self, of worldliness, and of "modernity"—were taking its place.

Cities and City Dwellers

The rapid economic expansion of earlier medieval Europe ended with severe depressions in the thirteenth and fourteenth centuries. A considerable change in the way that goods and money moved had taken place: the great mercantile fairs of the north had lost their place in direct trading because of safer and faster communications among buyers and sellers. Cities

FIGURE 8.3

A late-fifteenth-century painting of a circular theatre (?) for a performance of Terence, which seems to be mimed by masked actors as the figure with the book, Calliopius, reads. There was a medieval tradition that Terence had been so staged. The lower half of the picture is an interesting medieval rendering of a city. [From Pougin.]

themselves began to function as trading partners. In the south, Florence (the source of the first important international coinage), Venice, Genoa, and other Italian cities traded directly with Bruges, Hamburg, Bergen, and other cities of the north; the English wool towns dealt with those on the Continent; cities strung along the Baltic Sea formed the Hanseatic League, a commercial alliance powerful enough to wage war and engage in its own form of imperialism.

As with other institutions, the urbanization of the north differed from that of Italy—now (late fourteenth century) in its Renaissance. In Italy, the cities became independent earlier than in the north, whereas the cities of France and England more often retained a limited autonomy and found shelter under the monarchy, bypassing the feudal lords. Direct dealings between the king and the lord Mayor of London, for example, are part of the political maneuvering of Shakespeare's *Richard III,* and the royal "entries" into cities when the English and French kings made visits were occasions for great shows—many of which give us important data about theatrical practice.

City and countryside were devastated by the events of the fourteenth century—the Hundred Years' War on the Continent, a severe economic depression, and the plague, or Black Death. It is said that the plagues of mid-century took as many as one quarter to one half of the population.[2] Yet most medieval institutions survived, as did the cities, which may even have been strengthened by their isolation and by the slackening of competition for power during the period.

By the early fifteenth century, the cities of the north were independent (usually under the crown), proud, and assertive. They had wealth again. They felt strong mutual rivalry. They also rivaled the now declining medieval power structure: the barons, the Church, and the feudal order. They liked to make a show of their wealth and power, and they looked for opportunities for pomp. Often, these opportunities appeared in the form of vernacular theatre.

Islam, Byzantium, and the Crusades

The Crusades were effectively over by the end of the thirteenth century. A balance had been reached with Islam. Driven from its naval strongholds in the eastern Mediterranean and even attacked on its North African ground, Islam retrenched. It fragmented internally. Its scholars made a separate peace with Christendom and exchanged ideas and writings—before printing, the best versions of Aristotle came from Arabic sources.

Byzantium fell in 1453, overrun by the Seljuk Turks. It had been crumbling for at least half a century and had never really recovered after the Crusaders' occupation of 1204–1253. Its population had fallen to fifty thousand; its intellectuals fled to Europe.[3] The pressure on Byzantium was a gain for the West, at least in the short run; however, the obliteration of Byzantine civilization had great symbolic importance. It was the end of the longest continuum in the medieval world. Its end—coincident with the introduction of printing—would make a convenient end to a period if so many typical

institutions had not continued quite vigorously. As it was, the fall of Byzantium profoundly depressed many Europeans and made them feel that an era had ended.

Technology

Technological innovation did not revolutionize later medieval Europe, nor did it end the Middle Ages, but it contributed mightily to the changes we have noted. We need cite only two innovations—the compass and gunpowder—to symbolize their importance. The compass and the star-finding astrolabe made long-distance navigation possible, making it possible to exploit new developments in the hull shapes and

FIGURE 8.4

Map of Islam, Byzantium, and the Mediterranean about 1250.

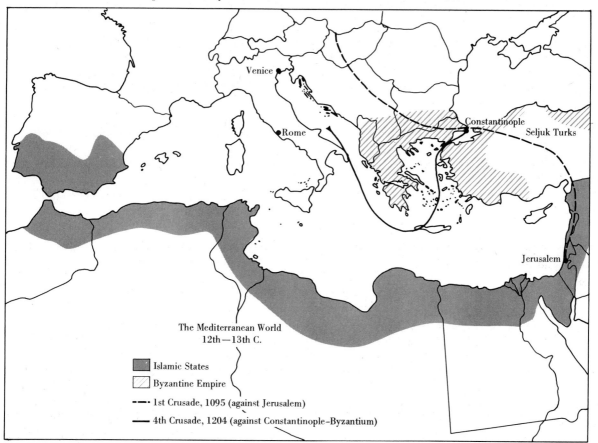

The Mediterranean World
12th–13th C.

■ Islamic States
▨ Byzantine Empire
- - - 1st Crusade, 1095 (against Jerusalem)
—— 4th Crusade, 1204 (against Constantinople–Byzantium)

the sails of ships. Scandinavians had sailed their "long ships" down to the Mediteranean and west to Iceland, Greenland, and perhaps Newfoundland in the tenth to the twelfth centuries, but the Atlantic was mostly a vast unknown. Now, exploration was possible. The printing press made better maps possible, using the new knowledge. Gunpowder appeared in the thirteenth century, followed quickly by the cannon and the hand cannon, with consequences for both the mounted knight and the walled city.

The effect of all these technological advances was to make the world of humans—*mundus*—more immediate and more important, and to make *ecclesia* more abstract.

Later Medieval Theatre and Its Drama

The theatre changed between the end of the twelfth century and the end of the thirteenth. There seems to have been a falling off of both numbers of new works and frequency of records. Liturgical music–drama in Latin continued, but there are fewer records of new texts after the twelfth century. Contemporary with this apparent decline, a vernacular drama in a new performance place came into being, reaching its zenith in the late fifteenth and the sixteenth centuries.

This new European drama was still a religious drama, but it was unlike the Latin music–drama in several ways:

1. *It was spoken, not sung*, although it used music at times.
2. *It was in the vernaculars, not Latin.*
3. *Its day and time of performance were independent of liturgical offices.*
4. *Its playing place was rarely inside a church.*
5. *Its performers were most often laymen,* although clerics and monastics were often involved.
6. *The church or monastic house was not the pro-*

ducer, although individual priests often wrote all or parts of the texts and sometimes oversaw the production, and the Church exercised considerable authority over plays and productions.

At the same time, certain important similarities to the earlier drama persisted:

1. *The plays were based on the Gospels, other parts of the Bible, or religious legend* (including the lives of the saints). Later allegorical plays were often entirely imaginative but fell within orthodox theology.
2. *The theatrical concept of space was much the same:* "simultaneity" of setting was almost universal. A nonspecific playing area was ordinarily used in which real distance was ignored, and it was usually backed or surrounded by locations analagous to *sedes.*
3. *Emblematic acting, costuming, and setting dominated.* Vernacular language and spoken drama are themselves closer to image than are Latin or song, but the dominant style was emblematic.
4. *Interpenetration of audience space and acting space was common.* It appears that actors and their characters were seen as different from the audience, and the theatre space was seen as different from nontheatre space. In certain important instances, however, audiences could enter into the theatrical action and the theatrical space (sometimes by invitation), as in the singing of hymns and perhaps the joining of processions.
5. *Until fairly late, anonymity of authorship continued,* although there were exceptions.

Early Religious Plays in the Vernacular

Certain plays in vernacular languages appeared as early as the twelfth century, one—a hybrid—as early as 1100. They were probably first staged in Normandy in the second half of the twelfth century. The Adam play (*Le Mystère d'Adam*) is

FIGURE 8.5

Time line: Latin and vernacular forms.

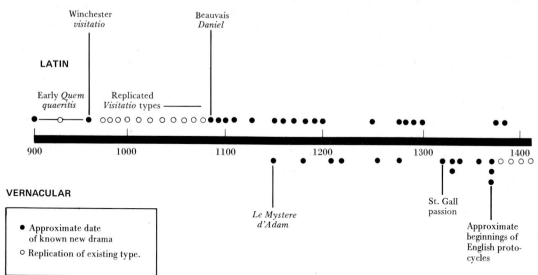

of interest because of its stage directions (*rubrics*), which seem to indicate a playing space outdoors in front of a church. A low platform for paradise, a central throne for God, and a hell were specified. Paradise was to be hung with a shoulder-high cloth that probably hid the actors' bodies and was decorated with emblems of paradise. The play's subject—the expulsion from the Garden of Eden—was different from the subjects of the Latin music–dramas, as was the use of *mystère* in the play's title.

Of slightly later date were a cluster of vernacular plays from the northern French city of Arras. The most famous of these were secular and were the products of a *puys*, a company formed to present such japes. However, there was also an early religious play from Arras, the *Play of Saint Nicholas* of Jean Bodel. It owes little, if anything, to the Latin Saint Nicholas plays. Like others of the Arras vernacular works, it was happily coarse and earthy, and much of it was surely recognizable to the citizens of Arras: "the play-world is always recognizably the streets and taverns of Arras, and the characters are intimate with local people and affairs."[4]

Bodel's play has a story line, but it is one that he seemed to pick up or toss aside as he chose, swinging between the miracles of Saint Nicholas and the ribaldries of Arras. Most certainly, such a play was very different from the Latin ones.

Later Vernacular Plays and the Great Cycles

There seems to be the same blank in the history of the vernacular plays in the thirteenth and fourteenth centuries as we have already noted in the Latin ones. The gap may be nothing more than a lack of evidence, or it may show a real break between early vernacular plays done under Church auspices (*Le Mystère d'Adam*) and later ones done under other auspices.

The exceptions are Passion plays, at least some of which were vernacular, in the thirteenth and early fourteenth centuries. There appears to have been a clustering of early vernacular plays away from those areas of northern Europe where the crises of the mid-fourteenth century hit hardest.

England

Modern scholars suggest rather late dates for even the earliest English plays—probably about 1370–1400—"and even those late dates may not refer to fully developed cyclic plays."[5] By *cyclic* is meant here the comprehensive span of these plays at their fullest, when their subject matter was the whole history of the world (according to the Bible and legend) from the Creation to Doomsday. Not all plays were so inclusive; in fact, complete cycles were probably outnumbered by partial ones. However, it is in the cycle (or *cosmic drama*, as some historians call it) that the vernacular theatre of the Middle Ages was to find its fullest expression.

In England, the cycles are associated with the names of towns and cities. Four such cycles survive in manuscript: those from Wakefield, York, Chester, and (probably) Lincoln. The surviving manuscripts were probably *registers*, or master copies. Over a hundred English towns and cities had such plays.

Current scholarship allows us to say the following:

1. The cycle plays were the property of the town or city, most often of the "corporation" (the town government), but occasionally of a religious guild or brotherhood.

2. Plays were kept in manuscript *registers*, from which "sides" were copied for actors' use. Because many of the actors would have been illiterate or nearly so, there must have been a mechanism for teaching them their roles. The registers were kept secure against unauthorized borrowing, suggesting that prestige and perhaps money were involved with them.

3. Cycle plays were products of accretion over quite long stretches of time—sometimes several generations. Although there is evidence of a late fourteenth-century origin for plays within the extant cycles, it appears that the ones we have were mostly late-fifteenth-century or even sixteenth-century works *in their final form*. On the other hand, two unnamed but recognizable dramatists of these plays—the so-called York Realist and Wakefield Master—were "mid-fifteenth-century writers."[6]

4. Cycles, or parts of them, were rented or lent. Smaller towns might get a play or plays for a fee. In some cases, plays from one cycle were incorporated into another. (Five of the York plays appear in the Wakefield cycle, for example.)

5. Cycles, or parts of them, were staged outdoors in the city on a special occasion each year, or every other year, or sometimes even less often. The most common performance days were the Feast of Corpus Christi and Whitsun, both warm-weather holidays; by the sixteenth century, the days were occasionally shifted to avoid conflict with other nearby cycles or fairs. The performance might last several days.

6. The plays in their complete (sixteenth-century) form consisted of a set of *banns* and the texts of the plays. The banns were used to advertise the plays days or weeks before their performance. The plays themselves, numbering from twenty to forty-two in the surviving texts, typically included plays of the Creation, Adam and Eve, and Cain and Abel; other Old Testament stories like Abraham and Isaac; a play of the prophets; and stories from the life of Christ—the Annunciation, the Nativity plays, John the Baptist, Christ among the doctors, the woman taken in adultery, and the raising of Lazarus, through the complex matters of the Passion, and Doomsday.

7. The cycles were not monoliths. The plays could be played individually or in various combinations; it is believed for example, that a "Marian Cycle" (of the life of Mary) was removed and played separately from one cycle.

The English cycles were collective art. Within them, there is considerable variety of style and quality. Some language was kept for so long that it must have seemed archaic by the sixteenth century. Despite internal inconsistency and contradiction, however, as a group these works represent some of the highest achievements of medieval art.

France

The vernacular religious plays of France are not markedly different from the English, although French historians have credited them with greater literary merit. Their history is similar, however: early emergence from what Gustave Cohen called the "aridity" of thirteenth-century drama, with rapid proliferation *at least of*

FIGURE 8.6

Speculative Stages in the Growth of an English Vernacular Cycle, Both Through Accretion (New Plays) and Through Division of Old Plays

"Protocycle"* (14th century?)	"N-Town" Banns† (late 15th century?)
Fall of Luficer	Fall of Lucifer
Creation and Fall of Man	Creation and Fall of Man
Cain and Abel	Cain
Noah	Noah
Abraham and Isaac	Abraham and Isaac
	Moses
	The Prophets
	The Betrothal of Mary ⎫
	Salutation to Mary ⎪ Possible
	Joseph's Lament ⎬ "Marian
	Trial of Joseph and Mary ⎪ Cycle"
	Joseph and the Midwives ⎭
The Nativity	Shepherds
	Magi and Stella
	Ordo Rachelis (with the Flight into Egypt)
	The Death of Herod
	Christ and the Doctors
	The Baptism of Jesus
	The Temptation
	The Woman Taken in Adultery
The Raising of Lazarus	The Raising of Lazarus
	The Entry into Jerusalem
	The Last Supper
	The Betrayal
The Passion	Caiaphas
	Judas
	Pilate's Wife's Dream and the Second Trial of Christ
	The Crucifixion
	Longinus and the Harrowing of Hell
The Resurrection	The Burial and the Watch
	The Second Harrowing and the Resurrection
	The Maries at the Tomb
	Mary Magdalene in the Garden
	The Castle at Emmaus
	Thomas of India
	The Ascension
	Pentecost
Last Things and Doomsday	Doomsday

*From Kolve, *Play Called Corpus Christi.*
†The "N-Town" plays are probably those of Lincoln.

records in the fifteenth century and a quite phenomenal outpouring just at the turn of the sixteenth century. Like the English plays, these were cosmic dramas. The later and most highly praised ones, however, were often the work of individuals and not of collectivity and accretion; as a result, they have more internal consistency of both language and idea. We may say of the French dramas, as well, that:

1. They were common by the mid-fifteenth century, although not necessarily in cyclic (cosmic) form.

2. They were frequently the property of *puys* or *confréries*. Of these, the most important to theatre history was the Confrérie de la Passion of Paris, formed in about 1400.

3. Indoor presentation of the plays was known in France from the fifteenth century. The Confrérie de la Passion, for example, had a succession of halls.

4. By the late fifteenth century, production in France seems to have been frequently more expensive than in England; also performances of greater length were often given—up to forty days, although the figure is rare. Some of the *confréries* might take months to perform a complete cycle, performing only once a week or even less often.

5. After the development of printing, the publication of French cycles was known—especially the Grébans' monumental *Mystère de la Passion*. Publication had several effects: the authors appear to have sought publicity, probably because they were paid to write the plays; published plays could no longer be jealously guarded as registers; and plays began to exist as literary works to be read, not simply as texts for performance.

Italy and Spain

Vernacular religious drama in both Italy and Spain appears to have been less common in early years than it was in the North. Spain suffered Moorish occupation until the last third of the sixteenth century; much of Italian dramatic interest was channeled into Renaissance work (see Chapter 11.) The Italian *sacra rappresentazione* were confined mostly to the north of Italy, and particularly to the area around Florence. However, there was a confraternity at Rome, and Rome saw a performance of a Passion play in the Colosseum. Other vernacular religious plays were much affected by the extreme localism of Italian dialects. Thus, it is wrong to suggest that there was no vernacular Italian religious drama, but little of it has survived and it is usually overshadowed by the plays of the Italian Renaissance.

The *autos sacramentales* of Spain correspond to the vernacular plays of the north. Despite the Islamic occupation, parts of Spain knew the same kinds of plays as did the rest of Europe. However, the real zenith of the Spanish *autos* did not come until the seventeenth century; before that, processional pageantry and traditional religious plays (Corpus Christi mysteries) were done. The later *autos* were works written by leading playwrights for what was by then a full-fledged professional theatre. Thus, the early Spanish plays may have more closely resembled the early English plays, although the leading authority on the Spanish theatre does not identify outdoor Corpus Christi plays before the sixteenth century.[7]

Northern Europe

Vernacular religious plays were known in the Low Countries, Germany, Switzerland, and elsewhere, although an early reference to a religious play in the eastern Baltic outpost of Riga must be taken as an oddity. The plays flourished in southern Germany, and one in German Switzerland (Lucerne) was at its height as late as the last quarter of the sixteenth century.

Vernacular cycle dramas, then, were pan-European. Their greatest concentrations were in eastern England, northwestern France, and modern Belgium. Northern Italy, central and eastern Spain, and southern Germany were also areas where they were common.

FIGURE 8.7

The Martyrdom of St. Appolonia, by Jean Fouquet (late fifteenth century). This famous miniature seems to show a saint's play in performance, with scaffolds for (left to right) heaven, music, the *sedes* of a king, two audience scaffolds (?), and hell. The figure with the white wand and the book may be the *devysor* or Master of Secrets. Many details are worth noting: the audience under the scaffolds and in the *place;* the rather literal treatment of torture and humiliation; the devil costumes; and the ambiguity about the theatre's shape. [Photo Giraudon. Courtesy of the Musée Condé.]

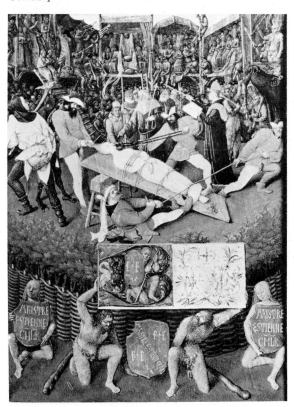

Other Vernacular Plays: Saints' Plays and Moralities

Although the cyclic dramas have deservedly achieved the most fame and have received the most attention from theatre historians, there were other forms that flourished. Two of these, saints' plays and moralities, are particularly important.

Saints' Plays

Plays on the lives of Christian saints, often based on legend, offered many opportunities for spectacle. Both the comic and the melodramatic are found in them, as are the grotesque, the cruel, and the miraculous.

The saints' plays also gave some scope to such secular matters as romance in dramatizations of the saints' lives before they left earthly concerns. Thus, although they undoubtedly had sincere goals and pious origins, these pieces offered opportunity for secular entertainment, and they allowed a play of imagination that the Scriptures did not.

Moralities

The allegory, an internally consistent and comprehensive symbolic work, was a familiar form. In the theatre, allegorical plays were called *moralities*. Of all the medieval forms, they are perhaps the least congenial to modern tastes. Nonetheless, allegory was a fruitful form for purposes as different as the sermon or the amorous tale, and it had the theatrical advantage of being expressible in every element of production—the more tellingly because of the importance of the visual in the theatre.

In what is probably the best known of the English moralities, *Everyman* (fifteenth century, based on an earlier Dutch work), the title character embarks on a journey to the grave, summoned by Death. He looks among his virtues and vices for those things that will accompany him: Fellowship, Kindred, Knowledge, Beauty, Strength, and so on. That none of these entities will go with him is part of a conceptual statement; that Good Deeds *will* go extends that statement. Confession gives Everyman "a precious jewel . . . called penance"; Knowledge gives him a "garment of sorrow . . . , contrition"; Beauty, Strength, Discretion, and Five-

Wits go with him until they recognize that the grave is their destination (after having given assurances that they will "never part you from"), and then they flee; Knowledge goes a little farther—until "ye to death shall go"; Good Deeds descends into the grave with Everyman to "speak for thee."

Although typical moralities are products of the fifteenth and the early sixteenth centuries, many were written well into the Reformation and figured as weapons in that intellectual battle. Sir David Lindsay's *Ane Pleasant Satyre of the Three Estatis* (1540) and John Bale's *Three Laws of Nature, Moses and Christ, corrupted by the Sodomytes Pharisees and Priests Most Wicked* (1538) are religious and political moralities.

The moralities extended the emblematic conventions of medieval theatre and made them the primary carrier of meaning. The gain in impact was sometimes remarkable, and for a brief period (ca. 1490–1540) the morality play was probably the favorite vehicle of polemicists. Although the form eventually lost much of its popularity, allegorical elements continued to be important in drama until the middle of the seventeenth century.

Theatrical Production of the Vernacular Religious Plays

Production of these plays was remarkably similar across most of Europe, whether the plays were cycles, saints' plays, parts of cycles, or moralities. The kind of set piece and the use of space were based on one of two dominant systems, but the same spatial convention underlay both: theatrical space was *abstract*, and theatrical place was *simultaneous*.

Simultaneous Place-and-Scaffold Staging

Of the two major staging systems, the more common, both geographically and numerically, was that arrangement best called *place-and-scaf-*

FIGURE 8.8

Diagram and instructions for *The Castle of Perseverance*, an English morality (15th C.). It clearly shows a castle in mid-place with a practical bed in or under it and five mansions around the circle. [From Sharpe.]

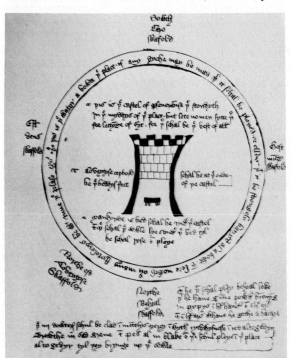

fold. The *place* was the unspecified area around or in or along which localizing units were sited. These localizing units were sometimes called *scaffolds* in English, less often *pageants*, by extension from a word for the plays that used them; they were *mansions* or *lieus* in French, *sedes* or *loca* in Latin. The *place* was the same as the *platea* or *placeam* of the liturgical plays, and these terms also continued in use.

Scaffolds had fixed locations for the duration of a performance. In some cases, plays that lasted more than one day changed scaffolds between performances or used a scaffold for two different locales. The scaffolds were in full view during the day's performance, although certain of them "unclosed" and "closed" with curtains. If they were elevated structures, they looked like little stages, but it is dangerous to assume that they were *used* as little stages. There are plenty of references to a character's speaking *from* his scaffold, and characters are often addressed *in* their scaffolds, but there is far less evidence that scenes were actually played in these covered and walled structures. Many *scaffolds, mansions,* or *loci* were not this sort of structure at all, of course, some being tiny houses, thrones, or even single objects like a pillar for the scourging of Christ or a tree on which Judas was to hang himself. At its simplest, the localizing unit of place-and-scaffold staging provided information about the locale of the scene; frequently, it also provided an essential property (a seat, a tree, a pillar). It did not provide a complete scenic background for theatrical action.

Staging "in the Round"

Richard Southern's influential book *Medieval Theatre in the Round* (1957) had the short-lived effect of making it seem that all medieval theatres were round. Scholars now recognize that the circle was only one of many possibilities.

"The Martyrdom of St. Appolonia "(Figure 8.7) provided Richard Southern with much of his evidence for theatre-in-the-round. The painting is a miniature by the artist Jean Fouquet, who is known to have staged at least one production himself. Southern also relied on a manuscript sketch in the morality play, *The Castle of Perseverance* (Figure 8.8). He reconstructed a theatre with scaffolds sited around a circular place. The audience was *in* this place, kept from interfering with the actors by *stytelers,* or ushers; a barrier—a raised dirt mound or a moat or both—surrounded the place to keep out those who had not paid. Where appropriate (as in *The Castle of Perseverance*), there was a structure in the center of the place for important action; Southern argued that it was specially constructed so that the audience could see through it to watch action on the far side.

Scholars have objected to some of Southern's conclusions. The problem of sight lines remains, despite his ingenious central struc-

ture. The rubrics of the *Castle* suggest that the theatre can be made in several ways, so that its sketch may show only one of several possibilities. French practice, contrary to Southern's interpretation, put the moat between the audience and the place; they were *around* the acting area, not in it. If the dirt mound were used, the audience would have had the advantage of being on a slope; in many cases in northern France, we know that bleachers and rows of enclosed boxes called *loges* were built. Thus, keeping the audience out of the place and elevating them on the hill, stands, bleachers, or *loges* would have solved sight-line problems better than the skeletal structure would, although sight-line problems would remain for those who sat right next to a scaffold. However, it is almost a truism of medieval theatre that some of the audience had poor sight lines some of the time.

It is not certain that putting a structure in the middle of the place was common. The English "N-Town Plays" (*Ludus Coventriae*) require a "council-house" located "in the midplace" for their Passion sequence; an old French play has a structure "en mi la place." These may be the exceptions, however, not the rule.

At any rate, there is no question that circular theatres were used in the period. They were not permanent structures, however, and some were put up for a single performance. On the other hand, there is evidence that circular locations were set aside in some areas and also that already-existing circular structures were used. For example:

1. *"Game places."* Permanent circles of dirt and/or stone seem to have been common in eastern England by the sixteenth century.[8]
2. *Cornish rounds.* Although highly localized (Cornwall), these structures have long been known. Their original purpose is a mystery, but their use as medieval theatres is likely.
3. *Premedieval hill forts* and similar structures.
4. *Roman ruins,* especially arenas. Although not common, they were available in some places.

Even in ruins, they were usable. A spectacular production of the *Actes des Apôtres* at Bourges (France) in 1536 used an arena with two-story stands and *loges,* part of the area covered with awnings against the sun.

It can be asked if the circular arrangement was an imitation of what was *thought* to be Roman practice, or if there was a tradition that the Romans used circular theatres because of circular sports arenas. In the twelfth-century English poem *The Vision of Thurkill,* a theatre in hell is described as round, with *sedes* and *platea* among the terms used to describe it.[9] Roman literature—as in Pliny, for example—included descriptions of circular arenas. Medieval theatre people, looking for an elegant solution to the problems of simultaneous staging, may have combined a hazy notion of Roman practice with their own experience—and perhaps with the availability of a ruin—to build theatres-in-the-round.

Such theatres were most common in eastern England and northwestern France and Flanders in the fifteenth and sixteenth centuries. If they were meant to be Roman, they were meant to be so in ways quite different from those in the Italian south, where Roman structures and Roman writings were better understood.

Irregular Theatres

Adaptation to existing shapes was the rule in an age that had no theatre buildings. The shape of a public place often determined the shape of the theatre. A plan from Villingen (Germany) is very crude but shows a rectangle divided into parts; one from Donaushingen (Germany) shows, again, a rectangle with *loci* scattered in it without symmetry or apparent pattern. Most instructive of all is the manuscript sketch from Lucerne (Switzerland). Here, we know from other records, the entire public square called the Winemarket was used. The square is not much changed today: at one end lies the House of the Sun, at the other a large fountain to which wires or lines were fastened for a flying effect. The

FIGURE 8.9

A late-fifteenth-century engraving of a theatre from an early printed Terence. This kind of (probably imaginary) theatre may have influenced the English public theatres: the audience are in galleries; there are *aediles* near the stage, more or less in the position of the lords' rooms in London; the theatre is polygonal. Architecturally, however, it makes little sense. [From Bapst.]

Winemarket is not a true rectangle, nor was the theatre. From the drawings, we see how irregular such a theatre could be, and how scattered its loci and how poor its sight lines. The playing area looks incoherent, in fact, if one is looking for symmetry or regularity. It is a true *place* or *platea,* however. Around it are locations for spectators; in and around it are the *mansions* or *scaffolds:* the enormous hell-mouth, Judas' tree, and the River Jordan. The actual place was about 125 feet long and 65 feet wide at one end, tapering to 35 feet at the other.[10]

It is worth noting that entrance to these irregular spaces could be blocked off. Those who did not pay could be kept out, as in Southern's theatre-in-the-round.

Linear Theatres

The rubrics of the Anglo-Norman *Adam* play suggest a line of three scaffolds or mansions in front of a church. It is unclear how the audience was to be oriented—on three sides, or facing from the one long side. The brilliant and artistic illustrations for the much later plays of Valenciennes (France) show very clearly a linear arrangement that the audience must have faced. The row of mansions is well extended, apparently on a raised stage. As many as thirteen locations were arranged in a row, with a place of sorts in front of them. The localizing structures

changed from day to day; the real distance in the place was of no importance, and hell, heaven, and Jerusalem existed simultaneously to the audience's eyes. Certainly, the scale of the Valenciennes stage was very large, and properties like a practical ship could be accommodated. The elevation of the entire playing space and the mansions was hardly typical, although other, similar platforms have been found in France.

Other Arrangements

One of the strengths of the simultaneous theatre was its great flexibility. One of the more interesting arrangements was at Romans, where an "alley" stage was created by putting a long audience structure on each side of a narrow acting area.[11] A somewhat similar stage was used at Paris and Mons, where bleachers and *loges* were built facing a single elongated playing area. We do not know what the arrangement of in-

FIGURE 8.10

The linear stage for the Valenciennes mystery plays in 1547. This representation appears to show a very large, raised stage with five large mansions, three city gates, a sea with a practical ship, a large hell-mouth, and hell. The mansions changed for different days' playing. The *feints* for this elaborate spectacle—the ship and the burning limbo, for example—moved directly into postmedieval theatre without a hiatus. [From Petit de Julleville.]

door spaces was, but the shape of the long and narrow halls occupied by the Confrérie de la Passion suggests that an "alley" may have been used.

The variety of yet other spaces was considerable. Besides open squares, churchyards, and prepared circles, there were cemeteries, tournament yards, courtyards, street crossings, and

FIGURE 8.11

Schematic of variations in simultaneous theatre shapes and acting–audience relationships.

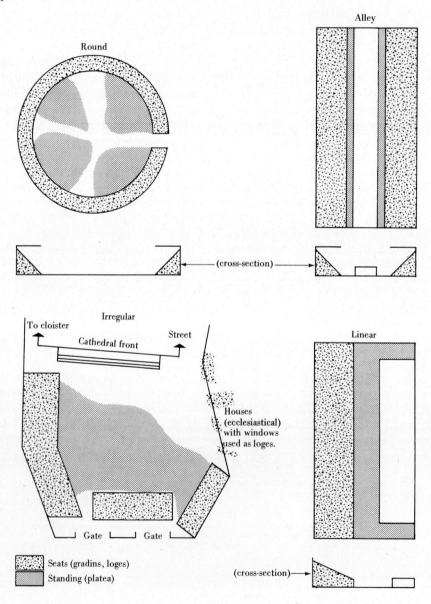

such usable structures as wellheads or "conduits," flat-topped structures in streets or crossings where public waterworks were located.

The Theatre of Procession and Pageant Wagon

"These pageants or carriages was a high place made like a house, with two rooms, being open on the top. [In] the lower room they appareled and dressed themselves, and in the higher room they played. And they stood upon six wheels." This seventeenth-century account, presumably based on the writer's father's recollections, is one of the principal pieces of evidence for our understanding of *pageant wagons*. There is no doubt of their existence and of their widespread use in certain areas. Precisely what they looked like, however, is uncertain.

Another version of the above account gives the pageant wagons four wheels, not six, and has them "all open on the top, that all beholders might hear and see them." An inventory from a Norwich (England) guild includes "A pageant, that is to say, a house of wainscott painted and builded on a cart with four wheels." A York list mentions a four-wheeled "Pagent" with a painted cloth "for the bakke of the pagent" and other cloths "for [two] sides of the pagent." Spanish accounts contain many references to *carros*, or wheeled wagons for religious plays. Gustave Cohen cited relatively rare examples of the use of wagons for religious plays in France and Belgium. The use of wagons for staging, then, although geographically limited, was important.

We are able to conjecture from a good deal of sometimes conflicting evidence that:

1. Wheeled pieces for processions, holy days, royal or noble entries, and such secular festivals as the Nuremberg (Germany) Fools' Day (*Schembart*) were common. There is sound evidence that in Spain, two wagons were used, sometimes with a third wagon as a stage.[12]

2. There may have been a direct connection between nondramatic processions and the presentation of dramas on wagon stages, although the point is disputed. The leading historian of the Spanish theatre says flatly that "the [Spanish] Corpus Christi drama began as a pageant, consisting of a series of static tableaux, with wooden figures. . . ."[13]

3. Wagon stages are things of the cities, not small towns or the countryside.

4. There is much dispute over the idea that wagons were two-storied. Problems of both weight and height are used to argue against the idea.

5. Most often in England, it appears that the wagons were used in sequence to present certain cycles, with a carefully regulated order of playing and a definite location for each stop.

6. English and perhaps Flemish pageant wagons were the property of craft guilds, who stored them year after year, sometimes at fairly high rents. The expense of building, decorating, and maintaining these wheeled pageants could be impressively high. In Spain, designs for wagons sometimes had to be submitted ahead of time in competition, and it appears that new ones were designed each year.[14]

7. One pageant was usually devoted to a play or to a major *locus* of a biblical story, for example, Herod's throne, the Nativity manger, or paradise. However, there are many plays that require more than one *locus*. It is unclear what sort of wagon was used for a play that required only a low hill or an altar—Cain and Abel, for example.

It was once believed that pageant wagons were, in effect, wheeled proscenium stages. It was believed that they were lined up at dawn and then sent off in order—Creation first, Doomsday last—to stop at each designated location along a route of city streets, to play each play at each of as many as twelve such stops. This theory has several problems, however:

1. The number of actors would have been large: for continuing characters like Christ, Mary, Joseph, and God, a new actor for each pageant wagon.

2. Each actor would have had to perform as many as twelve times a day—a strain on amateurs, although not impossible.

3. The plays of the extant cycles are of vastly different lengths. The short ones would have spent a good part of the day waiting while the long ones played.

4. The extant cycles are so long that it would have been impossible to begin at dawn, play every stop, and still have time to play the entire cycle at the last stop before dark. The York cycle has forty-eight plays and is known to have used wagons; scholars argue that it is incredible that an audience would have sat for the twenty hours

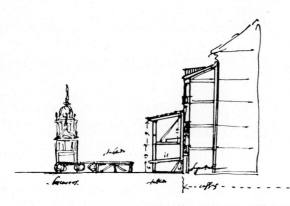

FIGURE 8.12

Left, a seventeenth-century sketch of a Spanish *carro* drawn up to a stage. The wagon has a set piece on its rear (left) half. Below, the plan for such a performance in Madrid in 1636, with two *carros* drawn up to a stage, top. [Courtesy of the Archivero de Villa, Ayuntamiento de Madrid.]

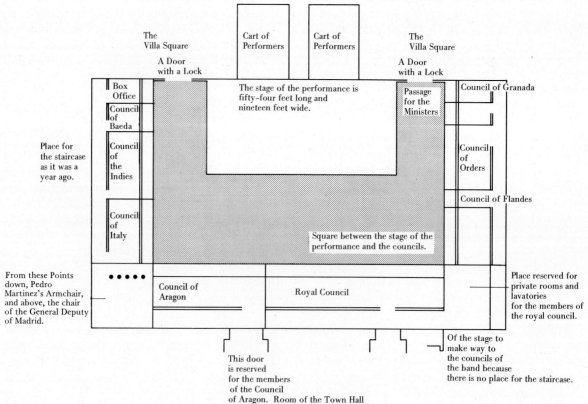

FIGURE 8.13

An early-nineteenth-century interpretation of an English pageant wagon. Although purely speculative, it satisfies certain of the traditional descriptions: upper and lower rooms, wheels, size, place of performance. It raises serious questions, however, about how the wagon was moved through narrow streets, how the performers kept from falling down in transit, how they got to the street to play (if they did), and so on. [From Sharpe.]

it would have taken to play this cycle—sunup to summer midnight.

Recent scholarship has given these questions great attention:

1. Perhaps the stops within the city were not for playing, but for showing off the pageant, with perhaps a tableau or a short dumb show. This theory does not explain fully why audience space at the stops was carefully reserved and money was charged, however.

2. Perhaps the pageant wagons were used for procession and for playing, but the two things were different—processing one day, playing the next. Many existing records seem to contradict this idea.

3. The cycles grew by accretion. Perhaps in their early years, they had so few pageants that they could play them all comfortably in a day's time; then as they grew, perhaps traditional stops were kept, but only dumb show or tableau was shown, with actual playing being done at only three, or even only one, location. This idea has considerable merit, for it explains many seeming contradictions, and it matches our knowledge of the history of the cycles' growth. It agrees, as well, with the complicated structures of a cycle like the "N-Town Plays," which shows not only accretion but also a mixture of place-and-scaffold and pageant-wagon staging. Chronology suggests that this cycle's earlier plays were processional (pageant wagon), the later ones fixed (place-and-scaffold).

Some historians now suggest that pageant wagons could have been drawn up in a public place and constituted the scaffolds of place-and-scaffold theatre. Many of the objections to theories of processional staging "temporarily disappear if we accept the theory that pageant-wagons were occasionally sited about the perimeter of a Place and used like scaffolds,"[15] but they do not disappear for very long because we have little evidence of such practice and a great deal of evidence of procession.

Medieval pageant wagons, therefore, remain vexing problems. We can say with certainty that they existed, and we can say that they probably grew from the pervasive medieval tradition of procession with emblems. We can point to analogues in royal entries, in secular festivals, and in certain rhetorical stages in the Low Countries. Using data from Spain and England in particular, we can say that:

1. The actions of pageant-wagon plays tended to be simpler and less interwoven than those of place-and-scaffold cycles because each played separately.

2. The pageant wagon probably provided, along with a localizing set piece, some kind of masking for entrances, storage for small properties, and perhaps a changing room for the actors. Some wagons may have provided the acting area, as well, either on that part of the wagon not occupied by decor or on another wagon

FIGURE 8.14
Map of geographical distribution of kinds of medieval staging.

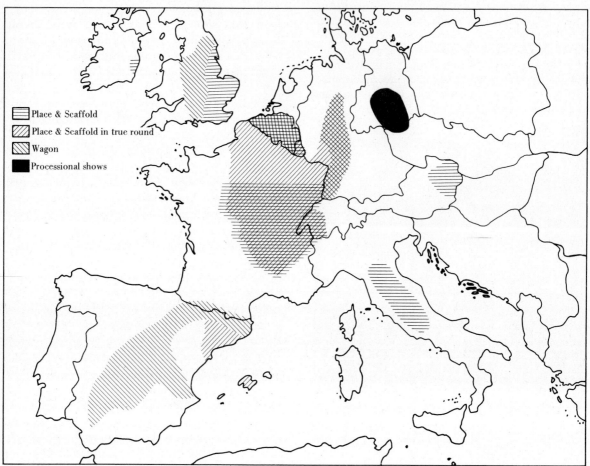

drawn alongside. Some acting, however, was done on the ground ("in the street").

3. There is little indication that staging on wagons preceded place-and-scaffold staging or that it was in any way more primitive. There were very sound reasons for wagons, particularly the tradition of procession; and there were very sound reasons for separate making and ownership of set pieces, particularly the guild structure of medieval cities. In parts of Spain, England, and the Low Countries, wagon staging was always the dominant mode.

Aspects of Vernacular Religious Production

Production Organization

Until well into the sixteenth century in northern Europe, perhaps later in the south, production was collective and actors were amateurs. The plays were done for the glorification of God, for didactic purposes, and for the self-aggrandizement of the cities. It is in the context of civic pageantry that they are best understood.

Production Responsibility

Pageant wagons—and, usually, their counterpart in place-and-scaffold staging, the "pageants"—remained in the possession of individual craft guilds from year to year, because in most countries it was the guilds that were the organizing units of production. Below them were the individual members; above them were either citywide religious guilds or the city corporation, or both. Whether through town government, religious guild, or craft guild, however, it is likely that the entire resources of a large town or city were involved. Freemen of means and workmen of the level of journeymen, and probably still lower, had a sense of identification with the city; craftsmen of all social levels belonged to a guild; and most also belonged to a religious guild. Thus, the medieval city was an interlocking net of structures that all impelled the individual toward the same goal: excellence of show, for the sake of the city, the guild, and the brotherhood.

Expenditures and Income

Producing these plays was not cheap. Gustave Cohen cited a yearly expense of 16,000 modern francs for a play—an enormous sum if the change in money values is considered. One northern French city almost bankrupted itself because of the magnificence of its cycle.[16] It has been suggested that such expenses were a major reason for the cycles' decline after the early sixteenth century.

Money for production came from two main sources: (1) subsidies from the city corporation and the guilds and (2) income from the plays. In France, nobles and men of wealth made large contributions (probably equivalent in their eyes to the worthiness of supporting a chapel or the building of a church). Civic officials were responsible for the plays' fiscal health, and deficits sometimes were made up from their own pockets.

Such attention to audience security as the walling in of the place, the closing off of streets, the selling of stopping places in the pageant-wagon cities, and the assigning of family names to the *loges* and stands at many continental plays suggests clearly that there were entrance fees for the plays. It is questionable if it was even possible to see them without paying. It is probable that a stratified system of payment was in effect, with the covered and private *loges* most expensive and standing room least.

Actors and Geniuses

It has been said that men of the Church were never far away from the plays. The statement is no doubt true of the writing of many, perhaps even most, of them; it is also true that some of the actors were clerics. After the mid-fifteenth century, monastic groups appear to have toured with plays, especially moralities. However, as the vernacular religious plays grew more complex, we see the rise in importance of men who specialized in organizing and staging these complex theatre pieces. Called variously *meneurs de jeux, masters of secrets, devysors, property players,* and *feinteurs,* they represented the increasing specialization that marks the late medieval period. On the Continent, they were joined by the first professional playwrights, a number of them rhetoricians from the universities.

The *meneurs de jeux* and *devysors* were not directors as we know them. They were technicians, organizers, and enablers. Sometimes they were little more than risk takers who were willing to take an entire cycle "to farm," that is, to pay a fee in return for taking all or most of the income. This situation, however, came rather late and was typical of cities with financial problems. More often, these men were highly skilled specialists with a knowledge of the effects, tricks, and machines that had been developed over centuries of theatre. They were theatrical jacks-of-all-trades who could schedule complicated rehearsals of large groups of amateurs, plan, budget, and build—a combination of the modern stage manager, technical director, and business manager. In a sense, they were the embodiment of the cycles' final phase, when

FIGURE 8.15

Speculative reconstruction of the Hôtel de Bourgogne, ca. 1550. Indicated by numbers are: 1. The playing-area, shown here as an "alley" stage; *gradins* (bleachers) may have been set up along the sides; 2. *loges;* 3. rear of the *loges,* with a narrow communicating passageway and individual doors; 4. a "tunnel" under the *loges,* both for actors' movement and for storage; this space, however, was often open and used for audience members, although they would have been blocked by *gradins;* 5. galleries above the *loges;* 6. the *paradis,* here used as a mansion; 7. support spaces and lobby behind the *loges* of the confraternity's masters. This was the street end of the building and the principal public entrance; there were probably shops here at some periods.

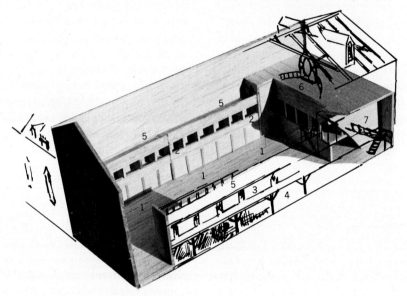

the plays suffered from success by becoming burdensome to their originators.

Thus, in its glory days, the vernacular theatre gave birth to a new man of the theatre, "a highly paid professional . . . whose services included supervising the physical staging and sometimes the economic organization of local plays. He probably directed players, and certainly saw to the orderly marshalling of costumes, props and other play gear."[17]

Machinery and Special Effects

Late medieval theatrical effects could be spectacular and were used to make visual the magical, the miraculous, and the sensational—flying, ascending into heaven, throwing bolts of lightning, appearing and disappearing. As the

Chronicler of Valenciennes wrote, "We saw Truth—the angels and others descend from very high. . . . Lucifer was brought from Hell on a dragon; the rod of Moses suddenly put forth flowers and fruit. Devils carried damned souls through the air. . . ."

Sophisticated machinery and gunpowder had appeared early in the period. Mechanical clocks were first made toward the end of the thirteenth century, and clockwork figures followed, to be used at times with or in place of actors for processional floats and pageants. As early as the tenth century, hydraulic machines had been used in Byzantium for "magical" animals.[18] A famous fourteenth-century French mansion held a room that was virtually a fun house of mechanical and hydraulic tricks: "a machine for wetting ladies when they step on it . . . a machine by which all who pass through will be struck and beaten . . . and a wooden hermit who speaks . . . and six personages . . . that wet people in various ways . . . and an owl that makes faces at people and gives an answer to everything that is asked of it. . . ."[19] In 1378, Charles V of France gave a banquet at which the conquest of Jerusalem was presented as a *mystère sans parolles* (pantomime or dumb show) with a boat large enough to contain thirteen people and capable of moving about the banquet hall; there was also a Jerusalem with walls and a siege using ladders, as in the battles of the liturgical drama, suggesting that the *artisans mécaniques* of the period were on their way to becoming *meneurs de jeux.*

The categories of machines and effects included the following.

Flying and Unusual Movement. Both actors and statues or cutout figures were flown; in some cases, the ropes and apparatus were entirely visible; in some, they were masked with clouds.

Opening and Closing Set pieces. Heavens opened to reveal God and angels; hell was inevitably represented as a head with a huge and horrible mouth that sometimes opened and closed. The face of heaven might be covered with curtains, with wool clouds, or with painted surfaces, sometimes with astronomical figures. In 1439, a visiting Byzantine bishop saw in a Florentine church a heaven fifty-six feet above the floor:

> On this platform was a circular opening about fourteen feet in diameter covered by a blue curtain decorated with a sun, the moon and stars. . . . At the right moment, the curtain was raised, or, one might say, the portal of Heaven opened. . . . The circular opening of Heaven was adorned with effigy images of angels painted on . . . discs. . . . These moved and turned separately. . . . From this opening in the sky, seven thin, strong ropes were stretched down to Mount Olivet. The young man who

portrayed Jesus Christ used these ropes and some small iron wheels, masterly made, in the action of the ascent. On the wall above the altar, there was a small room which measured twenty-one feet on each side. This was closed off from the church by a rose curtain and in front of this curtain a crown in a circle moved constantly from right to left and back again. . . ."[20]

Large Movable Properties. Ships were common. Sometimes it appears that they sailed on actual water; they were also wheeled. Because some of the Noah plays belonged to shipwrights' guilds, it is fair to conclude that these vessels were built like full-sized ships.

FIGURE 8.16

The Noah pageant at Grantham, England (1966), in a cycle that mixed fixed and wagon staging. [Photo by Chris Windows, Granthan.]

Sleight-of-Hand and Tricks.   The miracles were fertile ground for the imagination of the theatre technicians. Some Nativity plays included a legendary incident when, at Mary's bidding, a winter tree put out leaves and ripe cherries. Moses' rod flowered. Graves opened and the dead rose. The miracle of the loaves and fishes was made visible. Along with clockworks, the tricks of jugglers and traveling performers were probably used.

Light Effects.   Devils carried "squibs" (firecrackers or roman candles) in the orifices of their costumes (ears and anus). Rudimentary rockets were used for divine fire: "At the Conception there was a crash of thunder from the Heaven to the middle of the Stage . . . ; a flaming and crackling fire seemed to fill the whole church. This was accomplished by means of three ropes. As the thunder continued to rumble, the fire became more intense, lighting the lamps of the church."[21] Polished reflectors were common adjuncts to pageants, and were used for stars, beams of light, and divine rays. In a world that was very dark when the sun went down, such effects seemed remarkable.

Costumes

Medieval theatre was not time-bound. The cycles showed *all* time, and even timelessness beyond time, and they tolerated anachronisms of dress, language, and reference that a modern audience would despise. However, we cannot assume that the dress of the day sufficed for theatrical costume. Exceptions included:

1. Intentional Archaism.   Military dress was an example of intentional archaism. The 1378 show witnessed by Charles V of France featured performers dressed in outmoded armor that had been kept in storage, perhaps for just such use. There was no intention to reproduce the actual armor of the Crusades; rather, "differentness" was the goal. Such intentional archaism would have had to be understandable to the audience, of course.[22]

2. Exoticism.   There is ample evidence from painting and sculpture that there were conventions of foreign, especially Eastern, dress. Some of the performers before Charles V were costumed as Saracens, and one even exhorted his fellows in Arabic. Many of the plays called for pre-Christian Jewish officials and religious figures—"doctors after the old law," as one English cycle calls them. Furred robes and pointed hats were used; the Magi wore special crowns; Muslim kings and soldiers carried unusual weapons and unusual emblems.

3. Display.   Fabrics were often of the finest. Great kings were given the garb of kings, and in an age of pomp and pageantry, such things could hardly be stinted. "God's coat of white leather (6 skins)" is an entry at Coventry for one of the many costumes of God in this pageant-wagon cycle. Silks, satins, and furs were used; the costumes strove for theatrical beauty and not for mere functionalism.

4. Symbolism.   In the moralities, symbolic clothing was, of course, important; in the cycles, too, "an attempt to associate symbolic clothing was an important trait."[23] At Coventry, Christ's tormentors wore "jackets of black buckram with nails and dice upon them"; at York, Christ wore a "bloody shirt" in one play, white in another, and the purple of empire in another.

The most easily recognizable—and often the most spectacular—of symbolic costuming was that of the devils. Masks, even double-faced masks, were often used, many of the most grotesque and bestial sort, for it was the reduction to the beast that marked Lucifer's fall from the angelic. Some had faces at belly and pelvis. Other medieval devils had bat wings or pointed ears. As well, devils frequently carried implements, such as hooks, forks, and cooking utensils, that were emblematic of their calling.

Finally, the cycle plays, like the moralities, included a number of symbolic or allegorical characters who must have been symbolically

FIGURE 8.17

Medieval costume was often colorful and spectacular, as in this sixteenth-century German *Schembart* costume. The little pageant at the lower right appears to be a sled, not a wagon; its true size is unclear. [Courtesy of the Fitzwilliam Museum, Cambridge.]

costumed. One of the most spectacular of these was Death, seen in both German and English cycles, probably costumed in a black-and-white skeleton dress.

Audiences

The society was a varied but structured one. It is to be expected, therefore, that the audience was similarly varied and structured, and that audience areas in the theatre would provide a variety of places (and prices). The preferred audience spaces went to the wealthy and the noble, and the largest class excluded from the theatre was probably the rural peasantry. The theatre was not actually elitist, because it seems to have made room (standing room, at least) for sizable numbers of the urban lower class, but even then, it must have effectively shut out those who could pay nothing and those who could not travel from the country to the city. It was mass theatre in that it appealed to a wide part of the social spectrum, but it did not include the entire spectrum in its audience.

The *loges* of the elite were built with attention to comfort. At Angers in 1471, a scaffold twenty-four by thirty meters was built, with the *loges* in two parts, one for viewing and one for "retiring." (Performances that lasted all day for several days presented real problems of support systems—toilets, storage for foul-weather clothing and food, means of transport, and so on.) The converted amphitheatre at Romans had eighty-four *loges* in tiers, with awnings to protect the occupants. These were fairly expensive: 39 modern francs at Romans, 150 at Vienne for the eight days of playing. Seats in the *gradins*, or bleachers, were cheaper, but the seating was undoubtedly less comfortable, the support systems cruder, and protection from the weather nonexistent; the cheapest places probably offered nothing but room, and not too much of that.

Gustave Cohen's figures for the production at Romans tend to show that the audience, although large, was hardly comprehensive. He found a total of 13,947 attendees for three days; however, many of the same people must have returned on the second and third days, so that the total number of individuals was far below 13,000. He estimated that as few as 5,000 or 6,000 actually made up the audience.[24]

It would be wrong to suggest that the vernacular religious drama was elitist drama, even though fees were charged and the wealthy were favored. On the other hand, it would also be wrong to say that this was free drama for a mass society. It was a popular theatre, but not a universal one; it drew from a broad range of society, but probably not from the rural peasantry. It was truly loved at many levels: it was played before visiting kings and queens: it drew cathedral clergy and civic dignitaries; aristocrats and merchants paid handsomely to see it, while craftsmen, tradesmen and apprentices paid less (but may, proportionate to their earning power, have paid much more.) And when parts of the cycles were borrowed or rented by small towns or when a small touring troupe brought a morality, even some of the lowest rural classes had a chance to attend.

The performances were great events, uniting the best of spectacles with the excitement of a fair and the piety of a holy day. Virtually every urban class had representatives in the audience. Something of a cross between a revival meeting and a carnival, Corpus Christi Day thrilled a medieval city as few other events ever could have. It was the life of the society in little.

Ends and New Beginnings

Mysteries' End is the intriguing title of a book that explores the reasons for the rather sudden but almost complete disappearance of the vernacular religious theatre.[25] It is the book's hypothesis that the plays were put down intentionally—victims of the Reformation. Whether this explanation is the correct one or not, it is certainly true that between 1550 and 1590 most of the major cycles of northern Europe ended, to be replaced by a secular drama and by secular theatres that were very different.

Evidence of a suppression of the plays in certain countries is strong: "[S]uccessive [English] governments from 1535 to 1574 first undermined the Catholic stage by ridicule, censorship and threats and ultimately directly forbade its continuance."[26] In some cases, the valuable registers were called in for "examination" and then either returned with radical demands for changes or simply not returned at all. The Council of Trent (1545–1564) was called by the pope to deal, at least ostensibly, with the threat of the Reformation; one of its decisions was to discourage production of the cycle plays and related forms. In Paris, the Confrérie de la Passion was forbidden in 1548 to perform "religious mysteries." Thus, Protestant forces were attacking the plays as popish even as Roman Catholic forces were attacking them as heretical or secular or anticlerical.

However, the evidence of official suppression does not satisfy many historians: the Council of Trent was a highly politicized exercise in public relations that may simply have found the theatre a convenient target; the Confrérie de la Passion was forbidden to play because, it was said, its actors were incompetent and unlettered; and in England, as often as some officials called registers in, others gave permission for productions to go forward.

Rather than suppression, economic difficulties seem a better explanation to many scholars: "[E]ither just prior to, or early in the Reformation, some towns with cycle dramas had run into serious economic trouble."[27] The plays were enormously expensive, and after 1550 Europe suffered severe inflation. In a time of crisis, the great cycles may simply have proved more expensive than they were worth.

Or perhaps the plays seemed suddenly obsolete. Their theology was dated and inadequate to the challenge of the Reformation. Their language was sometimes archaic. And people had been seeing them for years and years; perhaps a living spectacle had turned into an empty tradition, although in Spain they were just entering on a new phase (that of the *autos sacramentales*) when they died in the north.

The northern vernacular religious drama reached its height early in the sixteenth century. A natural process may have already scheduled its death for a generation or two later, and the Reformation hastened it. Most certainly, it could not have survived the impact of the Italian Renaissance, even without the Reformation. There were already changes swirling around the plays even as they achieved their glory: the coming of new professionals, including the *meneurs des jeux* and the property players; the appearance of new kinds of drama; and the creation of new performance spaces.

ENDNOTES

1. Friedrick Heer, *The Medieval World, 1100–1350* (London: Weidenfeld and Nicolson, 1962), p. 299.

2. John Hatcher, *Plague, Population and the English Economy* (London: Macmillan, 1977), p. 25.

3. Steven Runciman, "Life in a Doomed City: Constantinople Before the Capture by the Turks," *Medieval and Renaissance Studies* (Summer 1966): 105.

4. Richard Axton, *European Drama of the Early Middle Ages* (London: Hutchinson, 1974), p. 131.

5. Stanely J. Kahrl, *Traditions of Medieval English Drama* (London: Hutchinson, 1974), p. 23.

6. Ibid. p. 20.

7. N. D. Shergold, *A History of the Spanish Stage* (Oxford: Clarendon Press, 1967), pp. 83 ff.

8. Kenneth M. Dodd, "Another Elizabethan Theatre in the Round," *Shakespeare Quarterly* 21 (Spring 1970):125–156.

9. Tom Cole Gardner, "The Theater of Hell: A Critical Study of Some Twelfth-Century Eschatological Visions" (Ph.D. diss., University of California at Berkeley, 1976), pp. 77 ff.

10. Glynn Wickham, *The Medieval Theatre* (London: Weidenfeld and Nicolson, 1974), p. 77.

11. Elie Konigson, *L'Espace Théâtrale Médiéval* (Paris: Editions du Centre National de la Recherche Scientifique, 1975), pp. 131 ff.

12. Shergold, p. 93.

13. Shergold, p. 53.

14. Shergold, p. 103.

15. Richard Hosley, "Three Kinds of Outdoor Theatre Before Shakespeare," *Theatre Survey* 12, 1 (May 1971):27.

16. Gustave Cohen, *Histoire de la Mise-en-Scène, . . .* rev. ed. (Paris: H. Champion, 1926), p. 91.

17. J. C. Coldewey, "That Enterprising Property Player," *Theatre Notebook* 31, 1 (1977):11.

18. G. Brett, "The Automata of the Byzantine. . . . ", *Speculum* 29 (1954):477–487.

19. M. Sherwood, "Magic and Machines," *Studies in Philology* 44 (1947):567–592.

20. Orville K. Larson, "Bishop Abraham of Souzdal's Description of Sacre Rappresentazioni," *Educational Theatre Journal* 9 (October 1957):208–213.

21. Ibid.

22. L. H. Loomis, "Secular Dramatics and Chaucer's 'Tregetoures,' " *Speculum* 33 (April 1958):242–255; and S. M. Newton, *Renaissance Theatre Costume. . . .* (New York: Theatre Arts Books, 1975).

23. Peter Holding, "Stagecraft in the York Cycle," *Theatre Notebook* 34, 2 (1980):57.

24. Cohen, p. 254; prices from p. 245.

25. H. C., Gardiner, *Mysteries' End* (Hamden, Conn.: Archon Books; Yale Studies in English, Vol. 103, 1946).

26. Glynn Wickham, *Early English Stages, 1300 to 1600*, 3 vols. (New York: Columbia University Press, 1967), Vol. 1, p. 117.

27. B. D. Bills, "The 'Suppression Theory' and the English Corpus Christi Play," *Theatre Journal* 32 (May 1980):159.

9

The Age of Shakespeare: London, Paris, and Madrid, 1500–1650

In 1500, the dominant European drama was religious and the dominant theatrical conventions were medieval. In 1600, the dominant drama was secular and the dominant theatrical conventions were a blend of the simultaneity of the Middle Ages and the new vision of the Renaissance. There were exceptions: Spain's drama continued to have a vigorous religious component, and Italy had had a distinctive secular theatre for many years (see Chapter 11). Thus, there was great overlapping, and it is necessary to remember that during this complex period, three strands coexisted: the medieval, the secular-professional, and the Renaissance.

The End of Medievalism

Vernacular languages had become the principal ones of discourse, government, literature, and record keeping by 1500. They were the verbal expression of nationalism, and national governments were increasingly centralized in national capitals. Both nationalism and urban centralization were symptoms of the death of the Middle Ages. Important in medievalism's final decline and in the appearance of new institutions were the following elements.

The Reformation

When, in 1517, Martin Luther published his theses demanding church reform, he was not doing anything radically different from several predecessors, and he certainly did not intend to split the Church of Rome. Such was the result, however; Calvin, Knox, Zwingli, and others gave new voice and focus to reform. The first printed, vernacular Bible gave authority. Henry VIII of England was "Defender of the Faith" for his early support of the pope, but by 1533, he had broken away from Rome. The Reformation came with enormous speed, often hurried by nationalism and expediency.

France, England, and Germany were internally split by religious factions. Spain and Italy reacted conservatively, Spain becoming an enemy of England, then an uneasy ally when England swung back to Catholicism under Henry's daughter, Mary. France experienced religious persecution and political assassination in the name of religion throughout the sixteenth century.

These events were not mere fashion. Religion was a passionate matter. And where there was official change, as in England, the entire national structure was shaken. In England, the monarch became the head of a new "established church" and installed his own bishops and priests, the "new men" of the age; the monasteries were closed, their wealth seized and sometimes used to pay off political debts; suspect persons in government, the universities, and the church were hunted down and forced out. Some of the nation's ablest people were lost:

Sir Thomas More, for years Henry VIII's chancellor, was beheaded for opposing the king. Not even poets were immune; the court dramatist John Heywood ended his life in religious exile.

The Reformation brought upheaval. When that upheaval ended, many—as in Elizabethan England—felt properly that a new age had dawned, and they wanted to celebrate that newness.

Knowledge and Education

Education and religious orthodoxy were very closely linked. The right to read the Bible in the vernacular, for example, became an important Protestant demand, and it was one of the reasons for the founding of sectarian schools.

The great medieval universities maintained their status through the Reformation period. In many cases, however, and most notably in England, they became part of the new establishment. Even in a nominally Protestant country, both Roman Catholics and Protestant sectarians found themselves at odds with universities dominated by new masters.

Within the universities, new ideas still found fertile ground. They had always seemed like havens of heresy to the orthodox; now, they were frequent nurseries for new ideas in many fields—including drama.

Cities

Powerful monarchies changed the role of the cities, emphasizing national capitals and large bureaucracies. No longer did the government move when the monarch moved; the "court" went along at least symbolically, but the bureaucracy was tied to its functional spaces and its records. National capitals became different from other cities: power and wealth flowed into them; increasingly, as the court and the parliament sat there, so did the lower law courts and the lawyers. The nobility built houses there; foreign ambassadors lived there; the center of the monetary system—the king's mint, goldsmiths, and banks—located there. Centralization was very important in France, England, and Spain, but far less so in Italy and Germany.

Technology and New Wealth

New technology revolutionized the very way in which people saw the world, which was suddenly larger, clearer, and more real. The world became hard-edged and knowable; time became linear, capturable, and comprehensible. Perhaps more important still, technology itself became important, and the rate of technological change increased geometrically.

By 1500, the Portuguese had gone down the coast of Africa to India; Columbus had reached the Caribbean; Cabot and others had reached Newfoundland. Over the next century, enormous wealth would come to Europe: gold and silver from the Americas, particularly to Spain; furs and fish from Canada, principally to France; timber, furs, and fish to England; slaves, gold, ivory, and foods from Africa and India to several nations. Governments and private capital combined to form great trading companies that, with public subsidy and private armies, explored and colonized.

The enormous influx of precious metal from the Americas caused drastic inflation after about 1550 and probably contributed to the cultural separation of Spain from the rest of Europe. For all that Spain was ruled by the house of Hapsburg and engaged in extensive adventures in the Low Countries and against England, it did not participate in the rush toward modern institutions as did northern Europe—partly, perhaps, because Spain's wealth came directly in the form of gold and silver, the very stuff of money, creating a surplus of money while not affecting either goods or labor; the new wealth brought back to *northern* Europe came largely as raw goods that had to be worked and traded, so that employment, new industries, and markets were created. The result was to fix Spanish medievalism in a protective shell of wealth, while

FIGURE 9.1

Tradesmen (ca. 1490). Increasing specialization and increasing urbanization marked the age. [From Besant, *Tudor*.]

the North had to create new, postmedieval institutions to cope with entirely new factors.

The Northern Renaissance

Renaissance means "rebirth," and the word is used specifically to refer to the rebirth of interest in classicism as the Middle Ages ended. The Middle Ages, however, having been a patchwork, ended in a patchwork fashion. The biggest pieces that can be defined in the patchwork are northern Europe and southern Europe, most particularly Italy. It is with Italy that the Renaissance is usually associated (Chapter 11).

This is not to say, however, that the north lacked a renaissance. On the contrary, it had Humanists of genius, like Erasmus (ca. 1466–1536); it had a rebirth of interest in classical writings; it had innovators like Gutenburg and Copernicus; and it had mercantile empires like the Hanseatic League. It had even had earlier "renascences" like the twelfth-century rena-

scence, which anticipated much of the Renaissance itself. Perhaps most obviously, northern Europe had the ferment of the Reformation and its typically Renaissance concern for individualism.

However, what the northern Renaissance did *not* experience in this period was a shift in its *dominant* theatrical convention from medievalism to something else. *In the theatre, the clearest Renaissance effects were seen first in Italy.* As a result, the northern theatre from about 1500–1650 was a theatre of conflict, compromise, and overlap, with aspects of both the waning medieval vision and the coming Renaissance one. It would be absurd to pretend that theatre people in northern Europe were ignorant of Renaissance tendencies or that they were indifferent to the Renaissance interest in classicism; on the contrary, as we have already seen, one explanation of the structure and arrangement of the theatres of the great *mystères* of northern France is that they tried to imitate the arenas of classical Rome.

Northern Europe *did* have a minor theatre in some of its courts that was similar to that of the Italian Renaissance. The public theatres seen by most people, and the performances created

FIGURE 9.2

French farceurs of the sixteenth century on a booth stage on trestles. [From Petit de Julleville.]

by most theatre people, however, remained more identifiably medieval.

The Elizabethan Age in England

Elizabeth I came to the English throne in 1558. Although her reign was stressful, it saw perhaps the most spectacular explosion of artistic genius that that nation had ever experienced, most of all in poetry and drama. The foundation of the international position of England was laid in Elizabeth I's reign; trade increased, overseas expansion began, and both personal and national wealth increased. A long and tortuous period of difficult relations with Spain ended with the destruction of the Spanish Armada in 1588. Stabilization of the crown and of the Protestant religion were both achieved. Almost until Elizabeth's death in 1603, an enormous optimism gripped English consciousness, expressed as a brilliant, sometimes brash sense of achievement. The national mood darkened after her death, but between about 1575 and 1600, England gloriously displayed the cheek and the hopefulness, the conceit and the genius, of youth in its first freedom.

The Background of Secular Theatre

In its developed form of about 1585, secular theatre can be identified as:

1. Professional.
2. Commercial.
3. Specialized.
4. Worldly in its concerns.
5. Critically self-aware.

This new secular theatre was so different from religious theatre that some scholars have looked for its sources outside the religious theatre. These sources have been thought to include:

Folk Theatre and Drama

Mummers plays, sword dances, morris dances, and similar events are either overtly theatrical or have theatrical elements. They have been particularly attractive to ritualists because of their frequent association with seasonal playing and because of their inclusion of what seem to be stories, symbols, or characters of death and resurrection. A recent scholar has associated them with an ancient European witch cult.[1] Nonetheless, it is difficult to find their direct bearing on the matter.

Games and Stories

Jokes, tales, and some games have strong affinities with drama; they have often provided characters, situations, and stories. Often-told jokes crop up in secular farce.

Ceremonies

Pageantry—the public show of elaborate emblems—was central to celebration, and ceremony and formalized behavior were part of such occasions. Many processional events, including royal visits, featured stops at stages or pageants where live or clockwork figures presented static tableaux, often allegorical ones, or dumb shows or even plays. In the Low Countries, "theatres of rhetoric" (*Rederykerkamers*) had rhetorical competitions on theatrical stages.

Professional Entertainers

Mimes and *jongleurs* are frequently mentioned in medieval records, from the *scop* of Anglo-Saxon times to the royal dwarves and jesters of the sixteenth century. Below the court level, these men and women were often wanderers and outcasts; sometimes, however, they had connections with royal or great houses and became official "members" as servants. By the fifteenth century, households included "waits" (usually musicians) singers, jesters, and even players. Traditional routines, jokes, and characters—especially the fool—were undoubtedly handed down by these entertainers and incorporated into plays.

Secular Entertainment Societies

The *puys* of cities like Arras, the Compagnies des Sots (Fools' Companies) of cities like Paris, and the Basoches of the French legal societies were all organized for secular fun. The Compagnies des Sots gave their name to the *sottie*, a play of wild and fantastic humor, often satirical, always ridiculous. Similar brotherhoods existed for the springtime fools' festivals of the north, like the Nuremburg *Schembart*; they, too, presented plays, and it was for their carnivals that the comedies of the early German playwright Hans Sachs (1495–1576) were written.

Dancing and Disguising

The love of music and dance was often joined with a love of "masking" or "disguising," in which the performers disguised their identities. "Disguising" frequently took the form of allegories and became a distinctive theatrical form using costume, mask, speech, dance, and (often) set pieces, and they gave birth to the later form called the *masque*.

School and University Drama

Drama was increasingly used as a teaching tool after the middle of the fifteenth century, especially in the German-speaking areas. The teaching of Latin and the teaching of morals were considered most important, and the Latin plays of Terence were staged. New plays were also written in both Latin and the vernaculars. Along with rhetoric, drama became the object of prize days and commencements.[2] The school drama neither left an important body of plays nor contributed importantly to staging, but it did introduce generations of influential men to nonreligious theatre.

FIGURE 9.3

The *Ballet de la reine*, France (1582). Simultaneous settings were used, here in a large room with the audience on three sides: galleries on the long walls and the king's seat at the bottom, facing the length of the hall. [From Lacroix.]

Related to school drama were the plays presented by the Society of Jesus (the Jesuits) on a rather simple platform stage with draped back and sides. Although opposed to the public theatre, the Jesuits used theatre as a teaching tool.

Universities staged both Latin classics and new plays in the sixteenth century. The staging, however, remained simultaneous, the houses of Plautus becoming "houses" in the medieval sense (*mansions*).

Three Stages of Secular Theatre (ca. 1500–1650)

Despite national peculiarities and differences of chronology, the secular theatre of the late Middle Ages can be divided into three stages:

1. Rising professionalism without permanent theatres.
2. Professional production with permanent theatres.
3. Stagnation, decline, and/or change.

Germany and Italy did not show the second and third stages; Spain did not show the third in the way that France and England did.

Stage One: Actors on the Move (ca. 1500–1575)

The wandering actor of about 1500 was a non-feudal being in a partly feudal world. As that world came undone, its conservative establishment tried to hold it together with more and more rigid laws. As late as 1572 in England, the "Act for the punishment of vagabonds" sought to deal with persons "having not land or Master, nor using any lawful craft or mystery" and including "Fencers, Bearwards, common players in interludes, and minstrels." It was the intent of this act that if such people did not belong to a household of the rank of baron or above, they were to be treated as "rogues, vagabonds and sturdy beggars."

The actor's rootlessness was a huge difficulty for late medieval institutions. Feudal society needed to know where people belonged (it has been said that the typical medieval person never traveled more than fifteen miles from home), but the actor could not afford to belong to one place. Until populations became centralized in large cities, actors could not find an audience in one place; when they took to the road, they were constantly crossing jurisdictions—parishes, towns, villages, manors, shires, and counties—that were jealous of their power and fearful of outsiders. In this first stage, actors moved uneasily, looking for holes in the medieval fabric, often suffering the penalties of "rogues, vagabonds and sturdy beggars." Some became *town players* or noble servants; as early as "the late fifteenth century [in England] players of more than fifty lords have been recorded."[3] When these actors took to the road, using their servant status as protection against local harassment, they were paid both for playing and for *not* playing, as some jurisdictions moved them quickly along, virtually bribing them not to play there.

We know little about who these early actors were or why they took up this seemingly precarious profession. Some, like the early Italian actors of the *commedia dell'arte*, became quite famous and even wealthy, but most left little record. Some of them were part-time actors; a lawsuit of 1530 includes the testimony of several "players," each of whom gave his profession as something else: latten (lead) founder, mason, and so on.

They were adventurers and risk takers, men of their time who reacted out of a new restlessness against a system grown too restrictive. Some were rogues; some were runaway servants; some were discontented apprentices; few were gentlemen. Nonetheless, they succeeded only if they had ability.

These actors organized into *sharing companies*, which were usually headed by one actor (usually a man, but sometimes a woman). These usually numbered only four to six people. The permanent members were *sharers*, with a part interest in the company's stock of props, costumes, and plays, as well as of each day's takings.

The best of these troupes played in wealthy houses, corporation halls, and guildhalls; at universities; and even at court. The worst played at fairs, in the open, and in taverns.

It is likely that some of these early actors

FIGURE 9.4

Time line: Toward permanent theatres.

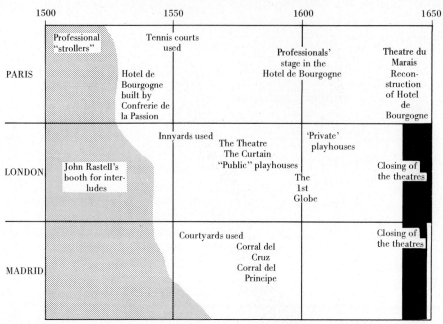

were the same property players, *meneurs des jeux, feinteurs,* and *devysors* of the religious theatre, which was then in its most vigorous period. Some of them also were hired to act in the religious plays. The Spanish theatrical figure Lope de Rueda served the religious stage as both actor and dramatist, and "it is probably no coincidence that [in Spain] the expansion of the Corpus Christi drama from about 1540 takes place roughly about the time that the professional actor makes his appearance."[4]

The early touring professionals often went far afield. An Italian troupe was found in "Bavaria, at the Emperor's court in Vienna, and at the court of the French kings, in England and elsewhere."[5] A Flemish company played in Nuremberg; the Italian Alberto Ganassa was in Madrid for two winters, and in Italy and Paris before and after; a slightly later English company played in Germany, France, the Spanish Netherlands, and the Low Countries. These ac-

tors learned at least the rudiments of the language of the countries where they played.

Impermanent Theatre: The Booth Stage

The actors could not carry an elaborate stage or massive scenery with them. The smallest troupes—"three men and a boy" (the last to play women's roles)—carried only what a swaybacked horse or mule or their own shoulders could hold.

Records and illustrations suggest that the most popular stage of these actors was the *booth stage.* This simple but elegant form had the following characteristics in late medieval use:

1. An elevated platform.
2. A curtained rear wall with entrance slits.
3. A curtained area behind the wall for dressing and storage.

The platform was set on barrels or trestles; sometimes a ladder was used in scenes to be played over the curtain—as if from a window, balcony, or wall. The audience surrounded such a stage on three sides, but the platform was high enough to enhance visibility and to keep the audience from climbing on the stage.

Like the space of the place or *platea,* space on the booth stage was nonspecific. The splits in the curtain could represent places that were miles apart or as close as two doors in the same room. There was no scenery, and there were merely essential properties. The focus was on the actor and the immediacy of the action; imagination supplied detail—if detail was needed, and it is even doubtful that the audiences of this time were accustomed to highly detailed backgrounds.

Traveling troupes often found playing spaces waiting for them. Wealthy houses were "halls" whose typical arrangement was linear; intended for eating, these had kitchens at one end, usually served by two doors, and a dais at the opposite end for the lord or master. Sometimes, there was a musician's gallery at an upper level; there were tables and seats down the long walls. The natural playing space, therefore, was between the kitchen doors and extending up the hall toward the lord's table. The resulting "theatre" had a back wall, like the booth, with two entrances; often an upper level (the gallery); a playing area thrusting out into the audience; and an audience that surrounded it on three sides.

Plays

Audiences varied from unlettered villagers to the monarchy. There was considerable variety in the plays done, therefore. At the lowest level, farces were popular; at the other extreme were plays of high seriousness and what was then the avant-garde. Playwrights were emerging as professionals, just as actors were, and the printing press gave the acting companies access to a constantly renewed stock of plays. Many of these printed plays of the sixteenth century have directions to show exactly how the roles can be doubled, so that a company of four or five could

FIGURE 9.5

Farceurs on the stage of the Hôtel de Bourgogne (?), early seventeenth century, interesting for costume and action but questionable for its setting. [From Loliée.]

play the fifteen or twenty parts. This is another example of the conflict in which these actors found themselves: many officials were trying to suppress them, but a tool as powerful as the printing press was urging them on.

This early secular drama can be divided into the following categories.

Popular Comedies and Farces. Often drawn from jokes and tales, the subjects were frequently domestic and sexual. The plays were generally short. Extant examples include the plays of the French farce-actors of Paris; Angelo Beolco's (Ruzzante's) *Ruzzante Comes Home from the Wars;* the festival comedies of Hans Sachs; and John Heywood's *John John, His Wife Tib and the Priest Sir John,* all from about 1500–1550.

Serious Long Plays. These plays were related to the moralities and the cycles. In trying to use the theatre for serious and yet secular purposes, playwrights tried a variety of subjects and approaches. The plays had in common their multiple plots, their mixed tone, and their serious moral intent. They included early history plays like the French *La Guisiade,* the first Spanish *comedias* (dramas), and plays like the English

Cambises, a "lamentable tragedy mixed full of pleasant mirth."

Renaissance and Humanist Plays.   These include school plays, some court entertainments, and classical imitations. Notable here are those plays that have Humanist subjects without following Renaissance dramatic theory. Of these, the plays called *interludes* (*entremeses* in Spain) are the most important. The word *interlude* came to be a catchall expression as vague as *play,* but in its early-sixteenth-century use, it meant a short play suitable for playing between the courses of a banquet; in a slightly extended meaning, it referred to a short play with serious (intellectual) intent but often comic tone and allegorical characters, as in *The Marriage of Wit and Science* and *The Four Elements.* The English interlude often included a trickster or seducer called the Vice, whose wit and comic energy made him an audience favorite and who persisted into the great plays of later years.

Costumes and Masks

Costumes were different from clothes—emblems rather than images. A lawsuit of about 1530 lists "player's garments" of silk and gilt leather, along with more common fabrics (including buckram and *fustian,* the latter a favorite theatrical fabric that gave its name to bombastic speeches); one costume was "green, lined with red, and with Roman letters stitched upon it of blue and red;" another was "spangled of blue satin of Bruges."

Comic actors, especially those of French farce and the *commedia dell'arte,* used costumes in association with stock characters, so that certain costumes were traditional; some of these apparently derived from the fool's dress of ass's ears and phallic prop.

Masks and other coverings of the face were common. They had been long used in the Spanish religious theatre; they are seen on actors in certain illustrations, and they were common in the *commedia dell'arte.* French farce-actors whit-

FIGURE 9.6

A fencers' show set up in a German innyard with the audience in the inn's balconies. Traveling actors of the sixteenth century would have performed in the same way. [From Weddigen.]

ened their faces with flour (and so were called *enfarinés*).

This first stage of the secular theatre, then, drew its conventions from the religious theatre, but in its staging, its company organization, and its plays, it contained the elements that would define the great theatre of the second phase.

Stage Two: Buildings and Greatness (ca. 1575–1620)

[I]t was not long [after the death of Lope de Rueda in 1565] before actors realized the desirability of having some kind of permanent playing-place. . . . The custom thus began of hiring from private individuals the yards or "corrales" at the center of blocks of houses, and of erecting stages in them.[6]

The desire to set up permanent quarters in the national capital did not always meet with success. Paris was disturbed by political and religious upheavals until the end of the sixteenth century; London kept up a seemingly perpetual attack on the theatre:

> Plays were first flatly forbidden, out doors or indoors, in 1542. Then they were allowed only in the Livery Halls, the private houses of Aldergate, on the open street. They were forbidden before three o'clock, forbidden after five o'clock, forbidden on Sundays, forbidden in Lent, forbidden in Cheapside. They were to be played only in open streets and not in close and secret places. Prentices and journeymen are forbidden to go to plays. At least five times plays are forbidden for plague. The City made three determined general attempts to put down plays—in 1574–6, in 1580–4 and 1597–1600.[7]

The theatre proved unstoppable, however. In 1576, the first permanent English theatre went up just outside the jurisdiction of the City of London. The venture was daring and risky, but like other ventures in Paris and Madrid, it paid off.

Many actors continued to tour, of course, their life as uncertain as their predecessors' had been. As well, conditions varied widely among the great capitals, and Germany continued without permanent theatres. London had the greatest number and variety, with both "public" (outdoor) and "private" (indoor) theatres; Madrid had two permanent *corrales,* although other Spanish cities also supported theatres in a way that English and French provincial cities did not; and Parisian actors were harried by a unique theatrical monopoly in the hands of the vestiges of the Confrérie de la Passion. In all three cities, the theatres owed much of their success to the court, from which some of their best-paying audiences came and where they played with some regularity; as well, some of the monarchs at times protected the theatres from other authorities.

Centralization made the theatre economically practicable; the consolidation of power in the monarchy made it legally so. It is no accident that, for example, "the story of the companies between 1572 and 1642 is one of increasing royal favor and protection."[8] This favor and protection included new institutions of control and often censorship—in London, the Master of the Revels; in Paris, the Confrérie de la Passion; in Madrid, the Alcalde—but made it possible for the companies to settle and to plan ahead.

Organization

Theatre companies continued to be sharing organizations under one or two strong leaders. Full and half shares were carefully parceled out among the most talented and the most experienced; lesser talents or newcomers were taken on as *hirelings.* New specialists joined the companies: scene keepers, prompters, and house personnel. By the end of the period (ca. 1620), one Parisian theatre had a resident *décorateur.*

A different kind of specialist appeared in the theatre, too: the entrepreneur, a man who was neither artist nor craftsman, a venturer willing to invest money and to organize. The most famous of these in London was Philip Henslowe (d. 1616), a producer–landlord–accountant–speculator who began as a pawnbroker.

Actors and Acting

In England, boys continued to play women's roles; in Spain, France, and Italy, women appeared on the stage. It is possible that English acting was different in other ways, as well; England, for example, had no masked and typed comic form like *commedia dell'arte* or the farce of the *enfarinés.*

Comedy. Comic actors in all countries seem to have assumed a line for long periods, often for life. The French farceurs were known by their characters', rather than their own, names, for example, Guillot Gorju or Gautier–Garguille. *Commedia* actors inherited or created a type and kept it. It is important to distinguish between low comedy and a higher comedy, however: in England, the clowns Will Kempe and Robert Armin were so different that their differing effects

FIGURE 9.7
Leading English Players, c. 1575–1642

Richard Tarleton (d. 1588)	clown	Wit, dancer, comedian
Robert Wilson (d. 1600)	comic actor	
Edward Alleyn (1566–1626)	tragedian	"The Roscius of our age" (Fuller); the original Faustus and Tamburlaine; founder of Dulwich College
Richard Burbage (ca. 1573–1619)	tragedian	Original Hamlet, Othello, Lear; Alleyn's equal and rival
Will Kempe (fl. 1600)	clown	Dancer, comic; Dogberry in *Much Ado*
Robert Armin (fl. 1610)	witty clown	Feste, *Twelfth Night;* Fool, *Lear*
Nathan Field (ca. 1586–ca. 1653)	comic actor	
John Lowin (1576?–1653)		Falstaff, Volpone
Joseph Taylor (1586–1653)	tragedian	Hamlet, Othello (after Burbage)
Hilliard Swanston (d. 1651)	leading player	Othello; Bussy D'Ambois
John Heminge (1556–1630)		Original Falstaff (?)
Henry Condell (d. 1627)		With Heminge, caused the publication of the First Folio edition of Shakespeare's works
John Shank (d. 1636)	clown, dancer	Followed Armin in roles
Timothy Reade (fl. 1626–1642)	clown, dancer	Boy actor, then adult clown; arrested for playing, 1647
Andrew Cane (fl. 1620–1642)	clown, dancer	

There were no actresses on the English stage in this period; women were played by boys who were apprenticed to adult actors. Their careers were fairly short unless they matured into adult players.

on Shakespeare's plays can be noted in the texts, Armin having been more poetic, more intellectual, and perhaps more melancholy. A strong strain of gusty, often vulgar comedy was inherited from the grotesquerie of medieval deviltry; on the other hand, a strain of trickery, verbal cleverness, and intellect came from certain devil figures, from the Vice of the interludes, and from Machiavellian tricksters, modified by exposure to Plautine comedy.

Serious Acting.   Size of gesture and of voice was important. As well, the oratorical tradition coupled with the plays' verbal demands seems to have created an acting style heavily weighted toward the voice. Both French and English tragedy, and the Spanish *comedias*, derived from traditions of highly colored acting and extreme situations. Immediately behind these plays was the theatre in which tyrants "raged" and, in Hamlet's phrase, "tore a passion to tatters." Yet,

closer to them was an erudite concern for elegance and subtlety. The result was probably a mixed tragic style, with an older one represented by the great English actor Edward Alleyn (1566–1626), a commanding, authoritative interpreter of Marlowe sometimes accused of bombast; and a newer one represented by Richard Burbage (1567–1619), interpreter of Shakespeare's great tragic protagonists, subtle, varied, intelligent—but such differences are also the differences between the plays in which they appeared.

Style.   Extreme subtlety would have been lost in the large theatres, but there was probably a movement toward subtler gesture and expression as theatres grew smaller and audiences more refined (after ca. 1615 in France and England). Undoubtedly, acting was a mixture of image and emblem. The playing of women by men is an example: sexually attractive young women, as played by men in England, were presented with enough imitativeness to seem womanly, yet with enough of either abstraction or irony so that the complex man-playing-a-woman-playing-a-man of several comedies was clear and funny. The playing of old women by men was a different matter; it had a long tradition on the Continent and in England, and it appears to have been a comic, sometimes grotesque, presentation of the un-womanly aspects of old and coarse women—sometimes even carried to the point of the actor's being bearded.

A later commentary in Spain mentions actors' representing "the mane of a horse, the wings of an eagle, the horns of a bull, the roar of a lion, the motions of a swimmer." This passage suggests an illustrating of poetic figures with pantomime—an element of at least the Spanish style.

In sum, then, although the professional acting of the period was varied, we may say that it was *oratorical;* that it was based partly on observation, but was *typical* rather than literal in its imitation; that it probably developed a *theatrical tone* in voice, gesture, and stance that were more formal in tragedy and more grotesque in comedy than in real life; that it emphasized *emblem* more than image; and that it was *large* in its effects rather than subtle.

Playing Conditions

Actors were now full-time professionals and were able, in at least the most successful cases, to devote their lives to the profession. They did not play every day, however. Sunday playing was very rare; playing during Lent, on religious holidays, and during certain periods (plague or official mourning) was forbidden. Many actors

FIGURE 9.8
Leading Spanish Actors, 1550–1650

Lope de Rueda (c. 1510–1565)	*autor* (troupe leader)	Usually called founding figure of professional stage, at least as symbol; dramatist, actor
Tomas de la Fuente, fl. last quarter 16th C.	*autor*	
Juan Granados, fl. last quarter 16th C.	*autor*	
Jeronimo Galvez, fl. last quarter 16th C.	*autor*	
Juan Batista Valenciano, fl. 1st quarter 17th C.	*autor*	
N.B. *Actresses legalized on Madrid stage, 1587.*		
Alonso de Riquelme	*autor*	
Maria Damiano Riquelme, d. 1656		daughter of Alonso; one of first actresses; praised as beautiful and "virtuous"
Manuel Vallejo, fl. 1620s	*autor*	husband of Maria
Josefa Vaca, 1589–1653		daughter of actress, mother of an actress; noted for breeches roles, despite laws forbidding them
Juan de Morales Medrano, fl. 1630s		husband of La Vaca; one of most noted actors of the period
Roque de Figueroa, ca. 1587–1667	*autor*	one of founders of the actors guild, the Cofradia de la Novena, 1631; noted for *The Trickster of Seville* (Tirso)
"La Calderona," Maria Calderon, fl. 1623–1633		Highly publicized royal affair
"Juan Rana," Cosme Perez, d. 1672	clown	Performer of comic *entremeses* (interludes) written for him by Calderon and others; publicly lauded in *The Triumph of Juan Rana,* 1672

Note: Thousands of actors are listed in the *Geneaologia, origen, y noticias de los comediantes de Espana* (c. 1700–1721) but details are scanty outside Spanish scholarship.

FIGURE 9.9
Leading French Actors, 1550–1650

Agnan Sarat, fl. 1570s	comic, masked or *enfariné*	Perhaps the first professional to make a name in Paris
Valleran LeComte, d. before 1634		Played major roles of Alexandre Hardy, whom he championed; led 1st "comédiens du roy" at H. de B.
Robert Guérin, "Gros-Guillaume," d. 1633	*farceur.*	
Hugues Guéru, "Gautier-Garguille," d. 1634	*farceur.*	These three often performed together; masked or *enfariné*; witty, bawdy*
Henry le Grand, "Turlupin," d. 1637	*farceur.*	
Rachel Trépeau, fl. 1607–1616		One of the first, if not the first, of professional French actresses
Marie Venier, "Laporte," fl. 1607–1610		
Colombe Venier, "LaFontaine," fl. 1603–1616		(sister of Marie)
Guillaume Desgillets or desGilberts, "Mont-dory," 1594–1653		First of leading actors at Marais; Brutus in *Mort de César* (Scudéry)
Pierre le Messier, "Bellerose," c. 1592–1670		Succeeded Valleran at H. de B.; major tragic roles; retired, 1647
Julien Bedeau, "Jodelet," 1600–1660	comic	Bridge between great *farceurs* and Molière; famous in *Le Menteur* and plays written for him
Zacharie Jacob, "Montfleury," 1600–1667		Leading tragic actor of transition to Neo-classicism
Josias de Soulas, "Floridor," 1608–1671		Tragedian; Oedipus (Corneille)
Madeleine du Pouget Beauchateau, fl. 1632–1674		Leading serious actress; Infanta in *Le Cid*
Marguerite Béguin de Villiers, d. 1670		Chimène in *Le Cid*

Note: French actors were known by, and are usually still discussed by, their stage names (in quotation marks). Such a list suggests that, while the mid-1630's marked an abrupt change in dramatic theory, they did not see the same abruptness in acting style; more probably, there was a shift c. 1630–40, or about the time of the establishment of the Théâtre du Marais.

*These actors also performed serious roles at times under other stage names—La Fleur, Fleschelles, and Belleville.

toured in the summer. During the London season, a leading actor may have played every other day, hirelings as often as they could find work. With new plays constantly being put into the repertory, however, all days were probably occupied.

In London, hirelings made about ten shillings a week at a time when laborers made six; in Spain in 1604, a man and wife made 16 *reals* per performance plus 6 *reals* for expenses, and a leading actor was said to make 3,000 *reals* per year at a time when the average total income for the company was about 400 reals per performance.[9] Only remarkable success could earn an

actor a secure life, and even large financial success was only relative: the house that Shakespeare bought with his life's earnings cost about the same as the average price of several doublets and cloaks bought by the Earl of Leicester.[10]

Actors performed in the afternoon and probably rehearsed in the morning. Rehearsals were limited in number but must have demanded concentration for technical work on cues, entrances and exits, coordinated movement, and fights and crowd scenes. The actor was expected to be able to create character; there seems to have been no director-*cum*-acting-coach. The playwright usually served his own play as interpreter, managing rehearsals through the prompter and the leading actor. What modern directors call *blocking*—movement, cued and planned—would have occupied the entire company, not just to create the realistic patterns of much modern blocking, but to create the emblematic patterns and the tableaux then common.

Theatres: Globe, Corral, and Hôtel

Despite the use of the booth stage on the road, early professional theatres were "found" spaces, and their audience areas were adapted to existing conditions, except for those of London. Elements of innyards, halls, and courtyards can be found in certain of the permanent theatres, but, whatever their antecedents, these theatres shared certain common features:

1. A high (five-foot to six-foot) platform.
2. A back wall or curtain pierced by entrances.
3. A raised, secondary acting area in or jutting from the back wall.
4. An audience area below and in front of the stage, and others in galleries above and around it.
5. Machinery inherited from the medieval religious stage, including floor traps and flying apparatus.

The shape of the London theatres may have been affected by ideas about Roman arenas, but there was nothing like the Italian imitation of Roman architecture, much less like the Italian invention of perspective scenery. Instead, the conventions and practices of the medieval stage continued, including:

1. Simultaneity.
2. Elasticity of distance in the playing area.
3. Multiplicity of viewing-points.
4. Identification of place by a sign, an emblem, or a set piece, or by the actor.

London: The First Globe.

The public theatre was one of the glories of the Elizabethan Age. Despite attempts to suppress it, despite plague, and despite temporary setbacks, the theatre flourished. Proportionally, theatre attendance must have compared well with that of fifth-century Athens and must have been out of all proportion to modern attendance. There were several reasons: the secular, professional theatre was new; it was urban in a highly self-conscious and growing city; and its plays were optimistic, often highly nationalistic, and frequently joyous in both the exuberance of their language and the showiness of their performance. It was a theatre that offered its audiences an image of their best selves; it was no accident that Hamlet called the players "the abstract and brief chronicle of the times." The London theatres of 1576–1600 were placed where Londoners could go to laugh, to be thrilled, to learn, and to understand themselves and their world.

The actor–entrepreneur James Burbage put up the first playhouse—the Theatre—in 1576, just outside the London city limits. For a generation before this, actors had been playing at London inns, and the more important innyards continued in use through the 1590s. The playhouses were preferred, however, and more of them were built (see Figure 9.19). These were all freestanding structures for fairly large audiences (two thousand or more). There were also smaller theatres, the so-called private ones converted from indoor spaces in buildings not subject to the City's rules (usually former monastic holdings). The private houses were at first associated with companies of boys that began as singing schools and ended in competition with the adults; The Blackfriars, "the house of greatest prestige,"[11] was finally taken over by an adult company for winter use.

The first Globe was the theatre of Shakespeare's greatest plays. Regrettably, we have no exact picture of it, but several kinds of evidence allow scholars to conclude that:

> It was . . . round or polygonal on the outside and more or less round inside. It had two narrow entry doors. . . . Its galleries were roofed with thatch. . . .

There is a large measure of agreement amongst the many scholars who have studied the Globe plays in detail, that like the Swan the Globe's stage area had a tiring-house facade; a stage extending to the middle of the yard; a large stage-trap . . . ; two pillars supporting the heavens; and two stage doors. The last item is less certain. . . .[12]

The *yard* was the ground level, paved; surrounding it in the Globe would have been three tiers of covered galleries like *loges*. The large stage (43 feet by about 23 feet) stood 5 or 6 feet above the yard and was backed by the wall of the *tiring house* ("attiring house," that is, the dressing rooms and support spaces). Two pillars stood on the stage and supported an overhanging ceiling, the *heavens*, in which it is believed machinery was housed.

The Globe was built of wood on stone foundations.

Controversy: Acting Areas, Entrances, Discoveries.

Evidence about other aspects of this theatre includes:

1. *Pictorial.* The best-known is the "Swan drawing" (see Figure 9.10). Its reliability is questionable, however, as is its accuracy.

2. *Stage directions.* Elizabethan plays were often stingy with stage directions. Nonetheless, there were enough to give evidence of an upper and a lower playing area, called "above" or "on the top" and "below" or "on the stage." There were also enough to give evidence of two doors in the tiring-house wall and perhaps three: "He goes in at one door and comes out at another," (*The Spanish Tragedy*); "Exit Hamlet tugging in Polonius. Enter King," presumably at a different door (*Hamlet*). We also find such stage directions as "At a window" and "Under the stage."

3. *Antecedents.* For some scholars, the question of whether the most important antecedent was Renaissance or medieval is crucial. It now appears that there were several antecedents and that the Elizabethan theatre was a re-

FIGURE 9.10

The Swan drawing, redrawn and with labels translated. A Dutch visitor made the original sketch. It raises many questions: Who are the people in the gallery behind the stage? What are the dark blocks under the stage? Is this a rehearsal or a performance? Where is the "discovery" space? Is the "plain or arena" used for audience or actors or both? Are the "nobles seats" (Lords Rooms) so labeled because of a knowledge of the London theatre or because of a tradition from the Terence theatres, as in Figure 8.9?

sult of complex forces, and that it was neither simply a medieval theatre-in-the-round nor a Renaissance attempt to copy a Roman theatre. The known or suspected antecedents include both of those things as well as tournament grounds, with their elevated *loges*; innyards, with their encircling galleries; other kinds of Elizabethan structures such as the bear garden, in which animals were made to fight and in which stages could be erected; banqueting halls, which were large and circular, with tiers of *loges* and open centers for entertainments; and, perhaps, metaphorical or fantastic structures like the "theatres of the world" that existed as poetic figures.

4. *Contracts, legal papers, plat maps, and so on.* These provide much of the information on dimensions and materials, but less on interior details and little, if any, on staging.

The way in which this evidence has been interpreted has led to several controversies. Important among these are

1. *Shape.* The Elizabethan theatre has been variously seen as round, polygonal, and square. Leslie Hotson postulated a complete theatre-in-the-round in his *Shakespeare's Wooden O*, whose title comes from the Chorus in Shakespeare's *Henry V*. Most scholars view Hotson's reconstruction as too radical, however, for it supposes a completely medieval stage.

FIGURE 9.11

A conjectural reconstruction of the Swan by Richard Leacroft. [Courtesy of Richard Leacroft. First published in *Theatre Notebook.*]

2. *Discovery space(s).* "Discoveries" are common in Elizabethan plays; they are the sudden appearance (to the audience) of people or objects. Sometimes, the things discovered are quite large—whole banquets, for example, or beds. As well, there are many references to hiding and particularly to hiding behind, or hiding things behind, a curtain or "arras." Polonius hides "behind the arras" (*Hamlet*); Hieronimo "knocks up the curtain" and later removes it to discover a grisly spectacle (*The Spanish Tragedy*).

However, we look in vain at the Swan drawing for any sign of either an arras or of what has come to be called a *discovery space*. Scholars have speculated, however, and three hypotheses dominate:

a. The inner below. J. C. Adams's influential book *The Globe Playhouse* postulates the existence of an inner stage below the gallery in the tiring-house facade, probably between the stage doors. It has been objected that the sight lines would have been dreadful into such a space; some critics have also objected that the very idea of an inner below is too much like a nineteenth-century proscenium stage. However, the "inner below" solves a great many of the problems raised by the evidence and the plays, and it had a counterpart in the Spanish theatre.

b. The pavilion. More recently, a theory associated with C. W. Hodges (*The Globe Restored*) has gained attention. It supposes that a "pavilion" was set up against the tiring-house wall and between the stage doors, if they were in the positions shown in the Swan drawing. Such a pavilion could have had an acting area on its roof, if necessary, and it could have been curtained, like many medieval scaffolds, for discoveries and hiding. Again, there would have been sight-line problems with such a structure, although it has been suggested that the curtains were usually left open so that the audience could look through it.

c. The variable mansion. George F. Reynolds (*The Staging of Elizabethan Plays at the Red*

Bull Theatre, 1605–1625) posited the use of structures that could go in various places on the stage, to be put up as needed. Such usage would have been medieval; it has some similarities to Hotson's concept; and it fits many of the requirements of the plays. However, the hard evidence is slim.

The Elizabethan Theatre in Use.

By 1590, several of the London public theatres were on the Bankside, across the Thames from London. The audience members reached them mostly by boat, coming in the afternoon for a daylight performance. The plays would begin with a spoken prologue or, less often, with an *induction* (a short scene with its own fictional situation); in the early years, plays may still have begun with *dumb shows*, pantomimes that summarized the action (as in the play-within-a-play in *Hamlet*). Musicians played in a gallery two levels above the stage. The performance was usually broken into acts.

The casts were large and spectacle was common: flags, processions, showy costumes, sword fights, and trumpet fanfares. Large as the audiences sometimes were, they were probably attentive to language, and the perfomances exploited the music of the human voice and the richness of English poetry. The plays were long and their plots often complex; things moved quickly, one character or group leaving as another came on, the place shifting with them. Emblems were necessary for quick identification. Often, the part stood for the whole: armies marched in the persons of twenty or so figures; battles were fought by half a dozen. Between the acts, other entertainments were performed: music, comic dances, and short pieces called *jigs*. Food and drink circulated; people gossiped, gawked, and waved. The audience was always visible, both during the acts and between them. This was great theatre—and it was great social interaction, as well, when simply *to be there* was to have one's place in a dynamic nation affirmed.

Paris: The Hôtel de Bourgogne.

In Paris, the Confrérie de la Passion had occupied two other buildings before leasing a plot of land in 1547 on the site called the Hôtel de Bourgogne. There, they put up a long, narrow structure several stories high; however, in 1548, the Parlement de Paris forbade them to play the religious dramas that were their reason for being, though it did allow "secular mysteries" (perhaps an intentionally vague expression) and also gave the Confrérie what amounted to a monopoly on theatre production in the city.[13] The times were extremely unsettled ones, and few troupes were able to find security in France. How the Confrérie managed to earn enough money from their building to pay for the lot and the construction, therefore, is not known, for their own performances were very sparse.

Their building can be partially reconstructed from plot dimensions, later contracts, and old maps. They appear to have had a structure 109 feet long by 44 feet wide (outside dimensions) with principal entrances at one end and along one side.[14] Inside, there were *loges*, but how many or in what arrangement is unclear.

The Confrérie's earlier repertory had included the *Mystère des Actes des Apôtres*, the *Mystère de la Passion,* and the *Mystère du Vieux Testament*. It is a fair assumption that their hall was built for such large spectacles. It is barely possible that they put a raised stage at one end, but it must be pointed out that their building was very narrow for such an arrangement, at least by medieval standards—especially if the *loges* were ranged along the long walls, as was likely, thus cutting off another twelve feet or more. A long, shallow stage with a linear arrangement, as at Valenciennes, was possible, although the likeliest arrangement appears to be that of the "alley theatres," with a long, narrow playing area down the middle and bleachers and *loges* on each side.

Such an arrangement would not have been congenial to the early professionals, however,

FIGURE 9.12

The Hôtel de Bourgogne, ca. 1625. Indicated by numbers are: 1. Stage (on which scenery of the Mahelot type would have been used); 2. *loges;* 3. rear of the *loges,* with narrow communicating passageway and doors to individual boxes; 4. a "tunnel" under the *loges,* probably used in this period for storage, although there are mysterious (and rare) references to the "tunnel *loges*"; 5. galleries; 6. the *paradis,* now a small audience area (which would have been railed); 7. the lobby on the street end, unchanged from the mid-sixteenth-century location; other support spaces, and perhaps shops and food booths were also here; 8. the *parterre;* 9. the "little stage" above the main one; access stairs not shown; 10. the *amphithéâtre;* 11. the *loges* on the stage, shown here as remaining from their original position and now used as dressing-rooms enclosing the scene- and acting-area. This illustration should be compared with the speculative reconstruction of the Hôtel de Bourgogne, ca. 1550 (Figure 8.15) which uses the same basic model. [Reconstruction by Kenneth Cameron.]

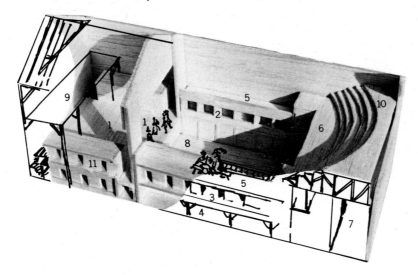

with their small troupes, their lack of large scene pieces, and their familiarity with the booth stage. They would probably have set up a booth in the building, probably at one end, where the thirty-two or so feet of width would have been adequate.

By 1600, the theatre at the Hôtel de Bourgogne was Paris's principal permanent theatre. (Other temporary ones were set up in tennis courts—also long, narrow buildings.) There was a major reconstruction of the Hôtel de Bourgogne in 1647. Between 1600 and 1647, we find references to audience areas in the Hôtel de Bourgogne called the *paradis* (perhaps a vestige

of the Confrérie's paradise mansion, or at least its location); to *loges* below this *paradis,* meaning that the *paradis* was at least two levels above the floor, as *loges* were at least one above it; to an *amphithéâtre* "under the gable at the end," apparently very high; to the *parterre,* or floor below the stage—standing room; and to a *petit théâtre,* or "little stage," reached by a flight of stairs, and therefore assumed to be a second stage (perhaps a machinery loft or an upper playing place, the *théâtre supérieure*) above the main one.

It appears, then, that the theatre of the professionals who settled at the Hôtel de Bour-

FIGURE 9.13

Interior of a Paris theatre, perhaps the Hôtel de Bourgogne (ca. 1630). This representation seems correct for the Hôtel: a long, narrow hall; a small stage; and a closed tunnel under the *loges*. The audience appears to be seated (not standing) in the *parterre*, however, and has an unusual proportion of women. [Courtesy of the Bibliothèque National.]

gogne was long and narrow, with a stage five or six feet above the *parterre* and a single rank of *loges* on each side; the stage was thirty or so feet wide and about thirty-five feet deep. It was probably trapped, had a smaller stage above it (presumably at the back) and undoubtedly had machinery overhead for flying—perhaps the machinery installed by the Confrérie for religious plays. The professionals perhaps inherited some of the Confrérie's setpieces as well. At the end of the *parterre* opposite the stage were, probably, a bank of facing *loges* with the *paradis* above them and the *amphithéâtre* behind that, rising steeply to the end gable. We know almost nothing of the support areas, although late references to old *loges* "on the stage" suggest that when the professionals' stage was built, the *loges* in place along the walls from the

back wall to the forestage were left, probably as dressing rooms. They would have been very small—perhaps six feet on a side.

Madrid: The Corral del Principe.   The first *corral* (interior courtyard among several houses) was used in the 1560s or earlier, but none apparently was made permanent for theatrical use until about 1580 (the Corral del Cruz). The second, the Corral del Principe, was adapted to a theatre in about 1584 and was so used until about 1735.

The features of the *corral* were peculiar to Spain: the use of large awnings over almost the entire yard; the use of windows in the rear walls of the surrounding houses, and of the balconies on those walls, for the audience; and the separation of men and women in distinct seating areas. A religious charity, the Cofradia de la Passion y Sangra de Jesucristo, rented the yards and made the alterations in order to raise money for its hospitals; thereafter, the connection between charitable hospitals and the professional theatre was close for many years. The association benefited the actors in that the charities came to depend on the actors' regular playing for income, thus giving them a legitimacy that they lacked in other capitals. (Madrid had just as much antitheatrical sentiment as did Paris or London.) In 1638, the two principal *corrales* were taken over by the city and became "municipal enterprises."[15]

No comprehensive reconstruction of the Corral del Principe exists, and knowledge of it comes from construction contracts, the plays performed in it, contemporary accounts, and eighteenth-century plans. It appears that the stage was only about twenty-eight feet wide and twenty-five feet deep; that it was flanked by covered bleachers (*gradas*) at or below stage level; and that a *patio* (a yard or *parterre*) about forty-nine feet deep and the width of the stage stretched back from it, with *gradas* on each side. Directly opposite the stage at ground level was the principal entrance; on each side of it was a small, roofed seating area. On the first floor

FIGURE 9.14

A speculative reconstruction of the Corral del Principe, ca. 1625. The numbers indicate: 1. the machine space over the stage; 2. the "backstage" *vestuario*; 3. the curtained discovery space; 4. the stage; 5. the *patio* with benches near the stage; 6. the sloping roof over the lowest rank of *loges,* with the grilled windows and *chica* in the wall above, and galleries above those; 7. the exterior (street) wall. [Reconstruction by Kenneth Cameron.]

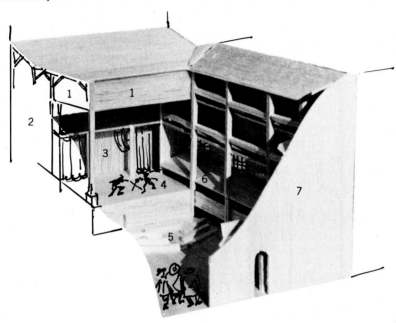

above the entrance was a gallery as wide as the *patio,* called the *cazuela*—the segregated seating for women. Two more galleries faced the stage above the *cazuela,* that on the second level having five *loges,* of which the center one was reserved for the officials of Madrid; on the third level was the *tertulia,* a gallery that may have had a curved back wall, making it perhaps similar to the *amphithéâtre* of the Hôtel de Bourgogne.

The sides of the rectangular *corral* also had upper seating areas at the second and third levels; at the first level, however, were certain grilled windows and balconies (*aposentos*), four on one side and two on the other. These provided audience areas for the houses on those sides, but they were probably rented out by the householders; for their own use, the house-

holders sometimes got special permission to break a small window (*chicas*) through the wall and cover it with a grill (as much to keep them from climbing into the theatre as to keep the theatre patrons from entering their houses).[16]

About eighteen feet back from the edge of the stage were two pillars that almost certainly supported a rear gallery; they probably also marked the line of the rear curtain that was characteristic of the Spanish stages. Thus, the principal acting area was about eighteen by twenty-five feet, backed by a curtain; when this curtain was open, an additional space seven by twenty-five feet (or narrower) was usable; at a second level, a gallery—also presumably seven by twenty-five feet—existed.

We do not know if there was any structure over the stage, although it is likely that at least

FIGURE 9.15

Schematic of comparison of acting–audience arrangements.

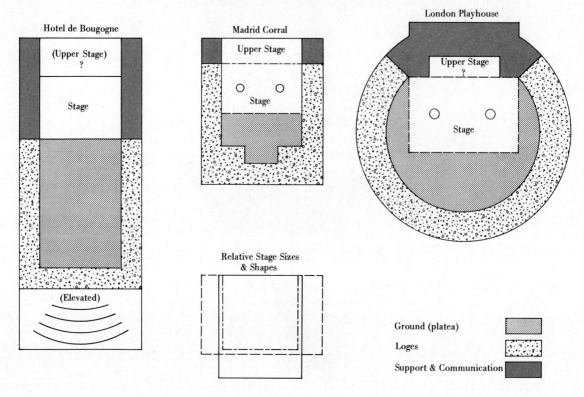

some of the stage was covered by a housing for machinery, as in the Globe.

The Corral del Principe, then, had roughly the same arrangements as the Globe and the Hôtel de Bourgogne, although its acting areas were smaller. An upper and lower level, an elevated stage, an audience in standing room and tiered galleries, a rear wall with entrances, and overhead machinery were probably common to all three. The differences in size and shape were significant, however.

Scenery

Settled into their permanent quarters, the professionals were able to invest in spectacle in a way that their earlier life had not allowed. Set pieces and complex machinery were now pos-

sible. The *devysors* and *feinteurs* had new employment.

In 1598, Henslowe made an inventory of "all the properties for my Lord Admiral's Men"; it included:

Item, 1 rock, 1 tomb, 1 Hell mouth
Item, 1 tomb of Guido, 1 tomb of Dido, 1 bedstead
Item, 8 lances, 1 pair of stairs for Phaeton . . .
Item, . . . the city of Rome
Item, 1 golden fleece, 2 rackets; a bay tree . . .

Spanish plays of the period required such pieces as a fountain, the upper rigging of a ship, the "castles" of a Moorish and a Christian ship, and tombs. The *décorateur*'s notes for plays at the

Hôtel de Bourgogne required a practical ship, a house with an upper window, and a cave. In short, these theatres quickly took over the scenic principles—and even the scenic units—of the religious stage.

However, it must be remembered that it was the theatre itself, and particularly the back wall of the stage, that was the principal "scenery" of the plays. Mostly, what the audience saw was apparently the tiring-house facade or the rear curtain. Even Henslowe's hell-mouth or the painted canvas picture of the "city of Rome" was limited in size, compared to the size of the stage. Often, the more spectacular of these pieces of scenery were small enough to be curtained or otherwise hidden at the back and then "discovered" by pulling a curtain (or opening the pavilion, if such a thing existed, between the doors of the Globe). In certain plays in all three theatres, set pieces were on the stage and in full view of the audience for long periods of time, even for the whole play, and medieval simultaneity was exploited in its full sense.

The permanent professional theatres were places of show and of spectacle, despite the visual isolation of individual pieces against the rear wall. Static spectacle in the form of large pieces—ships, a hell-mouth, castles, and caves—mixed with the kinetic spectacle of such traditional pageantry as crowds with banners, devils emerging from hell, and throned figures. With machinery, magical appearances and disappearances were possible; flying was, if not common, certainly possible. The very lack of scenery allowed for a rapid change of place and for the presentation of exciting events: battles, duels, love scenes, and murders.

Costumes

Increasing stability and increasing wealth allowed the most successful companies to match their elaboration of scenery with elaborate costumes. There was no substantive change from the principles of medieval and earlier costumes, however; intentional archaism, exoticism, and show continued to be important. Certain national dress was made recognizable on the stage, perhaps for comic purposes. The emblematic costuming of classical divinities was an extension of the ideas of costumes for God and the angels in Christian drama. Allegorical characters gave imaginative possibilities, and a pageant like the Seven Deadly Sins in Christopher Marlowe's *Doctor Faustus* was a visual feast. Some attempt was made to suggest classical costume, although the usual practice was to put rather vaguely Greek–Roman items (a breastplate or a piece of drapery) over the dress of the day.

Costume remained a mixture. Unity of design was probably not even considered. Often, actors supplied their own clothes—or bought clothes for the purpose from used-clothes dealers, where the cast-off finery of the gentry and nobility were available—without regard for what other actors would be wearing. Where the matter was considered, emblem prevailed over image, but theatricalism was probably more important than either. Pageantry—show, finery, and spectacle—was preferred over either historical accuracy or imitation of contemporary life.

The Audience

These theatres were popular, but not necessarily either democratic or universal. They had an ascending price structure, and they had segregated audience areas that gave preference to an elite, just as the religious theatre had. In London, the private theatres appear to have catered to an even narrower audience than the public ones.

The audience areas were differentiated by price. Admission to the yard, the *parterre*, or the *patio* was the cheapest (one penny in London) and was "general admission." In Madrid and Paris, it was this money that went to the actors, and so playing to the standing-room people was the actors' way of guaranteeing their bread and butter. Admission to the other audience areas was by additional payment at their entrances; in Madrid, there were also benches close to the stage on the *patio* that could be rented. There were various formulas during the period for dividing the income from these other areas between landlord and actors in both Madrid and Paris; by and large, the income from them was about the same as that from the standing room. New plays or special performances, of course, had different price scales and different formulas; often, when the court were not in the city, the prices were lower.

In London, a second penny was paid for "scaffold seating" and a third for a "quiet standing," although literal standing room was probably not meant. To sit on the stage or in one of the "lords' rooms" (special boxes) cost even more, in many cases payable directly to the actors because entrance was made through the tiring house.[17]

Women, as we have said, were given separate seating in Madrid, and there were police officials present to guarantee their secure exit from the theatre into the street. There is debate about the kind and number of women who went to the theatre in London and Paris. Certainly, they were far outnumbered by men, and, especially in London, the propriety of a "decent" woman's attending the public playhouse was questionable.

The standing-room areas allowed considerable freedom of movement; the presence of vendors made for motion and bustle. One historian's description of the patrons of the *parterre* as a "howling mob"[18] seems too strong; and although the regulars of the *patio* were called *mosqueteros* because of their sting, they cannot have been uncontrollable. These audiences were varied, lively, and demanding, but they loved the theatre.

Plays and Playwrights

This period (1575–1620) includes at least part of the great ages of drama in England and Spain. The French drama was inferior to the English and the Spanish in quality, although it would make up for that lack after about 1630. Italian drama was putting its energy into Renaissance forms, and German drama seemed locked into imitations of carnival plays, Fools' plays, and the works of touring English companies.

Elizabethan Drama. The time from the fairly crude dramas of the innyard professionals to the greatness of Shakespeare was short—barely a generation. There is no easy explanation for the spectacular heights that were reached, but the reasons include:

1. *Renaissance influence.* The English looked more to Rome than to Greece in this period, most of all to Horace, Cicero, and the Roman playwrights. From Cicero came oratory. From Horace, they took generic distinctions between comedy and tragedy, although they hardly were strict about them; they ignored the "Horatian file," the emphasis on time and care in composition. From Plautus, they took exuberance and complicated comic plotting; from Terence, elegance of language and an example of a graceful and high-minded, even romantic, comedy. From Seneca, some tragic playwrights took:

1. Powerful, often bloody subjects, such as revenge.
2. Ghosts, portents, curses, and doom sayers.
3. *Sententiae* (pithy statements).
4. Five-act structure.
5. (Perhaps) the chorus, although Elizabethan chorus figures were much like many of the "expositors" of medieval plays.

2. *Italian and continental vernacular literature.* Italy had become the symbol of worldly sophistication. On the positive side was the Petrarchan sonnet and works like *The Courtier*, which gave an ideal of manners; on the negative was Machiavelli's *The Prince*, whose cynicism made Machiavelli's name a synonym for the devil. Both continental poetry and continental romance gave character types, plots, and a poetic to English drama, and a work like the Spanish prose romance *Celestina* influenced

FIGURE 9.16
Leading Playwrights, 1500–1650

England

John Rastell, b. 1475	Interludes: *The Four Elements*, 1517
Henry Medwall, fl. 1490–1500	*Fulgens and Lucrece*, 1496; interludes
John Heywood, 1497–1580	Interludes: *The Four P's*, ca. 1520
Nicholas Udall, 1505–1556	*Ralph Roister Doister*, ca. 1551, comedy on Latin model
"Mister S." (William Stevenson, ca. 1521–1575?)	*Gammer Gurton's Needle*, ca. 1555; comedy with Vice, some Latin elements
Thomas Norton (1532–1583) and Thomas Sackville (1536–1608)	*Gorboduc*, 1562, 1st English tragedy
Robert Lyly, ca. 1554–1606	*Endymion*, ca. 1588
George Peele, 1556–1596	*The Old Wives' Tale*, 1596, chivalric burlesque
Robert Greene, ca. 1560–1592	*The Honorable History of Friar Bacon and Friar Bungay*, ca. 1591
Thomas Kyd, 1558–1594	Revenge tragedy, Senecan influence: *The Spanish Tragedy*, ca. 1588
Christopher Marlowe, 1564–1593	Sweeping tragedy in vigorous blank verse, the "mighty line": *Doctor Faustus*, 1589; *Tamburlaine the Great* (2 parts) 1587–1588; *The Jew of Malta*, 1589–1590
Thomas Dekker, ca. 1572–1632	City comedy: *The Shoemaker's Holiday*, 1599
Ben Jonson, 1572–1637	"Comedy of humours": *Volpone*, 1605–1606; *Epicene*, 1609; *Bartholomew Fair*, 1614; *The Staple of News*, 1626; tragedies: *Sejanus*, 1603
George Chapman, ca. 1560–1634	Senecan tragic melodrama: *Busy D'Ambois*, ca. 1602; popular for a century
John Marston, ca. 1576–1634	Cynical mixed genre: *The Malcontent*, 1604
John Webster, ca. 1580–1634	*The Duchess of Malfi*, 1614
Francis Beaumont (1584–1616) and John Fletcher (1579–1625)	Together, singly, and with other people wrote plays that remained popular through the century: *The Maid's Tragedy*, *Philaster*, both c. 1610
John Ford, 1586–1639	Dark, sometimes lurid tragedy: *The Broken Heart*, 1629
James Shirley, 1596–1666	Social comedy, bridge to next period: *Hyde Park*, 1632; *The Lady of Pleasure*, 1635

France

Etienne Jodelle, 1532–1573	Renaissance tragedy and comedy: *Eugène*, 1552
Jacques Grévin, ca. 1538–1570	Comedy: *Les Esbahis*
Paul de Larivey, ca. 1540–ca. 1612	*The Wits*, 1579 (*commedia* influence)
Théophile de Vian	*Pyrame*, 1621
Aléxandre Hardy, ca. 1575–ca. 1631	Usually called the first professional French playwright, with hundreds of plays
Jean de Rotrou, 1609–1650	First translation of Lope de Vega (1629); *Lost Opportunities*, 1633
Paul Scarron, 1610–1660	*Jodelet, or the Master-Valet* (for the comic actor Jodelet)

Spain

Bartolome de Torres Naharro, d. 1524	1st author of *comedias*: *Himenea*, 1517
Lope de Rueda, 1505–1565	Farces, religious *autos*
Gil Vicente, fl. 1514–1530	*comedias*
Miguel de Cervantes, 1547–1616	*The Siege of Numancia*, c. 1590
Lope de Vega, 1562–1635	As many as 500 plays; said to have originated the *comedias de capa y espada*; highly varied works: *Fuenteovejuna* (c. 1615); *Castelvines y Monteses* ca. 1608 (a version of the Romeo and Juliet story); *Punishment Without Revenge*, 1635; comedy, *Belisa's Tricks*, 1634
Juan Ruiz de Alarcon y Mendoza, ca. 1581–1639	27 Plays, including *La verdad Sospechosa* (*Suspicious Truth*) 1628
Tirso de Molina, ca. 1571–1642	*El Burlador de Sevilla* (*The Trickster of Seville*, i.e., Don Juan) before 1625
Jose de Valdevielso, ca. 1560–1638	Religious plays: *El Perigrino*
Pedro Calderon de la Barca, 1600–1681	Perhaps most famous of Spanish dramatists for poetic genius, intellectual depth. *La Vida es Sueno* (*Life is a Dream*) ca. 1636; *El Magico Prodigioso* (*The Wonder-working Magician*) 1637; *El Medico de Su Honora* (*Doctor to His Own Honor*) 1635; *autos*

Note; The Spanish Golden Age produced thousands of plays, many of which were imitated, translated or adapted in France, to have a subsequent influence in England (especially after 1660). The elements of intrigue in both *capa y espada* (cloak and sword) and English romance proved very durable.

many English plays. It is hardly accidental that so many English plays have foreign settings; the settings often reflect an origin, and at the same time—and more important—give an aura of the exotic and the romantic to the work.

3. *English tradition.* By the time of Elizabeth, English was a vernacular with a rich poetic tradition behind it. It abounded in lyric poetry with images drawn from nature; at the same time, it was rooted in sophisticated literary work like Chaucer's. The vocabulary was large and still growing; the poetic devices had been used but not overused; and metrical patterns were being explored, with blank verse already emerging as dominant. In addition, there was the rich tradition of native drama, which contributed:

1. Mixed tone.
2. Complexity and multiplicity of plot.
3. Large casts.
4. Interest in moral concerns (formerly religious ones) that lay at the center of the culture.
5. Characters from many social levels.
6. Symbolic and allegorical character, action, and figure.

Types of Elizabethan Drama. By the end of the Elizabethan period, English drama covered a broad range of types, including:

1. *Satiric comedy,* which mocked contemporary types and behaviors and whose tone varied from the savagery of Ben Jonson's *Volpone* to the good-natured fun of Francis Beaumont's *Knight of the Burning Pestle.*
2. *Romantic comedy,* a benign comedy of love and its follies and joys, of which Shakespeare's *As You Like It* is a superb example.
3. *City comedy,* satisfying the London audience's appetite for a mirror of itself, like Thomas Dekker's *The Shoemaker's Holiday.*
4. *Domestic tragedy,* a relatively rare form with an outstanding example in the anonymous *Arden of Feversham.*

5. *Revenge tragedy,* with numerous examples, from Thomas Kyd's *Spanish Tragedy* through *Hamlet* to Cyril Tourneur's *Revenger's Tragedy.*
6. *Villain tragedy,* a form of great vigor and popularity that focused on the Renaissance problem of how aggressive individual behavior could be balanced with Christian precept. One answer was to make the secular and aggressive individual a villain but at the same time to make him heroic in stature, as in *Macbeth.*
7. *History plays,* many of which were based on the *Chronicles* of Raphael Holinshed and showed English history in a light favorable to Elizabeth and the Tudors, as in Shakespeare's *Richard III.*

William Shakespeare **(1564–1616)** *and Other Elizabethan Dramatists.* Happily, this active theatre needed plays in quantity, and young men in need of money turned to it readily. Some were university-trained—the so-called University Wits (including John Lyly and Christopher Marlowe); some were intellectuals like Ben Jonson; some, like Shakespeare, were men on the make with some education and great ambition. They had certain things in common: they all came to early manhood at the time The Theatre was built, or after; their formative years saw the end of the medieval religious drama in England; their education, however scant, gave them access to the Latin classics; and they were all turned loose to make their own way in a world of competition and opportunism.

It is said that Shakespeare looms in the midst of English literature like a mountain. He is still the most widely produced dramatist in English, not only in England, but also throughout the English-speaking world, Germany, Russia, and even the Orient. His plays seem to speak outside of time to many audiences; they survived rewriting in the eighteenth century to dominate much of the nineteenth-century repertory, and that dominance continues.

FIGURE 9.17

A scene from Thomas Kyd's *Spanish Tragedy* from a seventeenth-century edition. If correct, it shows a simultaneous set piece (the arbor), a number of properties, a black mask, and representative costumes. However, it may be entirely invented. [From *Appleton's.*]

Shakespeare wrote in the forms already noted above, in most cases surpassing the forms, so that calling *Hamlet* a "revenge tragedy" is like calling a Rolls-Royce a car. He often built on plays of the recent past: *Hamlet* itself was a giant leap from an earlier *Hamlet* that may have been the work of Kyd. He was not remarkably different from his contemporaries in either form or treatment, with the considerable exceptions that he was an unquestionably greater poet and that he almost always created plays of great internal coherence. That is, he stamped a poetic integration on each work, so that his plays rarely seem as careless or as arbitrary as those of many others. They are just as exuberant, but the exuberance is part and parcel of the work.

Typically, the Shakespearean play has a central plot, plus a political or social "overplot" that gives it breadth, and several subplots that connect at points to the central one. Although the incidents themselves bind these levels together, they are also united through subject matter and through poetic imagery. Such an integrated but multilevel set of actions was one of Shakespeare's appeals to his own audience, for

whom the world—or at least England—was an integrated whole. Shakespearean drama, then, whether comic or tragic, was a coherent image of a coherent world, and in that coherence lay much of its impact. No other playwright of the period, with the possible exception of Ben Jonson, was able to achieve coherence so well.

After his death, Shakespeare's plays were gathered into a collection called by modern scholars the First Folio edition of his works (1623): its division of the plays into tragedies, comedies, and histories is still followed. These categories do not adequately express the breadth of his creative ability, however, and many of his plays defy easy categorization.

Shakespeare was a "Tudor apologist" in his history plays. The approach gives the plays the focus and shape that an objective history would lack; they may sometimes be poor history, but they are superior drama. Shakespeare's comedies range from the Plautine *Two Gentlemen of Verona* to the mature and poetic *Tempest*. They include some of the best-loved plays and the most desirable roles in English dramatic literature, ranging from low comics like Launcelot Gobbo in *The Merchant of Venice* to the witty Beatrice and Benedick in *Much Ado About Nothing* to the autumnal, bittersweet jester Feste of *Twelfth Night*.

It was in tragedy, however, that his late poetic genius seemed to find its fullest expression, and his concerns came from the very heart of the Elizabethan world: guilt and action in *Hamlet*, ambition and opportunism in *Macbeth*, and the very nature of the human animal in *King Lear*.

Shakespeare was an actor who played such roles as Adam in his own *As You Like It* and a comic part in Ben Jonson's *Every Man in His Humour*. His dramaturgy was of the stage and not of the study, probably because of his professional experience. He was a supreme welder of the dramatic and the poetic image, so that his plays abound in visual emblems that subtly and overtly coincide with the imagery of the language. They are the best examples of the legacy

FIGURE 9.18

The Plays of Shakespeare

Histories

The First Part of King Henry the Sixth, 1591–1592
The Second Part of King Henry the Sixth, 1592
The Third Part of King Henry the Sixth, 1592
The Tragedy of King Richard the Third, 1592–1593
The Tragedy of King Richard the Second, 1594–1595
The Life and Death of King John, before 1598
The First Part of King Henry the Fourth, 1597
The Second Part of King Henry the Fourth, 1598
The Life of King Henry the Fifth, 1599
The Famous History of the Life of King Henry the Eighth, 1613

Comedies

The Comedy of Errors, 1592–1593
The Taming of the Shrew, ca. 1594
The Two Gentlemen of Verona, ca. 1593
Love's Labor's Lost, before 1598
A Midsummer Night's Dream, 1594–1595
The Merchant of Venice, ca. 1595–1596
Much Ado About Nothing, 1598
As You Like It, 1599
Twelfth Night, or What You Will, 1600–1601
The Merry Wives of Windsor, ca. 1599
All's Well That Ends Well, ca. 1601–1604
Measure for Measure, 1601–1604
Pericles, before 1608
Cymbeline, 1610
The Winter's Tale, 1610–1611
The Tempest, 1611

Tragedies

The Tragedy of Titus Andronicus, 1593–1594
The Tragedy of Romeo and Juliet, 1594–1595
The Tragedy of Julius Caesar, 1599
The Tragedy of Hamlet, Prince of Denmark, 1600–1601
The Tragedy of Troilus and Cressida, 1602
The Tragedy of Othello, the Moor of Venice, 1602
The Tragedy of King Lear, 1606
The Tragedy of Macbeth, 1606
The Tragedy of Antony and Cleopatra, 1607–1608
The Tragedy of Coriolanus, 1607–1609
Timon of Athens, ca. 1606–1609

These categories hardly suffice to show the range of the plays. The list does reveal Shakespeare's remarkable productivity. *Pericles* is not entirely Shakespeare's; like other dramatists, he took a hand in other plays, including, perhaps, *A Yorkshire Tragedy* and, with John Fletcher, *The Two Noble Kinsmen.*

of medieval pageantry—great, speaking theatrical spectacles.

Spain and Lope de Vega. Although the actor–playwright Lope de Rueda set the precedent for the professional theatres, it was Lope de Vega (1562–1635) who was Spain's first great playwright. One of the earliest writers of *autos sacramentales,* he was also one of the most prolific authors of the secular tragicomedies called *comedias.* His play *Fuenteovejuna* is still frequently performed.

The behavioral code called by the Spanish *honor,* as well as the Christian and Catholic struggles of moral action, became the serious concerns of the *comedias.* Spain developed independently of the rest of Europe in this subject matter, which gives the *comedias* the "uniqueness" that some scholars find there. One of them has written that "the Spanish Theater of the Golden Age . . . is unique when seen within the cultural area of Western Europe. . . . Spain . . . sustained the theocentric concept of life and man. The rest of Europe changed to the anthropocentric view. . . ."[19]

Stage Three: The End of Simultaneity (ca. 1620–1650)

The period from about 1620 to 1650 marks the end of simultaneity in England and France and its ossification in Madrid. The furor surrounding the creation of the first permanent theatres was over. Actors were increasingly favored at court and often played there; in Paris, Cardinal Richelieu gave his important patronage to the theatre. There was pressure to change, however. The audience of English theatre became more exclusively upper class as the smaller, indoor theatres were favored; Richelieu and those around him were aggressive in trying to drive medieval elements from the French theatre and to drag in neoclassicism, almost by force.

The English theatres were closed in 1642 by an act of Parliament when the open conflict between Puritans and Loyalists was most bitter. The Loyalists lost; the king was beheaded; and the theatres remained closed. Sporadic and surreptitious playing went on here and there in London, but the regularity of theatregoing was shattered and the popular theatre was crushed.

When Paris's two leading theatres both converted to Italianate scene systems in about 1644–1647, the Paris theatre, like that in London, ceased to be medieval.

The years between 1615 and 1645 saw the following developments.

New Playhouses

The rate of building declined, but the theatres that appeared after 1620 were significant as perfected examples of their kind.

The Théâtre du Marais, Paris. Paris is supposed to have had at least two hundred build-

---

FIGURE 9.19

Permanent Playhouses, ca. 1575–1650

Madrid

Corral de Burguillos, 1574–ca. 1584
Corral de la Pecheca, 1574–ca. 1584
Corral de Puente, ca. 1576–1579 (but some use until 1584)
Corral de la Cruz, 1579–18th century
Corral del Principe, 1582–18th century

Paris

Hôtel de Bourgogne, 1547–1647	(major reconstruction) (first professionals c. 1578)
Théâtre du Marais, 1634–1644	(fire; rebuilt in non-simultaneous form)

London

(1st) Blackfriars, 1576–ca. 1584	Private (children)
The Theatre, 1576–1597	(demolition; timbers used to build 1st Globe)
The Curtain, 1577–ca. 1630	Public
The Rose. 1587–ca. 1610(?)	Public
The Swan, 1595–ca. 1632	Public (but little used)
Paul's, c. 1599–ca. 1608	Private (children; scanty information)
(1st) Globe, 1599–1613	Public (Shakespeare and Burbage's company)
(2nd) Blackfriars, 1600–c. 1655	Private (children until 1608; then adult company, winters, of Shakespeare)
(1st) Fortune, 1600–1621	(fire) Public
The Red Bull, 1605–c. 1665	Public (used after Restoration)
Whitefriars, c. 1608–1614	Private (children)
(2nd) Globe, 1614–1644	(demolition) Public
The Hope (Beargarden), 1614–1656	(demolition) Public (but little used)
Phoenix (Cockpit), 1617–after Restoration	Private
(2nd) Fortune, 1622–1649	(demolition) Public
Salisbury Court, 1629–1649	(demolition) Private

Amsterdam

Schouwburg, 1637–1664	(major reconstruction)

Note: There were more or less permanent theatres in London inns and less permanent ones in hotels and tennis courts in Paris; inns were also used in Madrid. The greater number of theatres in London has many causes: Multiplicity of jurisdictions; competitive enterprise and risk-taking (some of the theatres were failures and were little used); weather; and so on.

ings for the game of court tennis. Actors competing with the Hôtel de Bourgogne rented them as theatres. The courts' interiors were long (about a hundred feet) and narrow (thirty to forty feet), with boxes down one or both sides and the empty court taking up most of the building. A booth stage easily went up at one end. In the late 1620s, a troupe led by the actor Montdory rented a series of spaces, settling in 1633–34 in a tennis court in the section called the Marais (Marsh), where permanent alterations were made. The assistance of the playwright Pierre Corneille made the Marais "the leading troupe of Paris during the period."[20] The Marais appears to have been like the Bourgogne in its arrangement of *loges, paradis, parterre,* and *amphithéâtre,* but it may have held as many as fifteen hundred people.[21] It burned in 1644.

The Cockpit or Phoenix, London. Fashionable preference in London shifted from the public theatres to the private ones, which were smaller and more expensive, and where plays were done in the evening by artificial light. A number of these were built, including the second Blackfriars and the late (1629) Salisbury Court. Outstanding among the newcomers, however, was the Phoenix, also called the Cockpit in Drury Lane. Built about 1616–1617, it continued as "one of the two principal . . . theatres . . . after Blackfriars . . . the favorite resort of the gentry."[22] It had been built for cockfighting and was originally circular or polygonal. Recent scholarship has argued persuasively that drawings by Inigo Jones are the plans for this theatre, an elegant little structure with a semicircular end opposite the stage, and with seating that combined Renaissance and Italian models with the familiar theatres of the period. The former cockpit was apparently converted to the audience area; the stage, for all its embellishments, was of the established English type.[23] Like the Cockpit-in-Court that Jones designed in 1628, the Cockpit in Drury Lane "functioned like . . . an Elizabethan public theatre."[24]

FIGURE 9.20

A conjectural reconstruction by Richard Leacroft of a private theatre based on drawings by Inigo Jones in the Worcester College Collection. [Courtesy of Richard Leacroft. First published in *Theatre Notebook.*]

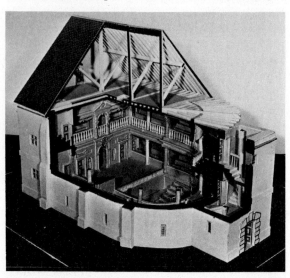

Plays and Playwrights

The word *mannerism* has been applied to English plays of this period, meaning a concern with form and style for their own sakes. A refinement, perhaps an overrefinement, of technique can be seen, sometimes at the expense of humanity and theatricality. One scholar finds "a narrowing of intellectual interest . . . a concern with manners and decorum . . . at the expense of larger moral and political issues, and . . . a marked critical bias toward the aesthetics of form, so that 'Nature' and 'Truth' become much less important than 'Art' as criteria of excellence."[25]

London. Shakespeare had died in 1616. Ben Jonson continued to write well into this last period for both the professional theatre and the court, but his best comedies were behind him. With increasing ferocity, the later plays of the second period had shown a cynicism that was almost offensive; now, that negativism was

FIGURE 9.21

Frontispiece to *The Wits*, published after the Restoration but believed to show an earlier stage. It has been called "The Interior of the Red Bull Playhouse," probably incorrectly. The thrust stage, the curtain, the upper level, and the footlights are very interesting elements; compare with Figure 9.20. [From Besant, *Stuarts*.]

translated into what one scholar has called "distrust." John Ford (1586–1639) and James Shirley (1596–1666) were probably the best of this final group. Ford's tragedies were sensational and were sometimes more interested in psychopathology than in tragic action; Shirley's comedies of the 1630s looked forward to the comedies of manners of the next age and, like them,

took much of their humor and genuine delight from the mores of "good society."

Paris.　In France, the prolific Aléxandre Hardy lived until 1631–1632, writing tragicomedies for the Hôtel de Bourgogne almost to the end (perhaps five hundred in all). He was eclipsed, however, by a cluster of younger writers, including Jean de Rotrou (1609–1650), who at nineteen was writing for the Hôtel de Bourgogne and who was the first to translate a play by Lope de Vega for French production; Jean Mairet (1606–1684), an early proponent of neoclassicism; and Pierre Corneille (1606–1684). Corneille was to be the one to carry French drama from medieval to neoclassical drama.

Madrid.　Pedro Calderon de la Barca (1600–1681) is generally conceded to have been the greatest of Spanish playwrights. In serious dramas like *La vida es sueno* (*Life Is a Dream*), he grappled with many of the same "theocentric" problems as Lope de Vega, but with a poetic genius perhaps equal to Shakespeare's. Calderon also wrote the plays called *cloak-and-sword plays*, highly charged dramas of love and honor in which dueling, trickery, and romantic passion were paramount. The cloak-and-sword play was an enormously popular form and continued to be so well into the eighteenth century. As well, Calderon was an author of *autos* and plays for the court. He left the professional theatre about 1640. With the extended closing of the Madrid theatre from 1644 to 1649 for royal mourning (and perhaps because of church opposition), the Golden Age was effectively over.

A Parallel in the Low Countries.　Although not producing an equivalent drama, Holland and parts of what are now Belgium saw a theatrical development not unlike that of France and England. In the late sixteenth and early seventeenth centuries, the chambers of rhetoric (*rederykerkamer*) built temporary, open-air stages for allegorical and rhetorical performance. Often embellished with Renaissance architectural de-

FIGURE 9.22

The Schouwburg, Amsterdam, ca. 1640. [Bodleian Library, Johnson Collection of Ephemera.]

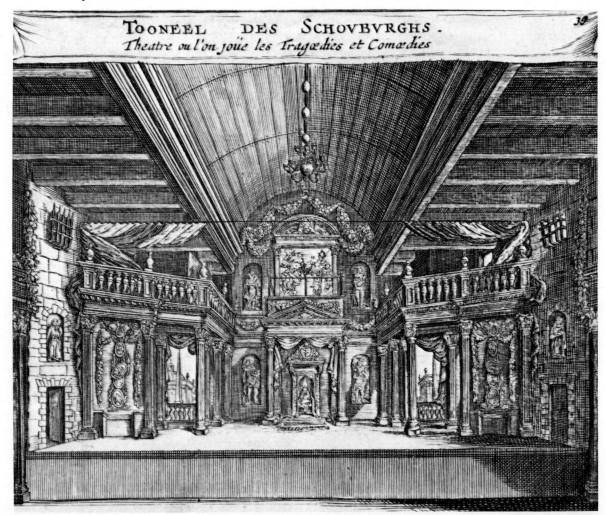

TOONEEL DES SCHOVBVRGHS.
Theatre ou l'on joüe les Tragœdies et Comœdies

tails, they showed some of the same blending of the Renaissance and the medieval that was seen elsewhere in Europe; the influence of both the booth stage (universal in the popular theatre of the area) and medieval simultaneity were readily seen. Therefore, when a permanent theatre was built in Amsterdam in 1637, it maintained the mixture. The first Amsterdam Schouwburg used simultaneous settings around a large, unlocalized stage; neo-Roman architectural details; an audience area of *loges*, curved benches, and a *parterre*.

Staging

Both France and Spain saw a considerable increase in so-called machine plays—spectacles for which the playscript was most of all a springboard for the use of stage machinery. Still, the

FIGURE 9.23

Simultaneous settings at the French court, Clermont (1656). [From Bourgeois.]

FIGURE 9.24

Simultaneous setting by Mahelot (probably 1630s). This redrawing shows the quite different mansions on each side downstage and the back scene, center, that may have filled the space between the stage and the upper level; if so, the clouds were probably on a separate hanging above and behind the upper stage. The unity that appears to have been achieved by relating all the scenes to a single vanishing point may merely have been Mahelot's wishful thinking in the sketch, or it may be an accurate reflection of a Renaissance impulse to unify the diverse medieval pieces visually. [From Bapst (see also Figure 3.8).]

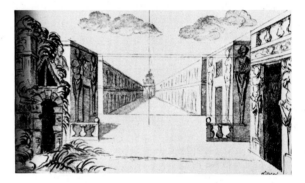

principle of simultaneity ruled, and in France, there was one remarkable application of it. At the Hôtel de Bourgogne, medieval set pieces were arranged in a scheme that was apparently more controlled artistically than any that had previously been used. Sketches of these settings by the *décorateur* Laurent Mahelot have been published as the *Mémoire de Mahelot*.[26] These are probably from the 1630s,[27] and many are for plays by Aléxandre Hardy. Many of the same set pieces are repeated in sketch after sketch—a cave, a ship, the same house. These were arranged, in Mahelot's drawings, into almost symmetrical groups with common perspective; if the drawings accurately show what the stage looked like, then the rather small stage of the Bourgogne had as many as seven different units in a U-shape around the sides and back, leaving a fairly sizable acting area (the place) in the center, with entrances at each side between the front of the stage and the first unit, as well as from or between the units themselves. The rearmost unit may have been some kind of painted back scene, and it has been suggested that it ran under the forward edge of the upper stage, although this cannot be told for certain from Mahelot's drawings.

Whatever their exact meaning, Mahelot's sketches are remarkable for what they symbolize about the persistence of medieval simultaneity in an age that was increasingly fascinated by Renaissance perspective and unity. The drawings themselves are definite attempts to give artistic unity to disparate elements, but we do not know if the unified perspective of the drawings was carried over to the settings.

These drawings mark, then, and fittingly, the end of a long theatrical tradition. Within twenty years, the London theatres would be closed, the Marais and the Bourgogne would be rebuilt with the raked stages of Italianate scenery, and the critical principles of neoclassicism would dominate French drama. The Middle Ages, which began with a simple three-line text sung in Latin and grew to magnificent dramatic spectacles of days' duration and the glory of Shakespeare and Calderon, were over.

ENDNOTES

1. Stephen D. Malin, "Four Doubled Figures in the Origins of English Folk Theatre," *Theatre Journal* 33, 1 (March 1981): 18–33.

2. F. J. Stopp, "Latin Plays at the Academy of Altdorf, 1577–1626," *Journal of European Studies* 4 (June 1974):189–213.

3. M. C. Bradbrook, *The Rise of the Common Player* (Cambridge, Mass.: Harvard University Press, 1962), p. 25.

4. N. C. Shergold, *A History of the Spanish Stage* (Oxford: Clarendon Press, 1967), p. 111.

5. W. Schrickx, "Commedia dell'arte Players in Antwerp," *Theatre Research International* 1 (February 1976): 79–86.

6. Shergold, p. 177.

7. Bradbrook, p. 44.

8. Andrew Gurr, *The Shakespearean Stage, 1574–1642* (Cambridge: Cambridge University Press, 1970), p. 19.

9. H. A. Rennert, *The Spanish Stage in the Time of Lope de Vega* (New York: Hispanic Society of America, 1909), pp. 183, 203.

10. Gurr, p. 9.

11. G. E. Bentley, *The Jacobean and Caroline Stage* (Oxford: Oxford University Press, 1968), Vol. 6, p. v.

12. Gurr, p. 95.

13. W. L. Wiley, *The Early Public Theatre in France* (Cambridge: Harvard University Press, 1960), p. 133 ff.

14. W. L. Wiley, "The Hôtel de Bourgogne," *Studies in Philology* 70 (December 1973): 85.

15. Shergold, pp. 384, 177 ff.

16. Shergold, pp. 395–396.

17. Bradbrook, pp. 57–58.

18. Wiley, "Hôtel de Bourgogne," p. 65.

19. Arnold G. Reichenberger, "A Postscript to Professor Thomas Austin O'Connor's article on the *comedia*," *Hispanic Review* 43 (Summer 1975): 290.

20. Wiley, *Public Theatre*, p. 173.

21. Ibid., p. 176.

22. Bentley, p. 47.

23. John Orrell, "Inigo Jones at the Cockpit," *Shakespeare Survey* 30 (1977): 157–168.

24. Leonie Star, "Inigo Jones and the Use of Scenery at the Cockpit-in-Court," *Theatre Survey* 19 (May 1978): 37, 47.

25. Michael Neill, " 'Wits Most Accomplished Senate': The Audience of the Caroline Private Theaters," *Studies in English Literature* 18, 2 (Spring 1978): 341–60.

26. Henry Carrington Lancaster, ed., *Le Mémoire de Mahelot* (Paris: E. Champion, 1920).

27. Wiley, "Hôtel de Bourgogne,"p. 69.

10

Simultaneous World, Simultaneous Stage

Introduction

In this chapter, we try to relate the simultaneous theatre to its world, although we risk damaging generalizations in speaking of a medieval world that embraced a thousand years of history. We cannot pretend that the medieval world was a monolith; we know that there were important class differences, craft and professional differences, geographic differences, and gender differences that made the world of medieval women different from that of men at all social levels.

Yet, we believe that there was a commonality that makes cautious generalization possible. Life was not compartmentalized in the way that modern life is; existence was integrated—the individual's home with his work, his work with his religion, his sense of self with the selves of others. Thus, dangerous as generalization is—and we urge attention to those problems discussed in Part One—the integrated nature of the period justifies a study of its common perception.

Medieval Stages

We tried to identify the common characteristics of medieval theatres over several centuries. We identified *simultaneity* of setting; the concept of the *emblem* in acting, costuming, and properties, as well as in character; and the use of *found spaces* rather than specialized theatre structures, until very late. As well, we cited the importance of *multiple audience viewpoints* and, in

the drama, *large* or *cosmic actions* with large casts, complex interaction and flexible time-schemes. Finally, we saw the importance of *religious subject matter* and an *elevated language*, usually poetry or sung lyric.

None of these characteristics itself defines a medieval theatre. Some medieval theatres lacked or altered some of them. At one extreme, Mahelot's settings of ca. 1630 were more medieval than Renaissance because of their simultaneity, which had more visual importance than his attempts to unify them. At the other extreme, the tenth-century *Visitatio Sepulchri* did not have a large cast or complex action, but its subject matter, its sung Latin text, its extreme emblemism, and the very earliness of its arrival in the theatre made it medieval. Yet, we cannot pretend that the theatre of Mahelot and the theatre of Bishop Ethelwold were identical. One was ready to leap to neoclassicism; the other had just emerged from ceremonial. Thus, medieval theatre must be seen as a spectrum, and its examples must be identified by their location on that spectrum. In the discussion that follows, we urge that different examples be considered and that thought be given to the different ideas that they inspire.

Question: What Defined Medieval Theatrical Space?

In modern use, *found space* is defined partly by our knowledge of formal theatrical space: it is a conscious alternative. Until very late in the

FIGURE 10.1

God's universe, with God at the center and larger than all other figures, and a huge and hideous hell-mouth at bottom. [Courtesy of the Fitzwilliam Museum, Cambridge.]

Middle Ages, however, found space was simply itself and had no implication of "differentness" or of being what is now called *alternative theatre*.

More basic than the idea of found space, however, was the matter of the control—the definition—of theatrical space in the Middle Ages. It appears that medieval theatre people felt no urgency to focus audience vision as modern theatres do, that is, with a darkened auditorium and a brightly lighted stage. The medieval audience understood the limits of the acting area *and* accepted the authenticity of what went on within it (a set piece here, a set piece there, a costumed actor) without, so far as we know, the intense lighting, the predetermined stage shape, or the extensive scenic backdrop that modern audiences usually find essential. Extreme digression from the definition of the acting area (open sky, a background of audience faces and bodies, city streets) was not very distracting, it seems.

Did the audience "fill in" the gaps imaginatively? By the time of the permanent public theatres, such filling in of space was being done, especially among the erudite (the density of descriptive language suggests this), but for most of the period, an irrelevant background was not filled in by either language or scenery. Whether, for some reason, the background began to intrude on the theatrical space, or whether it became necessary to authenticate the theatrical space with a background, it does seem to be true that one of the symptoms of the waning of medieval perception was the urge to have a background. This may have been a factor in the slackening of the cycles, especially those staged on wagons, where the size of the set piece was small in the field of vision. It may have been a factor, too, in the urge toward indoor spaces with focused playing spaces that, in their most extreme form (the Hôtel de Bourgogne, for example), put the stage at the end of a long space and completely enclosed it. The result was enforced focus on the rectangle within the enclosure (a frame). Within the enclosure—in the dimension away from the audience—Mahelot's settings provided a surround, which, although made up of diverse units, was complete.

If we look at the pre-Mahelot theatre, however, we see less and less of either framing or background before about 1500. What defined this earlier theatrical space? Obvious as it sounds, one answer is *the limits of found space* (a city wall, a church, a hall screen); another is *the audience itself*. In those theatres where the audience was around the playing area (the majority of medieval spaces, we believe), the audience was a defining factor, even when the audience moved back and forth to accommodate the action.

The actor also defined space. Although sometimes assisted by ushers (*stytelers*), he carried his playing area with him—which is to say, he carried his reality with him. A further question, however, is just how large the space between *two* actors could have been while remaining definable theatrical space. The single actor defined "the theatre" as being the space he needed to turn, gesture, and caper; two actors defined it, perhaps, as the space needed to interact. The actor and the set piece defined it as an elastic space between them; groups of actors in procession actually carried theatre space with them.

We may cite two conventions that we think were part of this sense of space. In one, *the actor created place*, sometimes by coming from an identifiable set piece, sometimes by announcing where he was. However, *in the absence of such localization, the space could remain unplaced*, and the audience seems to have felt no need for placeness. Many interludes occurred in this no-place, as did many scenes in the plays of Shakespeare and his contemporaries, as well as older plays, and it appears that *lack* of place was not thought "unreal" or "fantastic." In the broadest sense, the actor made the theatre in the Middle Ages, and even Hamlet can tell us all we need to know about situation and place: "Now I am alone." On the other hand, it is questionable that if an actor entered from an identifiable set piece, he was necessarily at that place unless he announced that he was. Most certainly, when the actor came from one set piece of a Mahelot simultaneous setting and announced that he was "at" that place, the visual presence of the other set pieces could be ignored. Such a practice made simultaneity not only a visual principle of medieval art but also a practical matter of staging.

Other Arts

If we look at other medieval arts, we note the following.

Framing

Medieval painting is often not organized to conform to the familiar rectangular frame of later art—it is not, as it were, a glimpse of something seen through a window. The tendency of the rectangular frame to create a plane to which the size of objects is related is usually obviated. The "correct" size of the objects is thus not all-important, and the objects (saints or angels, for example) are often sized in terms of their hierarchy, not their physical dimensions.

This is not to say that medieval art was without internal harmony. On the contrary, it always tried to show a harmonious universe. That harmony was achieved, however, in ways other than perspective, framing, and a rigid imitation of reality.

Lack of Background

Byzantine mosaic had an important influence on medieval visual art, as Byzantine music and costume did on other arts. In Byzantine mosaic, broad areas were more-or-less blank—often of metallic gold—or abstractly patterned. Human figures were important; background was not. In the painting derived from mosiac, environments sometimes appeared, but they were conventionalized (emblematic) and often existed without any real-life spatial relationship to the figures. (Buildings and even cities looked small enough to step over, for example.) The truth that such art sought to convey was not a physical truth, then, but a spiritual and philosophical one.

Use of Existing Surface

Much medieval art was created to fill spaces defined by other conditions, for example, an area over a doorway, a window, or the sides of a reliquary. Much medieval art was a handmaiden to function. On the other hand, there was a

FIGURE 10.2

Art finds its own space, as on this twelfth-century decorated letter. [From Willemin.]

strong urge to decorate otherwise blank space, like the undersides of roof bosses and the supports of choir seats. As a result, much of art's space was found space.

The Culture

Two relevant attitudes seem to spring from the culture.

The Idea of Purpose

Medieval art was *instrumental* rather than self-justifying (there was little "art for art's sake.")

The purpose was sometimes decorative (as in letters in manuscripts), behind which was another purpose, the glorification of God and his works. The monastic who labored at illumination was as surely praising God as his fellows who were singing the Te Deum in the choir.

Sometimes, the purpose was didactic. Much of the society was illiterate, and pictures told stories. For the more sophisticated, symbolism added dimensions of meaning to poetry, painting, and sermons. Many people saw existence itself as didactic and symbolic, so that the entire world was permeated with didacticism.

Medieval men and women were both practical and spiritual. They believed that they lived in a purposeful universe and that the things that they did had purpose. Perhaps far more willingly than we, they accepted the existence of entities and then went about looking for their reason for being where and as they were (rather than the other, modern way, which is to question the existence first). They may therefore have been able to accept art in found places and to accept art without "explaining" or "justifying" backgrounds because they accepted the givens of life.

The God-Centered Universe

God was the Creator and God was the center. The human world was an uneasy place where many lived dangerously, their environment not made understandable by even rudimentary science. Change and uncertainty were common—weather, famine, disease. A dominant image was the "wheel of fortune," turned by a capricious hand. There had to be a pattern, however, although humans could not understand it because they were mired in sin and change.

One explanation of the nature of things was that God had created them as lessons. From the fall of kings to the fall of the sparrow, events were cautionary tales. People's task (if they accepted it, and many people, despite a nominal piety, did not) was to understand the lessons and then to achieve grace by abjuring sin and

the world of things. Penance, atonement, forgiveness, and the imitation of Christ were rejections of the world of things. Life lived merely *for life*, on the other hand, was a rejection of God's lessons and a further miring in sin.

Of what relevance, then, could the representation of surface reality have been? Only such relevance as could offer a lesson. All else could be left out. Both artist and audience were able to understand that lesson better without the clutter of a background, and so they accepted easily either the neutrality of a golden surface or the easily ignored backdrop of a familiar street in which a play was being performed.

Question: What Are the Authenticating Devices of Medieval Theatre?

The medieval audience did not expect to find the principal authentication of realistic theatre, the literal imitation of the real world. What, then, made medieval theatre internally coherent and authentic to that audience? That is, what convinced the medieval audience of the truthfulness and importance of what happened in the playing area?

It is not enough to say that the fact of theatre was its own authentication (that art, in other words, was its own justification). Certain forms of entertainment *were* so perceived, probably— juggling or acrobatics, for example.

Nor is it enough to say that the medieval audience thought that the theatre was actual life. Even the most naive of medieval peasants, at least after his first experience of theatre, knew that what he saw was not actual life, but an emblem of certain aspects of life.

Was it, then, the presence of the living actor that brought authentication? Did the actor create truth, just as he created space and place? He certainly brought immediacy. Yet, in many cases, the actor was known to the audience (for example, in the cycles, guildsmen played many roles for their townspeople), and so there must have been a disjunction between the known person and the assumed role. There might have been pleasure in watching a friend perform, but such pleasure hardly helps in bringing authenticity.

Authentication came, most probably, from the subject matter itself. Medieval drama was a constant reference to known materials, not from daily life but from what we may call cultural truth. There was a constant recall of such old materials as biblical stories and ideas from sermons and homilies. Novelty was not welcome until the end of the fifteenth century; evocation, resonance, and reminder—figure and prefigure, emblem and type—were the devices of a reinforcing art, not of an innovative one. The stories and characters of the cycles were known; an audience seeing God with Adam was experiencing a "truth" that had been present since childhood. Conviction may well have come as much, then, from the fidelity of the subject to the known model (the Gospels) as from the presence of the living actor or the lifelikeness of behavior or properties. In the moralities, on the other hand, fidelity to *acceptable* ideas—the symbolic presentation of Greed, for example—was authenticating.

The problem is not an easy one. We cannot really know what happened between medieval audience and medieval work of art. Watching a play of Noah, a modern audience sees a man, animals, a flood, and the ark. The medieval audience may, at the first and most important level, have seen the lesson instead, looking, as it were, through the man and the animals and the ark at the referents. We know that in some performances, for example, the animals were represented by two-dimensional paintings. Did the audience believe that these were "real" animals? Certainly not. Did they believe that the actors were "really" Noah and his wife? Very probably not. But did they believe that the biblical events of the Noah story had really happened? Yes, they did—and therein may lie all the difference, for the events of the play could

then be made truthful by seeming to correspond to "history."

By the sixteenth century, things were changing. Shakespeare's history plays are very different from the example of the Noah play, not least because they changed "history." Thus, one of the significant things that was happening as the period ended was that theatrical authentication was changing—which is another way of saying that the idea of truth was changing, which is another way of saying that the paradigm (the perception of the nature of nature) was changing.

Other Art: The Image of Man

God made man in His own image; therefore, God was shown as manlike, and humans were often shown in an idealized way. Perhaps because of the prevailing didactic tendency to show what should be rather than what was, particularizing details were often ignored. Although limbs were clearly shown, and such defining details as the swell of the abdomen and the navel were depicted, along with hair, beards, and facial features, the specific and the idiosyncratic were ignored. Muscles were not emphasized, nor were bony structures like the rib cage. Even vigorous figures like men at war often appeared almost detached. Eyes were often shown as seen from the front (as in Byzantine mosaic). Even in a proto-Renaissance work like the Martini-Memmi *Annunciation*, the Virgin's body seems soft, almost boneless, and she withdraws gracefully from the angelic words that float toward her against a golden background. It is the moment that interests the painter, not either the human passion or its physical expression.

However, one area—torture and suffering—was sometimes given gruesome attention. A northern Gothic school of sculpture created skeletal Christs. Hell and its torments were graphically depicted. Pain was emphasized. The depiction of the Devil shared the style, his ugliness and bestiality shown in imaginative de-

FIGURE 10.3

The frame is not a window; the background is not important; anatomy is not literal. Simone Martini's *Annunciation*. [From Vasari.]

tail. Sometimes, this diabolical literalism approached the comic, and grotesques were the result—the famous gargoyles on Notre Dame cathedral, for example, with their sly, evil faces and their drooping tongues. The same grotesquerie found its way into the common metaphor of cooking for hell's torments and of cooking implements—pans, forks, and grills—for the demons' emblems.

There was literalism in some medieval art, then. It varied geographically and it varied chronologically: as we have said, the period was a patchwork. Overall, however, we may say that art divided itself between the two aspects of existence that it knew: the ideal, which was "real" through received wisdom, faith, and the constant reinforcement of the Church; and the painful and unpleasant, which were "real" because they were inescapable in a world that lacked medicine, sanitation, central heating, good food, and painkillers. There was some tendency of art to polarize at both extremes—an ideal, Byzantine positive depiction; and a grotesque, brutal Gothic one.

One may ask by corollary, however, if there

was a connection between the Gothic grotesque and the comic. No necessary connection seems to have existed, but it is true that when evil was shown in many works it was shown in terms of this Gothic grotesque, and in the theatre it was often laughable. Not all comedy dealt with evil, to be sure—popular farce cannot be considered didactic in that way—but the comic in the religious plays usually did. It would be easy to make a step from this point to a suggestion that the comic in the plays was therefore more literal (or even "more realistic") than the noncomic, but the idea would not be a productive one.

Detail and physicality were, then, important mainly for the presentation of a special subject matter. Behind this use was the prevailing sense that the world of the senses—the world of surface and of objects—was flawed, temporary, and allied with sin (and hence with pain and the diabolical).

The Culture

There was a frequent split between aspiration and performance in much of medieval life. The ideal figures of the age—Christ, the Virgin, the wise king, the good knight—were pious, calm, and good, but the achievers of the period were active and emotional and "evil"—warriors, cynical bishops, greedy nobles.

There is no proof that men and women were any less human than they are now. Ambition, greed, love, guilt, and fear impelled them then as they do us now. Still, these things were culturally suspect. People might struggle to achieve worldly goals, but they were constantly told to work for contrition, confession, and penance. Such conflict contributed to great spasms of self-hatred, like the rages of the Dance of Death and flagellation.

The culture often had a deeply divided picture of itself. Its public one was idealized and aspired toward God. Everybody lived in the world of the senses, however, and so there were two claims on truth: the physical and the intellectual/spiritual. Art, frequently linked with

FIGURE 10.4

The literal frequently goes to the grotesque and is used to show torment. A Mirror of the World with hell's cooking pot, grimaces of pain, snakes, and insects; above, Christ throned, with stigmata and the gaunt body of the suffering Crucifixion. [From Petit de Julleville.]

piety, often showed the ideal but was tempted toward the literal, especially in its depictions of evil and pain.

Question: If Medieval Theatre Was Didactic, Why Was Such Attention Lavished on Spectacle?

By the time of the Fleury plays, spectacle was an important component of theatre; it became far more so in the cosmic or cycle theatre.

Particular attention was given to the *feints*, especially in showing the supernatural (miracles). Was the impulse didactic or exploitative? Certainly, the supernatural was *not* made merely conventional: heaven really seemed to open; angels really seemed to fly; and lightning—within the technology of the age—really seemed to strike. The Chronicler of Valenciennes said that the audience saw "Truth." This "truth," however, was a truth that could not be verified in the literal world. In what may now seem a curious artistic decision, the miraculous was given the texture of that same experience that in daily life was superficial and tainted. As well, the truthfulness was achieved partly by working against the laws of observable nature—gravity, distance, time, and death.

In the *Visitatio Sepulchri*, the rising of Christ is not shown, and the miraculous is represented by the showing of the cloth and the cross. By the time of the *Stella* plays and the Fleury Play-Book *Herod*, such miracles (spectacles) as the Christmas star were popular. The later cycles abounded in supernatural spectacles: the cherry tree, the Ascension, the raising of Lazarus. As didacticism, these events may have reinforced the "truth" for the credulous, but there must have been a large part of the audience for whom the trickery involved was quite directly a form of entertainment like juggling.

Other Arts

In no art but theatre could the supernatural be embodied in a form that gave the viewer full substitute experience. Paintings of miracles gave many symbols to the age but could hardly have been of the same order of experience as the events in the theatre. Narratives of miracles—as in sermons, for example—may have approached the theatre in their impact. Still, we must remember that most people believed in these miracles to begin with.

The Culture

Although credulous people became the butts of jokes, even among the pious, belief in the divinely caused supernatural was common. It is unclear just how such belief affected the viewing of theatrical representations, however. It seems that there may have been a general movement from an early (eleventh-century) acceptance of merely emblematic representations (the paradise of the *Jeu d'Adam,* for example) through an integration of spectacle into the cosmic dramas (perhaps through the fifteenth century) to a period of decadence when spectacle for its own sake took over as the audience, no longer either credulous or pious, simply wanted entertainment. (One of the criticisms leveled at the Confrérie de la Passion just before their 1548 suspension was that they appealed to the lowest level of their audience's taste for such stuff.) At the fifteenth-century height, there was probably appreciation both of the spectacular and of the technical facility with which it was achieved: Bishop Souzdal, seeing the Florentine performances, was fully aware of lines and pulleys, and much of his enthusiasm came from his understanding of the abilities of the *feinteurs.*

It is a commonplace of theatre that an audience's admiration of tricks is based on its own awareness of how difficult the tricks are: in an age of electricity, a bolt of lightning on the stage is not much, but in an age of candles, it is a wonder. Technicians must always work at the edge of the technology, and the *devysors* and Masters of Secrets were no exceptions.

Question: Was Simultaneity a Theatrical Expedient?

Simultaneous settings were seen by neoclassicists as naive and quaint, and they have never reappeared in the theatre in any important way. The principle of simultaneity is so different from the principle of illusionism that many realists have been unable to see how simultaneous settings could have been anything but very poor compromises with a necessity like cost or limited space.

Simultaneous settings make the environ-ment that the audience sees around the actor irrelevant as a representation of the world; that is, simultaneous settings cannot be seen as forceful environment (in the modern sense that environment determines character). Each piece can be decorative; each piece can determine place; each piece can contribute to spectacle and can make certain kinds of action possible (entering, hanging, flying). Inevitably, however, they exist as pieces of theatrical art and not as a uniform sample of the real world. If one believes that theatrical setting should be as convincing as the actor's body is, then simultaneous settings are an embarrassment.

Other Arts

In painting, sculpture, glass, and tapestry, scenes that showed different stages of a story were commonly presented on the same surface. They were "simultaneous." However, their scenes were not meant to be coexistent, for they typically had a sequence (the beginning, middle, and end of the story). Thus, there was a double time-scheme at work: that of the viewer, who saw all the scenes at once, and that of the scenes themselves, which had sequence.

Medieval scenes were also sometimes simultaneous in that they were presented with equal attractiveness and in the same format. Also, their order was not necessarily determined by a left-to-right, top-to-bottom sequence (as in a cartoon strip).

True simultaneity is impossible in narrative: the narrator can say "meanwhile" or "at the same time," but the experience of two narrated scenes cannot be simultaneous. In pictorial narrative, a linear structure with built-in order (the cartoon strip) is common in our own time. Juxtaposition in such a linear form is part of the artistic effect and makes possible cumulative statements—preparation, climax, and punch line. The medieval viewer did not always seek such effects, however. In many medieval simultaneous works, each scene made a statement and the whole made a statement, but there was not necessarily any cumulative effect.

In the theatre, the settings were simultaneous but the narrative was linear. A double time-scheme again prevailed: the audience viewed from an "upper" time that embraced the entire drama, while the scenes went forward at a "lower" time. At least by analogy, an emblem of existence was created: God's overarching time (or timelessness) embraced limited human time.

The Culture

Medieval existence was probably not as time-conscious as ours, as the relatively late invention of the clock may suggest. On the other hand, life was short and pleasure was fleeting. The dichotomy of human world–divine world was evident.

The time that man perceived was itself an instance of sin. Timelessness had been one of the experiences of Adam and Eve before the Fall; in sinning, they had started the human clock going. The pious believed that eternal life was a Christian goal, and that escape from time was the reward of contrition. Little wonder, then, that simultaneity was effective in the theatre, for it was a figure of timelessness—a visible reminder of the double time-scheme. Given the set of the medieval mind, it can be seen that simultaneity was not a compromise or an expedient, but a brilliant device.

Question: Was Medieval Theatre Popular Art?

A broad spectrum of society attended the great cycles. A much narrower part had seen the Latin music–dramas. The audience for the vernacular secular theatre in the sixteenth century began as a restricted one, often with coterie attendance (members of one college or one of the Inns of Court, or the friends of the printer–playwright John Rastell, for example), but it expanded to include a wide band.

It has been said that "every able-bodied man" of a medieval town was involved in the plays. Was every able-bodied man and woman therefore a part of the audience? (Women certainly attended the plays—Chaucer's Wife of Bath was one of them.) Perhaps, in the mid-fifteenth century in the large cities, most people saw at least a procession connected with the plays, but by the time of the more commercialized religious plays of the sixteenth century, a good part of the society either may have been excluded or may have gone elsewhere.

Exclusion because of an entrance fee does not of itself make such an art nonpopular, however. The question remains: Did it appeal to the whole society, even if some could not afford it? The answer appears to be that (setting aside the rural peasantry in England and France and the nonfree populations of other areas) in the fifteenth century it did, but that after 1500 the broad base was lost. When the professional theatre reached its fullest popularity, it, too, appealed to a wide part of the society (ca. 1600 in England, 1630 in France, and ca. 1590–1650 in Spain) but then declined. One scholar has estimated that an astounding one person in every eight attended the theatre in London at the end of Elizabeth's reign.

Other Arts

Painting and sculpture cannot be thought of as having been popular, except insofar as they appeared where people could not miss them. There were few consumers of painting and art for domestic use because of cost, although beautiful objects were sought by the wealthy. Poetry had coterie audiences for the literary romance, the courtly lyric, and works like Chaucer's, which were passed about in manuscript before the time of printing; ballads and songs were handed down in oral transmission and were widely enjoyed.

Theatre, then, may have been the only truly popular medieval art, although it may have been not so much popular as inescapably public. Like choral songs and the artful sermon, it was didactic art in a public situation, with added visual and emotional appeal and the advantage of happening only once a year (or less), so that it built up the expectations of a great event.

The Culture: Hierarchies

From its feudal roots, medieval society was hierarchical. After feudalism was institutionalized, raw power was given respectability, and elitism and structures became universal. Wealth, clothes, knowledge, and crafts were all hierarchically organized. Titles were important. A person's exterior proclaimed him or her—clothes, texture of skin, amount of dirt, tools or weapons (which were virtual emblems).

Place was given an almost mystical importance. A few people managed to pass from level

FIGURE 10.5

Hierarchy, expressed as size of figure. [From Petit de Julleville.]

to level: lucky, intelligent peasants sometimes rose through the Church; some rose from so-called rich peasantry to a title and slipped back again in several generations. These were exceptions, however, and from the individual's viewpoint, place was fixed.

God existed at the top of a ladder, stair, or chain. His creatures attended in ranks below him. His right and his left hand marked even subtler degrees. He and this structure were the model for society.

Hierarchy had two implications for the theatre. First, the audience was hierarchically structured, and so the theatre was sometimes popular without being democratic. Second, the hierarchical structure made it possible for an entire level to drop out and to leave a discernible gap. In at least some areas, it appears that the upper hierarchy (the nobility) did not take part, although in France it made important financial contributions to the cycles. Then, toward the end of the religious drama's life, it appears that more of the upper social levels withdrew, apparently leaving the plays to an audience with less education or less imagination or perhaps simply less patience.

Failure of the upper hierarchy to attend is not proof of the theatre's decline. However, if that hierarchy included the people who had given spiritual and intellectual leadership to the society, then that theatre may indeed have been in trouble, especially when production depended on attendance. Then, the theatre would decline both from lack of cultural leadership and from declining revenues.

Did such a decline take place over much of Europe in the sixteenth century? Some evidence suggests that it did, although the strongest comes only from Paris (the Confrérie de la Passion) and from parts of England. Perhaps more important, the loss of the upper level of the social hierarchy did not take place in a vacuum; rather, this class moved toward the new secular theatre, taking their taste-making power there and leaving the late religious theatre to an audience unable to sustain it.

Revivals

Antiquarians have revived the medieval theatre temporarily, of course: William Poel revived the Elizabethan stage in the late nineteenth century; Gustave Cohen and his Théophiliens did productions of medieval plays in the 1920s; there were revivals of the great cycles in England after World War II; and there have been Shakespearean restorations in the United States.

These, however, were all rather self-conscious, even scholarly, efforts. Have there been unconscious revivals of medieval elements? Have the theatrical practices of the Middle Ages ever found new life? In that the theatre was part of the culture, it is unlikely that it could be revived without a complete revival of the Middle Ages. However, some elements have found new life, although usually in different ways and with different uses, such as the following.

The Theatre-in-the-round

In England and the United States, theatres in the round enjoyed a great vogue after World War II, and many are still in use. They were a reaction to the proscenium theatre and the box set, and they were attractive to the new regional theatres because of their relative cheapness. They were indoors, of course; they did not use simultaneity, nor was the stage a *platea;* and their audiences were hierarchically arranged, although not as rigidly as in the Middle Ages. Many did new plays, but not at all medieval ones, and they adapted readily to the conventions of realism.

FIGURE 10.6

The thrust stage at Stratford, Ontario, Canada, a brilliant modern use of several Elizabethan elements. [Courtesy of the Stratford Shakespearean Festival Foundation of Canada.]

Emblematic Theatre: Expressionism

The emblem was so central to medieval perception that it would be surprising if it had carried over into a different culture. Symbols are common, however, especially in ceremonial societies. The emblem had a radically different home, however, in the theatrical style called *Expressionism* in Germany before and after World War I. Its use of both commonly recognized signs (emblems) and sometimes mysterious or private symbols made it at least analogous to some medieval theatre.

Neutral Background: The Vieux Colombier

After 1650, the theatre became one of scenic backgrounds; only when a reaction set in against illusionism did an interest in neutral background reappear. The impulse was quite different from the medieval, however, defining itself in terms of what it tried to replace.

One interesting and influential modern use was the theatre conceived by the French actor–director Jacques Copeau. It had a permanent architectural unit backing the playing area; stairs, arches and a platform were combined to assure flexibility in a theatre analogous to that of Shakespeare.

Alley Stages

Several historical dramas staged outdoors in the United States have used the alley stage, probably without conscious imitation of medieval practice. They put a long acting area between ranks of bleachers, in at least one case in a gymnasium. One used a wagon at each end, as well.

This was medieval in plan, at least: multiple viewing-points, central action, and even the potential (the wagons) for simultaneous settings. There were other similarities: civic support; amateur actors; popular appeal; and historical, pageantlike dramas.

Early in the Soviet period, some Russian theatre people used the alley stage, too. There, a conscious desire to break away from the proscenium stage was an important impetus; the proscenium stage was seen as "aristocratic," the alley stage as "democratic and popular." Although these views may have been correct for the pre-Revolutionary Russian theatre (where the imperial theatres used the proscenium configuration), the medieval experience would seem to suggest that the alley was not of itself "democratic."

None of these afterimages was a true revival of medieval staging, of course. As we would expect, the medieval theatre perished with its culture.

FIGURE 10.7

The alley stage in revival, Leningrad (1934). [Courtesy of *The Drama Review.*]

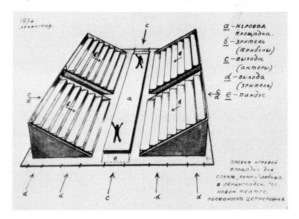

BIBLIOGRAPHY
Part Three

Adams, John C. *The Globe Playhouse,* 2nd ed. New York: Barnes and Noble, 1961.

Axton, Richard. *European Drama of the Early Middle Ages.* London: Hutchinson, 1974.

Bentley, G. E. *The Jacobean and Caroline Stage.* Oxford: Oxford University Press, 1968.

Bills, B. D. "The 'Suppression Theory' and the English Corpus Christ Play." *Theatre Journal* 32 (May 1980):157–168.

Bjork, David A. "On the Dissemination of *Quem quaeritis* and the *Visitatio sepulchri* and the chronology of their early sources." *Comparative Drama* 14 (Spring 1980):46–69.

Bogdanos, T. "Liturgical Drama in Byzantine Literature." *Comparative Drama* 10 (Fall 1976):200–215.

Bradbrook, M. C. *The Rise of the Common Player.* Cambridge: Harvard University Press, 1962.

Brett, G. "The Automata of the Byzantine. . . ." *Speculum* 29 (1954):477–87.

Bryan, George. *Ethelwold and Medieval Music-Drama at Winchester: The Easter Play, Its Author, and Its Milieu.* Berne: Verlag Peter Lang, 1981.

Cantor, Norman F. *Medieval History,* 3rd ed. New York: Macmillan, 1976.

Chambers, E. K. *The Medieval Stage.* London: Oxford University Press, 1903.

———. *The Elizabethan Stage,* 4 vols. Oxford: Clarendon Press, 1923.

———. *The English Folk-Play.* Oxford: Clarendon Press, 1933.

Clopper, Lawrence M. "The History and Development of the Chester Cycle." *Modern Philology* 75 (February 1978):219–46.

Cohen, Gustave. *Histoire de la mise-en-scène. . . .* rev. ed. Paris: H. Champion, 1926.

Coldewey, J. C. "That Enterprising Property Player." *Theatre Notebook* 31, 1 (1977):5–12.

Craig, Hardin. *English Religious Drama of the Middle Ages.* New York: Oxford University Press, 1960.

Craik, Thomas W. *The Tudor Interlude: Stage, Costume and Acting.* Leicester, England: University Press, 1958.

Deierkauf-Holsboer, Wilma S. *Le Théâtre du Marais,* 2 vols. Paris; Librairie Nizet, 1954 and 1958.

———. *L'histoire de la mise-en-scène dans le théâtre français de 1600 à 1673.* Paris: A. Nizet, 1960.

———. *Le théâtre de l'Hôtel de Bourgogne.* Paris: A. Nizet, 1968–1970.

Dodd, Kenneth M. "Another Elizabethan Theatre in the Round." *Shakespeare Quarterly* 21 (Spring 1970):125–56.

Edwards, Robert. *The Montecassino Passion and the Poetics of Medieval Drama.* Berkeley: University of California Press, 1977.

Evans, Marshall Blakemore. *The Passion Play of Lucerne.* New York: Modern Language Association of America, 1943.

Frank, Grace. *The Medieval French Drama.* Oxford: Clarendon Press, 1960.

Gardiner, H. C. *Mysteries' End.* Hamden, Conn.: Archon Books (Yale Studies in English, Vol. 103), 1946.

Gardner, Tom Cole. "The Theater of Hell: A Critical Study of Some Twelfth-Century Eschatological Visions." (Ph. D. diss., University of California, Berkeley, 1976).

Geanakoplos, D. J. *The Interaction of the "Sibling" Byzantine and Western Cultures. . . .* New Haven, Conn.: Yale University Press, 1976.

Griffith, G. P. *Population Problems of the Age of Malthus*, 2nd ed. New York: Kelley, 1967.

Gurr, Andrew. *The Shakespearean Stage, 1574–1642*. Cambridge: Cambridge University Press, 1970.

Harbage, Alfred. *Shakespeare's Audience*. New York: Columbia University Press, 1941.

Hardison, O. B. *Christian Rite and Christian Drama in the Middle Ages*. Baltimore: Johns Hopkins University Press, 1965.

Hatchet, John. *Plague, Population and the English Economy*. London: Macmillan, 1977.

Heer, Friedrick. *The Medieval World, 1100–1350*. London: Weidenfeld and Nicolson, 1962.

Hodges, C. W. *The Globe Restored*. London: Ernest Benn, 1953.

Holding, Peter. "Stagecraft in the York Cycle." *Theatre Notebook* 34, 2 (1980):51–60.

Hosley, Richard. "Three Kinds of Outdoor Theatre Before Shakespeare." *Theatre Survey* 12, 1 (May 1971):1–33.

Hotson, Leslie. *Shakespeare's Wooden O*. New York: Macmillan, 1960.

Hoyt, Robert S., ed. *Life and Thought in the Early Middle Ages*. Minneapolis: University of Minnesota Press, 1967.

Joseph, Bertram. *Elizabethan Acting*, 2nd ed. London: Oxford University Press, 1962.

Kahrl, Stanley J. *Traditions of Medieval English Drama*. London: Hutchinson, 1974.

Kernodle, George. *From Art to Theatre*. Chicago: University of Chicago Press, 1944.

Kolve, V. A. *The Play Called Corpus Christi*. Stanford, Calif.: Stanford University Press, 1966.

Konigson, Elie. *L'espace théâtral médiéval*. Paris: Editions du Centre National de la Recherche Scientifique, 1975.

Lancaster, Henry Carrington, ed. *Le Mémoire de Mahelot*. . . . Paris: E. Champion, 1928.

Larson, Orville K. "Bishop Abraham of Souzdal's Description of the Sacre Rappresentazioni." *Educational Theatre Journal* 9 (October 1957):208–213.

Leacroft, Richard. *The Development of the English Playhouse*. Ithaca, N.Y.: Cornell University Press, 1973.

———. "The Introduction of Perspective Scenery and its effects on theatre forms: a study by first year students of the School of Architecture, Leicester polytechnic." *Theatre Notebook* 34:1 (1980):21–4; and 2:69–73.

Loomis, L. H. "Secular Dramatics and Chaucer's 'Tregetoures.' " *Speculum* 33 (April 1958):242–255.

Malin, Stephen D. "Four Doubled Figures in the Origins of English Folk Theatre." *Theatre Journal* 33 (March 1981):18–33.

McConachie, Bruce A. "The Staging of the Mystère d'Adam." *Theatre Survey* 20, 1 (May 1979): 27–42.

Nagler, A. M. *The Medieval Religious Stage: Shapes and Phantoms*, trans. George C. Schoolfield. New Haven, Conn.: Yale University Press, 1976.

Neill, Michael. " 'Wits Most Accomplished Senate': the Audience of the Caroline Private Theatres." *Studies in English Literature* 18, 2 (Spring 1978):341–60.

Nelson, Alan H. *The Medieval English Stage*. . . . Chicago: University of Chicago Press, 1974.

Newton, S. M. *Renaissance Theatre Costume*. New York: Theatre Arts Books, 1975.

Orrell, John. "Inigo Jones at the Cockpit." *Shakespeare Survey* 30 (1977):157–168.

Prosser, Eleanor. *Drama and Religion in the English Mystery Plays*. Stanford, Calif.: Stanford University Press, 1961.

————. *Hamlet and Revenge.* Stanford, Calif.: Stanford University Press, 1967.

Reichenberger, Arnold G. "A Postscript." *Hispanic Review* 43:289–291.

Rennert, H. A. *The Spanish Stage in the Time of Lope de Vega.* New York: Hispanic Society of America, 1909.

Reynolds, George F. *The Staging of Elizabethan Plays at the Red Bull Theatre, 1605–1625.* New York: Modern Language Association of America, 1940.

Reynolds, L. D., and Wilson, N. G. *Scribes and Scholars.* London: Oxford University Press, 1968.

Roy, D. H. "La scène de l'Hôtel de Bourgogne." *Revue d'Histoire du Théâtre* 14 (1962):227–235.

Runciman, Sir Steven. "Life in a Doomed City: Constantinople Before the Capture by the Turks." *Medieval and Renaissance Studies* (Summer 1966):98–113.

Schrickx, W. "Commedia dell'arte Players in Antwerp." *Theatre Research International* 1 (February 1976):79–86.

Shergold, N. D. *A History of the Spanish Stage.* Oxford: Clarendon Press, 1967.

Sherwood, M. "Magic and Machines in Medieval Fiction." *Studies in Philology* 44 (1947):567–592.

Southern, Richard. *The Medieval Theatre in the Round.* London: Faber and Faber, 1957.

Star, Leonie. "Inigo Jones and the Use of Scenery at the Cockpit-in-Court." *Theatre Survey* 19 (May 1978):35–48.

Stopp, F. J. "Latin Plays at the Academy of Altdorf, 1577–1626." *Journal of European Studies* 4 (June 1974):189–213.

Tydeman, William. *The Theatre in the Middle Ages.* Cambridge and New York: Cambridge University Press, 1978.

Wickham, Glynn. *Early English Stages, 1300 to 1600*, 3 vols. New York: Columbia University Press, 1967.

————. *The Medieval Theatre.* London: Weidenfeld and Nicolson, 1974.

Wiley, W. L. *The Early Public Theatre in France.* Cambridge, Mass.: Harvard University Press, 1960.

————. "The Hôtel de Bourgogne." *Studies in Philology* 70 (December 1973):3–114.

Yates, Frances A. *Theatre of the World.* London: Routledge and Keegan Paul, 1969.

Young, Karl. *The Drama of the Medieval Church*, 2 vols. Oxford: Clarendon Press, 1933.

Zacour, N. P. *An Introduction to Medieval Institutions*, 2nd ed. New York: St. Martin's Press, 1976.

part four

The Theatre
of Illusionism

PART FOUR

Within the four-hundred-year period, the nature of illusion shifted noticeably, from single-point perspective, so typical of the seventeenth century (and multi-point perspective of the eighteenth), to aerial perspective in the nineteenth, culminating in the closed box set, filled with three-dimensional rather than painted details, by the twentieth century. To see the shift compare a machine play on the French stage, *Andromède* by Corneille (with sets by Torelli, 1640s, from Bapst) with the scenery for *As You Like It* [courtesy of the University of Rochester] and the New York production of *The Christian* in 1899 [from *Le Théâtre*].

11

Italian Renaissance, ca. 1350–ca. 1600

Europe and Europe's mind lay hid at night;
God said, "Renascence be!", and all was light.
[Alexander Pope]

Ask Everyman to name one golden age in world history and he will unfailingly come up with the Renaissance—*the* Renaissance.[1]

And indeed, *the* Renaissance was revolutionary—in politics, in social organization, in art, and in life. With the Renaissance came a new way of seeing, a new sense of time, and a new kind of theatre. Thus, the Renaissance provides one of those rare benchmarks in history where the *view* of the world shifted so dramatically that some argue that the very world itself shifted. The Renaissance was such a revolution. In the new social and artistic order that emerged from it, many scholars have found the beginnings of our modern world.

The Nature of the Revolution

The word *renaissance* means rebirth. *Italian Renaissance* is the name given to that period in Italy, from about 1350 to 1600, when there was a rebirth of interest in the ancient civilizations of Greece and Rome. The Italian Renaissance was not the first rebirth of interest in classical cultures (there was a twelfth-century renascence of northern Europe, for example). But the Italian Renaissance was different. It was no fleeting phenomenon. The discoveries that it made had

a permanent impact. The institutions that it developed continued beyond its own towns and its own centuries. The changes that it wrought were lasting and profound, and Italy's Renaissance (unlike those in northern Europe) changed theatre and drama in startling ways. It is probably for these reasons that the word *renaissance* has become almost synonymous with the Italian Renaissance and so usually designates that particular flowering of the fourteenth through the sixteenth centuries in Italy.

Humanism

Central to the Italian Renaissance was humanism, a cultural and educational program based on the study of Greek and Latin authors. *Studia humanitates* had described, for Roman scholars, a liberal or literary education (as opposed to a scientific or practical one). Renaissance schoolboys coined the word *humanista* to designate those professors who taught in such a program of studies. The point is important. In earlier renascences Latin authors had been studied, but usually in an attempt to reconcile their teachings with those of Christianity and the Church. Earlier renascences had involved study of the Greek authors as well—principally works of medicine, astronomy, astrology, and biology. The Italian Renaissance, however, emphasized *the study of Greek and Latin literary works for their own sake.* The exact reasons for this new interest in literary studies are unclear, but interest in Greek culture was so strong that Byzantine scholars were being brought to some Italian universities to teach Greek language and literature well before 1400.

The Italian Renaissance, then, stressed the *secular* traditions of classical antiquity. There was therefore a contrast between Christian authors (who placed God and His Church at the center of the world) and pre-Christian, classical authors (who extolled heroes and concentrated on human rather than divine accomplishments). Probably because of this contrast, the word *humanism* came to carry an additional connotation: humanism was marked by its commitment to the centrality of human beings within the universe and thus the importance of people as well as God, of this world as well as the next. Renaissance educational programs were neither dominated by the Church nor aimed at the training of churchmen. Increasing numbers of schools and universities were founded by secular units (towns and states) for the education of the laity and the promulgation of secular learning.

Political and Economic Shifts

At the time of the Renaissance, no political entity called *Italy* existed. Rather, the peninsula was a patchwork of independent city states, each with its own policies, government, and culture, based primarily on its economic needs and class rivalries. Although the individual histories of these cities are bewildering in their complexity, some patterns emerge. Five major city states (Venice, Milan, Florence, the Papal States, and the Kingdom of Naples) joined with four important minor states (Ferrara, Mantua, Siena, and Urbino) to dominate life and trade on the peninsula. Although occasionally at war, these units maintained a degree of peace and stability by maintaining an uneasy balance of power (see Figure 11.1).

For much of the Middle Ages, Italian feudal manors and trading towns had existed side by side. At the time of the Renaissance, however, feudalism was in decline, and the trading centers were prospering, just as in northern Europe. Commerce had joined (and in some places replaced) agriculture as the major source of wealth, and older systems of barter had given way to a new economy founded on money and credit. As in northern Europe as well, new alliances developed to facilitate trade and to minimize the financial risks of commerce, and these alliances gradually replaced the intricate network of feudal ties based on land and defense. As power shifted away from the country and into the growing cities, successful merchants and tradesmen gained financial leadership, social respectability, and political influence. Successful merchants, the richest among the small but expanding middle class, were able to form new alliances with old but impoverished noblemen to produce a new power bloc.

Travel became an accepted way of life for an unprecedented (if still small) number of people. Trade routes to distant, new markets were sought and opened by explorers on land and sea. The apparent size of the world increased as new lands were discovered and new products traded.

The new economy (based on trade, fluid assets, and shifting wealth) highlighted the mobility of life just as the old economy (based on land, inherited wealth, and noble birth) had emphasized its solidity and constancy. With the increased awareness of mobility and change came altered views of time and space. Time came to be viewed as limited, a precious commodity to be measured carefully and paid out wisely. The passage of time had come to be acutely sensed. Clocks assumed an increasingly important role in the workings of daily life, just as navigational aids proliferated to help order the business of voyaging. Maps became ever more precise, and with this precision came a new awareness of the size and the relationship of earthly masses and celestial bodies. The sciences of mathematics and optics joined to raise a new breed of artist–engineer with tools for seeing, analyzing, and depicting proportion and depth with greater accuracy than ever before.

FIGURE 11.1

Map of major Italian states during the Renaissance.

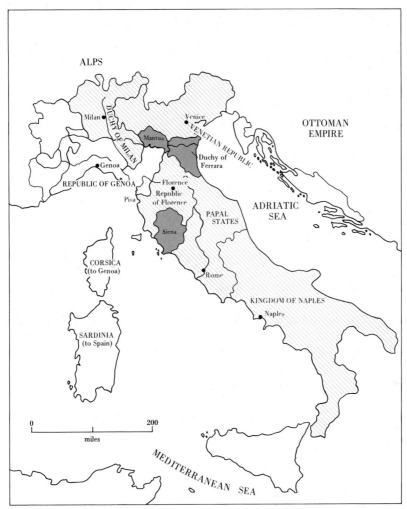

Triumph of the Vernacular

Latin, once the universal language of the vast Roman Empire, had been gradually replaced by an array of local dialects. Scholars and churchmen still read Latin; schoolmen might still write in Latin; but the language of the marketplace, the home, and the literatures was one of the many dialects that had emerged from the disintegrating empire. Dante wrote his *Divine* *Comedy* (ca. 1300) in a Tuscan dialect. Latin remained the official language of the Church, which meant that its liturgy unfolded in a language unfamiliar to the majority of its congregation. For some, this disjunction between the language of the Church and the language of daily life became a metaphor for the increasing separation of the Church from the daily lives of its members.

The Religious Reformation and CounterReformation

As Protestantism erupted in the north with Luther, Henry VIII, John Calvin, and others, the established Church (led by the Italian popes) struggled to reform and reassert itself. Thus, both the Reformation and the Counter-Reformation were part of the intellectual ferment of the Italian Renaissance. Probably because the Papal States formed both the spiritual center of the Church and the geographical center of the Italian peninsula, religious conservatism was more pronounced in Italy than in northern Europe.

None of these changes, however, was unique to the Italian Renaissance. As we have seen, the "rediscovery" of classical texts had occurred throughout the Middle Ages. Universities and schools had been organized to instruct the young; towns had grown up and traded abroad. Whenever a strong middle class had emerged in a town, feudalism in its surrounding area had been weakened. Schisms and heresies of many kinds had plagued Christianity from the outset. Never before, however, had such circumstances resulted in a major cultural shift of the sort witnessed between 1350 and 1600. Never before had the changes been so widespread or so far-reaching.

Printing

The uniqueness of the Italian Renaissance rests, at least in part, with a technological innovation that produced a revolution in communication. The Italian Renaissance, unlike the several renascences that predated it, participated in the advent of printing.[2] With printing came the opportunity to collect and systematize large masses of information, to compare variant texts, and to build on the past in ways never before possible. With printing came new ways of transmitting knowledge and also, as importantly, new ways of seeing knowledge. The printing revolution cut across all areas of life and assured the permanence of the new ideas and practices launched by the Italian Renaissance. The printing revolution was, in fact, not only a part but also a purveyor and perpetuator of the Italian Renaissance.

John Gutenberg in Germany printed his first book (probably a Bible) only one year (1454) after the fall of Constantinople. The timing may be significant, for Byzantine scholars fled west and set up major Greek communities in Crete, Venice, and Naples, and lesser ones in Florence, Siena, and Rome. Some of these émigrés brought manuscripts with them. Indeed, one result of the exodus from Constantinople was the establishment of a major library of Greek manuscripts at Venice.

By 1464, a printing press had been brought from Germany to Italy. By 1500, print shops could be found in Rome, Florence, Milan, Naples, Ferrara, Vicenza, and, most of all, Venice. By 1500, Rome had no fewer than thirty-eight presses, and Venice had more than two hundred, several run by Greek émigrés from Constantinople.[3]

The advantages of the press over older systems of hand copying were quickly evident. In Florence in 1483, for example, a press charged three times what a scribe did for duplicating a single work by Plato; the press turned out 1,025 copies, however, while the scribe produced only 1.[4] In Venice alone, over two million books had been printed by 1500; during roughly the same period throughout western Europe, "about eight million books had been printed, *more perhaps than all the scribes in Europe had produced since Constantine founded his city in* A.D. *330."* [5] This sudden availability of multiple copies of various texts can be described only as revolutionary, and the revolution invaded all areas of life, for the printed texts touched all fields of learning.

Printing facilitated trade (and thus, emerging capitalism) by the massive dissemination of correct and precise maps and navigational charts. Medical practices improved because more than six hundred editions of Galen were quickly published (Galen [ca. 130–ca. 200] was the age's best source of medical knowledge). New principles of art were popularized when a book on perspective drawing was printed (1545); new principles of stage design were popularized when new publications of Vitruvius appeared with perspective drawings (1547). New information about the chronology of the past became available as masses of historical data were sifted, reconciled, codified, and published for the first time.

Religion and the Church were drastically affected. The Church early seized on printing as a valuable tool of education, and so it early published devotional tracts, instructional booklets for priests, schoolbooks, and propaganda. But on the other side, the questions of theology became proportionately more troublesome. Textual scholars, examining the different manuscript versions of the Bible that now appeared in print, found it difficult to ignore the discrepancies and contradictions that had, before print, gone largely unnoticed. As the discrepancies among the various editions became clearer, the argument for the ultimate authority of the Bible became dimmer: How could the several contradictions be reconciled, or could they? If not, which of the several Words of God was, in fact, His? When Martin Luther issued his ninety-five theses in 1517, the power of print was evident, for within three years, more than 300,000 copies of his indictment had been printed and distributed.[6]

Vernacular Bibles had begun to assume a new importance, for wherever Bibles were translated into the vernacular and printed, daily Bible reading by laypeople was encouraged. Such reading prompted a personal and direct religion rather than a formal and hierarchical one. Bible reading among the laity thus flourished in Protestant lands. In strongly Catholic areas, on the other hand, Bible reading and Bible printing were severely discouraged by successive papal decrees (1515, 1559, and 1564). Both literacy rates and habits of reading were thus shaped, in part, through geography and religious affiliation.

Humanism was likewise affected, for manuscripts long available in limited supply were now available in large numbers. As well, Greek manuscripts brought to Italy and housed there in libraries quickly found their way into print, both in Greek and in Latin. Plautus, Terence, and Seneca were published by 1475, within ten years after printing reached Italy. By 1480, Greek books were being printed in Italy, including dictionaries that could facilitate later translations. By 1490, Vitruvius' *De Architectura* was published; within sixty years it had been combined with recent illustrations in single-point perspective and reissued. By 1520, the major texts from Constantinople were in print, including all the known texts of Aristotle, and all the known plays of Aeschylus, Sophocles, Euripides, and Aristophanes (see Figure 11.2).

Education changed. Students could for the first time learn directly from books. Intellectuals soon flocked to print shops, which in many areas rivaled schools and universities as centers of erudition. Indeed, the introduction of printing began a new age, an age after which the acquisition and dissemination of knowledge would never be as before: "The effects of printing seem to have been exerted always unevenly, yet always continuously and cumulatively from the late fifteenth century on."[7]

It is well to underscore the word *unevenly*. The Renaissance, like the Middle Ages, was a mosaic of cultures, often contradictory, placed side by side in a crazy patchwork. For example, trading towns sat next to manors; Protestant enclaves formed in Catholic lands; astronomy was often indistinguishable from astrology and religion from witchcraft. In the theatre, new practices unfolded side by side with the old—often in the same country, occasionally in the same city.

FIGURE 11.2
Publication Dates of Major Classical Authors

Author	Publication in Original Language	Publication in Italian
Terence	1470	1488
Plautus	1472	1486, *Menaechmi*
		1550, Most other works
Seneca	1474–1484	1497
Vitruvius	1486	1521
Aristotle	1495–1498 (*Poetics*, 1508)	1549
Aristophanes	1498	1545
Horace	1501	1536
Sophocles	1502	1532, *Oedipus Rex*
		1566, Complete works
Euripides	1503	1540s–1550s
Aeschylus	1518	After 1600

Renaissance Theatre

Before the greatest cycles and cosmic dramas of the Middle Ages were produced, Renaissance plays and productions were heralding a new kind of theatre in Italy. Almost seventy-five years before the Valenciennes Passion Play in France (1547), for example, students in Florence in 1476 had performed Terence's *Andria* at school, at the home of the Medici, and in the palace of a leading aristocrat. Over eighty years before the great promptbook of Lucerne (Switzerland) was devised (1583), Plautus' *Menaechmi* was staged at the Vatican by Pope Alexander VI in honor of a visit from his daughter Lucrezia Borgia (1502). For a de Medici wedding in 1565–1566, an Italian comedy provided the excuse for several *intermezzi* that used cloud machines (flying platforms decorated to look like clouds) to tell the story of Cupid and Psyche, and later in the same festivities a religious drama of the Annunciation unfolded inside a church and used cloud machines to display a celestial paradise filled with angels and heavenly hosts.

Although Renaissance productions existed for a time side by side with medieval ones, the two traditions were vastly different. The Renaissance theatre was aimed at a different kind of audience, a fact reflected both in the arrangement of its playing spaces and in the architecture of its theatres. As well, Renaissance dramas and theories of drama departed radically from those of the Middle Ages, again a reflection of the audiences for whom the Renaissance theatre was intended (see Figure 11.3).

Audiences

The great vernacular cycles and liturgical dramas of the Middle Ages were inclusive. They were generally aimed at large audiences of the faithful, whether inside or outside the church building. Renaissance performances, on the other hand, were typically intended for small, restricted, and elite groups, for Renaissance theatre was initially nurtured in the schools and academies of Italy's cities and in the homes and courts of her aristocrats. Its performances were occasional and festive affairs whose goals were as much educational or political as diversionary.

In several city states, academies were formed during the Renaissance in order to complement and extend the work of the universities. In them, selected intelligentsia gathered to

FIGURE 11.3

Time line: Interpenetration of Italian Renaissance and medieval theatres.

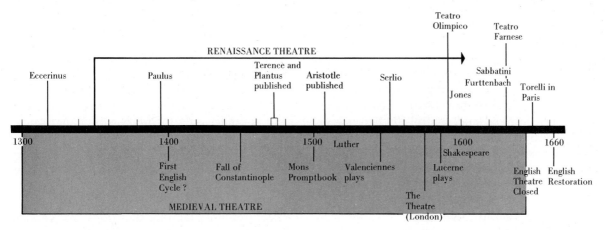

investigate particular fields and to gain outlets for their findings. For example, the stated goal of the Florentine Academy was to encourage the use of the vernacular, or, as they said, to interpret, compose, and translate "all knowledge in whatever language into our own."[8] On the other hand, some academies were devoted to the revival of classical culture, including its language: Latin. Thus, members of the celebrated Roman Academy took Roman names, studied Roman art and literature, and practiced the rites and mysteries of the pagan city (for which Pope Paul II jailed them). Founded by Pomponius Laetus (1428–1498), the Roman Academy promoted not only the literature of Rome, but also "Latin compositions written in antique form by its [own] members."[9] By 1485, the Roman Academy was producing plays by Plautus, Terence, and Seneca—in Latin—for the edification of its members.

Like the Roman Academy, some schools and universities regularly produced plays, in keeping with their commitment to humanism. Renaissance students and faculty read, produced, and attended plays as a part of their education in classical literature. The plays were therefore often given in Latin rather than in the vernacular in order to allow the actors to refine their pronunciation and the audiences to hone their listening skills. As well, the plays were often given in settings intended to reproduce the "ancient manner" so that a better appreciation of the classical art could be shared by Renaissance students (see Figure 11.4).

Theatrical presentations at court were likewise aimed at an elite audience—this one consisting of the ruler, the courtiers, visiting dignitaries, and invited guests. Their purpose was

FIGURE 11.4

Taken from a woodprint of G. P. Trapolini's *Antigone* (Padua, 1581), this picture may be a real or imagined theatre of the day. Notice that the actor is playing well in front of the perspective scenery. [From Walker.]

political: to reflect the majesty, power, and liberality of the ruler and to teach the subjects of the realm the bounty that they received through his power. Artistic patronage therefore became simply another aspect of government, a position that found classical support in the writings of Vitruvius.[10] The planning of theatrical pageantry became a matter of government policy, with the political content of the presentations carefully contrived and controlled. Because of their political nature, the theatrical presentations of one court were closely watched by another, and the rivalries among the courts were keen, a condition that encouraged accelerating splendor and innovation.

Participation in these courtly theatres was carefully controlled and rigidly hierarchical. At the center of the event were the ruler and his family. Others were ranged about him in keeping with their own importance. The ruler watched the performance; others watched the ruler *and* the performance. When ordinary people glimpsed the proceedings (as they often could when performances unfolded in several parts of a city), they watched the magnificence of the courtiers as much as the splendor of the performances. The court itself thus became a part of the pageantry as well as a witness to it.

Records of a *secular* theatre aimed at a *general* audience did not appear regularly until the mid-sixteenth century (in conjunction with the surfacing of professional players, the *commedia dell'arte*). Audiences throughout most of the Italian Renaissance were made up mostly of academicians and courtiers who sought to recapture both the literary and political glories of the ancient world.

Scenic Conventions

Humanism found its expression in the visual world—through the introduction of perspective. Perspective was, in the words of John White, "the final crystallization of the increasingly close connection between the observer and the pictorial world."[11] Or as an early Renaissance theorist of perspective explained, with perspective all appearances became relative to the *human* figure, and so the *human* observer provided the measure of what the *human* artist created.[12] The invention of a mathematically based system of perspective early in the fifteenth century revolutionized painting and architecture. During the sixteenth century, perspective seized the imagination of theatre artists and audiences. By the end of the Renaissance, perspective scenery and its attendant conventions dominated the theatre of the Western world, a domination that was to last for over three hundred years.

Early in the Renaissance, however, staging rested on more familiar traditions. As we have seen, Italy, like the rest of western Europe, had a strong tradition of medieval drama throughout the 1400s. It was therefore not surprising that medieval staging practices were often applied to early productions of classical and Renaissance plays. For example, a series of productions at the court of Ferrara between 1485 and 1491 used medieval mansions; the production of another Renaissance play at the court of Bologna in 1487 used a version of processional staging from the medieval theatre.

At about the same time scholars were encountering descriptions of the ancient facade stage, and so some productions strove to recapture its traditions. For example, in 1502, at the court of Ferrara, five Plautine comedies unfolded before a classical facade. Again, in 1513 in Rome, the pope offered a production of Plautus' *Carthaginian* to celebrate a political victory. For the event, a theatre was erected out-of-doors in the Campidoglio, a large square. Constructed of wood treated to resemble marble, the theatre featured a "ceiling" of blue and white cloth and a series of classical columns separated by painted scenes drawn from history and mythology. The stage jutted out from an end wall. Although painted like the others, this end wall was pierced by three doors through which the actors entered and exited. No further scenery was used. Clearly, this staging rested squarely on the traditions of the facade stage "in the ancient manner."

Yet another staging tradition *may* be represented by illustrations accompanying early editions of Terence's plays. As problematical as they are provocative, these illustrations from the 1493 edition published at Lyons show a stage that combined elements of a medieval theatre with those of a classical facade. As well, some scholars have imagined that the columns and statues appearing at each end of the linked mansions marked a tentative step on the way to a proscenium arch—a position allowed but certainly not encouraged by the evidence (see Figure 11.5). Because the editor of the plays was briefly associated with Pomponius' Academy, some have argued that the Lyons illustrations recorded practices that he had actually observed in Rome. Because subsequent editions of both Plautus and Terence (1511 and 1518) carried similar illustrations, some have argued that these Terence stages (so-called) became standard throughout western Europe. On the other hand, no real proof exists that such stages were ever used in theatrical production, and so they

FIGURE 11.5

A Terence stage that offers a curious mixture of medieval-style mansions and a classical facade. [From Bapst.]

may record nothing more than the artistic imagination of their illustrator.

The first certain reference to a perspective setting was in 1508. The account of an enthusiastic eyewitness to a performance of a Renaissance comedy related, "But what has been best in all those festivities and representations has been the scenery. . . . a view in perspective of a town with houses, churches, belfries, and gardens, such that one could never tire of looking at it."[13] By 1513, the court at Urbino had also used perspective sets (which apparently combined three-dimensional with painted detail): its stage "was designed to look like a very beautiful city, with streets, palaces, houses, towers, and real streets, and everything in relief, but helped by excellent painting expert in perspective."[14] The same play revived in Rome the following year also used a perspective setting, this time one designed by Baldassare Peruzzi (1481–1536), one of the age's leading architect–painters and the teacher of Sebastiano Serlio (1474–1554). By 1519, the new perspective style had appeared at the Vatican: in a room painted by the great artist Raphael, and behind a curtain whose design was also attributed to him, lay a stage that reproduced the town of Ferrara. By the 1520s, perspective scenes were no longer merely a novelty; the revolutionary changes in theatre were well under way. Indeed, as Allardyce Nicoll observed in 1966, it is still almost shocking to realize "how far the stage had travelled within a space of less than twenty years."[15]

By 1545, then, when Sebastiano Serlio published his manual of practical architecture, *Architettura*, perspective techniques were regularly used in painting, architecture, and theatre. Because court architects were expected to supervise the design and building of stages and scenery for all courtly entertainments, Serlio devoted a short section of his book to the special problems of perspective in stages and scenery. Although his *Architettura* only codified practices already familiar, the book had an immediate and profound influence because it was one of the first systematic presentations of the techniques and uses of perspective for the stage. New editions and translations followed almost immediately. By 1611, several Italian editions had been joined by publications in French, Dutch, Latin, German, Spanish, and English. The influence of Serlio's work increased even more after 1547, when his drawings regularly accompanied editions of Vitruvius. By many, Serlio's perspective drawings were assumed to illustrate the practices of classical architects as set forth by Vitruvius. Thus Serlio's work, while seeming to describe ancient practice, focused attention on perspective stage design. Its publication led to a spate of subsequent treatises on theatrical architecture, design, painting, and technology. Taken together with Serlio's, these treatises set forth those practices in staging that were to dominate Western theatre throughout most of the nineteenth century.

In those sections of *Architettura* dealing with theatre, Serlio provided instructions and illustrations for meeting a wide range of problems. For his solutions, he seems to have drawn heavily on his experiences with Peruzzi (they both designed together and collaborated on a book treating classical architecture) and on his own experiences as a court architect and painter at Vicenza. The theatre that he described was based on classical precedents, but it could be built inside an already-existing hall (the usual practice in Italian courts). Its auditorium was planned in keeping with court protocol, with the important people in the best seats. The seat that provided the best view of the perspective scenery was reserved for the lord.

The stage of the theatre consisted of a flat platform in front of one that was raked (slanted front to back). The actors and dancers were to work on the flat portion, whose floor was painted in perfect squares. Scenery occupied the raked portion, whose floor was decorated with squares painted in perspective to increase the sense of distance.

The scenery was a combination of architectural and painted units. The side houses toward the front of the stage were built of angle flats, whose front face was a rectangle, but whose side face was trapezoidal, with top and bottom slanted to assist the perspective. On the front houses, as well, three-dimensional details made of wood were added to enhance the sense of depth. For the side houses farther back, ordinary flats with painted details sufficed. The perspective scene was closed at the back of the stage by a scene painted in perspective. Neither a curtain nor a proscenium arch was mentioned by Serlio. Because a front curtain was customary during this period, Serlio probably assumed its presence and merely neglected to mention it. The masking function of the proscenium, on the other hand, was probably fulfilled by the first pair of houses.

Clearly making use of Vitruvius' earlier work, Serlio described three kinds of settings: tragic, comic, and satyric. Serlio elaborated considerably on Vitruvius, however, as the following comparison makes clear:

> Vitruvius: Satyric scenes are decorated with trees, caverns, mountains, and other rustic objects delineated in landscape style.[16]

> Serlio: Hence Vitruvius in dealing with scenery recommends that these [satyric] scenes be composed of trees, rocks, hills, mountains, herbs, flowers, and fountains,—together with some rustic huts, such as those in the illustration. And since in our times these performances are generally given in the winter when few trees and bushes have flowers and foliage, these will have to be made artificially of silk, and will receive more praise than the natural objects.[17]

Serlio obviously thought that he was reviving ancient practices, but he clearly brought assumptions to his designs that were probably not shared by Vitruvius. Because Serlio's illustrations often accompanied Vitruvius' words after 1547, however, Serlio probably helped to shape later interpretations of the classical work (see Figure 11.6). Serlio also popularized the use of three stock sets that were constructed and painted in single-point perspective and were set on a raked stage.

Before the end of the sixteenth century, some designers were including the final feature of the "Italianate scenic system"—a proscenium arch—as a part of their scenic designs. By 1618, a proscenium arch had been included as a permanent architectural feature of a theatre building. With the development of the proscenium arch, the first phase in the development of the Italianate system of staging was complete.

Machinery and Special Effects

Renaissance court theatres vied with one another for preeminence in the splendor of their special effects as well as their scenery. Neither revivals of classical works nor productions of original Renaissance plays allowed lavish scenic displays, and so the most spectacular effects usually occurred *between the acts* of regular dramas (where they formed the basis of entertainments called *intermezzi*), as a part of court ballets, tournaments (including pageant jousts and equestrian ballets), and triumphal processions. In the case of the *intermezzi*, the usual pattern was for a drama to be played in front of a perspective setting (in the manner of Serlio); the *intermezzi* would then use the same space but alter it by means of an ingenious variety of stage machinery. Although much of the technology

FIGURE 11.6

The three scenes that had been earlier described by Vitruvius have been here elaborated and rendered in perspective by Serlio. [From Serlio. Courtesy of the Rare Books Room, Bowling Green State University.]

for the special effects was taken from the stage-craft of the Middle Ages, its classical justification could be found in Pollux' list of machines and in Aristotle's inclusion of spectacle as one of the six parts of drama.

The most common effect used by Renaissance designers was a cloud machine or its more elaborate cousin, the glory, on which supernatural beings, bathed in heavenly light, could fly up and down. Whereas in the medieval theatre such heavenly chariots customarily bore Christian saints and angels aloft, in the Renaissance theatre the riders were pagan gods and various allegorical figures from the art and literature of Rome or Greece. A particularly spectacular example of such machinery can be found in the sixth *intermezzo* that accompanied a production of the comedy *La Pellegrina* in honor of a de Medici wedding:

> After the last lines of the comedy had been spoken, the stage was filled with clouds. . . . The heavens opened, revealing a consistory of some twenty pagan deities which shone so radiantly. . . . Five clouds descended to earth, and two remained hovering aloft. The cloud in the central aperture was larger than the others and held Apollo, Bacchus, Harmony, and Rhythm. On a second one, next to the first but somewhat lower, stood the three Graces. The Muses were scattered over several.[18]

Adding to the splendor of many clouds and glories were the many lights that burned and reflected off special polished basins (see Figure 11.7).

Traps allowed for the appearance and disappearance of scenic units as well as people. Indeed, it was primarily by means of traps that stage designers enlivened the regular settings and transformed them into views suitable for the *intermezzi*. Following the first act of a comedy in 1586, for example:

> Suddenly the floor of the stage opened . . . a horrible cavern gaped wide, and as the boulders vanished behind it, the city of Dis emerged

in a fiery glow, amidst flames and billows of smoke, dismal mires, and muddy streams. The Furies howled shrilly on the battlements of the burning towers, brandishing tangled serpents. . . . A bark plowed through the lead-colored sludge, ferried by Phlegyas. . . . As soon as he dipped his flaming rudder into the Stygian flood, smoke billowed up, and the current soon bore him off in all directions [sic]. . . . At length the boat was moored fast. . . . the city of Dis was swallowed up, and the cavern closed. Thus ended the second intermezzo.[19]

Along with flying and trapping, the usual special effects included thunder, lightning, smoke, fire, waves, and various kinds of monsters:

> New sea monsters with wild eyes, scaly ears, and puffed cheeks emerged, agitating the sea, so that ships in the distance seemed to dance on the billows. Neptune angrily ascended, shaking his head and his trident. . . . The twelve sea-nymphs on the chariot of the god transmitted his order to the monsters, who promptly submerged, causing the sea to be serene once again.[20]

For tournaments, processionals, and mock *naumachia* (staged in an echo of Rome), both costumes and theatrical scenery were used. For example, a marriage celebration in 1589 included a processional entry, several musical programs, several comedies, at least six *intermezzi*, an animal baiting, a tournament, and a mock sea battle. The scenery for the comedies and the *intermezzi* were clearly Renaissance perspective scenery. For the tournament, a series of processional cars were drawn by "dragons," "lions," "bears," and "crocodiles" and were decorated with fountains, clouds, shrubbery, animals, ships, boulders, sirens, giant birds, and elephants. A brilliant fireworks display closed the tournament. While the spectators dined, the courtyard filled with water (to a depth of about five feet), and then a round of cannon fire called the spectators back. They watched as eighteen galleys engaged in a mock battle be-

FIGURE 11.7

Special effects formed an integral part of the Renaissance court theatre. Here, the special effects include: above, a sorceress flown aloft in a golden chariot drawn by winged dragons and surrounded by a dazzling crescent of clouds, lights, and costumed spirits; below, a flaming, smoking stage whose open trap reveals demons, devils, Furies, Charon, and the tormented, trapped souls of the damned, as described by Dante in his *Inferno*. Notice the single point perspective scenes arranged in wing and drop. Bernardo Buontalenti's *Inferno,* for the fourth intermezzo accompanying Girolamo Bargagli's comedy *La Pellegrina* (1589), for a de Medici wedding. [Engraving by Epifanio d'Alfiano, courtesy of Biblioteca Marucelliana di Firenze.]

tween the Turks and the Christians for the possession of a fortress. The Christians won, and the guests were dismissed for the evening.[21]

Renaissance stages were filled with spectacular effects. Although the technology for most (or perhaps all) of the effects had come from the medieval stage, the effects had been refined and converted for use by Renaissance artists, who sought and found ancient authorities to support such effects.

Lighting

Lighting had seldom been a problem in Greek, Roman, or medieval cycle productions, for they were usually out-of-doors. In the Renaissance, however, because performances were regularly held indoors, illuminating the actors and the scenery posed a challenge. Although both candles and oil lamps could be used, candles were usually preferred because they produced less smoke and odor.

For general illumination, Serlio advised placing a large number of candles in several overhead chandeliers and "leaning at the front of the scene" (probably a reference to footlights). Designers regularly treated such sources of light as a part of the overall design of the theatrical space. For example, at a de Medici wedding in 1565–1566, twelve chandeliers were used: three suspended at one end of the room resembled papal crowns (a reference to the three de Medici popes); three at the other end of the room resembled imperial crowns (a reference to the bride's illustrious family); and at the center of the room were two royal crowns,[22] surrounded by four smaller coronets.

In addition to general illumination, Serlio paid attention to ways of securing various special effects. To alter both the color and the intensity of light, Serlio recommended using colored water housed in special containers. He gave specific directions for coloring the lights blue, emerald, ruby, topaz, and diamond. To increase intensity, Serlio advised placing a torch behind glass but in front of a metal reflector; to show something aflame, he suggested soaking it well in strong aqua vitae and setting fire to it with a taper; to make lightning, igniting powdered resin in a high place; and to produce a thunderbolt, igniting "a rocket or ray ornamented with sparkling gold on a wire. . . ."[23]

The opening of the Uffizi theatre (1586) included an *intermezzo* that required a number of such effects: "[T]he sky grew dark over Florence. Flashes of lightning stabbed through the clouds. Subsequently, a bright cloud appeared. . . . the spokes of the [chariot] wheels glinted like sunbeams as they turned. Bolts of lightning streaked like incandescent arrows through the rain and hail. At last the storm subsided, and a most convincing rainbow formed about Juno's cloud."[24]

Renaissance designers had obviously begun to exploit the theatrical potential of light as well as its illuminating properties. Their techniques, when refined and extended by the designers of the seventeenth century, would serve as the standard practices until the nineteenth century, when first gas and then electricity became available.

Costuming

A paramount function of Renaissance costuming, as of medieval costuming, was the identification of characters, a function that took precedence over historical or geographical suggestiveness. Thus, for a Renaissance spectacle, the character Fame had "her whole person covered with peacock feathers and human faces" (a holdover from medieval symbolism), and the character Midas wore "armour such as at one time used to be made . . . all in gold" (a reference to the mythical king's golden touch).[25] In Florence, in 1566, nearly sixty thousand people may have watched as more than four hundred costumed figures represented both allegorical and mythological figures, a dizzying mixture of medieval and classical lore. For each character, the details of costume provided the major clues to the identity. Thus, Hercules wore a lion skin and carried a club, and Velocity wore a dolphinlike headdress (because Aristotle had declared the dolphin the world's swiftest animal).[26]

A second major function of Renaissance costuming was the heightening of visual splendor. The costumes were commonly made of the finest materials available: furs, silk, and fabrics thickly embroidered with jewels. In Florence, in 1539, the costumes of the nine classical Muses were particularly sumptuous. For example, the first Muse wore a helmet "ornamented with crystals and beryls and, as a crest, a chameleon. . . . A panther-skin was flung across her breast and her little classical boots were covered with cat skin." The costume of the second included a hyena skin, a parrot, decorations of agate and topaz, and boots of monkey skin. Yet another wore boots of white lambskin, whose gilded faces matched her dress of doeskin.[27] Clearly, no expense was spared.

It should perhaps be noted that for tournaments and processions connected with the courts, the participating horses and mules were often elegantly "costumed." Some were covered to resemble exotic animals like lions, bears, sea monsters, unicorns, or stags; others were merely outfitted in livery of the most splendid sort, whose decorations commonly included precious metals and jewels.

With the Renaissance's interest in antiquity came some vague gestures in the direction of historical and geographical identification. A point might be made about the national origins of characters by having them clothed in exotic garments faintly reminiscent of Greek, Oriental, Turkish, or some other foreign people—at least, as popularly envisioned. Occasionally, some unspecified "olden days" might be evoked by dressing characters in fashions of an earlier age, an age not yet forgotten but one definitely out of phase with current fashion.

Most common of all, however, were costumes intended to suggest classical antiquity. Indeed, by the late 1400s, costumes were often described as *all'antica* or as *alla greca*. This classical garb for men consisted of flesh-colored tights (to simulate naked arms and legs), distinctive boots (*socci*), and a distinctive shirt (*camicia*), to which might be added appropriate armor or a mantle. For women, the classical dress regularly included short skirts and boots that extended to mid-calf, a fashion that departed considerably from historical accuracy.

By about 1565, the Renaissance had produced a systematic discussion of the principles of costuming in the *Quattro dialoghe* of Leone de Sommi (ca. 1525–ca. 1592). In this unpublished work, de Sommi described suitable theatrical costumes. First, they should be as sumptuous and as noble as possible. Even servants should dress elegantly, as long as their masters appeared even more lavishly garbed. Second, costumes should vary in order to help differentiate characters. The variety might be achieved

through changing colors, altering lines, or adding details like hats, capes, feathers, and ornaments. Third, exotic and colorful costumes should be used because they enhanced spectacle. A sprinkling of soldiers and gladiators was especially helpful in this regard. For exotic costumes, designers might well follow the styles set forth in painting and sculpture. Modern dress should always be avoided.

By the end of the sixteenth century, several published books were available. Ferdinando Bertelli's book of Italian fashion, published in 1563, was reissued in 1569. By 1589, Caesar Vecellio had published the first book of costuming to try to recapture international fashions of the past as well as the present. Although often inaccurate, the book nevertheless provided a new base from which historical dress might be attempted. And in 1597, a Frenchman, Robert Boissard, published a novel book—not of fashion but of original designs for Oriental, fantastic, and historical costumes. The publication of these books doubtless made information about costuming more widely available than ever before. Probably, too, the books moved costuming practices in the direction of more, rather than less, standardization by offering approved models for emulation.

Before the seventeenth century, then, costuming as an element of theatrical design for the erudite theatre was acknowledged and its current practices were available for study by anyone who could read.

Theatre Buildings

Before about 1550, the production of plays by the academies and the courts was so occasional that temporary theatres sufficed. By about 1550, however, productions were offered regularly enough to warrant the erection of permanent theatre buildings. An examination of these early permanent theatres reveals that, as in staging, a tension existed between the desire to replicate classical (usually Roman) practices and the need to express the vitality of the new age. In the case of architecture, this tension expressed itself in a spatial conflict between the precedents of the older facade stages of Greece and Rome and the contemporary fascination with perspective techniques in architecture and painting.

The first permanent theatre of the Italian Renaissance was the Teatro Olimpico, begun at Vicenza in 1580 for the Olympic Academy.[28] Founded in 1555 to study Greek drama, the academy had periodically staged plays in temporary theatres for the edification of its members, an elite group of connoisseurs and scholars that included the great architect Andrea Palladio (1518–1580). Before Palladio undertook the design of the Teatro Olimpico, his last major work, he had already completed many *pallazzi*, villas, churches, and government buildings, drawing heavily for all of them on Roman classical precedents. Palladio was quite familiar with both the monuments and the traditions of classical architecture, for he had written a book, *Antichita di Roma* (1554), and had illustrated a contemporary study of Vitruvius (1556). Indeed, Palladio had even boasted that Vitruvius had been his "maestro e guido," his inspiration.[29]

For the Teatro Olimpico (which was to be erected inside an already-existing building), Palladio planned an architectural facade pierced by five doorways and adorned with assorted columns and statuary. He planned, in short, some version of the imperial Roman stage. The auditorium, as in the Roman theatre, was to include a semicircular *orchestra,* around which was wrapped the seating, built up in stadium style and ending in a columned aisleway at the back. In fact, except for being smaller and being indoors, the theatre designed by Palladio fulfilled well his wish "to construct a theatre according to the ancient use of the Greeks and Romans."[30]

Palladio died within months after the beginning of construction, however, and the completion of the theatre fell to younger architects. For *Oedipus Rex,* the choice for the theatre's official opening in 1585, Vincenzo Scamozzi (1552–1616) added street scenes (in perspective) be-

hind each doorway: "streets of the city of Thebes, represented with a show of lovely houses, and palaces and temples, and altars in the antique style, of most fine architecture, and of solid wood so that they may last always. The expense for this came to 1500 ducats."[31] These vistas were cleverly arranged so that every seat in the house had a view into one of the doorways, thus permitting every member of the illustrious Academy to enjoy the delights of perspective. Thus was the replication of the old facade stage wedded with the age's interest in illusion (see Figure 11.8).

After his work at the Teatro Olimpico, Scamozzi was hired to design a complete theatre, this time for a nobleman in the town of Sabbi onetta. For the stage of this indoor court theatre, Scamozzi abandoned Palladio's classical model, eliminating the ornate *scaena frons* in favor of a stage that represented the vista of a single street, in the manner of Serlio. Although lacking a proscenium arch, the stage did provide a series of angled wings whose diminishing size gave the illusion of increasing distance when seen by the audience. For the audience area of this small court theatre, Scamozzi observed strict social protocol. The duke and his family had seating in an elevated area at the back of the auditorium (from which the view of the perspective was best); his most important visitors had seating on raised benches around part of the *orchestra* area. Scamozzi's design moved clearly in the direction of the contemporary interest in perspective and away from the classical facade.

The still later Teatro Farnese (begun 1618, opened 1628) affirmed this shift in taste by providing a permanent proscenium arch and two additional framing devices that accentuated the illusion of depth. Designed by Giovanni Battista Aleotti (for a time, painter and architect at the court of a Farnese duke), this court theatre retained the traditional duke's box and raised benches arranged in a semicircle (later remodeled into a U-shape). The *orchestra* area was left open to permit court dances or other spectacles.

The stage, in addition to this permanent proscenium arch and other framing devices, contained a variety of scenic machines that Aleotti noted in his final report to the duke: Mercury's flying machine, Aurora's machine, several wing carriages, "which make the side scenes go forward and backward," a central drum "for moving the wings forth and back," and a machine for imitating the waves of the sea.[32] The contemporary courtly interest in perspective and spectacular effects was thus accommodated by a well-equipped theatre with a permanent

FIGURE 11.8

The Teatro Olimpico was an inventive blend of a classical facade and a Renaissance interest in perspective vistas. Note the vomitories, the steps into the orchestra, and the covered aisle at the top of the audience area, all based on classical precedent. Compare the plan (from Walker) with the two views (from Streit) to understand just how suitable for use by an academy this theatre was.

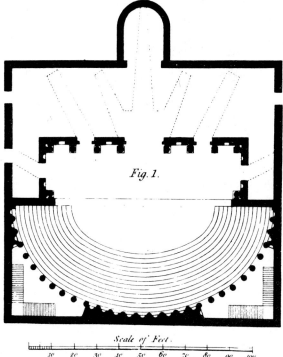

Fig. 1.

Scale of Feet.
10   20   30   40   50   60   70   80   90   100

FIGURE 11.9

The Teatro Farnese was a more typical Renaissance theatre, with a permanent proscenium arch and a large space for dancing and other courtly entertainments. [From Streit.]

proscenium arch—as far as we know, the first in the world (see Figure 11.9).

Renaissance theatre, then, was mostly a courtly and academic enterprise aimed at educated and wealthy patrons. Its most spectacular displays were given primarily in temporary court theatres built to accommodate scenery arranged in a series of angle wings and terminating in a back shutter or drop, all painted in single-point perspective (drawn for the view of the most important member of the audience). These displays relied on an array of machines and special effects and most often occurred between the acts of a regular drama. At court, the displays were usually more applauded than the dramas in which they were imbedded, a situation better understood if we consider the nature of Renaissance drama.

Renaissance Drama

Renaissance drama arose from a literary rather than a theatrical impulse. Its early playwrights were humanists who strove to recapture aspects of classical culture, and so they read and studied classical literature, including classical drama.

Most often studied were the Latin plays of Seneca, Terence, and Plautus. Although locally available throughout the Middle Ages, the plays became more widely known and consulted after their first printings: Terence in about 1471, Plautus in 1472, and Seneca in about 1485. During the 1480s and 1490s, plays by Plautus and Terence were being regularly performed at courts; by about 1485, Seneca's *Hippolytus* had been performed by the Roman Academy. Less readily available and therefore less well known were the Greek models, none of which was published in Greek before 1500 nor in Latin before the 1540s (see Figure 11.2).

By 1500, some humanists were writing original plays, usually in Latin and with unmistakable reliance on classical models. For example, Albertino Mussato's tragedy *Eccerinus* (ca. 1315), the earliest known Italian tragedy, was written in Latin with five acts, a chorus, and a messenger, all echoes of Senecan practice. Pier Paolo Vergerio's early comedy *Paulus* (ca. 1390) was written in Latin and in five acts. The acts were even labeled *protasis, epistasis,* and *catastrophe,* in the manner of Terence.[33]

These early humanists were affected by Italy's other traditions, however. The subjects of fourteenth- and fifteenth-century plays, for example, drew from native as well as classical sources. Although many plays dramatized events of Greek or Roman mythology or history, *Eccerinus* told of an event in Italian history, and *Paulus* of life in a medieval Italian university. *Orfeo* (1472), the first surviving nonreligious play written in Italian, drew its story from Greek mythology, but its rambling and actless structure owed more to the *sacra rappresentazione* than to classical tragedy. Italian farce, a popular entertainment that was neither classical nor literary, flourished in and around several cities and helped shape some plays that followed. Thus, by the sixteenth century in Italy, a cleavage had already formed between popular drama (mostly religious plays or rustic farces) and erudite drama, or *commedia erudita* (mostly done in courts and schools). The cleavage was only partly bridged with the flowering of *commedia dell'arte* late in the century.

Erudite Drama (Commedia Erudita)

Throughout the sixteenth century, erudite (learned) dramas, now written in Italian rather than Latin, drew inspiration from classical sources.

Learned comedies most often adapted or imitated the works of Terence, although Plautus and (rarely) Aristophanes might serve as models. As the century progressed, increasing numbers of comic writers turned to Italian life and fiction (novels and romances mostly) for their stories, and by the century's end, some were drawing inspiration from earlier erudite comedies as well. From the outset, the comedies appeared in prose as well as verse, perhaps because in the medieval manuscripts of Terence, verse had been copied out as if it were prose. A list of the major comedies is provided in Figure 11.10.

Early tragic writers were divided among those who desired to follow Greek models (especially Sophocles and the advice of Aristotle) and those who preferred Seneca. The leader of

the Grecian advocates was Giangiorgio Trissino (1478–1550), who argued that Senecan tragedies were "for the most part fragments of Greek matter, put together with very little art."[34] In 1515, Trissino completed the first important erudite tragedy written in Italian: *Sofonisba*. Although quite successful with other humanists, the play failed to capture the public. After its first publication in 1524, it had nine additional printings before 1620; it was not performed, however, until 1562, twelve years after Trissino's death. The leader of the Roman adapters was Giambattista Giraldi Cinthio (1504–1573), who argued that Seneca surpassed "in prudence, in gravity, in decorum, in majesty, in sentiments all the Greeks who ever wrote."[35] His famous tragedy *Orbecche* was produced in 1541 to such great public acclaim that it set the standard against which later tragedies were evaluated. Thus, the controversy between Greek and Roman adherents was clearly resolved in favor of Rome. A list of the major tragedies is provided in Figure 11.11.

Late in the century, a third kind of erudite drama grew popular. *Pastorals* (often tragicomedies) probably grew both out of the romantic traditions of Italian fiction and out of a desire to emulate a Greek satyr play (the understanding of which rested largely on Vitruvius' description of its setting). Based on the love affairs of shepherds and shepherdesses, the plays typically formulated actions of only fleeting seriousness and thus ended happily. The vogue for such plays was set by Torquato Tasso's *Aminta* (1573) and Giovan Battista Guarini's *The Faithful Shepherd* (1590).

The erudite drama of the Italian Renaissance, like its Roman predecessors, was probably more important for its influence than for its intrinsic merit. The erudite comedies were replaced both on the stage and in the bookshops by the *scenarii* of the professional actors, and tragedy gave way to a rising interest in opera, an art developed by an academy seeking to reproduce Greek drama, with its chorus: "Indeed by the end of the seventeenth century in Italy

FIGURE 11.10

Notable Italian Comedies of the Renaissance

Date	Title	Author	Comments
ca. 1390	*Paulus*	Pier Paolo Vergerio	First known Italian comedy (in Latin)
1483	*Epirota*	Thomas Medius	Best comedy of the fifteenth century?
1503	*Formicone*	Publio Filippo Mantovano	First erudite comedy in prose
1508	*La Cassaria*	Lodovico Ariosto	Major author; wrote also *La Lena, I suppositi* (1509), *Il Negromanta* (1530), and *Scolastica;* major influence on English authors
1513	*La Calandria*	Bernardo Dovizi da Bib-biena	Perhaps the most influential comedy of the sixteenth century
1513–1520(?)	*Mandragola*	Niccolò Machiavelli	Author noted for *The Prince;* wrote another comedy *La Clizia*
1524–1542(?)	*La Cortigiana*	Pietro Aretino	Major author; other comedies include *Marescalco, Ipocrita, Talanta,* and *Filosofo*
1536	*L'Amor Costante*	Alessandro Piccolomini	Major humanist; wrote also *Alessandro* (ca. 1543)
1550(?)	*L'Assiuolo*	Giovanni M. Cecchi	Major author; most prolific writer of the sixteenth century; wrote at least twenty-one comedies
1550s	*Il Ruffiano*	Lodovico Dolce	Prolific writer; five comedies and several tragedies
1556	*Flora*	Luigi Alamanni	Strict neoclassical comedy
1606	*L'Astrologo*	Giambattista Della Porta	Major author; fourteen extant comedies
1613	*L'Idropica*	Giovan Battista Guarini	Major author; noted for *The Faithful Shepherd* and for theoretical statements in support of tragicomedy
1582(?)	*Il Candelaio*	Giordano Bruno	Major humanist; best play of the last half of the sixteenth century?

traditional [erudite] comedies and tragedies were unperformed, unread, unprinted."[36]

Secular Popular Drama

Popular Italian farces varied widely in subject, length, and form, but in general, they aimed to entertain city people by displaying the foolish antics of ignorant rustics. Although such farces flourished around Naples, Siena, Florence, and Venice, they probably reached their zenith at Padua, where Ruzzante (né Angelo Beolco, 1502–1542) both wrote and acted in farces. The importance of farce declined after 1600 as its position was taken over by the growing popularity of the *commedia dell'arte.*

The origins of *commedia dell'arte* have been endlessly debated. Among the sources most commonly cited are Atellan farce, Roman comedy, Italian farce, and Italian erudite comedies. All or none of these precursors may have shaped the *commedia dell'arte.* The available evidence about its early history is too sparse and scattered to permit sure answers. Whatever its source, however, *commedia dell'arte* was clearly established by 1550.

Organized as sharing ventures, *commedia* troupes typically toured with about a dozen players—seven or eight of whom were men. The relatively small size of the troupes was possible in part because most of the players wore masks, but unlike the masks of the ancient theatre, those of the *commedia* lacked a single defining expression and covered only a part of the head and face. Made of leather and linen, the masks allowed the actors considerable freedom of

FIGURE 11.11

Notable Italian Tragedies and Pastorals of the Renaissance

Date	Title	Author	Comments
ca. 1315	*Eccerinus*	Albertino Mussato	Earliest known Italian tragedy (in Latin)
ca. 1390	*Achilles*	Antonio Laschi	Earliest known Italian tragedy based on mythology
1472	*Orfeo*	Angelo Poliziano	First pastoral drama; first surviving nonreligious play in Italian
1515	*Sofonisba*	Giangiorgio Trissino	First regular tragedy; Greek model; written in Italian
1541	*Orbecche*	Giambattista Giraldi Cinthio	Major author of comedies and tragedies (*Didone*, *Cleopatra*), as well as a theorist (*Discorsi*, 1554); Roman models
1547	*Didone*	Lodovico Dolce	Major writer; five comedies; tragedies include *Marianna* (1565), *Thyeste* (1543), *Hecuba* (1543), *Giocasta* (1549), *Ifigenia* (1551), *Medea* (1558), and *Le Troiane* (1566); influenced several English authors
1581	*Aminta*	Torquato Tasso	Influential pastoral; also wrote *Torrismondo* (1573?); best-known "gothic" tragedy of the sixteenth century
1590	*Pastor Fido*	Giovan Battista Guarini	Influential pastoral; major writer of theory; supporter of the genre tragicomedy
1593(?)	*Semiramis*	Muzio Manfredi	Best example of Italian "tragedy of blood"

movement and permitted communication through facial expression, the mouth and lower jaw being unmasked. Both masks and costumes served primarily to identify the characters wearing them, and in time they tended to become standardized, reflecting the nature of the *commedia* characters.

Commedia characters tended to repeat from play to play—and even from troupe to troupe. The usual stock types for women were lovers, mothers, maids, nurses, bawds, and courtesans; for the men, they were lovers, old men (usually fathers, merchants, soldiers, and doctors), and servants (*zanni*). Depending on the particular performer and troupe, the stock types displayed somewhat different traits and took different names. Thus, the female lovers (*innamorate*), might be named, for example, Cornelia, Isabella, Lucinda, Flaminia, Lucrezia, or Lavinia, and soldiers might be named, for example, Capitano, Cocodrillo, Matamoros, or Spavento.

A typical troupe retained one or two sets of lovers, two servants, and two old men; the troupe then added some combination of the remaining characters in keeping with the preferences and abilities of its members. Although the individual traits of a stock character often varied radically among the several performers, some general traits were repeated from performer to performer and even from troupe to troupe. These traits have been briefly summarized in Figure 11.12.

Commedia players might gain considerable fame during their careers. The leading actress of *commedia* was an *innamorata* named Isabella Andreini (1562–1604), whose acting, singing, dancing, and fluency in several languages earned her an international reputation during the sixteenth century. Her skill as a poet and her general erudition earned her a place, as well, in a prestigious Italian academy. One of the best-known actors was Flaminio Scala (fl. 1575–1620), whose role as the lover Flavio earned him

FIGURE 11.12

Major Character Types of the *Commedia dell'arte* During the Sixteenth and Seventeenth Centuries

Type and Common Names	Noted Italian Performers	Major Traits	Appearance
Lovers			
Innamorata			
Cornelia, Isabella, Lucinda, Flaminia, Lucrezia, Lavinia	Isabella Andreini Vincenza Armiani Vittoria degli Amorevoli	Beautiful; sophisticated; innocent and noble, or wench saved by noble love	Unmasked; dressed in latest fashion
Innamorato			
Flavio, Ottavio, Orazio, Silvio, Leandro, Lelio, Mario, Fulvio	Flaminio Scala G. B. Andreini Domenico Bruni	Handsome; dapper and engaging but faintly ridiculous, foolishly passionate	Unmasked; dressed in latest fashion
Comic Masked Characters			
Capitano			
Spavento, Spezzafer, Cocodrillo, Matamoros, Rinoceronte, and later Crispin	Francesco Andreini Fabrizio de Fornaris Girolamo Garavini	Originally young Italian lover; later and more commonly a foolish Spanish braggart; pompous, ineffectual coward; unwelcome suitor	Extravagant dress that usually included cape, sword, and plumed hat; mask with menacing nose and bristling mustache; changed with changing military fashions
Dottore			
Gracian Baloardo, Plusquamperfetto, Dottor Gratiano, Partesana da Francolin	Ludovico de Bianchi Luzio Burchiella Ludovico (of Bologna)	Professor or physician; speaks Bolognese dialect peppered with inaccurate Latin; credulous pedant; friend of Pantalone	Black academic robes with small black toque; black or flesh-colored mask covering forehead and nose; often pointed beard and rouged cheeks
Pantalone			
Cassandre, Zanobio, Facanappa, Bernardone	Il Braga Bruni Luigi Benotti	Greedy and lustful merchant; speaks Venetian dialect; if married, a cuckold; if not, an unwelcome rival; a dupe or meddler	Brown mask with hook nose and white beard; sometimes glasses; long red legs, loose black cape; Turkish slippers
Pulcinella			
Cucurucu, Meo-Patacca, Marco-Pepe, and later Punch and Hanswurst	Silvio Fiorilli Andrea Calcese	Varied characteristics; often Neopolitan bachelor; a cruel sensualist; glutton; feigns stupidity but crafty; often vulgar	Humpback; protruding stomach; big hooked nose; pantaloons, wooden sword, and fat wallet
Scaramuccio	Tiberio Fiorilli	Varied; began as soldier; occasionally a servant; loves women and booze; a friend of Pulcinella	Masked or heavily powdered; all in black

FIGURE 11.12 (continued)

Type and Common Names	Noted Italian Performers	Major Traits	Appearance
Servants (Zanni)			
Arlecchino			
Truffaldino, Bagatino, Trivelino, Guazzeto, Harlequin, Arlequin	Alberto Ganassa Tristano Martinelli J. B. Andreini	Extremely varied; foolish yet shrewd; resilient; supple body of acrobat or dancer	Black mask; often a padded phallus; usually a slapstick; at first a patchwork costume and later the formal colored diamond garb
Brighella			
Bagatino, Flautino, Beltrame, later Scapin	Niccolo Barbieri Giovanni Gherardi	Often companion of Harlequin; a rascally intriguer, thief, liar, drinker, swaggerer, insolent jack-of-all trades	Olive-tinted mask, sloe eyes, hooked nose, prominent chin, thick lips, mustache; full trousers and jacket with green braid; carried purse and dagger; later, servant's livery
Pedrolino			
Piero, Pagliaccio, Peppe Nappa, Giglio, later Pierrot	Giovanni Pellesini Giuseppe Giratone	Valet often in love with soubrette; a sympathetic though comic character	Heavily powdered but played without mask; similar to Pulcinello's garb but better fitting and less exaggerated
Soubrette			
Fantesca, Licetta, Betta, Nina, Gitta, Olivetta, Fiametta, and later Columbine	Battista da Treviso (man) Silvia Roncagli Catherine Biancolelli	Often in love with another servant—occasionally the wife of Harlequin; often waits upon *innamorata*	Buxom; large apron; diverse costumes; often is disguised as doctor, cavalier, Harlequin, etc.

less fame than did his early publication of a collection of *commedia scenarii*. More famous as an actor was Tristano Martinelli (ca. 1557–1630), player of the famous servant Arlecchino.

In addition to their professional status, use of masks, and reliance on stock characters, *commedia* players were also noted for their improvisatory playing, at least after 1568. Although *commedia* troupes occasionally played erudite comedies, tragedies, and pastorals, more commonly they worked from story outlines, called *scenarii*, outlines that they filled in during the performance. The *scenarii* were often drawn from situations found in Plautus and Terence or in the erudite comedies of the day.

To flesh out the *scenarii*, the performers re-lied heavily on stock comic turns (*lazzi*) to enliven the scenes. *Lazzi* might be as simple as catching and eating a fly or turning a flip, but they might be as complex as a small skit to be tucked inside the larger skit. The *lazzi* were generalized enough so that they could be transferred among several plays and used for many different situations. They became so familiar and so standardized that often a *scenario* would call for a *lazzo* by name—the lazzo of nightfall or the lazzo of begging—without further elaboration. *Lazzi* were cued by specific lines that one character spoke to initiate the business; the other actors, on hearing the lines, knew to begin the comic turn. Most of our information about the *lazzi* comes from extant *scenarii*, actors' memoires, audiences' reports, and surviving manuscripts of collected *lazzi* (see Figure 11.13).

As well as the *lazzi*, other practices tended to diminish the amount of improvisation used by the troupes. The actors were encouraged to memorize suitable lines to utter on entering the action and clever couplets with which they could effect an exit. Such memorized bits were reused among several plays and were joined by other memorized snippets of dialogue, monologues, conceits, poems, songs, and set speeches that might be suitable for various sorts of recurring

---

FIGURE 11.13

Representative *Lazzi* of *Commedia Dell'Arte* Held at the Library of Perugia (As Translated by Herschel Garfein and Mel Gordon)*

---

2) *Lazzo of the pellegrina* (*a special, short cloak worn by travelers*): The lovers, supplicating Coviello, fall to their knees, and Coviello, bending to speak to one, sticks his ass in the other's face.

4) *Lazzo of crying and laughing*: The old man and his son have each tricked the other. The old man is crying over the departure of his son; at the same time, he is laughing in anticipation of sleeping with his son's mistress. Thinking the reverse, the son is also laughing and crying.

13) *Lazzi of water*: The mistress has fainted and the servant-girl cries for water. Pulcinella brings her all kinds of water: rosewater, jasmine water, orange water, mint water, lily water. Finally, he pisses in a cup and splashes it on his mistress. This revives her, and he sings the praises of "the water distilled by our rod."

34,35,36) *Latin lazzi*: The doctor, or the pedant, makes a number of statements in Latin that the Neapolitan Pulcinella misunderstands. For example, the Vergil line, "The queen for some time had been pressed by love," becomes in Pulcinella's head, "The queen, being pregnant, twice ate raw sausage." Or, Vergil's "The ship cast anchor by the curved shore" is interpreted as "The anchor broke the bottom of the boat and sent a letter with a crow." Or Pulcinella thinks that *rumpe moras* ("break off"; "end delay") means "Your ass hurts."

---

*List taken and quoted directly from Herschel Garfein and Mel Gordon, "The Adriani Lazzi of the *Commedia Dell'Arte*," *The Drama Review* 22, 1 (March 1978): 8, 12.

situations. These memorized parts and the *lazzi*, as well as the ensemble playing that resulted from years of acting together, obviously meant that the performances were not entirely improvisational.

On the other hand, improvisation was a skill of which the players themselves were very proud. A seventeenth-century Harlequin boasted:

> The Italian comedians . . . need but to glance at the subject of a play a moment or two before going upon the stage. It is this very ability to play at a moment's notice which makes a good Italian actor so difficult to replace. Anyone can learn a part and recite it on the stage, but something else is required for Italian comedy. For a good Italian actor is a man of infinite resources and resourcefulness, a man who plays more from imagination than from memory; he matches his words and actions so perfectly with those of his colleague on the stage that he enters instantly into whatever acting and movements are required of him in such a manner as to give the impression that all that they do has been prearranged.[37]

Renaissance Performers

For the most part, the actors in the courts and schools were not professionals but amateurs. Drawn from among students, teachers, courtiers, and friends, such performers engaged in acting for pleasure or fulfillment or education, but not for money. Some groups of young nobles, like the *compagnie della calza* of Venice, were formed specifically to sponsor plays and to provide the spectacles required for noble celebrations. They regarded the planning and financing of such pageants as training for higher civic responsibilities. The social status of such amateurs was never downgraded; they were considered ladies and gentlemen—not actors. Whenever unseemly behavior was required, a professional player was hired to perform it.

Professionals were brought into the courts to perform—sometimes erudite tragedies, comedies, and pastorals but more often their own *scenarii*. While at court, the players often used the intricate perspective scenery and elaborate machines available, but while playing in the public streets and squares, these same players might play just as comfortably on a temporary and flimsy facade stage, one especially built for the occasion out of a platform and a painted curtain. By playing both at court and in public, the *commedia dell'arte* formed an important link between the popular theatre and the courtly and academic theatres.

Professional troupes were usually organized as sharing companies in which responsibilities and expectations were clearly stated. Personnel within the companies often shifted as actors came and went, and troupes dissolved, combined, and re-formed. An early contract illustrates the point well. Eight men agreed to form a company of actors from Easter 1545 to Carnival 1546. The members of the troupe were forbidden to gamble with one another—except for food. They were to play comedies "from place to place" under the leadership of an actor known as Zannino. In case of illness, the sick actor would be supported by the common funds—which would also buy a horse to carry the troupe's luggage. These common funds were to be kept in a small chest with three keys, each held by a different member of

the troupe. This chest was to be opened and the funds were to be disbursed only with everyone's consent. If any member, "to his great dishonor and shame," should run away, he would lose all rights and privileges and all use of the money. He would as well be fined, with one third of the fine going to the "governors (*rettori*) of the place where we are," one third to the poor, and one third to the company. Any money left in the chest was to be divided in Padua in June.[38]

The troupes traveled—if not constantly, still very regularly—in order to tap new audiences among the still small and scattered towns; they traveled as well to avoid the pockets of persecution that they encountered among church and civic leaders, many of whom believed professional actors to be socially and morally unfit. The popularity of the best players led their troupes to be taken under the protection of courts and noblemen, thus gaining a measure of financial stability but losing a measure of independence (see Figures 11.14 and 11.15).

Renaissance Dramatic Theory

In dramatic theory, as in other fields, the men of the Italian Renaissance were determined to

FIGURE 11.14
Notable *Commedia Dell'Arte* Troupes of the Sixteenth and Seventeenth Centuries

Name	Dates Flourished	Comments
Ganassa's Troupe	1568–1583	Alberto Ganassa may have been the first Arlecchino
Gelosi ("zealous")	1569–1604	Troupe of Isabella Andreini; *scenarii* are extant, preserved by F. Scala
Confidenti ("trusting")	1574–1621	Protégés of the Medici family for a time
Desiosi ("desirous")	1580–1595	
Uniti ("united")	1585–1620	Formed by actors from other troupes? Associated for a time with the duke of Mantua
Accesi ("inspired")	1590–1630	Troupe of Tristano Martinelli, famous Arlecchino; associated with Mantua; played in France regularly
Fideli ("faithful")	1598–1650	Leader was son of Isabella Andreini

FIGURE 11.15

Commedia dell'arte was arguably the most successful dramatic entertainment of Italy during the seventeenth century. What cultural factors changed to cause its declining importance before 1800? [From *The Theatre,* London.]

Pullicimiello·   Sig.ª Lucretia·   Scaramucia.   Fricasso·

profit from the wisdom of the ancients. Both Horace and Aristotle were available, although knowledge of the latter had been impeded by bad Latin translations and the transmission of corrupt manuscripts. Nevertheless, Aristotle (often misinterpreted) formed the basis for much Renaissance thinking about the purpose and nature of drama. A series of commentaries on Aristotle and some original formulations began to appear around the middle of the sixteenth century, and their tenets finally coalesced into the doctrine now called *neoclassicism* (literally, "new classicism"). As in design, architecture, and drama, the Renaissance Italians devised a new system even while insisting they were reviving ancient practices. Neoclassical theorists declared that they were making Aristotle clear to their own age.

The major doctrines of neoclassicism can be briefly summarized. Basic to the system was a commitment to *verisimilitude* (literally, "truth-seemingness"), a concept far more complex than its facile definition suggests. The "truth" that the neoclassicists sought to reproduce in the drama was one based on the typical—or general—attributes of a class rather than on unique or particularizing details of individuals. Thus,

characters should behave with *decorum;* that is, they should behave as befit their age, sex, and social class. The aberrational person or situation was not really "true" and should therefore be avoided. If such a person had to be included, she or he should be roundly punished for the peculiarity.

Similarly, supernatural events were to be eschewed unless they formed a necessary part of the story received from myth, history, or the Bible. If supernatural happenings had to be included, they should be minimized—perhaps by having the event or character offstage and merely reported to the audience. Because people did not really talk to themselves, soliloquies and monologues were avoided; in their place were dialogues facilitated by *confidants* or messengers. Because in God's world (the true world), good was rewarded and evil punished, dramas should likewise dispense justice; that evil occasionally appeared to go unpunished in this world was an aberration and thus an unsuitable subject for drama.

A late Roman commentary on Terence and a misinterpretation of Aristotle combined with the neoclassicists' commitment to verisimilitude to produce the curious doctrine of the "three unities," according to which playwrights were to observe the unities of time, of place, and of action. Aristotle advocated only unity of action, but the Renaissance theorists (following the lead of early Renaissance dramatists) reasoned that an audience seated in the theatre for a short time to watch a play would not accept as true a rapid change of place or an extended period of time.

Depending on the particular theorist, unity of time could mean anywhere from a twenty-four-hour period to the actual playing time of the drama, and unity of place could vary from a single site to the walking distance of a single day. Whatever the particular form of the rules, their general intention was clear: plays were to depict a single action within a restricted time and place. By 1540, the setting of some plays included a mechanical sun that rose at the beginning of the first act and set at the end of the last act, suggesting that the day and the duration of the performance coincided. As well, the widespread use of single-point perspective to create the illusion of a real place provided an impetus for considering the stage a single space.

Because verisimilitude depended on essence or generality, a commitment to purity of form (or genre) arose. Tragic elements should not mix with comic ones because tragedies were *essentially* different from comedies. Tragedies depicted affairs of state that were conducted by noble characters speaking an elevated and poetic language; they had unhappy endings. Comedies, on the other hand, depicted domestic affairs among ordinary people speaking a pedestrian verse or prose; they ended happily. Purity of form meant, then, not only that funny scenes or happy endings should be avoided in tragedies but also that prose tragedies written about the daily problems of the middle class were unacceptable.

In a clear departure from Aristotle, the neoclassicists insisted that the purpose of drama was to teach and to please. This echo of Horace probably assumed importance as a consequence of the need felt by Renaissance theorists to justify the existence of a drama and a theatre that were not religious. When secular theatre began, the problem of justification assumed an importance unknown to the medieval theatre, where the justification was clear: the plays were a glorification of God and a teaching of His word to His people.

Finally, following what seemed to be the practices of Seneca and the advice of Horace, the neoclassicists advocated five acts for the drama. With minor variations, then, neoclassical doctrine was complete: the drama should be verisimilar; it should have decorous characters; it should observe the three unities and display purity of form; it should be written in five acts; and it should both teach and please its audiences.

Despite its acceptance in educated circles in Italy from about 1550 to about 1750, neoclassicism did not capture general audiences. Attacks on it by some playwrights and critics continued throughout the period, and many audiences paid no attention to it whatever, demanding spectacles and mixed genres. Nonetheless, the impact of neoclassical doctrine was significant and must be acknowledged. For a summary of the major theorists of the period, see Figure 11.16.

The Aftermath of the Italian Renaissance

By 1600, Italian theorists, playwrights, and designers were influencing theatre and drama in other parts of western Europe. The tenets of neoclassicism triumphed in France after about 1636 (see pp. 291–294). By the 1700s, German dramatists were being urged by German intellectuals to adopt French neoclassical models. In England, comic writers like Ben Jonson, George Chapman, and John Marston used Italian comedies as models for their own; and as Marvin T. Herrick has reminded us, "every student of Elizabethan drama . . . knows that English tragedy between Gascoigne and Shirley is

FIGURE 11.16
Major Theoretical Writings of the Renaissance

Date	Author	Comments
Early Translations of the **Poetics**		
1498	Giorgio Valla	First Latin translation
1536	Alessandro Pazzi	First good Latin translation published
1549	Bernardo Segni	First Italian translation published
1576	Anonymous	Second Italian translation published
Commentaries on the **Poetics**		
1548	Francesco Robortello	Advocated unity of time, interpreted as a twelve-hour day; extended Aristotle to comedy
1550	Vicentio Maggi	
1560	Victorius Vettori	
1570	Lodovico Castelvetro	First to formulate the *three unities;* stressed the importance of *verisimilitude;* together with Minturno and Scaliger, established neoclassicism
Treatises on the Art of Poetry That Showed Aristotelian Influence		
1527	Vida	Influence of Horace dominated
1529	Giangiorgio Trissino	Published in three parts; first not dependent on Aristotle; last two,
1562		published posthumously, were clearly derivative
1536	Bernardino Daniello	Influence of both Horace and Aristotle
1543	Giambattista Giraldi Cinthio	*Discourse on Comedies and Tragedies;* cited Aristotle but did not follow slavishly
1559	Antonio Minturno	Along with Castelvetro and Scaliger established authority of Aristotle in Italian dramatic theory
1561	Julius Caesar Scaliger	Very authoritarian view of Aristotle, but sided with Horace in the view that poetry should teach as well as please, advocated the importance of *verisimilitude*
1599	Giovan Battista Guarini	*Compendium of Tragicomic Poetry;* knew but did not strictly follow Aristotle; argued for the legitimacy of a third genre, *tragicomedy*

teeming with Italian plots, characters, and stylistic devices."[39]

In no area, however, were the contributions of the Italian Renaissance greater or more lasting than in the area of scenic design and theatre architecture. The earlier phase of Italianate staging was over by about 1600, when Serlian settings behind proscenium arches had become standard. Serlio's system of design, although productive of illusion, did not permit rapid changes of setting. As the architectural details of Serlio's system began to be replaced by painted details, however, scene changes could be more easily effected, and the courtly audience's appetite for lavish scenic displays led to considerable experimentation in movable scenery.

By 1638, when Nicola Sabbattini (1575–1645) published his *Manual for Constructing Theatrical Scenes and Machines*, three systems were apparently in use: one, relying on classical precedent, adapted *periaktoi* for use on Serlian perspective stages; the other two involved changing the appearance of angle wings, by either covering them up or replacing them.

Of more lasting consequence was Sabbattini's advice about changing the flat wings located at the back of the Serlian stage. He showed how they might be rapidly changed either by being slid along grooves placed overhead and on the floor or by being turned like the pages of a book. Clearly, the changing of flat wings was more efficient and quicker than the manipulation of angle wings.

By 1600, improved techniques in perspective painting allowed flat wings to be used in place of wings at all stage positions (except the first house, which remained an angle wing like later *returns* or *tormentors*). These flat wings could be easily and quickly changed by the use of grooves and "nests" of flats. When the flats were placed one behind another, old scenes could be quickly pulled from view to reveal new scenes already in place. Such nests and grooves dominated scenic practices until about 1650 on the Continent. America, England, and Holland retained this groove system of scene changing until wings and drops were abandoned altogether—mostly during the nineteenth century.

This Italianate system of wings, drops, and grooves was taken to the English court by the designer–architect Inigo Jones (1573–1652). Like many upper-class Londoners, Jones went to Italy to study. Beginning in 1600, he worked at the Florentine court with one of Italy's leading court architects and painters, Giulio Parigi (ca. 1570–1635). There he had access not only to Parigi's productions and advice, but also to the writings of Serlio, Palladio, Scamozzi, and others. When he returned to the English court in 1604 as its architect–painter, he knew well the latest Italian practices.

Jones first designed a theatrical event for James I in 1605. He provided scenery for *The Masque of Blackness* (English court masques were roughly the equivalent of Italian court *intermezzi*). For this piece, Jones abandoned the English medieval practices, *which were still popular in England.* Instead of medieval mansions dispersed throughout the hall, Jones introduced a perspective scene on a small stage built at one end of the hall. Also in the manner of the Italian court, he hid the scenery until the audience was assembled and ready, so that he could reveal the spectacle instantly by dropping a front curtain.

For masques produced in 1608, he introduced Renaissance cloud machines to increase the spectacle; he used a proscenium arch designed as a part of his scenery to help with the masking; and he used a kind of inner stage to increase still further the apparent sense of depth. In 1609, for the *Masque of Queens*, Jones used *periaktoi* to change from an "ugly Hell" to "the House of Fame" and then to "fama Bona."

Following a series of experiments during the decade of the 1630s, he revolutionized English staging at court in 1640 when he used a series of nested flat wings, overhead borders, and back shutters, all changeable by means of grooves, before the eyes of the audience. Through Jones, all major Italianate practices in staging had reached the English court before the Puritans seized control of the government in 1642—and closed the court as well as the theatres.

What Jones did for English staging, Joseph Furttenbach (1591–1667) did for German practices. Like Jones, Furttenbach studied at the court of Florence with Parigi, whom he regarded as his "patron, master, and teacher."[40] After Furttenbach returned to Germany, he wrote and published three books that contained extensive descriptions of contemporary scenic and lighting techniques: *Civil Architecture* (1628), *Recreational Architecture* (1640), and *Noble Mirror of Art* (1663). In his works, Furttenbach outlined the construction of stages, scenery, and seating. In addition to techniques for painting curtains and angle flats, he described ways of changing sets by using *periaktoi* (a technique already long out of date by the time Furttenbach's book was published). He described the construction and rigging of several kinds of cloud and flying machines as well as techniques for making fire, lightning, wind, hail, rain, ships, a fiery bush, and four different kinds of waves. Finally, Furttenbach described in considerable detail different kinds of lighting instruments and their proper placement (see Figure 11.17).

Furttenbach's books were important for

FIGURE 11.17

Joseph Furttenbach's theatre, showing *periaktoi* used in wing positions in front of a backdrop. [From Weddigen.]

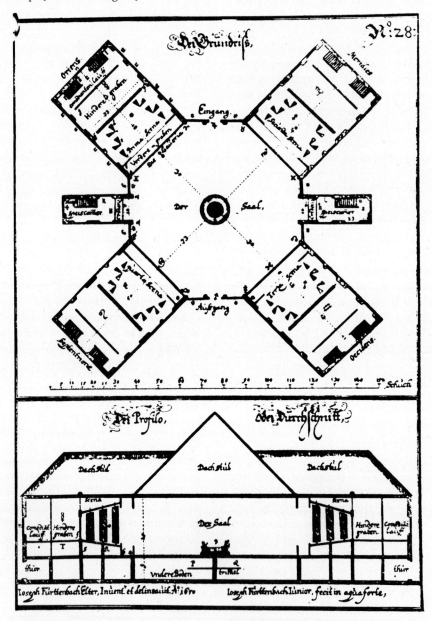

several reasons. They provided details of Italianate practices unavailable elsewhere, and they showed that these practices had been carried out of Italy and into Germany by the middle of the seventeenth century. As well, they suggested the state of lighting design and practice just after the Renaissance, and they did so in greater detail than was elsewhere available. Indeed, the innovations in lighting described by Furttenbach may have been his own, for contemporary Italian records give little attention to lighting, perhaps suggesting that the Italians regarded it as less important or that they had failed to discover ways of controlling its use.

The final major technical advance in stagecraft came in Italy between 1641 and 1645—after both Jones and Furttenbach had returned home. Giacomo Torelli (1608–1678) perfected a system known as the *chariot-and-pole.* Beneath the stage, a series of chariots ran on tracks parallel to the stage. Long poles attached to these chariots ran up through the stage floor (which was slotted for this purpose). The poles then extended several feet in the air. The scenery attached to the poles above stage level moved onto the stage whenever the chariots below the stage moved toward the center of their tracks; and the scenery disappeared into the wings as the chariots below the stage moved toward the outside edge of their tracks. By an elaborate system of interconnecting ropes, pulleys, and winches, all the scenery could be changed at once. By a coordination of the chariots with the machinery that controlled the borders and the flying, a rapid transformation of the entire setting could take place as if by magic before the eyes of the audience. Once perfected, the magical transformation became a major delight for courtly audiences and therefore an integral part of the spectacle of operas, ballets, and *intermezzi,* not only at court but in the new public theatres after about 1650.

The chariot-and-pole system did not remain long confined to Italy. In 1645, Torelli was summoned to Paris from Venice by the queen of France. For his first Parisian production (1645), Torelli converted a French court theatre (the Petit Bourbon) into an Italianate house— complete with a proscenium arch and a chariot-and-pole system for changing the sets. This production was a total triumph; thereafter, the Italianate system of staging dominated French theatres. And so, by about 1650, the chariot-and-pole system of scene changing joined the other

elements of the Italianate perspective setting in both Italy and France. By the eighteenth century, the system was widely adopted throughout the rest of western Europe, except in Holland and England (see Figure 11.18).

Renaissance innovations in theatre architecture also had repercussions. By 1600, there were several public theatres built along the lines previously adopted in the court theatres. (Venice had the first public Renaissance theatre in 1565, probably because her strong merchant

FIGURE 11.18

Illustration of a chariot-and-pole system published in the Diderot *Encyclopédie* during the mid-eighteenth century. [Courtesy Rare Books Room, Bowling Green State University.]

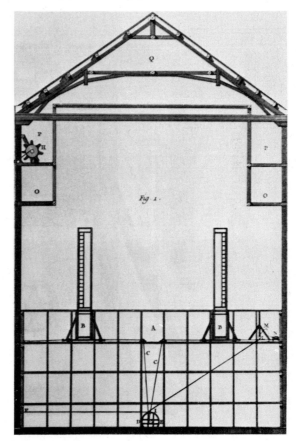

class was capable of supporting a theatre and no king exerted the power to monopolize theatrical entertainments for his court.) By 1637, opera in Venice was being performed for the general public, who thereafter regularly enjoyed those elaborate scenic displays previously restricted primarily to the Italian courts.

The public opera house, like the earlier court theatres, had a permanent proscenium arch and a complete complement of scenic equipment and machines. Unlike the court theatres, however, the audience areas in these opera houses were arranged for a large number of people and for people of various social classes. The box, pit, and gallery (similar to the arrangement in Shakespeare's playhouse) thus became standard for most public playhouses before 1650. As Italy exported its operatic productions throughout western Europe, it exported as well the major features of its public opera theatres: Italianate staging; chariot-and-pole methods of scene changing; proscenium arches; and box, pit, and gallery arrangements for the auditoriums (see Figure 11.19).

In almost every area of theatre and drama, then, the practices of the Italian Renaissance had touched the rest of Europe by 1650. And in almost every case, the Italians, while seeking to revive ancient practices, had produced an art more of their own times than of antiquity.

FIGURE 11.19

Illustration of a cloud machine in use (upper right) and the stage machinery of cloud borders published in the Diderot *Encyclopédie* during the mid-eighteenth century. [Courtesy Rare Books Room, Bowling Green State University.]

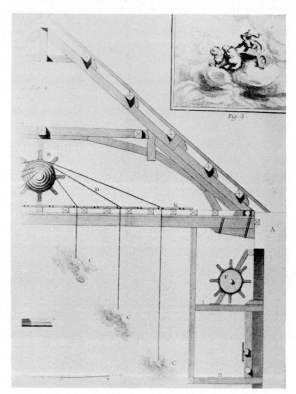

ENDNOTES

1. Robert Nisbet, "The Myth of the Renaissance," *Comparative Studies in Society and History* 15, 4 (October 1973): 473.
2. The significance of printing is excellently presented by Elizabeth L. Eisenstein, *The Printing Press as an Agent of Change*, 2 vols. (Cambridge: Cambridge University Press, 1979). Sections of this chapter rely heavily on her work.
3. Deno John Geanakoplos, *Interaction of the "Sibling" Byzantine and Western Cultures in the Middle Ages and Italian Renaissance (330–1600)* (New Haven, Conn.: Yale University Press, 1976), pp. 179–81, 203–212.
4. Eisenstein, p. 46.
5. Eisenstein, p. 45, who cites Michael Clapham. Emphasis ours.
6. Eisenstein, p. 303, who cites Arthur Geoffrey Dickens.
7. Eisenstein, p. 158.
8. Richard S. Samuels, "Benedetto Varchi, the Accademia degli Infiammati, and the Origins of the Italian Academic Movement," *Renaissance Quarterly* 29, 4 (Winter 1976): 629.
9. Samuels, p. 606.
10. Edward Muir, "Images of Power: Art and Pageantry in Renaissance Venice," *The Ameri-*

can Historical Review 84, 1 (February 1979): 19.

11. John White, *The Birth and Rebirth of Pictorial Space* (New York: Thomas Yoseloff, 1958), p. 120.

12. Leon Battista Alberti, as cited by White, p. 122.

13. George R. Kernodle, *From Art to Theatre: Form and Convention in the Renaissance* (Chicago: University of Chicago Press, 1944), p. 177.

14. Bonner Mitchell, "Circumstance and Setting in the Earliest Italian Productions," *Renaissance Drama*, n.s., 4 (1974): 193, cites a letter of Baldassar Castiglione.

15. Allardyce Nicoll, *Development of the Theatre* (New York: Harcourt, Brace and World, 1966), p. 73.

16. Vitruvius, *The Ten Books of Architecture*, trans. Morris Hicky Morgan (Cambridge, Mass.: Harvard University Press, 1926), p. 150.

17. Bernard Hewitt, ed., *The Renaissance Stage: Documents of Serlio, Sabbattini, and Furttenbach* (Coral Gables, Fla.: University of Miami Press, 1958), p. 32.

18. A. M. Nagler, *Theatre Festivals of the Medici, 1539–1637* (New Haven, Conn.: Yale University Press, 1964), p. 89.

19. Nagler, p. 63.

20. Nagler, p. 65.

21. Nagler, pp. 71–92.

22. Nagler, p. 15.

23. Hewitt, p. 35.

24. Nagler, p. 66.

25. Stella Mary Newton, *Renaissance Theatre Costume and the Sense of the Historic Past* (New York: Theatre Arts Books, 1975), pp. 152–153.

26. Nagler, pp. 24–33.

27. Newton, pp. 202–203.

28. There may have been earlier theatres (at Ferrara, perhaps) but none of them remains.

29. Ludwig H. Heydenreich and Wolfgang Lotz, *Architecture in Italy: 1400 to 1600*, trans. Mary Hottinger (Baltimore, Md.: Penguin Books, 1974), p. 304.

30. Kernodle, p. 169, who quotes a letter from Filippo Pigafetto.

31. Ibid.

32. Nagler, p. 153, who cites *Argomento, e ristretto dell torneo*.

33. Marvin T. Herrick, *Italian Comedy in the Renaissance* (Urbana: University of Illinois Press, 1960), p. 16.

34. Marvin T. Herrick, *Italian Tragedy in the Renaissance* (Urbana: University of Illinois Press, 1965), p. 45.

35. Herrick, *Tragedy*, p. 73.

36. Beatrice Corrigan, "Italian Renaissance Drama in the Eighteenth Century," *Comparative Drama* 10, 2 (Summer 1976): 102.

37. Pierre Louis Duchartre, *The Italian Comedy*, trans. Randolph T. Weaver (New York: Dover, 1966), pp. 30–32.

38. Winifred Smith, *Italian Actors of the Renaissance* (New York: Coward-McCann, 1939), pp. 23–24.

39. Herrick, *Tragedy*, p. 277.

40. Hewitt, p. 179.

12

Neoclassicism and the Baroque: Rules and Rule Makers, 1650–1750

Neoclassicism was an element of the Italian Renaissance. It was delayed in coming to the mainstream theatre of the north, but when it did, it came with a rush, and it came most of all to France. It then became a new phenomenon, a mix of truly classical ideas, of Italian understanding and misunderstanding of those ideas, and of French building on all of these as foundation. French neoclassicism had important qualities of order, authority, and grandeur that matched well with the ascendancy of France to the cultural leadership of Europe.

At the same time, Italian stage designers and machinists were carrying the theatrical techniques of Renaissance spectacle from Italy all over Europe. Originally advertised by private letters and ambassadorial reports, the lavish, often fantastic entertainments of Venice, Rome, Florence, and other Italian cities were envied and desired by northern rulers in an age of competitive opulence. Through the second half of the seventeenth century and the first half of the eighteenth, Italians created court spectacles in France, England, and the principalities of Germany, and in Spain, Hungary, Poland, and Scandinavia. Usually, the vehicle for these spectacles was Italian opera or specially written material like the masque. It was in these courtly and Italianate performances that the style called *baroque* was seen at its best—ornate, fanciful, and lush. At the very end of this period, the baroque style was lightened and often trivialized and sometimes became *rococo*, a mannered baroque.

The Period 1650–1750

The national boundaries that mark modern Europe were only roughly in place, but intensely national struggles were under way. Europe seemed in constant turmoil: Spain had engaged in a major adventure in the Low Countries, ultimately losing them and leaving the Netherlands without a crown, opening it for both federalism and a democratic theatre in which the baroque played no important part. Outside the Netherlands, however, royalty created national images in this age of absolute monarchy. Louis the XIV of France was the model for all.

Alliances shifted quickly. England had three wars with the Netherlands in the 1660s but accepted the Dutch Stadtholder as its king in 1689. France and England, enemies in the sixteenth century, were politically close at the royal level from 1660 until the late 1670s, only to break apart completely by 1700.

The French Century

"L'état, c'est moi," Louis XIV is supposed to have boasted ("I am the state"). He took the sun as his symbol. He proclaimed the *gloire* that still dazzles France. His long reign (1659–1715) saw France move from political turmoil to apparent stability. He and the court that he assembled at Versailles dominated the period as no imperial court had dominated since the fall of Byzantium.

Early in his life, Louis was seen as a lively figure with a love of the theatre, of art, and of beautiful women. The companion of his old age, Madame de Maintenon, symbolized in her narrow piety his shift from youthful exuberance to aged conservatism.

After Louis's death, the *gloire* remained, but assertions of royal power began to hinder, rather than to help, France's movement into the modern age, especially in competition with the "nation of shopkeepers" across the Channel.

England: Restoration, Revolution, and a German Succession

Charles I was beheaded in 1647; his son Charles II was "restored" to the throne in 1660 after years of Cromwellian rule (the Interregnum). This *restoration* of the monarchy gave the period its name through about 1685, although some scholars extend the period to 1700. Historians once viewed Charles II as a lightweight amoralist who did little but indulge in the pleasures he had learned in France, but he is now seen as a wily politician who brought England through a critical period. He was excellent at playing factions off: he accepted a secret pension from Louis XIV in 1670 but postponed indefinitely the concessions Louis wanted in return; he flirted with Catholicism during all of his reign but kept a nominal Protestantism.

Charles II loved the theatre. He also loved actresses and made an official (pensioned) mistress of Nell Gwynn, although, in the royal fashion of the day, he was a proper husband to his Portuguese queen. He was witty. He was a model to his court of what a courtier should be— verbally deft, cool, elegant, and self-indulgent. He may have wanted to take Louis XIV as his own model, but he was king by the invitation of a Parliament whose power was on the increase.

Charles's dour (and Catholic) brother James II ruled for only three years after Charles's death in 1685; he was replaced by his Protestant daughter Mary and her Protestant Dutch husband, William of Orange, in a parliamentary "bloodless revolution" that brought England both a sternly Protestant king and a written Bill of Rights. Thereafter, France and England went different ways. English power flowed toward Parliament and the increasingly important parliamentary political parties, but French power centered in the monarchy and a smaller cluster of upper nobility.

In 1714, the English crown passed (with Parliament's agreement) to James I's grandson, George, the Elector of Hanover, a German state; his son became George II in 1727. Thus, 1689 was a watershed, after which Parliament had increasing power as successive monarchs needed its support.

Science and Technology

The rational humanism of the Renaissance gave new life to science. One revolution in scientific thought derived from the work of Galileo Galilei (1564–1642), which accepted the Copernican idea of the sun's, rather than the earth's, centrality in our astronomical system, but which went much farther in defining a "new Nature," one almost without either God or man and "pictured . . . not as an organism, but as a machine, engine, or clock."[1] Thus, the Galilean heavens were *mechanistic*, and—despite the retraction forced on Galileo by the Inquisition— the machine gave one image to the age.

The scientific revolution was climaxed by the work of Sir Isaac Newton (1642–1727), whose *Principia* (1686–1687) set out a complete and intellectually elegant paradigm of the new Nature. Newton's laws of motion described completely the mechanistic universe, and they would continue in force until Einstein. They

FIGURE 12.1
Time line: 1636–1750.

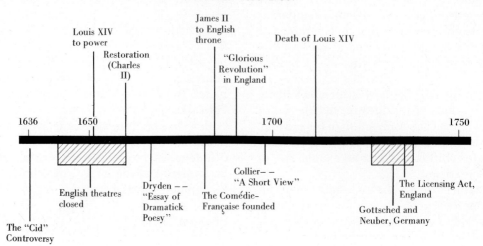

changed the way human beings thought about both themselves and nature. First, these laws removed the need for any cause other than the workings of the machine; that is, they worked without divinity. Second, they provided the theoretical base for advances in technology. And finally, they gave support to secular, rational thinking in other fields.

Secular Philosophy

Important to upper-class ideas of man and nature was the philosophy of Thomas Hobbes (1588–1679). Hobbes, in his *Leviathan* and other works, supported the idea of absolute monarchy: he saw man as, by nature, selfish, and as in a state of war, with "every man against every other man." In forming societies, humans could escape this ceaseless war only through submission to a "mortal God," a king or other absolute power. Hobbes's was not a cheerful philosophy, and perhaps not even a popular one, but it represented important new tendencies in thought: first, the primacy of the secular mind; second, the extension of mechanistic (that is, Galilean and Newtonian) concepts into psychology and behavior; and third, the attempt to justify social organization on a scheme neither inherited from the past nor given by God.

Economics

The period's comedies were often obsessed with money, and they reflected the times. Particularly after 1700, there were large amounts of money to be made in foreign trade, industry, and speculation. Titles had to have money to perpetuate them; the courtly style needed money to exist. Beyond the courts, newly rich "nabobs" and entrepreneurs were becoming wealthy enough to buy their way into upper society. The absolute monarchies had controlled wealth through royal monopoly and taxation, but in the eighteenth century, private enterprise competed with inefficient monopoly.

Manners

This was the great century of manners. France gave the rest of Europe behavior as well as style. Court life at Versailles was so mannered as to be compared by some with theatre. The way in which things were done became more important than what was done. Beyond the courts, however, aggressiveness and plain speaking were needed, a difference in manners that accentuated a difference that was social and moral. Particularly in France, the difference was maintained and court manners became even more artificial after 1700; in England, on the other hand, court and city approached a common code.

The European Theatre (1650–1750)

France led northern Europe in neoclassical theatre, which fanned out from Paris under the double impetus of French prestige and baroque example. In many areas, the similarities in theatrical practice were more important than the differences; therefore, we shall look first at a pivotal French debate over neoclassicism itself, and then at the common elements of that theatre. In a later section, we will look in more detail at France, Germany, and England individually.

A Pivotal Debate: The *Cid* Controversy

Neoclassical theory was already an influence in many of the northern European court theatres when the brilliant Cardinal Richelieu became First Minister of France (1624–1642), but it had had little effect on public and professional theatres until then.

Although not himself the ruler of France, Richelieu had almost a ruler's power, which spread far beyond the arts but was certainly felt there. Richelieu was a neoclassicist, a believer in order, reason, and rules.

Richelieu gave encouragement to the founding of the French Academy in 1635. The Academy gave at least symbolic order and central authority where the fading medieval arts had had none. Thus, when a controversy swirled around Pierre Corneille's play *Le Cid*, the Academy (and Richelieu) took on themselves the task of settling it. Whether the incident had been sought—even instigated—to give the Academy a cause remains open to dispute. The year was 1637; the literary world of Paris was a small and self-conscious one. A hothouse atmosphere was unavoidable, especially at a time when a few playwrights felt that they were at the leading edge of a new movement, neoclassicism. There is no doubt that Corneille thought of himself as a neoclassicist, so that, in writing *Le Cid*, he made many changes to adapt its Spanish source to the new "rules." He was already a playwright of proven ability, with both comedies

FIGURE 12.2

The End of Simultaneity: Public Theatres Using Italianate Scenery*

Paris	
Reconstruction, Théâtre du Marais	1644–1645 (after fire)
Reconstruction, Hôtel de Bourgogne	1647
London	
Lincoln's Inn Fields	1661, "the first regular theatre [in England] to use movable scenery"†
Theatre Royal, Bridges Street	1663
Amsterdam	
Reconstruction, Schouwburg	1664–1665 (new stage and scene space, new audience auditorium)

*Except in the Netherlands, Italianate public theatres were inevitably preceded by court theatres, sometimes temporary, usually intermittent in their performances.
†Leslie Hotson, *Commonwealth and Restoration Stage*, p. 120.

FIGURE 12.3

The theatre in the Palais Cardinal (*ca.* 1641), the king and Richelieu in chairs. Compare these two long galleries and the *parterre* royal seating with Figure 9.3. [From Petit de Julleville.]

and serious works behind him; he had for a short time been part of Richelieu's collaborative group.

Le Cid was an immediate popular success. It became, in fact, one of the most popular plays of the century, and it remains one of the few neoclassical plays given fairly regular production—and probably the only one from the first half of the century. It was staged with the multiple settings we have noted in association with the *Mémoire de Mahelot.* Thus, *Le Cid* would have looked quite familiar to its audience in its simultaneous settings and quite the opposite of neoclassical; ". . . in the background the royal palace, perhaps both the throne room and the king's 'cabinet.' . . . On one side of the stage must have been the Infanta's apartment, the house of the Count and his daughter on the other."[2] However, it was not because of its staging that the play created a furor.

The play was attacked by Corneille's rivals because of what they saw as its violation of *vraisemblance*—"truth-seemingness," or verisimilitude—with particular attention to the believability of certain incidents. The most telling attack came from the playwright–critic Georges de Scudéry; to him, the play was badly flawed because the heroine, Chimène, agreed to marry the protagonist, Rodrigue, even though he had killed her father in a duel—a violation of both verisimilitude (her behavior was unbelievable) and propriety (the morality of it was shocking). As well, the play crowded too much incident into its twenty-four hours, preserving unity of time at the expense of clarity and verisimilitude. There were also other violations by other characters, and some of the play's events were improbable, although based on history: "Scudéry's conclusion is that the subject is worthless, that the play violates dramatic rules, is poorly constructed, has many bad verses, and owes almost all its beauty to its Spanish source."[3]

The controversy was taken up in other

FIGURE 12.4

Frontispiece to Scudéry's *La mort de César* (1636). The author was the most outspoken critic of *Le Cid;* his play is shown here as if staged in a neoclassical theatre. However, it was presented at the Hôtel de Bourgogne, which is not believed to have been Italianate at this time. The clothes do not look like what we know of theatrical costume of the period; on the other hand, the mustaches and hairstyles look more or less of the period. The picture is probably of little use as evidence, but it shows the intellectual tendency of the period. [From Pougin.]

pamphlets and finally came to the official attention of the French Academy. A committee headed by the critic Jean Chapelain considered it for months and delivered its judgment: Scudéry had been wrong in his criticisms, but *Le Cid* was flawed in other ways. Citing Aristotle frequently, the Academy said that *Le Cid* lacked verisimilitude: Chimène should not have married her father's murderer, and the fact that her historical prototype had done so was beside the point; putting such an event into a play was a "deplorable example" (Lancaster). The Academy subjected the play to exhausting analysis and found it wanting; more important, it gave voice to "the first literary discussion in the seventeenth century of large proportions in which the general question of the rules of art was brought out."[4] Most important of all, the Academy articulated for a large public the principles that would underlie not only subsequent tragedy but also much of acting, costuming, and scenery. What would henceforth be sought on the stage was "a *possible* reality" (our italics) "as [an] essential feature of the drama."[5]

Le Cid was staged at the Marais *before* the mid-century reconstruction that probably turned that theatre into an Italianate scenic house. When that reconstruction was made, unified perspective scenery would bring the new *visual* equivalent of neoclassicism's "possible reality" to the theatre. That visual equivalent would be far from a literal representation of the surface of contemporary life, however, for one of the most important points that the *Cid* controversy revealed was that the *appearance* of truth was to be sought, and not the literal, materialistic truth.

In 1637, the French Academy ruled decisively in favor of truth's appearance ("truth-seemingness"), which could communicate the morally desirable without dealing in those "exceptions" that were, although truthful, morally monstrous. As the critic d'Aubignac said, "[T]here are many things that should not be shown, and many things that cannot be staged." Chapelain went still further by saying, "Bad examples are contagious, even in the theatre; artistic representation can lead to actual crime. . . . We must be careful to beware of accustoming our eyes and ears to actions that they ought to ignore. . . . There are monstrous truths that it is either better to suppress for the good of society or, if they cannot be hidden, to point out as monstrosities.''

Chapelain's words pointed toward the very heart of the theatre's uneasy relationship with external reality. Both theoreticians and artists would wrestle with aspects of the question for the next three centuries: Should we "ignore" some aspects of truth or emphasize them? Who determines what is a "monstrosity" and what is a truth? Should the selection among "possible realities" emphasize the morally correct? Are some aspects of life better left unnoticed, or are they the very things that theatre should feature?

The answers in France committed her to neoclassicism. With France as the cultural leader of Europe, neoclassicism became paramount in European theatre.

State of the Theatre (1650–1750)

France's public theatres had a continuous line from the sixteenth century. England, despite the Puritan interruption (1642–1660), was able to pick up again with vigor at the Restoration.

In Russia, theatre was hardly known outside the court, although Russia had evidently had a meager medieval drama that extended well into the seventeenth century; during the reign of Peter the Great (1672–1725), foreign troupes were sporadically brought in, but there appears to have been no permanent theatre building, no permanent theatre company, and no drama of any significance in Russian.[6]

Spain's *corrales* were replaced by more conventional theatres of the Italianate type in the eighteenth century, and theatrical activity continued with some energy, but the Spanish drama of the period had fallen from the Golden Age (to "the depths of absurdity," according to one scholar[7]—a rather harsh judgment).

Holland had an active theatre but limited native drama. German theatre was split among court theatres preferring Italian opera, itinerant companies playing farce and popular drama, and embryonic imitations of French neoclassicism.

The Italian theatre remained geographically splintered, like Italian politics; the *commedia dell'arte* continued but seemed more and more to be imitating itself, while the new form of Italian opera dominated the repertory of many court and urban theatres, so that "spoken poetry . . . like spoken formal prose, had almost disappeared from the Italian stage by 1700, and the plays which had been discussed so fiercely by Renaissance critics . . . were forgotten."[8] In America, scattered records of performances can be found in the coastal communities before 1700, and the far-ranging English actor Tony Aston said that he performed there early in the eighteenth century.

A Layered European Theatre

A division among court, public, and popular theatres was accentuated early in the period and was perhaps modified toward the end. All three contributed to the period's style.

Baroque Theatre

Louis XIV tried to surpass other princes in the splendor of his entertainments. *Les Plaisirs de l'Ile Enchantée*, given at Versailles in 1664, was an exemplary baroque spectacular: "events, plays, banquets, ballets, fireworks displays and mock combats . . . conceived as a single work of art." Based loosely on the fantastic *Orlando Furioso*, the *Ile Enchantée* lasted for three days: on the first day, "the king led the enchanted knights through the park of Versailles to take part in a *quadrille*" followed by a banquet; the second day ended with a play by Molière; the third day saw "an artificial island bearing a witch's palace. Whales and sea-monsters swam in the lake; giants, dwarves, spirits and demons hindered the knights' escape. . . . Her palace vanished amid thunder and lightning . . . ."[9] Subject, effects, and costumes were fan-

FIGURE 12.5

Baroque opera house, Dresden (late seventeenth century). [From Weddigen.] Compare with Figure 12.3.

tastic; the very excess of decor, color, and inventiveness was at the heart of such theatre.

These shows could be only of the court because of their expense and because of their taste. Playful and elitist, fanciful and decadent, they were *not* neoclassical. Few rules confined or ordered them. Yet it must be understood that the very people who made and enjoyed them were,

FIGURE 12.6

Sample Highlights of Baroque Design*

Giacomo Torelli	*La Finta Pazza*	Paris, 1645
Francesco Santurini	*Fedra Incoronata*	Munich, 1662
Israel Sylvestre	*Les Plaisirs de l'Ile Enchantée*	Versailles, 1664
Carlo Vigarini	*Alceste*	Versailles, 1676
Oswald Harms	*Musikalische Opera und Ballet . . .*	Dresden, 1678
Jean Berain	Sets and costumes, French court (*Armide*)	Late seventeenth century
Marcantonio Chiarini	*La Forza della Virtu*	Bologna, 1694
Filippo Juvarra	Perspective flats throughout the stage; *per angolo* setting	Rome, 1708
Giuseppe Galli-Bibiena	*Costanza e Fortezza*	Prague, 1713

*Although only a sample, this list serves to show how baroque scenery spread directly from Italy, usually as designed by Italians; native baroque designers in other countries appeared in greater numbers in the eighteenth century.

in the public theatre and in the drama, fervent neoclassicists.

Specialized theatres were built for baroque operas and entertainments. "Hedge" theatres were built outdoors in gardens, their wings made of living greenery; there were also grotto theatres, cave theatres, and, rather late, "ruin" theatres—their intentionally ruined classical lines perhaps a sentimental acknowledgment of time's passage. Baroque opera houses were built throughout Europe. Opera was particularly favored at the court of Vienna, and it was to Vienna and other operatic centers that the great Italian designers of baroque scenery were drawn.

Public Theatres

Under the absolute monarchies, of which France's was the model, public theatres lived for a while as adjuncts of the court theatre. However, economic necessity quickly drove most theatre troupes to seek larger audiences. It was the increasing dependence on the support of these "citizens," *bourgeois,* or *gens* that made it possible for noncourtly tastes to exert pressure. It was this public theatre that remained the home of neoclassicism but that was also the testing place of new drama.

Popular Theatre

Beyond the influence of the courts and outside the capital cities, theatres flourished that were often continuations of archaic forms. The booth stage still appeared everywhere at fairs, inn-yards, and public gatherings; mountebanks traveled, often accompanying quack salesmen; troupes of actors who could not make it in the capitals had whole lifetimes of touring in the provinces. It was during this period that later touring "circuits" were laid down. Even established professionals from the capitals toured during the seasons when their theatres were closed, taking new plays—often in altered forms—into the country and to the great fairs.

Plays and Playwrights

Many people wrote plays (far more of them men than women), but there were very, very few professional dramatists. There was no copyright, and authors of new plays generally received nothing until a third performance. Some playwrights—for example, John Dryden in London and Molière in Paris—associated themselves with one company for a long period.

Playwrights made no bones about using others' works. Originality was not all-important, and individual genius was less prized than either neoclassical regularity or verbal facility. Both French and English dramatists went frequently to the Spanish work of the Golden Age for materials; in England, revising and "regularizing" Shakespeare was common.

Plays did not have long runs in the modern manner, but successful plays were revived season after season, putting new playwrights into competition with the repertory.

Audiences in the Public Theatres

Perhaps the most important single thing to be noted about European public theatres of this period was their intimacy. Although the first Restoration houses held only a few hundred, and the operatic houses of the eighteenth century held several times that number, not even these figures suggest how small many interiors were. The audiences were not spread over a broad floor, as in modern theatres; they were piled up in two or three tiers around a crowded central pit, so that the distance from box front to box front may in extreme cases have been as little as twenty-five feet—the length of many modern living rooms. From the front of the forestage to the box opposite may have been no more than forty feet. The sense of community in such a space, especially on crowded evenings, must have been remarkable. Intra-audience communication was very easy; there are many anecdotes of flirting, conversation, and even insults from box to box and from pit to box. The rectangular shape of the house made many people as much performers as observers.

The view of the stage, and especially of the scenery, may not have been very good from the sides, but the conditions for listening were excellent. Despite the importance of the new scenery, these were theatres of the ear more than of the eye.

The audience itself was sometimes obstreperous. There were duels and even deaths in theatres. Some members of the audience sat on the stage. Normally, they were restricted to the sides of the forestage below the scenery (at the Comédie Française in the eighteenth century the areas were enclosed with railings), but on crowded nights, they sometimes formed a solid backdrop of humanity to the action. Again, their presence makes us wonder how important the scenery was, and the *regular* presence of audience members along the sides of the playing area should caution us to be wary of expecting too much strict illusion. There are many references that indicate that a seat onstage was favored by show-offs, many of whom competed with the play for attention.

Nor was the rest of the audience particularly demure. At the top of the house, a gallery often taken over by footmen, or *lacquais*, was a source of uproar. Their masters sat in the pit or the lower boxes, and the servants—anonymous in the dim light—often tyrannized, with noise and even missiles. In 1737, one London gallery was so obstreperous that the pit "led a revolt" and evicted them; they returned by breaking down a door, and a war began that lasted for weeks and ended only with the sentencing of the gallery ringleaders to prison.[10]

By early in the eighteenth century, an audience might include "persons of quality in the front and side-boxes; the pit and first gallery occupied by wealthy tradesmen, their wives and families; the upper gallery inhabited by 'the Mob.' "[11] However, the pit and the sides of the stage also contained critical young gallants, and the gallery probably did not represent the great

mass of people so much as sophisticated servants.

It was an audience in an age "becoming more conscious of the problems of self-government, especially of the overriding problem of equilibrium between the demands of the many and the demands of the one, between maintaining public peace and security and affording a maximum of individual liberty."[12] The remark seems truer of England than of the Continent.

Scenery

Baroque scenery swept both the court and the public theatres. The outstanding elements were

1. Changeable scenery.
2. Mechanical spectacle.
3. Perspective scenery.

Even in the public theatres, the scene that "changed like magic before our eyes" was popular. Machinery, however, was expensive, and the "machine plays" of baroque spectacle disappeared from London before 1700 and from Paris some years later.

Simple perspective scenery using rows of

FIGURE 12.7

Mirame at the Palais Cardinal, (1641) Cardinal Richelieu's early use of Italianate scenery in Paris. [From Loliée.]

wings was established in Paris after Torelli (1645) and in London shortly after the Restoration (probably 1661). In many cases, however, it was applied to stock settings: the so-called *palais à volonté* ("a palace") for tragedy and the *chambre à quatre portes* for comedy. In public-theatre use, elements of stock settings were often interchanged, the first two wings of a palace being combined with a backdrop of an ocean or with rear wings of a park or garden.

Front curtains became common before 1670; they were typically raised at the beginning of the play and not lowered until the end. On the Continent, "transformations" or changes of scene were accomplished with Torelli's chariot-and-pole system, in England with grooves. "Shutters" that met in the middle of the stage came into general use, most often upstage but sometimes down almost to the proscenium; "prospects" or views of great apparent depth

were made possible by "relieves"—cutouts through which other shutters were seen.

Settings were not "dressed" in the modern way. The seeming luxury of a *palais à volonté* was not carried into luxurious furniture; only the objects essential to the action were included: for Racine's *Phèdre*, the *Mémoire de Mahelot* called for one property—a chair. It was used because of the play's only stage direction: "she sits." Thus, settings were often austere. This spareness reflected the real interiors of the period, but more important, it was consistent with neoclassical theory, which stressed inclusion of the necessary; what was left out was often as important as what was put in.

An Eighteenth-Century Development of Perspective

About 1700, Italian baroque designers began to work with so-called *per angolo* perspective, in

FIGURE 12.8

The baroque magnificence of a *per angolo* setting by one of the Bibiena family, using three pairs of downstage wings, angled wings, and upstage wings and back scene. [Courtesy of the Billy Rose Theatre Collection, the New York Public Library at Lincoln Center, Astor, Lenox and Tilden Foundations.

FIGURE 12.9

A candle-lit French stage (1670) in the Palais Royal. Molière is at far left, Fiorilli (Scaramuccio) in black, lower right. The others are farceurs, *enfarinés,* and *commedia* actors who had appeared in Paris since about 1600. It is perhaps a sign of Molière's status as comic actor that he was included. [Photo Laniepce. Collections of the Comédie Française.]

which the vanishing points were placed off the center line of the stage. Credit for the development is often given to Ferdinando Bibiena (or Galli-Bibiena), although the point is disputed, but it is incontestable that the Bibienas became the most famous family of baroque designers. Their *per angolo* settings were notable for magnificence, size, and seemingly infinite space down corridors that opened at angles to the stage. *Per angolo* settings became common for opera and were used in the public theatre.

Lighting

Theatre had moved indoors. (The exception, of course, was the Madrid *corral,* in use until almost the end of the period.) The hours of playing had been moved back to the hours of darkness, and artificial light was now needed.

The best light sources were the candle and the oil lamp. No matter how ingeniously they were used, however, they were grudging sources of light. As a rule, both stage and audience area were lighted throughout the performance. This lighting of the audience bound them visually into the same world as the actors and invited the audience's attention to itself as well as to the stage.

Candles were located in holders between the boxes and in chandeliers, which dropped wax on people sitting in the pit. On the stage, the principal locations were

1. Chandeliers hanging over the stage—as few as two or as many as eight.
2. Candle footlights at the edge of the fore-stage, sometimes made as buoyant lights floating in a trough of water.
3. Candles in brackets attached to the backs of the wings.

Illumination was improved on the Continent, especially in France, long before it was in England. Separate stands of lights were placed where needed between the wings; chandeliers could be lowered and raised. Devices were used to enhance illumination: polished reflectors, with spring-loaded candleholders to keep the flame always at the same level; prisms in the chandeliers, for both reflection and diffraction; and bottles of water to function as lenses. These never raised the power of the candles to that of modern lamps; on the other hand, the eyes adjusted to the low level, and an actor or a piece of scenery very close to a light source would have been fairly well lighted.

Modern opinion is much divided on this illumination. Some historians have argued for a warm, soft, but adequate bath of light. Others have suggested that the audience must have been in a perpetual squint, trying to find the actors. Donald Mullin has analyzed a London theatre's lighting, and he believes that the level was very low, finding, for example, a total illumination of eighty-eight candles, "perhaps the equivalent of one modern 75-watt bulb." The effect would have been to push the actors' makeup toward white and their movements toward a constant centering on the bright spots between (not under) the chandeliers: "Chalk and rouge, women's jewels, and men's spangles, tinsel and silver lace, must all have served to add sparkle and brightness to what would otherwise seem—to us at least—as an appalling gloom."[13]

It may have been that the low lighting was balanced by the smallness of the interior and by the thrust stage. Nonetheless, the unevenness of the lighting had an important effect on the actors' placement and movement.

Actors and Acting

Like lighting, the presence of audience members on the stage affected acting, not only by restricting the area but also, perhaps, by forcing actors to make themselves different. More important, however, were the social emphasis on manners and the neoclassical emphasis on decorum. Particularly in tragedy, the idea of the great figure (hero or heroine, personified in life by absolute monarchs) was strong. The life around kings was highly formal, and the kings in their formal roles gave examples of *public* behavior that affected the stateliness, spareness of gesture, and formality of tragic actors. Moreover, education in rhetoric and oratory made declamatory speech the rule in tragedy, with the French developing a style that some have called "sing-song" in its extreme form (Mlle. Champmeslé, Beaubour) (see Figure 12.11).

Molière (*The Versailles Impromptu*) mocked some of the tragic actors of competing companies for their artificial gait and delivery. His play suggests both that comic style was less formal

FIGURE 12.10

An eighteenth-century French tragic actress, Mlle. Dumesnil as Athalie (ca. 1750). [Authors' collection.]

and that some tragic style was almost operatic: attention was given to poetic rhythms for their own sake; decorum of gesture ("dignified indifference" as an English critic called it) was more important than passion of gesture; and tragic costume, gesture, and voice were intentionally divorced from real life. This view of tragic style was an extreme one, however, and in both France and England there was tension between more- and less-formal actors, with shifts toward the less formal among *some* tragedians following the "first wave" (after Montfleury and Floridor in France, Mohun and Hart in England) and again about 1720, when Baron (one of the less formal) returned to the stage.

Too, it must be remembered that during this period actors increasingly limited themselves to *lines of business*—a single kind of role; and *possession of parts* meant that a successful actor held a role for an entire career. Lines of business tended to generalize character (i.e., one specialized in a type, not a particular), and possession of parts tended to limit variety and to accentuate differences among generations.

Comic acting changed. At the beginning of the period in France, it was connected closely to the farce of the *enfarinés*, then evolved through the socially accurate playing of Molière and Raisin to the elegance of Mlle. Dangeville; in England, it built on the powerful tradition of the great witty clowns and the social comedies of before and after the Interregnum. Leading actors who played in the Restoration comedy of manners and the French social comedies were sometimes tragic actors, as well, but their comic style was less formal; it was based far more in observation, was highly verbal, and, where appropriate, studiedly elegant in gesture.

Many low comic actors mastered balletic movement and tricks of voice and body similar to those of *commedia dell'arte*. Both male and female comedians often sang and danced—and, indeed, many actors, both tragic and comic, were also highly talented singers.

The social position of actors in 1700 was little better than in 1600. In France, actors took stage names until well into the eighteenth century; actors married actors; and the children of actors often went into the profession—all of these symptomatic of an outcast group. In France, the excommunication of actors remained in force. Acting was an unstable profession: companies merged, split, failed; they were silenced, suppressed, closed for plague, for royal mourning. Yet, a leading actor could earn a handsome income, and by 1700, there was a tendency for outstanding individuals to command higher salaries as the old sharing system broke down. Thomas Betterton, for example, was paid 150 pounds to act and another 50 pounds to teach young actors in 1703—good money, but nothing like the sums that the stars of later centuries would get.[14]

Costuming

Tragic costume was formal rather than imitative; in its way it, too, was *à volonté*, its outlines defined far more by the serious occasion than by the fictional situation. A generalized sense of antiquity defined the *habit à la romaine*, whose silhouette on both men and women was similar down to the hips: a tight upper garment with tight sleeves and puffed or flared elbows, and a raised headdress, sometimes with enormous plumes. The male costume below the hips included a stiff, short skirt called a *tonnelet* and tights, with a calf-high soft boot. The female used a long skirt, sometimes with a thigh-length overskirt, almost a softer and shorter *tonnelet*. These general lines were varied with fabrics and trims for tragedies and tragicomedies set in places as exotic as Mexico, North Africa, Turkey, Persia, and the East Indies, as well as Greece and Rome: "Ingenious designers . . . were able to develop variations suggesting Turks, Indians, and mythological gods."[15]

Costume for contemporary comedy was basically contemporary dress, with the protagonists in variations of genteel clothes and other characters in various degrees of heightening or abstraction. Comedies satirized dress along with

FIGURE 12.11
Leading French Actors, 1650–1750

"Laroque" Pierre Regnault Petit-Jean ca. 1595–1676	Led Marais after Floridor
Madeleine Béjart 1618–1672	Mentor, then associate of Molière
"Mlle. Desoeillets" Alix Faviot 1621–1670	Tragic actress, Marais, then H. de B.
"Molière" Jean-Baptiste Poquelin 1622–1673	Consummate comic actor; *commedia* influence
"DuCroisy" Philibert Gassot 1626–1695	With Molière; original Tartuffe
François Lenoir de la Thorillière 1626–1680	With Molière, then H. de B.; scion of theatrical family
"Belleroche" Raymond Poisson ca. 1630–1690	Comedian, often played valet *Crispin;* scion of theatrical family
"Mlle. du Parc" Marquise-Thérèse de Gorla 1633–1668	Tragic actress, with Molière, then H. de B.; wife of "Gros-René," comic
Isaac François Guérin d'Etriche ca. 1636–1728	Comic (Molière's Miser); married Molière's widow; founding member, Comédie-Française
"LaGrange" Charles Varlet 1639–1692	Lovers, leads with Molière; his *Register* a major historical document
"Mlle. Molière" Armande Béjart 1642–1700	Played major roles for Molière after c. 1664; his wife; Madeleine's sister; led company after his death
"Champmeslé" Charles Chévillet 1642–1701	Lead, played with Marais, Bourgogne, Comédie-Française
"Mlle. Champmeslé" Marie Desmares 1642–1698	Tragedian, Marais, Bourgogne, C-F
Michel Baron 1653–1729	Protègé of Molière; great tragedian; retired 1691, returned 1720
Jean-Baptiste Raisin 1655–1693	"The little Molière"—comedian; original C-F; of theatrical family
Paul Poisson 1658–1735	Son of Raymond; comedian; C-F
Pierre Trochon de Beaubour 1662–1725	Tragedian, high declamatory style; retired 1718

FIGURE 12.11 (continued)

"Mlle. Duclos" Marie-Anne de Chateauneuf 1668–1748	Tragedian, declamatory style; came to be seen as old-fashioned; retired 1740
"Mlle. Desmares" Charlotte Desmares 1682–1753	Tragedian taught declamatory style by aunt (Mlle. Champmeslé); retired 1721
Adrienne Lecouvreur 1692–1730	Tragedian; debut, 1717; less formal style
Abraham-Aléxis Quinault Dufresne 1693–1767	Debut 1712, less formal style; more suited to *comédie larmoyante* than predecessors
"Mlle. Dangeville" Marie-Anne Botot 1714–1796	Comedian; major roles of Marivaux

NOTE: Among tragedians, the early ones on this list were forging a style first defined in the previous generation (Montdory, Bellerose, Floridor) and mocked by Molière; Baron seems to have made the tragic style less artificial (in part because of Molière?) and his return to the stage in 1720 marks a shift from a second "high" style (Beaubour, Mlles Duclos and Desmares). See also Figure 9.9.

Women were often known by married names with "Mlle." Married couples and whole families of actors were common, perhaps because of social rejection of actors.

manners, and the fops of the English stage and the "little marquis" of Molière wore costumes made ridiculous with ribbons and excesses of contemporary fashion. Stock costumes, like that of Harlequin, were still common. Masks were less common than they had been in 1600. Where specific professions were important to comic effect—especially medicine, the law, and the church—their costumes and costume props were given outlandish emphasis; in Molière's medical comedies, for example, physicians' assistants were identified by their enormous clysters (syringes for giving enemas).

The Growth of Three National Theatres: France, Germany, and England

France

French Theatres (ca. 1645–1750)

We marked the end of the medieval simultaneous system in Paris by three events of about

1645–1650: the introduction of his machines to a French theatre by Giacomo Torelli; the rebuilding of the Théâtre du Marais; and the rebuilding of the Hôtel de Bourgogne, both of these theatres being rebuilt, presumably, so that wings, borders, and shutters could be used.

In 1650, then, there were three then-modern playhouses in Paris for the use of perspective scenery: the Marais, the Bourgogne, and the theatre in the Palais Cardinal, now called the Palais Royal. The latter had been the first one converted for Renaissance scenery (for Cardinal Richelieu) and was subsequently rebuilt for Torelli. In addition, there were two other spaces sometimes used as theatres: the Grande Salle du Louvre, a vast space used mostly for court ballets; and the hall in the Petit Bourbon, used for court performances, ballets, and appearances by visiting acting troupes.[16] Finally, there were seldom-used court halls (for example, the Guardroom of the Old Louvre Palace, where Molière first acted for the court), a number of tennis courts sometimes used as playhouses, and an irregular collection of fair booths and street-corner stages.

FIGURE 12.12
Leading English Actors, 1650–1750*

William Beeston (ca. 1605–1682)	Son of Christopher Beeston, one of Beeston's Boys (ca. 1637); may have acted during Interregnum
William Cartwright (ca. 1606–1686)	Pre-Commonwealth player; Falstaff after Restoration
Charles Hart (d. 1683)	Leading tragedian until the Union; acted before Interregnum
John Lacy (d. 1681)	Comic actor, original Bayes in *The Rehearsal*; minor dramatist
Michael Mohun (ca. 1620–1684)	Leading actor until Union; had acted before Interregnum
Nicholas Burt (ca. 1624–1690)	Played women with Beeston's Boys before Interregnum; Othello after restoration
George Jolly (fl. 1630–1673)	Persistent tourer; played in Germany during Interregnum; secured license at Restoration; ran Nursery
Henry Harris (ca. 1634–1704)	Leading actor; singer; Yeoman of the Revels
Cave Underhill (1634–1710)	Comedian: gravedigger, *Hamlet*; Feste, *Twelfth Night*; Sancho, *Don Quixote*
Thomas Betterton (ca. 1635–1710)	Long career as leading figure—Hamlet, Lear (Tate version), many Restoration roles; led secession from Rich
James Nokes (d. ca. 1692)	Low comedian: "Nurse Nokes" for female role
Edward Kynaston (ca. 1640–1706)	One of last male players of women: Epicene, 1661, then male roles
Jo Haines (ca. 1647–1701)	Low comedian: prologues and epilogues; Sparkish, *Country Wife*
Katharine Corey (fl. 1661–1692)	"She was the first and is the last of all the actresses . . . constituted by King Charles the Second at His Restauration" (petition, 1689)
Margaret Hughes (d. 1719)	Tragic actress; may have been first actress, as Desdemona, 1660(?), but see Katharine Corey
Elizabeth Barry (1658–1713)	A voice "full, clear and strong"; Cordelia (Tate's *Lear*) other leads
Anne Bracegirdle (ca. 1663–1748)	Both comedy and tragedy; a noted figure. Cordelia; Almeria in *The Mourning Bride*
William Mountford (ca. 1664–1692)	Emerged as major tragic actor at Union; murdered
Robert Wilks (ca. 1665–1732)	Comic leading actor: Horner in *The Country Wife*
Susanna Verbruggen (ca. 1667–1703)	Leading comic actress
John Coysh (fl. 1667–1697)	"Strolling Coysh"—tourer
Thomas Doggett (ca. 1670–1721)	Actor and singer; strolled on Coysh's license, played fairs; comic Shylock; Fondlewife
Colley Cibber (1671–1757)	Excelled as fops: Sir Fopling Flutter in Etherege's *Man of Mode*; also dramatist, manager
Barton Booth (1681–1733)	Tragedian: first Cato in Addison's *Cato*, 1713
Anne Oldfield (1683–1730)	Comedy and tragedy; buried in Westminster Abbey
James Quin (1693–1766)	"No actor ever greater heights could reach In all the labour'd artifice of speech." But see Figure 13.4
Charles Macklin (ca. 1697–1797)	First serious Shylock See Figure 13.4
Susanna Maria Cibber (1714–1766)	Tragic actress and operatic singer, "probably the last of the great actresses who retained the tragic elocution in vogue under Charles II." (Summers, *Playhouse*, p. 47)

*No women appear in the early part of this list because they did not go on the stage until 1660–1661, and far fewer trained women were available at the Restoration than men. In considering changes in style, note should be taken of the perseverance of pre-Restoration actors in the 1660s and 1670s; of the rather sharp break at the Union, when the number of roles decreased and certain kinds of actors may have been dropped; and of the probable increase in the need for actors early in the eighteenth century.

FIGURE 12.13

Principal Paris Theatres*

Hôtel de Bourgogne	"King's Company" to 1680; Italians, 1680–1697, 1716 and after	Rebuilt, 1716
Théâtre du Marais	Noted for tragedy until 1670s	
Palais Royal (formerly, Palais Cardinal)	Molière's troupe, shared with Italians, 1661–1680	
Petit Bourbon	Italians to 1658, then shared with Molière's troupe, 1658–1661	Demolished, 1661
Grande Salle du Louvre	Ballets and baroque spectacles	
Théâtre Guénégaud	The first Comédie Française (Molière's troupe and the remnant of the Hôtel de Bourgogne), 1680–1689	
Théâtre du rue des Fossés-St.-Germain des-Prés (the "Old Comédie Française")	Comédie Française, 1689–1770	

*Temporary theatres were erected for the fairs and became both more complex and more permanent after 1700. By 1750, the *"théâtre des foires"* was a separate type. Some "fair theatres" set up temporary quarters within the city.

The principal theatres appear to have had certain similarities:

1. Some variation of a *loge*-and-*parterre* audience space.

2. A rectangular shape, with a good part of the audience on the long sides so that they faced each other as much as they faced the stage.

3. A stage without an important acting area forward of the structure (usually a proscenium arch) that framed the scenery. The point is debatable, and the situation did change in the eighteenth century, but existing accounts and pictures do *not* suggest that the seventeenth-century Parisian theatres used large forestages.

The sizes of these theatres varied; estimates of capacity range from five hundred to over a thousand. In fact, these estimates are based on modern standards of capacity and do not take into account the remarkable elasticity of bench seating, which could be made to hold up to three times as many people on rare occasions, when people squeezed together.

Later in the seventeenth century, a number of other theatres came into use, notably that called the Guénégaud, the home for sixteen years of the then-new Comédie Française; and that called the Théâtre du rue des Fossés-St.-Germain-des-Prés, which the troupe occupied until well into the eighteenth century (the "old Comédie Française").[17]

The Hôtel de Bourgogne was refitted—and perhaps rebuilt—in 1716; thereafter, it appears that its *amphithéâtre* was in the usual position for the period, between the *parterre* and the *loges* facing the stage; as well, its side *loges* may have been angled in slightly, to give the occupants a better view of the stage. It had three tiers of *loges*, or two *loges* and one gallery; and its capacity may now have been almost twelve hundred, with six hundred of those in the *parterre*.[18]

It is generally assumed that all of these theatres, insofar as they used movable perspective scenery, used the Torelli chariot-and-pole system.

FIGURE 12.14

The "old Comédie Française," actually new in this period (1689). Note the sloping stage; the *parterre, loges,* and *amphithéâtre;* and the extensive support spaces. [From Diderot. Courtesy of the Rare Books Room, Bowling Green State University.]

Parisian Troupes

Early in the seventeenth century, there had been two troupes known somewhat casually as "the King's": the Italians, actually the first on the scene, perhaps because of the Italian influence of the queen, Marie de'Medici; and the "King's Comedians" (*Comédiens du Roy*) at the Hôtel de Bourgogne. After about 1625, there was competition from the company under Mondory, at the Marais after ca. 1634. These three, then—the Italians, the King's, and the Marais company—were the permanent troupes of the first half of the seventeenth century. By 1648, the Marais had enjoyed great success, having been the producer of *Le Cid* and other important plays; it had survived the burning of its theatre and had rebuilt it as a modern house with modern

machines. By just after mid-century, however, it had gone into decline, and the King's Company at the Bourgogne was in the ascendant.

In 1658, however, a new company appeared to change this balance. It had spent thirteen years in the provinces; it had the protection of "Monsieur" (the king's brother); and it had thoughts of leasing the Marais.[19] In October of 1658, it performed for the king in the Guardroom of the Old Louvre, its offering an established tragedy by Corneille and a brilliant short farce by the troupe's leader, Jean Baptiste Poquelin, who called himself Molière. The tragedy was competent; the farce made the company's future.

Instead of using the Marais, therefore, the new troupe was installed at the Petit Bourbon theatre, but in alternation with the Italians. The Italians, led by Tiberio Fiorilli ("Scaramuccio"), had their established days: Tuesday, Friday, and Sunday. Molière's company had the other days. With the demolition of the Petit Bourbon palace in 1661, however, Molière took up sole possession of the theatre in the Palais Royal—the old Palais Cardinal of Richelieu.

Again, the situation seemed balanced: Molière, master of comedy, at the Palais Royal; a company now noted for tragedy at the Hôtel de Bourgogne; and the Italians. The Marais company were a remnant. Another new troupe was forming, however; an ambitious and talented musician, Jean Baptiste Lully was court master of performers of music and ballet. He often worked with Molière in an uneasy collaboration, but he was intensely jealous of his own art. His Royal Academy of Music came on the scene in 1669; in 1672, Lully was given sole control of music in Paris, including opera, and his monopoly led to the permanent separation of his company, called most simply The Opera (*L'Opéra*).

Molière died in 1673. His theatre continued, however, absorbing the remnant of the Marais. In 1680, they were commanded to combine with the tragedians of the Hôtel de Bourgogne to form the Comédie Française. The institution and the name still exist, not only having survived the French Revolution, many changes of government, foreign occupation, and changes of taste, but also having prospered: "During the eighteenth century the Comédie Française was responsible for the production of almost all new plays of any importance," and from the time of its formation onward, it "occupied a dominant position in the theatrical life of Paris."[20]

The Italians were ordered to leave Paris in 1698 and were not invited back until after the death of Louis XIV. (It was for that return that the Hôtel de Bourgogne was redone in 1716.) The reasons for their banishment are still argued; they range from charges of impropriety to suggestions that they were victims of a bud-

FIGURE 12.15

Armide at Lully's Opéra, as designed by Bérain (late seventeenth century). [From Bapst.]

get cut. Certainly, the end of their long association with the French court was a sign of changing times. They had come in with the gusty and pleasure-seeking reign of Henri IV; they were driven away by the stuffy, overheated piety of Louis XIV's declining years.

Thus, the Parisian theatre, which had had five troupes at its fullest expansion, had shrunk to merely two in 1700; these two became three with the Italians' return. Thereafter, the three official theatres had to vie increasingly with a new rival, the fair theatres (*théâtres des foires*), especially after mid-century.

French Drama

The principal kinds of French drama included the following.

Neoclassical Tragedy. Neoclassical tragedies were, originally, plays written in accord with the principles articulated by the French Academy and other critics. The unities, five-act structure, verisimilitude, decorum, and linkage of scenes were demanded. In tragedy, these plays usually focused on conflicts between individual and general imperatives, that is, love versus duty, love versus honor, honor versus reputation, and so on.

At the center of this controlled but powerful form was a concern about the dominant quandary of the age: What is the balance between order and individual will? The universe had been defined as a machine; on the other hand, the human being had been defined as a kind of animal, perhaps one with angelic attributes, but one selfish and striving, nonetheless. In Jean Racine's *Phèdre*, images of monstrosity contrast with those of order; Phedra describes her compulsive love for her stepson as "madness"; by implication, a woman without such a love would be sane. Her world is dominated by her husband, Theseus, "killer of monsters"—the bringer of order, the rule giver. Racine's exploration of this situation is very complex and gives no easy answers, and the tragedy, like the other great tragedies of the period, projected for its audience a compelling image of their own situation.

Neoclassical Comedy. The comedies, like the tragedies, explored the relationship between order and anarchy, but because they were comedies, they made both anarchy and wrong (or false) order funny. The greatest of France's comic playwrights, Molière, created characters who frantically try to impose order on disorderly situations—old men wanting to force young women to love them; miserly fathers wanting their children to be obedient and thrifty; a husband wanting his household to submit to the rules of a religious fanatic (and hypocrite). Contrarily, there were comedies of trickery, with their roots in *commedia dell'arte* and medieval farce, in which a trickster destroys order to establish happy disorder (or, more properly, a new order—the marriage of young lovers, a son's inheritance of money, or the uniting of long-lost relatives.)

In comedy, neoclassicism generally had neither the influence nor the importance that it exercised on tragedy, although much French comedy of about 1650–1700 was very regular. Plautus and Terence provided many plots and examples. Comedies in five acts were usual, and those using rhymed alexandrine verse, scene linkage, and the three unities were common; Molière's *Le Misanthrope* is a good example. At their best, these plays satisfied both neoclassical ideals and their audiences, showing characters below the highest rank engaged in actions involving love, reputation, wealth, and other worldly matters.

Musical Forms and Machine Plays. Neoclassical dramatic principles and Italianate scene technology were in fundamental conflict: one demanded unity of place and verisimilitude, but the other had great potential for rapid change, movement, and magical effects. The conflict was never adequately resolved, but there was a tendency to move the more spectacular scenic effects into a separate category of so-called machine plays. Many excellent dramatists, including Corneille, wrote such plays, which usually required less verbal facility and far more spectacle. The machine play was expensive to produce, and, despite its great appeal, it did not really survive the turn of the eighteenth century as a distinct category, merging instead with opera and ballet.

Molière and Lully created a hybrid form called *comédie-ballet*, a composite of drama, dance, and spectacle, and some of their *comédies-ballets* (*Le Bourgeois Gentilhomme*, for example) rank among the best work of the period.

Playwrights

Pierre Corneille (1606–1684). Much of Corneille's early life was spent in Rouen, where he made a connection with the actors who became the company of the Marais, and his association with them lasted for a decade in Paris. His important works included, besides *Le Cid*, the comedy *Le Menteur* (1643) and the tragedies *Horace* (1640), *Cinna* (1641), and *Polyeucte* (1642). His career spanned the formative years of the French neoclassical period, and it was he, above all, who gave an example of tragic size and solemnity to both the French and the English theatre.

Jean Baptiste Poquelin, Molière (1622–1673). Born into a bourgeois Parisian family, Molière disappointed them by turning to the theatre. With the actress Madeleine Béjart, he formed the Illustre Théâtre in 1643 and then spent years in the provinces, much of the time at Lyon, where the Italian *commedia* influence was strong. After his Paris debut in 1658, he was a successful but controversial actor–dramatist–manager with many enemies at court. Not notably successful

at tragedy as either an actor or a playwright, he excelled in a broad range of comedies, from *Le Misanthrope* (1666) to the satirical *Tartuffe* (1669) and *Les Femmes Savantes* (1672) and the farcical *Scapin* (1671) and *Le Malade Imaginaire* (1673). Molière was neoclassical in temperament, but not doctrinaire; "the great rule" for him was "to make people laugh." Molière was not a member of the French Academy, probably as much because he was an actor as because he was not a rigid respecter of the rules.

Jean Racine (1639–1699). Although Molière's troupe produced his first play, Racine moved to the Hôtel de Bourgogne, whose style was better suited to his plays. For clarity of diction, no French dramatist of the period equals him except Molière; none even approaches him for the brilliant union of theatrical vision and neoclassical form. Racine represents the paradox of French neoclassical tragedy at its greatest: absolute passion in an absolutely rational form.

FIGURE 12.16

French Playwrights (1650–1750)

Pierre Corneille	1606–1684	Neoclassicist; comedies and tragedies; also machine plays	*Le Menteur*, 1643 *Le Cid*, 1636
Paul Scarron	1610–1660	Comedies; also a novelist	*The Foolish Heir*, 1650
Jean Mairet	1616–1664	Early neoclassicist	*Sophonisba*, 1634
Jean Baptiste Poquelin ("Molière")	1622–1673	Greatest of French comic dramatists; actor; manager; *commedia* influence	*Le Misanthrope*, 1666 *Scapin*, 1671 *The Bourgeois Gentleman*, 1671
Thomas Corneille	1625–1709	Brother of Pierre; opera libretti for Lully	*The Mock Astrologer*, 1650
Jean Racine	1639–1699	Greatest of tragic dramatists	*Phèdre*, 1677
Jean-François Regnard	1655–1709		*Harlequin, Lucky Fellow*, 1690
Florent-Carton Dancourt	1661–1725	Social comedy	*Les Bourgeoises à la Mode*, 1692
Evaristo Gherardi, editor	1663–1700	Collected plays written for the Théâtre Italien by French authors	*Le Théâtre Italien de Gherardi*, 1721
Alain-René Lesage	1668–1747	Social comedy	*Turcaret*, 1709
Prosper de Crébillon	1674–1762	Tragedy trying to recall the great age	
Phillipe Néricault Destouches	1680–1754		*The Philosopher Married*, 1727
Pierre Caret de Chamblain de Marivaux	1688–1763	Rococo comedy	*Love's Surprise*, 1722
Pierre Claude Nivelle de la Chausée	1692–1754	*Comédie larmoyante*	*The School of Friends*, 1737

His tragedies were of a remarkably consistent quality—*La Thébaïde* (1664), *Andromaque* (1667), *Britannicus* (1669), and others—but it was *Phèdre* (1677) that was his masterpiece. Thereafter, Racine did not write for the public stage, becoming Louis XIV's historiographer and returning to playwriting only with his "biblical tragedies" *Esther* (1689) and *Athalie* (1691), which had important musical elements, perhaps in imitation of Greek tragedy.

Germany: Hanswurst versus Gottsched

A medieval disorder prevailed in German-speaking areas long after it had ended in France and England. Germany was a patchwork of small states and duchies—more than three hundred of them at one point—and the disorganized state of the German theatre is often blamed on the situation. After about 1600, even the religious theatre of the Middle Ages had faded, and what was left was socially split: on the one hand was a popular theatre of gross effects and low comedy and, on the other, a court theatre dominated by Italian opera. Thus, although by 1700 there were court theatres throughout the German-language region, there was no German drama to speak of; and, although there were itinerant German professionals, they were never able to perfect their art.

English professional actors continued to affect German theatre through their tours, which had a spurt of new life during the Interregnum. English actors quickly made concessions to German audiences, adapting plays (including Shakespeare), translating and paraphrasing into German dialects, and absorbing German actors; they are also accused of pandering to the lowest level of German taste by introducing clowning and buffoonery into everything. The use of comic pantomime, of course, would have been natural to actors performing in a foreign language; there were probably infusions, too, from the familiar *zanni* of the *commedia dell'arte* companies that played in Germany. A stock clown

figure emerged, typically named Hanswurst or Pickle-Herring, a figure so popular that he became an almost inescapable element of performances in Germany. Throughout the seventeenth century, then, German audiences saw plays of decidedly mixed tone, often with a Shakespearean flavor, and all too often with no pretentions to art or literature. This drama existed virtually without critical examination, and except for Andreas Gryphius (1616–1664), it had no serious playwrights.

By the beginning of the eighteenth century, German theatre was still itinerant, and its repertory was dominated by Hanswurst and an indigenous genre called *Haupt- und Staats-aktionen* ("high-and-mighty stuff," as it were), "bombastic melodrama . . . mere mixtures of gory incident, meaningless mouthings and such conceits as clowuage keeps in pay."[21] It has also been described as a form that "reflected the idle fancies of the lower ranks in a society with well-marked classes."[22] The alternative was still the baroque opera of the court theatres.

Johann Christoph Gottsched (1700–1766) was an educated man of the middle class who approached the German theatre with a missionary's zeal. Fired by exposure to Aristotle and French neoclassicism, he set about to formulate principles for the reform of the German theatre; the actual execution of his ideas was far more the work of theatre artists, particularly of the actress Carolina Neuber (1697–1760). As critic, commentator, and organizer, sometimes as playwright and translator, Gottsched was identifiably the first major theoretical figure of the postmedieval German theatre. Although subsequent theorists overshadowed him, it is Gottsched who can be credited with the transformation of German theatre from seventeenth-century disorder to the beginnings of order.

Although Gottsched failed in many of his goals, his most important aims were

1. To end the domination of Hanswurst, and thus of vulgarism.
2. To raise the level of production.

3. To bring the rules of French neoclassicism to Germany.

Gottsched's thinking was not without contradictions, not least because he was trying to impose French neoclassicism on a distinctly different culture. He is not to be blamed too severely, however, for having had difficulty in dragging a national drama—kicking and screaming—from 1600 to 1725 in one quick yank.

Like his French models, Gottshed's ideas had two basic principles:

1. *The representational nature of art.* Gottsched went much further than the French

FIGURE 12.17

A German Hanswurst (seventeenth century). [From Weddigen.]

FIGURE 12.18

A German theatre of the seventeenth century, with a Hanswurst(?) left. [From Weddigen.]

Academy had, however, in his idea of what constituted a convincing representation; *vraisemblance* was not enough, and more literal representation and more literal adherence to the unities were desired.

2. *The moral purpose of art.* Comedy, especially, was seen as normative and corrective. The only kind of laughter that Gottsched acknowledged was the laughter of ridicule.[23] The morals of Gottsched, however, were "an expression of middle-class ideals. The comedies written by Gottsched's admirers . . . aim at a closer relationship between the theatre and society."[24]

For more than a dozen years, Gottsched had the enthusiastic support of Carolina Neuber. She and her husband were actors in Leipzig when Gottsched first became interested in the theatre; thereafter, usually with her own company, she worked to apply Gottsched's reforms: proper rehearsals, the learning of lines (instead of paraphrasing or improvising), the regularizing of the actor's personal lives, and improvement of the repertory. She ultimately broke with

FIGURE 12.19
Playwrights of Germany, Holland, Denmark, and Italy
(1650–1750)

Germany

Andreas Gryphius	1616–1664	*Cardenio and Celinda,* 1647
Daniel Caspar Lohenstein	1635–1683	*Sophonisba,* 1680
Johann Christian Hallman	1640–1704	*Theodoricus,* 1666
Christian Weise	1642–1708	*Abraham and Isaac,* 1682
Johann Christoph Gottsched	1700–1766	*Cato,* 1737

Holland

Joost van den Vondel	1587–1679	*Iphigenia in Tauris,* 1666

Denmark

Ludvig Holberg	1684–1754	*Jeppe of the Hill,* 1723

Italy

Scipione F. M. Maffei	1675–1755	*Merope,* 1713
Pietro Metastasio	1698–1782	*Cato in Utica,* 1721

Gottsched over the necessity of wooing an audience, which required that she keep some of the old repertory. Nonetheless, her name is linked with his whenever the foundations of the postmedieval German theatre are discussed. Her historical significance is hampered by the ephemeral nature of the actor's art, while Gottsched's was assured by his access to print, yet her work was courageous and had enduring effects, and it was her later work that inspired Gottsched's critical successor, Gotthold Ephraim Lessing.

Gottsched and Neuber tried to do too much in too short a time. Their impact, however, was lasting. Gottsched (and Neuber) "favoured and introduced such novelties as rehearsing a play and making the actors learn their parts . . . and he [they] generally brought the theatre into line with serious and polite literature. . . . And it meant getting rid of [Hanswurst], the ubiquitous figure on the popular German stage, the symbol of unruliness and low entertainment."[25]

England

London Theatres
Theatrical activity had begun again in England shortly after the Restoration (1660); indeed, preparations had begun when it was clear that a restoration was likely. One entrepreneur, William Davenant, had been staging "operas" privately since 1656. With Thomas Killigrew, another courtier, Davenant secured from the crown two *patents* (permanent royal authorizations) that were to give perpetual legitimacy to a succession of English theatres. These were granted in the names of the king and of his brother the Duke of York. (There was a third document granted under somewhat different circumstances to George Jolly, who had spent most of the Interregnum touring the Continent; this license eventually became the basis for the Nursery, the common training ground of the two major companies. It had an up-and-down existence for some years.)

After a brief joint venture at one of the pre-Commonwealth playhouses, Killigrew and Davenant set out separately. Each installed a company in a converted tennis court. Their actors were drawn from the veterans left from before the closing of the theatres and from newcomers. For the first time, women were recruited, and England joined the rest of Europe in accepting women on the stage in 1660–1661.

It is significant that both Killigrew and Davenant rejected the old playhouses, a few of which were still usable. Without doubt, the decision to use a tennis court had something to do with the new scenery, and it may have been influenced by French example; however, it cannot be supposed that elaborate machines were installed immediately.

The Duke's Company began at the converted tennis court called Lincoln's Inn Fields, which remained a useful theatre well into the eighteenth century. The King's Company, after a brief stay at a tennis court, built the Theatre Royal, Bridges Street (1663), which burned in 1772. By that time, the Duke's had built a new "machine house" at Dorset Garden (1671). The King's Company performed at Lincoln's Inn Fields until their new theatre in Drury Lane was completed in 1674.

From 1674 until early in the eighteenth cen-

FIGURE 12.20

Interior of Dorset Garden Theatre, one of the illustrations for Settle's *The Empress of Morocco* (1673). The shaded parts on each side seem to be later additions but may be correct. This representation seems to show a musicians' gallery (?) above a forestage (not shown); a sloping inner stage with Italianate scenery in forced perspective; and two or three rows of boxes. [From Thornbury.]

FIGURE 12.21

A conjectural reconstruction of the Theatre Royal, Drury Lane. Note the stage doors; the enclosed area for the onstage audience; and the pronounced forestage. [Courtesy of Richard Leacroft. First published in *Theatre Notebook*.]

tury, then, there were three principal theatres in London that were capable of using movable, perspective scenery; they shared some characteristics:

1. A rectangular plan, with box-and-pit seating.
2. A proscenium arch to frame the scenery and, projecting in front of it, a forestage, or apron, estimated at about twenty feet in Dorset Garden and Drury Lane.
3. Wing-and-groove, rather than chariot-and-pole, scenery.
4. Highly elastic capacities, with estimates ranging from five hundred to twelve hundred as base figures. Conservative judgment suggests that the smaller figures are the likelier.

The converted tennis courts of 1660–1671 were smaller, although one estimate of twenty-five by seventy feet seems too small. They had capacities of perhaps four hundred, with perhaps only a single row of boxes around the pit.

One conclusion about these London theatres of the Restoration seems clear, however: familiar as their builders may have been with Parisian theatres, the most important model for them was the pre-Restoration court stage of Inigo Jones: "The early Restoration stage . . . is the result of the attempt to impose features of the scenic stage, associated with the court masque, upon the stage of the private playhouse. . . . [It] elaborates upon the earlier private playhouse, combining with it the arrangement of wings and shutters evolved by Inigo Jones for his court masques."[26]

The interiors of the English playhouses were probably not fundamentally different from those of the French, except where the long forestage was used, causing some scholars to use the word *tripartite* to designate the English arrangement (scenic space, forestage, and audience space). The use of the English forestage before 1700 required that the actors have access to it without having to come down from the proscenium; this access was given through doors below the proscenium, of which different theatres had one, two, or possibly even three on each side. Before 1700, one door was replaced at at least one theatre by "stage boxes"— a continuation of the side boxes at each of their levels to embrace the forward part of the forestage with audience. Thus, although the forestage remained as an important feature of the eighteenth-century stage, the audience area, in a sense, encroached on it; the doors retreated upstage, reaching the proscenium itself until, by the end of the eighteenth century, the forestage itself was shrinking.

Parisian and London theatres had a common arrangement of box, pit, and gallery. Although they may have placed the actor differently in relation to the scenery between 1660 and 1690, after the turn of the century the difference disappeared, and a recent reconstruction of the Hôtel de Bourgogne of 1716 looks like an English theatre.

London Theatre Companies (ca. 1660–1700)

London began with two companies, the King's and the Duke of York's. Until the "Bloodless Revolution" of 1689, the perpetual patents of 1660 were the only legal authorization. Foreign troupes visited London but were not given patents. Opera was staged, but no opera company was created. By 1677, however, the King's Company was in trouble, and in 1682 the King's and the Duke's combined into the United Company. For thirteen years, London had only *one* patent company. It had strengths: the best actors of both troupes; the combined repertory; and the use of both theatres. But there were drawbacks for dramatists, whose outlets were reduced; for the actors themselves; and for the audience. Financial control had been taken over by Christopher Rich, who was so offensive to many that in 1695 the actor Thomas Betterton "defected" with some of the United Company actors and set up a new troupe at the very old theatre in Lincoln's Inn Fields. He had, not a patent, but a license, which was not permanent and which existed at the will of the Crown.

The theatre—like the society itself—was trying to thrash out the implications of the great change of 1689. At this point, with the London theatre divided, weak, and disorganized, its very existence was attacked from a quite different quarter.

The Collier Controversy (1698–1720)

The primary weapon was a publication titled *A Short View of the Immorality and Profaneness of the English Stage, Together with the Sense of Antiquity upon this Argument* (1698). Its author was Jeremy Collier, an intelligent and eloquent "nonjuring divine" (a sectarian cleric outside the established church). Collier wanted to do nothing less than crush the theatre: "Tis my business rather to kill the Root than Transplant it."

Collier failed and the English theatre survived; however, the controversy had much of the importance of the French battle over *Le Cid*, although the issues were different. The English dispute had far more to do with a deep-seated distrust of pleasure than with dramatic theory.

Collier stated that the theatre had "debauched the age." He listed the "Particulars" of

FIGURE 12.22
Principal London Theatres (1650–1750)

Lincoln's Inn Fields (had been Lisle's tennis court)	Duke of York's, 1661–1671 King's, 1672–1674 Betterton's, 1695–1705 John Rich's, 1714	(1714)*
First Theatre Royal (had been Gibbon's tennis court)	King's Company, 1661–1663	(1663)
Theatre Royal, Bridges Street	King's Company, 1663–1671/2	Burned (1671/2)
Dorset Garden	Duke's Company, 1671–1682 United Company, 1682–1695 (but little used)	"Machine house" (1709)
Theatre Royal, Drury Lane	King's, 1674–1682 United Company, 1682–1695 Christopher Rich, 1695–1709 Thereafter, a succession of managements, usually of several partners	(1792–this building)
The Queen's, called the King's after 1714 (the Haymarket)	Vanbrugh, Betterton, et al., 1705; mostly opera after 1711	(1789)
Second Lincoln's Inn Fields	John Rich, 1714–1732	*The Beggar's Opera,* 1728 (1744)
Little or Second Haymarket	1720	(1820)
Goodman's Fields	1720; rebuilt, 1732	"Third regular company," 1729 (1742)
Covent Garden	John Rich, 1732	(1808–this building)

*Dates in parentheses indicate last year as theatre.

this debauchery: "Smuttiness of Expression: Their Swearing, Profaneness and Lewd Application of Scripture; Their Abuse of the Clergy; Their making their Top Characters Libertines, and giving them Success in their Debauchery . . . ." Collier wrote with zeal, and there is no denying that the *Short View* was "receiv'd by the world with generous applause, and stood the shock of some of the greatest wits of the age."

The "wits" who responded to Collier did so through pamphlets, dramatic prologues, and their own plays, but the responses were "beneath [their authors'] literary ability both in argumentative and rhetorical force."[27] The wits may have recognized that Collier was attacking from a powerful position of established critical theory. His moral argument coincided with fundamental dramatic theory: the goal of art is moral instruction.

His main contention [was that] the end of art is morality. . . . [He cited] Horace's praise of poets for reforming manners, . . . Aristotle,

. . . Jonson's 'it being the office of a comic poet to imitate justice, and to instruct life,' . . . a quotation from Rapin, and the following from Boileau . . .

I like an author that reforms the age;
And keeps the right decorum on the stage:
That always pleases by just reason's rule. . . .[28]

Thus, Collier made his points with many of the arguments of the neoclassical theorists: appeals to authority (Horace, Aristotle, et al.); appeals to reason and decorum; and an assertion of the moral end of drama, including comedy.

The best-reasoned response to Collier came from John Dennis (1657–1734), who sought to explain the pleasure of theatre as a self-justifying one: "Pleasure is not in itself an evil, but . . . mankind lives for happiness." The weight of authority was on the side of Collier, however: art must instruct *and* delight; delight alone would not suffice. Despite Dennis's reasonable arguments, it was Collier's that prevailed; and although he lost the war against the theatre, Collier certainly won the battle for a moralizing drama throughout the next generation.

The Theatres (ca. 1700–1737)

The Collier controversy did not close the theatres. Rather, there were new attempts to reform old companies or to start new ones: Christopher Rich was forced to suspend his Theatre Royal because of a profound dispute with the actors (1709). New theatres were built, and old ones occupied by new companies, as when Rich's son John began playing at Lincoln's Inn Fields in 1714. Licenses were granted anew, and one theatre seems to have operated with no license or patent at all.[29] The accession of George II led to the revivification of a patent thought legally dead. The two Restoration patents proved inadequate, and new temporary "licenses" became examples of the Crown's power to control the theatre by giving or withholding the permission that had once been perpetual. The period was chaotic, although the activity itself was a sign of increasing health. It was a health, however, that seemed to threaten order and authority, and it ended with a parliamentary law that greatly changed both theatrical organization and censorship.

The Licensing Act of 1737

In the highly politicized atmosphere of the early eighteenth century, the direct exercise of royal power was under parliamentary attack. Political parties took strong stands on the matter. Political satire abounded, much of it highly—to our sensibilities, even offensively—personal. In a sense, satire is the unwanted child of restriction, for, as expression is limited, satire becomes attractive as the expression of truth in disguise. Although there were laws limiting such expression, they were very difficult to enforce, and poets and playwrights found a haven in satire. In the theatre, verbal satire was often augmented by mimicry of personal characteristics.

Henry Fielding (1707–1754) was the author of strong political satire in such plays as *The Author's Farce, The Grub Street Opera,* and *Pasquin, A Dramatick Satire on the Times.* In 1728, his plays were joined by one of the most popular works of the century, John Gay's *Beggar's Opera,* a satire on the politics and personalities of the day that is unusual in also being able to stand alone as a theatre piece.

The main object of both Fielding's and Gay's attacks was Robert Walpole, the prime minister. Walpole, unable to suppress them, pushed through the Parliament a new law that is now known as the Licensing Act of 1737. The new law did not end theatrical satire, but it radically changed the English theatre. Its clauses:

1. Limited the king's power by allowing him to grant theatrical patents only in the City of Westminster (i.e., a part of London).
2. Required that all new plays be licensed by the Lord Chamberlain.

FIGURE 12.23

Patents and licenses in London (1650–1750)

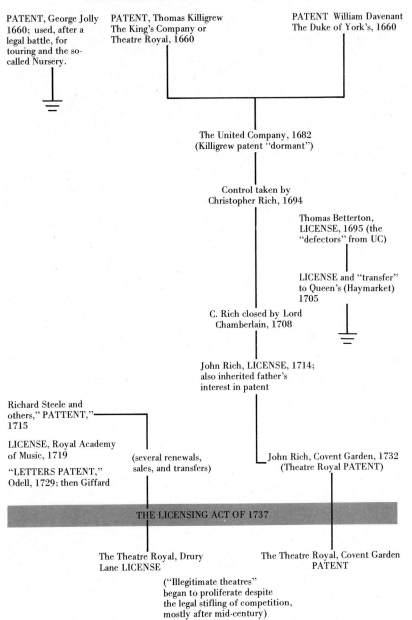

PATENT, George Jolly 1660; used, after a legal battle, for touring and the so-called Nursery.

PATENT, Thomas Killigrew The King's Company or Theatre Royal, 1660

PATENT William Davenant The Duke of York's, 1660

The United Company, 1682 (Killigrew patent "dormant")

Control taken by Christopher Rich, 1694

Thomas Betterton, LICENSE, 1695 (the "defectors" from UC)

LICENSE and "transfer" to Queen's (Haymarket) 1705

C. Rich closed by Lord Chamberlain, 1708

John Rich, LICENSE, 1714; also inherited father's interest in patent

Richard Steele and others," PATTENT," 1715

LICENSE, Royal Academy of Music, 1719

"LETTERS PATENT," Odell, 1729; then Giffard

(several renewals, sales, and transfers)

John Rich, Covent Garden, 1732 (Theatre Royal PATENT)

THE LICENSING ACT OF 1737

The Theatre Royal, Drury Lane LICENSE

The Theatre Royal, Covent Garden PATENT

("Illegitimate theatres" began to proliferate despite the legal stifling of competition, mostly after mid-century)

317

3. Required that theatres have patents.
4. Authorized the Lord Chamberlain to inter-
   fere in performances.[30]

The immediate effects included Fielding's
abandonment of the theatre for other forms (a
happy event for the novel) and the withdrawal
from London of several marginal and now ille-
gal companies. These included the troupe of
Lewis Hallam, which ultimately moved to
America (1752).

Subsequently, the Licensing Act would affect the kinds of theatre, the number of theatres, and even the forms of drama that would
exist in England. At the time of its passage,
however, it was important as a symbol of a fundamental change in English society: power had
shifted from the throne to Parliament.

English Drama

Just as the pre-Restoration playhouses were an
influence on the Restoration theatre, so pre-
Restoration drama was an influence on Restoration drama. Nonetheless, neoclassicism had
a powerful impact, particularly as understood
in John Dryden's *Essay of Dramatick Poesy* (1666).

The repertory of the two patent companies
remained mixed, composed of the following
forms.

Neoclassical Tragedy. The same contest between personal and public motives that marked
French tragedy also marked English tragedy.
Dryden's *All for Love* (1678), a neoclassical treatment of the story of Antony and Cleopatra, was
a masterful work. Later neoclassical tragedies
included Joseph Addison's *Cato* (1713), an
enormously popular play, and Samuel Johnson's *Irene* (1749). An offshoot of English neoclassical tragedy was "heroic tragedy," written
in heroic couplets, the equivalent of the French
alexandrine. Dryden's *Conquest of Granada*
(1670–1671) was the best of the heroic tragedies,
whose values were those of the court.

Shakespeare Revised and Imitated. Shakespeare was "improved" to bring him closer to
neoclassical lines, the most notable of the revis-
ers being Nicholas Rowe and Nahum Tate.
Other dramatists tried to turn back to the Elizabethan drama itself, the best result being
Thomas Otway's *Venice Preserved* (1682).

Restoration Comedy. A blend of pre-Restoration comedy and French influence produced
some of the best comedies in English drama.
Sometimes questioned for their "immorality,"
these plays were often topical, witty, and direct. The "city comedies" of the Elizabethans
were a precedent: scenes were often laid in recognizable London locales. They varied from the
bawdy, almost journalistic crudeness of Thomas
Shadwell's rewriting of Molière's *Miser* to elegant flights of wit like George Etherege's *Man
of Mode*.

The comedies were usually five acts long,
they involved characters below the highest rank
in mundane actions, and many of them had a
loose unity of time and place. Theirs was an
open neoclassicism, not too much burdened by
morality—so they were open to the attacks of
Collier in 1698.

At the heart of Restoration comedy was the
struggle between individual desire and social
constraint. It sometimes took extreme comic
forms; for example, in William Wycherly's *The
Country Wife* (1674–1675), the protagonist,
Horner, pretends to be a eunuch so that he can
seduce the women of London. Stratagems and
tricks abounded, although they depended less
often than French comedy on the cleverness of
servants; here, the courtiers and gentlemen were
themselves tricksters. Restoration comedy has
been called both a comedy of manners and a
comedy of wit, and different examples justify
both titles: many drew laughter from the manners of those who did not belong (servants,
country people, the bourgeoisie), and many
drew laughter both from witty expression and
from mockery of witless behavior and the exposure of fools.

Sexuality and money were common subjects. Sex was treated as sex, not as love; money was considered a perfectly respectable object of desire. As a result, the plays often seem hard-hearted, their characters selfish. In that they spoke to their age, we must assume that these were genuine concerns of the time.

Restoration comedies drew on many sources—French and Spanish plays, classical plays and stories, and continental romance—and often mixed several in one play. They had complex plots, large casts, and, frequently, multiples of mirror images of a protagonist, so that several versions of the same action went forward at once.

After 1700, a change appeared in comedy, and new forms made a significant appearance. The important developments included sentimental comedy and bourgeois tragedy.

Sentimental Comedy.   Perhaps as early as 1700, but certainly by 1720, comedy began to abandon the apparent heartlessness of manners and wit and began to move toward "sentiment." At its furthest extreme, *sentimental comedy* seemed all sentiment and no comedy, arousing tears and feelings of moral piety rather than laughter.

Sentimental comedy employed the happy ending as defined by the working out of poetic justice—punishment of the wicked and reward of the virtuous. As practiced by many dramatists, sentimental comedy was an expression of the post-Restoration age: the audience now included many of the people who had been the objects of laughter in the comedy of manners and wit, and they were of a new, "sentimental" mind.

The values of eighteenth-century mercantilism created a new code of behavior that gave weight to such new, rather pragmatic virtues as dependability, honesty, and restraint, instead of the courtly virtues of creativity, wit, and enlightened self-indulgence. Thus, sentimental comedy was a drama appropriate to its age, emphasizing virtuous statements and behavior instead of wit and manners. It accepted changes

of heart (if for the better) and moral conversion, which the comedy of manners had been too cynical to tolerate; it believed in sexual chastity, marriage, and, at least in principle, love; and above all, it believed in human goodness, not Hobbesian savagery.

In its extreme form in France, sentimental comedy was called *comédie larmoyante,* "weeping comedy."

Bourgeois Tragedy.   There had been a few examples of a serious drama without noble characters before the neoclassical period, but they

FIGURE 12.24

The character George Barnwell from Lillo's *London Merchant* in a later eighteenth-century frontispiece. The relative simplicity of costume and hair should be noted. [Authors' collection.]

did not comprise a distinct genre. Early in the eighteenth century, however, bourgeois tragedy presented the solemn concerns and the sufferings of nonnoble characters. In that such characters did not begin at a height of power or position, it was difficult to bring them visibly low, except in a materialistic or a moral way. The great example of the type in England was George Lillo's *London Merchant* (1731), which was played for many years after as an example to apprentices and young businessmen. On the Continent, the type was not important until after mid-century.

Musical Drama.   Later combinations of music and drama were more often attempts to circumvent legal restrictions on the performance of "legitimate" or nonmusical theatre; of these, the English ballad opera was the most important. In 1728, John Gay's *Beggar's Opera* was performed at the Lincoln's Inn Fields theatre of John Rich; so popular was its combination of satire, new lyrics, old tunes, and comic plot that audiences flocked to it, and it was said to have made "Rich Gay, and Gay Rich." Although many of the musical-dramatic pieces were ephemeral, they sometimes drew large audiences, and they, or other and similar forms, persisted into the period of the modern musical comedy.

Prologues, Epilogues and After-pieces.   Plays opened and closed with specially-written, sometimes satirical poems. After *ca.* 1720, *afterpieces* were increasingly added to plays. Often farcical, sometimes musical, these existed outside the ideas of neoclassicism. The *pantomime* developed, often featuring an Anglicized Harlequin, and it and other after-pieces became an important locus of new trends in scenography—toward local color, rural scenes, and romantic tone.

FIGURE 12.25
English Playwrights (1650–1750)

William Davenant	1606–1668	Theatre patentee, 1660; Interregnum producer	*The Cruelty of the Spaniards in Peru*, 1658
John Dryden	1631–1700	Critic, theorist, outstanding literary figure other than Milton	*All for Love*, 1678
George Etherege	1634–1691	"Gentle George"; ideal courtier, wit	*Marriage à la Mode*, 1671 *The Man of Mode*, 1676
William Wycherley	1640–1716	"Brawny Wycherley"; harshest of Restoration comic dramatists	*The Country Wife*, 1674–1675
Thomas Shadwell	1642–1692	Jonsonian comedies of humours	*Bury Fair*, 1689
Thomas Otway	1652–1685	Tragedies, much influenced by Elizabethans	*Venice Preserved*, 1682
Nathaniel Lee	1653–1692		*The Rival Queens*, 1677
John Vanbrugh	1664–1726	Architect of King's Theatre	*The Provoked Wife*, 1697
William Congreve	1670–1729	Superlative comedies of manners	*The Way of the World*, 1700
Colley Cibber	1671–1757	Actor, memoirist, manager, author of early sentimental comedies	*Love's Last Shift*, 1696
Richard Steele	1672–1729	Critic; coauthor of *Spectator* papers; dramatist of best sentimental comedies	*The Conscious Lovers*, 1722
Joseph Addison	1672–1719	Critic; coauthor of *Spectator* papers	*Cato*, 1713
Nicholas Rowe	1674–1718	"She-tragedies"; Shakespeare reviser	*The Tragedy of Jane Shore*, 1714
George Farquhar	1678–1707	End of Restoration comedy	*The Recruiting Officer*, 1706
John Gay	1685–1732	Poet, satirist	*The Beggar's Opera*, 1728
George Lillo	1693–1739	Bourgeois tragedy	*The London Merchant*, 1731
Henry Fielding	1707–1754	Satirist, novelist	*The Tragedy of Tragedies, or . . . Tom Thumb*, 1731
Samuel Johnson	1709–1784	Critic, novelist, wit, man of letters	*Irene*, 1749

ENDNOTES

1. Franklin L. Baumer, *Modern European Thought* (New York: Macmillan, 1977), p. 49.

2. Henry Carrington Lancaster, *A History of French Dramatic Literature in the Seventeenth Century* (Baltimore: Johns Hopkins University Press, 1929–1942), Part II, Vol. 2, p. 126.

3. Ibid., pp. 136–137.

4. Ibid., p. 141.

5. H. Phillips, "Vraisemblance and Moral Instruction in Seventeenth Century Dramatic Theory," *Modern Language Review* 73 (1978): 267–277.

6. B. V. Varneke, *History of the Russian Theatre* (New York: Macmillan, 1941).

7. Allardyce Nicoll, *World Drama from Aeschylus to Anouilh* (New York: Harcourt Brace, n.d., rev. ed. of 1976), p. 298.

8. Beatrice Corrigan, "Italian Renaissance Drama in the Eighteenth Century," *Comparative Drama* 10 (1976): 101–15.

9. Margarete Baur-Heinhold, *Baroque Theatre*, trans. Mary Whittall (London: Thames and Hudson, 1967), p. 10.

10. Leo Hughes, *The Drama's Patrons* (Austin: University of Texas Press, 1971), pp. 19–20.

11. Harry W. Pedicord, "The Changing Audience," in *The London Theatre World*, ed. Robert D. Hume (Carbondale and Edwardsville: Southern Illinois University Press, 1980).

12. Hughes, p. 175.

13. Donald Mullin, "Lighting on the Eighteenth-Century Stage: A Reconsideration," *Theatre Notebook* 34, 2 (1980): 73–85.

14. Judith Milhouse, "Company Management," in Hume, p. 21.

15. Douglas A. Russell, *Period Style for the Theatre* (Boston: Allyn and Bacon, 1980), p. 232.

16. S. Wilma Holsboer, *L'histoire de la mise en scène dans le théâtre français de 1600 à 1657* (Geneva: Slatkine, reprint edition, 1976), pp. 46–52.

17. Henry Carrington Lancaster, *The Comédie-Française, 1680–1701* (Baltimore: Johns Hopkins University Press, 1941), p. 9.

18. Graham Barlow, "The Hôtel de Bourgogne According to Sir James Thornhill," *Theatre Research International* 1, 2 (Feb. 1976): 89–94.

19. John Palmer, *Molière* (New York: Brewer and Warren, 1930), p. 125.

20. John Lough, *Paris Theatre Audiences in the Seventeenth and Eighteenth Centuries* (Oxford: Oxford University Press, 1957), p. 3.

21. Nicoll, p. 298.

22. Walter H. Bruford, *Theatre, Drama and Audience in Goethe's Germany* (Westport, Conn.: Greenwood Press, reprint edition, 1974), p. 21.

23. Betsy Aikin-Sneath, *Comedy in Germany in the First Half of the Eighteenth Century* (Oxford: Oxford University Press, 1936), p. 25.

24. Ibid., p. 29.

25. Gertrud Mander, "Lessing and His Heritage," in *The German Theatre*, ed. Ronald Hayman (London: Oswald Woolf, 1975), p. 19.

26. Colin Visser, "Killigrew Folio: Private Playhouses and the Restoration Stage," *Theatre Survey* 19 (1978): 119–38.

27. Sister Rose Anthony, S.C., *The Jeremy Collier Stage Controversy, 1698–1726* (New York: Benjamin Blom, reprint edition, 1966), p. 293.

28. Joseph Wood Krutch, *Comedy and Conscience After the Restoration* (New York: Columbia University Press, 1949), p. 109.

29. Emmett Avery, *The London Stage, 1700–1729, A Critical Introduction*, Vol. 2 (Carbondale: Southern Illinois University Press, 1968), p. xli.

30. Arthur Scouten, *The London Stage, 1729–47, A Critical Introduction*, Vol. 3 (Carbondale: Southern Illinois University Press, 1968), p. li.

13

The Enlightenment, 1750–1800

The Period

By the middle of the eighteenth century, a surge of intellectual activity was sweeping western Europe. Variously known as the *Enlightenment*, the Aufklarung, and the *siècle des lumières*, this intellectual movement began the shift from a tradition-centered, absolutist world view to an individual-centered, relative one in government and in art.

Undergirding the Enlightenment were ideas developed somewhat earlier in England. The doctrine of *sensationalism*, formulated by the English philosopher John Locke (1632–1704), proposed that knowledge comes as a result of the physical environment acting upon the five senses; therefore, Nature (rather than reason) was humanity's proper teacher. The cause of *libertarianism* gained currency from an idealized view of the English Constitution and the writings of Locke, who argued that government was a kind of social contract that existed between the ruler and the ruled, a contract broken by either only at great peril. From the still revolutionary views of Sir Isaac Newton (1642–1727) came the view that physical laws govern nature (both external and human) and that human minds could discover such laws. The world, accordingly, could work on its own, without the personal and continuing attention of God.

Although the basic ideas of the Enlightenment were English, their widespread dissemination came from France. The early champions of this new intellectualism were the *philosophes*, the most important of whom were Voltaire, Denis Diderot, and Jean Jacques Rousseau. Their remarkable influence came, in part, merely because they were French at a time when the world still looked to France for cultural and intellectual leadership. It came in part, too, from the breadth of their interests and the excellence of their writing. They wrote clear, vivid, and persuasive French, and they set forth their ideas on topics, ranging from education and science to art and drama, in a wide variety of genres: political tracts, plays, poems, letters, and satire. But probably the reputation and influence of the *philosophes* was due mostly to their publication of a massive (thirty-five-volume) *Encyclopédie* (1748–1772), in which they set forth the current state of knowledge in all major fields—interpreted, of course, in light of their own beliefs. Through their writings, the *philosophes* popularized ideas previously known only to a few, and so they prepared the way in the last half of the eighteenth century for the more radical romantics, who were to follow in the nineteenth.

Politics

Toward the end of the seventeenth century, Louis XIV had spoken with confidence of the rightness of absolutism and had declared himself synonymous with the State of France: "L'état, c'est moi." But by 1748, Montesquieu, a *philosophe* and author of *The Spirit of the Laws*, argued for the importance of both the king *and* the noble class in a stable government: "No monarchy, no nobility; no nobility, no monarchy."[1] Thereafter the political ideas of the *philosophes* steadily gained advocates among the powerful. Frederick II, ruler of Prussia and admirer of the *philosophes,* wrote that the king was "only the first servant of the people."[2] Catherine II of Russia, George II of England, Maria Theresa of Austria, and Louis XV of France were all captivated, although to varying degrees, by the newly popular ideas of the *philosophes.* They all considered themselves "enlightened" and believed that their power could work for the good of their subjects. They prided themselves, therefore, on their modest improvements in agricultural methods, tax structures, seignorial obligations, and legal codes.

The first wholesale implementation of the reforms advocated by the *philosophes,* however, came not in Europe but in America. The American Revolution of 1776 was a major experiment in government, for as its result, the United States established a society that had no hereditary aristocracy, no titles, and no primogeniture; indeed, the United States established a government that had no king at its head. The success of the experiment seemed to prove that the abstract ideas of the *philosophes* were practical after all—and that republican governments could survive and prosper.

Economics

By the middle of the eighteenth century, a massive technological revolution was under way that was to change the way people made, transported, and exchanged information about goods.

For centuries, civilization had relied on power produced by humans, animals, wind, or water. With the invention in the eighteenth century of the first steam engines, however, civilization had a massive source of power that was for the first time steady and continuous. For centuries, as well, individual craftsmen had used a limited number of tools to produce single items of exceptionally high quality. By 1800, however, tools had been devised for making

other tools. With such machine tools, standard items could be turned out in large numbers, and mass production became practical for the first time in human history.

The mass production of goods whetted trading appetites: new sources of raw materials were needed in order to feed factories, and new markets were needed in order to sell the finished products. As developed countries sought such raw materials and markets, both trading and imperialism flourished. Transportation became both more certain and more rapid as barge canals and roads were built in increasing number.

One important result of this technological revolution was to intensify and accelerate some shifts begun in the Renaissance. The basis of wealth continued to shift insistently away from agriculture and toward commerce—and now an embryonic industry. With changing patterns of wealth and population came those in political power and social respectability. Money, rather than pedigree, came to be socially prized; and money, at least theoretically, was available to anyone with ambition and drive. The size, importance, and confidence of the middle class grew as the economy changed from rural and agricultural to civic and commercial.

Social Reforms[3]

Reforms were necessary because a gap had opened up between the lives of many people and the institutions that had long ago been organized to order those lives. People sought protection from exploitation, and more sought access to power. Several antislavery societies sprang up before 1790, and in 1792, Mary Wollstonecraft wrote her *Vindication of the Rights of Women.* Although these efforts did not always produce immediate, tangible benefits, they did focus public attention on inequities and thus served to promote, as well as to express, a spirit of humanitarianism that would carry throughout the nineteenth century and into the twentieth. The Enlightenment set forth in a con-

tained form what erupted in the French
Revolution.

The Theatre of the Enlightenment

The years 1750–1790 were years of contradictions and competing interests in theatre and drama, as in society. Some tendencies surfaced that can help to define the period generally, and several major theatrical figures can help to underscore national distinctions.

General Trends

Audiences and Theatres

The number of theatregoers generally increased after 1750. Two examples can illustrate the trend. London's population, about 676,000 in 1750, grew steadily, reaching almost 900,000 by 1800. Regular playgoers increased from about 8,500 per week in 1742 to 12,500 in 1776 and almost 15,500 by 1800 (holding steady at about 1.7 per cent of London's population).[4] Average attendance at Paris's Comédie Française grew from about 177,000 in 1750 to about 187,000 in 1777, reflecting an increase in that city's population.[5]

FIGURE 13.1

Information About London's Audiences During the Enlightenment

Architectural Changes to Accommodate Increased Numbers*

Drury Lane		Covent Garden	
Date	Seating capacity	Date	Seating capacity
1674	700?		
1732	ca. 1,000	1732	1,335
1747	ca. 1,300	1750s (?)	?
1762	ca. 2,400		
1775	?	1782	2,170
1792	Torn down	1792	3,013
1794	3,611		

Work, Wages, and Prices of Potential Audience Members†

Wages/Week in Shillings		Entertainment Costs	
Day laborer	7–14	Patent Houses (shillings)	
Average shopman	7–8	Upper gallery	1
Journeyman mason	12–14	Gallery	2
Journeyman saddler	12–15	Pit	3
Journeyman printer	14–1g.	Boxes	5
Experienced clerk	19–20		
		Minor Houses (shillings)	
Working Hours/Occupation		Gallery	½
Tailor	6 A.M.–7/8 P.M.	Pit	1
Bookbinders	6 A.M.–8/9 P.M.	Boxes	2½
Bldg. trades	6 A.M.–6 P.M.	Pot of beer	3 pence
Shopkeepers	7/8 A.M.–8/10 P.M.	Cheap dinner	3½ pence
		Small book	3 shillings

*Information taken from Pedicord, pp. 3–6
†Information derived from Pedicord, pp. 22, 32, 27, 37.

Audiences still tended to distribute themselves by class both inside a theatre and among several theatres. For example, the aristocrats gravitated to the boxes, the lesser classes toward the galleries; and those in power tended to support the established theatre, whereas working people often favored neighborhood theatres, minor houses, spectacle theatres, and the like. Still, after 1750, these distinctions appeared to be less rigid than before.

To accommodate the increase in patrons, old theatres were remodeled and new ones built. In England, for example, both patent houses were remodeled several times between 1750 and 1800, and after 1776 the Haymarket became London's third patent house. During the same period, not only were Paris's major theatres remodeled, but several troupes that had been playing the fairs now moved to the Boulevard du Temple, a popular recreational area in Paris. As well, the number of private theatres in the city burgeoned, reaching almost two hundred before the century's end.

As the Western world's population increased, more towns grew large enough to support permanent theatres, and new theatres sprang up outside the traditional capitals. For example, in England between 1768 and 1779, seven provincial theatres received royal patents. In 1774, a theatre calendar in Germany listed fourteen permanent theatres; during the 1790s, the number had grown to nearly forty.[6]

Plays

Probably related to these shifts in audiences—but in ways yet to be satisfactorily explained—were shifts in the drama. In England, the most profound change was a surge of new plays. In 1750–1751, for example, only 28 per cent of the plays produced in England's major theatres had been written within the past forty years; in 1790–1791, however, 68 per cent had been written after 1760 (within the past thirty years). For the first time in the eighteenth century, new plays dominated the English repertory[7] (see Figure 13.2).

In Germany, the most significant change was the growing interest in native dramatists. Germany's repertory in 1750 was both conservative and derivative. In a theatre devoted to promoting native dramatists, for example, fewer than one third of the plays were by German authors; most were French (neoclassical), with a smattering of English and Italian pieces. In 1776, however, the most popular plays produced at Germany's fourteen theatres (as judged by the total number of performances) were French, 90; English, 83: Italian, 64; and German, 413.[8]

In France, interest centered on new kinds of drama. The Comédie Française remained stubbornly neoclassical. Such innovations as there were sprang from practices at the Comédie Italienne and on the boulevard. Shortly after 1750, for example, comic operas in France dropped their *commedia dell'arte* characters, substituted original music for familiar tunes, and increased the sentimentality of their stories. Following these innovations, the popularity of comic opera surged. Perhaps as a result, the Comédie Italienne secured a monopoly on its production (1762), forcing the boulevard theatres to rely on other entertainments. Chief among the boulevard offerings were transplanted English pantomimes (introduced around 1750 when comic opera was temporarily forbidden), French tragedies of the middle class (also

FIGURE 13.2a

English Drama of the Enlightenment.
Percentages of Plays by Period Performed at
Major London Theatres*

When Plays Were Written	Seasons Under Study		
	1750–1751	1770–1771	1790–1791
New	5 ⎫	15 ⎫	33 ⎫
1760–1800	⎬ 28	30 ⎬ 45	35 ⎬ 68
1710–1760	23 ⎭	20	10
1660–1710	38	22	13
Pre–1660	34	18	10

*Information taken from Hannaford, p. 100.

FIGURE 13.2b
English Drama of the Enlightenment. Major English Authors and Works
Arranged in Rough Chronology

Authors	Major Works
Edward Moore (1712–1757)	*The Foundling* (1748), a sentimental comedy *The Gamester* (1753), a domestic tragedy

David Garrick
(1717–1777)
	Plays and adaptations number forty or more, among the most important of which are
	  Miss in Her Teens (1747), a farce, from Dancourt
	  Catherine and Petruchio (1756), a farce, from Shakespeare
	  The Country Girl (1766), a comedy, from Wycherley

Samuel Foote (1720–1777)	Wrote numerous farces (*The Knights,* 1749) and occasional sentimental pieces (*The Minor,* 1760)
Oliver Goldsmith (ca. 1730–1774)	*The Good Nature'd Man* (1768), a comedy *She Stoops to Conquer* (1773), a comedy
George Colman, the Elder (1732–1794)	More than thirty plays, including adaptations (*King Lear*), and famous original works (*The Clandestine Marriage,* 1766, sentimental comedy, with Garrick)

Richard Cumberland
(1732–1812)
	Prolific author, with fifty or more plays to his credit, the most important of which are
	  The West Indian (1771), a sentimental comedy
	  The Fashionable Lover (1772), a comedy

Isaac Bickerstaff (1735–1812)	*The Maid of the Mill* (1765), comic opera *Lionel and Clarissa* (1761), comic opera
Hugh Kelly (1739–1777)	*False Delicacy* (1768), a sentimental comedy
John O'Keeffe (1747–1833)	*The Poor Soldier* (1783), a comic opera *Wild Oats* (1791), a comedy
Richard Brinsley Sheridan (1751–1816)	*The Rivals* (1775), a comedy *The School for Scandal* (1777), a comedy *The Critic* (1781), a burlesque

called *drames,* dropped from the repertory of the Comédie Italienne during the 1770s), and *co-médie-en-vaudeville* (short, satiric pieces that resembled comic opera before it drifted toward sentimentalism). Spectacular effects, appropriate musical accompaniment, and sentimental stories of virtue rewarded and evil punished became the mainstay of the boulevard theatres and the forerunners of that quintessential nineteenth-century entertainment, the melodrama. By the end of the century, then, French drama was developing in two separate trends: neoclassicism at the Comédie Française and new forms on the boulevard (see Figure 13.3).

Two other trends deserve attention: a resurgence of laughing comedy and a renewed interest in Shakespeare.

Although pathos, virtue, and sentiment remained popular throughout the century, interest in "laughing comedy" increased significantly during the 1770s. In 1773, in England, Oliver Goldsmith printed his famous critique of sentimental comedy, "Comparison Between Laughing and Sentimental Comedy." Within four years of the essay, three successful examples of laughing comedy had appeared in England: Goldsmith's *She Stoops to Conquer* (1773) and Richard Brinsley Sheridan's *The Rivals*

(1775) and *The School for Scandal* (1777). The abruptness of the shift may be better appreciated if one recalls that in the thirty years before the appearance of the essay, only three successful laughing comedies had appeared in England. At about the same time in France, Beaumarchais' two satiric comedies *The Barber of Seville* (1775) and *The Marriage of Figaro* (1783) appeared, boosting the popularity of laughing comedy there before the century's end.

Shakespeare's plays were increasingly revived after 1750, in versions closer to their originals than the bastardizations of neoclassicism. In England between 1747 and 1776, for example, four of the five tragedies most often produced were by Shakespeare. Among all serious dramatists, he led the list, with thirteen tragedies, more than twice the number of the author who was second. Likewise in comedy, Shakespeare led the list with nine titles, followed by Colley Cibber with seven.[9] In 1769, David Garrick organized the first great Shakespearean Jubilee at Stratford, which, despite its financial failure, "proved truly international: in France and Germany it became the very symbol of romantic philosophy, giving 'substance to the vi-

sion of Poet as creator, prophet, and national hero.' "[10] The English rage for Shakespeare gripped France soon after mid-century, where the interest was confined mostly to reading and discussing his plays, newly translated and explicated by the prolific Voltaire. And in Germany, Gotthold Ephraim Lessing urged his countrymen to adopt Shakespeare as a model of playwriting, thus beginning a new interest in Shakespeare among German-speaking people.

Acting

Acting, too, was in transition. Although the precise nature of the change is difficult to reconstruct, the likelihood is that the old style placed greater stress on voice and declamation and the new on movement and variety. In England in 1755, for example, an observer commented, "Of old, the delivery of speeches in tragedy was regulated by certain musical notes. . . . the recitation was a kind of singing";[11] only a year later, another Englishman complained about the new actor's "overfondness for extravagant Attitudes, frequently affected Starts, convulsive Twitchings, Jerkings of the Body, sprawling of the Fingers, flapping of the Breast

---

FIGURE 13.3

Major French Dramatists of the Enlightenment (Arranged in Approximate Chronological Order)

Authors	Major Works
Voltaire (François-Marie Arouet, 1694–1778)	Wrote fifty-three plays, the most important of which are *Merope* (1743) *Oedipe* (1718) *The Orphan of China* (1755) *Sémiramis* (1748) *Tancrède* (1760) *Zaïre* (1732)
Bernard-Joseph Suarin (1706–1781)	*Beverlei* (1768), from Edward Moore's *Gamester*
Charles Simon Favart (1710–1792)	Wrote more than sixty pieces, among them *Acajou* (1744), *Le Coq du Village*, *Bastien and Bastienne*, and *The Three Sultans*
Denis Diderot (1713–1784)	*The Illegitimate Son* (1757) *The Father of a Family* (1758)
Michel-Jean Sédaine (1719–1797)	*A Philosopher Without Knowing It* (1765)
Beaumarchais (Pierre-Augustin Caron, 1732–1799)	*The Barber of Seville* (1775) *The Marriage of Figaro* (1783)
Louis Sebastian Mercier (1740–1814)	*Jenneval* (1769), from Lillo's *London Merchant*

and Pockets. . . . the Caricature of Gesture''[12] (see Figure 13.4).

French actors tended to be even more conservative than English actors, and they typically depended even more heavily on declamation, to the exclusion of movement. But by 1753, a leading actress, Mlle. Clairon, was persuaded to abandon her declamatory delivery in favor of a more conversational style. With the actor Henri-Louis LeKain and others, Mlle. Clairon led French acting toward a ''natural'' style (although most historians agree that French ''natural'' acting remained considerably more formal than English ''natural'' acting even then); (see Figure 13.5).

During these years of transition, it was apparently not unusual to see the old and the new styles of acting together in a single performance. The following account describes James Quin (an actor of the old school) in performance with David Garrick (the leading English representative of the new):

FIGURE 13.4

Major English Actors of the Enlightenment (Arranged in Rough Chronology)

Actors	Actresses
John Rich ''Lun'' (ca. 1692–1761)—famous pantomimist and player of Harlequin and teacher of other successful Harlequins of the period; as manager at Covent Garden, popularized the afterpiece	Kitty Clive (1711–1785)—farce player
James Quin (1693–1766)—master of the old school; noted for roles like Coriolanus, Cato, Brutus, ghost in *Hamlet*; in comedy, Falstaff and Sir John Brute	Hannah Pritchard (1711–1768)—new school of acting; noted for natural style; Lady Macbeth; finest tragic actress of the age
Charles Macklin (1697?–1797)—actor and teacher of acting; founder of the ''natural school''; noted for reforms in costume as well as acting; specialized in eccentric characters and hearty old men; Shylock	Peg Woffington (1714–1760)—good coquette; breeches roles; played both comedy and tragedy with some success
David Garrick (1717–1779)—age's leading actor; some say greatest English actor ever; noted for extreme versatility; pantomimic quality; facial expressions and use of eyes; the ''new'' school of natural acting	George Ann Bellamy (ca. 1727–1788)—noted as Garrick's Juliet
Harry Woodward (1717–1777)—student of Rich; major pantomimic player and Harlequin at Drury Lane	Mary Ann Yates (1728–1787)—tragic actress
Spranger Barry (1719–1777)—Garrick's major rival; noted for portrayals of Othello, Antony, and Lear; major romantic lead	
Samuel Foote (1720–1777)—specialized in satiric farce; studied with Macklin; wrote as well as acted; opened Haymarket Theatre	
Edward Shuter (1728–1776)—comic actor specializing in old men	
Thomas Sheridan (1719–1788)—actor and teacher of acting; father of Richard Brinsley Sheridan; scholar of elocution and rhetoric; impressive declaimer	
William Powell (1735–1769)—leading actor at Drury Lane in Garrick's absence; noted for emotional impact on audiences and may have anticipated romantic style of early nineteenth century; strongest in pathetic roles: Lear, Othello, and George Barnwell	David Garrick

FIGURE 13.5
Major French Performers and Designers During the Enlightenment
(Arranged in Approximate Chronological Order)

Actors	Actresses
Charles-François de Grandval (1710–1784)—inherited roles of Quinault-Dufresne; leading actor at Comédie Française until 1768	Mlle. Dumesnil (Marie-Françoise Marchand, 1713–1803)—tragic actress noted for powerful roles; Diderot discussed in his *Paradox sur le Comédien;* Garrick disliked her artificiality
Préville (Pierre-Louis Dubus, 1721–1799)—leading comic actor after mid-century; began in provinces, then went to *opéra comique,* and finally to Comédie Française; changed earlier low-comic interpretations to more human, natural ones; Garrick admired him	Marie-Anne-Botot Dangeville (1714–1796)—comedienne; favorite actress of Garrick
Henri-Louis LeKain (1729–1778)—greatest tragic actor after retirement of Grandval; instrumental in costume reforms and in acting reforms, with Mlle. Clairon	Mlle. Clairon (Claire-Josèphe-Hippolyte Léris de la Tude, 1723–1803)—acted at Opéra and Comédie Italienne before joining the Comédie Française; began in old style but changed around mid-century to new style of acting; discussed in Diderot's *Paradox* and admired by Voltaire; Garrick considered too stilted; leader in costume reforms
François-René Molé (1734–1802)—played young comic heroes, fops, comic valets, and some of LeKain's serious roles, but moved into dramas of Diderot, Sédaine, Beaumarchais; used the "English style"	Marie-Justine Favart (1727–1772)—reputation rests entirely with work at Comédie Italienne; leader in costume reform
Larive (Jean Mauduit, 1747–1802)—successor to LeKain	Mme. Vestris (Françoise-Marie-Rosette Gourgaud, 1743–1804)—studied with LeKain
	Mlle. Raucourt (1756–1815)—understudied Mme. Vestris

Designers

Giovanni-Nicolas Servandoni (1695–1766)—introduced angle perspective to France; worked at opera and Salle des Machines; joined Rich at Covent Garden; specialized in reproduction of well-known places

François Boucher (1703–1770)

Louis-René Boquet (1717–1814)—notable for Chinese motifs

Quin presented himself upon the rising of the curtain in a green velvet coat embroidered down the seams, an enormous full-bottomed periwig, rolled stockings and high-heeled, square-toed shoes: with a very little variation of cadence, and in a deep full tone, accompanied by a sawing kind of action, which had more of the senate than of the stage in it, he rolled out his heroics with an air of dignified indifference, that seemed to disdain the plaudits, that were bestowed upon him. . . . [Then came Garrick] alive in every muscle . . . heavens, what a transition!—it seemed as if a whole century had been stept over in the transition of a single scene: old things were done away, and a new order at once brought forward, bright and luminous, and clearly destined to dispel the barbarisms and bigotry of a tasteless age, too long attached to the prejudices of custom, and superstitiously devoted to the illusions of imposing declamation.[13]

Although the causes of the changing style of acting remain obscure, at least two related movements may be relevant. There was a revolution in rhetoric that paralleled the revolution in acting.[14] Major classical texts of rhetoric were being translated (Longinus, Cicero, and Quintilian), and an unprecedented number of new works were being published on oratory, elocution, and speech. This new rhetoric, drawing on current philosophical and psychological theories, conceived of the passions as internal sensations and activities that remained under control of the soul. Thus conceived of, the passions were passive; they could be analyzed and class-

ified and recreated rationally. Scholars of rhetoric (and acting) therefore set about discovering
ways of identifying and then notating them. The
resulting acting style, according to one scholar,
featured "distinct passions separated by spectacular transitions."[15] Actors sought *points*
(movements of brilliant and artful display designed to call forth applause) rather than an
overall characterization (a spine or overarching
objective).

As the rational dimension (the science) of
acting gained powerful adherents, the interest
in teaching acting increased. Successful actors
gave lectures and opened schools. Several books
on acting were published. Both actors and ora-

FIGURE 13.6

Each passion had an appropriate gesture, and illustrated studies were published to teach about them.
Here, for example, are pride, terror, and sublime ad-
oration. [From Siddons. Courtesy of the Rare Books
Room, Bowling Green State University.]

tors of the day were increasingly enjoined in these lectures and books to study and follow nature: students should examine the passions themselves and not rely merely on imitating the performance of a predecessor. John Hill published an essay in England that, when translated into French in 1769, provided the impetus for Denis Diderot's consideration of the apparent contradiction between the art and the science of acting, "The Paradox of the Actor."

Design

At the same time that acting styles were in transition, practices in scenery, costuming, and lighting began to change in the general direction of greater historical accuracy, greater internal consistency, and more emphasis on mood.

The Italian designers continued to export their preferences for angle perspective, monumentally scaled sets, and designs that separated the stage from the auditorium, techniques that the Bibienas had popularized during the first half of the century. The rediscovery of Pompeii (1748), however, rekindled an interest in Italy's past glories. Classical settings grew newly popular (often depicted in a state of deterioration, as if returning to nature). Also, medieval and Gothic settings became popular as designers experimented with light, shadow, and mass to achieve various atmospheric effects and to suggest mood within their stage pictures. The recent popularity of comic opera led to a spate of rustic settings, and new plays based on domestic situations (as well as new sentimental comic operas) doubtless contributed to the development of an embryonic box set shortly after 1750. These new preferences were quickly exported to other countries.[16]

In France, scenic innovation came mostly in the boulevard theatres, where spectacle often replaced language as the major appeal of the evening. At the Comédie Française, change was slow and erratic because of the continuing power of neoclassicism (with its insistence on unity of place) and the financial policies that put actors in charge of all monies (actors who were disinclined to vote large sums for scenic display). Still, shortly after 1750, onstage seating was eliminated and some moves in the direction of historical accuracy and details of local color were made for certain productions. For most, however, a version of the *palais à volonté* or the *chambre à quatre portes* continued to serve.

In 1750, German scenery still had to tour, and so a few stock sets sufficed: a palace, a street, a rustic scene, an assortment of domestic interiors, and a village. Sets were changed behind a curtain drawn at midstage. When permanent theatres arose, however, chariot-and-pole systems were installed, and interest in consistent and authentic settings began to assert itself. *Ritterstücke* (chivalric plays) led the way, seeking "historical accuracy" by the 1770s (in fact, all were set in the sixteenth century, regardless of their historical surround). By the 1770s, embryonic box sets were also in use.

In England, a well-equipped theatre of 1750 had a stock of scenes: "1st, Temples. 2dly, Tombs. 3rdly, City walls and gates. 4thly, Outside of Palaces. 5thly, Insides of Palaces. 6thly, Streets. 7thly, Chambers. 8thly, Prisons. 9thly, Gardens. And 10thly, Rival [sic; Rural] prospects of groves, forests, desarts, etc."[17] These conventionalized sets were supplemented by occasional properties, like a pedestal for *The Winter's Tale* and a bridge for *The Rehearsal*. Such stock sets and particularizing pieces provided the background for almost all plays: only four productions at the Drury Lane between 1749 and 1759 used newly created sets.

By the 1770s, a far greater variety of scenery was offered and far more attention was paid to its authenticity. Designs for pantomimes and entertainments led to changing practice, and eventually innovations appeared in the design for certain main bills. Baroque landscapes gave way to rustic scenes of English peasant life and to moody, picturesque, and finally romantic scenes of nature—with craggy rocks, forbidding mountains, and gnarled trees. Symmetry gave way to assymmetry, regularity to irregularity (perhaps because of the baroque Italian influence of *per angolo* scenery). Attempts were made to reproduce actual scenes—both those seen in England and those reproduced in paintings and prints. Lighting experiments sought to capture various atmospheric effects within a scene. Landscape painters became favored theatrical designers.

The trends in costuming paralleled those in scenery. In 1750, the stock of costumes in a theatre still consisted largely of modern (or recently modern) garments, supplemented by several other types of costumes ("Persian," "Roman," and so on). Among the stock would be some few costumes built especially for a single production (in England, most often for a pantomime). Leading actors wore what they wished and what they could afford. Shortly after mid-century, in country after country, however, inaccuracies and inconsistencies began to receive unfavorable notice: "Alexander and Cato were not masters of the snuff box, nor Greek women of French Heels" [18] and "What business has a party of English footguards to attend upon a Persian emperor? . . . [Why should] the persons of one single family [be] drest in the manner of a dozen countries?" [19] The complaints began to be answered. In France, Mlle. Clairon abandoned her paniers, and in England, David Garrick introduced another category of costumes (the "Old English Manner") when he used slashed Elizabethan costumes for revivals of pre-Restoration plays. By 1773, the English

FIGURE 13.7

Mlle. Clairon in her supposedly authentic Chinese costume. Note the paniers and the plumed headdress. [From Laumann. Courtesy of the Rare Books Room, Bowling Green State University.]

FIGURE 13.7
Pivotal Productions Promoting New Trends in French Theatre

Date	Production	Innovation
1753	*The Loves of Bastien and Bastienne*	Mme. Favart wore an "authentic" peasant dress
1755	*The Orphan of China*	Mlle. Clairon appeared in an "authentic" Chinese costume; sets were also Chinese
1756	*Sémiramis*	LeKain scandalized audiences by appearing with bare arms in a modified *habit à la Romaine*
1760	*Tancrède*	Both costumes and setting were "authentic" reproductions of the Middle Ages
1761	*The Three Sultans*	Mme. Favart wore a dress imported from Constantinople to assure its authenticity
1767	*Eugénie*	The setting sought to recapture the details of a domestic background

actor Charles Macklin had attempted a production of *Macbeth* in which even minor characters wore historically appropriate costumes (see Figure 13.7).

As a result of lighting changes during the same years, the scenery (compared with the acting platform) was better lit and more visible than ever before. By the 1770s, the chandeliers over the acting platform had been eliminated in several theatres, and there were more wing lights than before. The intensity of both wing lights and footlights had been increased by the use of reflectors. Experiments were being undertaken to control the color of lighting (by means of cloths and water) and their intensity (by turning and tilting the "scene ladders" that held the wing lights). Such experiments pointed to a growing awareness of the artistic potential of light and to a renewed interest in using it to achieve "natural" effects.

Again, the reasons for such shifts are unclear, but several factors doubtless contributed.

First, an increase in foreign trade made foreign artifacts familiar to more people. Thus, whereas the playgoers of 1700 might have known little of the customs of distant peoples, those of 1750 and later probably recognized discrepancies that had earlier passed unnoticed.

Second, antiquarianism (the study of antiquity) was flourishing by 1750, and the antiquaries increasingly published their findings. For example, David Garrick's library contained five books on the dress of different countries and different ages; their publication dates were 1653, 1723, 1757, 1768, and 1776.

Third, the increased use of act drops after 1750 in theatres not outfitted with chariot-and-pole systems made more elaborate changes of scenery possible. Such drops performed two functions: they provided an appropriate background for the actors' performance, and they concealed the stagehands as they manipulated scenery. Once scenery could be changed in a leisurely fashion, out of sight of the audience,

FIGURE 13.8

The stage of Covent Garden in 1763 at the time of a riot. Notice the chandeliers over the stage, the side boxes at the forestage, and the position of the actors well in front of the scenery. [From *Magazine of Art*.]

the temptation of ever more elaborate settings perhaps grew irresistible.

Fourth, shifts in seating, perspective, and lighting led to a changing definition of stage space: acting could now (at least theoretically) take place behind as well as in front of the proscenium. The elimination of onstage seating made more acting space available; the increased illumination of the area made the space visible; and the use of angle perspective and box settings made a close relationship between performer and scenery possible. Although the upstage acting area was not regularly used until the nineteenth century, certain productions (like Macklin's 1773 production of *Macbeth* in London) exploited its possibilities.

Fifth, the changes within all of the production areas were probably mutually reinforcing. That is, moves in the direction of greater accuracy in costumes probably encouraged moves toward greater accuracy in scenery and greater naturalness in acting. Discrepancies in scenery may have been more noticeable as a result of the increased visibility caused by improved lighting.

Obviously, the percentage of a theatre's budget required for the visual aspects of production increased markedly as a result of such changes, and the importance of designers rose proportionately. For example, in England, Garrick more than quadrupled the cost of lighting Drury Lane within thirty years, from about 400 pounds in 1747 to about 2,000 pounds in 1776. Designers were now often permanently attached to theatres and were paid handsome salaries: when Garrick hired his major designer, he paid him 500 pounds a year, an amount earned by leading actors.

National Distinctions

England
Between 1741, when he made his phenomenally successful acting debut at Goodman's Fields, and 1776, when he retired from the management of Drury Lane, London's theatre

FIGURE 13.9

Major English Scenographers During the Enlightenment

At Covent Garden	At Drury Lane
George Lambert	Robert Carver
Nicholas Thomas Dall	John French
John Inigo Richards	Pierre Royer
Giovanni Battista Cipriani	Thomas Greenwood
Giovanni Nicholas Servandoni (1695–1766)	Philippe Jacques de Loutherbourg (1740–1812)

"despite its teeming variety, was dominated in spirit and in practice by one man—David Garrick."[20]

Garrick was the leading English actor of the period—some say of all time. He changed the way his art was practiced. During his lifetime, he played ninety-six different roles, in tragedy, comedy, and farce, moving easily among them. Often, he played in both the main bill and the afterpiece, and he regularly offered the prologue or epilogue. In all, he is said to have given more than twenty-five hundred performances throughout his career.

Garrick was also a prolific author and adapter, drawing heavily from the dramas of France as well as those of England. He led the Western world to a new understanding and appreciation of Shakespeare, and he emerged as one of the most successful theatrical managers in London. During his almost thirty years as co-manager of Drury Lane, Garrick cleared the stage of spectators and established a system of regular rehearsals. He vastly improved the physical theatre and introduced new practices in costume, lighting, and scenery. He stabilized the financial situation of the theatre in order to support a large acting company and a strong production staff—all of whom were regularly paid. Finally, he established an insurance fund for the "support of those performers who through age, infirmity, or accident should be retired from the stage; and also for the relief and support of the widows and children of deceased performers."[21] It is a tribute to his managerial ability that Drury Lane prospered under his leadership, a situation that occurred neither before nor after his management for many years.

Through the force of his own intellect and personality, Garrick raised the reputation of the English theatre both at home and abroad. As early as 1750, a student at Oxford could boast, "since Mr. Garrick's Management, the Stage is become the School of Manners and Morality; Ribaldry and Prophaneness are no longer tolerated. Sense and Nature exert their Influence . . . and the British can now vie with the Athenian Drama, when in its Severest State of Purity."[22] In France, he was a regular visitor at the homes and salons of the *philosophes*. The French sought his advice on theatre management; they came to London to watch him act; they sought his advice on new plays; and they profited from his instruction in Shakespeare.

Finally, by introducing Philippe Jacques de Loutherbourg to England in 1771, Garrick established English preeminence in the new, romantic scenery so popular after the turn of the century. De Loutherbourg succeeded in part because he brought the innovations of others to a new level of accomplishment: his act drops were masterfully painted; his placement of ground rows gave an increased sense of depth; his use of irregularly shaped pieces heightened the sense of the picturesque; and his careful reproductions of actual places established a new standard for scenic illusion. But he succeeded, too, because of his own experimentation, particularly with lighting. In his specially built model theatre, the Eidophusikon, de Loutherbourg experimented with Argand lamps and devised techniques for simulating sunrises, sunsets, mists, and moving clouds through the judicious use of tinted glass, cloth, gauzes, and revolving cylinders. According to a modern historian,

> The significance of his tiny show-place [the Eidophusikon] lies in the fact that it is a kind of microscopic prophecy of the nineteenth-century theatre to come when gas and electric illumination allowed an absolute control to the technician. Here is a framed picture which, being small, could be brightly and colourfully lit; here is an auditorium in which the spectators, being few in number, could easily be seated in semi-darkness.[23]

As a designer, de Loutherbourg produced at least forty-nine rural scenes, twenty-three rural and architectural scenes, and thirty-six cloud and water scenes. Because these designs were widely copied in the provincial theatres of England, de Loutherbourg's influence was widespread, and with it, his interest in romantic scenery.[24]

Through his genius, then, Garrick "raised the character of his profession to the rank of a liberal art, not only by his talents, but by the regularity and probity of his life. . . . His memory will long be honoured by all who are sensible how much a solid, refined, and moral taste, in its public pleasures, contributes to the improvement and glory of a great nation."[25]

France

Just as Garrick presided over the shift away from neoclassicism and toward romanticism in England, Voltaire and Diderot embraced and popularized the new ideas about art in France.

Voltaire, the older and more conservative of the two, had a deep and long-lasting interest in theatre. As an educated Frenchman interested in theatre and drama, Voltaire supported most of the basic tenets of French neoclassicism and most of the traditional practices of the French stage. For example, in his *Preface to Oedipus* (1719), Voltaire confidently reaffirmed the rightness of the three unities, and in his *Preface to Semiramis* (1748), he reasserted his belief that tragedy should both teach and please. Sprinkled through various letters can be found Voltaire's support of other neoclassical rules: decorum should be observed; violence should not be shown onstage; tragic verse should be elevated; and actors should declaim tragic verse with pomp and magnificence.

FIGURE 13.10

Philippe Jacques de Loutherbourg's Eidophusikon (ca. 1782), from a watercolor by Edward Francis Burney. Consider its similarity to a modern movie theatre. [Photograph courtesy of the Trustees of the British Museum and reproduced with permission.]

But by 1750, Voltaire had concluded that the French theatre was decadent, a condition he attributed in part to overreliance on mechanically applied rules (*The Temple of Taste*). His impatience with the thoughtless application of ill-understood regulations was probably exacerbated by his own frequent encounters with the French censors, who seemed bent on stifling innovation, whether political or artistic. Still, the new art that Voltaire sought was certainly not to be one that was free of rules; rather, it was to be governed by less rigid rules—by rules improved and perhaps even perfected by the thoughtful.

As a start, he thought the French theatre could be improved by adopting some (but certainly not all) of the practices of the English stage. In fact, he argued that both French and English theatres might be improved if they were to learn from one another:

Would each Nation attend a little more than they do, to the Taste and the Manners of their respective Neighbours, perhaps a general good Taste might diffuse itself through all *Europe* from such an intercourse of Learning. . . . The *English* Stage, for Example, might be clear'd of mangled Carcasses, and the Style of their tragick Authors, come down from their forced Metaphorical Bombast to a nearer Imitation of Nature. The *French* would learn from the *English* to animate their Tragedies with more Action, and would contract now and then their long Speeches into shorter and warmer Sentiments.[26]

In opposition to strict neoclassical practice, Voltaire argued for the use of ghosts on stage (even introducing them into his own plays, *Ériphyle* and *Sémiramis*). In keeping with recent English practice, too, Voltaire helped to ban spectators from their onstage seats in 1759. For his play *Tancrède* (1760), he abandoned the strict alexandrines of traditional neoclassical tragedy in favor of a freer verse form; but for as long as he lived, Voltaire opposed prose for tragedy, calling it "the *coup de grâce* given to the fine arts."[27]

Voltaire developed a familiarity with England, its language, and its literature at a time when otherwise the French remained almost wholly ignorant of English life and customs. He introduced Shakespeare to France through his translations and his criticisms, and he popularized, as well, the works of Dryden, Pope, Addison, Milton, Locke, and Newton. Almost single-handedly, Voltaire launched that Anglophilia that swept France during the late eighteenth and early nineteenth centuries: between 1450 and 1750, only a few hundred English works had appeared in the French press; between 1750 and 1800, roughly fifteen times as many were listed. Thus, through his introduction to the French of English language and literature (which was much freer, much less rule-bound than the French), Voltaire unwittingly took a first step in eroding not only French religion and government but also French neoclassicism.

Denis Diderot, Voltaire's junior by some twenty years, was not so prolific as his colleague, but he was a good bit more extreme in his views. Although he joined Voltaire in accepting the unities of action and time (finding them both quite natural), he confessed that he longed for a theatre in which unity of place was unnecessary. Although he agreed with Voltaire and the neoclassicists that drama had a moral purpose, Diderot was convinced that the best plays were those that moved spectators, not those that followed the rules: "What do the rules matter to me so long as I am pleased?"[28]

He differed from Voltaire in asserting that the theatre should look to nature rather than to its own past or its own conventions. Diderot sought greater "truthfulness" in costumes, stage settings, acting, and playwriting. He urged actors and playwrights to rely more on gesture and pantomime and less on poetry and to substitute natural speech for declamation, prose for verse (even in tragedy).

In his most significant work on the art of acting, "The Paradox of the Actor" (1769), Diderot explored the proper balance between technique and feeling and seemed to conclude that only through a careful control of his or her own feelings could the actor arouse those of the spectators. Finally, in anticipation of the fourth-wall theatre of the late nineteenth century, Diderot seemed to argue that acting was best when it ignored the presence of the audience in the theatre: "Whether you write plays or whether you play them, do not think any more about the spectator than you would if he didn't exist. Imagine on the edge of the stage a large wall that separates you from the audience and write or act the play as if the curtain had not risen."[29]

Diderot's most radical proposal, however, was for liberalizing the dramatic genres, kept so pure in neoclassical theory. He proposed that neoclassical comedy and tragedy were insufficient to the needs of late-eighteenth-century theatregoers, and so he advocated two additional genres, serious comedy and domestic tragedy: "Here then is the entire range of the dramatic scale: Happy Comedy, whose subject is ridicule and vice, Serious Comedy, whose subject is virtue and the duties of man; that Tragedy whose subject may be our domestic misfortunes, and that Tragedy whose subject is public castastrophes and the misfortunes of the great."[30] In support of these views Diderot wrote *The Illegitimate Son* (1757) as an example of domestic tragedy and *The Father of the Family*

(1758) as an example of serious comedy. As well, he set about translating one of the most popular English examples of middle-class prose tragedy, Edward Moore's problem play *The Gamester* (1753).

Thus, through their plays, their translations, and their writings about the theatre, Voltaire and Diderot moved France away from the authority-centered neoclassicism prized in the days of Louis XIV and toward a more democratic art of the sort later practiced by the romantics. The significance of these two men extended far beyond France. During his lifetime, Voltaire wrote over fifteen million words (roughly the equivalent of twenty Bibles), including over twenty thousand letters to persons throughout Europe, among them Gottsched, Frederick the Great, and Catherine of Russia. By 1800, over six hundred of his works had appeared in England, and his plays formed an increasing part of the German repertory, beginning with the troupe of Neuber and Gottsched. Similarly, Diderot's writings found their way to the leaders of western Europe, both through the *Encyclopédie* and through the *Correspondence littéraire*, an early cultural newsletter circulated for twenty years among selected European courts outside France. Diderot's library, like Voltaire's, was purchased by Catherine the Great, and both *The Father of the Family* and *The Illegitimate Son* gained favor with eighteenth-century Russian audiences. In Germany, largely through the efforts of Gotthold Ephraim Lessing, Diderot's views of theatre eclipsed those of the more conservative Voltaire and helped to set German theatre on a course quite different from that imagined by Gottsched.

Germany

Gotthold Ephraim Lessing (1729–1781) occupied roughly the same position in the history of German theatre as Voltaire and Diderot did in the French theatre. A creature of the German *Aufklarung*, Lessing began as a supporter of Gottsched in calling for a German theatre based on French models. Soon, however, he rejected

such a rigid neoclassicism and embraced the ideas of Diderot and the genius of Shakespeare.

Lessing early developed an interest in theatre and drama. Before he was twenty, he had written his first play, *The Young Scholar*, which was performed by Carolina Neuber's troupe in 1748. In 1750, Lessing, still "a docile disciple of Gottsched,"[31] launched a journal dedicated to the exploration of international drama and theatre of the past and present. The death of the journal's coeditor in 1754, however, caused Lessing to deemphasize reviews of contemporary performances and stress instead scholarly essays on dramatic and theatrical practices in a second journal. During this period of his life, two events marked Lessing's turn away from Gottsched and the French theatre: he wrote his first successful play, *Miss Sara Sampson*, a prose tragedy based on the life of an English woman of the upper middle class; and he translated John Dryden's *Of Dramatick Poesie, An Essay*, a work from which Lessing's understanding of the greatness of English drama is said to date (see Figure 13.11).

When in 1759 this second journal ceased publication, Lessing turned his attention to other matters, among them a serious study of aesthetics that culminated in the publication of

FIGURE 13.11

The Major Works of Gotthold Ephraim Lessing (Arranged in Approximate Chronological Order)

The Young Scholar, 1748
The Jews, 1748(?)
Beytrage zur Historie und Aufnahme des Theaters, first journal, 1749–1754
Theatralische Bibliothek, second journal, 1754–1758
Miss Sara Sampson, 1755
Epistles Concerning the Most Recent Literature, 1759
Laokoön, 1766
Minna von Barnhelm, 1767
Hamburg Dramaturgy, 1767–1769
Emilia Galotti, 1772
Nathan the Wise, 1779

The Laokoön and the translation of Diderot's *The Illegitimate Son* and *The Father of the Family.*

By then, the chief theatrical center in German lands had shifted from Leipzig, the home of Neuber's troupe, to Hamburg, the wealthiest and most populous city in northern Germany. Between 1767 and 1769, Hamburg was the site of Germany's second major theatrical experiment, the Hamburg National Theatre, Germany's first "national theatre." (The title is somewhat inappropriate, because at the time there was no German nation and the theatre was not state-owned.)

Nominally headed by a consortium of twelve Hamburg businessmen, the Hamburg National Theatre set out to reform current theatrical practices. It strove to eliminate the power of the "principal" (the leading actor–manager), to institute fixed salaries for company members, and to provide old-age pensions. It tried to improve the quality of acting by establishing a training school and to encourage native playwrights by offering prizes for original works. None of the goals was met, and the theatre closed within two years, the victim of internal squabbles and continuing financial problems. But it left two legacies of lasting importance: a body of critical writings on the drama (Lessing's *Hamburg Dramaturgy*) and a model for the establishment of other permanent theatres.

Probably Lessing's growing reputation as a playwright, a critic, and an aesthetician had earned him the offer to become literary adviser (*Dramaturg*) to this Hamburg National Theatre in 1767. The appointment assured Lessing of a lasting international reputation. For it, he wrote *Hamburg Dramaturgy*, "without question, the greatest treatise on the theory of drama which that century [the eighteenth] produced. . . . it represents in general the most advanced thinking which Europe had attained at the close of the third quarter of that century."[32]

In *Hamburg Dramaturgy*, Lessing showed himself to be freed from the influence of Gottsched and battling against the conservatism of the early Voltaire. He argued for a national, truly German, theatre in contrast to the pale, French-inspired imitation proposed by Gottsched. Lessing spoke out against the rigid adherence to false rules: "The only unpardonable fault of a tragic poet is this, that he leaves us cold; if he interests us he may do as he likes with the little mechanical rules."[33] He also spoke of the importance of genius in art. A genius might make a mistake, but he could rise above it and create a world of art, a world not necessarily in correspondence with the real world or with rules of dramatic composition. Shakespeare was, for Lessing, an excellent example of genius: he knew little of the rules of dramatic composition, and yet his plays were better than those of Voltaire or of any other Frenchman. In fact, Lessing observed, Shakespeare more closely followed Aristotle than did any of the French dramatists, for Shakespeare understood the essence of Aristotle's theory and did not err, as had the French, in misplacing emphasis on incidental remarks. Shakespeare, Lessing concluded, would be a better model for German writers than were the French.

Lessing also applauded the ideas of Diderot, whom he cited when he spoke out in favor of both sentimental comedy and domestic tragedy: "the names of princes and heroes can lend pomp and majesty to a play, but they contribute nothing to our emotion. . . . if we pity kings, we pity them as human beings, not as kings."[34] With a domestic tragedy already to his credit, Lessing next wrote a comedy of virtue, Germany's first national comedy, the sentimental *Minna von Barnhelm.*

Like Diderot, then, Lessing wrote plays against which his theories could be tested. In both his plays and his theoretical statements, Lessing sided with Diderot against Voltaire on the issue of the language ("There can never be feeling with a stilted, chosen, pompous language. . . . feeling agrees with the simplest, commonest, plainest words and expressions"[35]) and on the art of acting (concluding that the actor's ability to give expression to the necessary emotions was more important than her or his personal feeling of them). Finally, Lessing shared with Diderot (even though he may not have borrowed from him) a great interest in gesture and pantomime, and he condemned actors who relied on conventional and artificial movements rather than natural ones.

Permanent theatres modeled on Hamburg's sprang up during the 1770s and 1780s. Although called *national* or *state theatres* (to distinguish them from *court* theatres or *touring* companies), they were seldom maintained by the state; they were, instead, privately owned and managed. Originally, of course, the court theatres had catered to the aristocracy and the new state or national theatres to the bourgeoisie. Soon, however, these distinctions blurred, with some theatres even taking the name *Hof und Stadtstheater* ("court *and* state theatre"). Good theatre thereafter became a source of pride and rivalry among the cities, just as good opera had been among the courts a century before. By 1800, most German towns had such a theatre, establishing the model for decentralized theatres that still exists in Germany (see Figure 13.12).

The location of a town exerted an effect. For example, in Hamburg, the influence of the English was strong; in Vienna, French and Italian models were more important. In commercial Hamburg, the bourgeoisie was strong; in Vienna and Dresden, the influence of the (French) court dominated. In some cities (like Vienna and Dresden), French and Italian troupes competed with German troupes for the support of theatre audiences. As well, certain cities early became associated with certain styles of production and acting. For example, Weimar was known for its simplicity, Berlin for its elaborate staging, and Hamburg for its attention to individualizing detail. Vienna continued two competing traditions: one in foreign plays and operas, another in folk entertainments. Important artists often changed troupes and cities, however, and styles tended to move with the strengths, weaknesses, and preferences of the artists currently in residence.

FIGURE 13.12

Leading German Actors During the Enlightenment (Arranged in Roughly Chronological Order)

Actor	Cities Often Associated With
Johann Friedrich Schöne-mann (1704–1782)	Leipzig, Schwerin, Hamburg
Gottfried Heinrich Koch (1703–1775)	Leipzig, Schwerin, Hamburg, Weimar, Berlin, Vienna
Konrad Ackermann (1710–1771)	Hamburg, Konigsberg
Sophie Schröder (1714–1792)	Hamburg, Konigsberg
Hans Konrad Dieterich Ekhof (1720–1778)	Schwerin, Hamburg
Susanna Mecour (1738–1784)	Vienna, Hamburg, Gotha
Sophie Hensel (1738–1789)	Hamburg
Johann Michael Bock (1743–1793)	Hamburg, Gotha, Mannheim
Friedrich Ludwig Schroeder (1744–1816)	Hamburg, Vienna
David Borchers (1744–1796)	Hamburg

Of special interest now are the theatres of Strasbourg and Frankfurt, where, in the late 1770s, a radical literary movement sprang up. Called the *Sturm und Drang* ("storm and stress"), this movement took its spiritual leadership from the *philosophe* Jean Jacques Rousseau and its dramatic inspiration from the English poet Shakespeare (who had recently been translated into German). Within it, a group of angry young men, clustered around Johann Wolfgang von Goethe, wrote plays in defiance of neoclassical forms and socially acceptable subjects. They stressed the importance of genius over training, of emotion over reason, and of individuals over types.

Because writers of the *Sturm und Drang* shared little except their contempt for the current state of the German drama, their plays differed remarkably from one another. Some maintained the French unities and the five acts of neoclassicism but brought to the stage actions like incest and murder, subjects previously considered unsuitable; others treated polite subjects but in sprawling structures that defied neoclassical respect for the unities. Some took as their heroes men of action; others focused on sensitive, withdrawn, subjective, and misunderstood artists. Few of the plays were successfully produced, but they were widely discussed and therefore influential. They may thus indirectly account, at least in part, for the increased number of German plays performed in German theatres during the decade (see Figure 13.13).

When Goethe, its central figure, renounced the excesses of the movement and moved to Weimar, the *Sturm und Drang* withered away, its existence bounded by the decade of the 1770s. Its influence, however, extended far beyond. In addition to enhancing the position of native dramatists, it also promoted historicism and consistency in the visual elements of production. Members of the *Sturm und Drang* seemed to enshrine Shakespeare as a genius and thus accelerated German interest in his work. As a revolt against the philosophy of the Enlightenment, the movement inspired bold, new artists

who infused a fresh spirit into the German theatre. Finally, probably because of their diversity, the plays of the *Sturm und Drang* harbored the seeds of most of the dramatic experiments of the next two hundred years, and so, in retrospect, the movement has assumed an importance for theatre historians that it perhaps lacked for its contemporaries.

Italy, Spain, Russia, and the United States

Theatrical conditions in other countries, although similar in certain respects to practices in England, France, and Germany, remained for different reasons outside this mainstream. Italy's artists had fallen from the preeminence they had enjoyed during the Renaissance, Spain's from the heights of their Golden Age. Russia and the United States, on the other hand, were only just developing a public theatre and lagged far behind.

Italy. Like Germany, "Italy" at the middle of the eighteenth century was still a collection of independent cities, major among which were Venice, Naples, and Rome. Their literary and intellectual world was split between those people determined to maintain the grandeur and purity of Italy's past traditions and those whose affection for the ideas of Voltaire, Diderot, and Rousseau led them to scoff at the conventions of baroque opera, unrelieved neoclassical tragedy, and *commedia dell'arte*. Opera rather than theatre was the major art, and design rather than playwriting the major theatrical contribution that Italian cities made to the rest of the world.

Only three playwrights of the period gained international significance: Vittorio Alfieri, Carlo Goldoni, and Carlo Gozzi.

Alfieri tried to reform the old *tragedia erudita* by using fewer characters, simpler actions, and unsingable blank verse. His influence was limited, however, for his plays were seldom performed in public by professional actors; rather, they were read aloud by amateurs in aristocratic salons. Opera, rather than tragedy,

FIGURE 13.13
Representatives of the *Sturm und Drang*
(Arranged Alphabetically)

Major Authors	Major Works
Johann Wolfgang von Goethe (1749–1832)	*Götz von Berlichingen* (1773) *Werther* (a novel, 1774) *Urfaust* (early version of *Faust*)
Friedrich Maximilian Klinger (1752–1831)	*Sturm und Drang* (1776)
Johann Anton Leisewitz (1752–1806)	*Julius von Tarent* (1776)
Jacob M. R. Lenz (1751–1792)	*Die Soldaten* (1776)
Maler Müller (1749–1825)	*Fausts Leben* (1777/8)
Friedrich Schiller (1759–1805)	*Die Rauber* (1782) *Fiesko* (1782) *Kabale und Liebe* (1783)

continued to dominate the interest of those seeking seriousness in the theatre.

Around 1750, serious opera began to move away from its old style (which featured virtuoso singers against highly polished and artificial musical settings) and toward a new style (which stressed simplicity, naturalness, and balance between the singers and the orchestra). The shift came in part, no doubt, from the age's new interest in feeling and emotion, but it came in part, as well, from the increasing popularity of comic opera, newly sentimentalized. The new Italian comic opera, like the old, was exported—to France, Germany, and even Russia.

Goldoni and Gozzi were both popular, comic playwrights. Their rivalry epitomized the split within Venice's intellectual community. Goldoni, a liberal, sought to change traditional *commedia dell'arte* by eliminating the masks, using stories of common people in contemporary life, and providing written texts. The immediate popularity of Goldoni's new-styled comedies provoked Gozzi, a literary conservative, to write plays that featured the conventions of traditional *commedia:* he returned to masks, used *commedia* characters as heroes of fantastical stories, and relied heavily on improvisation. The jealous rivalry of these two writers, fueled by a flurry of pamphlets and poems as well as plays, spilled out of Italy and into France (where Voltaire took the side of Goldoni) and England (where Dr. Johnson's circle supported Gozzi). Although the rivalry remained heated for a while, by 1800 plays modeled after Goldoni's "natural" comedies had all but replaced *commedia*, thus exposing Gozzi's efforts as only a doomed attempt to recapture an outmoded theatrical style (see Figure 13.14).

Spain. Spain remained even further from the centers of theatrical power. Whereas Italy continued to partake of European culture and even continued to contribute to it, Spain held aloof, occasionally receiving but seldom giving ideas outside her own borders.

By 1750, the Spanish intellectual commu-

FIGURE 13.14

Major Italian Theatre Artists During the Enlightenment

In Design	
Gian Battista Piranesi (1720–1778)	Interest in mood, light, shadow, and mass began a movement toward romantic treatment of classical settings
In Playwriting	
Vittorio Alfieri (1749–1803)	Sought to simplify tragedy. Most famous works: *Oreste* (1776), *Saul* (1782), *Antigone* (1783)
Carlo Goldoni (1707–1793)	Moved Italian comedy toward the sentimental; most famous works are *The Servant of Two Masters* (ca. 1746) and *The Mistress of the Inn* (1753)
Carlo Gozzi (1720–1806)	Sought to retain traditions of the *commedia dell'arte*. Most famous works: *The Love for Three Oranges* (1761), *King Stag* (1762), *Turandot* (1762)

nity had split into two increasingly hostile camps: those who sought to regularize Spanish theatre through the application of French neoclassical precepts, and those who sought to affirm the superiority of Spain and the genius of Spanish authors through an appeal to her past. Taunts about the ignorance of Spanish critics or the barbarousness of her plays only inflamed the nationalists into a vigorous defense of Spain's past glories. Probably because of the political climate in Spain, this literary struggle quickly assumed jingoistic overtones. The defense of authors like Lope de Vega and Calderon became a defense of Spanish honor: the *"comedia* represented the pinnacle of perfection and any attempt to change it could only be construed as evidence of a lack of patriotism."[36]

The power of the nationalists was such that, whereas much of western Europe was struggling to throw off neoclassicism by 1750, Spain was only just beginning to feel its major impact. Events of the mid 1760s seemed to favor reform: two popular performers of the old style died, removing one obstacle to change; a translation of Voltaire's *Zaïre* appeared and proved a popular play; the *autos* were finally suppressed; and most important of all, the Count of Aranda gained political power and worked to reform Spanish theatre and drama.

To disseminate the tenets of neoclassicism, Aranda established theatres in royal residences, where French plays (in translation) were performed in careful productions before audiences favorably disposed to receive them. Thus encouraged, the neoclassicists reformed the repertory of the public theatres by removing all plays harmful to morality and all plays whose irregularity might invite the scorn of foreigners, particularly the still influential French. Because few original Spanish plays had been written in a neoclassical style (and fewer still had gained public support), the reformers set out both to translate foreign neoclassical plays and to rework old Spanish *comedias* to bring them into closer accord with neoclassical principles. As well, these reformers sought to banish all comedies of magic (still the most popular kind of play on the Spanish stage). Following such guidelines, the censors examined the old comedies and drew up a list of about seventy plays that would form the basis of a provisional repertory (see Figure 13.15).

By the 1780s, Spain already seemed anxious to move from rigid French neoclassicism and toward the works of Shakespeare and Diderot, but the French Revolution frightened her into a posture of careful conservatism based on central authority in both government and art.

Russia.　During the second half of the eighteenth century, rulers like Catherine the Great were still trying to modernize and westernize Russia, as had Peter the Great before them. The result was a Russia whose society was essentially medieval with elements of eighteenth-century western European culture grafted on it.

Theatre, like the other arts, was still confined largely to the courts, where Italian, French, and German professionals entertained the aristocracy with operas, plays, ballets, and specta-

FIGURE 13.15

Major Figures in the Spanish Theatre
(1750–1800; Arranged in Alphabetical Order)

Ramon de la Cruz	*Manolo* (1769)
Vincente Garcia de la Huerta	*Raquel* (1778)
Tomas de Iriarte	*The Busybody* (1770)
Nicolas Fernandez de Moratin	Major writer of the period, of both plays and tracts. *The Fashionable Lady* (1762, a comedy), the *Censure of the Spanish Theatre* (1762–1763, three pamphlets), *Lucrecia* (1763), *Hormesinda* (1770), *Guzman the Good* (1777).
Mariano Nipho	*The Spanish Nation Defended Against the Insults of the Thinker and His Followers* (1764)

cles. Not until 1756 was a company of *Russian* performers attached to the court at Petersburg and, in the same year, regular theatrical performances begun in Moscow. In that year, as well, a legislative decree gave status to Russian actors and laid the foundation for permanent imperial theatres. Thereafter, interest in native theatre apparently grew, for the number of private theatres increased (some now sponsored by wealthy merchants as well as aristocrats), as did the number of public provincial theatres.

The repertory remained largely derivative, with plays by Molière, Racine, Corneille, Voltaire, Beaumarchais, and Diderot representing France; those of Goethe, Schiller, and (later) August von Kotzebue, Germany; and Shakespeare and Lillo, England. Although a number of native authors arose during the latter half of the eighteenth century, none gained international fame and none successfully competed with foreign authors, even in Russia.

As the Russian repertory rested on foreign models, so, too, did its theatrical practices. Performers were an odd mixture of professionals (usually foreign) and amateurs (usually Russian). After the court decided to sponsor Russian professionals, it took steps to upgrade their quality and reputation. Schools for performers were opened, and experienced actors were encouraged to instruct beginners. Some Russian actors traveled abroad to learn from the likes of Garrick, Clairon, and LeKain, but Russian professionals continued to be held in lower esteem than foreign artists. Before 1800, in the large cities, private theatricals, serf companies, and foreign troupes regularly competed for public and imperial support. In the provinces, however, any performance might mingle professionals (one or two) with amateurs and serfs, the latter marked by the absence of a titled initial before their names in the program.

At the end of the eighteenth century, then, Russian theatre remained in an embryonic state (see Figure 13.16).

The United States.   Before 1750, there was almost no theatre in what is now the United States. Although there are scattered records of

performances by professional strolling players and ambitious amateurs dating back to 1664, not until 1749 did America have a relatively stable company of actors who regularly toured a series of towns to offer dramatic entertainments. Although this first company (headed by Walter Murray and Thomas Kean) effectively disappeared after 1752, its role was quickly assumed by Lewis Hallam's company of English actors, who left London following the Licensing Act of 1737. Hallam's company organized as a sharing venture and, in 1752, began to tour the English colonies' major cities (New York, Philadelphia, and Charleston, S.C.) and Jamaica. After amalgamating with another English troupe headed by David Douglass in 1755, the troupe apparently grew more confident of its future in the colonies, for it both expanded the number of cities that it served and built permanent playhouses in the major ones. As in any *traveling* troupe, scenic displays were probably minimal; and, as in any English *provincial* troupe, the

FIGURE 13.16
Russian Theatre Artists of the Enlightenment (Arranged by Area and in Rough Chronology)

Playwrights

Alexander Petrovich Sumarokov 1717–1777	Considered the age's leading playwright
Yakov Borisovich Knyazhnin 1742–1791	Son-in-law and successor of Sumarokov; charter member of Russian Academy; wrote seven tragedies
Denis Ivanovich Fonvizin 1744–1792	Noted for satirical comedies like *Coryon, The Brigadier* (1766)
Peter Alekseyevich Plavilshchikov 1760–1812	Noted for bourgeois dramas and tearful comedies

Actors

Fyodor Grigoryevich Volkov 1729–1763	Considered the founder of the Russian professional theatre
Ivan Afanasyevich Dmitrevsky 1733–1821	Leading actor of the age, with major roles in Sumarokov's tragedies as well as roles in high comedies
Agrafena Mikhailovna Musina-Pushkina ? –1788	Specialized in Molière's soubrettes
Tatyana Mikhailovna Troyepolskaya	Leading tragedienne in tragedies by Sumarokov and adaptations of Shakespeare
Anton Mikhailovich Krutitsky 1751–1803	Comic actor, especially noted for roles in Molière
Yakov Yemelyanovich Shusherin 1753–1813	Leading actor, excelling in domestic tragedies and sentimental comedies

FIGURE 13.17

Leading Managers (and Performers) of the Eighteenth-Century Theatre in America

Dates	Events
1703	*Anthony Aston*, first professional actor in America; played Charleston and New York
1752–1755	*Lewis Hallam* (1714–1756), his wife, and three children arrived with other not-very-successful English actors, organized as a sharing company, to tour the provinces; said to be the beginning of professional theatre in America
1758–1764 1766–1775	*David Douglass* (? –1786), with troupe in Jamaica, joined forces with that of Hallam, whose widow he married; major tours of the provinces (this time including Rhode Island) interrupted by stays in Jamaica
1775–1783	American Revolution sends Douglass back to Jamaica. After revolution, four major theatrical centers emerge, many drawing personnel from Hallam and Douglass troupes, others directly from England
1783–1800	After American Revolution: *Philadelphia*—the major theatrical center of the late eighteenth century; *Thomas Wignell* (1753–1803) and *Alexander Reinagle* assemble a superior troupe of English players, including Eliza Kemble Whitlock (1761–1836), James Fennell (1766–1816), Anne Brunton Merry (1768–1808), Thomas Abthorpe Cooper (1776–1849), and John Bernard (1756–1828); management passes later to *William Warren* (1767–1832) and *William Wood* (1779–1861) *New York*—"The Old American Company" weakened by internal squabbling; major personnel included Lewis Hallam, Jr., John Henry (1738–1794), John Hodgkinson (ca. 1765–1805), *William Dunlap* (1766–1839), T. A. Cooper, and Joseph Jefferson (1774–1832) *Boston*—probably the weakest of the four; difficulties with censorship; major personnel included Charles Stuart Powell, Snelling Powell (1774–1839), and John Bernard (1756–1828), the actor *Charleston, S.C.*—heavy French influence; major personnel included John Joseph Sollee and Alexander Placide (ca. 1750–1812)

quality of acting was probably not up to London standards. Nonetheless, the Hallam–Douglass troupe seemed to be bringing English theatre and drama to a generally receptive and growing audience when the American Revolution loomed in 1774, forcing the company to retreat to Jamaica (see Figure 13.17).

From the revolution's outbreak in 1775 until the ratification of the peace treaty in 1783, the theatre in the colonies was again limited to occasional performances by amateurs (both British and American soldiers staged plays, for example). Amateurs, as well, wrote a number of plays, mostly didactic pieces aimed at promoting the American version of the revolution (see Figure 13.18). When the conflict simmered down and English actors from the old Hallam and Douglass troupes began dribbling back into the colonies (now called the United States), they wisely paid tribute to the current chauvinism, calling their newly organized troupes the "American Company" and "Old American Company." Although American in name, both the repertory and the practices remained solidly English (except in Charleston, S.C., where the French had gained an important foothold during the revolution).

By 1800, the American theatre was healthy and growing. The pattern was to live and perform in a home city from which tours could be launched at certain times each year. There were by now four major theatrical centers, the most important of which was Philadelphia, whose troupe also served Annapolis, Baltimore, and (after its establishment in 1802), Washington, D.C. The troupe based in Boston served most of inhabited New England; the troupe in New York served its environs; and the one in Charleston toured the populated areas of the Southeast. As the population of the United States grew and new territories opened for settlers, the number of troupes grew. The size and permanency of the company determined the elaborateness of the scenery. In all troupes, English actors con-

FIGURE 13.18
American Plays and Playwrights of the Eighteenth Century

Dates	Works and Authors	Significance
1714	*Androborus*, Robert Hunter	First extant American play
1759	*The Prince of Parthia*, Thomas Godfrey (1736–1763)	First American play to be produced professionally (1767)
1767	*The Disappointed, or the Force of Credibility*, Thomas Forrest	First American comic opera
1773	*The Adulator* and	
1775	*The Group*, Mrs. Mercy Otis Warren (1728–1814)	Political satires, the first tragic, the second farcical; part of a spate of pro-American plays to appear at the time of the Revolution
ca. 1776	*The Patriots*, Robert Munford (ca. 1730–1784)	Satire on false patriotism
1776	*The Fall of British Tyranny, or American Liberty Triumphant*, anon., possibly Joseph (John?) Leacock	
1776	*The Battle of Bunker's Hill* and *The Death of General Montgomery*, Hugh H. Brackenridge (1748–1816)	
1787	*The Contrast*, Royall Tyler (1757–1826)	First American comedy to be produced professionally; first successful American play
1787	*Modest Soldier*, unproduced.	Dunlap was America's first professional playwright; wrote or
1789	*The Father, or American Shandyism*	adapted about sixty plays; managed a New York theatre; wrote
1798	*Andre*	the first (often inaccurate) history of the American theatre
1832	*History of the American Theatre* William Dunlap (1766–1839)	

tinued to outnumber Americans, and foreign plays (especially English) dominated the repertory. As with most English provincial troupes, all of the companies had originally been organized as sharing ventures, but by 1800, many actors preferred to work for a fixed salary, and so entrepreneurs took over the management of the main troupes, leaving only small, unimportant companies as sharing ventures.

ENDNOTES

1. Louis Gottschalk and Donald Lach, *Toward the French Revolution: Europe and America in the Eighteenth-Century World* (New York: Charles Scribner's Sons, 1973), p. 116, quoting *The Spirit of the Laws*. We have drawn heavily on the ideas presented in this book for the discussion that follows.

2. Gottschalk and Lach, p. 215, quoting Frederick's *Anti-Macchiavel* (1740).

3. Excellent summaries of the major shifts in the so-cial, economic, technical and scientific fields can be found in Guy S. Metraux and Francois Crouzet, *The Nineteenth-Century World: Readings from the History of Mankind* (New York: New American Library, 1963).

4. Harry William Pedicord, *The Theatrical Public in the Time of Garrick* (Carbondale: Southern Illinois University Press, 1954), pp. 16 ff., summarizes the major attributes of the audience.

5. John Lough, *Paris Theatre Audiences in the Sev-

enteenth and Eighteenth Centuries (London: Oxford University Press, 1957), is the standard work, from which much of the following discussion is drawn.

6. W. H. Bruford, *Theatre, Drama, and Audience in Goethe's Germany* (London: Routledge & Paul, 1950; reprint ed., Westport, Conn.: Greenwood Press, 1974), pp. 174 ff.

7. Stephen Hannaford, "The Shape of Eighteenth-Century English Drama," *Theatre Survey* 21 (November 1980): 97–98.

8. Bruford, p. 199.

9. Hannaford, pp. 97–98 ff.

10. Allardyce Nicoll, *The Garrick Stage* (Manchester, England: Manchester University Press, 1980), p. 15, who in turn quotes Martha Winburn England, "Stratford Jublilee," *Shakespeare Survey* 9 (1956): 90–100.

11. John Hill, *The Actor* (1755), as quoted by Cecil Price, *Theatre in the Age of Garrick* (Oxford: Basil Blackwell, 1973), pp. 14–15.

12. Theophilus Cibber, *Two Dissertations on the Theatre* (1756), as quoted by Price, pp. 14–15.

13. As reproduced by A. M. Nagler, *A Sourcebook in Theatrical History* (New York: Dover, 1959), pp. 363–364.

14. The matter is well summarized in George Taylor, " 'The Just Delineation of the Passions': Theories of Acting in the Age of Garrick," in Kenneth Richards and Peter Thomson, *Essays on the Eighteenth-Century English Stage* (London: Methuen, 1971).

15. Taylor, in Richards and Thomson, p. 62.

16. The best available work in English on the Italian theatre of the period is Marvin Carlson, *The Italian Stage from Goldoni to D'Annunzio* (London: McFarland & Co., 1981).

17. *The Case of the Stage in Ireland* (1758) as quoted by Price, p. 65.

18. A contemporary as quoted by Nicoll, p. 170.

19. Price, p. 55.

20. Nicoll, p. 1.

21. George Winchester Stone, Jr., and George M. Kahrl, *David Garrick: A Critical Biography* (Carbondale: Southern Illinois University Press, 1979), p. 607.

22. As quoted in Price, p. 197.

23. Nicoll, p. 119.

24. Sybil Rosenfeld, "Landscape in English Scenery in the Eighteenth Century," in Richards and Thomson, pp. 171–177.

25. From Garrick's epitaph as quoted in Stone and Kahrl, p. 648.

26. Quoted in Trusten Wheeler Russell, *Voltaire, Dryden, and Heroic Tragedy* (New York: Columbia University Press, 1946), p. 77.

27. Quoted in Russell, p. 123.

28. As quoted in Joseph Royall Smiley, *Diderot's Relations with Grimm* (Urbana: University of Illinois Press, 1950), p. 37.

29. "On Dramatic Poetry" (1748), as reproduced in Bernard F. Dukore, ed. *Dramatic Theory and Criticism: Greeks to Grotowski* (New York: Holt, Rinehart and Winston, 1974), pp. 292–293; p. 293 for the quotation.

30. Dukore, p. 292.

31. J. G. Robertson, *Lessing's Dramatic Theory* (London: Cambridge University Press, 1939; reprint ed., New York: Benjamin Blom, 1965), p. 334.

32. Robertson, p. 491.

33. Lessing, as reproduced in Dukore, p. 431.

34. Dukore, p. 430.

35. Dukore, p. 434.

36. John A. Cook, *Neo-classic Drama in Spain: Theory and Practice* (Dallas: Southern Methodist University Press, 1959), p. 106.

14

The Romantic Age, 1800–1850

The Period

Politics

The last decade of the eighteenth century and the first decade of the nineteenth were dominated by the French Revolution and its aftermath. The revolution played out, in miniature, the major social and political questions of the age.

By the time the French Revolution began in 1789, the major *philosophes* had died, and with them the moderating emphasis on rationalism and "enlightened despotism." Cries for Liberty, Equality, and Brotherhood were cries for a democracy more far-reaching than that envisioned by the *philosophes* or achieved by the Americans. By late in the French Revolution, only the most radical views prevailed, and restraint of any kind was looked on suspiciously. The revolution that began as a search for equality ended as a slaughter. France was in chaos.

Out of this bloody confusion emerged the military hero Napoleon Bonaparte, who gradually restored order by limiting freedom. As dictator and later emperor, Napoleon redrew the political boundaries of Europe and changed their ruling houses. Clearly a man of his times, Napoleon fatally undermined any lingering beliefs in the divine right of hereditary kingships, for he successfully made and unmade kings using raw power; and he rose to his emperorship out of the middle class, that increasingly powerful segment of French society.

Napoleon's rule had three major effects: it temporarily reversed the political (and artistic) movement toward democracy; it temporarily brought several countries under France's political (and artistic) control; and it encouraged nations toward internal unity in order to oppose him.

Because England was separated from France by the channel, it was able to maintain a somewhat aloof position from the revolution and Napoleon and so could respond to French political and artistic convulsions with a reason born of distance. As neighbors, both Italy and Spain watched the proceedings with alarm, and because most of Napoleon's battles were fought on German lands, Germany's relationships with France during the period were unusually intricate.

After Napoleon's final defeat in 1815, autocratic governments in Europe were increasingly on the defensive, and popular democratic governments went on the attack. A series of revolutions swept Europe in 1820 and again in 1830 and yet again in 1848. In each instance, there was bitter fighting in nearly every European country and even in Asia and the Americas. The goals were clear: to overthrow foreign domination and to replace despotic regimes (domestic as well as foreign) with more representative ones.

The revolutions of 1848 conveniently mark the end of a political era during which conservatism and autocracy had momentarily interrupted the move toward representational gov-

FIGURE 14.1

England, the most quickly industrialized of Western nations, was the first to recognize and write about the attendant problems. Here, an illustrated exposé describes women and children pushing and pulling heavy loads of coal through passageways only sixteen to twenty inches high. [From Cobden.]

ernments that had begun in America in 1776. Thereafter, new alliances and new leaders shaped Europe. England forged ahead as leader in a race toward industrialization. Prussia replaced Austria in speaking for German interests. France strove to rebuild a stable country following the military disasters of foreign wars and domestic revolts. Italy was on the verge of unification, and the United States was on the verge of greatness.

Population Growth and Shift

The early nineteenth century saw a massive breakthrough in the biological and health sciences.[1] The word *biology* was first used in 1802, at about the same time that the introduction of a vaccine against smallpox ended the worst health scourge of the preceding hundred years. Death in London from smallpox had averaged about twenty thousand deaths per decade during the years 1770 to 1800. Between 1800 and 1830, however, the death rate plunged to about nine thousand per decade. In the English provinces of 1800, there were only 38 general hospitals; by 1840, there were 114. As scientific discoveries and statistical observations revealed the importance of cleanliness, disinfectants, and ventilation in the prevention of diseases, deaths from infections within hospitals declined and fever-related deaths in the cities dropped. In the first decade of the century, one newborn English child in about two hundred was expected to die; in the second decade, only one child in five hundred. As people survived infancy—to have families of their own—and as people lived to older ages, the population increased significantly, and a changing economy tended to bring them increasingly into cities.

Economic and Social Changes

During the years 1790–1850, the Western countries finally threw off the remaining vestiges of the courtly world epitomized by Louis XIV and began their emergence as modern industrial societies. England, the most quickly industrialized, for example, completed nearly twenty thousand miles of paved streets and highways between 1800 and 1830, and before mid-century was laying trans-Atlantic cable. In 1801 only about 20 per cent of England's populations lived in towns; by 1850, almost 40 per cent lived there. As the earlier cottage industries declined and factories opened in the cities, masses of working poor became concentrated in urban centers. There, by 1850, the workers had begun to comprise a group capable of wielding political influence. New alliances were forged. Wealthy merchants, once antagonists of the aristocrats, became their supporters in opposing the demands of the urban workers. Thus, conflicts between workers and industrialists began to join the more traditional struggles of landholders with peasants.

The views of money and property rights proposed by Locke and embraced by the *philosophes* in the middle of the eighteenth century were under attack by the middle of the nineteenth. In 1848, one of the most influential critics of capitalism, Karl Marx, drew up his *Com-*

munist Manifesto. Later, he examined history as a series of inevitable economic transformations. Just as the middle class had overcome the aristocrats, he argued, the workers would overthrow the (often middle-class) capitalists.

The Arts

A number of changes, dating from about 1750, had gradually coalesced into something resembling a coherent system of beliefs by the 1790s. The system came to be called *romanticism* (and its adherents *romantics* or *romanticists*). The new system perceived and promoted a view of the world very different from that of neoclassicism, which had preceded it and which it opposed. The romantics sought a new kind of truth and a different sort of beauty.

Some Assumptions of Romanticism

Romanticism assumed many different forms from artist to artist and from country to country.[2] Its diversity was in part an outgrowth of its own emphasis on individuality, for there was in romanticism not a single, clearly defined doctrine but several clusters of attitudes. The strengths of these various clusters rose and fell, and the emphasis among them changed, so that the parts of the system were forever rearranging and reemerging as slightly altered beliefs and practices. Nonetheless, some basic attitudes seemed to characterize Romanticism:

1. *Romantics exalted nature.* The point, although important, is not simple. The single word *nature* had so many meanings that one scholar called it a "verbal jack-of-all trades."[3] Most romantics, however, understood nature in roughly the same way: whether used of the external world or of human beings, the term *nature* for the romantics referred to unsullied states unspoiled by human intervention. Thus, romantics, unlike neoclassicists, used the word

FIGURE 14.2

Edwin Forrest as Metamora, one of the most popular of America's Noble Savages. [From *Century,* an engraving by T. Johnson from an early photograph by Brady.]

nature to contrast with words like *reason, education, civilization, society,* and *artifice.*

2. *Romantics tended to distrust reason.* Seizing on the earlier doctrine of *sentimentalism,* most romantics believed that humanity was basically good and each individual innately moral. Thus, if people would follow their instincts (their *natural* feelings), they would behave properly. People should therefore follow instincts and feelings rather than reason and example, for their innate goodness would never betray them although their education might.

3. *Romantics tended to distrust society and civilization.* Natural and primitive people were glorified. The Noble Savage, a person untouched by civilization, became an ideal. Artists extolled common people (peasants and workers) over aristocrats, because the former were less polluted by the artifices of civilization. Among societies, those that were simple were exalted, for they were the most in tune with nature and the least encumbered by artificial trappings. *Primitivism,* a belief in the superiority of the simple way of life, led to the careful study of past peoples. *Antiquarianism* flourished as scholars sought a new understanding of Rome and (especially) Greece. *Medievalism* thrived as newly powerful nations sought their own historical roots.

For many romantics, the past and not the future was the hope of humanity: *humanity itself was seen as a long process of decline and decay rather than of improvement and progress:* "the melancholy evidence [is] that we might have avoided almost all the ills we suffer from, if we had kept to the simple, uniform, and solitary existence prescribed to us by nature. . . . the state of reflection is a state contrary to nature. . . . the man who thinks is a vitiated animal."[4]

4. *Romanticism promoted the equality of men.* If undeceived by false education or bad example, all men would strive to do right and struggle toward truth; therefore, one man's intelligence was—for all practical purposes—as good as another's. By extension, one man's opinion was as good as another's. In matters of religion, morals, taste, and politics, the trend for the romantics was toward democratization and tolerance. The quest for equality did not extend to women, except in the rarest instances.

5. *Romanticism stressed the importance of details.* Most romantics were not so interested in the general, the typical, and the normal as in the particular, the specific, and the unique. To establish uniqueness was to affirm identity and significance, and so the romantics tended to reveal and cultivate the personal and the idiosyncratic. History and geography were important because, by appreciating the details of remote times and places, people could identify the specific and defining qualities of their own time and place.

Details were important, too, because they offered paths to Truth. Because all creation was one, all created things were integrally linked. Thus, an understanding of any part of creation could lead to an improved understanding of the whole. Each detail could lead toward an apprehension of truth, and many details could offer a fuller apprehension yet. Nature, in its abundant complexity, was the only necessary teacher.

6. *Romanticism taught that all people must search for truth and perfection, even though they knew that neither was attainable in this life.* The unending search for the unattainable brought sadness and melancholy to the lives of sensitive people. Particularly vulnerable to despair were artists and philosophers, because they possessed unique insights that ordinary people were unable or unwilling to understand. They found themselves, Cassandra-like, blessed with penetrating discoveries about the world but cursed with their inability to communicate these discoveries convincingly to their fellows. Thus arose the romantic view of the artist as misunderstood genius.

7. *Romantics reserved a special place for art and artists.* "The ideal of earnest poetry," said Samuel Taylor Coleridge, "consists in the . . . fusion of the sensual into the spiritual." Beauty, again according to Coleridge, "is that in which the many, still seen as many becomes one . . . [it is] Multeity in Unity."[5] Romantic theorists believed that art could eliminate the tensions between the physical and the spiritual, the material and the ideal. Artists (better than other people) could see the truth, but their vision was based on personal revelation and individual insight rather than on rational study or traditional authority: their vision and their art were subjective, and, because subjective, not learnable by the mastery of a set of principles. Art was introspective, for each individual artist could finally find truth only within.

8. *Romantics argued that criticism, like art, was personal and subjective.* Because the purpose of art was to offer spiritual solace to humankind, its value depended on its ability to affect individuals. In a revolutionary leap, romantic criticism removed the basis for judging art from the work itself to the perceiver of the work. The result, of course, was to democratize art, for if any person was stimulated to feel and understand better the nature of existence through a work of art, then that work of art was good for that person, regardless of its adherence to external criteria. Indeed, because common, unlettered people were capable of having an open and honest response to art, such people might finally be better judges than sophisticated, learned receivers, whose honest responses might be blocked by their intellect or education.

The Theatre of Romanticism

Through the early decades of the 1800s, the romantics were in a constant struggle with those wanting to reassert the primacy of authoritarianism and classicism. Consequently, the romantics and the neoclassicists existed side by side well into the 1830s. As early as the 1840s, however, romanticism was itself under attack by those espousing yet another view of life and art, one later called *realism.* As a result, the period seemed always in artistic conflict, with competing styles found in different countries, different theatres, and different productions. Some trends first seen during the Enlightenment continued, but national differences grew stronger than before.

France

The official acceptance of romanticism was slow in coming to France. The powerful association between neoclassicism and privilege (the king, the aristocrats, the French Academy) had served to institutionalize neoclassicism in France more than elsewhere. Also, just as romanticism began to flourish in England and Germany, France first plunged into the chaos of the Revolution and then recoiled to appoint Napoleon, who sought to re-create an empire based on Roman models. Perhaps because of the strength and persistence of neoclassicism in France, the attacks on it were often rancorous, and its overthrow violent.

Regulations

In France at the time of the revolution, the Comédie Française split into two camps almost from the outset of hostilities. The young actors (led by a promising newcomer named François Joseph Talma) tended to support the revolution, and the old actors tended to support the old order, resisting any changes that might threaten their pensions, their possession of parts, or their control over costumes.

Weakened by dissension, the Comédie lost its privileged position in 1791, when a new law authorized an unlimited number of theatres in Paris. The boulevard rejoiced. Newspapers stopped talking of Paris's three theatres and began to speak of all theatres as though they were equal. Within a year of the decree, twenty-three new theatres had opened, bringing to almost sixty thousand persons *a day* the number of people who had to attend the boulevard theatres in order to support them financially.

Competition had already caused the failure of many of the new theatres when the emergence of Napoleon and his recentralization of authority (and power) intervened. Napoleon decreed in 1807 that only eight theatres, four major and four minor, would be tolerated in Paris. To the three official prerevolutionary theatres, he added a "second Comédie," formed from a troupe housed at the Odéon. The repertory of each major theatre was roughly what it had been before the revolution: the Théâtre de S. M. l'Empereur (the former Comédie Française) offered regular comedy and tragedy; the new Théâtre de l'Impératrice, considered an annex to the Comédie, offered comedy only; the

Académie Impériale de Musique (the old Opéra) produced opera, dance, and other works that were entirely in music; the Théâtre de l'Opéra Comique presented comedies or dramas that mixed music and dialogue. The repertories of the four approved minor houses were likewise controlled: The Ambigu with melodramas and pantomimes; the Gaieté with pantomimes, harlequinades, and farces; The Variétés with short parodies and peasant plays, perhaps including songs, and the Vaudeville with *vaudevilles,* short (often satiric) pieces that featured songs with new lyrics set to familiar tunes. For Parisian theatres, then, the result of the bloody revolution had been almost to triple the number of privileged theatres—not to eliminate privilege altogether.

With the return of the monarchy following Napoleon's fall in 1815, restrictions on the boulevard houses were again lifted. Theatres popular before the Decree of 1807 reopened and were soon joined by new theatres devoted to popular entertainment. Now, as at the time of the revolution, most theatrical activity was on the boulevard.

When genre restrictions were again lifted in 1831, the competition intensified, for the Odéon and Opéra could threaten the Comédie Française directly for the first time. By the time of the Revolution of 1848, the once unassailable Comédie was seriously ailing. Too many of its practices were of another age. A creation of Louis XIV and his court, the Comédie Française became, with the triumph of romanticism, an anachronism. The future of the French theatre after 1850 rested with the once-maligned boulevard.

Audience

In France, the revolution and its aftermath were reflected by the audiences in the theatres. As long as the king remained in favor, the fashion in dress and drama remained with the court, and the seating arrangements defined the controversies (aristocrats in the boxes fought with patriots, in the pit).

With the coming of the Reign of Terror, extremism triumphed. By 1793, the revolutionaries had taken over all of the theatres. Several were closed, and others were remodeled to eliminate boxes and balconies, thus giving architectural concreteness to the revolution's increasingly shrill demand for democracy and equality. Both audiences and actors adopted appropriate revolutionary dress, often consisting of tattered rags that avoided any suspicion

FIGURE 14.3

An entr'acte at Nicolet's theatre, an early theatre to settle on the boulevard, and a picture of the boulevard during its prime, shortly after mid-century. [From Pougin.]

of prerevolutionary wealth. The financial panic of 1795–1796, which caused the price of a single balcony seat to shoot from 10 to 1,000 francs within a single year, was echoed in the dress and the manners of the audience. While the nation recoiled in revulsion against the excesses of the Terror, dandyism and foppery abounded. Elegance of language required that certain letters (*q* and *r*) be avoided, for they sounded harsh. Acting style became mannered, and playwrights like Pierre Carlet de Chamblain de Marivaux replaced those like Molière in public favor.

When Napoleon became emperor, stability returned to the audiences, and many old patterns reemerged. Napoleon reinstituted official theatres and reserved for himself an imperial box. He required the members of his government to maintain boxes at the Comédie Française and required the actors to give command performances so regularly that the state theatre threatened to become (once again) the plaything of a ruler.

Napoleon's interest in the theatre indirectly led to an audience convention that was to plague French theatre for years to come, the paid claque. The new emperor hired people to applaud the performances of his mistress; the empress hired others to applaud a rival actress. The power of organized response was readily apparent, and so the claque quickly became an accepted part of the French theatre. By the 1820s, the chief of the claque was an exceedingly important person in the theatre: he attended rehearsals, planned appropriate responses, and, during performances, sat in the middle of the pit to orchestrate the behavior of his employees. The presence of a paid claque, however, seemed to discourage audiences' response and may help to explain the increasing power that critics exercised over the success or failure of a play. By the 1830s, the vocal audiences of 1800 had quieted noticeably.

Drama and Theory

By the time of the revolution, French theatre was split, with neoclassical plays dominating the repertory of the major houses and various minor genres blossoming on the boulevard: comic operas, animal acts, harlequinades, circus entertainments, farces, spectacles, panoramas, peasant plays, parodies, and pantomimes. Out of this cauldron of dramatic activity came the most popular genre of the nineteenth century, the melodrama.

Developed from a combination of several elements—sentimentalized comic operas, *pantomimes dialogués*, English gothic tales, and German domestic dramas, to name the most important—French melodrama grew in popularity and sophistication under the authorship of Guilbert Pixérécourt and emerged to dominate first the popular stages of France and then those of the Western world for the next half century.

Melodramas, as developed by Pixérécourt and his emulators, were plays in which music underscored the actions and the emotions of the scenes. Exotic settings and spectacular effects were often substituted for carefully crafted dialogue and elevated language. The moral universe was simple. Good and evil were clearly separated, and stock characters were aligned accordingly: a hero and heroine were opposed and threatened by a villain, whose desires and actions propelled the actions of the play. After a series of increasingly extreme reversals, the hero and the heroine gained happiness, and the villain received his well-deserved punishment.

Melodrama deviated from neoclassicism in several important ways. Scenes of comic relief were sprinkled throughout the otherwise serious action. The episodic plot unfolded in three (or one, two, or four) acts, not usually in five. The exotic settings were detailed enough to pander to the current interest in travel and history. Special effects—fire, explosions, and earthquakes—emphasized the visual elements of the production even as prose dialogue decreased verbal interest. Because onstage disasters were often required to bring the play to a resolution (by foiling the villain or saving the hero), their successful execution in the theatre placed an increasing emphasis on the role of the designer and the director, who had to ensure the careful timing of the effects in order to guarantee the conclusion of the play.

The French intellectual community remained deeply divided: Should practices tolerated at popular houses on the boulevard be sanctioned at France's major theatre? Before the revolution, the answer was clearly no. At the time of the revolution, however, drama and theatre became political acts, and the revolutionaries sought and secured control of the repertory of all theatres. As the revolution wore on, therefore, the boulevard theatres and the major houses mingled their offerings. Increasingly, all turned to patriotic pieces: historical spectacles in support of freedom, anticlerical plays in opposition to the church, and outright propaganda that interpreted contemporary events. Throughout the revolution, the subjects of plays lurched wildly as they chased after first one and then another political fad. In the name of patriotism, for example, the word *citizen* replaced titles like *king*, *duke*, and *marquis* in plays by Racine, Corneille, and others.

When Napoleon emerged as the nation's leader, the drama regained some stability, for he outlawed all political dramas. Given his desire to encourage comparisons between his empire and Rome's, it is not surprising that Napoleon favored neoclassical plays over the newly popular romantic ones. Paris thus soon found itself once again split, with neoclassical plays languishing at the major houses and various minor genres flourishing on the boulevard. Napoleon's downfall did little to disrupt this pattern. Between 1815 and 1830, for example, the boulevard offered over two thousand new plays; the Comédie, during the same period, produced fewer than one hundred tragedies (see Figure 14.4).

Despite its clearly moribund tradition, the Comédie Française resisted the incursions of romanticism until 1827, when Alexandre Dumas *père's Henry III and His Court* opened. With its loose dramatic structure (reminiscent of German and English plays), several violent onstage acts, and a set change during the first act, the play stunned traditionalists, who complained to

the king about artists who sought "to exclude tragedy from the stage and to substitute for it plays composed in imitation of the most eccentric dramas that foreign literature affords—dramas which no one ever dared to produce before except in our lowest theatres."[6] On the other hand, growing numbers of people began to seek reform, even within the Comédie, perhaps because several French intellectuals had begun to write persuasively in favor of accepting romanticism (see Figure 14.5).

Among the earliest to promote the values of the new style was Mme. de Staël, who had emigrated to Germany for political reasons and there had encountered the works of the German romantics. Her books *On Literature* (1800) and *On Germany* (1810) introduced to France the major ideas of romanticism that were then sweeping Germany.

Others sought inspiration not in Germany but in England, particularly in the works of Shakespeare (who was enjoying a new vogue). In *Racine and Shakespeare* (1823, 1825), for example, Stendhal argued that Shakespeare was a better model than Racine for writers of tragedy. "The entire dispute between Racine and Shakespeare," he observed, "comes down to whether, while observing the two unities of *time* and *place*, one can write plays that vitally interest nineteenth-century audiences—plays that make them weep and shudder or, in other words, that give them *dramatic* pleasures."[7] His answer to the implied question was a resounding no, and so he moved to attack neoclassical tenets like the three unities and the alexandrine line.

In time, French dramatists with romantic leanings took up the fight. Victor Hugo introduced almost all of his plays with prefaces that explained his abandonment of the neoclassical conventions in favor of romantic techniques. The most influential of those prefaces, because the earliest, was the preface to *Cromwell*, which opened with the eloquent: "Behold then a new religion, a new civilization; upon this twofold foundation a new school of poetry must inevitably spring into life." The new poetry, according to Hugo would "take a great step forward,

FIGURE 14.4
Major French Playwrights (1800–1850; Arranged in Approximate Chronological Order)

Authors	Plays
Louis Caigniez 1756 or 1762–1842	Melodramas: *The Judgment of Solomon* (1802)
Marie Joseph Chenier 1764–1811	Revolutionary playwright: *Charles IX* (1789)
Népomucène Lemercier 1771–1840	Neoclassicist: *Christopher Columbus* (1809, which caused a riot for violating the unities and mixing genres)
René Charles Guilbert de Pixérécourt 1773–1844	"The Corneille of the Boulevards"; over 120 melodramas: *The Wife of Two Husbands* (1802), *Pizarro* (1802), *The Mines of Pologne* (1803), *The Hermit of the Black Rock* (1806), *William Tell* (1828)
Victor Ducange 1783–1833	Melodramas: *Thirty Years, or The Life of a Gambler* (1827)
Eugène Scribe 1791–1861	Well-made plays: *Bertrand and Raton* (1833), *The Independents* (1837), *The Secret Passion* (1834), *A Glass of Water* (1840), *Adrienne Lecouvreur* (1849)
Casimir Delavigne 1793–1843	Mixed neoclassicism and romanticism: *Sicilian Vespers* (1819)
Alfred de Vigny 1797–1863	*The Moor of Venice* (1829), *Chatterton* (1835)
Victor Hugo 1802–1885	Major romantic; *Cromwell* (1827), *Hernani* (1830), *Marion de Lorme* (1831), *The King Amuses Himself* (1832), *Ruy Blas* (1838), *Les Burgraves* (1843)
Alexandre Dumas, *père* (1802–1870)	Major romantic; *Caligula* (1847), *Terea* (1832), *Henry III and His Court* (1829)
Alfred de Musset (1810–1857	Romantic: wrote for publication, not production; *Lorenzaccio* (1830), *No Trifling with Love,* (1861), *A Door Should Be Shut or Open* (1848)
François Ponsard 1814–1867	The "School of Good Sense": *Charlotte Corday* (1850)
Emile Augier 1820–1889	"School of Good Sense" and early realist: *Good Man* (1845), *The Adventurer* (1848), *Gabriel* (1889)

FIGURE 14.5
Major French Theoretical Statements (1800–1850; Arranged in Approximate Chronological Order)

Title	Author
De la littérature (1800) and *De l'Allemagne* (1810)	Mme. de Staël (née Germaine Necker, 1766–1817)
Quelques refléxions (1809) and *Refléxions sur la tragédie* (1829)	Benjamin Constant (1767–1830)
Cours de littérature générale (1817)	Népomucène Lemercier (1771–1840)
Racine et Shakespeare (1823, 1825)	Stendhal (Marie-Henri Beyle, 1783–1842)
Various *Prefaces* and *William Shakespeare* (1864)	Victor Hugo (1802–1885)
Various *Prefaces*, *Mémoires* (1852–1854), and *Souvenirs dramatiques* (1868)	Alexandre Dumas, *père* (1802–1870)
Tableau historique et critique de la poésie française et du théâtre au XVIe siècle (1828)	Charles Augustin Sainte Beuve (1804–1869)

a decisive step, a step which, like an earthquake shock will change the whole face of the intellectual world. It will strive to do as nature does, to mingle in its creations, but without confounding them, light and darkness, the sublime and the ridiculous, in other words, the body and the soul, the animal and the intellectual."[8] So much for purity of genres.

Although *Henry III* had introduced serious romantic drama to the stage of the Comédie, the test case for the acceptance of romanticism was the production of Victor Hugo's *Hernani* in 1830. Already considered the official spokesman of the new romantic school because of the principles of drama that he set forth in his preface to *Cromwell* (1828), Hugo anticipated trouble and so had insisted that his friends and supporters receive those tickets normally reserved for the Comédie's paid claque. These friends began to gather at the theatre at two o'clock in the afternoon and were ready to fight by the time the curtain opened on the play at about ten. Demonstrations repeatedly interrupted the performance, with Hugo's friends loudly supporting all departures from neoclassical practice and traditionalists just as loudly opposing them. Whether out of curiosity or commitment, audiences flocked to the theatre. Romanticism finally won its battle for acceptance on the stage of the Comédie. The style that had dominated the minor houses since the 1790s had finally gained critical acceptance at the major house in 1830.

The triumph of romantic drama in France was short-lived, however, for times were changing rapidly. When Hugo's *Les Burgraves* failed at the Comédie in 1843, romanticism ceased to be critically significant in France. Although many of its features continued to dominate plays offered on the boulevard for another fifty years or more, its philosophical basis was so trivialized that it was only an image of its former self. The theatre of spectacle became only a banal shadow of the formerly vital romantic drama.

England

Regulation

In England, as in France, the trend was away from monopoly and privilege. The theatrical monopolies instituted by Charles II (following the model of Louis XIV) were anathema to the new democratic spirit of the age. Although in existence in England during the late eighteenth century, minor theatres had been licensed only outside the city until 1804, when a new Lord Chamberlain permitted them inside Westminster as well. According to their licenses, they could not compete directly with the three major houses, which meant, in effect, that they could not do regular spoken drama. The attempts of the major houses to eliminate this new competition met with only intermittent success, for public opinion generally favored the minor houses whenever legal action was taken against them.

A parliamentary investigation opened in 1832 under the direction of the Select Committee on Dramatic Literature of the House of Commons. After a lengthy study, the committee concluded that "the interest of the drama will be considerably advanced by the natural consequences of a fair competition in its representation"[9] and recommended that all existing minor houses be permitted to operate and to offer, if they wished, legitimate drama. Although the committee report did not cause an immediate change in the laws, the minor houses had clearly won. By the time the legal restrictions were finally removed in 1843, there were already about twenty "illegitimate" companies operating openly in the environs of London. But after 1843, any theatre could legally perform any play that had passed the censor.

Audience

London's population more than doubled between 1800 and 1850, and so it is not surprising that theatre audiences continued to grow. As a result of remodelings during the 1790s, Covent Garden in 1800 seated about 3,000 and Drury

FIGURE 14.6

The vast size of Drury Lane in 1804 contrasts with the somewhat smaller Haymarket of 1821. In the Haymarket, note the stage boxes, the proscenium doors, and the divided stage behind the acting platform. [From Thornbury and *The Theatre* (London).]

Lane about 3,600; the Haymarket theatre was considered intimate at 1,500 seats. (Probably theatre historians have paid far too little attention to the effect of these cavernous spaces on the period's acting style, the resulting relationship between actors and audiences, and the public's apparent preference for spectacle rather than language; see Figure 14.6.) New theatres opened to serve the expanding audience. By 1800, nineteen provincial theatres were operating more-or-less regularly; by 1820, another six had opened. Several new minor houses appeared in London shortly after 1804, with another spurt of theatrical building around 1830, when the construction of docks in England's East End spawned a number of new theatres in that area. Theatrical seasons were lengthened to expand capacity so that theatres (including the Haymarket) played almost year round and com-

peted directly with the major houses for support.

Although incompletely documented, some shift in the social class of theatrical patrons—a democratizing—almost certainly occurred. Many upper-class patrons abandoned the theatre in favor of the opera, their places taken by members of the middle and working classes then flooding into London. Although box, pit, and gallery continued to reflect social class, they apparently did so less rigidly than before. Although the major houses tended to attract a somewhat higher class of clientele, they did so less consistently than they had before. All classes might be found in all theatres, but some theatres (like those in the East End) tended to appeal mostly to working-class, neighborhood patrons.

Gallery audiences (with all that the gallery

implies about class and educational level) were the backbone of the English theatres between 1800 and 1850. Their tastes affected repertory, acting style, production values, and even theatre architecture. They massed to enter the theatre (queuing, or lining up, did not become English practice until after mid-century); they crowded onto benches; they loudly expressed their approval and disapproval. They regularly affected onstage performances. They, not the boxes, dominated the theatrical event.

Not all theatre managers were entirely happy with this turn of events. The major houses, in particular, tried to woo aristocratic patrons back by adjusting the opening hours, changing the evening's bill, and increasing the number of private boxes, the entrances to which did not require mixing with the general audience. The newly powerful gallery audiences, however, resisted such changes and usually prevailed. Although not the only example, the most dramatic is the famous Old Price (or OP) Riots. Turmoil reigned for sixty-seven nights in 1809 when the manager tried to raise ticket prices and increase the number of private boxes at the expense of gallery seating. At issue was a power struggle between the frequenters of the galleries and those of the boxes (complicated, no doubt, by the hiring of an Italian singer at a time when English patriots favored native talents). The riots ended (as had riots in 1792) with the restoration of gallery seating and the reduction of ticket prices.

Repertory

The repertory in the major and minor houses reflected both the changing audience and the ambiguous legal setting. Before 1843, the licensed minor houses could not give regular comedies and tragedies, for such plays remained the exclusive property of Drury Lane, Covent Garden, and the Haymarket. The major houses, on the other hand, could offer all kinds of entertainments, including those given at the minor theatres. To decrease their competitive disadvantage, the minor houses quickly devised a variety of strategies for circumventing the laws governing repertory. The major device became the ubiquitous burletta.

Originally brought to England from Italy during the eighteenth century, the burletta, like the comic opera, consisted of recitative accompanied by music. As the only dramatic form given at the major houses that did not contain spoken dialogue, it seemed vulnerable to plundering by the minor houses, and so late in the eighteenth century, Astley's Equestrian theatre sought and secured specific permission to perform burlettas. At first the term *burletta* described entertainments "written in a sort of doggrel verse, . . . accompanied by a pianoforte, the person playing in the orchestra."[10] By early in the nineteenth century, however, the term *burletta* could be used to refer to almost anything that contained music, including melodrama. Regular (five-act) tragedies could be redivided into three acts, interrupted occasionally by music, and converted into burlettas.

The form thus became a legal umbrella under which minor houses could hide performances of regular plays: there were burletta versions of *The Beggar's Opera* and *Macbeth* at the Royal Circus, and French works were "rendered burletta" and performed at the Sans Pareil. The process by which burlettas were transformed from something akin to comic opera into something virtually indistinguishable from regular drama was described by a contemporary: the minor houses had "made their Recitative appear like Prose, by the actor running one line into another, and slurring over the rhyme;—soon after, a harpsichord was touch'd *now and then*, as an accompaniement to the actor;—sometimes once in a minute;—then once in five minutes;—and last—not at all;—till in the process of time, musical and rhyming dialogue has been abandoned."[11] By the time the Select Committee gathered in 1832, the burletta had made the repertory of the major and minor houses virtually identical.

FIGURE 14.7

Puss in Boots was a popular one-act burletta, offered in 1838 at the Olympic Theatre under Mme. Vestris. [From an engraving by Pierce Egan, said to be sketched "during the performance." Reproduced in Dolby's. Courtesy of the Rare Books Room, University of South Carolina.]

As the minor houses infringed on the repertory of the major houses by means of the burletta, the major houses attempted to meet the competition of the minor houses by including more popular fare in each evening's bill. In an attempt to appeal to the widest possible range of tastes, evening bills were lengthened so that in the five or six hours of performance, a patron might see two full-length plays, numerous variety acts, and an afterpiece. To support such bills, the theatre had a voracious appetite for materials.

The most successful dramas during the period displayed little literary excellence. Melodramas of August von Kotzebue and Pixérécourt succeeded well in translation and held the stages throughout most of the century. English imitators soon joined the translators, and native English melodramas became the rage. Domestic melodramas in the manner of Kotzebue flourished, as did exotic melodramas like those of Pixérécourt. Gothic melodramas came into vogue following the success of the gothic novels of the period. Nautical melodramas, equestrian melodramas, canine melodramas, melodramas of urban life—all held the stage.

In addition to the melodrama and the burletta, probably the most popular minor form was pantomime. Originally, pantomimes were fantasy pieces that opened with several short scenes in verse and moved to a longer, mute spectacle featuring Harlequin cavorting through scenes of classical legend. Early in the nineteenth century, however, pantomime changed to a topical satire sandwiched between opening and closing scenes of fantasy. Featuring Clown rather than Harlequin and urban fantasy rather than classical legend, the pantomime became a sophisticated political satire aimed at strictly adult audiences. Leigh Hunt, a leading critic of the day, considered pantomime the best dramatic literature available.

Together with these three forms, various comedies with music, burlesques, operatic farces, regular farces, interludes, circus acts, animal acts, extravaganzas, spectacles, and a host of incidental entertainments were also popular original works.

Revivals of Shakespeare were well received during the period. Not only did they offer stunning roles for starring players, they also provided ample opportunity for dazzling visual effects. Some were played on horseback; some were "rendered burletta." Scenes were regularly added, subtracted, or rearranged in order to increase the opportunity for spectacle. In whatever bowdlerized form, however, "illustrated Shakespeare" became a hallmark of the

FIGURE 14.8

"Spirits of the British Drama" rewards close study, for it suggests the wide variety of entertainments that invaded the major theatres, threatening to drive the legitimate drama into oblivion. [Courtesy of the Print Collection, Art, Print and Photographs Division of the New York Public Library, Astor, Lenox, and Tilden Foundations.]

SPIRITS of the BRITISH DRAMA, or the legitimate GHOST'S horrified.

theatres during the early part of the century. Particularly popular were the tragedies like *Hamlet* that featured introspective (romantic) heroes and those like *Richard III, Othello*, or *Macbeth* that contained strong melodramatic elements. Revivals of eighteenth-century plays formed a significant portion of the remaining repertory: comic operas, comedies by Sheridan and Goldsmith, and Garrick's morally improved renditions of Restoration comedies joined such perennial favorites as *The Beggar's Opera, The London Merchant*, and *The Gamester*.

Oddly, the best romantic writers were not successful as dramatists. Although the major authors—Keats, Byron, Shelley, Wordsworth, and others—occasionally wrote plays, few succeeded. The reasons for their failure have tantalized scholars. Some suggest that the romantic writers were overwhelmed by the genius of Shakespeare and expended their creative energies trying to recapture his style. In blank verse and about past times, such plays seldom approached the greatness of the originals and suffered from the very comparison that they invited. Others argue that the romantic writers were sorely ignorant of the particular requirements of the theatre. Successful as lyric poets or novelists, they offered plays whose introspective or narrative qualities resisted all attempts to bring them to dramatic life on the stage. Several of the poets actually preferred to write closet dramas aimed at the single, discriminating reader rather than at the audiences found in theatres of the day. Beginning with the romantics, the literature and the stage suffered a division uncommon in England before their time (see Figure 14.9).

This disjunction between "literature" and "the stage" may be explained in part by the changing role of print within the society. En-

FIGURE 14.9

Major English Authors (1800–1850; By Category and in Approximate Chronological Order)

Literary Drama

William Wordsworth 1770–1850	Major lyric poet; *The Borderers* (1795–1796)
Samuel Taylor Coleridge 1772–1834	Major lyric poet and theorist of romanticism; *The Fall of Robespierre* (1794, with Robert Southey)
Sheridan Knowles 1784–1862	*Virginius* (1820)
George Gordon, Lord Byron 1788–1824	Wrote eight plays, five of which were produced, one during his lifetime: *Manfred* (1817), *Sardanapalus* (1821), and *Werner* (1823), a vehicle for Macready
Percy Bysshe Shelley 1792–1822	Major lyric poet; *The Cenci* (1819)
John Keats 1795–1821	*Otho the Great* (1819, with Charles Brown)
Robert Browning 1812–1889	*A Blot on the Scutcheon* (1843)

Popular Authors and Plays

Thomas Holcroft 1745–1809	*The Road to Ruin* (1792); *A Tale of Mystery* (1802, after Pixérécourt; the first English play to use the title *melodrama*)
Elizabeth Inchbald 1753–1821	Adapted widely from French and German; favored sentimental comedies
George Colman, the Younger 1762–1836	*The Iron Chest* (1796), *The Heir at Law* (1797), *Blue-Beard, or Female Curiosity* (1797–1798), managed the Haymarket
Pierce Egan 1772–1849	*Life in London* (1821), later dramatized to great success as *Tom and Jerry;* began a fad for similar urban plays
Matthew Gregory "Monk" Lewis 1775–1818	*Ambrosio, or the Monk*, novel from which successful dramatizations were drawn (1795); *The Castle Spectre* (1797), *Timour the Tartar* (1811)
Isaac Pocock 1782–1835	*The Miller and His Men* (1813), *Rob Roy Macgregor* (1818, a great success for the actor William Charles Macready)
Edward Fitzball 1792–1873	Wrote melodramas; specialized in nautical melodramas and crime plays like *Jonathan Bradford* (1833), based on actual murder; dramatized novels of Sir Walter Scott
John Baldwin Buckstone 1802–1879	Wrote or adapted more than 200 plays, mostly farces and melodramas, including *Luke the Laborer* (1826); skilled comedian
Edward George Bulwer-Lytton 1803–1873	Gentlemanly melodramas, like *The Lady of Lyons* (1838), *Richelieu* (1839), and *Money* (1840), which may have helped bring middle classes back into the theatre
Douglas William Jerrold 1803–1857	*Black-Eyed Susan* (1829) and other nautical melodramas; *The Rent Day* (1832); and edited magazine *Punch*
H. M. Milner	*Masaniello* (1829) and *Mazeppa* (1831, from Byron's poem)

gland's reading public was growing, and with it, the power of the printed word. Published works influenced theatre practice in a variety of ways. For example, as histories of costume, illustrated editions of Shakespeare, records of archaeological finds, travel accounts, and so on were published, the relevant information became readily available to artists who wished to achieve accurate settings and costumes. The effect extended as well to the theatre patrons, however, for with their education came changed expectations with respect to accuracy and consistency. For another example, more people had begun reading plays, at first as a supplement to playgoing and later (for some) as an alternative to it. Some authors then aimed works directly at the discriminating reader, the famous "audience of one." As a final example, public interest in theatre prompted a number of publications devoted solely to it. Between 1800 and 1830, approximately 160 different *theatrical* periodicals appeared in England; by 1825, 19 periodicals dealt with theatrical issues on a *daily* basis. The role of the theatre critic thus became as powerful as it was demanding. During the period, three in particular rose to deserved prominence: William Hazlitt, Leigh Hunt, and Charles Lamb. Of the three, Lamb openly argued the superiority of play reading to playgoing: "The Lear of Shakespeare cannot be acted. . . . On the stage we see nothing but corporal infirmities and weakness, the impotence of rage; while we read it, we see not Lear, but we are Lear." [12]

Germany

Because "Germany" still consisted of many separate states, "German" theatre unfolded in many different cities. Between 1800 and 1850, four were particularly significant: Weimar, where Goethe and Schiller worked; Dresden, supported by Tieck and the Schlegel brothers; Berlin, managed first by the actor Iffland and later by Bruhl; and Vienna, with its four thea-

tres. Although all partook of some aspects of romantic beliefs and practices, each developed differently (see Figure 14.10).

Weimar

With only a few stocks sets and costumes and an unpromising mixture of amateur and second-rate actors, the theatre at Weimar seemed an unlikely candidate for greatness when Johann Wolfgang von Goethe reluctantly assumed its directorship in 1791. Friedrich Schiller joined him there in 1798, and from then until Schiller's death in 1805, Weimar's theatre was the most important in German lands. There developed a style now called *Weimar classicism.* Although from the distance provided by history, it is clear that Weimar classicism shared philosophical assumptions and dramatic practices with romanticism, Goethe and Schiller emphasized the distinctiveness of their work. Goethe explained, "I call the classic *healthy,* the romantic *sickly.* . . . Most modern productions are romantic, not because they are new, but because they are weak, morbid, and sickly; and the antique is classic, not because it is old but because it is strong, fresh, joyous, and healthy." [13]

As in all German theatres of the day, at Weimar the same actors performed an astonishing array of works: operas, comic operas, domestic melodramas, farces, and so on. Because the most popular were the musical offerings and the domestic dramas, these had long formed the bulk of Weimar's repertory. Goethe and Schiller, however, had come quite independently to the conclusion that German audiences lacked taste and that current German drama was demeaned by pandering to their preferences. Goethe and Schiller set out at Weimar, therefore, to improve audiences by offering them (and training them to appreciate) better plays.

In developing their views of art, Goethe and Schiller used as their models the great masterpieces of the past. Both translated widely, and both composed original plays that conformed to their emerging views. Characters should be no-

FIGURE 14.10
Map of Germany showing major theatres.

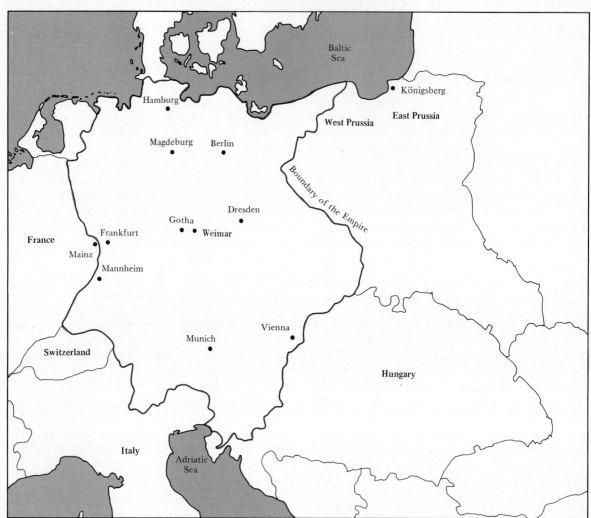

ble; language, elevated through verse; and dramatic actions, significant. For art, they sought an ideal harmony achieved through a careful blend of all elements: "the highest problem of any art is to produce by appearance the illusion of a higher reality."[14]

Gradually, works of literary significance formed an increasing part of Weimar's repertory, but financial pressures required an income from the box office, so that in even its best years, the repertory of Weimar was divided among operas and musical offerings (given on Tuesdays), classics and experimental plays (on Thursdays), and light entertainments (mostly domestic melodramas, on Saturdays).

To perform such a repertory required actors of great skill, but those that Goethe inherited at Weimar were decidedly mediocre. On assuming control of the theatre, therefore, Goethe determined to mold the generally inferior actors into an ensemble in which each performer gave an acceptable (if not inspired) performance. To build his ensemble, Goethe eliminated the customary lines of business and reduced the individuality of his actors. To improve the quality of the individual actors, Goethe instructed each in every aspect of voice and movement, both through rehearsals and through an enforcement of his ninety-one *Rules for Actors.*[15]

Goethe, following the practices of F. L. Schroeder earlier, instituted reading rehearsals in which the primary goal was the proper speaking of the lines. He instructed actors in clear and proper enunciation (insisting that they eliminate their regional dialects) and in effective control of pitch, volume, and rate. All punctuation marks, for example, carried a prescribed pause: commas, one beat; semicolons, two beats; colons, four beats; and so on. Although initially Weimar's most experienced ac-

tors could not even *memorize* plays written in verse, by 1800 many of them were able to *improvise* in verse.

Goethe's emphasis was clearly on declamation, but he by no means ignored stage movement. To aid in blocking, the stage was marked off into squares for rehearsal, and each movement was plotted in advance to assure a pleasing picture for the audience. Goethe paid attention to stage groupings, rehearsing even minor actors so that the total picture might succeed. He supplemented onstage voices with others, offstage, to suggest the large crowds that his small acting troupe could not provide. He forbade certain activities (Rule 74: "The actor should not produce a handkerchief on stage, nor blow his nose or spit"); and he encouraged others (Rule 48: "The two middle fingers should always stay together; the thumb, index and little finger should be somewhat bent").

Goethe's success in training actors is open

FIGURE 14.11
Artists at Weimar During Its Greatest Period (1790s–1800s)

Artistic Leaders and Two Major Authors

Johann Wolfang von Goethe 1749–1832	In addition to early works of *Sturm und Drang*, major dramatic works included *Egmont* (1788), *Tancred* (1801), *Iphigenia in Tauris* (1802), *Faust, Part I* (1808) and *II* (1831), and *Rules for Actors* (1803)
Friedrich Schiller 1759–1805	In addition to early works of *Sturm und Drang*, major dramatic works included *Don Carlos* (1787), *Wallenstein's Camp* (1798), *The Piccolomini* (1799), and *Wallenstein's Death* (1799), a trilogy, *Mary Stuart* (1800), *The Maid of Orleans* (1801), *The Bride of Messina* (1803), and *William Tell* (1804)

Leading Designers

George Melchior Kraus 1762–1827	Costumes
Heinrich Meyer 1760–1832	Scenic painting
Anton Genast 1765–1831	Stage manager and memoirist of company

Leading Performers

Amelie Malcomi 1780–1851	For a time, the company's leading tragedienne
Pius Alexander Wolff 1782–1828	Actor to whom Goethe dictated his *Rules;* with wife Amalia Wolff (1780–1851), was hired at Berlin to act with Ludwig Devrient
Karoline Jagemann 1777–1848	Singer, dramatic actress and duke of Weimar's official mistress

to dispute. Several accounts praised the ensemble, but one thought it an ensemble only in the sense that the actors could have exchanged roles without effect. When the company toured to Leipzig in 1807, they were enthusiastically praised; but when actors from Weimar attempted to join other companies, they were seldom successful.

Although the visual elements of production were also conceived of in terms of ideal beauty and classical values, they were never considered very important: "I did not look to magnificent scenery, and a brilliant wardrobe," said Goethe. "I looked to good pieces." [16] His view may have been as pragmatic as theoretical, however, for the small stage of Weimar had only five sliding wings per side and a single back cloth; there was no fly loft. Neither the property nor the costume stocks of the theatre were extensive. Indeed, when August Wilhelm Iffland played at Weimar in 1796, the theatre was unable to provide him with a chair in which to collapse during his emotional scene. An imitation velvet cloak was apparently the most valuable piece in the costuming stock, and it served for several years as the standard royal garment for all productions.

After Schiller's death, Goethe's interest in the theatre faltered. As his influence waned, the repertory shifted toward those dramas that he and Schiller had deplored. He finally resigned in 1817 rather than support the production of a canine melodrama by Pixérécourt at Weimar. With Goethe's resignation, Weimar's theatre declined. Although Goethe occasionally returned to the theatre for productions of his own works thereafter, his influence—and Weimar's glory—was at an end.

Weimar's importance to its contemporaries was limited, for its work lay outside the mainstream of Germany's theatres. Its subsequent fame however, has outstripped that of all other German theatres of the time. Several reasons for this reversal can be suggested. First, the work of Goethe and Schiller at Weimar reduced the gap between Germany's theatrical and literary traditions. It demonstrated that there was a German audience for serious, artistic work, a lesson not lost on those who came later. Second, Weimar's ensemble offered an alternative to the system of traveling stars then enveloping the German theatre, an alternative that triumphed at the end of the century. Third, at Weimar, Goethe (like others in Germany) tried techniques of directing that culminated in the work of later German *régisseurs* like the Duke of Saxe-Meiningen and Max Reinhardt. Fourth, the plays and the theoretical statements of Goethe and Schiller at Weimar remain among the most important documents in the German language.

Why Goethe and Schiller succeeded where others had failed is not entirely clear, but their artistic partnership proved an unusually happy symbiosis, merging Goethe's theoretical and literary strengths with Schiller's grasp of the practical requirements of theatre. Weimar's audience was probably more amenable to experimentation than the average, for among its six thousand inhabitants was a substantial core of amateur performers, educated aristocrats, and wealthy bourgeoisie. To this group were regularly added students from the university in nearby Jena. Finally, Goethe's rank as a government official gave him a position of power unusual for theatre managers. He viewed the theatre as a cultural resource and himself as the manager of the resource. He could (and did) reprimand—or even arrest—people whose behavior did not conform to his standards.

Dresden

As Weimar's fortunes waned, those of Dresden waxed. The central figure in this theatre's rising importance was Ludwig Tieck, a romantic who joined the theatre in 1820, became its *dramaturg* in 1824, despaired of its potential by 1830, and in 1842 left for Berlin, where he undertook two radical experiments in staging before his death in 1853. During the decade of the 1820s, however, he led Dresden to artistic prominence as a center of serious romantic theatre.

Tieck was already renowned before coming

to Dresden. While Goethe and Schiller worked at Weimar, Tieck, along with the Schlegel brothers (August Wilhelm and Friedrich), belonged to a group of young writers a few miles away at Jena. The Schlegels' publication of the literary periodical *Athenaeum* is said to mark the beginning of German romanticism, but their major contribution to German drama may well have been August Wilhelm Schlegel's translations of Shakespeare, sixteen of which appeared between 1797 and 1801 (he also later translated a seventeenth; the remainder, the work of others, appeared between 1825 and 1833). Not only did these translations make available the first relatively accurate versions of Shakespeare in Germany, but they also exerted a clear influence on the style of later German playwrights. They provoked intense study of Shakespeare's drama and theatre and intensified that Shakespeare-philia that marked the early years of the nineteenth century. In addition to translations, both brothers published widely on romantic theory, popularizing its tenets in Germany and influencing French authors (like Mme. de Staël) and English writers (like Coleridge). Each, as well, wrote one (unsuccessful) play.

By 1800, Tieck was Germany's major romantic playwright. His work, according to Marvin Carlson, "forms a sort of compendium of reasons why this movement produced no major dramatist."[17] Tieck's plays were wildly idiosyncratic. In them, fairy and folk tales served as vehicles for ridiculing political, social, and artistic conventions of all kinds. The characters were contradictory, the structures sprawling and confused. In *Zerbino*, for example, the hero tries to destroy the play by forcing it to run backward, allowing editors, readers, and critics to work on it. For some, Tieck's plays are anarchy rather than art. Although his most original plays were completed before 1800, Tieck made his major contributions as a romantic theorist, historian, and translator after he settled in Dresden in 1820.

The recently established court theatre at Dresden was specializing in popular French and German comedies and domestic plays when Tieck reluctantly agreed to serve as drama critic for the local paper. Soon after his arrival, he began promoting the works of two young and unknown playwrights: Heinrich von Kleist and Christian Dietrich Grabbe. Reminiscent of earlier *Sturm und Drang* authors, both Kleist and Grabbe offered black views of the human condition. In preposterous comedies and despairing tragedies, both authors provoked from critics descriptive terms like *tormented, cynical, irrational, chaotic, demonic,* and *wayward*. Both seemed obsessed with the illusory nature of this world and with the (often malevolent) forces that appear to control human lives.

The theatrical public did not share Tieck's enthusiasm for either author, and so their reputations are largely posthumous. Various experimental styles (especially expressionism) have found their old techniques and bleak visions compatible, and so the fame of both surged during the twentieth century (see Figure 14.12).

Tieck improved the repertory in other directions, as well. During the 1820s, his own translations and criticisms of English drama, his histories of English and continental drama, and his encouragement of other scholars focused attention on masterpieces from the past. Dresden produced more Shakespeare than had ever before been attempted at a German theatre, and it offered plays by Calderon and Lope de Vega, Grillparzer, and Goethe, including a production of *Faust, Part I* in honor of the author's eightieth birthday.

As literary adviser, Tieck indirectly influenced acting style and visual production. In essays published during the 1820s, he spoke out against the declamatory style popularized by John Philip Kemble in England and promoted by Goethe in Germany. He preferred a "natural" style that respected poetic rhythms without introducing contrived pauses. He decried the use of conventional neoclassical costumes and symmetrical, Italianate settings. He objected as

FIGURE 14.12

Leaders of Germany's Romantic Movement in Theatre and Drama (1800–1850; Arranged in Approximate Chronological Order)

August Wilhelm Schlegel 1767–1845	Seventeen masterful translations of Shakespeare (1797–1801) a single play, *Ion* (1803); translations of Calderon (1803–1809); lectures on dramatic art (1809–1811)
Friedrich Schlegel 1772–1829	Force behind *Athenaeum* (1799); single play, *Alarcos* (1802)
Ludwig Tieck 1773–1853	Plays *Bluebeard* (1782–1786), *Puss in Boots* (1797), *Zerbino* (1799), and *Life and Death of Tiny Thomas* (1811); Shakespearean staging; critical essays include *Costume* (1825), *Decor* (1825), and *About Tempo* (1825)
Heinrich von Kleist 1777–1811	Works collected and published by Tieck in 1826; plays include *The Broken Jug* (1806), *Amphitrion* (1807), *Penthesilea* (1808), *Kate of Heilbronn* (1808), and *The Prince of Homburg* (1810)
Christian Dietrich Grabbe 1801–1836	Plays include *Jest, Satire, Irony, and Deeper Significance* (1827, first performed in 1907), *Marius and Sulla* (1823), *Nannette and Maria* (1827), *Henry IV* (1828), *Don Juan and Faust* (1828, the only play performed during his lifetime)

well to elaborate visual elements that sought historical accuracy or local color. He proposed, as an alternative, costumes and settings that sought poetic rather than historical truth, that used simple and suggestive rather than detailed and correct elements. Although his ideas on physical production were never tested in Dresden, the court theatre at Potsdam in the 1840s invited his experimentation. For productions of *Antigone* and *Medea*, Tieck supervised the construction of a Greek-inspired performing space. For productions of *Romeo and Juliet* and *Macbeth*, he designed permanent architectural spaces based on his understanding of the theatre in which Shakespeare worked. For *A Midsummer Night's Dream*, he created a version of an Elizabethan theatre: two levels with a musician's gallery, no scenery, and no curtain. Although considered odd in his own day because so far removed from contemporary practice, Tieck's ideas of staging reemerged late in the nineteenth century and triumphed during the twentieth.

With Tieck's departure, Dresden's theatre lapsed for a time back into comparative obscurity.

Berlin

Although as capital of Prussia Berlin was a large and important city, its theatrical traditions were decidedly unstable before the arrival of the famous actor and author August Wilhelm Iffland. During the years of his management (1796–1815) and those of his successor Count Karl Bruhl (1815–1828), Berlin's theatre grew in importance. It offered, in miniature, a view of the mainstream of German theatre during the early nineteenth century. If Weimar and Dresden are important because of their unique contributions to theatre, Berlin claims our attention primarily because of its typicality (see Figure 14.13).

Its repertory was dominated by domestic dramas. Popular with German audiences since the days of Lessing, family plays now took over the stage, largely because of the popularity of Iffland and his younger contemporary August von Kotzebue (who also lived for a time in Berlin). Both playwrights avoided political questions and public affairs in favor of domestic stories based on the interests and values of Germany's middle class. They offered a sentimentalized and comfortable picture of virtue rewarded and reputation upheld. Kotzebue was both the more prolific and the more popular. Although uniformly scorned by critics, his plays dominated the stages of Germany throughout the century and appeared in translations throughout the Western world. After the deaths of Iffland and Kotzebue, imitators carried on the traditions of the domestic melodrama and found a comfortable home in Berlin's theatre.

Supplementing the domestic dramas was a fairly wide range of plays already successfully produced elsewhere. Plays by respected German authors like Goethe, Schiller, and Lessing were offered. Translations of popular contemporary French melodramas, *vaudevilles*, and comedies far outnumbered the production of foreign authors like Shakespeare, Molière, or Calderon. Any box-office success was likely to produce echoes; thus, when Zacharias Werner's fate tragedy *The Twenty-Fourth of February* prospered, similar fate plays were produced in such profusion that Berlin became known as the home of fate tragedies. The repertory was, in a word, safe. Although spoofs of current literary

fashions might be produced, controversial authors and plays were not.

An actor himself, Iffland exerted considerable influence on acting style in Berlin. He was a "natural" actor, building his (mostly domestic) heroes one meticulous detail at a time. His performances infected others in the company. "The influence of natural playing still dominates [a Berlin actress] so that her delivery approaches conversation and every phrase becomes realistic in her mouth. This is Iffland's school and it gives a general tone to Berlin's productions," reported Schiller.[18] Just before his death, Iffland recruited Germany's leading Romantic actor, Ludwig Devrient, to Dresden; and Bruhl later hired stars from Weimar. Thus, Berlin's acting style steadily lost its distinctive-

FIGURE 14.13

Artists Linked to Berlin (1800s–1820s)

Authors

August Wilhelm Iffland 1759–1814	Germany's leading "natural actor" after F. L. Schroeder; major essays on the art of acting (1785–1815); managed Berlin's theatre (1796–1814); wrote family dramas, including *The Bachelors* and *The Foresters*
August von Kotzebue 1761–1819	Wrote more than two hundred plays, specializing in domestic and romantic melodramas; most popular playwright in the world during the early nineteenth century; popular plays included *The Stranger* (1789), and *Lover's Vows* (1790)
Zacharias Werner 1768–1823	*Martin Luther* (1807); and *The Twenty-Fourth of February* (1809)
Ernst Raupach 1784–1852	Successor to Iffland and Kotzebue; wrote over one hundred plays

Actors

Johann Ferdinand Fleck 1757–1801	Contemporary of Iffland; preferred romantic style, causing a mixture of styles in Berlin from the outset
Friedrich Wilhelm Lunn 1792–1837	"Natural" actor who succeeded Iffland
Ludwig Devrient 1784–1832	Leading romantic actor in Germany
Auguste Stich-Crelinger 1795–1865	Favorite interpreter of domestic plays of Raupach

Critic

Friedrich Schulz	Berlin's first systematic theatre critic; *Berlinisher Dramaturgie* (1799); opposed the new romantics

Designer

Carl Friedrich Schinkel 1781–1841	Leading romantic designer; known especially for designs for Mozart's *Magic Flute* (1816), Schiller's *Maid of Orleans* (1817), and Kleist's *Kate of Heilbronn* (1824) and *Prince of Homburg* (1828)

ness, as romantic, classical, and natural actors performed in the same productions.

After Iffland's death such unity as was achieved on the stage came not from the acting but from the costumes and scenery. Berlin had long been noted for its elaborate settings and costumes, its pageantry and spectacle. A theatre fire in 1817, however, gave Bruhl a unique opportunity to exploit his own interest in costumes and scenery and to rebuild the theatre's stock in keeping with his own antiquarian interests. The opportunity was the greater because he had been told by Berlin's ruler to "make the best theatre in Germany, and then tell me what it costs."[19] Accordingly, Bruhl hired Germany's leading romantic designer, Carl Friedrich Schinkel, who encouraged Bruhl to costume his actors in historically accurate garments, preferring correct fabrics and trims, and proper hair styles and makeup. Although not all productions nor all elements within a single production were accurate, the goal was (romantic) particularity rather than (classical) generality.

After Bruhl left the theatre, its company declined for a time, emerging later as an important home of realistic theatre around mid-century.

Vienna

Vienna's national theatre (called the *Burg-theater*) rose to prominence during the 1820s because of its excellent acting company and solid repertory. Part of the credit for this theatre's excellence doubtless rested with its ability (after 1810) to specialize in spoken drama, a luxury not shared by other German companies, which continued to do ballets and operas as well as plays. Part of the credit for the achievement, however, clearly rested with Josef Schreyvogel (1768–1832). After assuming its management in 1814, he recruited and retained some of Germany's best actors, shaping them into an acting ensemble of uncommon merit (he dismissed even superior actors who wrenched the total effect). As well, he developed a repertory that included artistic as well as popular fare.

To Schreyvogel must go the credit for introducing to the German repertory the works of Franz Grillparzer (1791–1872). Self-described as "that middle thing between Goethe and Kotzebue which the times need,"[20] Grillparzer explored, in an astonishing variety of styles, the conflict between a person's natural place in a harmonious order and the loss when he or she necessarily enters the world of conscious decision and action.

The Burg-theater did little that was innovative: its sets and costumes, for example, were spectacular but not "accurate" or "unified" or any other "experimental" thing. The theatre's reputation came simply because what it did, it did better than most theatres of the day.

More unusual were Vienna's three folk theatres. Influenced both by Germany's Hanswurst and Italy's *commedia dell'arte* traditions, Vienna had long been a center for folk comedies. In 1800, three folk theatres existed. Although all offered standard popular fare—Kotzebue, Iffland, French *vaudeville*, and (if the theatre permitted) equestrian spectacles—all depended heavily on works by native authors. Out of this tradition developed two authors who raised the folk play to a position of literary respectability: Ferdinand Raimund (1790–1836) and his younger contemporary Johann Nepomuk Nestroy (1801–1862). Although separated by only a few years, the authors were separated widely by points of view. Whereas the plays of Raimund (written during the 1820s) tended to be innocent, mirthful, and romantic, those of Nestroy (written during the 1830s) were satirical and biting, anticipating the literary turn that dominated after 1850 (see Figure 14.14).

Other Theatres

Each of Germany's theatres had a history, and each was to a degree unique. Munich, for example, was noted for its exceedingly talented but idiosyncratic actors. To its theatre can be credited the tradition of virtuoso stars. Dusseldorf's theatre, on the other hand, ranks promi-

FIGURE 14.14
Artists Linked to Vienna (1810s–1820s)

National Theatre, the Burg-theater

Josef Schreyvogel
1768–1832 — Viennese literary critic who managed theatre 1800–1804 and again, more successfully, 1814–1831

Anton de Pian
1784–1851 — Scenic artist

Philip von Stubenrach
1784–1848 — Designer, with interest in historical costumes and setting

Actors

Maximilian Korn
1782–1854 — Specialized in dashing young lovers

Sophie Schroeder
1781–1868 — Major tragic actress, specializing in dark and heavy roles like Lady Macbeth and Medea; probably influenced by F. L. Schroeder

Ludwig Lowe
1795–1871 — Specialized in demonic young heroes of romantic tragedies, including Schiller's works

Sophie Müller
1803–1830 — Often partner of Lowe; specialized in innocent tragic heroines like Ophelia, Desdemona, and Emilia Galotti

Franz Grillparzer
1791–1872 — Major author; promoted by Schreyvogel; major works include *Die Ahnfrau* (1817), *Sappho* (1818)

Folk Theatres

Joseph Alois Gleich
1772–1841 — Prolific author; works dominated the folk theatres around 1800

Carl Meisl
1775–1853 — Prolific author for folk theatres with over 200 plays to his credit

Ferdinand Raimund
1790–1836 — First author of folk play to achieve literary distinction; *Thinking of the Alps* (1828) and *The Spend Thrift* (1834)

Johann Nepomuk Nestroy
1801–1862 — Dominated folk theatres after 1830; actor turned playwright; over 60 plays, many adapted from French farce; only play translated was *Ein Jux will er sich machen* (1842), the inspiration for Thornton Wilder's *The Matchmaker* and thus indirectly for *Hello, Dolly!*

nently in any history of directing, for at Dusseldorf during the decade of the 1830s, Karl Leberecht Immerman (1796–1840) continued and elaborated the practices established by Goethe at Weimar. From Prague came Germany's first complete pension plan for actors. Bamberg's stage earned its reputation for spectacular romantic scenery and special effects. It is neither possible nor necessary to offer the framework of fact for each German theatre during the period; instead, certain general trends can be summarized.

First, political fortunes weighed heavily on German theatres during the period. Buffeted between the promises of the French Revolution and the rise of Napoleon, the German states developed a nationalistic fervor at the same time that Napoleon unwittingly began the process of German unification (by reducing the number of states to fewer than forty). Revolutions in 1830 managed to liberalize some of the smaller states, but not until the Revolution of 1848 were large states like Austria and Prussia affected. Thereafter, German politics, culture, and art pursued a new direction.

Second, censorship was an intermittent problem in most German states, its strictness fluctuating with current political conditions. When strict, it kept some works off the stage altogether and caused others to be presented only in sanitized versions. Obviously bland works, of the sort offered by Iffland and Kotze-

FIGURE 14.15

Interior of the Hamburg Theater early in the century. Note the orchestra, the stage boxes, and the prompter's box. [From Weddigen.]

bue, were favored over potentially controversial plays, like many of Schiller's.

Third, the period favored the development of native dramatists. An increased national pride brought about by Napoleon's invasions caused patriotic Germans to give preference to plays and playwrights with German connections. Gottsched had condemned the gap that existed between Germany's stage and its literature. Through authors like Goethe, Schiller, Tieck, Grabbe, Kleist, and later Friedrich Hebbel, this gap lessened steadily between 1800 and 1850.

Fourth, the power of critics and claques increased. Printed materials were cheaper and more available than ever. New sorts of patrons were attending the theatre, and many of them had little acquaintance with its traditions. In the absence of the experiences from which to draw artistic conclusions confidently, such patrons relied on the opinions of the growing press.

Fifth, in most theatres, especially after 1830, the trend was toward traveling virtuoso performers.

Sixth, allowing for notable exceptions, the trend throughout the period was toward increasingly elaborate sets and costumes, often seeking (if not achieving) a measure of antiquarian exactness. When considered with the fourth and fifth trends discussed above, this trend had implications for the health of the theatre. As the costs of production were mounting (for stars and spectacle), the potential box office receipts were dwindling (because of the free tickets for reviewers and claques). Indeed, financial problems plagued many German theatres as the century wore on.

Italy

Italy, like Germany, remained a number of small, independent states, and its theatre was as diverse as its many political units. Some general patterns can be noted, however.

In part because of the censorship and in part because of history, opera rather than theatre continued to dominate Italy's art and culture. The romantic age was the age of Rossini, Bellini, Donizetti, and Verdi. Italy (with Russia) also led in the development of ballet, that quintessentially romantic art, with ballet masters like Vigano and ballerinas like Fanny Cerrito and Maria Taglioni. Theatre and drama, alas, had no such luminaries. A respected contemporary observed in 1827, "Among the other miseries of our Italy is that it has no theatre worthy of the name."[21] Although somewhat overstated, the description was essentially correct. Theatre and drama were a poor second to opera and ballet.

During the period of the French occupation (1790–1815), Milan's theatrical activity overshadowed that in Venice, Naples, and Rome, a situation probably explained by its location. In imitation of France, an official state-subsidized theatre was organized there (the Compagnia Reale Italiana), and contests were instituted for original dramas (judged, of course, according to neoclassical standards).

Although the defeat of Napoleon in 1815 was greeted in some quarters with enthusiasm, it had several unhappy consequences for the peninsula, because France's somewhat enlightened regime was replaced by a far more repressive Austrian one (1815–1830). Austria encouraged the reestablishment of courts modeled on Vienna's, and so subsidized theatres sprang up in almost every state. Although acting companies achieved stability, the new conservative regimes instituted exceedingly severe censorship, and most repertories became necessarily blander. In several areas, radical undergrounds arose to organize opposition to Austria's rule—artistic as well as political. It was out of this ferment that Italian romanticism arose.

An article by Mme. de Staël in 1816 initiated the romantic movement in Milan. A heated literary debate between classicists and romantics culminated in several romantic manifestos and a literary journal, *Il Conciliatore* (1818), devoted to the promotion of romantic ideals. More than elsewhere, romanticism in Italy was a political position. To be a romantic meant to be fired with liberal idealism, to be a supporter of freedom and an advocate of Italian unification.

The growing struggle between classicists and romanticists was soon recognized for what it was: the sublimation of a political struggle between forces favoring the status quo and those seeking change. Accordingly, Austria increased its control: censorship was tightened; leading romantics were jailed; and artists (including Milan's fine acting company) went into exile—to Naples, Florence, and Turin, all of whose theatres gained from Milan's loss.

The curious but close relationship between Italian literature and politics was nowhere clearer than in the years between 1830 and 1850, when Giuseppe Mazzini and Gustavo Modena dominated Italian theatre and drama. Mazzini was the driving force behind Young Italy, a radical organization dedicated to securing Italy's unification and freedom. A theorist and translator as well as a revolutionary, Mazzini was a major spokesman for Italian revolution and romanticism. Modena, his friend and supporter, was Italy's leading actor. He stressed "truth" and "spontaneity" and encouraged all

FIGURE 14.16

Major Italian Artists (1800–1850; Arranged in Approximate Chronological Order)

Designers	
Antonio Niccolini 1772–1850	Designer at Naples; opened school of scenography that trained leading designers of the next generation
Alessandro Sanquirico 1777–1849	Designer at Milan's La Scala; considered Italy's best
Authors	
Allesandro Manzoni 1785–1873	Leading author; self-proclaimed classicist
Silvio Pellico 1789–1854	Romantic author; *Francesca da Rimini* (1815), *Ester d'Engaddi* (1832), *Tommaso Moro* (1833), and *Corradino* (1835)
Giuseppe Mazzini 1805–1872	Leader of Young Italy; romantic theorist and apologist
Actors	
Carlotta Marchionni 1796–1861	Leading tragic actress of the romantic period; tutor of Ristori
Gustavo Modena 1803–1861	Follower of Mazzini; leading actor of the age; trained the next ˌration of actors in Italy
Adelaide Ristori 1822–1906	Italy's first international star; career reached height after 1850

actors to discover for themselves the best details for a characterization. Because his troupe
was largely composed of young actors, Modena's
influence on Italian acting extended beyond the
brilliance of his own performances to his development of a new generation of Italian actors,
some of whom would earn fame as Italian companies undertook international tours after 1850.
With Modena ended the declamatory style of
Italian acting (see Figure 14.16).

Spain

Romanticism and constitutional monarchy ar-
rived at about the same time in Spain—around
1830. The two previous decades had been chaotic. Power seesawed between liberal and conservative elements, with the liberals in control
from 1804 to 1814 and again from 1820 to 1823,
and the conservatives backlashing to power from
1814 to 1820 and again from 1823 to 1833. One
important result of these power swings was a
massive Spanish emigration (perhaps as many
as forty thousand). When the émigrés returned
to Spain, they brought with them the current
political and literary ideas of France, England,
and (to a much smaller degree) Germany. At the
same time, two foreign invasions of Spain (1808–
1811 and 1823) also served to open Spanish culture to the books and ideas of Europe, whose
countries were then deeply immersed in romantic theories and practices.

The resulting intellectual revival resulted in
a flood of translations and adaptations and an
explosion of critical essays and journals. Byron,
Keats, Shelley, Wordsworth, Coleridge, and especially Sir Walter Scott were well represented
among the English authors; Schiller and Goethe
among the German. Alexandre Dumas *père* was
the favorite French romantic author, but almost
all received attention. At the same time that
Spanish interests were expanding to embrace
other Euopean cultures, Spanish artists and intellectuals were also rediscovering and reassert-
ing the glory of their own Golden Age.

The first production of *Don Alvaro* (1835)

marked the beginning of romantic drama in
Spain. Written by Angel de Saavedra, later Duke
of Rivas (1791–1865), while he was exiled in
France, the play incorporated most of those elements now commonly associated with romantic
drama: violence, melodramatic action, scenes of
local color, picturesque settings, and a brood-
ing sense of fate. The care that the author took
with details of setting was considered revolutionary in Spain at that time.

Once introduced, Spanish romantic drama
prospered for the next twenty years. Not since
its own Golden Age had Spanish theatre and
drama shown such vitality. A craze for Italian
opera set in. Literary dramas appeared at public
playhouses. Melodramas and plays with melodramatic elements were popular. Historical
plays, especially those with medieval settings,
attracted new interest, as did plays with strong
nationalistic ties. Plays mingled prose and verse,
the ugly and the beautiful, the sensual and the
spiritual. Traveling stars became popular.

By mid century, dramatic production was
abundant, and romanticism was entrenched (see
Figure 14.17).

Russia

Russian theatre, like its culture, remained conservative, lagging a few years behind its French
model.

Early in the century, Moscow joined Petersburg as a theatrical center when an imperial
theatre was authorized there in 1805 and a state
school of drama in 1809. Although important
thereafter, Moscow still received less financial
support and remained subordinate to Petersburg. By the period's end, Petersburg had three
theatres: the Bolshoi (for opera and ballet),
the Maly (for drama), and the Mikhailovsky
(for foreign works). Moscow had two: the Bolshoi and the Maly.

The Russian repertory featured works from
Germany, France, and England, all considerably adapted to satisfy the tastes of Russian audiences, which were still largely aristocratic.

FIGURE 14.17

Major Dramatists in Spain (1800–1850)

Angel de Saavedra, Duke of Rivas 1791–1865	Major poet and novelist; introduced Romantic drama to Spain with *Don Alvaro* (1835)
Manuel Breton de los Herreros 1796–1873	Major comic writer, offering 177 comedies, of which 103 were original, 64 translations, and 10 adaptations; numerous essays and critical reviews; specialized in presentation of bourgeoisie
Antonio García Gutiérrez 1813–1884	Sixty-eight plays including translations; most successful was *El trovador* (1836), later set as Verdi's opera *Il trovatore*
José Zorilla 1817–1893	Lyric poet as well as prolific and popular romantic dramatist; *comedias,* historical plays
Tomas Rodriguez Rubi 1817–1890	Director of Teatro Espanol and Spanish Academy member; prolific author of comedies, within which he explored a number of different types; considered a progenitor of modern comedy based on more realistic portrayals of society

Among the German authors, Schiller and Kotzebue were the best represented. From the French, the works of Molière and Voltaire found favor. Still more popular, however, were contemporary pieces. *Vaudevilles* were the rage for a time, serving as vehicles for bland social satire and offering dilettantes an opportunity to establish a reputation for cleverness by writing them. Melodramas became popular in Russia almost immediately after Victor Ducange's *Thirty Years* appeared in 1818. A brisk business in translations and adaptations followed thereafter and was in turn followed by a number of Russian imitations. From the English repertory, Shakespeare was often produced, although his works usually appeared in adaptations from the French rather than from the original English.

Censorship was a continuing problem, and so produced plays tended to be either politically innocuous or blatantly supportive of the country's conservative rulers. In general, serious neoclassical and romantic works, although written during the period, were kept from the stage until after mid-century. (For example, both *Woe from Wit* and *Boris Gudonov,* respectively the best neoclassical and romantic plays to come from Russia, were written about 1825; neither was produced, however, until about 1870.) During the 1830s, however, one Russian dramatist appeared to earn an international reputation, and his most famous play found a con-

tinuing place in the dramatic repertory of the Western world: Nicolai Gogol wrote one of the greatest Russian plays of the century, *The Inspector General.* With Gogol came attention to techniques and subjects that would dominate the Russian theatre and drama at the century's end.

Russian actors operated very much under the conditions of the eighteenth century. They were still considered socially inferior, and many were serfs. All were subject to regulations that governed casting, rehearsals, costumes, performances, illnesses, leaves of absence, and so on. If the rules were broken, the actors could be fined, fired, or even arrested. In 1839, their conditions improved somewhat when a statute categorized actors into three groups according to seniority and awarded specific rights accordingly.

Acting companies were still organized according to lines of business, and actors were paid a salary that was supplemented by benefit performances. To help assure success, the actors customarily made rounds to the homes of their patrons before benefit performances, and those with small children often paraded them before the audience in a bid for sympathy and support (as in other countries).

Between 1800 and 1850, then, Russia's theatre and drama followed roughly the patterns observed in France, Germany, and England. By

FIGURE 14.18

Major Russian Theatre Artists (1800–1850; in Approximate Chronological Order)

Authors

Alexander Griboyedov 1795–1829	Neoclassicist in the manner of Molière; adapted French *vaudeville* and comedies: *The Student* (1817), *Feigned Infidelity* and *The Married Fiancé* (1818), and *The Rehearsal of an Interlude* (1819); greatest success was *Woe from Wit* (1825), a play combining classical forms with biting satire on contemporary Russian character types—first circulated in manuscript to avoid censors; then produced in mutilated version to unenthusiastic audiences in 1830; it has been in the active repertory since its successful revival in 1869
Alexander Pushkin 1799–1837	Early romantic dramatist and theorist; influence of Shakespeare clear in *Boris Gudonov* and of Schlegel in theories; abandoned drama for more agreeable literary pursuits, on which his major reputation rests
Mikhail Lermontov 1814–1841	Russia's major romantic dramatist; influenced by Shakespeare, Byron, Scott, Schiller, and Hugo in plays like *The Masquerade* (1834, censored until 1852) and *The Two Brothers* (1836, first produced after 1900)
Nikolai Gogol 1809–1852	Major playwright and theorist; a prerealist; with the actor Shchepkin strove to encourage ensemble acting; in addition to *The Inspector General* (1836), his most successful play was *The Marriage* (1842)

Performers

Yekaterina Semyonova 1786–1849	Classical actress noted for declamatory style: "Speaking of Russian tragedy, one mentions Semyonova—and, perhaps her alone," said Pushkin
Paul Mochalov 1800–1848	A contemporary of Shchepkin; preferred romantic interpretations of standard roles in tragedy and melodrama at Moscow; epitomized romantic acting for Russian audiences
Mikhail Shchepkin 1788–1863	Prerealist whose attention to familiar detail and commitment to ensemble playing won support of Gogol and admiration of Stanislavski; played many of Molière's old roles in adaptations of the French as well as a wide range of contemporary pieces

1850, its artists had begun to close the gap that had long separated them from their counterparts in the countries of western Europe. In another fifty years, artists from the West would turn to Russia for inspiration and guidance and find both in artists like Konstantin Stanislavski, Anton Chekhov, and Maksim Gorki (see Figure 14.18).

The United States

The fifty years between 1800 and 1850 saw an explosion of growth in the United States. The population mushroomed, giving rise to new states (thirty-one by 1850) and new cities. Transportation improved. Increased industry led to economic prosperity. American lands more than tripled in size with the addition of Louisiana, Texas, and Florida, and sophisticated cities on the eastern seaboard existed simultaneously with primitive mining towns in the West.

Theatre sprang up everywhere, but under radically different conditions.[22] During the half century, three different levels of theatrical organization existed simultaneously. In the smallest and most primitive locations, six to ten strolling players, usually amateurs, organized to offer a repertory of about a dozen plays to local residents. Because they had to tour almost constantly, the players usually performed in found spaces (like barns and stores) or in small structures of less than thirty-six hundred square feet. Such companies could be found during the half century in small towns and out-of-the-way places like the Mississippi Valley, Upstate New York, and the Midwest.

Somewhat larger communities gave rise to more stable theatrical conditions. Typically, one or two dozen performers, most with prior theatrical experience, offered two or three dozen plays in spaces built especially for theatrical performances (square footage averaged 4,000–8,000). These companies toured a definable circuit, which they repeated with few modifications year after year. Albany (Georgia), Memphis, Chicago, Buffalo, Detroit, and Sacramento housed such companies during the 1830s and the 1840s. An interesting variation on this structure was the floating theatre, or showboat. As early as 1817, a boat was transporting actors down the Ohio and Mississippi rivers to play river towns. By 1831, a special ship named, ap-

propriately, the *Floating Theatre*, had a permanent stage and seating for two hundred. By the 1840s and 1850s, dozens of such showboats played the river systems of the Midwest, bringing theatre to towns that lay outside all other established circuits.

Major metropolitan areas hosted resident companies permanently housed in relatively sophisticated theatres. Employing several dozen actors and offering a repertory of three or four dozen plays, these companies generally played three times a week, ten months a year (often touring the remaining two). Philadelphia, New York, Boston, and Charleston, S.C. boasted such companies in 1800.

The importance of Charleston began to de-

FIGURE 14.19

Interior of New York's Old Park Theatre in 1805. Notice the proscenium doors and the accented proscenium arch. The moves toward an ovoid rather than a rectangular auditorium probably paralleled the increasing attention being given to scenery at the expense of poetry in the theatre. [From *Appleton's.*]

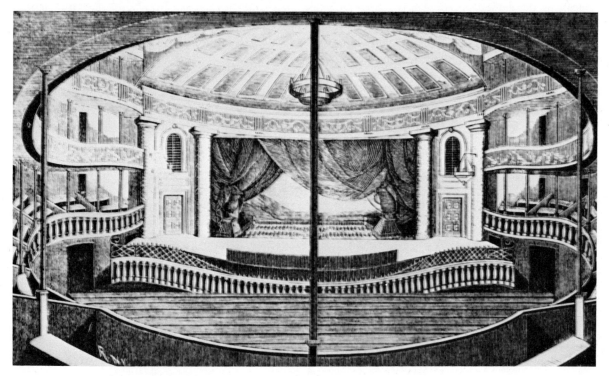

cline after Alexandre Placide died in 1815; within ten years, it had ceased to be a major theatrical center. Boston, on the other hand, continued a steady growth throughout the period, reaching 1850 with four healthy theatres. Although Philadelphia remained the leading theatrical center until almost 1850, destructive competition among three rival companies weakened its theatre at the same time that New York experienced a phenomenal growth in its population. By about 1850, therefore, New York replaced Philadelphia as America's most important center of theatre.

As these (and other) cities grew, so did the theatres. Throughout the period, the trend was to enlarge existing buildings and to establish rival companies. Thus, Philadelphia's Chestnut Street Theatre was remodeled to increase capacity, first to 2,000 and then to 2,500; and two new theatres, the Walnut Street and the Arch Street, arose to compete with it. In New York, the Bowery Theatre opened with a capacity of 3,000 and before 1850 could seat 4,000.

Production practices were governed more by the level of theatrical organization and the amount of touring required than by the date of the activity. The very sophisticated and the very primitive existed side by side in 1850 as well as in 1800. For example, in 1816, Philadelphia's theatre was the first in the world to convert to gas lighting; gas did not reach Denver, however, until after mid-century. Moving dioramas were used in New York for *A Trip to Niagara* in 1828 and in 1833 for a production of *Mazeppa*; in a California mining town at approximately the same time, a stage was being improvised from boards laid atop billiard tables. Urban theatres strove to emulate English practices. Mme. Vestris toured the States in 1838 and earned praise for her careful interior sets; in 1841, a box set appeared in New York's production of Anna Cora Mowatt's *Fashion*. Charles Kean brought antiquarian productions of Shakespeare to New York in 1845; thereafter, historical and geographical accuracy became American ideals as well.

The audiences varied with general conditions as well as with dates. In found spaces, little separation by class was sought or achieved. In established theatres, however, box, pit, and gallery carried social implications, though perhaps less rigid ones than in Europe.

Between 1800 and 1850, most actors in America were English. Most American resident companies had few or no American actors in them before 1830 (see Figure 14.20). As in England, metropolitan actors were paid salaries and were hired according to lines of business. In small companies, sharing arrangements continued. As in England, some actors stressed dignity and declamation, while others emphasized passion and impulse.

When traveling stars became the rage during the 1820s, English actors flooded to the United States: Junius Brutus Booth, George Frederick Cooke, Edmund Kean, Charles Kean, Charles and Fanny Kemble, the younger and elder Mathews, Mme. Vestris, William Charles Macready, and others. As elsewhere, the eventual result was a decline in the quality of the resident companies, a situation that became particularly acute in the United States after mid-century.

A very few significant American actors began to appear by the 1820s. Three deserve comment: Edwin Forrest, Charlotte Cushman, and Ira Aldridge.

Forrest, with little formal education, had performed in various frontier theatres as well as in Philadelphia and New York before achieving status as a star. Influenced by T. A. Cooper (a follower of Kemble) and Edmund Kean, Forrest popularized the American or "heroic" style, a style that blended elements of dignified declamation with vigorous physical activity. Perhaps because of his magnificent physique (of which he was perhaps inordinately proud), Forrest gravitated toward roles that permitted its advantageous display. Through prizes, he encouraged American playwrights to provide him with suitable materials, and by this means, he found two of his favorite roles: Metamora and

Spartacus. Despite the scorn of some critics, Forrest was unequivocally popular with American audiences. Although his later reputation was marred by a scandalous divorce and an outrageous rivalry with Macready (a rivalry that culminated in 1849 with the bloody Astor Place Riots), the trust that he established to support indigent actors remains today a mute testimony to his former success.

Charlotte Cushman was America's greatest

FIGURE 14.20

Major American Performers (1800–1850)

Early actors from England:	
Eliza Kemble Whitlock (1761–1836)	Philadelphia company; a Kemble
James Fennell (1766–1816)	Philadelphia company
Anne Brunton Merry (1768–1808)	Philadelphia; leading actress of the day
T. A. Cooper (1776–1849)	Follower of Kemble; America's leading tragedian; acted in Philadelphia and New York; manager in New York
Mary Ann Duff (1794–1857)	Best tragedienne of her day; acted with Kean and emulated him
American Actors	
Henry J. Finn ca. 1790–1840	An eccentric comedian; minor playwright
William Wood 1779–1861	First significant American-trained actor; sophisticated comedy roles; acted and later managed (with Warren) Chestnut Street Theatre; married the former Julianna Westray, the company's leading actress
Ira Aldridge 1807–1867	"The African Roscius"
Charles Burke 1822–1854	Elegant comedy; half-brother of Joe Jefferson III
Edwin Forrest 1806–1872	Leading tragedian; developed "American style"; Metamora, Spartacus
Charlotte Cushman 1816–1876	Leading tragedienne; international reputation; heavily influenced by Macready—called by some "The Female Macready"
Specialty Performers	
Charles Matthews 1776–1834	English actor, toured America in 1820s and 1830s; in a series of "at homes," popularized the "specialty tradition"
James H. Hackett 1800–1871	Given credit for establishing the Yankee character, Solomon Swap in *Jonathan in England* (1828)
George Handel "Yankee" Hill 1809–1849	Yankee character; more sentimentalized version than Hackett's
Dan Marble 1810–1849	Another Yankee character: Sam Patch
Joshua Silsbee 1813–1855	Another Yankee character, broadly caricatured
John E. Owens 1823–1886	The last of the great Yankee characters; vogue ended around mid-century
Thomas D. "Jim Crow" Rice 1808–1860	"Stage darky"; helped create the minstrel show; popularized the "Jim Crow" dance
Dan Emmett 1815–1904	"Stage darky"; put together early Virginia Minstrels, 1843
E. P. Christy 1815–1862	Perfected the form of the minstrel show
Frank S. Chanfrau 1824–1884	Mose the Bowery Boy; first seen in *A Glance at New York* (1841) and embroidered well into the 1860s

international star. After an undistinguished debut in 1834, followed by a training period in the theatres of upstate New York, Cushman joined the Park Street Theatre in New York and then the Walnut Street Theatre in Philadelphia. When Macready toured the United States in 1843, she played leading roles opposite him and was thus encouraged to try a tour of London, where she enjoyed an immediate success. Like Macready, Cushman paid meticulous attention to each detail of a performance. Because of her powerful voice (she had trained as a singer) and her stately body, she excelled in female roles like Lady Macbeth and Meg Merrilies or in such male parts as Hamlet and Romeo (which she often played to her sister's Juliet). When Cushman returned to the United States in 1849, she was hailed as American's leading tragedienne, a position she held without rival until her final retirement in 1875.

Ira Aldridge was born in America, but, because he was black, he could not secure suitable roles in its theatres. He left this country around 1825 and toured England, successfully performing Othello (the mainstay of his repertory), Lear, Macbeth, and Shylock (in white makeup), and black heroes in several antislavery plays. His twenty-five years of success in England prompted him to undertake a European tour in 1852. Called the African Roscius, Aldridge was acclaimed in almost all of Europe's capitals before he died on tour in Poland in 1867. He remained at his death still largely unknown and unheralded in his native America.

Like American acting, the American repertory was highly derivative. In 1800, only about 2 per cent of the plays in the urban theatres were American. In 1850 that figure hovered around 3 per cent in Charleston and 15 per cent in Philadelphia. The number of American plays, then, increased over the half century, but the repertory remained decidedly foreign. Most popular among the imports were plays recently popular in England. Shakespeare played regularly. In Philadelphia, between 1816 and 1831, for example, *Richard III* was most often played, followed by Kotzebue's *Pizarro*.

FIGURE 14.21

Ira Aldridge as Aaron in *Titus Andronicus*, from a daguerreotype. [Authors' collection.]

In general, American dramatists produced little of lasting merit, for they tended merely to imitate recent English and continental successes. William Dunlap, America's first professional playwright (and theatre historian), for example, is credited with over fifty plays, roughly half of which were adaptations. Some playwrights of the period did introduce distinctly American characters, which quickly became "types" that reappeared frequently thereafter: the noble Indian, the Negro, the Yankee, the city boy, the Irish immigrant.

The only play of the period that still finds occasional production is Anna Cora Mowatt's *Fashion* (1845). A successful satire of social pretension, the comedy played in several American cities to sustained applause before opening in London to enthusiastic audiences. Toward the end of the period, the only distinctly American dramatic form arose: the minstrel show. Developed largely by northern, urban, middle-class white men (presumably drawing on observations of black plantation life), minstrelsy quickly developed a strong set of conventions: blackfaced performers, end men, jokes and music, and walkarounds. Its (originally) all-male cast performed for largely male audiences, treating controversial social and cultural issues in a satiric and often raucous fashion. Its popularity erupted in the 1830s, so much so that black performers (also with cork-blackened faces) formed their own minstrel companies. After peaking during the 1850s and 1860s, minstrelsy's popularity was largely dead by 1900, the victim of changing tastes (see Figure 14.22).

General Trends

Some general trends in design, acting, and directing cut across national boundaries and helped to define the romantic theatre.

Scenery, Costumes, and Lighting

The trends toward more spectacle, greater accuracy, and more consistency that surfaced during the Enlightenment accelerated in the romantic theatre. Italian designers continued to point the way, for they regularly created a new setting for each scene and so achieved a consis-

FIGURE 14.22
American Dramatists (1800–1850)

William Dunlap 1766–1839	New York manager, theatre historian, and dramatist; wrote or adapted fifty-six plays, the best of the originals being *Andre* (1798), later revised and retitled *The Glory of Columbia; Her Yeomanry* (1803); also wrote *The History of the American Theatre* (1832), a standard, if flawed, source
John Daly Burk d. 1808	*Bunker Hill, or The Death of General Warren* (1797), best of a spate of patriotic pieces
George Washington Parke Custis 1781–1857	*The Indian Prophecy* (1827) and *Pocahontas* (1830) began fad for Indian plays—more than fifty written; John Brougham's parody of the same name (1855) ended the vogue
James Nelson Barker 1784–1858	Wrote ten plays, five extant; *The Indian Princess* (1809) was earliest surviving Indian play; best play, *Superstition* (1824), was a dramatization of novel by Sir Walter Scott
Samuel Woodworth 1785–1842	*The Forest Rose* (1825) was America's first hit show; introduced the famous Yankee character Jonathan Ploughboy; wrote seven other plays but none so successful
Mordecai M. Noah 1785–1851	*She Would Be a Soldier* (1819), a patriotic piece ridiculing British pretension; offered Forrest his first Indian role and may have influenced *Metamora*; other plays included *The Siege of Tripoli* (1820), *The Hero of Lake George* (1821), and *The Grecian Captive* (1822)
John Howard Payne 1791–1852	An expatriot living in England; child star and playwright; adapted numerous foreign works; wrote *Brutus* (1818), perhaps best of his sixty plays; wrote song, "Home, Sweet Home" for his musical play *Clari* (1823)
John Augustus Stone 1800–1834	Wrote *Metamora* (1829) especially for Forrest; the role of the noble red savage remained in the repertory of heroic actors throughout the century; other plays, but none successful
Robert Montgomery Bird 1806–1854	*The Gladiator* (1831), written for Forrest, was also acted by others in heroic tradition; *Oraloosa* (1832) and *The Broker of Bogota* (1834)
W. H. Smith 1808–1872	Reputation rests on the great temperance melodrama *The Drunkard* (1844), an urban problem play
Anna Cora Mowatt 1819–1870	The best play of the period, *Fashion* (1845), was a satiric comedy of social life in New York; Mowatt had a successful career as an actress, playing starring roles in London and America, before retiring in 1854; a second play, *Armand* (1847), was less successful

tency uncommon in France, for example, where stock sets were used and reused. Such consistency earned the admiration of foreigners, who continued to travel to Italy to study design. Combining their classical and architectural interests with their new attention to color, light, nature, and mood, Italian designers developed many qualities of design that defined the romantic style. They also perfected many of the techniques that won praise on the stages of Paris. For example, contemporaries who saw them both considered Pierre-Luc-Charles Ciceri's volcanic eruption in Paris a poor imitation of the Italian original, the spectacular eruption of Vesuvius at Milan's La Scala. Although Italy's best designers worked more often in opera and ballet than in spoken drama, their styles and techniques quickly found a place in the (dramatic) theatres of the West. In fact, it could be argued that one characteristic of the romantic theatre was its transference of the designs and stagecraft of spectacle (formerly the province of baroque court theatres and opera) to the public theatres, where (altered to suit popular taste), they formed the mainstay of the nineteenth century's "theatre of marvels."

Interest in spectacle found its initial and most consistent expression in melodrama and pantomime, forms that at first, by law, depended on visual representation rather than words. Stories in pantomime often merely provided the excuse for scenes of transformation and magic; the action of melodrama regularly progressed from thrill to thrill, where accelerating reversals of the hero's fortune culminated in a catastrophic event that foiled the villain. Even after language was permitted in the two forms, it overlaid rather than substituted for the music and spectacle.

Sophisticated stagecraft swiftly grew up to accommodate the new interest. From pantomime, particularly, came elaborately painted scenes of romanticized nature, techniques for rapid set changes, and machines for the magical flights of fairies and sprites (without evident mechanical aid). From melodrama came mechanisms for fires, floods, and explosions: in an English melodrama, for example, the characters "escape through the flames over the burning bridge, a part of which falls blazing into the river," or "the [ship] sinks—the sea covers the wreck—the moon emerges from the heavy clouds—green fire is lighted up, and a raft . . . floating, passes from the extreme corner, and when it reaches the centre, the scene closes." [23] Pixérécourt's melodramas in France were notorious for their special effects: a flood for *The Exile's Daughter* (1819), a volcanic eruption for *Death's Head* (1827), a waterfall transforming into burning lava for *Bijou* (1838). The popularity of these effects goaded other authors to even greater marvels, so that before 1830, promptbooks regularly described in detail the scenery and special effects required for a production and even included suggestions for simplifying the effects where necessary.

As lavishness increased, so did the cost of mounting productions. In 1830, for example, a single production at the Odéon cost 100,000 francs and required twenty-three separate scenes, including the burning of Moscow. In 1832, forty settings appeared in a play at the Cirque Olympique, whose regular company now numbered about one hundred people and thirty horses. Battles on horseback (at the Cirque Olympique and the Royal Circus) were matched by those at sea (in a real water tank at Sadler's Wells). Gothic melodramas regularly featured ghosts and apparitions in gloomy, medieval castles. So pervasive and popular were the visual effects in theatres that after 1835 some journals regularly carried articles devoted to the successful execution of such effects.

The popularity of such scenes led to their inclusion in a variety of plays—like Shakespeare's—where they had not appeared before. Fairy scenes from pantomime found their way into *The Tempest* and *A Midsummer Night's Dream*, storm scenes from melodramas into *King Lear* and *Julius Caesar*, cavalry battles into *Macbeth*, and so on. Whereas before, a few actors had sufficed for crowd scenes, now several hundred actors represented the senators in *Coriolanus* and the soldiers in *Richard III*.

The usefulness of new panoramas and dioramas for theatrical settings was quickly recognized. With only slight adjustments, panoramas could be used to provide the illusion of distant landscapes and to mask stage spaces (in the manner of modern-day cycloramas). Alternately, a panorama (a continuously painted canvas) could be unrolled at the back of the stage (transferred from one giant spool to another) and thus offer a *moving* picture against which stage action might play. Thus, panoramas and dioramas (the words quickly came to be used interchangeably) helped to meet the public's demand for ever-greater scenic wonders in the theatre.

Along with spectacle, accuracy and consistency of details became increasingly important. Germany's leading romantic designer, Carl Friedrich Schinkel, explained:

> The ideal designer will have certain indispensable assets: a basic knowledge of the general and specific stage history of all times and peoples, the utmost skill and accuracy in perspective, a knowledge even of archeology, a thorough acquaintance with all the schools of painting, particularly landscape painting, and the actual colors of things, yet even with botany and other studies which describe the various forms of trees, plants, rocks, and hills in every country.[24]

And the minister of the interior of the imperial court in Russia ordered:

> I have observed that in many plays produced in the local theatres, stage sets and costumes do not conform to the period in which the action takes place. . . . henceforth, when new plays are staged, more attention should be paid both to stage sets, which must harmonize with the period and the place of the action, and to costumes, in which the strictest exactitude must be shown.[25]

In France, Pixérécourt regularly identified sources from which he drew historical information, and he often argued for their accuracy:

> I was particularly concerned with retaining technical words and . . . the customs of the ship. . . I took the same care in the customs, dress, and actions of the savages. All conform strictly to truth.[26]

The desire for accurate details extended to contemporary times as well. For interior scenes, the box set became common in France and Germany during the 1820s and in England and Russia at least by the 1830s. For a revival of Diderot's *The Father of the Family* in 1834, the Comédie Française featured an accurate contemporary setting for the first time. By 1837, accuracy in settings and costumes was not only accepted but also expected: Moreover, *and this goes without saying*, there is not in *Ruy Blas* a detail of private or public life, of interiors, of furnishing, of sound, of manners, of character, or of topography, which is not scrupulously exact"[27] (italics ours). Even the conservative Comédie eventually succumbed and, for its classical repertory, replaced the traditional *palais à volonté* with detailed settings after 1842. By 1850 the enormous gap in production values that had existed between the Comédie and the boulevard houses for almost a century had begun to close.

In England, de Loutherbourg and Garrick had introduced authentic scenes of local color and history to an approving public in the 1770s; such illusions now became a craze. First as independent entertainments and soon as added attractions within plays, actors reproduced favorite paintings onstage by striking appropriate positions in the manner of "living statues" and "tableaux vivants." The first panorama opened in London in 1796; this form proliferated thereafter to indulge the public's interest in accurate reproductions of specific locations. Dioramas soon added the elements of sunlight and weather. To improve the staging

FIGURE 14.23

This scene from *Plot and Passion* at London's Olympic Theatre at mid-century shows the now-popular box set and the three-dimensional properties with which stages came to be increasingly dressed. [Authors' collection.]

of *Mazeppa* (1831), a horse ran on a treadmill as a panorama unfolded behind.

In the 1790s, John Philip Kemble earned praise for his relatively careful and accurate settings and costumes for Shakespearean productions. He always favored the theatrically effective over the accurate and archaeological, however. By 1823, his younger brother Charles had joined with J. R. Planché to produce a completely accurate *King John*. The playbills proudly announced: "every Character will appear in the precise HABIT OF THE PERIOD, the Dresses and Decoration being executed from indisputable Authorities, such as Monumental Effigies, Seals, Illumined MSS. & c."[28] The production was so successful that it set the fashion for ever greater attention to historical details in productions that followed. By the 1830s, William Charles Macready was continuing the tradition and seeking "to transfer [Shakespeare's] picture from the poet's mind to the stage, complete in its parts and harmoniously arranged as to fig-

ure, scene, and action."[29] He therefore consulted antiquaries for productions of *Romeo and Juliet*, *The Merchant of Venice*, and *Two Gentlemen of Verona*.

By 1850, then, most theatres in the West had accepted in principle the importance of visual production and the desirability of its fidelity to historical truth or (less often) contemporary reality, with the consistency that such fidelity assured.

Major technological breakthroughs in lighting contributed to the visual elements of the period. Gas lighting came to London's theatres in 1817 and to the French Opéra in 1822 (and the Comédie Française ten years later). Gas offered several advantages: it was cheaper than candles and oil; it could provide more light than either; and it could be better controlled. Because a gas table (perfected during the 1840s) allowed a single operator to adjust (selectively) the intensity of the lights, new kinds of special effects became possible. The use of gas lighting

FIGURE 14.24

The quest for pictures in the theatre extended to staged reproductions of famous paintings and famous statues. Here actors perform a tableau vivant of Pio Fedi's *Resurrection of Polixene*. [From Pougin.]

was therefore commonplace by mid-century. Thereafter, certain conventions based on candlelight gave way to others more suited to lighting with gas. For example, because the use of gas increased the visibility of both the scenery and the actors, scenic paint, makeup, and costumes had to be adjusted to accommodate its more intense and bluer light. The increased visibility of the stage allowed the actors to move away from the footlights and the position or-

biting the chandelier and into areas behind the proscenium that had previously been too dim for use.

Limelight appeared in 1837, and carbon arcs in 1848. Each represented an improved opportunity for visual display and special effects, and each was cautiously assimilated into the atmospheric changes, ghostly apparitions, gothic shadows, fires, storms, explosions, eruptions, and apotheoses that formed such an integral part of the stagecraft of the romantic theatre.

An English critic summed up complaints that were heard in many countries by the end of the romantic period: theatres everywhere were "theatres for spectators rather than playhouses for hearers. . . . The splendour of the scenes and the ingenuity of the machinist . . . in a great degree superseded the labours of the poet"[30] (see Figure 14.26).

Actors and Acting

Between 1790 and 1850, acting was in transition. There were at least two sets of forces at work: first, new styles of acting opposed old (classical) styles; and second, the rise of traveling stars undermined the organization of actors in sharing companies.

Acting Style

As the nineteenth century opened, French acting remained the most conservative in Europe. Although Talma, since the time of the French Revolution, had experimented with novel interpretations of standard roles (even adopting historically accurate dress for many), his impact was limited. Older, more conservative members of the Comédie Française opposed his attempts at innovations, and Napoleon's preference for Neoclassical plays gave Talma limited opportunities for romantic display. At the time of his death in 1826, therefore, French actors at the Comédie still formed a line or a semicircle at the front of the stage and declaimed their lines to the audience.

From 1782, Sarah Siddons was the undis-

FIGURE 14.25

The illustration of Shakespeare was a hallmark of the romantic theatre throughout the West. Here, a street scene designed by William Capon for John Philip Kemble in 1809 (from *Magazine of Art*) and a sketch of a scene in which William Charles Macready appeared as Macbeth. [From *English Illustrated Magazine*.]

FIGURE 14.26

Major Scenic Artists in England and France (1800–1850; Arranged by Country in Approximate Chronological Order)

England

William Capon 1757–1827	Architect and painter at Drury Lane strove for suggestion of historical accuracy; Gothic settings
Colonel Hamilton Smith 1776–1859	Antiquary consulted by Macready for exactness in costumes and scenery on a regular basis
James Robinson Planché 1796–1880	Antiquarian; worked with Charles Kemble on landmark production of *King John* (1823) and *Henry IV, Part I* (1824); his *History of British Costume* (1834) was for years a standard work in the field
William Roxby Beverley ca. 1814–1889	English scene painter; perfected transformation scenes in pantomime

France

Pierre-Luc-Charles Ciceri 1782–1868	Landscape artist; interest in history, spectacle, accuracy; designs include *Aladin, ou la merveilleuse lampe* (1822, using Opéra's first gaslights), *La muette de Portici* (1828, with famous volcanic eruption), *Robert le diable* (1831, with famous medieval cloister), and established own scenic studio (1822) and trained a generation of designers who dominated French design after 1850
Louis-Jacques Daguerre 1787–1851	Théâtre Pittoresque (1804), where scenes of nature rather than plays were featured; Panorama Dramatique with Ciceri; dioramas, Daguerrotype (see pp. 403–404)

puted tragic queen of the English stage. With her younger brother John Philip Kemble, she perfected and popularized the "classical" style of acting in England, a style described by critics with words like *studied, noble, grand, elevated, lofty, declamatory,* and *distant.* Both excelled in stately roles: for Siddons, Lady Macbeth, Mrs. Haller in *The Stranger* and Euphrasia in *The Grecian Daughter,* for example; for Kemble, roles like Coriolanus and Wolsey and the Stranger. Both Siddons and Kemble apparently shaped their performances into a consistent unit, avoiding "points" in the manner of Garrick. Consistency thus became a trait associated with English classical actors, but some found the result wearying: "The tragedy, five acts of declamatory, unimpassioned verse . . . did not tend to dissipate or enliven [and] was a tax upon the patience of the hearers."[31]

In Germany, the classical style of acting was most often associated with the theatre at Weimar, during the 1790s. There Goethe urged his actors to seek "beauty first, then truth." They were to find the ideal that underlay the actual: "The player must consider that he should not only imitate nature but also portray it ideally. . . ."[32] The search for such ideal truth led to experiments designed to distance the stage from life: masks were used in some productions and choruses with scored voices in others. All critics associated the Weimar style of acting with declaiming, distancing, and idealizing. In fact, Goethe's goal with actors may have been to produce a kind of spoken opera, for he regularly called on musical analogies to instruct actors about voice, pitch, and rate, and he often used a baton to direct them during rehearsals.

Although the classical style had adherents until the middle of the century, its popularity was in decline before 1815, overcome by a taste for a new, romantic style.

Even while the classical style of Siddons and Kemble dominated London's Covent Garden, a new style of acting was developing in the provincial theatres of England under the influence

of George Frederick Cooke and Edmund Kean. Cooke was already past his prime when he brought the new style to the stage of Drury Lane in 1800. Although critics praised his feeling, energy, originality, and passion, they found his acting "uneven." His challenge to Kemble was therefore only partially successful. He served as a harbinger of things to come, however.

The debut of Edmund Kean in 1814 at Drury Lane marked a turning point in stage history. With Kean, England's greatest romantic tragedian, the new romantic style triumphed: "Kean did extinguish Kemble," concluded Leigh Hunt. "It was as sure a thing as Nature against Art, or tears against cheeks of stone." Watching Kean act, said Coleridge, was "to read Shakespeare by flashes of lightning."[33] The new romantic style

FIGURE 14.27

Edmund Kean as Macbeth. [From *English Illustrated Magazine.*]

was passionate, emotional, flashy, and seemingly erratic (actually, all the effects were carefully calculated). It found its most comfortable expression in intense roles: Richard III, Lear, Macbeth, Shylock, Sir Giles Overreach (in Philip Massinger's *A New Way to Pay Old Debts*), roles in which both Cooke and Kean excelled. As Cooke before him, Kean lost much of his tragic power to his alcoholism. By the late 1820s, he seemed unable to memorize lines and so could not offer new roles to his public, who were tiring rapidly of his old ones. The great era of romantic acting was already in decline when Kean died in 1833 at the age of forty-five.

Germany's leading romantic actor, Ludwig Devrient, likewise sought intense effects. He preferred to portray villains and to emphasize moments of great emotional intensity. "Through the dazzling points of light that [Devrient] places before us he leads us to guess what lies hidden in the deepest shadows," a contemporary critic remarked.[34] His acting was reminiscent of the style of his contemporary, Kean, with whom he was often compared. Like Kean, he was called "demonic," and his effects were described as "spectacular." For some, this new and exciting romantic style was preferable to the older techniques: "immeasurably far removed from what is ordinarily called acting, so that everything else in comparison seemed but artifice and make-believe."[35] Despite Devrient's power, romantic acting did not triumph in Germany, where romantic and classical actors continued to perform in the same productions.

The turning point in France did not come until 1828, when a company of English actors, enlivened by stars like Edmund Kean, electrified Parisian audiences with their novel interpretations of English plays. Almost immediately, French actors adopted some of the English techniques. For *Hernani* (1830), actors at the Comédie Française (at Hugo's urging) left their positions downstage by the prompter's box and moved freely about the stage. Within a few years, boulevard actors were regularly employing English mannerisms and using stage furniture in their performances.

For the next twenty years, the new romantic style gained its greatest advocate in the "fiery, passionate, violent, and proud"[36] Frédérick Lemaître, "the Talma of the boulevards." Although a very versatile actor, Lemaître especially excelled in roles that allowed him a wide range of emotions, roles like Hugo's *Ruy Blas*, where he could combine "the actions of Kean with the emotion of Talma,"[37] and as the gambler in Ducange's *Thirty Years or the Life of a Gambler*, where he could portray many ages.

The extravagance of romantic acting did not earn universal acceptance in France, however, for neoclassical traditions remained strong. As Lemaître's popularity waned, that of Rachel grew. Following a successful debut at a boulevard theatre, Rachel moved to the Comédie Française in 1838, where she quickly excelled in the major roles of the classical repertory: *Andromaque, Cinna, Iphigénie en Aulide, Mithridate, Phèdre,* and so on. She excelled, as well, in a few contemporary plays written especially for her statuesque body and rich voice, most notably Eugène Scribe's only tragedy, *Adrienne Lecouvreur*. Most critics agree that Rachel's concentration on the classical repertory and her avoidance of romantic works hastened the decline of romanticism and romantic acting in France during the 1840s.

Even in conservative Russia, the classical style of acting declined after 1825 with the increasing popularity of Paul Mochalov. The epitome of the romantic actor, he was "a man of impulse and of unruly inspiration."[38] The intensity of his acting was matched by the turmoil of his personal life, where alcohol too often was in control. Although a versatile actor, Mochalov succeeded best, apparently, in contemporary melodramas and romantic plays, in which his startling effects gripped audiences. Although he was personally successful, his idiosyncratic style produced few imitators.

Styles of acting were further complicated by

FIGURE 14.28

Rachel as Phèdre. Her commitment to the classical repertory helped end the domination of romanticism in France before mid-century. [From the authors' collection.]

the popularity of the "natural" style. In Germany, its major practitioner was Iffland, in Russia Mikhail Shchepkin, and in England William Charles Macready, England's leading tragedian from Kean's decline until his own retirement in 1851. Natural actors stressed the commonplace, the familiar, and domestic detail. They did not seek dizzying emotional heights nor play for flashes of lightning; rather, they sought to fit the character into the rhythms of the play and those of the other performers. They sought a consistency of style. Not all critics, of course, liked the "natural" style. For example, supporters of Kean found Macready's style too ordinary: "Mr. Macready seems afraid of the poetry of some of his greatest parts."[39] On the other hand, in Russia, Konstantin Stanislavski credited Shchepkin with establishing the basis of Russia's dramatic art, in part because his style of acting is said to have caused Russian writers to turn to more realistic characterizations in their plays (see Figure 14.29).

Before we leave the subject of actors, a word about novelty performers seems warranted. A craze for child stars began in England with Master Betty. In roles like Romeo, Hamlet, and Richard III, the fourteen-year-old boy seized the imagination of both provincial and London audiences. Thereafter, a spate of young boys and girls, ranging in age from seven through fourteen years, appeared in a variety of plays, trying to cash in on Master Betty's success. Astley's equestrian and circus acts produced their own imitators. The Cirque Olympique featured trained horses in dramatic as well as nondramatic works. Dumas *père*, for example, agreed to write a play, *Caligula*, in which the leading role would be Caligula's horse, played, of course, by a member of the Cirque's resident troupe.

Mounted military spectacles, hippodramas, equestrian melodramas, burlettas, and pantomimes soon flourished. In *Mazeppa*, one of the age's most successful pieces, an actor, lashed to the back of a horse, was galloped over mountains and through rivers while being attacked by a (mechanical) vulture. The successful performances of the pachyderm Mlle. Djeck led to a rage of elephant dramas during the 1830s. When trained lions won applause, a predictable number of imitations featured "wild jungle cats." Pixérécourt wrote a melodrama called *The Dog of Montargis*, in which a trained dog finally brought the villain to justice. At one of the minor houses, a company of trained dogs regu-

FIGURE 14.29
Major English and French Performers (1800–1850; Arranged by Country in Approximate
Chronological Order)

England
Actresses

Sarah Siddons 1755–1831	The undisputed tragic actress of the day; an older sister of John Philip Kemble
Dorothy Jordan 1761–1816	Leading actress of comedy in Siddons's company; breeches parts
Eliza Whitlock 1761–1836	Another Kemble; a classical actress; joined Philadelphia company after career in the English provinces
Eliza O'Neill 1791–1827	Successor to Siddons
Mme. Vestris (Lucia Elizabeth Bartolozzi) 1797–1856	Breeches roles and light comedies; husband Armand Vestris (1788–1825) was a dancer; later married Charles Mathews, the Younger (1803–1878), a light comedian; together they managed the Olympic theatre, Covent Garden (1835–1842), and the Lyceum (1847–1856)
Frances Anne "Fanny" Kemble 1809–1893	Daughter of Charles Kemble; married an American landholder; her diaries are useful source of information on American slavery and women's issues
Helen Faucit 1817–1898	Classical actress; often worked with Macready

Actors

George Frederick Cooke 1756–1812	Romantic star; London debut 1800; first English star to tour America
John Philip Kemble 1757–1823	Classical actor dominated English stage at opening of century; "he is the very still life and statuary of the stage . . . an icicle upon the bust of tragedy"; managed Drury Lane (1788–1802) and Covent Garden (1802–1817)
Stephen Kemble 1758–1822	Brother of John Phillip Kemble; his corpulence suited him for roles like Falstaff
Joseph Munden 1758–1832	Low comedian specializing in drunk scenes
Robert Elliston 1774–1831	Leading comedian; managed Surrey and Drury Lane
Charles Kemble 1775–1854	Classical actor; brother of John Philip Kemble; more famous as a manager; became Examiner of Plays after retiring from acting and management
John Liston 1776–1846	First comic actor to earn more than a tragic actor; leading comedian for thirty years
Charles Mathews, the Elder 1776–1836	Specialist; "at homes" set vogue for specialty performers in America, where he toured, 1822 and 1834
Charles Mayne Young 1777–1856	Actor in the style of John Philip Kemble
T. P. Cooke 1786–1864	Specialized in nautical melodramas—four hundred consecutive performances of *Black Ey'd Susan*
Edmund Kean 1787–1833	Romantic actor and star; child performer under name of Master Carey; provincial career until London debut in 1814, a turning point in English acting style
J. M. Vandenhoff 1790–1861	Continued traditions of John Phillip Kemble
James William Wallack 1791–1864	London and New York; follower of John Philip Kemble's classical style
Robert Keely 1793–1869	Low comedian admired by Dickens; first hit was in *Tom and Jerry*; with wife, Mary Ann Goward (1806–1899), managed the Lyceum
William Charles Macready 1793–1873	"Natural actor"; sought common, conversational details of performance; considered Kean's rival by 1816

FIGURE 14.29 (continued)

Tyrone Power 1795–1841	Provincial and minor actor until 1826, when portrayal of comic stage Irishman made him a star
Samuel Phelps 1804–1878	Actor at Haymarket and Covent Garden with Macready; management at Sadler's Wells, where Shakespearean productions earned lasting reputation
France	
François-Joseph Talma 1736–1826	Flourished during revolution and empire; major tragic roles in *Charles IX*, *Hamlet, Manlius Capitolinus, Germanicus, Marie-Stuart, Sylla, Brutus*
Mlle. Duchesnois (Catherine Josephine Rafuin) ca. 1777–1835	Tragic partner of Talma; rival of Mlle. George; "natural and spontaneous"; noted for *Phèdre*
Mlle. George (Marguerite-Josephine Weymer) 1787–1835	Mistress of Napoleon; rival of Mlle. Duchesnois; "classic" delivery; defection from Comédie Française caused a scandal
Mlle. Mars (Anne Françoise Boutet) 1779–1847	Playing "first roles, first loves, and grand coquettes"; original Dona Sol in *Hernani*; rivalled by Mme. Dorval
Mme. Dorval (Marie Delaunay) 1798–1849	Boulevard actress; best in romantic plays and melodramas; together with Lemaître is credited with "a complete revolution in the art of drama"; a "natural" actor
Bocage (Pierre-François Touze) 1797–1863	Boulevard actor; best as melancholy heroes of romantic plays and melodramas; a "natural" actor
Frédérick Lemaître 1800–1876	Greatest romantic actor of France
Rachel (Elizabeth Felix) 1821–1858	Early great star; classical repertory; "revived a moribund classical tradition"

larly presented mock melodramas in which the villain was a large bull dog and the heroine a tiny poodle.

Although such novelties were often short-lived, they appeared in major as well as minor houses as long as the fad continued.

Traveling Stars

In 1790, acting companies still operated with lines of business and possession of parts. The growing popularity of individual performers like Kean, Lemaître, Devrient, and Rachel, however, undermined sharing companies and lines of business. The stars' public acclaim allowed them to command roles and salaries without regard to past traditions. Lemaître, for example, was a versatile actor who refused to be limited by traditional lines of business. Rachel demanded (and received) an annual salary equal to that of France's prime minister, and she regularly abandoned the Comédie Française to go on international tours.

After 1830, the trend was away from sharing companies and lines of business and toward traveling virtuoso performers. Gradually, to meet the public's demand for novelty, the length of the stars' residency declined. Therefore, stars tended to specialize more, some keeping only two or three roles in their repertory and playing these roles in an increasing number of cities for a decreasing number of days. Consequently, rehearsals with the resident company declined and, with them, the company's contributions to the event. At its worst, the practice resulted in a virtuoso performer's trying to dazzle audiences with highly idiosyncratic interpretations of a few favorite roles, supported by a lackluster resident company that tried to stay out of her or his way. Improved roads, new railroads, and steamships made touring easier and may indirectly account for the lowered quality of resident acting companies. The touring star system, according to an Englishman of the day "has been the ruin of the theatre, and the ruin of the drama."[40]

FIGURE 14.30
During the romantic period, railroads helped stars to travel from place to place. [From *The Mirror*, 1837.]

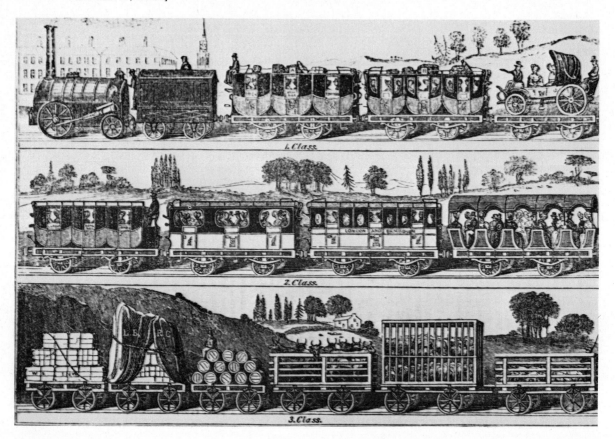

Directing

As accuracy and consistency in production became valued, someone was needed to assure its coordination. An early director explained, "The poet's work springs from a single mind. Therefore the reproduction of it obviously must also come from a single mind."[41] The idea that a single artistic vision should control the whole production found embryonic expression with Goethe at Weimar, and subsequent, stronger expression with Karl Immerman at Dusseldorf. In France, the playwright Pixérécourt pointed the way. Perhaps because the successful conclusion of his melodramas often required well-

timed spectacular effects, Pixérécourt insisted on overseeing all aspects of his productions, a practice that has caused some historians to call him the first modern French director. After 1830, playwrights like Hugo and Dumas *père* began to direct actors as Pixérécourt had directed visual effects.

In England, Macready earned attention as an early stage director. When he became manager of first one and then the other of England's major theatres, Macready regularly sought visual accuracy and consistency in production, paying careful attention to even small details of costume and business. He was the first to seek historical accuracy in set and costumes on a reg-

FIGURE 14.31

William Charles Macready as Macbeth. [From *English Illustrated Magazine*.]

ular basis. He insisted that all actors practice their performances during the required rehearsal periods (rather than merely mouthing their lines, as was then customary). He orchestrated stage pictures, taking care with the minor as well as the major actors and seeing that each contributed to the whole. In short, he strove to offer the public a work unified by the force of his own vision. Thus Macready undertook with greater consistency what Garrick and John Philip Kemble had attempted only intermittently, pointing the way toward those stage directors and antiquaries who would dominate the English theatre after mid-century.

Prerealists

During the decades of the 1830s and 1840s, new plays and practices began to suggest that romanticism was not meeting the needs of all theatre patrons.

In England, the actor Macready eschewed both the nobility of the classicists and the eruptive passion of the romantics in favor of a prosaic, conversational rendering of tragic roles. As a director, he sought a unified production, shaping his actors and mise-en-scène accordingly. Gentlemanly melodramas appeared. Designed to appeal to middle-class rather than working-class tastes, the plays avoided the extreme language and action of earlier romantic pieces in favor of more restrained approaches and more familiar settings. Plays like *The Lady of Lyons* and *Money* (both by Edward George Bulwer-Lytton) held the stage for the remainder of the century. As drama became less exotic, settings and costumes followed suit. For example, at the Olympic Theatre, Mme. Vestris (an actress turned manager) not only regularly enclosed the acting areas with box sets, she also furnished them so that they resembled rooms in contemporary homes. Following the same impulse, she eliminated the exaggerated comic costumes previously associated with various minor forms of drama in favor of garments more like those worn in daily life. In another appeal to middle-class families, the evening bill was shortened, first at the Olympic and then elsewhere. Rather than ending at one or two in the morning, performances now were "so regulated as to enable families to reach their homes before midnight."[42] The popularity of this innovation led to a bill that included only one play per evening, a pattern that triumphed after mid-century.

In France, when both Dumas *père* and Hugo had abandoned the Comédie Française, after 1843, their places were taken by two playwrights whose romantic inclinations were muted or absent: Casimir Delavigne wrote plays that offered a commonsense compromise between controversial romantic practices and conservative neoclassical ones; Eugène Scribe, the more important of the two, developed a tightly wrought drama called the well-made play (*pièce bien faite*).

Scribe was extraordinarily prolific, his works accounting for more than one tenth of the sixteen hundred new comedies and *vaudevilles* played in the theatres of Paris between 1805 and 1830. By his death, he had more than three hundred works to his credit—opera and comic opera libretti, melodramas, *vaudevilles*, and most important of all, comedies. The volume and success of his works helped change the direction of the French drama.

Scribe generally replaced the remote with the familiar, nature with society, and noble savages with pragmatic urbanites. He wrote plays noted for their careful construction, in which antecedents always seemed to produce appropriate consequences. Scribe adopted several techniques to achieve the appearance of dramatic unity based on action: (1) extensive exposition and careful preparation early in the play; (2) interlocking (and often mutually complicating) lines of action creating suspense and strong climaxes; and (3) single items (persons, places, or objects) to establish and explain a relationship among otherwise unrelated entities. Audiences so delighted in the well-crafted dramas that the well-made play joined melodrama as the major popular genres for the rest of the century. Because Scribe often sacrificed development of character and beauty of language to the intricacies of incidents, his plays by 1900 came to seem too obviously contrived. Thus, the term *well-made play*, so obviously intended as a compliment, became a condemnation applied to plays considered shallow and obviously artificial.

Comedies like those written by Scribe were continued by playwrights like Victorien Sardou after mid-century; and serious plays adapting Scribe's techniques were popularized by writers like Dumas *fils* and even Henrik Ibsen. Thus, Scribe and others like him (in the so-called school of good sense) helped turn the public's attention away from sprawling dramas unfolding in exotic settings and toward simple dramatic structures based on apparent cause and effect, everyday situations, and unaffected language.

Some German artists were also chafing under the idealism of the romantics before 1850. Inspired by the revolutions of 1830, Ludolf Wienbarg, in a book dedicated "to Young Germany," called for an art that fulfilled three requirements. First, it should possess a national spirit and "engage [people] in the conflicts of

the time."[43] Second, art should be national in the sense that it should be of value and interest to the whole nation. Third, art should be well suited to its own time, opposing conservative and reactionary elements and heightening a nation's social awareness. Underlying this new view of art was a changed perception of the middle class. From the Renaissance, the middle class (presumably speaking on behalf of those even less fortunate) had attacked the privileges of the aristocracy. With the movement known as Young Germany came the conviction that the middle class had joined with the upper class to block the masses from power.

Young Germany produced no major playwrights, but it set the stage for those realistic writers who would dominate the late nineteenth century (see Figure 14.32). By introducing the works of Scribe and other contemporary French authors, it brought to Germany the techniques of the well-make play and laid the foundations for later realists (as well as for playwrights like Gustav Freytag). Also, Young Germany introduced the works of Georg Büchner and Friedrich Hebbel. Although neither was listed among the members of the movement, both were tied to it philosophically.

George Büchner (1813–1837) wrote only three plays before his untimely death at the age of twenty-four. Championed by Young Germany because of his radical (early socialist) views, Büchner declined to affiliate with the group, believing that literature was incapable of ameliorating the problems of society. His plays, considered unstageable even by Young Germany, were marked by disillusionment, pessimism, and finally complete despair. All but ignored during his lifetime, Büchner has been hailed during the twentieth century as a forerunner of styles as diverse as naturalism, expressionism, and epic theatre. His plays, long unproduced, have now earned a position in the active repertory of the West.

Many critics now consider Friedrich Hebbel (1813–1863) the best German playwright between Schiller and Gerhart Hauptmann. For Hebbel, problems were both the source and the

FIGURE 14.32
Major Works of Young Germany (1840s)

Heinrich Laube 1806–1884	Author and theatre director (of Burg-theater and later at Leipzig); plays include *Monaldeschi* (1840), *The Karls Schoolboy* (1846), and *Graf Essex* (1856)
Karl Gutzkow 1811–1878	*Zopf and Schwert* (1843) and *Uriel Acosta* (1847); from 1847–1859 was Dresden's chief playwright and *Dramaturg*
Georg Büchner 1813–1837	A revolutionary; major plays were *Danton's Death* (published 1835, with Gutzkow's help), *Leonce and Lena* (1836), and *Woyzeck* (1836, published 1879)
Friedrich Hebbel 1813–1863	Playwright and critic; plays include *Judith* (1839), *Maria Magdalena* (1844), and *Agnes Bernauer* (1852); major critical essays: *My Word on Drama* (1843), foreword to *Maria Magdalena* (1844), and *On Style in Drama* (1847)
Gustav Freytag 1816–1895	Playwright and critic; plays include *The Valentine* (1846) and *Graf Waldemar* (1847); major critical work is *The Techniques of Drama*, (1863) based on techniques of the well-made play
Otto Ludwig 1813–1865	*The Forest Warden* (1850, still a popular tragedy of peasant life), and *Shakespeare Studies* (1871), a valuable contribution to dramatic theory

life of art. Ideas and issues already complete or perfect were for the artist, said Hebbel, no more interesting or productive than a healthy body to a physician. Like Ibsen (with whom he is often compared), Hebbel presented problems in which the society seemed as much at fault as the individuals who strayed from its conventions. Again and again in his plays, Hebbel depicted humanity at an ethical crossroads: in order for society to progress to a higher moral plane, an individual had to be sacrificed. Whether in the past or the present, his heroes were destroyed by the moral rigidity of the culture in which they lived; their destruction gained significance, however, because it might contribute to the ethical development of the society as a whole. Although one play (drastically censored) appeared in Berlin in 1840, most of his works did not reach the stages of Germany until after 1850, a fate he shared with the far less successful playwrights of Young Germany itself.

Although the causes of romanticism's decline were doubtless varied and complex, several factors were clearly important.

First, the idealistic words of the romantics did not correspond with the ugly realities of an increasingly industrialized society. The bucolic visions of an unspoiled past were in painful contradiction to the urban squalor that surrounded increasing numbers of city workers.

Second, the improvement of life seemed to be coming from scientists, who were rigorously applying the methods of science, rather than from people of emotions who were searching for forms of abstract truth.

Third, liberty, equality, and brotherhood were proving exceedingly difficult to achieve. The wealthy manufacturers were as distant from the workers as had been the earlier landholders from their serfs. The economic gap between the haves and the have-nots was all too clear.

Fourth, by the middle of the nineteenth century, disturbing philosophical questions were being raised. Certain scientific discoveries threatened to dethrone humans from their former place as God's special creations. Others seemed to argue that only the strong survived, a view that spilled out of biology and into other areas of life, where it was often corrupted into some version of "might makes right."

In sum, the exalted and optimistic view of the romantics, when tested against the realities of an emerging industrial world, was found wanting. Thus, the romantic wave that collected around 1750 ebbed after 1850.

ENDNOTES

1. Excellent summaries of the major shifts in the social, economic, technical and scientific fields can be found in Guy S. Metraux and Francois Crouzet, *The Nineteenth-Century World: Readings from the History of Mankind* (New York: New American Library, 1963).

2. The standard work on the cultural and artistic phenomenon now called *romanticism* is Arthur O. Lovejoy, *Essays in the History of Ideas*, originally published in 1948. Quotations in our text refer to the Capricorn Books edition (New York, 1960).

3. Lovejoy, p. 69.

4. Jean Jacques Rousseau, as translated and cited by Lovejoy, pp. 19–20.

5. Samuel Taylor Coleridge, in his essays "Greek Drama" (1812) and "On the Principles of Sound Criticism Concerning the Fine Arts" (1814), as collected by Bernard Dukore, *Dramatic Theory and Criticism: Greeks to Grotowski* (New York: Holt, Rinehart and Winston, 1974), pp. 581, 583.

6. Petition submitted to the king by classicists: Arnault, Lemercier, Viennet, Jouy, Andrieux, Jay, and Leroy, as cited in Marvin Carlson, *The French Stage in the Nineteenth Century* (Metuchen, N.J.: The Scarecrow Press, 1972), p. 62. Carlson's book is the standard source in English, and our discussion draws heavily on his work.

7. Stendhal, *Racine and Shakespeare*, quoted in Dukore, p. 677.

8. As reproduced in Dukore, pp. 683–684.

9. Select Committee on Dramatic Literature of the House of Commons, cited in Jan Williamson, *Charles Kemble: Man of the Theatre* (Lincoln: University of Nebraska Press, 1970), p. 200.

10. Charles Kemble's recollections before the Select Committee, quoted in Joseph Donohue, *Theatre in the Age of Kean* (Totowa, N.J.: Rowman and Littlefield, 1975), p. 46. Our discussion of English theatre draws heavily on this standard source.

11. George Colman, as cited in Donohue, pp. 49–50.

12. As quoted in Donohue, p. 162.

13. From *Conversations of Goethe with Eckermann and Soret*, quoted in Dukore, p. 491.

14. Goethe, as quoted in A. M. Nagler, *A Source Book in Theatrical History* (New York: Dover, 1959), p. 435.

15. Many of Goethe's rules are reproduced by Nagler, pp. 429–433.

16. As quoted in Nagler, p. 426.

17. Marvin Carlson, *The German Stage in the Nineteenth Century* (Metuchen, N.J.: Scarecrow Press, 1972), p. 24. Carlson's is the standard source in English, and our discussion draws heavily on his work.

18. Schiller, in a letter quoted by Carlson, *German Stage*, p. 41.

19. Staatsminister von Hardenberg to Bruhl, cited by Carlson, *German Stage*, p. 45.

20. In a diary quoted by George Witkowski, *The German Drama of the Nineteenth Century* (n. p., 1909; reprint ed., New York: Benjamin Blom, 1968), p. 33.

21. Giovanni Pindemonte, quoted by Marvin Carlson, *The Italian Stage from Goldoni to D'Annunzio* (London: McFarland, 1981), p. 73.

22. For the analysis of theatrical patterns, we are indebted to Douglass McDermott, "The Development of the Theatre on the American Frontier, 1750–1890," *Theatre Survey* 19, 1 (May 1978): 63–78.

23. Stage directions from *The Woodman's Hut* (1814) and *The Anchor of Hope* (1847), as reproduced in Michael R. Booth, *Victorian Spectacular Theatre: 1850–1910* (Boston: Routledge & Kegan Paul, 1981), pp. 61–62.

24. Quoted by Carlson, *German Stage*, p. 50.

25. Instruction to the Central Management Committee, quoted by B. V. Varneke, *History of the Russian Theatre* (New York: Macmillan, 1951), p. 277.

26. As quoted in Carlson, *French Stage*, p. 45.

27. As quoted in Carlson, *French Stage*, p. 44.

28. Playbill, as reproduced by Booth, p. 44.

29. Macready's *Diaries*, as cited by Booth, p. 39.

30. Playwright Richard Cumberland's *Memoires*, as cited in Linda Kelly, *The Kemble Era* (London: Bodley Head, 1980), p. 99.

31. Macready, cited in Nagler, p. 452.

32. Nagler, p. 429.

33. Hunt and Coleridge, quoted in Nagler, p. 453.

34. August Lewald quoted in Carlson, *German Stage*, p. 47.

35. August Klingemann's description, quoted in Carlson, *German Stage*, pp. 44–45.

36. J. Janin, as cited by Carlson, *French Stage*, p. 83.
37. Victor Hugo, as cited by Carlson, *French Stage*, p. 113.
38. A. I. Hertzen, quoted by Varneke, p. 259.
39. Leigh Hunt, quoted in Nagler, p. 472.
40. W. T. Moncrieff, as quoted by Donohue, p. 81.
41. Karl Immerman, quoted in Carlson, *German Stage*, p. 95.
42. J. R. Planche's tribute to Mme. Vestris, reproduced by Nagler, p. 463.
43. Wienberg, quoted by Carlson, *German Stage*, p. 102.

15

Realism and the Realistic Theatre, 1850–Present

No equivalent period has seen the degree and rate of change of the one from 1850 to the present. While successive revolutions in communications have created an information glut, parallel changes in other areas have also occurred, and we have been faced not only with change itself, but also with vastly increased information about change. Two effects have been the *compartmentalization* of knowledge and the coincident *fragmentation* of activity. It is no longer possible for an individual to grasp all of a field of knowledge, and specialization has become increasingly narrow. So, too, have the languages of specialization, so that specialists communicate more and more only with each other.

Fragmentation has not been limited to knowledge, however. Popular magazines appeal to narrower and narrower audiences; cable television is able to appeal to narrower and narrower tastes; politics shows signs of retreating from consensus democracy and moving toward narrow constituencies. The theatre has not been immune to fragmentation, and so it must be understood that realism has been simply one tendency among several.

Certain aspects of our world have their origins in romanticism, others in earlier movements back to the Renaissance, even to the late Middle Ages. However, it appears that there has been at least one major shift since 1850, and that some aspects of our world are radically and essentially different from anything before 1850.

The theatre of realism epitomizes those elements that have their roots in the past, particularly in romanticism. Although it is modern in that it makes excellent use of modern technology, realism as an artistic style is the latest expression of the illusionism that appeared in the Renaissance.

The Period

The revolutions of 1848 deeply shook established governments, and the immediate aftereffect was a reactive assertion of governmental controls. France suffered the most direct changes: the Second Republic lasted only from 1848 to 1852 and was replaced by popular choice with the Second Empire. Germany, under the aggressive leadership of Otto von Bismarck (1815–1898) found a national identity and was able to isolate France. Italy remained divided for many years; Russia continued as the ambivalent last outpost of feudalism and the most foreign of European cultures; the United States, expanding westward, had relatively little European involvement; Japan and China were "opened" to the West but were isolated by distance. The next century, however, would see remarkable reversals.

War: Toward Mass Death

War had always been a political tool; for the first time, it became a menace from which even civilians could not escape. To be sure, there had

FIGURE 15.1

Time line: 1850–present.

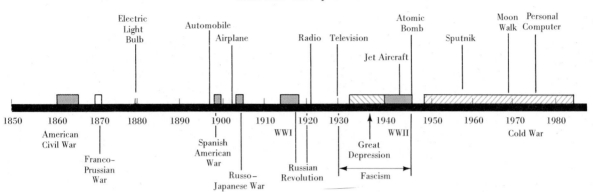

been long wars that had devastated civilian populations, but now even short wars could spread disaster. The American Civil War (1861–1865) had huge battles, and European observers saw in them the first use of the machine gun. The Franco-Prussian War (1870) saw France overwhelmed by a unified and powerful Germany; the Spanish-American (1898) and the Russo-Japanese (1905–1906) wars saw two emerging powers defeat two tottering ones.

In 1914, the planet embarked on its first "world" war—not truly a global one, but one understood as such. The Western Front settled into a three-year stalemate that gobbled up millions of men. The machine gun, now "perfected," slaughtered indiscriminately, taking officers and privates alike. Mounted cavalry were rendered instantly obsolete, ending one of the significant distinctions of the landed gentry. New weapons ended the colorful uniforms of the past, banishing them to balls and dress parades because of their high visibility, and thus stripping war of some of its glamor.[1] The slaughter was enormous: by the time that Russia withdrew from the war in 1917, it alone had lost 5.5 million men.

World War II (1939–1945) was more truly global, although South America and much of Africa were spared. Air power now made saturation bombing possible. Civilian populations

suffered, from the London Blitz through the Dresden fire-bombing to the atomic bombing of Hiroshima and Nagasaki. Millions died, but the figure that would be judged most horrible was the six million Jews who perished in gas chambers and death camps.

With the development of atomic and then hydrogen bombs, so-called limited wars were fought in the belief that any third "world" war would be cataclysmic. "Overkill" and "doomsday machines" were discussed, and it was clear that technology had moved war from mass death to universal death.

The Population Revolution

Even while war became more lethal and more universal, however, mortality from natural causes was decreasing and fertility was increasing, although there was a marked trough in European fertility between about 1900 and World War II.[2] England's population grew to 41.5 million in 1939, even while 8 million were lost to emigration.[3] The experience of continental Europe was about the same; the growth of the United States was significantly higher. However, world growth was not the same at all social levels, and since about 1850 growth has been much greater at lower income levels. Thus, while populations were growing, lower-income populations were growing disproportionately, a phenomenon once welcomed as an increase in the labor force but one now distrusted.

The massive shift from nonurban to urban populations continued: in 1851, less than half of England's people lived in urban areas; in 1931, more than three quarters did.[4] The great majority of people who moved to the cities were soon packed into small areas of often depressing ugliness and dangerous living conditions.

The city had been the glory of the late Middle Ages and the Renaissance; after 1850, it was to become a modern problem. There had always been slums; now slums went on for miles, and some people spent their entire lives in them. Cities grew beyond human scale.

Industrialization

Advances in metallurgy and tool making made precision machines possible about 1850. Steel making became a science. The early trades of the Industrial Revolution were joined by new heavy industries. Whole regions—for example, the Ruhr and southwestern Pennsylvania—were devoted to coal and steel. Industries clustered

because of natural affinities such as transportation, access to materials, and cheap labor. Heavy industry polluted heavily, but environmental effects were not understood and problems were flushed downstream. "If the creek don't stink, the men ain't workin'," as one pragmatist said.

After World War II, some countries began to shift their industrial base to a new technology; they included Germany and Japan, whose heavy industries had been destroyed by the war. These new industries were far less labor-intensive and far less polluting. More recently, the growing use of robots has begun to change industrialization again.

Mass Participation

The movement toward equality that had marked romanticism accelerated. For the first time, however, it truly reached all social levels. The romantics, whether poets or politicians, had operated mostly from an upper-class or upper-middle-class point of view. After 1850, a tendency toward egalitarianism spread slowly to all levels of society. It must be understood that this *mass* equality was very different from the romantics' concept. New elements included the following.

Labor Movements
England had its first national trade union in 1851 and its first major strike in 1889. Germany legalized trade unions in 1881, France in 1884; Samuel Gompers organized the American Federation of Labor in 1881. Union membership in England increased from 1.5 million in 1895 to 9.5 million in 1955; in Germany, it went from .25 million in 1890 to 3.5 million in 1914.

Suffrage
The vote had been extended in small increments in the eighteenth and early nineteenth centuries, but only to men. An international women's movement gained momentum after the mid-nineteenth century; women suffragists

FIGURE 15.2
The factory system involved thousands of people in identical work, made family life go by the factory clock, and revolutionized social organization. [From *Appleton's*.]

agitated for half a century to get women the vote. In the United States, black men had been enfranchised after the Civil War, but black women remained "slaves twice over." Women finally got the right to vote in England in 1918, in Russia in 1917, and in the United States in 1920. Parts of many populations remained effectively disenfranchised, however, through disaffection, isolation, or extralegal blocks. The American Voting Rights Act of 1965 and its aftermath have extended enfranchisement in the United States; in Europe, racial minorities are sometimes still outside the mass.

Education

The education of children had gained new importance with the romantics, for whom childhood was special and education a key to liberty. Prussia became the first state to require compulsory primary education and the first to sponsor widespread state schooling (ca. 1810). France embarked on such a system only in 1870. In England, a commission report of 1861 found one seventh of the population being schooled, compared with one ninth in France and one sixth in Prussia. British parliamentary grants for education increased from 30,000 pounds in 1839 to 396,000 in 1855 and 2.2 million in 1881. By 1907, the figure had risen above 11 milion pounds, and there were more than five million children in school. Generally, throughout Europe and America, the intention was to make primary schooling free after about 1880, and compulsory at about the same time. Compulsory secondary education became common as World War I approached. After World War II, higher education was increasingly "massified," in the United States by community colleges and by greatly expanded state university systems; in England, by the creation of many new "concrete" colleges (added to the "red brick" colleges of the late nineteenth century). University education was made available to a larger and larger proportion of the population. The older connection between education and class was

ended, at least in name, as university degrees became widespread.

Humanitarianism

The organized humanitarianism of the later Victorian period was partly an outgrowth of sentimentalism, and it became a powerful force. International and often run by women, the Red Cross, the Salvation Army, and child-welfare leagues went where there was suffering and tried to correct it (Marxists contended that they went and placated the sufferers to keep them from revolting). Such organizations have twentieth-century counterparts in environmentalism, pacifism, and race relations. Their emergence marked a new social consciousness after the laissez-faire attitudes of a century before. In a sense, too, they marked a new secularism, for they were secular replacements for the social action of the medieval and Renaissance Church. They attempted to "massify" comfort.

Internationalism

Technology shrank the world. At the same time, changes in communications made the world more aware of itself. Quite different cultures reached out toward each other and interpenetrated—for both good and ill. Such efforts included the following.

Imperialism

After 1880, central Africa became an imperial focus of France, Germany, Belgium, and England. The United States understood its "manifest destiny" and, after expanding to the Pacific, leapfrogged across it in the 1890s. France gained colonies in Indochina. By the 1920s, however, many of these colonies were dissatisfied; after World War II, they slipped their bonds with a speed that would have astonished the men and women of the 1890s. Perhaps predictably, many of these former colonies became the battlegrounds between major world powers as

FIGURE 15.3

The railroads brought cultures into collision and made institutions like theatre national and international as the great stars toured. [From *Appleton's*.]

ideological, rather than physical, colonialism became the new issue.

International Organizations

The predecessor of the World Court was set up at The Hague in 1899 as an international arbiter. After World War I, the League of Nations was created as a nonbinding, unarmed international parliament; it was crippled by the absence of the United States and then by the withdrawal of the totalitarian states in the early 1930s. Dissolved in 1946, it was replaced by the United Nations, which has been able to exercise more real power through various police forces, censures, mandates, and vetoes, although its real importance is probably symbolic.

Politics

The romantics had already exported their political ideals, as evidenced by the revolutions of 1848. Karl Marx's *Das Kapital* (1867) gave the theoretical base for a radically new but truly international politics. The First International (of socialist activism) was based in London and rather bumblingly represented the new working-class movement; the Second International, founded in 1889 and headquartered in Paris, was both better organized and more influential. Socialist and Social Democratic parties appeared in Germany, Scandinavia, and the countries of Eastern Europe, with analogues in the English Labour and the French Socialist parties.

The Russian Revolutions of 1905 and 1917

were in part the results of this international ideology. The latter revolution overthrew Russia's monarchy and set up the state now called the Soviet Union. The export of Communist doctrine has become commonplace. It has been countered by exported democratic capitalism, principally by the United States. Since the 1950s, nations aligned with neither Communism nor democratic capitalism have comprised a "third world" of common international goals.

Technology

Nineteenth-century discoveries in science were translated into new technology with unprecedented speed, and the philosophical implications of the new science spread almost as quickly. A new generation of "technophiles" appeared who thought that science and technology would solve all problems; these men and women came to maturity between about 1870 and 1930 and believed in progress and an ever brighter future. The basis of their technology was mostly Newtonian physics, and their creed of progress ran head-on into Einsteinian physics.

Technological innovation encouraged the movements toward internationalism and mass culture. Improved transportation shrank distance: the automobile appeared before 1900, the airplane in 1903, the rocket in the 1930s, and supersonic air travel after World War II. New sources of energy seemed to promise a much higher standard of living: petroleum was found in the 1850s; electricity, long understood in the laboratory, could be generated in quantity by 1880; and nuclear energy became practical less than a century later.

Two areas of the new technology were of particular importance: communications and photography.

Communications
The first Atlantic cable linking Europe and America was put down just before the American Civil War. The telephone became practical in 1877. The "wireless telegraph" came with the new century, and commercial radio in the 1920s. With it, the world penetrated the home. Television followed in the 1930s but was delayed in general use by World War II.

In the field of printing, changes in typesetting increased productivity from fifteen hundred to as many as twelve thousand pieces an hour. When engraved plates were adapted to rotary presses, Victorians were bombarded with *pictures* of their world. Between 1850 and about 1890, "sketch artists" labored for daily newspapers and magazines, and the great illustrated periodicals appeared, such as the *Illustrated London News* and *Harper's Magazine.* Color printing was possible by the 1890s. By 1900, pictures of things and places—*accurate* pictures—covered surfaces wherever the eye looked, not merely in newspapers but also on business cards, advertising posters, souvenirs, walls, and even some articles of clothing.

Photography
In 1839, Louis Daguerre in France and William Price Fox Talbot in England found ways of chemically fixing the lens-projected image of the *camera oscura* ("dark room"), a device in use since the Renaissance. Daguerre's process became immediately popular, and "daguerreotypists" produced cheap, exact images of individuals, as the upper-class portrait was massified by technology. Daguerreotypes on their metal backing appeared all over Europe and America, and even reached Japan in 1840. Fox Talbot's process became the basis of photographic printing from a negative and later of printing on metal for mechanical reproduction with type.

The photograph epitomizes nineteenth-century technology: it is entirely *of* the world and it deals entirely *with* the world. Although it began as an art, it almost immediately became a commercial craft. (Its enormous artistic potential remained.) It recorded what was: "The camera never lies." With the invention of moving pictures at the end of the century, it may be said to have reached its fulfillment: the speed with which people flocked to the nickelodeons and the new "motion-picture palaces" (often deserting the theatre in the process) was proof of its potency.

Did photography create the appetite for pictures of the real world, or did that appetite already exist? There is evidence that the answer to both questions is yes. The explosion of hand-drawn, machine-printed pictures after 1850 suggests that the appetite for visual information was already there; on the other hand, when photographic illustrations became feasible, they replaced hand-drawn ones within two decades. It seems that a widespread hunger for pictorial accuracy led to the invention of photography, and the accuracy of photography almost instantly raised the level of expectation of all illustrations.

Realism

Photography is perhaps the most spectacular example of the period's passion for *accuracy* and *detail*. Every age, as we have seen, has its passion for "truth," but the expression of that truth varies enormously. For the period of 1850–1900, and for literalists after 1900, it may be said that "truth" was photographic, if *photographic* is understood as a metaphor for a cluster of perceptions and expectations.

It must be emphasized that some of this passion for the photographic was rooted in romanticism. Daguerre had painted and shown romantic *dioramas*, and Fox Talbot had tried to record his travels in Italy with the help of a *camera oscura*. Dioramas had a great vogue in the nineteenth century: long paintings of famous events or of scenes were set up, often in a circle, and revealed to the audience through ingenious lighting. They could be made to seem to move and to pass from dark to daylight. They were a form of theatre, but one whose great appeal was their much-advertised fidelity to the

FIGURE 15.4

A *camera oscura* for the precise drawing of natural detail. [From *The Saturday Magazine.*]

real scene, "optical illusion endowed with the character of reality."[5]

Fox Talbot's use of the *camera oscura* repeated what sketchers had been doing for centuries: on a glass plate, the artist traced the image projected by lens and mirror. Fox Talbot was a poor draftsman, however, and he may have been philosophically dissatisfied with the intervention of the human hand. He wanted the device's image, not man's interpretation of it.

Daguerre's and Fox Talbot's concern with landscape was romantic. The desire to go to a machine instead of to human interpretation was not. Therein lies one of the great differences between the realistic and the romantic periods. On the one hand was the individual—sensitive, inspired, and capable of penetrating to the real to sense the ideal behind it; on the other hand was the technophile—analytical, scientific, and interested in recording the real *because it was the real.*

Realism in Art

"Rightly viewed, no meanest object is insignificant; all objects are as windows, through which the philosophic eye looks into Infinitude itself," wrote Thomas Carlyle, expressing the prerealistic idea of the importance of the object. Later in the century, however, Matthew Arnold would say, "The main effort, for now many years, has been a critical effort; the endeavour . . . to see the object as in itself it really is."[6] We must see how different the two statements are from each other.

Materialism

Above all, the realism of an attitude like Arnold's depends on an idea of man and of nature that is essentially *materialistic*. It does not look through objects and it does not look beyond them; it looks *at* them. To some extent, this view was the natural heir of the Enlightenment, and to some extent it was an extrapolation from the scientific method. It was also, however, the product of new ideas that had a profound impact in the nineteenth century. The most important of these came from responses to three seminal thinkers: Karl Marx, Charles Darwin, and Sigmund Freud. They challenged the "great man" concept of the romantics and earlier ages, undermined the idea of a benign Nature, and cast a shadow over the romantic idealization of childhood and the Victorian concept of rationalism.

As an artistic style, realism thus partook of both the optimism of the technophiles and the pessimism of some thinkers. Its principal characteristics in art were the following.

Rendering of Surface

Oliver Wendell Holmes called photography "a mirror with a memory." It is this same quality of total reproduction of surface reality that is important to realism. The mirror of neoclassicism and the mirror of realism are quite different. The first was concerned with making an illusion of its idea of the real; since the

FIGURE 15.5

The great American actress Charlotte Cushman, shown in an engraving made from a daguerreotype. Even before photographs could be reproduced in print, engravings of this kind brought new detail and accuracy to pictures. [Authors' collection.]

Renaissance, it had used devices like perspective, verisimilitude, and the unities. It embraced a number of means of giving its audiences effective illusions, usually of generalized places (for example) achieved through frankly conventional means: the *palais à volonté* had generalized "palace-ness" in a scenic system (wings and borders) quite unlike the walls of a real interior; eighteenth-century kitchens might have "kitchen-ness," with their pots and pans painted on the scenery.

Realism, however, bore down hard on the exact rendering of the materialistic surface, with great attention to precise rendering of detail and fidelity to authentic subjects.

The first of these meant re-creating objects in their appearances and in their real-life profusion. The second involved a sometimes curious idea of what was authentic in life itself: the present, for example, was "real"; the past, by and large, was not (although *antiquarianism* was concerned with precise historical reconstruction). Kings and queens were rarely "real" (they fell outside the experience of most people), but the middle class was very "real." After about 1870, audiences and dramatists found the working class to be more "real" still, and this class came to form a good proportion of realistic subject matter and still does. Although such an idea of the "real" seems highly subjective, it is still honored by those who speak of "real" people and mean, usually, those outside the suburban middle class. Many people still see suffering as more "real" than contentment, country music as more "real" than Bach, urban ghettoes as more "real" than suburban country clubs.

Clarity and Self-containment

Realism did not deal in mysteries and it did not leave loose ends. In these respects, it was a product of the science of the later nineteenth century—very practical, and yet optimistic enough to believe that all problems could be solved. In narrative art, this meant that the problem set out early in the work would be solved before the end of the work. Plots were to have beginnings, middles, and definite ends; casts of characters would not include large numbers of peripheral figures. One realistic writer advised that if a gun was shown in the first act, it must go off before the final curtain. In drama, there was a fairly straight line back to the plays of Eugène Scribe, whose "well-made plays" were important precursors of the structure of much realistic drama.

Utility

Usefulness was a prized postromantic attribute, perhaps as a result of the greatly increased value given to material things. Inventiveness, "Yankee ingenuity," and technophilia were admired. All useful objects were highly decorated, but the decoration came after the usefulness.

In order for art to be useful, it had to do something (other than hang on a wall or give pleasure). George Bernard Shaw said that a play had to "do its work in the world," by which he seems to have meant that it had to persuade in favor of an idea. Paintings told stories, often sentimental or moral ones; music, too, told stories, and the period was one of "program music."

Just what the usefulness of any given play or performance was depended on circumstances. The usefulness of plays with middle-class subjects and middle-class audiences lay in presenting a middle-class social "problem" or "question": the question of the divorce laws, the question of prostitution, the question of reputation, and so on. At least in theory, these plays were useful because they presented honest ("truthful," "real") treatments of the subject, which the audience had not been able to see in such a light before.

At least in the middle and upper classes, hiding things was as much a part of art as was showing things. The notorious example of the American woman who put a skirt on her piano to hide the legs may be apocryphal, but it is a fact that many aspects of life were carefully hidden. The middle- and upper-class worlds were dominated by well-to-do males who treated women and children as lesser beings. Social issues like labor conditions, slums, illiteracy, prostitution, starvation, venereal disease, infant mortality, and sanitation were called "improper"; that is, they were not to be matters of knowledge to women and children of the middle class and above. And even men who knew all about such things often kept them out of public discourse, especially in mixed company.

Art, then, made itself socially useful by dealing hesitantly with these subjects in ways made safe by censorship, by the special nature of art itself, and by the restricted access to art.

At least in theory, then, the realistic theatre had a significant knowledge-giving function.

Middle-class Frame of Reference

By 1850, industrial Europe and the United States had powerful middle classes, social groups dependent on industrialized capital, with access to education and political power, and with a large amount of discretionary income. Religious piety, a work ethic, sexual chastity, family solidarity, patriotism, ethnocentrism, and (sometimes) political conservatism bound them together; they were often allied with the smaller, richer, and more powerful classes above them, but rarely with the larger and poorer classes below.

It was the middle class for whom realism seems to have been most important. Realism was an artistic style that was accessible to its rather hardheaded, rational sensibility. Realistic artists frequently came from the middle class. We are not certain, but it appears that audiences in the major metropolitan theatres were middle-class.

The middle-class relevance of realistic theatre was shown through the following.

Middle-class Settings, Characters, and Actions.

Both the *palais à volonté* and the romantic landscape gave way to the upper- and middle-class interior, most often the drawing room. The characters generally lacked noble titles, but they had position and income. Their desires and fears frequently turned on money or social reputation.

Middle-class Values and Ideas.

Realists did not preach revolution; if they preached change, it was change of a sort that did not affect basic structures. Plays that did challenge basic structures were either refused a license to play or were called "scandalous." Inevitably, such plays—those of Henrik Ibsen and George Bernard Shaw, for example—became acceptable as the communications revolution made knowledge of their subjects inevitable. Many of the realists—the English playwrights Arthur Wing Pinero and Henry Arthur Jones, for example—avoided an actual confrontation with a fundamental social issue by using it as a background for a play's action, which would then be resolved by one of the devices of melodrama; thus, they avoided the issue while seeming to deal with it.

Middle-class Viewpoint.

Even when realistic theatre interested itself in social levels other than the middle class, the perceptions were usually middle-class perceptions, and the plays were still aimed at middle-class audiences. As a result, such plays were powerful revelations to their audiences, but they usually stopped short of confrontation with basic issues. The rare realistic artist who was able to surpass this limitation was not automatically successful, however: George Bernard Shaw's *Pygmalion* (1912), for example, showed real understanding of the harsh permanence of poverty and suggested that no amount of good works or individual effort could correct it. Audiences, however, have always preferred to see the play in a rosier light, as a romantic comedy with a "happy ending" that ignores the very issues that Shaw raised—a softening seen best in *My Fair Lady*, the musical made from the play.

The same middle-class viewpoint that limited the treatment of subjects also restricted language, behavior, and choice of subject. Sex and the language to describe it, as well as swearing and obscenity of the sort to be heard on the street, did not exist on the stage. Religion was almost untouchable. Restrictions were enforced by censors like England's Lord Chamberlain and Moscow's Orthodox Metropolitan; internal censors stopped many artists before the matter ever reached government offices. The moral basis, familiar since the *Cid* controversy, was that there were some things it was better not to show, no matter how true they were.

Strengths and Weaknesses of Realism

The unquestioned popularity of realism in the late nineteenth century and our own time attests to its appeal. It was perfectly matched to

FIGURE 15.6

Melodrama and realism were common allies as realism sought to escape the problems inherent in it and melodrama sought a new authentication. An 1861 production of *The Octoroon* by Dion Boucicault. [Authors' collection.]

its moment of industrial, technological, middle-class utilitarianism. Its strengths were the following.

Accessibility

Whether in painting, poetry, or theatre, realism needed little audience preparation. It did not lean heavily on literary or historical allusion, for example. Realism was accessible without any exercise of imagination, and its artfulness (in acting or playwriting, for example) was understandable without knowing anything; that is, the standard was that it was "just like life."

Clarity

Realism seemed to say that its world had no mysteries. Large, even unanswerable questions were banished from it. As a result, many of the subjects of great drama were ignored, and those subjects that were left were defined as rational and solvable.

Emotional Sympathy

Since the eighteenth century, appeals to supposed identities between audience and characters have been made, and sentimentalism is a popular strain that came through romanticism and into realism. With the banishing of transcendental subjects and their larger-than-life characters, much of the universality of the older theatre was lost; in its place, smaller, more easily understood, personal appeals appeared. The subject is not well understood, but it does seem that one of the things that happened during the realistic period was a change in the objects of emotional response—from the large and universal (the heroic) to the individual and personal (the sentimental). Without doubt, the emotions of sentimentalism are easier both to arouse and to deal with; in place of the tragic, there is the pathetic, for example. Serious realism, then, typically depended on emotional sympathy between audience and character ("just like me"), and it should not be surprising to find that the form of many realistic plays is that of melodrama.

Like other styles, realism was not without its weaknesses. These included the following.

Limited Subject Matter

The very accessibility that was an advantage produced a matching weakness. Playwrights, actors, and designers who yearned to express the mystery and the irrational complexity of life had either to look elsewhere or to redefine realism. Audiences that grew weary of readily solved problems and drawing rooms and people just like themselves had either to look elsewhere or stop going to the theatre.

Reduction to Anomaly

Georg Lukacs, the Marxist critic, said that the problem of realism was that its ultimate end was "pathology," that is, mere idiosyncrasy. When realism turned its back on the heroic, it had to see the individual; however, the individual had to be interesting to an audience and somehow significant. The result, with increasing frequency in the twentieth century, was a concentration on characters and situations individualized by their abnormality—social abnormality like drunkenness in Émile Zola's *L'Assommoir*, sex-role independence in Ibsen's *A Doll's House*, or psychopathology in Arthur Miller's *Death of a Salesman* or Tennessee Williams' *A Streetcar Named Desire*. Twentieth-century realism gave its audience psychological victims, usually asking it to pity them (in the belief that pity would lead to social change). In this sense, realistic drama had the same weakness as the realistic novel: " 'The novel is a form of gossip,' says Virginia Woolf, and this clearly expresses the basic direction . . . : towards personality, towards personal history and psychology."[7]

Too, because realistic characters were from the middle or lower classes, they were rarely figures of great power. Dramatic characters became not the doers of the world, but those who were done to—not heroes or villains, but victims. The result in narrative realistic art was a sameness and a parade of "sympathetic normal characters whose tales turn out to be loser's stories, stories about the common person's inevitable powerlessness."[8]

Significant Emptiness

Objective reality was a fine subject for scientists. After its novelty had changed to familiarity in the theatre, however, a problem of significance arose. It was all very well for scientists to see objects as neutral, for their goal was an understanding of the object itself; artists and audiences often wanted something different: they wanted meaning.

Few realists were content (or even able) to show the world precisely "as it is." Instead, most tried to bring significance to art—through the overt discussion of ideas (as in the plays of Ibsen and Shaw), through the arrangement of events (as in Pinero), through symbolism (as in Chekhov), and so on. Such efforts usually resulted in an altered picture of the object and so raised questions about the realism of the works; more important, they raised a large question about the potential for significance of realism itself.

Dullness

A theatre that presented literal representations of the objective surface of life would run the dangers of repetitiveness, poor timing, meaninglessness, drabness, and, finally, utter untheatricality. For example, there is a great difference between dramatic dialogue and real speech: the first is pointed, clear, and cumulative; the second is often meandering, vague, repetitive, and undirected. The language of real life, with its repressions, its long pauses, its personal symbolism, can be meaningless to an audience. Audiences want to hear actors and to understand their diction; in life, neither volume nor diction are of much concern. The events of real lives rarely wind themselves up into neat endings, nor do they have three-act structures.

People in real houses live in several rooms and come and go on their own business, not according to the needs of a plot or the actions of a "central character" (every real person being the main character of his or her own play).

Realistic playwrights tried in many ways to cope with these basic differences between reality and realism. They wrote short plays that were called "slices of life," to change the audience's expectations about structure and ending; they reduced the importance of language, in order to approximate some of the inarticulate, nondirected language of life; Chekhov brought his characters on and off the stage almost at random, making of the fact that everybody is his or her own protagonist a new dramatic tension;

and naturalistic works like Gorki's *The Lower Depths* almost did away with plot in order to try to approximate life's structure.

In order to be authentic, realism must ape life in its details; but if it apes life in all its details, it ceases to be art—and then why should an audience watch it?

Varieties of Theatrical Realism

Like other styles, realism was subject to outside influence. We will identify five major kinds of realistic theatre, but it must be understood that these often overlap, and that they can and do coexist.

FIGURE 15.7

Belasco's *Girl of the Golden West* (1905). [Courtesy of the Billy Rose Theatre Collection, the New York Public Library at Lincoln Center, Astor, Lenox and Tilden Foundations.]

Realism

The word *realism* is used to describe both the largest category, which embraces all the others, and the earliest and perhaps the simplest variety of it. Although the first in time, it has also been returned to a number of times. Its primary identifying marks are

1. Self-contained structure.

2. Middle- or lower-middle-class setting and characters.

3. Recognizable imitation of contemporary behavior, furniture, clothes, and so on, in great detail. Nineteenth-century realistic settings still had large amounts of painted (not three-dimensional) detail, and the costumes were made of fabrics that merely looked authentic at audience-viewing distances. Realistic makeup, too, looked authentic only at certain distances and under theatrical lights. Throughout the period, the lighting was always conventional.

Examples: Robertson, *Caste* (1867): Ibsen, *A Doll's House* (1879).

Naturalism

Naturalism was sometimes called *scientific naturalism* from an essay by Émile Zola. This form of realism had a vigorous life from about 1885 to 1910 and is still seen. Its primary identifying marks are

1. Sequential, but not necessarily self-contained, structure. Naturalism saw its characters as impotent products of forces, and the plays often lack the neat plotting of realism, substituting instead a narrative about the progressive effects of a force.

2. Lower-class characters and settings. Naturalism sometimes seemed to glory in revelations of squalor.

3. A recognizable imitation of contemporary settings, behavior, clothes, objects, and so on. Real objects were preferred. The extreme example that is usually cited is the use of real sides of beef in a stage butcher shop. The use of real people rather than actors, of real furniture, and of settings copied from real places in every detail were tried. Naturalistic actors

turned their backs on the audience; they tried behaviors—scratching, picking their noses, and spitting—appropriate to the setting but until then thought inappropriate to the stage.

Example: Maksim Gorki, *The Lower Depths* (1902).

"Reactive" Realism

Realism incorporated elements of other styles, maintaining its own broad outlines. Under the influence of impressionism, for example, it embraced a degree of symbolism; under the influence of the post–World War I expressionists, it was sometimes dreamlike and allowed exaggeration of certain elements.

Example: Chekhov, *The Seagull* (1896).

Commercial Realism

A commercialized romanticism (neoromanticism) was the dominant mainstream style in Europe and America until about 1900, and it remained strong until World War II; after 1900, a somewhat trivialized realism was also taken into the commercial theatre—"trivialized" because the style was adopted for its popularity and not for any strong theoretical position taken by its commercial producers.

Realistic drama became the dominant commercial form in England and the United States, and to a lesser extent in France, from World War I until at least 1960. Run-of-the-mill comedies and melodramas were crafted in more or less the style that Ibsen had pioneered. Usually, they had three acts, one set, and small casts; they tended to have a very clean and clear story line; and they tied up all loose ends before the final curtain. They achieved *authentication* by being realistic: they seemed to be so much like life that they commanded credibility.

When these techniques were carried over into television soap opera, it may be said that commercialized realism had reached its fulfillment: a perfected style in the service of utter trivia.

Example: David Belasco, *Madame Butterfly* (1900).

Socialist Realism

Socialist realism is realism conceived from a Marxist point of view, in which the real is seen as that which is presented with Marxist social truthfulness.

The distinction is not a casual one. Socialist realism is not mere propaganda, although at its baldest it may seem so. Becoming the dominant style of the Soviet Union after about 1930, it was defined by the First All-Union Congress of Soviet Writers in 1934 as "the basic method of Soviet literature and literary criticism. It demands of the artist the truthful, historically concrete representation of reality in its revolutionary development. Moreover, the truthfulness and historical concreteness of the artistic representation of reality must be linked with the task of ideological transformation and education of workers in the spirit of socialism."[9] The dissident Abram Tertz (Andre Siniavsky) has said that the defining characteristic is Purpose, that is, an almost religiously conceived Communist statement. He wrote bitterly that

> each work of socialist realism . . . is . . . assured of a happy ending. The ending may be sad for the hero, who runs every possible risk in his fight for Communism, but it is happy from the point of view of the superior Purpose . . . . lost illusions, broken hopes, unfulfilled dreams, so characteristic of literature of other eras and systems, are contrary to socialist realism.[10]

A sincere Marxist critic like Georg Lukacs, however, finds a complex aesthetic and a broad range of art possible in the style. For Lukacs, "socialist realism differs from critical realism, not only in being based on a concrete socialist perspective, but also in using this perspective to describe the forces working towards socialism *from the inside*."[11] Lukacs seems to differentiate between the realism we have identified with the middle class and the socialist realism that he identifies with socialist society: "Socialist realism is able to portray from the inside human beings whose energies are devoted to the building of a different future, and whose psychological and moral makeup is determined by this."[12] Lukacs argues for a truth revealed by the "typical," especially in character. Realism focuses on psychology, socialist realism on sociopolitics. "Man becomes aware of his nature as an ineluctably social animal," said Lukacs.

Perhaps no variation of realism shows its relativity more clearly than socialist realism. Its truth is a carefully defined political one. Its principal characteristics are

1. Concentration on surface, objective reality in acting, setting, and elements of production.

2. Narrative structure, usually causal.

3. Rationally conceived character, although the socialist-realist protagonist tends often toward the heroic, and truth of character is not psychological, but social.

Example: Vsevolod Vishnevski, *The Optimistic Tragedy* (1934), a play "in which the heroine dies at the end but Communism triumphs" (Tertz).

An Analogue to Realism

One theatrical style that preceded realism also shared its roots and had many affinities with it. This was *antiquarianism*, the accurate re-creation of historical moments; since about 1900, it may be said to have merged with realism.

In London, the Princess's Theatre seasons of Charles Kean from 1851 to 1859 represented the crest of this movement. Kean was praised for his "archaeological exactness," in which he combined such spectacles as a superbly painted diorama with historical and geographical accuracy, providing "a feast of spectacle, sentiment, scholarship, education and some Shakespeare."[13] It remained to be asked, what the importance of a historically correct Venice was to *The Merchant of Venice,* an English play whose Venice was an imagined place; however, this question did not torment the Victorians. Antiquarian correctness became a public relations

FIGURE 15.8

Charles Kean's antiquarian production of *The Merchant of Venice* at mid-century. [Authors' collection.]

point later in the century, when lavish historical settings and costumes were used by Sir Henry Irving in his Lyceum Theatre management in the 1870s and 1880s, by Herbert Beerbohm Tree for his *Julius Caesar* with settings and costumes by the establishment painter Sir Lawrence Alma-Tadema, and in New York and London by Augustin Daly. Daly "is reported to have sent a scene painter to France to make an exact copy of the Forêt d'Ardennes [for *As You Like It*], and for the final act of *The Taming of the Shrew* he used a backdrop based on a painting by Paolo Veronese."[14] Antiquarianism in historical films and plays has now become standard.

Another antiquarian tendency was one toward a reconstruction of exact *theatrical* conditions. In London, a young actor named William

Poel performed the uncut First Quarto *Hamlet* on a stage without scenery in 1881; he became the founder of the English Stage Society in 1895, which lasted until 1905, producing old plays in antiquarian reproductions of their original staging—for example, Marlowe's *Doctor Faustus* in an interpretation of the Fortune Theatre (1896). This form of antiquarianism has been particularly important in the production of medieval and Elizabethan plays and has had considerable influence on both Shakespearean production and on modern theatre design and the thrust stage.

The work of Poel and others was a reaction against late-nineteenth-century over-production, and it therefore seems very different from the work of antiquarians like Kean and Irving. At base, however, the impulse was the same.

FIGURE 15.9

Leading Figures in Antiquarianism (1850–World War I)

Name	Dates	Function
James Robinson Planché	1796–1880	Costume history and design
Charles Kean	1811–1868	Shakespearean production
William Telbin (father)	1813–1873	Scenery
George II, Duke of Saxe-Meiningen	1826–1914	Production
Victorien Sardou	1831–1906	Drama
Henry Irving	1838–1905	Production
Hawes Craven	1837–1910	Scenery
William Telbin (son)	1846–1931	Scenery
William Poel	1852–1934	Theatrical reconstruction
André Antoine	1858–1943	Production (at Odéon)
David Belasco	1859–1931	Dramas and production

Three Major Realistic Theatres

We have selected three pioneering theatres to epitomize important moments in realism's emergence. Each was headed by a theatrical person or group of persons who were themselves outstanding artists. These three theatres should in no way be thought of as the "causes" of realism or even as the "firsts" of realism; rather, they are recognizable artistic high points in realism's history.

A Triumvirate at the Meininger (1873–1890)

The Prussian-led unification of Germany swept many little duchies into its net, and one of the least of these was that of Saxe-Meiningen. The town of Meiningen was a spa; the duchy was ruled from a ducal palace and maintained a public theatre, a small opera company, and a chapel orchestra. Before 1866, the ruler had had the bad judgment to side with Austria against Prussia; when he was deposed by Bismarck's ambitions, his title and his power passed to his son, Georg II, Duke of Saxe-Meiningen (1826–1914).

Georg II had been trained as a soldier, but he had also been trained as a painter in the dominant school of antiquarianism. "Energy, which in earlier centuries might have found expression in significant acts of high politics, became re-directed."[15] Georg II moved actively into art as earlier rulers might have moved actively into politics. It was not the art of painting that now drew Georg II, however, but the art of the theatre.

He took on two colleagues in this task: his third wife, the former actress Ellen Franz (1839–1923) and a comic actor in the Meiningen company, Ludwig Chronegk (1837–1891). The duke was the oldest of the three and by nature and position its ruler and its source of money. Ellen Franz was the youngest and probably had the least power. Chronegk was a nobody—a Jew in an anti-Semitic era, a former comedian. From its formation in 1873, this triumvirate guided the company (colloquially called the Meininger) to an astonishingly successful season in Berlin and then to year after year of international tours that ended only with Chronegk's final illness in 1890. Without question, they were seen by virtually every important theatre person in Europe, and their influence was acknowledged from England to Russia: "Like a surprising meteor they rose in the theatre heaven. . . . I have never heard a more powerful storm of applause than that which first roared through the Freidrich-Wilhelm-Stadtisches-Theater on the first of May, 1874."[16]

A London review of 1881 suggests what was startling about this "surprising meteor": "the beauty of the costumes, the picturesque grouping, the thoroughness with which the intentions of whoever presided . . . were carried out. . . ."[17] In other words, historical correctness, groupings, and unity of production, to which we may add two other often-cited accomplishments: rejection of the star system and dependence on a repertory of traditional literary quality whose cornerstone was Shakespeare. (In its seventeen seasons on tour, the Meininger gave *Julius Caesar* 330 times, along with four other Shakespeare plays; its second most frequent title was Schiller's *William Tell* (223 performances), the third his *Maid of Orleans* (194), with the great proportion of its 38 other plays from Schiller, Goethe, and Kleist).[18]

It was the Meininger's use of crowds that most influenced later realists. Coupled with it was the rejection of the star system, which later realists would also espouse because they wanted to cast roles according to individual need and not according to lines of business.

For which, if any, of these accomplishments could the triumvirate have laid claim to originality?

Antiquarianism

"A richly decorative and scrupulously accurate historical realism was much the style of the Meininger period, rather than the personal style of Georg II and his company."[19] It was, in fact, Kean's London productions that had inspired Georg II. Antiquarianism had already figured in German productions of Shakespeare done by Franz Dingelstedt in the 1860s.

Groupings and Crowds

Careful control of stage crowds had been attempted before; as early as the first quarter of the century, stage crowds had been divided into units, and each unit had been given a leader for rehearsal and performance.[20] The Meininger used this same technique but went further in requiring all its actors to serve as extras when not in important roles. Above all, the care taken in stimulating each individual in a crowd to visual focus, gesture, and sound must be noted. Some critics felt that the Meininger overdid such reactions and that their crowds were hyperactive. They were judging, however, in terms of the stage crowds of stolid extras that they were accustomed to seeing, in theatres where extras were hired for the night and were barely rehearsed. The Meininger crowds appear to have had some slight precedent in Germany, but they were new elsewhere.

Unity

Stylistic unity had informed some German productions after about 1800. One theatre manifesto of 1808 dealt in some detail with what it called "*Total-effekt*."[21] Both the star system and scenic practice worked against unity, which could be achieved only by the exercise of a single will. Thus, while other theatres were using as many as three scenic artists in a single production, Georg II designed his own settings and had them executed by the same scenic studio that did Richard Wagner's Bayreuth settings. In costumes, he divided centuries into parts to mark historical differences, taking his examples from paintings and actual clothes, and making his own detailed and highly professional sketches of what he wanted. He and Chronegk then rehearsed the actors on these settings and in these costumes for what were long periods by the standards of the day.

Rejection of the Star System

Although the Meininger sometimes added leading actors from outside the company for its tours, it did not use stars of the first rank. These outside actors were sometimes startled by the company's rigid rules and by its absolute insistence that they wear the costumes given them and not supply their own. Not hiring stars ac-

FIGURE 15.10

Control of crowds and "kinetic space" marked the Meininger's style, as in this drawing by Georg II for Friedrich Schiller's *Maid of Orleans*. [From *Theatre Arts*.]

complished three things: the removal of competitive egos; an increase of audience attention on the total production; and a saving of money.

Quality of Repertory

The Meininger did perform contemporary plays for its home audience, but it made its international reputation with classics. It did not give a "Meininger look" to contemporary plays, as far as we know; except for their seasons at home, their repertory virtually ignored the preceding half century. Their international repertory was aristocratic and reflected the taste of Ellen Franz, who had a large part in selecting the plays. (The duke, it must be said, was interested in the work of Ibsen and others, and the company gave two performances of Ibsen's *Ghosts*, the first to an all-male, invited audience in its home theatre.)

By and large, the Meininger was not the very first company to introduce any of these theatre practices; however, it was the first to use them all simultaneously and well. Also, it was the company that benefited from the information explosion: through nineteenth-century

technology, its work was broadcast, in widely published engravings as well as in print. These two points, taken together, explain the considerable reputation of the company; we would suggest that there were two more underlying accomplishments that were of even greater importance to modern theatre:

The Example of the Director

There had been directors before, of course. *Régie* and *régisseur* were early-nineteenth-century terms for "direction" and "director." Figures as diverse as Goethe and Pixérécourt functioned in ways as directors, and rules putting German actors under the control of a single figure go back well into the eighteenth century;[22] David Garrick has also been called a director by some historians. With the Meininger, however, we see stage direction intimately linked with the very spirit of a company for the first time. Why?

Grube tells us that the triumvirate ran rehearsals. Ellen Franz was more or less responsible for the choice of plays and for vocal coaching; Chronegk managed the rehearsals and usually gave the directions to the actors; the duke made detailed sketches and designs and lengthy notes. Yet, surprisingly, there was no *Regiebuch*—no prepared promptscript from which the rehearsal was run. The lack of a promptscript suggests that blocking and business were not planned before rehearsal. Scenes were tried, changed, rejected, and tried again— this we know from contemporary accounts. Suggestions came from all three of the triumvirate and from the actors. Rehearsals were open-ended, often running late into the night. In other words, the Meininger, authoritarian as it was in many respects, was not created by a single authority. *Rehearsal was not the product of directorial work; it was the* process *of directorial work.*

Kinetic Theatrical Space

In a lengthy memo to Chronegk's successor, Georg II laid down his ideas about the use of stage space:

The middle of the scene does not correspond with the middle of the stage. [Symmetry] will appear wooden, stiff and boring. . . . the principal requirement of the stage is to reveal *motion* and *the impetuous progress of action . . .* [our italics]. The middle of the stage . . . should serve for the actor only as a passageway from right to left, or vice versa.

FIGURE 15.11

Three *Julius Caesars:* top, a frontispiece of 1824; left, the Meininger in 1879; right, Beerbohm Tree's production of 1898. The Meininger's *Julius Caesar* was its most-performed production, and it changed the way in which Europe saw crowd scenes. [From Dolby's, courtesy of the Rare Books Room of The University of South Carolina; from *Die Gartenlaube,* courtesy of the Libraries of the University of Rochester; from *Le Théâtre.*] (See also Figure 3.6.)

More attention should be paid to a pleasing relationship between the actors' positions and the set decorations. . . .

It is a real mistake to place the actors in positions parallel to one another. . . . The actor [should avoid moving directly] across the stage . . . instead, he should move unobtrusively at an angle to break the straight line. . . .

If three or more actors . . . are on the stage . . . they should avoid above all else standing in a straight line. . . .

The lack of beauty resulting from poor placement of individual artists in relation to one another is specially disturbing in crowd scenes. . . .

To give the impression that a very large crowd of folk is on the stage, groups should be so arranged that those standing on the edge of the group extend into the wings. . . .

Beauty meant romantic beauty, as taken from a Nature that abhorred symmetry and straight lines. The duke's stage designs show this same concern; his settings, like his crowds, seem to run off the stage into a real world of their own, into which the audience looks through the proscenium arch, which functions as a frame does on a painted landscape. George II and Chronegk, however, understood that the picture seen through the proscenium arch was a *moving* one, an "impetuous progress of action," and that the director's art was to give beauty to that ever-shifting spectacle. The proscenium arch became the *camera oscura* with which the duke captured the "impetuous progress" of life itself. Before his death, other directors would be working in the medium that was the perfect metaphor for his vision: the motion picture. "Progress in the invention of the cinema came," wrote A. Nicholas Vardac, "when the need for pictorial realism in the theatre was at a peak."[23] The ascent of that peak began with the Meininger.

André Antoine and the Théâtre Libre (1887–1894)

André Antoine (1858–1943) was born into the working class; without formal education after the age of thirteen, a conscript soldier for four years in North Africa, he must have seemed identical with millions of his generation. He represented quite a different social experience from that of the Duke of Saxe-Meiningen, but he had an insight into the needs of theatrical art that was equally a product of genius: he saw that the theatre of his time, in order to be free, had to be treated wholly as an art and not as commerce.

The Parisian theatre was stalemated. Its natural conservatism—caused by a mixture of commercial caution, official censorship, and the presence of the state theatres—worked to perpetuate a theatre split between an official wing (the Comédie Française, the Opéra, and the Opéra Comique) and an unofficial one, the theatre of the boulevards (and, increasingly, of working-class neighborhood theatres). The first was traditional, elitist, and often artistically reactionary; the second was contemporary and slick but neither daring nor serious. Playwrights like Alexandre Dumas *fils* (1824–1895) and Émile Augier (1820–1889) wrote plays with contemporary settings and the appearance of realism, but they challenged little in the society. Victorien Sardou (1831–1908) wrote both well-made comedies and fashionable melodramas, as well as historical spectacles (*Theodora*, 1884) in the antiquarian movement. The aggressively serious work being done in the novel by writers like Émile Zola and the Brothers Goncourt had little counterpart on the stage, a writer like Henry Becque (1837–1899) having great difficulty in finding a producer who would take one of his plays. In the mid-1880s, it seemed that there was no theatre for plays with powerful contemporary statements—particularly realistic and naturalistic plays—or for poetic and neoromantic avant-garde plays with limited audience appeal. Such plays existed, without question—they had existed since the 1860s, unproduced—but they did not exist in live performance.

André Antoine seems an unlikely figure to have turned this situation upside down, but he brought unique qualities to his mission:

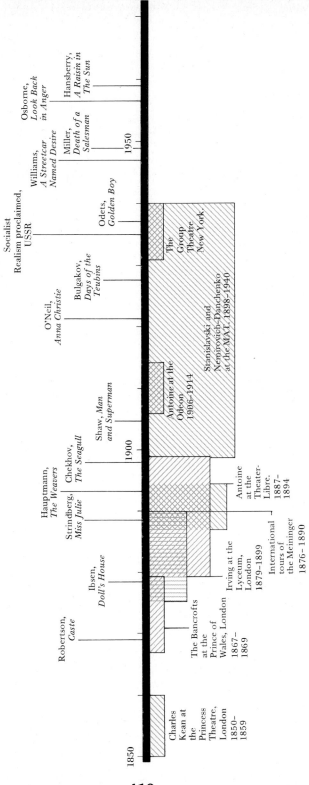

FIGURE 15.12

Time line: Realism and antiquarianism.

1850

Charles Kean at the Princess Theatre, London 1850–1859

Robertson, *Caste*

The Bancrofts at the Prince of Wales, London 1867–1869

Ibsen, *Doll's House*

Irving at the Lyceum, London 1879–1899

International tours of the Meininger 1876–1890

Strindberg, *Miss Julie*

Antoine at the Theater-Libre. 1887–1894

Hauptmann, *The Weavers*

Chekhov, *The Seagull*

1900

Shaw, *Man and Superman*

Antoine at the Odeon 1906–1914

O'Neil, *Anna Christie*

Bulgakov, *Days of the Teubins*

Stanislavski and Nemirovich-Danchenko at the MAT, 1898–1940

Socialist Realism proclaimed, USSR

Odets, *Golden Boy*

The Group Theatre New York.

Williams, *A Streetcar Named Desire*

1950

Miller, *Death of a Salesman*

Osborne, *Look Back in Anger*

Hansberry, *A Raisin in The Sun*

1. *An enormous capacity for work.* Antoine had been earning his living since he was thirteen. Sheer drudgery neither frightened nor offended him.

2. *An appetite for risk.* Whatever his private worries, he was able to work on, often without any assurance that a project would succeed. He paid for his first production by using his month's paycheck from the Paris Gas Company, not bothered by how he would live.

3. *Theatrical experience and perceptiveness.* Antoine, who was self-taught, was widely read and a regular patron of theatres and art exhibitions. He had studied stage diction, had worked as a stage extra, and had had ambitions to be an actor, even trying out for the Paris Conservatoire, where it appears that he was rejected by a split vote.[24] He knew the theatre of his time and he sensed its untapped potential.

4. *Understanding of the moment.* Antoine was *not* a doctrinaire realist; he was a doctrinaire artist. He saw that what was needed was a theatre devoted to theatrical art, not one devoted to a particular cause.

Formation of the Théâtre Libre

Antoine was released from military service in 1883; the day after, he married, against his family's wishes. He settled in Paris and supported himself by working at the Paris Gas Company.

In 1884–1885, Antoine joined the Cercle Gaulois, an amateur theatre that rehearsed in the evenings, rather like a modern community theatre. Its offerings were the popular commercial plays of the time; its theatre was privately owned. Antoine acted regularly, beginning with Scribe's *Bataille de Dames* in June 1885.[25] (He would later describe these as "works of completely lifeless nonsense."[26]) Antoine's association with the Cercle Gaulois lasted for almost two years; however, it is impossible to say how much of the attraction was artistic and how much personal and amatory, for his marriage was in ruins and the Cercle became the meeting place for him and his new lover. When he broke with the Cercle's patron in 1887, he wrote of his regret at leaving, but it was over: "The Cercle Gaulois was finished [for me] and I can only regret that they were not ready for a metamorphosis that would have transformed it."[27]

The "metamorphosis" began as a desire to modernize and elevate the group's repertory. It ended as a fierce commitment to the transformation of French theatre. In two years, Antoine moved from being what we would call an amateur actor in a community theatre to being the artistic director of an internationally influential avant-garde theatre. To see him as an amateur, however, is to suggest that he was really an employee of the Gas Company and by avocation a man of the theatre, when, in fact, he was an amateur Gas Company clerk who was really a man of the theatre, one who had to "reconcile two irreconcilable things: working at an art . . . and earning without too much trouble indispensable bread."[28]

His attempts to improve the Cercle's repertory had led to a search for previously unproduced plays. By the winter of 1886, determination and luck had brought him four plays—by the influential critic Paul Alexis; Arthur Byl, a newcomer; Jules Vidal; and, most remarkably, the established Léon Hennique, with an adaptation of Zola. The bill was played at the end of April 1887; by the first of May, Antoine had been asked to leave the Cercle Gaulois. The name of Zola had frightened the real amateurs in the group, as well as their patron. Also, Antoine's inclusion of non-Cercle actors was unacceptable; and, doubtless, Antoine's ruthless dedication rather destroyed the pleasure that the amateurs took in playing at theatre.

The morning after the first performance, Antoine wrote of his *Théâtre Libre* and his hope that it would find a place among the theatres of Paris.[29] A month later, he had the attention of artistic and literary Paris for his second bill, a play by the poet–critic Bergerat and an "ultra-naturalistic" afterpiece by Métenier.[30] Three weeks later, he quit the Gas Company: "I have burned my boats. Here I am, then, smack in the middle of the great adventure!"[31]

Life and Death of the Théâtre Libre

Antoine's creation lasted seven years under his leadership. At the end of that time, it was deeply in debt, and he decided to leave it, taking responsibility for the debts. In those seven years, the Théâtre Libre never had a permanent house of its own, never was financially successful, never ran its plays for more than a few nights (although it occasionally did revivals and tours), and was never a public theatre, surviving always by subscription. Its greatest impact was not from stage to audience, but rather from stage to media to audience. Relatively few people saw the Théâtre Libre, but *everybody* heard about it.

Antoine saw the Meininger in 1888 in Brussels; he was dazzled. The crowd scenes especially impressed him, as did actors who played with their backs to the audience. On the other hand, he did not like their "garish and oddly designed settings," their "abuse of practical [i.e., usable] elements, cramming them in everywhere," their "foolishly rich" costumes, and the "epic naiveté [of their] lighting effects." He had the realist's eye for detail: "All the mountaineers had the white hands and clean knees that we associate with the Opéra Comique." There was a great deal for Antoine to learn from the Meininger, however: "The actors are strictly forbidden to go outside the [proscenium] frame . . . and to look into the house, which is kept in darkness. . . . Why don't we try to appropriate what is good among [these things]?"[32]

He did so.

Antoine sought out fresh new French works, old, neglected ones, and a few foreign ones, among which were Ibsen's *Ghosts* and *The Wild Duck*, August Strindberg's *Miss Julie*, Giovanni Verga's *Cavalleria Rusticana*, and Gerhart Hauptmann's *The Weavers* and *The Assumption of Hannele Mattern*. In introducing these then-shocking foreign masterpieces to the French theatre, Antoine was as surely altering the traditional repertory as when he staged new French works by Henry Becque, Jean Jullien, or Eugène Brieux.

By 1894, he wrote, "I lack the material strength to continue. . . . I lack even a hint that new efforts would be useful, for young dramatists are no longer appearing. The upcoming generation has made its contribution. . . . From now on, we would be struggling in a vacuum."[33]

The Accomplishment of the Théâtre Libre

Antoine's most enthusiastic supporters compare his importance to that of Molière and Diderot. Even without granting him such eminence, one must acknowledge the following:

1. *Improvement of the repertory.*

2. *The example of an art theatre.* Eclectic programs, noncommercial structure, and dedication to quality gave a model to theatre all over Europe and the United States.

3. *Popularization of a realistic acting style.* "Here, I believe, are the actors we have needed for a long time," Zola is supposed to have said of the Théâtre Libre.[34] When a number of the plays that had been premiered at the Théâtre Libre failed in commercial productions, Antoine saw that one reason was the wrongness of the boulevard acting style:

> *One cannot play works based on observation . . . as one would play the traditional repertoire, or comedies based on the imagination* [our italics]. A work which is *true* must be played *truly*, just as a classic play should above all be *recited*. . . . The characters [in realistic plays] have voices like ours; their language is that of our own daily life, with its elisions and familiar turns, and not the rhetoric and noble style of our classics.[35]

4. *Creation of a realistic directorial style.* As his comments on the Meininger show, Antoine had a keen visual sense. He seems to have been most deeply interested in:

a. *"Fourth-wall" realism,* that is, the isolation of the event by the proscenium arch. It is said that for at least some of his productions, Antoine worked out the architecture of an entire building, placed the ground-plan of the

FIGURE 15.13
Realism at the Théâtre Antoine: *Monsieur Vernet* (1903). [From *Le Théâtre.*]

room he would use within it, and then decided from what direction the audience would look in. The term, a "fourth wall, opaque to the actors and transparent to the audience", was applied to his work by Jean Jullien but was an older idea dating to Diderot.

b. *The relationship of environment to action.* Antoine understood the effect on voice (and, by implication on movement) of real spaces, both in size and in symbolism.

c. *The use of real objects and abundant detail.*

d. *Observation as the basis of theatre.* He understood clearly what we would now call blocking, ground plans and actor coaching, with life as the standard. His casting was done on this basis, too—not by type or reputation, but by suitability, as suitability is a product of observation.

e. *Control of production.* Like Georg II and Chronegk, and like the German *régisseurs* before them, Antoine reached instinctively for control. It was his control that made the audacity and freshness of the Théâtre Libre possi-

ble—a complete vision that unified new text, acting, and production.

From 1897 to 1905, Antoine ran the Théâtre Antoine in Paris; from 1906 until 1916, he was head of the state theatre at the Odéon. At the latter house, he experimented with productions of French classics in their historical styles as William Poel had experimented with English ones. He continued as a major figure in French theatre until his death; however, his most immediate influence was on theatres in other major cities. These included:

1. The Freie Bühne of Berlin (1889), led by Otto Brahm, who in 1894 became the director of the prestigious Deutsches Theater; Brahm pioneered German production of realistic and naturalistic plays at both theatres, was an important realistic director, and encouraged the theatre work of Max Reinhardt.

2. The Volksbühne, Berlin, 1890, associated with the German socialist and union movements; interrupted by the Nazis but still vigorous.

3. The Independent Theatre, London (1891–1897), headed by Jacob Grein; very short runs, on the Théâtre Libre model, of plays by Shaw, Ibsen, and other realists and naturalists.

4. Le Théâtre d'Art, Paris (1891), headed by A.-M. Lugné-Poë, briefly an actor with Antoine; an art theatre interested in nonrealistic works as the Théâtre de l'Ouevre (1893).

5. The Teatre Independent, Barcelona (1896).

6. The Moscow Art Theatre, Moscow (1898).

A Duo and the Moscow Art Theatre (1897–present)

There is a considerable problem of evidence in dealing with the third of these important realistic theatres. Although the evidence is recent and some of the recorders of it are still alive, it is not fully reliable for at least two reasons: first, the principals wrote their accounts long after many of the events and at a time (shortly after the Russian Revolution) when their survival was possibly at issue; and second, the events and the records were and are prisoners of a repressive political and social climate whose distortion of history is notorious. In dealing with the Moscow Art Theatre, we are dealing with the Russia of both the revolution and the Stalinist purges, and we cannot hope for objective records of it.

In 1897, we are told, two Russian theatre men held what has become a legendary meeting. Vladimir Nemirovich-Danchenko (1858–1943) was a playwright, director, and teacher. Konstantin Sergeyivich Alexeiv (stage name, Konstantin Stanislavski; 1863–1938) was an amateur actor and director, "before everything . . . an amateur, i.e., one who did not occupy any kind of position in the theatrical service and was not connected with any theatre."[36] Nemirovich-Danchenko was teaching acting at the Philharmonic Institute in Moscow; Stanislavski was the leader and teacher of the Society of Art and Literature, a theatre of fairly well-to-do amateurs in Moscow. The meeting of these two men celebrated the coming together of two creative minds with the same goal: the reforming of

FIGURE 15.14

Leading Figures in European Realism Other Than Playwrights (1850–1900)

Name	Dates	Function
Georg II, Duke of Saxe-Meiningen	1826–1914	Producer, director, and designer
Ludwig Chronegk	1837–1891	Director
Henry Irving	1838–1905	Actor–manager and director
Marie Wilton	1839–1921	Actress and producer } "drawing-room
Squire Bancroft	1841–1926	Actor–manager } realism"
William Archer	1856–1924	Critic
Otto Brahm	1856–1912	Director
George Bernard Shaw	1856–1950	Critic (also dramatist)
Eleonora Duse	1858–1924	Actress
André Antoine	1858–1943	Director and producer
Viktor Simov	1858–1935	Designer (Moscow Art Theatre)
Vladimir Nemirovich-Danchenko	1859–1943	Director and producer
Elizabeth Robins	1862–1952	Actress, proponent of Ibsen in England
Annie E. F. Horniman	1860–1937	Financial supporter
Jacob Grein	1862–1935	Director and producer
Konstantin Stanislavski	1863–1938	Director and producer
Firmin Gémier	1865–1933	Actor and director

Russian theatre. The result—most of it settled in that first long meeting—was the Moscow Art Theatre.

The individual qualities of the two men were important:

Nemirovich-Danchenko

Nemirovich-Danchenko had had some success as a playwright and had won a prestigious Russian prize. As a teacher of acting, he was working with young students who did not yet have what he saw as the vices of commercial acting. He was a friendly rival of the playwright Anton Chekhov and appears to have understood better than anyone else the unique genius of Chekhov.

Stanislavski

Owner of a factory, Stanislavski had independent means and was solidly of the bourgeoisie. An indulgent father had provided him, as a child, with a small theatre in their house; he had studied acting briefly and had done considerable acting in amateur groups and a little with commercial companies (hence the stage name). Widely traveled, cultured, and enormously talented, he had a strong ego and a strong commitment to theatre as art.

The Russian Theatre in the Nineteenth Century

The Russian theatre of the end of the nineteenth century was somewhat different from that of the rest of Europe.

Commercialism. In Moscow and St. Petersburg, at least, the actors were professionals. Concepts of the art of theatre differed widely and had little effect on the conduct of theatres. A form of star system prevailed, with all its drawbacks, stressing imitation in actor training, inhibiting creative rehearsals, and making stage direction subordinate to star performing. The theatres still used stock settings and the actors still supplied many costumes.

Censorship. The theatre was subject to at least three kinds of censorship in Moscow: that of the church, that of the imperial government, and that of the city. Any of the three could close a play.

Russian Theatrical Tradition. The Russian tradition shared that of western Europe, but it had its own vigorous kind of prerealism, like Nikolai Gogol's *The Inspector General* (1836), Leo Tolstoy's *The Power of Darkness* (1886), and Alexander Ostrovski's *The Storm* (1860). The great mid-nineteenth-century actor Mikhail Shchepkin (1788–1863) had counseled that life was the great teacher of the actor. Both the Russian upper classes and the Russian intelligentsia looked to the West for artistic authority, however, and the native tradition was much affected by the foreign one.

Reformist Beginnings of the Moscow Art Theatre

"The working out of a plan in all its details was not difficult," Nemirovich-Danchenko wrote in the early 1920s, "because the organized forms in the old theatre had grown decrepit to such a degree that they seemed to implore change to new forms."[37] In his recollection of that plan, those "new forms" included:

1. Art must rule bureaucracy and business: "The office should yield . . . to the stage."

2. "Every play must have its own setting."

3. The performance must be given all courtesy by both audience and actors: no noise backstage, no noisy late arrivals.

4. Production preparation, especially rehearsals, must be changed. The two men took their examples from their own mode of work: preliminary discussions of the play among director and actors (itself an innovation in Russia), the frequent repetition of even small bits of scenes, the rejection of binding schedules and routine, and an adequate number of rehearsals, including dress rehearsals. "The first dress rehearsal in the history of the Russian theatre had

taken place only three years before," Nemirovich-Danchenko wrote.

5. The *régisseur* would control rehearsals and the production. Stanislavski had seen the Meininger and he had watched its rehearsals (under Chronegk, not Georg II), and he believed in the dictatorial director who worked by what his colleague would later call "martial law."

6. The repertory must be serious and artistic. This reform did not mean an immediate espousal of realism or any other style. Nemirovich-Danchenko knew what was happening in Russian drama. Stanislavski had had considerable experience with the traditional drama and with the new European drama. One must see the similarity to Antoine: here was no obsession with one style, but a commitment to art of several styles.

The History of the Moscow Art Theatre

It would be a year before the new theatre actually performed. Money had to be raised, actors chosen (mostly from the two founders' circles), and hundreds of details worked out. Stanislavski had his responsibilities at his factory and also spent part of the winter in Nice. Nemirovich-Danchenko continued to teach. The following summer, they gathered their company at a country place and began the rehearsals that would change the Russian idea of theatre.

The company announced a repertory to include Tolstoy's *Czar Fyodor* (formerly prohibited by the censor), *The Merchant of Venice,* Ibsen's *Hedda Gabler,* Hauptmann's *Hannele Mattern,* and Chekhov's *The Seagull.* (A little later, they tried to add Oscar Wilde's *Salome* and Lord Byron's *Cain* and were turned down by the censor.) The first season of the company, now called the Moscow Art Theatre (or the Moscow Accessible Art Theatre, according to some accounts, because it was meant to be accessible to all classes, but this may be a postrevolutionary editing of history), was mixed until they per-

formed Anton Chekhov's *The Seagull,* with whose performance they found their identity and their destiny.

After that first season (1899), the theatre's history can be broken into the three following periods.

Beginning to ca. 1906. According to Stanislavski's *My Life in Art,* he and the theatre reached a crisis after eight seasons (not unlike the Théâtre Libre). The theatre was more successful than they had dared to expect: they had had a stunning audience response to some productions; their financial arrangements had been reorganized; and they had moved into a newly refurbished, permanent home (which is still the Moscow Art Theatre's stage). Chekhov had died in 1904, but his plays were the heart of the repertory, and a seagull was now their symbol. The theatre had toured internationally and had discovered new Russian dramatists, of whom Maksim Gorki and his play *The Lower Depths* (1902), was most significant.

Stanislavski, however, was dissatisfied. Writing in 1921, when he had the benefit of hindsight, he said that he had come to the theatre in the autumn of 1906 determined to seek new answers to the problems of acting. The result—monumental for the Moscow Art Theatre and Western acting—was his lifelong search for what has come to be called the *Stanislavski System.* In a sense, what marks this first period in the theatre's history was actually an internal realization by Stanislavski; the theatre's repertory and its practice did not change markedly, although the nature of its acting evidently did.

From ca. 1906 to World War II. Stanislavski died in 1938, Nemirovich-Danchenko in 1943. Despite being "two bears in one den," as one put it, they successfully ran the theatre together for forty years, sometimes codirecting, sometimes taking over for each other. With their deaths, the links with the prerevolutionary origins of the Moscow Art Theatre were lost.

FIGURE 15.15

The early Moscow Art Theatre in Gorki's *Lower Depths* (1902) with Stanislavski on the table. [From Sayler, *Series.*]

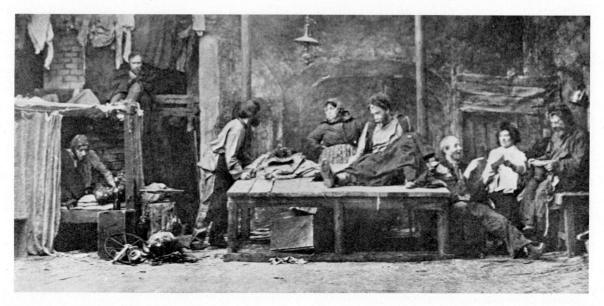

In those crucial years between 1906 and 1943, the theatre had had to cope with the replacement of one despotism by another and the artistic upheaval that culminated in socialist realism. We do not know what compromises the two directors had to make, nor what responses they made in dealing with the new censorship after they had learned to deal with the old, but we do know that the following happened:

1. The number of new productions per year (normally four) declined during the revolutionary years and then went up again.

2. The theatre was forced to open its doors to a mass audience when Lenin declared that art was an educational weapon of the revolution; oddly, the theatre responded by producing Byron's *Cain* for this mass audience.[38]

3. Both Stanislavski and Nemirovich-Danchenko published autobiographies in the early 1920s, perhaps as defensive justifications of their work, which was seen by many as reactionary and bourgeois.

4. Russian theatre was in a ferment in the 1920s. Both Stanislavski's and Nemirovich-Danchenko's autobiographies are aggressively critical of these experiments as untheatrical and deviant. Clearly, they felt that they were in a battle.

5. The Moscow Art Theatre produced its first modern works since the revolution with Mikhail Bulgakov's *Days of the Turbins* (1926) and Vsevolod Ivanov's *Armored Train 14–69* (1927).

6. Actors like Richard Boleslavsky, Maria Ouspenskaya, and Mikhail Chekhov emigrated, teaching Stanislavskian acting and becoming international voices for the Moscow Art Theatre.

7. The theatre made tours in the early 1920s, including one to America. They gave focus to the sentimental politics of the 1920s and 1930s, especially in the United States, which came to love all things Russian until the Hitler–Stalin pact of 1939.

After 1930, the Moscow Art Theatre began to emerge as the international exponent of Russian theatre. On the one hand, it was the principal bridge to the old drama and to classic European drama. (Stanislavski's last production, unfinished at his death, was Molière's *Tartuffe*.) On the other hand, it managed to suit the modern demands of socialist realism. The two directors achieved these two, possibly contradictory, successes through dedication, luck, and guile. Stanislavski's acting system, now perfected, was no small contributor, for it was perfectly tuned to realistic drama, such as plays by Chekhov and Gorki. The Stanislavski system was rational and even "scientific," at least on paper, and it was in accord with the official Soviet psychology of the time.

With socialist realism, the experimental forms of the 1920s came to be seen as decadent. During Stalin's purges, some rival theatre people disappeared. The Moscow Art Theatre survived.

From World War II to the Present. "The Art Theatre depended on its two founders as children depend on strict but loving parents. Deprived of them, the offspring felt lost. . . . Today [1962], it is run by a colloquium, or council of ten people."[39] It appears that this contemporary Moscow Art Theatre is a victim of its history, even in danger of becoming "the sort of 'academic' theatre that the Comédie Française has until recently been in France, a monument to tradition, a museum that contains some of the nation's most valued art treasures."[40] Nonetheless, the Art Theatre has enormous artistry, expressed particularly in its older actors, "ripe in years, robust as oaks, beaming in their beards and their supreme authority. . . . The power and the glory of the Soviet theatre resides in its older actors, who are by far the finest I have ever seen."[41] Thus, the Moscow Art Theatre continues today as one of the world's great theatres, with Stanislavski's acting system, although in a form somewhat different from the one best known in the United States.[42] If, in the eyes of more extreme Marxist critics, it is "bourgeois," it is so because the founders were men of their time and their class, and because the realism that they understood was "bourgeois."

Afterimage: The Group Theatre

The Moscow Art Theatre had one conscious imitator in the United States. The Group Theatre, founded in 1931, featured a group of young realists for a decade. These people became leaders of the American theatre from World War II through the early 1960s; they included the directors Elia Kazan and Harold Clurman; the actors Morris Carnovsky, Luther and Stella Adler, Lee J. Cobb, Sanford Meisner, and Lee Strasberg; the director–producer Cheryl Crawford; and the playwrights John Howard Lawson and Clifford Odets. Serious about their art, committed to a realism of ideas in the tradition of Ibsen, and enthusiastic about Stanislavskian acting, they became the makers of American post–World War II theatre.

The Realistic Theatre

The remarkable vigor of realism in the theatre since about 1850 can be followed along several tracks:

1. A new drama and new dramatists.
2. The union of illusionism and new technology.
3. Changes in scenery.
4. New systems of acting.
5. The emergence of the director.

New Drama and New Dramatists

Most obviously identified with Henrik Ibsen, new realistic drama was so offensive to many censors and moralists that it had to be staged in private (independent) theatres. It had precedents in some elements of romanticism and in plays that were called realistic before the appearance of Ibsen. In fact, what distinguished

FIGURE 15.16

Early gentlemanly melodrama (mid–1850s), using many of the devices of realism: the box set and detailed set dressing. [Authors' collection.]

the censorable plays of Ibsen and others was not a sudden leap in their degree of realism, but their binding of the visual truthfulness of realism with a truthfulness of language and character, as well as their unrelenting treatment of forbidden subjects. The pre-Ibsen realists had been willing to trivialize their plays by letting their resolutions turn on *coups de théâtre*, mere tricks, coincidences, or clever twists. Ibsen and those who followed him refused this easy way out.

A picture of this pre-Ibsen realism in London can be gained from an article of 1884:

> I may be permitted to attempt a brief sketch of the rise and progress of Realism upon the London stage. The late Mister Planché [James Robinson Planché, costume antiquarian] seems to have been the first. . . . Mister Phelps [Samuel Phelps, actor–manager] did much. . . .

Charles Kean followed on the same track, but he went too far. . . .

> After a while a new prophet arose whose original talent wrought a lasting change on the face of affairs. Hitherto Realism had taken the form of production from [antiquarianism]. . . . Mister [Thomas W.] Robertson founded a school of dramatic entertainment which at first sight threatened disaster to the stage. . . . At the little Prince of Wales's Miss Marie Wilton produced a comedy [of Robertson's] called *Society*. . . . Ordinary gentlemen and ladies strolled within Grosvenor Square railings, and talked platitudes. Bohemianism stole from its upper floor in Maiden Lane and flaunted before the astonished Upper Ten. . . . This was the realism of to-day in all its minute and trivial detail. "We don't go to the theatre to see what is to be seen in any drawing-room," sneered the old Playgoer.

To many the "Teacup and Saucer Drama,"

as it was in derision styled, seemed the acme of puerility. . . . Mister Robertson did for the modern stage what Mister Ruskin did for pictorial art. His plays were so slight and small (I except *Caste,* which was in its way a masterpiece), of such gossamer-tissue, that a breath of unreality would have blown the fabric to the winds. Without the tricks of fashion, the cigarette-cases, the display of the latest costumes, his plays would have fallen to pieces out of sheer feebleness and want of stamina. . . . Necessity taught the [actors] that the performers in a play of modern life should behave exactly as well-bred ladies and gentlemen ordinarily behave, and that their surroundings must be exactly those of the boudoir or smoking-room.

Mister [Dion] Boucicault [next] produced a play—though play, indeed, it can scarcely be called—in which a real cab and a real fire-engine performed the two principal parts. Nothing could be more mean than the whole affair, but it paid. Everyone ran to see the real hansom driven by a real licensed driver, drawn by a real cab-horse with real broken knees. That which might any day be seen in the street became a marvel. . . .

Others imitated Boucicault and produced [the play of the slums]. . . .

The Old Play-goer looked on and grumbled; the modern lover of the stage groaned in unison. Things were really going to the dogs.[43]

This account is accurate in its general outlines for much of the theatre of the time. It touches on three kinds of pre-Ibsen, realistic drama:

1. The drawing-room play, with upper-class or higher setting, fashionable characters, fashionable costumes, and fashionable problems.

2. The play of city life, sometimes of slum life, as seen from above. In working-class theatres, these appeared as crime plays.[44]

3. Gentlemanly melodrama, acted in the best theatres by top actors. In a play like *The Bells* (1871), in which Henry Irving made his first great success, artistic skill was given to plays that were more carefully written than earlier romantic melodrama, but that had no more idea. (Another version of *The Bells* was popular on the Continent and was played by Stanislavski in 1896.)

To those forms mentioned in the article we may add a fourth:

4. The working-class play, or the "factory play." Plays with titles like *The Factory Lad* had been staged in England since the 1830s. They very occasionally touched a raw nerve by dealing with working conditions and unionism; however, a combination of censorship, managerial caution, and the playwrights' insecurity caused few such plays to be staged, even in working-class theatres. By the time they might have been acceptable, it appears that their subjects had been absorbed into plays about city life.[45]

It was the Ibsenite realists' great achievement to make drama an effective vehicle for idea. Above all, it was, to be sure, *idea* that was feared by those who would censor, but the independence of the theatres that first staged the plays weakened that "absolute power [of the censor] that had prevented the theatre [from] dealing seriously with sex, religion and politics."[46] By the mid-1890s, the European theatre was opening to these new, tough-minded realistic plays in which idea was so important, and the realistic drama quickly reached its fulfillment.

The outstanding playwrights of the new drama included the following.

Henrik Ibsen (1826–1906)

Born into a lower-class family in a small Norwegian town, Ibsen grew up in an atmosphere that appears to have been stultifying in almost every way. He left home early, and his life was a series of self-imposed exiles. Early plays like *Catalina* (1848) brought him a number of theatrical jobs in Bergen and Oslo, where he worked on scores of productions in stage management and production. His plays of this period were large-scale historical dramas, some based on Scandinavian history and the sagas—works well within the late romantic tradition. In the early

FIGURE 15.17
Leading Playwrights of Realism (1850–1960)

Name	Dates	Language	Example
Precursors			
Émile Augier	1820–1889	Fr.	*Olympia's Marriage*, 1855
Dion Boucicault	1820–1890	Eng.	*The Poor of New York*, 1857
Alexander Ostrovski	1823–1886	Russ.	*The Storm*, 1859
Leo Tolstoy	1828–1910	Russ.	*The Power of Darkness*, 1888
Victorien Sardou	1831–1908	Fr.	*A Scrap of Paper*, 1860
Thomas W. Robertson	1829–1871	Eng.	*Caste*, 1867
James A. Herne	1839–1901	Eng. (Am.)	*Margaret Fleming*, 1890
Steele Mackaye	1842–1894	Eng. (Am.)	*Hazel Kirke*, 1880
Bronson Howard	1842–1908	Eng. (Am.)	*Shenandoah*, 1888
Henry Arthur Jones	1851–1929	Eng.	*Michael and His Lost Angel*, 1895
Arthur Wing Pinero	1855–1934	Eng.	*The Second Mrs. Tanqueray*, 1893
William Vaughn Moody	1869–1910	Eng. (Am.)	*The Great Divide*, 1906
Realists			
Henrik Ibsen	1828–1906	Nor.	*A Doll's House*, 1879
Bjornstjerne Bjornson	1832–1910	Nor.	*En Handske*, 1883
Henry Becque	1837–1899	Fr.	*The Vultures*, 1882
Giovanni Verga	1840–1922	Ital.	*Rustic Chivalry*, 1884
Émile Zola	1840–1902	Fr.	*Thérèse Raquin*, 1873
August Strindberg	1849–1912	Swe.	*Miss Julie*, 1888
George Bernard Shaw	1856–1950	Eng.	*Man and Superman*, 1903
Eugène Brieux	1858–1932	Fr.	*Damaged Goods*, 1902
Anton Chekhov	1860–1904	Russ.	*The Seagull*, 1896
Gerhardt Hauptmann	1862–1946	Ger.	*The Weavers*. 1893
Arthur Schnitzler	1862–1931	Ger.	*La Ronde*, 1900
John Galsworthy	1867–1933	Eng.	*Strife*, 1909
Maksim Gorki	1868–1936	Russ.	*The Lower Depths*, 1902
John Millington Synge	1871–1909	Eng. (Ir.)	*The Playboy of the Western World*, 1907
Somerset Maugham	1874–1965	Eng.	*Our Betters*, 1917
Sean O'Casey	1880–1964	Eng. (Ir.)	*Shadow of a Gunman*, 1923
Henry Bernstein	1876–1953	Fr.	*The Claw*, 1906
Susan Glaspell	1882–1904	Eng. (Am.)	*Alison's House*, 1930
Eugene O'Neill	1888–1953	Eng. (Am.)	*Anna Christie*, 1921
Sidney Howard	1891–1939	Eng. (Am.)	*They Knew What They Wanted*, 1924
Mikhail Bulgakov	1891–1940	Russ.	*The Days of the Turbins*, 1926
Vsevolod Vishnevski	1900–1951	Russ.	*The Optimistic Tragedy*, 1934
Paul Vincent Carroll	1900–1968	Eng. (Ir.)	*Shadow and Substance*, 1937
Lillian Hellman	1905–	Eng. (Am.)	*The Little Foxes*, 1939
Clifford Odets	1906–1963	Eng. (Am.)	*Golden Boy*, 1937
Sidney Kingsley	1906–	Eng. (Am.)	*Dead End*, 1935
Tennessee Williams	1911–1983	Eng. (Am.)	*A Streetcar Named Desire*, 1947
William Inge	1913–1973	Eng. (Am.)	*Come Back, Little Sheba*, 1949
Arthur Miller	1915–	Eng. (Am.)	*Death of a Salesman*, 1949
Brendan Behan	1923–1964	Eng. (Ir.)	*The Hostage*, 1958
Robert Bolt	1924–	Eng.	*Flowering Cherry*, 1958
John Osborne	1929–	Eng.	*Look Back in Anger*, 1956
Arnold Wesker	1932–	Eng.	*Roots*, 1959
Lorraine Hansberry	1930–1965	Eng. (Am.)	*A Raisin in the Sun*, 1959

1860s, he left Norway altogether, spending the next quarter century in Italy and Germany. Two plays of the mid-1860s—*Brand* and *Peer Gynt*—were highly important, and along with *Emperor and Galilean* (1876) they cemented Ibsen's reputation but were hardly revolutionary. It was not until he was fifty that Ibsen produced the works that changed the theatre: *Pillars of Society* (1877), *A Doll's House* (1879), and *Ghosts* (1881). They seemed unbearably harsh to many theatregoers; their subjects were sometimes bitterly offensive (the effects of syphilis in *Ghosts*, for example), their treatment of the clergy impious, their uncompromising endings almost terrifying. Nora's final exit in *A Doll's House*, it was said, was the closing of a door that was "heard all over Europe." The work poured from Ibsen: *An Enemy of the People* (1882); *The Wild Duck* (1884); *Rosmersholm* (1886); *Hedda Gabler* (1890); and *The Master Builder* (1892). "Ibsenism" became as immediate and passionate a cause as "Wagnerism" had been. By the turn of the century, Ibsen's plays had been performed in most major Western capitals, and they were already being imitated—or the liberating effects of their

FIGURE 15.18

Ibsen's *Rosmersholm*, with the great Italian actress Eleonora Duse at the National Theatre of Christiana (1906). [From *Le Théâtre*.]

presence were being celebrated—by other writers. Ibsen's Scandinavian middle class proved to be international in its concerns: greed, repression, sexism, love and the lack of it, small-mindedness, ambition, and spiritual emptiness. Ibsen's form, although hardly new, became the form of drama for the next fifty years: three acts, tightly knit plots, prosaic language, and resonance achieved through rare symbols or his perception of resonant situations.

August Strindberg (1849–1912)

Born and raised in Sweden in a lower-middle-class family, Strindberg turned early to writing as a profession. His early plays, like Ibsen's, included historical dramas; he also published novels and stories. Strindberg's life swung between periods of relative stability and periods of great instability, and he was institutionalized for some time. Extreme paranoia marked his later life. He was married several times. His psychological concerns, including his misogyny, showed in his plays; although he was a realist in some, he was also often a symbolic dramatist of the inner, rather than the outer, world. The harrowing *The Father* (1887) and the sexually explicit *Miss Julie* (1888) are outstanding realist plays; the preface to the latter is an important document in the history of realist (some would say naturalist) staging. In his later life, Strindberg turned to mysticism, and his late plays are elliptical, symbolic, and often mysterious: *A Dream Play* (1902), for example, and the "chamber plays," which included *The Ghost Sonata* (1907).

George Bernard Shaw (1856–1950)

Like Ibsen, Shaw was a late bloomer, coming to his full power as a dramatist in his late forties. Born in Dublin, Ireland, he moved with his mother to London when he was sixteen. He worked for a time as a book and music critic, then as a dramatic critic, while writing novels that were monumentally unsuccessful. A dedicated Socialist, he helped to found the Fabian Society. In 1891, he published his long essay on

Ibsen and realism, *The Quintessence of Ibsenism;* thereafter he began to write realistic plays of his own, from *Widower's Houses* in 1892 to a final volume of burlesques in 1950. In between, he produced the most significant English comedies of his time, as well as some of the most influential plays of ideas, from the light-hearted *Arms and the Man* (1894) through *Man and Superman* (1903), *Major Barbara* (1905), *Pygmalion* (1912), *Heartbreak House* (1917), and *Saint Joan* (1923). His lengthy prefaces and his philosophical five-play set, *Back to Methusaleh* (1921) made him important as a thinker as well as a playwright. He was awarded the Nobel Prize in 1925. Essayist, polemicist, lecturer, director, playwright, he was quintessentially a late-nineteenth-century giant, believing in progress, reason, enlightened socialism, and himself. It must be pointed out that Shaw was above all a writer of comedy; although he was no less a realist than others, he may seem so, for his characters are often witty and remarkably articulate (although they represent the articulate English at a period when talk was most prized). The gloomy seriousness of Ibsen's or Strindberg's characters may seem more "real" than Shaw's characters' comedy, but the difference is one between comedy and serious drama, not between realism and another style.

Anton Chekhov (1860–1904)

Grandchild of a serf, Chekhov was raised as the son of a shopkeeper. His father's business failure threw him early on his own resources. Even while a medical student, he earned money as a writer, mostly of short humorous pieces. A practicing physician for years, he was himself a victim of tuberculosis. His first long play, *Ivanov,* was staged in 1887, but his literary reputation depended largely on his stories. In 1896, *The Seagull* was staged unsuccessfully in St. Petersburg, and Chekhov vowed to write no more plays; however, in 1898 the same work was produced by the Moscow Art Theatre and was a

FIGURE 15.19

Chekhov's *Three Sisters* in its original production at the Moscow Art Theatre, 1901. [From Sayler, *Series.*]

success. Thereafter, Chekhov's name was linked with the Art Theatre's and further plays were staged successfully: *Uncle Vanya* in 1899, *The Three Sisters* in 1901, and *The Cherry Orchard* in 1904, the year of his death. Chekhov's realism, a little like Shaw's, does not neatly fit a mold (Shaw called his *Heartbreak House* a "fantasia in the Russian manner" for its affinity with *The Cherry Orchard*). Chekhov was neither so witty nor so ideological as Shaw, and his realism embraced symbolic elements. His work was often funny, and he differed with Stanislavski over the seriousness of his plays, especially *The Cherry Orchard*. Ibsen's causality and tightness of plot are missing from Chekhov, and much of his realism is psychological and social. The influence of the impressionists (see Chapter 17) is clear, so his is very much a reactive realism.

Gerhardt Hauptmann (1862–1946)

Born and raised in Silesia, Hauptmann knew well the peasants and workers, as well as the industrial conditions he sometimes wrote about. His best-known naturalistic play, *The Weavers* (1892), was first produced by Brahm, then by Antoine, then by the Volkesbühne, and then all over Europe. It was very unlike Ibsen: it had a group protagonist (the Silesian weavers), a looser, less Scribean plot, and a deep concern about a mass of victims of society. Much of Hauptmann's other work, however, was far from naturalistic, including *The Assumption of Hannele Mattern* (1894) and *The Sunken Bell* (1896). Hauptmann was awarded the Nobel Prize in 1912.

The realistic masters discussed above had many followers. As is so often the case with artistic innovation, those at the first crest seem the greatest; those who follow often perfect details and make modifications but do not always seem as monumental. In the case of realism, a period of consolidation, of acceptance, and of cooption by the commercial theatre followed. By 1920, realism was virtually the new establishment (except in Russia), against which other movements reacted. The push and pull of several styles in the highly eclectic period 1920–1960 brought the emergence of a new group of realists.

Eugene O'Neill (1888–1953)

The son of a neoromantic star, O'Neill became associated early with the Provincetown Playhouse (one of the "little theatres" of the American movement that imitated the independent theatres of Europe around World War I) and then with the Theatre Guild. Until World War II, O'Neill seemed to tower over American drama, not least because of his wide range of styles and his profound—some would say heavy-handed—seriousness. His realistic plays include *Anna Christie* (1921), *Desire Under the Elms* (1924), *Moon for the Misbegotten* (1943), *The Iceman Cometh* (1946), and the posthumously produced *A Touch of the Poet* and *Long Day's Journey into Night*. O'Neill's childhood and much of his later life were bitter and wretched, and their darkness touched many of the realistic plays. Many of his domestic scenes share Strindberg's ferocity. Utterly lacking in Shaw's wit, Chekhov's compassion or Ibsen's objectivity, O'Neill nonetheless wrote plays that are overpowering in their battering, drawn-out mercilessness. O'Neill won the Nobel Prize in 1936, although not solely for his realistic work.

Mikhail Bulgakov (1891–1940)

A child of the middle class, Bulgakov saw his world torn apart by the Russian Revolution of 1917. He survived rather as Chekhov had, as a "feuilletonist," or writer of ephemeral pieces, and then as a novelist. He adapted *The White Guard* as *The Days of the Turbins,* staged at the Moscow Art Theatre in 1926, the first "modern" play to be done there since the revolution. The play was later withdrawn, probably for political reasons (it was not markedly pro-Bolshevik) and then restored, becoming finally a casualty of World War II when the sets were destroyed by bombs. Bulgakov became a *Dramaturg* at the Moscow Art Theatre, where he was responsible for the adaptation of Gogol's *Dead Souls*; in the early 1930s, he went to the Bolshoi. His forceful play about Molière, *The Cabal of Hypocrites* (1936), was not satisfactory to the censors.

One of Bulgakov's last works, the *Theatrical Novel*, was not published until the 1960s and appeared in English as *Black Snow* (1970); it is a satire on Stanislavski, the Art Theatre, and the corrupt world of Moscow artists. Bulgakov was never a socialist realist; like many writers faced with severe censorship, he was often not a realist at all. However, two of his plays identify him as a master in the later mutation of the style. He remains that rarity, a realistic Soviet playwright who transcended Soviet aesthetics.

Arthur Miller (1915–   )

An American who came of age in the Great Depression, Miller has combined the populists' interest in the "little man" with an Ibsenite clarity of vision that has kept him from being sentimental. His first successful realistic play was *All My Sons* (1947); it was followed by the remarkable *Death of a Salesman* in 1949. Later realistic plays included *A View from the Bridge* (1955), *Incident at Vichy* (1964), and *The Price* (1968). Many critics consider *Death of a Salesman* the greatest of American serious plays. It is a striking example of latter-day American realism as it adapted to expressionism. Its characterizations and most of its dialogue and behavior are realistic and have provided fertile material for the realistic actor and director, but the scene arrangement is non-causal and the settings are partial and symbolic. Other Miller plays are closer to those of Ibsen; he adapted *An Enemy of the People*, although his version lacks Ibsen's comic edge.

Tennessee Williams (1914–1983)

Born and raised in the American South, Williams has set most of his plays there. His first success was *The Glass Menagerie* (1945), another play that shows realism's shift toward symbolism and impressionism and away from three-act structure. Direct audience address and non-realistic aspects of staging move the play away

from nineteenth-century realism, as well. *A Streetcar Named Desire* (1947) made Williams both famous and notorious, its treatment of sex then being shocking to some. *Cat on a Hot Tin Roof* (1954), *Sweet Bird of Youth* (1959), and *Night of the Iguana* (1962) followed, with other plays. Williams' are less plays of ideas than of psychology, and their plots are less dependent on causally linked actions than on the interplay of psyches. Unlike Miller's, Williams' characters are psychological rather than social victims. His are "loser's stories," often, and their effect is one of pathos.

John Osborne (1926–   )

An Englishman who grew up during World War II and its aftermath, Osborne was one of the leaders of the "Angry Young Men" of the 1950s. England's abrupt decline from world power caused many difficult reappraisals. A serious writer with serious things to say, Osborne turned to hard-edged realism, just as some English painters turned to "kitchen-sink" painting, as if realism (as Shaw had suggested a generation earlier) could cleanse an art of decadence. With *Look Back in Anger* (1956), Osborne thrust a new naturalism under English noses—a brutally anti-Establishment tone, social honesty, and sometimes sordid actions. He put the frustrations of a generation on the stage. Later plays like *Inadmissible Evidence* (1964) extended his reputation, but, with some other English playwrights, he moved to a more Brechtian style later. Osborne represents a second wave of English realism.

Realism continues to be a major style in the commercial theatre of England and America, and rather less so in France and Scandinavia; it has never seemed of dominant interest in Spain or Italy, and as one moves eastward, its grip seems to weaken—except, of course, in Russia. The style is everywhere in television and commercial film. It is embedded in the consciousness of much of the theatre education establishment, perhaps most of all in acting and directing.

Many contemporary theatre people discount it, but it has shown continued attraction for new movements like the black arts movement of the 1960s and 1970s, and it may prove true that groups seeking their own self-image will find it most readily in realism. It should not be surprising if other emerging minorities find fresh vigor in the style.

The Union of Illusionism and Technology

Realism is the most recent and most literal stage of illusionism. It is so in part because of its own commitment to materialistic detail, but in part, as well, because technology made new kinds of illusion possible. The impact of technology affected:

1. Energy sources and their use.
2. The structure of theatre buildings.
3. The structure and shifting of scenery.

These need to be considered in detail.

New Energy Sources and Their Impact

Gas, steam, electricity, and petroleum were the energy sources that drove nineteenth-century industry—steam before 1800, gas shortly thereafter, and petroleum and electricity after 1850. Steam was not of great importance in the theatre, although steam as a driving force for some heavy machinery and as a special effect for steam curtains had some application; after the development of complete electrical systems, steam was used to drive generators in some theatres before metropolitan electricity was available. Petroleum had limited importance. Gas and electricity, however, were very important, most of all for illumination.

Gas.   Although gas had come into quite widespread use in theatres by 1850, it was really after mid-century that technological improvements exploited its advantages over candles and oil lamps. These included greater illumination per unit, greater safety (when precautions were taken), and a dimming capability. Gas had its drawbacks, however: burning gas produced heat and water vapor in noticeable amounts; its open flame was always a fire hazard; units were not easily portable; and the single light source was neither powerful enough to project a beam through a lens nor confined enough to make the best use of either a lens or a reflector.

On the stage, gas after mid-century was used in several configurations:

1. On *battens* hung over the stage, casting light down on actors and scenery.

2. In *footlights* (still called *floats,* although the water-trough system was abandoned with gas) along the front of the stage floor, casting light up and back on actors and scenery.

3. In *sidelights* or wing lights placed vertically in the wings, casting light from the sides on actors and some scenery.

4. In *striplights*, smaller, portable strips of gas jets used mostly on the stage floor, horizontally, to light scenery.

5. In *bunchlights*, portable units on a stand with several jets, usually in a circle in front of a reflector.

Originally set alight by an open flame carried on a pole, all of these units eventually incorporated either a gas pilot or an electrical spark-igniter after about 1870, at least in large theatres. The light that they cast was pale yellow and diffuse. Clearly, they made the stage a very warm place.

The gas era also had *limelight.* A block of lime was made incandescent by hydrogen burning in oxygen, the two gases being piped to the block. The resulting light was brilliant, pale green in color, and capable of being focused by a lens. It gave the theatre its first effective spotlight and a metaphor for the center of attention. Although available by 1850, it seems not to have been widely used until the 1870s.[47] While used mainly for the spotlighting of individuals, limelight was also used for effects, and a few theatres used it for washes of light over part or all of the stage.

Limelight needed constant attention from an operator at the light's position. Gaslights were controlled at a distance from the *gas table*, where banks of controls could change the amount of gas reaching the banks of jets. Gas tables grew increasingly complex as battens, footlights, and sidelights were broken into smaller units. In the last two decades of the century, it became possible to dim areas of the stage independently or to color areas by using lacquered glass as a medium. The most noteworthy of these uses was made, it appears, by Henry Irving in the 1870s.[48] (Much of Irving's work with color was applied to limelight, however.)

In the audience part of the theatre, gas made possible an almost dark auditorium. It brought heat and vapor but was an improvement over dripping wax and smelly wicks. Gaslights were usually placed in the old wall-sconce position between boxes or in a concentrated "sun" high overhead, where heat and vapor could be vented. It appears to have been Irving who first put the audience into relative darkness, at least in England.[49]

At the time of the invention of electric light, then, the stage was brighter, but illumination was general, and some of it came from angles known only in the theatre and not, as a rule, in life: from below (footlights) and from the sides (sidelights). Color was rudimentary. Directional light was rare, except in the case of limelight. Light could be controlled from the gas table, but only by areas.

Electricity.   Edison's electric incandescent lamp appeared in 1880, Swan's English incandescent only months later.[50] The technology for the production of adequate electricity had not been available until 1870. Nonincandescent electric light had been known in principle since 1808, when the carbon-arc lamp was conceived; however, "the limitations of energy sources were so great that most workers had abandoned the field of arc lighting by 1860," and the uses of arc lights before the late 1870s were "scattered."[51] In 1880, however, energy, carbon-arc, and incandescent

lamps were all practicable, and a theatre was equipped almost immediately:

Mr [Richard] D'Oyly Carte, having determined to light the Savoy Theatre [London] by the Swan incandescent electric light, intrusted the work of installation to Messrs. Siemens Brothers and Co. The theatre is lighted by no less than 1194 Swan lights. . . . Of these . . . the auditorium is lighted by 150 lamps attached in groups of three, supported by threefold brackets projecting from the different tiers and balconies. . . .

Two hundred and twenty lamps are employed for the illumination of the numerous dressing-rooms, corridors, and passages . . . while no less than 824 Swan lamps are employed for lighting the stage.

The stage lights are distributed as follows:

6 rows of 100 lamps each above the stage			
1 "	60	"	"
4 "	14	"	fixed upright
2 "	18	"	"
5 "	10	"	ground lights
2 "	11	"	"

The lamps are at present worked in parallel circuit in six groups, five of which comprise 200 lamps each. . . .

[A]ny of the series of lights can in an instant be turned up to their full power or gradually lowered to a dull red heat as easily as if they were gas lamps. . . .

All risk of fire is avoided by the leading wires being thoroughly insulated. . . .

The small lamps worn by the fairies . . . are rendered incandescent by the current produced from a small "secondary" battery, which is carried on the back like a small knapsack.

The system of electric lighting has now been working at this theatre for about a year and a half, and has proved to possess many advantages over gas as applied to the illumination of buildings of this description. Not the least amongst these are the total absence of heat and vitiated air in the house, and the length of time during which the illuminations will retain their freshness and colour instead of becoming quickly faded and tarnished, as would be the case were the old system of gas adopted.

(*Nature*, March 1, 1883)

FIGURE 15.20

Gas footlight (1884). From *Scientific American Supplement.*] Electric footlight (1886). [From *Scientific American.*] Early lighting equipment. [From *Scientific American Supplement.*]

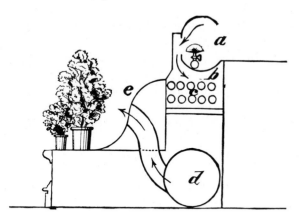
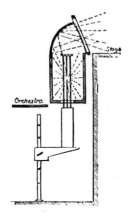
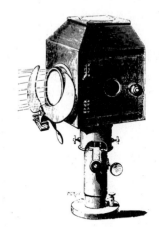

The similarities to gaslight are striking: the lamps were arranged in battens, footlights and sidelights, and they could be dimmed "as easily as if they were gas." There was an arc light set up outside the theatre, presumably as advertising.

Early incandescent stage lighting, therefore, mimicked gas. It was safer, brighter, and eventually cheaper than gas, but for years it was not used differently: individual lamps were combined in gas configurations, while powerful spotlights (now carbon-arc) were used as "specials."

"Simple spotlights" were available by the time of World War I. By the 1920s, "simple plano-convex lamps (condenser spotlights in the U.S.) in 500-watt and 1000-watt sizes "had been developed.[52] A division in lighting practice had appeared—one German, using clustered spotlights, and the other Anglo-American, using battens, footlights, and specials.

By the 1930s, spotlights with ellipsoidal reflectors and lenses had been developed, thanks in part to the invention of more powerful incandescent lamps that burned base up and had a point filament. It became possible to light a stage entirely with hard- and soft-focus spotlights; and a system of lighting with pairs of instru-

ments, one of each pair of which was usually differently colored, their beams at 45 degrees from the horizontal and 90 degrees from each other, became possible. (Such a system was made known in the United States by Stanley McCandless of Yale University before World War II.) The theory of lighting from a 45-degree angle had been known since the mid-nineteenth century, however.

Early electrical dimming used variable resistance between energy source and lamp. Resistance dimmers were durable, but they were large, inefficient, and hot. They were mechanically linked as gas tables had been, and the early models looked like gas tables. The direction of development thereafter was toward smaller and more flexible units, first with variable-voltage units and then, after World War II, with electronic units that sliced portions of the energy cycle. These used vacuum tubes and then thyristors.[53] In contemporary theatres the banks of battens, footlights, and sidelights have completely disappeared, and entire productions are lighted with hundreds of small instruments individually controlled by remote dimmers that are programmable by computer and highly flexible.

After 1920, then, electricity gave the theatre

the potential for *directional light*, for carefully defined *area light*, for *colored light* of great range, for more *intense light* than any ever before known, and for *dimming flexibility*.

It would be convenient for history if the realists had immediately used electric light to enhance the illusion of reality, but in many cases they did not, probably because, first, the technology was so limited, and, second, the convention of theatrical light was so ingrained. In order to have been highly illusionistic, theatrical light would have had to imitate environmental light in color, direction, and intensity, but such lighting was not possible until the 1920s and 1930s.

FIGURE 15.21

Early resistance-dimmer bank (nineteenth century). [From Ginisty.]

In fact, what electric light did in the nineteenth century—like gas before it—was to supply new tools for the spectacular, neoromantic theatre. Projections, dissolves, transformations, scrims, and mood effects became possible. Realistic lighting, however, would not have come from effects but from great subtlety (to bring it, for example, to the level of illusionism of stage properties). It is true that there was a debate with realistic overtones about the *direction* of lighting. It centered on the use of footlights, which were among those things argued against by Strindberg in his preface to *Miss Julie*. In London, this debate appeared in the 1890s as a controversy over footlighting versus sidelighting (essentially a false issue left over from gas and candles). The whole matter had been anticipated before mid-century by a J. E. Dove, who had installed gaslights with reflectors over the auditorium of a small theatre to illuminate the forestage without footlights in 1847; others, including the American David Belasco, had tried similar experiments before 1880. Footlights cast a warm light on the actors as they approached the audience, and both actors and audiences liked them. Only a great change in the amount of illumination available from some other position would eliminate them (and then, in many cases, there would be a new problem with shadows under hats, eyebrows, chins, and noses).

Gaslight, and then electric lighting used like gaslight, was the illumination of early realism. Realistic lighting would be available only to the second generation of realists. However, it must be said that even quite early uses of electric light may have *seemed* more "real" to audiences because of their conditioned expectations: the new light was brighter than gas, it *could* be colored, and even primitive incandescent instruments were strikingly different from unfocused gaslight.

The Structure of Theatre Buildings
Theatre buildings changed during the period of realism, but it cannot be proved that realism was

the cause of those changes. The principal directions of change were (1) the enlargement of scene space; (2) the suppression of galleries and side boxes in favor of flown (cantilevered) balconies; and (3) the withdrawal of the performance behind the proscenium, with the consequent union of scenic and acting areas and the end of the tripartite structure. Realism, as a cause of these changes, must share responsibility with the use of new materials and the continuing taste for neoromantic spectacle.

Scenic Space.   Theatre enlargement brought in money while also satisfying the Victorian artistic desires for spectacle. Expansion was also required to satisfy new technology: steam curtains, hydraulic lifts, elevator stages, revolving stages (Karl Lautenschlager, 1896), "wagon" or "slip" stages, and massive machinery for flying and shifting. Steele Mackaye's Madison Square Theatre (New York, 1880) had the entire acting area on a lift so that settings could be lowered and rolled off and new ones could be rolled on; his Lyceum Theatre (New York, 1885) had steam engines both to generate electricity and to provide mechanical power.

Under such pressure, the theatrical scene-space grew higher and wider and sometimes went deeper into the ground: "As machinery for lifting scenery was perfected, the fly-tower over the stage grew higher. Other pieces of machinery could move whole sets from the wings, or from below the stage, or cause the entire stage to revolve."[54]

Audience Space.   The box, pit, and gallery configuration had been under assault from two quite different directions. One was Wagnerian theory, the other the appearance of new materials.

With Gottfried Semper, Richard Wagner had made plans as early as the mid-1860s for "continental seating," an arrangement that would put the entire audience on an incline facing the stage, without boxes or galleries. The plan was realized in the theatre at Bayreuth

FIGURE 15.22

The Madison Square Theatre, New York (1884). Although gaslighted, it was innovative in its huge elevator stage. [From *Scientific American Supplement.*]

(1876). This system is sometimes called *democratic* because it removes many of the privileged locations of box, pit, and gallery and gives all members of the audience a fairly equal view of the stage; however, it was also aesthetically "serious" because Wagner and Semper wanted the audience to concentrate on the performance and not on each other. Continental seating was used in Germany; Wagner's "leading disciple," Max Littmann,[55] designed theatres using it in Weimar, Berlin, Munich, and other cities. Existing theatres elsewhere often resisted it because of the cost of the change.

Even existing theatres, however, did not

resist the influence of new materials. With the use of structural steel, deep and steeply raked balconies could be cantilevered over the orchestra or stalls, providing many more seats that faced the stage; almost accidentally, they wiped out many boxes and, of course, the galleries. "In the auditorium, the most important innovation was the steel cantilevering of balconies, which became general by the 1890's."[56]

In some newly built theatres, continental seating was combined with flown balconies: the Adler–Sullivan Auditorium Theatre in Chicago (1889) seated more than four thousand on this plan. Somewhat oddly, it kept two tiers of boxes at the side, as many theatres (including movie houses) were to do until after World War I. Metropolitan theatres remaining from that period still show this plan, with their side boxes now often used for lighting or sound equipment.

Theatres built since World War I show other influences, for example, greater size and greater "democratization" (Radio City Music Hall, New York City); the placement of the performance in the center of the audience (the Berlin Grosses Shauspielhaus, 1920); and trade-offs between size, acoustical excellence, and cost (the new Metropolitan Opera House at Lincoln Center, New York City).

Assertion of the Proscenium. Withdrawal of the performance behind the proscenium had been going on for two generations. In the last part of the nineteenth century, it was marked by a well-defined proscenium "picture frame"; by the disappearance of the forestage; and by the marked separation between the acting area and the auditorium.

Both realism and Wagnerism encouraged these changes. Wagner's "mystic abyss . . . heightening the illusion of another world . . .

FIGURE 15.23

Interior of the festival theatre, Bayreuth (ca. 1899), showing the double proscenium and the "mystic abyss" between performance and audience. [From *Le Théâtre.*]

the perfecting of the picture-frame idea"[57] accomplished its ends in the name of mythic illusion, however, not of realism. The gains in audience space also encouraged suppression of the forestage.

With batten lighting and sidelighting, overhead light was now located behind the proscenium, where it would not spill into the house, and the brightest spot for an actor was no longer on the forestage, under or between candelabra, but behind the proscenium. When lighting with powerful spots from beam and balcony-front positions became possible, the reassertion of the forestage became feasible (after ca. 1930).

The combined influences of realism, Wagnerism, new materials, and new scenic technology, then, led to the changed structure of the theatre. On the other hand, many metropolitan theatres kept their configurations long after the changes could be seen in new buildings; therefore, many important theatres in New York, London, Paris, and elsewhere still look structurally like theatres of about 1900. The "new" theatre building of realism and Wagnerism, modified by economics and purpose, can be seen in many schools and colleges built since about 1930.

Changes in Scenery

The scenic change most important to realism was the widespread adoption of the box set. Although versions of it may have appeared as early as the Renaissance,[58] the box set joined nineteenth-century scenery about 1840 and became common in the 1860s. By 1894, the English stage painter William Telbin wrote that "the stage is now in most theatres a big box, in which you can set a picture up in any way you please at any angle. The grooves, the flats, the wings made by the dozen pairs, are all gone."[59] In realistic (rather than spectacular) use, this stage housed a box set—three walls and ceiling, the fourth wall open to the audience (although the siting of the box at all sorts of angles was an

early development, so that many box sets did not have three walls or a symmetrical siting).

A movement toward broken planes, angles to the proscenium line, and masterly painting went back to de Loutherbourg and the baroque designers, and the movement toward "practicables" and vertically broken planes went back to the early years of the century. All were seen in the work of Irving and Saxe-Meiningen. Despite the abandonment of wings and grooves, this scenery was still tied to its Renaissance origins, both in its painted illusionism and in its materials, canvas and wood and paint. Built-up scenery was now common, as were painted drops and act curtains. The moving panorama, in front of which actors "traveled" on foot or on horse or by boat; the "transformation" that used scrim and flexible light; the rapid shifting of scenes by hydraulic lift and wagon stage or revolve—all had replaced the once-magical scene changes of the chariot-and-pole or wing-and-groove systems. Some very old problems remained, however—the masking of margins, for example. Exterior scenes were still difficult, especially now that audiences expected authenticity; sky borders were a wretched compromise. Belatedly, the curved *cyclorama* proved a workable solution; perfected in Germany after 1900, it became effective in the 1920s with incandescent spotlighting. By that date, projected scenery, pioneered by Adolf Linnebach in Munich (but anticipated by limelight magic lanterns) had become practical.

Realism's first wave, from about 1850 to 1890, found a theatre whose scenery was adequate to domestic interiors and to antiquarian and contemporary exteriors, but one with masking problems. As well, the realists' belief that each play must have its own setting could not be met, except in rare instances. By about 1920, however, most commercial theatres routinely made new sets for each new play, and their sometimes photographic illusionism was impeccable.

It should not be thought that any of the changes in lighting, scenery, or architecture

FIGURE 15.24

Masking of outdoor scenes was a major problem of realistic scenery, as in this production of *Les Deux Grosses* (Paris, 1900). The water, the lock, and the "drowning" were presented fairly convincingly, but the sky borders remained sky borders. [From *Le Thé-âtre.*]

happened everywhere at the same time or that the new easily or quickly drove out the old. Some theatres were using wings and borders into the twentieth century, and gaslighting overlapped electricity.

The theatres of the age of realism, then, were highly varied. If we try to generalize, we have to say that they were nineteenth-century theatres and that their realism was based in the scenic materials and techniques of illusionism.

Antoine staged many of his plays in borrowed settings. The early plays of Ibsen were sometimes performed in settings whose details were painted on and whose canvas doors shook when they were closed. Chekhov's exteriors were sometimes seen with strips of blue cloth for the sky. Often, the plays were seen by audiences in tripartite theatres, with some of the audience seated along the sides, straining their necks to see in auditoriums that had been designed for hearing.

Acting

Realistic theories of acting have certain criteria in common:

1. Rejection of the traditional.
2. Rejection of playing for effect.
3. Insistence on the individuality of the role (and of the actor in the role).
4. Concern with truth as distinct from language (i.e., text).
5. Belief in observation of life (including memory) as a source or test of truth; belief in generalization from observation.
6. Distrust of artifice of voice or gesture and, by extension, of obviously trained voice and gesture. A social bias against the artificiality of manners and upper society led often to a belief that all artifice is bad. It is hardly an accident that realistic acting rose as the star system and lines of business declined. Nor was it an accident that Antoine and Stanislavski both used amateurs as many of their actors, in part because the amateur actor lacked the trained voice and gesture of the professionals of the time. Nor was it an accident that certain actors and actresses found their careers in realism as their innate qualities matched the new style—Eleonora Duse in Italy and Elizabeth Robins in London and the United States, for example.

Stanislavski was and is the greatest theorist of realistic acting. Another highly influential theorist of the nineteenth century, François Delsarte, was important in much actor training, however.

François Delsarte (1801–1871)

Of the systems that preceded Stanislavski's, none gained the reputation, especially in the United States, of Delsarte's. A largely self-taught singer, Delsarte had had a brief career in Paris before losing his voice and turning to the teaching of elocution, movement, and acting. His most famous American pupil was Steele Mackaye (1842–1894), producer, playwright, actor, and theatrical inventor.

Delsarte's method rested on certain assumptions:

1. Observation can lead to the perception of universal laws about the relationship between feeling and gesture.

FIGURE 15.25
Leading Actors, 1850–World War II

Got, Edmond-François	French	1822–1901	Classic roles, Comédie Française
Ristori, Adelaide	Italian	1822–1905	Tragedian: Mary Stuart (Schiller)
Fechter, Charles	French	1824–1879	Pre-realist; tragedian: Hamlet in Paris, New York, London
Sothern, E. A.	American	1826–1881	Romantic; contemporary roles
Jefferson, Joseph	American	1829–1905	Pre-realist, genre actor: Rip van Winkle
Salvini, Tommaso	Italian	1829–1916	Shakespearean roles, London, New York, Continent
Janauschek, Francesca	Czech	1830–1904	Romantic; tragedian
Toole, John Laurence	English	1830–1906	Leading light comedian
Booth, Edwin	American	1833–1893	Shakespearean: Hamlet, Othello, latter with both Irving and Salvini; own theatre and company, New York, 1869–1873, but failed
Irving, Henry	English	1838–1905	Actor–manager; first English actor to be knighted; famous for *The Bells*, but great Shakespearean
Modjeska, Helena	Polish	1840–1909	Wide repertory, especially Shakespeare
Coquelin, Constant-Benoit	French	1841–1909	Neoromantic: Comédie Française; first Cyrano
Mounet-Sully, Jean	French	1841–1916	Tragedian, Comédie Française
Bernhardt, Sarah	French	1845–1923	Neoromantic; media star; classic and contemporary roles: L'Aiglon, Tosca, Hamlet; intrepid tourer
Terry, Ellen	English	1847–1928	Irving's leading lady; Shakespearean; mother of Gordon Craig
Yermolova, Maria	Russian	1853–1928	Tragedian
Gillette, William	American	1855–1937	Lead in own melodramas: *Sherlock Holmes; Secret Service.*
Mansfield, Richard	American	1857–1907	Neoromantic early, but played important roles of Ibsen, Shaw
Réjane (G.-C. Réju)	French	1857–1920	Boulevard, especially comedy
Duse, Eleonora	Italian	1858–1924	Versatile: D'Annunzio and Ibsen; Scribe and Dumas; rival of Bernhardt
Leno, Dan	English	1860–1904	Music-hall, pantomime
Rehan, Ada	American	1860–1916	Augustin Daly's leading lady; neoromantic; Shakespearean
Robins, Elizabeth	American	1862–1952	Realist: Ibsen
Achurch, Janet	English	1864–1916	Realist: Ibsen, Shaw
Kommisarzhevskaya, Vera	Russian	1864–1910	Neoromantic; art theatre; experimenter
Fiske, Minnie Madern	American	1865–1932	Realist: Ibsen, new American plays
Marlowe, Julia	American	1866–1950	Shakespearean
Yablochkina, Alexandra	Russian	1868–1964	Classic and modern Russian repertory, Maly Theatre
Knipper-Chekhova, Olga	Russian	1870–1959	Moscow Art Theatre; wife of Chekhov; Ranevskaya in *Cherry Orchard*
Adams, Maude	American	1872–1953	Neoromantic: Peter Pan
Moskvin, Ivan	Russian	1874–1946	Moscow Art Theatre: Realist: Chekhov, Gorky
Grasso, Giovanni	Italian	1875–1930	Realist: Othello, roles of Pirandello
Kachalov, Vasili I.	Russian	1875–1948	Moscow Art Theatre

FIGURE 15.25 (continued)

McCarthy, Lillah	English	1875–1960	Roles of Shaw
Anglin, Margaret	American	1876–1958	Tragedian: Shakespeare, Greeks
Barrymore, Ethel	American	1879–1959	Queen of America's "Royal Family": modern comedies and dramas
Hampden, Walter	American	1879–1956	Cyrano; Stage Manager, *Our Town*
Nazimova, Alla	Russian	1879–1945	Realist: Ibsen; in U.S. after 1906
Barrymore, John	American	1882–1942	Noted Hamlet, Richard III; brother of Ethel
Thorndike, Sybil	English	1882–1976	Shaw's Saint Joan; Old Vic; classic repertory
Allgood, Sara	Irish	1883–1950	Abbey Theatre: Synge, O'Casey
Fontanne, Lynn	English	1887–1983	Neoromantic: with Alfred Lunt, a Theatre Guild star: *The Guardsman, Idiot's Delight;* Shaw, Shakespeare
Jouvet, Louis	French	1887–1951	Copeau disciple; Comédie Française; roles of Molière
Chevalier, Maurice	French	1888–1972	Musical comedy
Evans, Edith	English	1888–1976	Old Vic; Shakespearean; classic roles, noted Lady Bracknell
Lunt, Alfred	American	1893–1977	Husband of Lynn Fontanne, with whom he made America's greatest acting duo
Anderson, Judith	American	1898–	Tragedian: Lady Macbeth, Medea; *Mourning Becomes Electra* (O'Neill)
Cornell, Katharine	American	1898–1974	Neoromantic: modern roles, Shakespeare's Cleopatra
Lawrence, Gertrude	English	1898–1952	Light comedy, especially that of Noel Coward
Robeson, Paul	American	1898–1976	Othello; Emperor Jones
DeFilippo family: Titina (1898–1963); Eduardo (1900–); Peppino (1903–)	Italian		Dialect and Italian theatre, Naples
Coward, Noel	English	1899–1973	Brilliant light comedian, especially in own plays
LeGallienne, Eva	American	1899–	Founded Civic Repertory, New York, 1926; Ibsen, Chekhov
Babanova, Maria	Russian	1900–	Versatile: in Meyerhold's company, then (1938) classic Russian and Soviet roles
Hayes, Helen	American	1900–	Realist: *Victoria Regina,* modern roles
Paxinou, Katina	Greek	1900–1973	Tragedian: Greeks, Ibsen, Shakespeare
Waters, Ethel	American	1900–1977	Singer, actress: *Mamba's Daughters, Member of the Wedding*
Richardson, Ralph	English	1902–1983	Old Vic; character roles: Falstaff, Peer Gynt
Rénaud, Madeleine	French	1903–	Classic French repertory; Comédie Française, then own company (1946) with husband, Jean-Louis Barrault
Gielgud, John	English	1904–	Actor-director; Old Vic; noted Hamlet; Shakespeare; voice
Ashcroft, Peggy	English	1907–	Old Vic; Shakespeare, Wilde, moderns
Olivier, Laurence	English	1907–	Actor-director; Old Vic; head of National Theatre (1963); wide range: Hamlet, Oedipus, Justice Shallow, moderns

FIGURE 15.25 (continued)

Barrault, Jean-Louis	French	1910–	Comédie Française; adaptations of Kafka, Faulkner; own company with Madeleine Rénaud (1946); broad repertory
Guinness, Alec	English	1914–	Old Vic; versatile; character actor, but respected Hamlet, other major roles; noted film actor

The truly international stars until about the time of the silent film often played either in languages unfamiliar to their audiences (Booth in Germany, Bernhardt in America) or learned new languages (Fechter, Modjeska, and Janauschek, English). The great roles of Shakespeare were the common denominator. After about 1900, they were joined by the great roles of Ibsen and Chekhov; however, the classic international repertory remained small. After about 1930, Soviet actors were rarely seen outside Russia or foreign actors in it. Theatrical internationalism ended by World War II, largely replaced by the internationalism of film and then television.

As a reading of the list will show, however, there was also a group of actors who excelled outside the great companies (Old Vic, Comédie-Française, Moscow Art Theatre) and outside the classic repertory: Sothern, Jefferson, Gillette, Mansfield in America, then the great actors of modern realistic theatre: Hayes, Allgood, Moskvin, Babanova, and others.

2. Gesture can induce feeling: "A perfect reproduction of the outer manifestation of some passion, the giving of the outer signs, will cause a reflex feeling within."[60]
3. Gesture is more potent than speech: "There are three forms of expression by which man outwardly reveals his inward experience. The first is pantomimic; the second is vocal; the last is verbal."[61]
4. All inner states have specific outer manifestations; their exact reproduction is the basis of acting: proper analysis of a play, poem, or recitation will lead to perfect outer expression if the laws noted by Delsarte are obeyed.

Delsarte himself was described as a master of pantomime who applied his own "laws" with skill and selectivity. His system, however, was easily made mechanical in less skilled hands. It is because the method tried to be "scientific" that it was vulnerable, for it seemed to offer laws that, if followed, would produce art. With students of great natural ability like Mackaye, Delsarte's method produced good actors; with those of little ability, it produced mere posturing, as any other method would have.

The Stanislavski System

The Stanislavski system is still the most important modern concept of acting, acknowledged in most major nations of the West, in Russia, and even in cultures where the theatre is vastly different (for example, the experimental theatre of modern Poland). It is realistic in its assumptions; its truth is the truth of the late nineteenth century; and it works best for realistic plays, with a sometimes distorting effect on plays of other styles. One must always ask how much its enormous fashion from the 1930s through the early 1960s depended on political or social sentiment; and one must remain aware that the system is actually two systems from different periods of Stanislavski's life, and that modern proponents are themselves split into factions.

Elements of the system include:

1. *Analytical consistency.* Stanislavski postulated a "through line of action" in every play and every performance, a consistent "spine" without inconsistent "tendencies" that would diverge fruitlessly from it. Essential to the idea of the through line was that of a "superobjective" of character—the actively stated life goal that subsumed every gesture, line, and bit of behavior of the character. The superobjec-

tive defined and tested the actor's analysis, and it was the superobjective that made the totality a coherent one.

2. *Motivational psychology.* In Stanislavski's theory, all human action was motivated. Every result had a cause, every act of consciousness a goal. The terms *motivation* and *objective* entered the actor's vocabulary. Stanislavskian acting gave meaning (of objective and motivation) to all roles, however small; however, it could also give false meaning to roles without meaning in other styles: "The thought that Chekhov's pauses might be empty, his tears motiveless,

FIGURE 15.26

The great American actor Edwin Booth as Iago. Son of the actor Junius Brutus Booth, he excelled as a neo-romantic interpreter of Shakespeare in London and New York and on international tours. [Courtesy of the Libraries of the University of Rochester.]

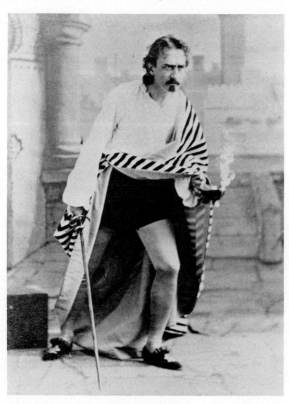

and his characters unchanged at the day's end never occurred to Stanislavski."[62]

3. *Subsurface emotional life.* Partly because of the unique rhythms and pauses of Chekhov, Stanislavski gave attention to the problems of character that were not overt in the text. The term *subtext* came into the actor's vocabulary to describe a network of memory, objective, awareness, and unexpressed feeling. One of the side effects of this concept was the reduction of the importance of the text itself, although Stanislavski did not so intend it: the insistence on a second level of life below the text lowered the text and, with it, the playwright if the play was a new one. Although the idea of the subtext was not a result of Freud's influence, it represents a "remarkable case of parallel evolution. Freud and Stanislavski hold the common assumption that beneath our superficial social transactions a subconscious life exists which is more real than the surface actions we perform."[63]

4. *Affective memory.* For Stanislavski, the connection between art and life was not merely one of "going to life" for truth, as Mikhail Shchepkin had said half a century earlier, but of merging the life of the actor with the art of the role. The most important tool for this work was "affective memory," the calling up from the actor's own memory of specific or analogous feelings related to an event in the role. Affective memory is important to the American Stanislavski system but was downgraded by Stanislavski himself late in his life. It has the attraction for many would-be actors of allowing them to make their own lives, rather than the role, the raw material of their work (something that Stanislavski himself never intended) and of defining truth as an inner experience rather than an outer performance.

5. *Life as data: given circumstances.* According to Stanislavski, age, sex, health, social class, and other "given circumstances" of character pointed the actor toward the life of the role.

6. *The method of physical actions.* After about 1930, Stanislavski deemphasized the psychological aspects of his system and emphasized

instead physical behavior. The actor Vasily To-porkov recorded his experiences with the system during this period; he quoted Stanislavski at this time as saying, "Don't *act* anything, just play each action." They worked, not on "exalted objectives" but on "the simplest stage tasks."[64] He still defined "high art" as "that in which there exists a superobjective and a through-line-of-action. Bad art is that in which there is neither superobjective nor through-line-of-action."[65]

It is hardly coincidence that the method of physical actions appeared at a time when Soviet psychology was concerned with physical behavior. One authority has written that the method of physical actions was "the result of Stanislavski's life work; it is the answer to what he was searching, it is the 'Conscious Means toward the Subconscious' and the solution for spontaneous behavior on stage."[66]

Stanislavski Outside Russia. In England, Stanislavskian methods have been incorporated into actor training and performance without replacing the tradition of technical preparation. It may be said that although Stanislavski did not provide a total system for British actors, he provided strength and modernism for an acting tradition that might have become precious without him. A cautious early Russian proponent in England was Theodor Kommisarzhevsky, brother of the actress Vera.

In the United States, by the late 1940s, an American Stanislavski system, dubbed the *Method,* was well known, its reputation reinforced by work at the Actors Studio of Lee Strasberg, where many much-publicized actors came to study. The American Method had the reputation of emphasizing inner work, often at the expense of technique, and of giving great importance to improvisation. Actors trained in the Method *and no other* have shown technical inadequacy in some cases and a lack of interest in nonrealistic theatre.

Stanislavski Today. The Stanislavski system penetrated academic theatre departments in the United States and Canada by the late 1950s and was dominant by 1970. In the Soviet Union, on the other hand, the system is treated respectfully at the Moscow Art Theatre, with far more emphasis given to the method of physical actions. A recent comparison of American and Soviet systems suggests that the Art Theatre does not share the American enthusiasm for inner work.[67]

The Emergence of the Director

The true director, as distinct from the stage manager, *devysor,* Master of Secrets, and others, appeared at about the same time as realism, but not necessarily because of realism; central authority was also being shown, for example, in the emergence of the orchestra conductor.

We can identify two lines of the director's history. One is a German tradition, which began to emphasize *regie* and *total-effekt* by 1800. The other is the emphasis on a single perception that seems to have begun with romantic spectacle at about the same time.

The German Tradition
Centralization of authority reached a theoretical height in Richard Wagner and his "master artist." It was through Wagner that both a German theatrical tradition and a romantic concept of individual genius flowed. The master of both play and stage appeared, a superior sensibility bent on creating a total artwork. The Meininger reinforced the idea, and it was of course Chronegk and the Meininger who gave Stanislavski the image of the authoritarian director. By 1890, in Germany, Otto Brahm at the Freie Bühne and the Deutches Theater gave important examples of directorial work in realism and naturalism. Those examples influenced protégés like Max Reinhardt (see Chapter 17).

The Organizer of Spectacle
The period's enthusiasm for spectacle encouraged central organization, which became clearest in the work of the antiquarians. The anti-

quarian productions of Charles Kean were influential on Saxe-Meiningen, and those of Irving influenced Stanislavski. Kean and Irving, however, were "actor–managers" rather than directors—stars who also financed and produced, but who were artistically concerned with the centrality of their own performances rather than the centrality of a "master artwork." Kean's great concern was historically authentic costume and scenery; Irving's concerns were those, as well as lighting and spectacular effects. He is reported to have said, "Stage lighting and groupings are of more consequence than scenery."[68] These actor–managers, along with Herbert Beerbohm Tree, William Poel, and others, came at the end of a form of theatrical organization (actor-management) that would be

FIGURE 15.27

Henry Irving, England's greatest actor of the second half of the nineteenth century and a pioneering actor–manager. The woodcut is by Gordon Craig. [From *The Dome*.]

replaced by one headed by nonacting entrepreneurs, but their example flowed smoothly into the work of the directors who appeared after 1900.

Realistic Directors

Stanislavski, Nemirovich-Danchenko, and Antoine were true directors of realism. The German and the spectacular tradition met in them. They worked from artistic rather than commercial impulse; they chose their own plays; they staged them with attention to integrity of style rather than fashion, working out such problems as the angle of the setting to the audience, the degree of authenticity of properties, matters of accent and the vocal quality of the actors, levels of light, casting, and so on; they sometimes rehearsed for long periods on seemingly small details (less true of Antoine than of the others); and they left as little as possible to accident.

Increasingly, as the work of Stanislavski became known and his system became widely used, actor coaching in the Stanislavskian fashion became common. The pictorialists' fascination with crowds turned into a standardized practice in forms as diverse as opera and film.

Other important early directors of realism included the following.

William Bloch (1845–1926). Bloch directed a number of Ibsen's plays at the Danish Royal Theater, including *An Enemy of the People* (1883) and *The Wild Duck* (1885), serving as stage director there from 1881 to 1893 and from 1899 to 1909.[69] Bloch's *Enemy of the People* was "one of the earliest and most characteristic examples of stage naturalism in Scandinavia."[70] Bloch appears to have developed his own style independent of Antoine (as he of Bloch).

Augustin Daly (1839–1899). A manager in New York and later in London, Daly staged contemporary melodramas with great attention to effect. In plays like his own *Under the Gaslight* (1867), he carefully coordinated the action and the effects. He became an antiquarian in his

FIGURE 15.28

Augustin Daly's *Under the Gaslight* (1867). It was for the coordination of such moments as this one that a central authority was needed. [From Appelbaum.]

production of Shakespeare. He was a commercial manager whose realism was the product of his acute sense of the times, and a neoromantic who "permitted no voice but his own to be heard in the preparation of a play."[71]

David Belasco (1859–1931). Belasco epitomized trivialized realism in America, for he managed to put on the stage everything but the dangerous ideas most crucial to it. His own plays were sentimental and trivial but enormously popular, for example, *DuBarry, Madame Butterfly*, and *The Girl of the Golden West*. Like Irving, he was deeply concerned with technical problems, especially lighting. Like Daly, he ruled his productions, with the same result: he created neoromantic spectacle. His often-cited use of an exact replica of a Child's restaurant in one play and of the historical Madame du Barry's actual furniture in *DuBarry* may be seen as examples of the best realism that money could buy.

The Commercial Theatre (1850–Present)

There had been "commercial" (public and professional) theatre since the Renaissance. The romantics, however, began to see an opposition between commerce and art that seemed new. Before the end of the nineteenth century, the sense of a difference between commercial theatre (which depended on income for its existence and which was aimed at making a profit for somebody) and artistic theatre (which aimed at the idealization of the artistic product and which rejected a dependence on income) became acute, and it still exists. In many societies, commercial theatres practice the highest standards of technique, but "little" or "avant-garde" or "art" theatres continue to think of themselves as working in opposition to commercialism. Although it remains difficult to separate the two impulses neatly (a deeply entrenched nonprofit theatre like the Moscow Art Theatre now being as conservative and cautious as a West End producer) it is generally true that money and not quality has become a final criterion in many commercial theatres.

Innovation in the period, although usually made outside the commercial theatre, was quickly absorbed into or coopted by it, although commerce has tended to mute or prettify what it coopts. In twentieth-century commercial theatres, one tendency has been to "massify" new tendencies in theatre art and to shorten greatly the time between the appearance of an innovation and its widespread acceptance. Thus, commercial stage design easily incorporated the most revolutionary and even anticommercial design elements of the early realists, simply leaving out the theoretical underpinnings that had made them revolutionary; and both playwriting and production easily assimilated realism without absorbing its social theory.

Since World War II, cross-seeding between commercial and art theatres has intensified in the West. Artists pass back and forth between the two easily; plays, especially in Great Britain and America, move from nonprofit theatres (some government-supported, some not) into the commercial theatre as if along a seamless web.

From the mid-1880s until World War I, so-called independent and art theatres introduced most new drama and new production styles. The majority of these came from Europe, with America lagging about a half-generation behind. The European situation actually varied greatly from country to country, sometimes from city to city, but where there was commercial production (as opposed to private, court, or government theatre), it was one of the following types.

Actor–manager or Star Management

Most common in England, the great actor–managers picked their own plays, hired and ran their own companies, and often took the responsibility for all phases of production. The great example was Henry Irving, whose two decades at London's Lyceum Theatre (1879–1899) were the high point (and about the end) of English actor–manager organization. Actor–managers leased a theatre from its owner, although in cases like that of the American Edwin Booth, they sometimes built their own (which, in Booth's case, resulted in financial disaster). In France, much commercial production of the same period was organized around a star like Sarah Bernhardt and was a continuation of the star system from earlier in the century; however, the provincial companies that had served star tours were disappearing, and so even the great, charismatic continental stars were forced into a form of managership. Both it and actor–management in England were actor-centered, and the plays were chosen either for their suitability to the actor–manager's talents or for their long-established appeal.

Entrepreneurial Sponsorship

Overlapping and then succeeding the actor–managers were businessmen, although there were examples of director–managers (Augustin Daly and David Belasco, for example), who were somewhat like the actor–managers. It was the

FIGURE 15.29

Sarah Bernhardt, perhaps the greatest of the international neoromantic stars, in *L'aiglon* (1900). [From *Le Théâtre*.]

businessmen without production involvement who eventually dominated, however, and their appearance marked the beginning of the modern commercial theatre. At their worst, they were cynical money-men who took up the theatre because it was a business that turned a profit. Often their primary interest was theatrical real estate, and they simply booked into their theatres whatever would fill them with the largest and longest-continuing audience. At their best, they were organizers who stood above the hurly-burly of production and who brought efficiency and unity to an often chaotic business.

In the United States, the early entrepreneurs included Charles and David Frohman before the turn of the century and the Shubert brothers (Sam, Jacob, and Lee) just after. Theatres outside New York were numerous and could earn huge amounts of money. The tendency to combine, which is seen in other businesses at this time, also afflicted the theatre, and the biggest of the combinations became the infamous Theatrical Syndicate (ca. 1896–1905). It controlled a large proportion of America's theatres and used the power of monopoly to close out rivals, regulate bookings, and exercise a form of censorship by making it impossible for some artists and plays to find theatres. The Syndicate has been blamed for the death of both the decentralized theatre and the touring system:

> The "syndicate" adopted the methods common to lawless "big business" of that day. . . . After a short campaign so few rebels remained that the American theater lay practically helpless in the hands of a few New York speculators. . . . Experiment was eliminated, profits formerly scattered to a hundred independent agencies now flowed regularly to the one headquarters in New York, and price-raising was possible on a cornered commodity."[72]

As the laws of business came to dominate matters of art, to be sure, the climate became increasingly dangerous (and as costs went up geometrically after World War II, it became even more so). The result in most commercial theatres has been the "hit-or-flop" mentality of New York's Broadway. It has tended toward the long run, the tying up of theatres for very long periods, and the emphasis on the tried-and-true rather than the new, with a liking for plays that are long on razzmatazz and short on mind.

Funded Sponsorship

Various forms of underwriting have existed since Athens of the fifth century B.C., but in the period since 1850, underwriting has been complicated by the supremacy of commercial thea-

tre, by a preference in Western nations for capitalistic arrangements, and by the private-enterprise emphases of many democratic governments. Nonetheless, the trend has been toward some kind of funding of certain theatres. These have included:

1. *"Workers' theatres."* The great example is the German Volksbühne, founded in 1890 and now the sponsor of hundreds of productions in West Germany. Originally connected with socialism and the labor movement, it was crushed by the Nazis but reappeared after World War II.
2. *Government theatres.* The national theatres of Great Britain, France, and the Soviet Union are government-funded; there are many civic theatres in Germany and Italy.
3. *Private funding.* Especially in the United States, philanthropic foundations have underwritten theatres.
4. *Tax incentives to nonprofit theatres.*
5. *Association with educational institutions.*

Style and the Commercial Theatre

Commercial theatre has tended toward conservatism in both repertory and style. It is usually porous, however—artists come and go to and from it—and there is a constant influx of ideas. Perceived changes in audience taste lead some commercial producers to try innovations. Nonetheless, commercial theatre since 1850 has been dominated by only two major styles: realism and neoromanticism.

Coming to the fore about mid-century, neoromanticism (ca. 1850–1930) absorbed the popular aspects of romantic drama and production without insisting on romantic theory. Its primary characteristics included:

1. Spectacle.
2. Mixing of genres.
3. Sentimentality and emotionalism.
4. Upper-class settings and characters, or lower-

FIGURE 15.30
Leading Playwrights of Neoromanticism (1850–Present)

Name	Dates	Language	Example
Richard Wagner	1813–1883	Ger.	*The Ring* (cycle of four operas), 1869–1876
Oscar Wilde	1854–1900	Eng.	*The Importance of Being Earnest,* 1895
Gabriele d'Annunzio	1863–1938	Ital.	*Francesca da Rimini,* 1902
Jacinto Benavente	1866–1954	Span.	*The Bonds of Interest,* 1907
J. M. Barrie	1860–1937	Eng.	*Peter Pan,* 1904
Edmond Rostand	1868–1918	Fr.	*Cyrano de Bergerac,* 1897
Percy Mackaye	1875–1956	Eng. (Am.)	*The Scarecrow,* 1908
Ferenc Molnar	1878–1952	Hungar.	*Liliom,* 1909
Rachel Crothers	1878–1958	Eng. (Am.)	*Susan and God,* 1937
Jean Giraudoux	1882–1944	Fr.	*The Trojan War Will Not Take Place,* 1935
Robinson Jeffers	1887–1962	Eng. (Am.)	*Medea,* 1946
Maxwell Anderson	1888–1959	Eng. (Am.)	*Winterset,* 1935
Philip Barry	1896–1949	Eng. (Am.)	*The Philadelphia Story,* 1939
Robert Sherwood	1896–1955	Eng. (Am.)	*The Petrified Forest,* 1934
Noel Coward	1899–1973	Eng.	*Private Lives,* 1930
Jean Anouilh	1910–	Fr.	*The Lark,* 1953

class settings and characters within a properly sanitized context.

5. Elevated character defined by values rarely found in an industrial and mercantile society, such as self-denial and unselfish love.

Neoromantic plays provided an unusual number of roles to actresses, and there was a noticeable shift toward female "leads" (although they were still outnumbered by male leads). A great many of the characters were females who erred and repented or who were punished for early sins that they had covered up (divorce, a "scarlet past," an illegitimate child); quite a number were "bad women" or outright villainesses. It may be that neoromantic drama expressed an unease with the women of its society.

After World War I, neoromantic drama tended to give up its upper-class qualities in favor of middle or lower-class ones, but the values remained the same (as in plays like Robert Sherwood's *The Petrified Forest* or Ferenc Molnar's *The Guardsman*). Historical drama continued to be popular, from Sardou's *Theodora* through Maxwell Anderson's *Elizabeth the Queen*. A neoromantic acting style persisted through World War II (coexisting in most countries with a realistic one) and was evident in the work of such leading performers as Sarah Bernhardt, Vera Kommisarzhevskaya, John Barrymore, and even the youthful work of John Gielgud and Laurence Olivier.

A Commercial Theatre Original: The American Musical Theatre

A signal contribution to world commercial theatre has been the American "musical," which has evolved since the mid-nineteenth century into an identifiable type that some historians consider America's sole innovation in drama.

A curious mélange called *The Black Crook* (1866) is usually cited as the starting point of a distinctly American musical theatre. Behind it were several traditions: French *vaudeville,* melodrama, and ballad opera, and, most immediately, displays of female bodies that presented themselves as extravaganzas, ballets, and "shows." (Even the great Charlotte Cushman seems to have appeared in one in Philadelphia in the 1840s.) *The Black Crook* attached a melodramatic plot to some spectacular scenery and some provocative costumes and ran for months. One of its heirs was American burlesque, the comic, musical form that turned into a vehicle for striptease; the other was the form we now call the musical. Also important to it were comic operetta and Viennese operetta.

Both the French *opéra-bouffe* and the English comic operetta were influential. The leader of the French strain was Jaques Offenbach (e.g., *La Belle Hélène*, 1864), and of the English, Sir William Gilbert and Sir Arthur Sullivan (e.g., *Patience*, 1881) whose operettas are still widely performed in virtually their original staging.

Johann Strauss is linked to the waltz and to the Viennese operetta, the musical form made popular in Vienna from his own *Fledermaus* (1874) to Franz Lehar's *Merry Widow* (1907). It was a neoromantic mixture of lush music and amorous action; popular in America, it influ-

enced composers like Victor Herbert (e.g., *Naughty Marietta*, 1910). It is significant that all of these are remembered for their music, not for their texts; as in opera, the composer was the dominant artist. In most cases, a dramatic text existed to give the music opportunity, offering stock neoromantic characters, rather glamorous plots, and happy endings.

By World War I, American musical comedy had split into two large categories, the *review* and the *book musical*. The most spectacular reviews were the *Ziegfeld Follies*, presented annually by Florenz Ziegfeld; they had no plot and no connected scenes, but a mixture instead of comic turns, skits, and lavish "production numbers" involving the beautiful Ziegfeld Girls in costumes noted for their luxury. Satirical reviews were popular in England, especially in club theatres, where they avoided the Lord Chamberlain; in America, smaller reviews like

FIGURE 15.31

Contemporary commercial realism. *A Thousand Clowns* at Brown County Playhouse, Indiana University. Directed by Jeffrey Huberman.

The Little Show (1929) brought many comic and musical performers to the stage.

The book musical became the more important type, however. The book was the dramatic script; in American hands, it lost its more obviously neoromantic qualities and grounded itself in American life. From World War I onward, the book musical provided a large proportion of America's best popular music and engaged her best popular composers (although seldom, with the exception of George Gershwin, her serious composers): Gershwin (*Of Thee I Sing*, 1931); Jerome Kern (*Showboat*, 1927); Cole Porter (*Kiss Me Kate*, 1948); Richard Rodgers (*Oklahoma!*, 1943); Frederick Lowe (*My Fair Lady*, 1959); and Stephen Sondheim (*Sweeney Todd*, 1979). The stages in the enrichment of the book musical have been:

1. Integration of book and music so that the songs do not stand out but are continuations of the book (*Pal Joey*, 1935).
2. Greater seriousness of subject and treatment (*Showboat*, 1927).
3. Integration of serious dance (*Oklahoma!*, 1943).
4. Contemporaneity of music (*Sweeney Todd*, 1979).

The American musical is the mainstay of the American commercial theatre. Expensive as musicals have become to produce, they are the most consistently attractive form to producers and audiences, and paler reflections of them can be seen everywhere in the nation in community theatres, educational theatres, and schools. For many, American musical theatre *is* American theatre.

Conclusion

Realism was and is a shifting concept. The realism of Belasco's *Girl of the Golden West* was different from the realism of Bloch's 1883 production of Ibsen's *Enemy of the People*, and both were different from the realism of Elia Kazan's production of Miller's *Death of a Salesman*. John Gassner pointed out perceptively that realism has become the established style of our age—the received tradition, the benchmark, and paradoxically (now) the most traditional of styles.

The situation that had existed since at least 1700 was suddenly reversed with realism: similarity to life had once been a notable departure from convention, but it now became the convention from which other styles must depart.

After 1900 the number of such departures multiplied rapidly. Realism, even though its definition shifted somewhat, was accepted by the commercial theatre and by mainstream popular criticism as stable. Other forms were "experiments," but realism was not, a scant few decades after its inception. Such is the nature of revolution.

The revolution in ideas that was epitomized by Ibsen did not turn the bulk of drama as topsy-turvy as the revolution in physical production did that of staging. The great majority of plays continued to offer mere imitations of lifelike problems that were then solved by improbable means—they continued to be romantic rather than becoming realistic. They were staged in the style of realism, however, and so became "authentic."

Perhaps realism—the mainstream style of both the United States and the Soviet Union—is the style most accessible to mass industrial societies.

ENDNOTES

1. John Ellis, *The Social History of the Machine Gun* (1st American ed., New York: Pantheon, 1975).
2. Neil Tanter, *Population Since the Industrial Revolution* (London: Croom Helm, 1973), p. 41.
3. Ibid., pp. 41–42.
4. D. Friedlander, *Population Studies* XXIV, 1970, quoted in Tranter, p. 51.
5. Andre Jammes, *William H. Fox Talbot* (New York: Macmillan, 1972), p. 5.
6. Quoted in Jerome Bump, "Manual Photography," *Texas Quarterly* 16 (Summer 1973): 104.
7. Jovan Hristic, "The Problem of Realism in Modern Drama," *New Literary History* 8 (1977): 314.
8. Gary Stephens, "Haunted Americana: The Endurance of American Realism," *Partisan Review* 44 (1977): 71–84.
9. Abram Tertz (Andre Siniavskii), *On Socialist Realism,* trans. George Dennis (New York: Pantheon, 1960), p. 24.
10. Ibid., p. 44.
11. Georg Lukacs, *Realism in Our Time,* trans. John and Necke Mander (New York: Harper & Row, 1964), p. 93.
12. Ibid., pp. 95–96.
13. Richard Southern, *The Victorian Theatre* (New York: Theatre Arts Books, 1970), p. 50.
14. Garff B. Wilson, *Three Hundred Years of American Drama and Theatre* (Englewood Cliffs, N.J.: Prentice-Hall, 1973), p. 249.
15. J. Osborne, "From Political to Cultural Despotism. . . .," *Theatre Quarterly* 5 (March 1975): 41.
16. Max Grube, *The Story of the Meininger,* trans. Ann Marie Koller (Coral Gables, Fl.: University of Miami Press, 1963), p. 5.
17. Anonymous, "The Meiningen Company and the London Stage," *Blackwood's Magazine* (1881), reprinted in *Appleton's* (1881): 357.
18. Grube, appendix.
19. Osborne, p. 42.
20. John H. Terfloth, "The Pre-Meiningen Rise of the Director in Germany and Austria," *Theatre Quarterly* 6 (Spring 1976): 69.
21. Ibid.
22. Ibid.
23. A. Nicholas Vardac, *Stage to Screen* (Cambridge, Mass.: Harvard University Press, 1949), p. xxiii.
24. Francis Pruner, *Les Luttes d'Antoine au Théâtre Libre* (Paris: Minard, Lettres Modernes, 1964), vol. 1, p. 32.
25. Francis Pruner, ed., *Lettres à Pauline* (Paris: Société des Belles Lettres, 1962), p. 160.
26. André Antoine, *Memories of the Théâtre-Libre,* trans. Marvin A. Carlson (Coral Gables, Fla.: University of Miami Press, 1964), p. 9.
27. Pruner, ed., *Lettres,* p. 306.
28. Ibid.
29. Pruner, ed., *Lettres,* p. 307.
30. Ibid., p. 313.
31. Ibid., p. 321.
32. Antoine, pp. 85–86.
33. Ibid., p. 226.
34. Ibid., p. 56.
35. Ibid., pp. 150–151.
36. Vladimir Nemirovich-Danchenko, *My Life in the Russian Theatre,* trans. John Cournos (New York: Theatre Arts Books, 1968; reprint of Little, Brown edition of 1936), p. 81.
37. Ibid., pp. 89–100.
38. Konstantin Stanslavski, *My Life in Art,* trans. J. J. Robbins (New York: Theatre Arts Books, 1948), p. 556.
39. Norris Houghton, *Return Engagement* (New York: Holt, Rinehart and Winston, 1962), p. 68.
40. Ibid., p. 60.
41. Kenneth Tynan, quoted in James Roose-Evans, *Experimental Theatre,* rev. ed. (London: Studio Vista, 1973), p. 11.
42. Jack Poggi, "The Stanislavsky System in Russia," *The Drama Review* 17 (March 1973) .
43. Lewis Wingfield, "Realism Behind the Footlights," *Fortnightly Review,* New Series 35 (January–June 1884): 474–479.
44. Sally R. Vernon, "Trouble up at 'Mill," *Victorian Studies* 22, 2 (Winter 1977): 137.
45. Ibid.
46. Michael R. Booth, "A Defense of Nineteenth Century Drama," *Educational Theatre Journal* 26, 1 (March 1974): 9.
47. Frederick Penzel, *Theatre Lighting Before Electricity* (Middletown, Conn.: Wesleyan University Press, 1978), p. 59.
48. Ibid., p. 60. On the subject of Irving's work with

light, see Allan Hughes, "Henry Irving's Artistic Use of Stage Lighting," *Theatre Notebook* 33, 3 (1979): 100–109.

49. Hunton D. Sellman, *Essentials of Stage Lighting* (Englewood Cliffs, N.J.: Prentice-Hall, 1972), p. 18; Hughes, p. 102.

50. Arthur A. Bright, Jr., *The Electric-Lamp Industry* (New York: Macmillan, 1949), p. 55.

51. Ibid., p. 24.

52. Frederick Bentham, *The Art of Stage Lighting*, 3rd ed. (London: Pitman House, 1980), p. 40.

53. Sellman, pp. 27–28.

54. Simon Tidworth, *Theatres, An Architectural and Cultural History* (New York: Praeger, 1973), p. 182.

55. Ibid., p. 174.

56. Ibid., p. 182.

57. Kenneth MacGowan, *The Theatre of Tomorrow* (New York: Boni and Liveright, 1921), p. 188.

58. See, for example, B. H. Lee, "Origins of the Box Set in the Late 18th Century," *Theatre Survey* 18 (November 1977): 44–59; and Orville Larson, "New Evidence on the Box Set," *Theatre Survey* 21 (1980): 79–91.

59. W. Telbin, "Art in the Theatres: The Question of Reform," *The Magazine of Art* (1894): 45.

60. Genevieve Stebbins, quoted in *The Delsarte Recitation Book,* 4th ed., ed. Elsie M. Wilbor (New York: Werner, 1905), p. 9.

61. Steele Mackaye, quoted in *Delsarte Recitation,* p. 7.

62. Timothy Wiles, *The Theater Event* (Chicago: University of Chicago Press, 1980), p. 31.

63. Ibid., p. 27.

64. Vasily Osipovich Toporkov, *Stanislavski in Rehearsal,* trans. Christine Edwards (New York: Theatre Arts Books, 1979), pp. 86–87.

65. Ibid., p. 213.

66. Sonia Moore, "Critical Response," *Theatre Journal* (December 1981): 527.

67. Poggi, p. 126.

68. Quoted in Penzel, p. 62.

69. Lise-Lone Marker and Frederick J. Marker, "William Bloch and Naturalism in the Scandinavian Theatre," *Theatre Survey* 15 (November 1974): 85–104, and "Bloch, Ibsen and Nineteenth-century Rehearsal Practice: A Note," *Theatre Survey* 16 (May 1975): 89–92. See also Carla Waal, "William Bloch's *The Wild Duck,*" *ETJ* 30 (December 1978): 499–512.

70. Marker and Marker, p. 90.

71. Wilson, p. 246.

72. Sheldon Cheney, *The Art Theater* (New York: Alfred Knopf, 1925), p. 25.

16

Illusionistic Stages in Review

Introduction

From the Italian Renaissance to the 1950s, illusionistic stages dominated theatre in the West. The facade stages of the classical period lasted about one thousand years; the emblematic, simultaneous stages of the medieval era lasted only six hundred years; the illusionistic stages prevailed for a relatively modest four hundred years. Their four-hundred-year history is nonetheless difficult to embrace. Like any period, it is complex, diverse, and contradictory. Moreover, its events are closer to us in time than those of the classical or medieval worlds and so more difficult to render coherent. Finally, the massive number of facts, the sheer bulk of information (available largely because of printing) makes the selection and ordering proportionately more difficult.

The past several chapters have stressed differences among illusionistic theatres in various centuries and countries. This chapter, by contrast, focuses on the similarities among illusionistic theatres, downplaying for the moment their differences in order to illuminate their important shared features. Once identified, these shared features can then be usefully contrasted with the qualities of the earlier facade and simultaneous stages.

Question: What Were the Major Features of Theatres From about 1550 to about 1950?

They were *private* or *commercial* rather than civic, public, or religious. The performances were *regularly scheduled* rather than occasional, *professional* rather than amateur. They took place *indoors,* in spaces designed specifically as *theatre buildings*. There, a *proscenium arch* separated the scenic space from the audience space; and the scenery, thus framed, presented an *illusion* of a real world. Audiences were encouraged both by the shape of the auditorium and the placement of the scenery to *watch performances from one direction.*

Within the four hundred years, however, some significant shifts occurred. Renaissance theatres were most often places of private entertainment for aristocrats at court; after the eighteenth century, however, most theatres were commercial enterprises serving all classes of society. Drama changed: tragedies stopped featuring state issues enacted by aristocratic characters and began treating domestic or private matters played out by ordinary people; comedies placed less emphasis on social correction and more on simple diversion; and a variety of new forms earned first critical interest and then critical acceptance. Early in the period, the actors played well in front of the scenery (as in the earlier facade stages), forging a link between the world of the audience and that of the stage. Late in the period, however, the actors retreated behind the proscenium arch and played within their scenic environment, a shift that found architectural expression through changing treatments of the forestage and the proscenium doors. The nature of the world behind the proscenium changed: from a painted reproduction of a classical world (as interpreted by the *literati*) to a three-dimensional reproduction of a contemporary one.

Question: What Was the Role of Art in Society?

As we have seen, theatre in the Classical Age was well-integrated with civic life. Plays were presented during special days, at great festivals that all people could attend; work stopped while the citizens watched plays that depicted public—even cosmic—actions. Likewise, during the Middle Ages, great cycles, performed only occasionally, were community events held at any convenient public place: inside a cathedral, outside on the church steps, alongside the buildings of a public square. Here ordinary people worked together to produce plays that depicted the great mysteries of the Christian religion, binding this world to the next.

After the Renaissance, the theatre was not integrated into civic life in that way. Theatre buildings were now usually privately owned (either by a ruler or by an entrepreneur). They were located on privately held lands, generally situated close to the specific audiences that they served (near the court or, later, near commercial centers). Theatres opened on a regular basis, typically in the evenings (after work) several times a week for several months of each year. The theatre was professional, with some men and women earning their living through performances that others paid to watch. The plays that they performed, indoors and in private spaces, were as apt to deal with personal or domestic questions as with public or cosmic ones, and they were as likely to offer contemporary as historical or mythical references. The theatre had thus been transformed from an unusual public event in the life of a community to a common social event in the daily lives of individuals able and willing to pay for it. Going to the theatre became, for urban people, a welcome diversion from their workaday world, an embellishment with which to end a day rather than an event around which to build a year.

Other Arts

The visual arts, like the theatre arts, became less civic and religious. Artists did not work for cities or churches but for individual patrons. Art patronage often took on political and economic overtones, for courts vied with one another for the latest and best art. When Louis XIV embarked on his construction of Versailles, for example, he hired over one hundred sculptors to embellish his palace and gardens; the court of Versailles then became the standard against which all were measured. After new materials and techniques increased the efficiency with which artworks could be produced, decorative paintings and statues could—and did—adorn the living spaces of all who could pay for them. When techniques of mass production emerged, art objects became available for the first time to common people, for they were suddenly affordable. Throughout the four hundred years, artworks—paintings, sculptures, and even buildings—expressed the personal tastes of those who bought them: they were seldom the communal expression of religious awe or civic pride.

Society

There is obviously no simple reason for art's new role in society. Certain changes in society itself, however, offer tantalizing parallels.

FIGURE 16.1

Like the other arts, sculpture changed, becoming more accessible and more democratic between the seventeenth and the nineteenth centuries, as this comparison of a sculpture from Louis XIV's Versailles and a popular Rogers group (ca. 1880) shows. Note changes both in the subject matter and in the materials used. [Sculpture from Bourgeois, and Rogers group from a contemporary catalog.]

First, *capitalism* replaced feudalism as the basic economic system, and capitalism stressed the exchange of commodities for profit. It encouraged competition rather than cooperation and stressed private rather than communal ownership. Its emphasis on travel and trade rather than agriculture probably caused a changed sense of time and space, as rather precise instruments like clocks and compasses replaced the leisurely cycles of harvests and seasons in human affairs. Commercial times and spaces existed alongside the natural cycles without partaking directly of them.

Second, theatre depends on audiences and therefore on centers of population. The period of illusionistic theatre was one in which *cities*— rather than manors or villages—dominated the political and social landscape, for in a trading economy, cities were crucial, forming the hubs where money and goods could be conveniently collected and exchanged and, in an industrial economy, providing a massive work force to operate the machines of the factories. The inhabitants of these cities had disposable income. As soon as the early Renaissance trading cities of Italy developed the staging conventions of illusionism, these conventions were easily exported to other major cities. Thereafter, both the increasing world population and the growing capitalistic economy favored the growth of cities and therefore the spread and survival of theatres.

Question: How Were Artistic Space and Time Defined?

Both architecture and setting defined theatrical space in the theatre of illusion. Audiences gathered inside a building to watch actors perform either before or within a framed picture, which was created by the scenery within a proscenium arch. The proscenium itself was seldom designed as part of the stage world; rather, it was a neutral frame, separating the world of the stage from that of the auditorium. By convention, audiences ignored the proscenium arch, yet agreed to define the proscenium doors as appropriate; that is, they could be doors into a room or entrances to the forest. The scenery behind the frame either suggested or reproduced the specific places called for in the scripts, striving—for the first time as far as we know—to achieve the illusion of a real place.

Other Arts

The overriding visual convention of the four hundred years was perspective.

The discovery during the Renaissance of the scientific and mathematical principles that allowed artists to give the illusion of three dimensions on a two-dimensional surface revolutionized the art of painting and significantly altered architecture and sculpture. Perspective made it possible to render a clear and consistent picture of things in space. Not only was the result to offer an illusion of the real world but also to promote a new principle of artistic unity. A work of art was framed. It was seen from a single viewpoint, and its unity depended on the proper placement of elements in relation to that viewpoint. The picture as a whole became more important than any one of its parts. Painting represented a specific place at a specific time seen from a specific point of view: the medieval presentation of simultaneous places and times, all capable of being seen from several directions, was no longer acceptable. By introducing the illusion of depth, the painter could make a viewer look through the canvas, as it were, into the world beyond.

Architects were equally fascinated by the possibility of perspective and also sought to achieve the effect of depth in their work. Through a combination of barrel vaults and painted details, architects introduced the illusion of greater depth within parts of a building. By designing landscapes carefully, they sought to increase the sense of distance, even out-of-doors, within formal gardens whose rows of trees seemed to stretch into infinity. Even sculptors experimented with the manipulation of apparent distance, producing reliefs that partook of painting and earned praise as "pictures in bronze."

Theatre

Beginning with the Renaissance, theatre artists used scientific principles, mathematically expressed, to produce the illusion of depth on a stage. This introduction of perspective linked the stage and the audience in new ways by defining a single appropriate relationship between the viewer and the scenery. As well, perspective allowed the stage picture to offer an illusion of a real place. Thus, the stage now depicted a single place at a time. When the place changed (between plays or within a play), the scenery—the appearance of the stage—changed. The visual unity of a production came, then, from the completed stage picture, which was itself an illusion of a single place seen from a single point of view. Perspective settings, in turn, defined and limited the nature of artistic time. Because the scenic space produced an illusion of a real place existing at a given time, dramatic space and time were tied together and to the audience. Only between acts and scenes could dramatic time pass quickly; within an act, as the audience confronted the illusion of a real place, dramatic time was limited by audience (real-world) time.

The visual conventions of the stage had be-

FIGURE 16.2

Perspective invaded all aspects of art. One can see it at work with a barrel vault in St. Peter's Church, Rome [from Lubke], and in the landscaping of Louis XIV's Versailles [from Bourgeois].

come those of painting rather than those of theology (the medieval period) or architecture (the classical period). The choice should not be surprising, for art historians generally agree that since the Renaissance, painting has been the principal means of expressing the Western perception of visual reality.

Society

Although Christianity remained a powerful and binding force throughout the four hundred years, attention definitely shifted away from God and His Universe to people and their world. Natural laws that governed the operation of this (physical) world received at least as much attention as theological pronouncements about the nature of the next (spiritual) one. Individuals gained renewed importance, not only as special creatures of God but also as important participants in social, political, and economic systems. Although this new *Christian humanism* differed from both its medieval and its classical precedents, it clearly partook of both. Although certainly not denying the importance of religion and God, Christian humanists were rugged individualists, interested in life here on earth.

"With the invention of perspective the modern notion of individualism found its artistic counterpart. Every element in a perspective representation is related to the unique point of view of the individual spectator,"[1] argued Sigfried Giedion in his influential book *Space, Time, and Architecture*. Doubtless, as Giedion proposed, the *humanism* of modern society contributed to its adoption of a visual convention like perspective. Another influence was equally significant, however: reliance on *scientific observation and mathematical formulations*.

The Middle Ages had relied heavily on received wisdom, to which logic might then be applied. Wisdom came from the authority of the Bible and certain approved classical texts, notably those of Aristotle, who stressed qualitative categories. Reasoning proceeded from the accepted proposition to its logical outcome.

With the rediscovery of classical texts (especially scientific texts) and the emerging interest in the physical world came new modes of thinking. Careful observation and measurement showed that logic did not always agree with fact. It was logical, for example, that heavy objects should fall faster than light ones; careful observation showed that they did not, however. Theology taught and logic seemed to support the proposition that the earth stood still in the center of the universe while heavenly bodies moved around it; careful observations combined with sophisticated mathematical reckoning proved that, on the contrary, the earth moved around a fixed sun.

Empiricism and inductive reasoning were increasingly respected as ways of knowing. Before the end of the seventeenth century, the works of Copernicus, Galileo, Kepler, Newton, and others had effected a major scientific revolution. Among the assumptions on which this new scientific system rested was the assumption that space and time are absolute and that phenomena like time and mass and length are independent of an observer. This scientific model—of an independent, fixed observer whose observations do not affect the course of the phenomenon—was well suited to a visual system that depended on a single point of view from which to see and to reproduce what was seen. It was the scientific model that dominated until the work of Einstein and Heisenberg in our own century.

Perhaps more important, the scientific revolution of Copernicus and Newton had shown clearly that observable phenomena could be mathematically described and that, once described, they could be understood, systematized, and taught. As a part of this emerging world of scientific observation, it is not surprising that artists grew determined to uncover and codify the principles by which they perceived distance. Once understood, these principles (reduced to mathematical certainties and thus expressed) could be taught. Thereafter, the ability to reproduce the illusion of reality in works of art could be systematic rather than haphazard.

Question: How Were Perceptions of Space Manipulated?

Early, with designers like Serlio and Torelli, the stage was seen as an extension of the auditorium. The single vanishing point at upstage center encouraged audiences to look beyond— to extend the world of the stage into the distance at the back of the stage. During the eighteenth century, designers like Piranesi and the Bibieni multiplied the vanishing points so that the stage was no longer perceived as an extension of the auditorium. Moreover, they altered the apparent scale of the scenery by manipulating the vanishing points and extending the sets out of sight into the wings and flies, making the stage space seem vaster. From the Renaissance until the late eighteenth century, the emphasis was on linear perspective—the use of receding lines to suggest depth.

With the coming of romanticism, these perspective lines were deemphasized. Irregularly shaped wings (trees, bushes, and rocks) and irregularly placed pieces (groundrows) obscured rather than underscored the perspective lines. Now, light and color were manipulated to achieve the sense of distance—and to suggest a mood. As aerial rather than linear perspective began to dominate the stage, unity seemed as much tied to color, texture, and mood as to line and symmetry. Painted backdrops still encouraged audiences to include space beyond the stage as a part of the illusion, for landscapes and horizons seemed to stretch off to infinity.

Box sets, increasingly important after 1850, brought another shift in visual perception. Distance was not sought through perspective. The stage was virtually self-contained, confined on four sides and often at the top (through a ceiling piece). A couple of doors or windows might offer a timid suggestion of a world beyond the stage, but its vastness was not indicated, as designers stressed its limits rather than its infinity. The stage world had become smaller—some would say, claustrophobic.

Other Arts

Not surprisingly, painters and architects displayed similar shifts in their manipulations of space. During the Renaissance, painters used a perspective that depended on a limited range of distance and required a measurable point of optical interest. They offered a static view of the world, one that relied on receding lines to achieve a sense of distance. Fascinated by the mathematical principles that allowed them to suggest distance, the painters typically painted inside a studio from sketches made beforehand. Romantic landscape painters, by contrast, used multiple vanishing points and a seemingly limitless field of vision to capture the qualities of change through the manipulation of color, light, and texture. They painted as they observed. With the coming of photography and moving pictures, the literal (mechanical and thus unselected) reproduction of surface reality became possible. The goal of illusionistic painting seemed realized at last.

Because architects manipulate volumes rather than surfaces, their approach was somewhat different. Their solutions were equally instructive, however, for they demonstrated similarly changing conceptions of space. Renaissance architects abandoned the plan of medieval cities, whose streets formed bands around the center, in favor of star-shaped cities whose streets radiated out from a single center. Certainly this pattern resulted in part from the requirements of military fortification, but it also seemed to be simply another expression of the visual convention that dominated that period: single-point perspective: "The central building in the midst of a star-shaped city fulfills the same role—that of a symbolic observer standing at the focal point."[2] Before the nineteenth century, more complex conceptions of space caused city planners to organize cities around streets that connected all major points of interest within them and to integrate nature with the city. First at Versailles and then in cities like Rome, Paris, and London, a complicated arrangement of natural and man-made elements were forced into a new unity as parks and gardens, buildings and streets were laid out in planned spaces. By the end of the nineteenth century, some city planners arranged individual suburban houses, warrenlike, each with its own small garden (a still more complex and compartmentalized vision of space). Through the four hundred years, then, architects abandoned the spatial unity provided by a single point of view in favor of a more complex, more fragmented, and more confined vision of space.

Society

The various manipulations of space within a tradition that remained firmly illusionistic can serve as useful metaphors for a variety of social shifts that occurred contemporaneously. Obviously, we do not assert that one caused the other; rather, we observe that they happened at about the same time and therefore may have complex relationships only dimly understood.

Single-point perspective dominated theatrical art at a period when authority (usually classical or biblical) was sought to justify many (perhaps even most) practices. Not only past authorities but also general principles (rules) were sought as guides to behavior. Once discovered, such rules were codified, their transmission was centralized, and adherence to them was required. Academies were established to teach mathematics and anatomy to artists so that they could master the theories and techniques of perspective and figure drawing and thus achieve an illusion of the real world. It was a world where autocratic governance was the rule rather than the exception, and where the rulers mattered far more than the people ruled:

> The space art of perspective, which depended on a single fixed eyepoint, was possible only

FIGURE 16.3

The treatment of space in cities changed during the period from the seemingly accidental banding of a medieval town like Marseilles [from Lacroix], to the complex, radiating patterns found in Louis XIV's Versailles [from Farmer], to modern modular towns. [Oklahoma City, ca. 1900, courtesy Prints Division, Astor, Lenox, and Tilden Foundations, New York Public Library.]

 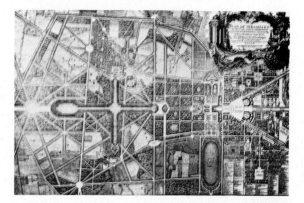

when duke and cardinal in the Renaissance were rich enough and important enough to create an aristocratic theatre just to please themselves. For the first time, the architect could build a scene for a small ducal party and forget completely such other people as were permitted to look on at the princely entertainment. . . . The rich Italian princes, at the beginning of an age of absolutism, made themselves the center of the circle: the scenic elements were on the arc of the circumference.[3]

At the end of this age of authority and authoritarianism, we find Louis XIV, the Sun King, the center of the world as the sun was center of the universe and a single building the center of the city. His is perhaps the most conspicuous example of the desire to centralize and codify artistic as well as political authority. He established his Royal Academy, in which a complete system of instruction prepared artists to achieve previously formulated and approved artistic standards.

As political authority dissipated, so did artistic authority. When Louis XIV died, the nobility left Versailles in great numbers and began to build their own residences. To decorate their homes and gardens, they hired painters and sculptors who had *not* been trained at the Royal Academy. At the same time, scientific and mathematical advances were offering more complex ways of depicting space: the techniques of multipoint perspective emerged alongside the development of calculus. Merchants and tradespeople were forming an increasing part of the cities' social and political life—and of their theatre audiences. For these audiences, some of the old aristocratic rules seemed predictably irrelevant. The authority of the classics was increasingly questioned. Indeed, when some of the new intellectuals compared classical and modern art, the ancient models were judged inferior.

By the early nineteenth century, the population of the cities was increasing significantly because of rising birth rates, declining death rates, and the accelerating immigration of workers from the countryside. City dwellers—merchants and workers—clamored for more representative governments. They asserted the rights of individuals against those of absolute rules and rulers. Artists turned their attention from the rules of art to the emotions produced by the artistic experience, from precise mathematical formulations to subjective manipulations of light and color: aerial perspective overtook linear perspective. Likewise, the test of good art shifted from adherence to a set of external criteria (devised by a literary elite) to the arousal of an emotional response among all individuals who saw the work.

By the early twentieth century in the West, representative and democratic governments were the rule rather than the exception. By then, too, the theatres had adopted a more democratic visual experience: box sets replaced perspective scenery, and so all people sitting within the sight lines of a theatre had an equally good view of the stage setting. Plays now more often had urban settings than outdoor (or rural) settings, and so in the theatre, as in real life, spaces that had once seemed so vast now seemed quite limited and confined. Industrialization had already resulted in uniformity; spaces, times, and even experiences had grown modular, often seemingly interchangeable. Mechanical arts—photographs and movies—placed new limits on the role of the artist and the audience. Rugged individualism—a view that saw individual human actions as important—had given way to the fear that individual human actions were powerless in the path of outside forces. As human action seemed more inconsequential, human personality seemed more essential to identity. One contemporary critic described the shift this way: "Renaissance [drama] was drama of great individuals, today's is that of individualism. . . . The realization and maintenance of personality has become . . . pressing and urgent. . . . survival as an individual, the integrity of individuality, [thus] becomes the vital center of drama."[4]

Question: Why Were Details So Important in the Theatre of Illusion?

Theatre artists had always used details to decorate and to signify. Illusionistic artists used them for these purposes; but they also used them to *authenticate*—to make more believable the illusion of reality. They therefore included many details whose sole function was to bolster the correspondence between the real world and the stage world. They used details to increase the *sense of distance*. Serlio, for example, called for converging lines to be painted on the stage floor and for architectural elements to be added to the first set of wings as an aid to perspective. Torelli regularly repeated similar or identical scenic elements—a series of arches or pillars or houses—in order to accentuate the receding (perspective) lines. Designers added details to transform the stage into a *certain kind of space* suitable for the action of the play. Serlio, for example, painted public buildings for tragedy and private houses for comedy; the Bibieni introduced ornately encrusted baroque halls for operas that seemed to demand interior spaces suggesting wealth and vastness. Later designers sought not a certain kind of place but a certain, *specific* place—even an actual place. De Loutherbourg therefore included enough painted details for his audience to recognize the specific London site that he had reproduced. Antoine hung real sides of beef on a stage to achieve the illusion of an actual butcher's shop.

Throughout the four hundred years, the purpose of artistic details remained unchanged: to decorate, to signify, and to authenticate. Their number and kind, however, changed, as did the manner of rendering them. Sculpture, painting, and theatre all followed roughly the same patterns.

At the Renaissance, sculpture broke away from its medieval and architectural moorings. Statues were no longer attached to buildings, as embellishments to the architecture. Freestanding, three-dimensional sculpture, in the manner of the ancients, offered an imaginative blend of classical and Christian motifs and from the outset aimed for a lifelike, if idealized, human body. Similarly, Renaissance painters largely abandoned the religious, symbol-laden, and flat art of the Middle Ages. Working in their studios, they rigorously selected details according to the mathematical and anatomical principles that governed the representation of idealized reality. Their details, like the mathematical principles on which they rested, were sparse and elegant. Their subjects, scenes from classical and Christian mythology or idealized subjects of the ruling classes, all but guaranteed that their details would be selected for their contribution to an illusion of a world that was beautiful. In the theatre, both drama and scenery sought the authenticity of the classics.

By the end of the eighteenth century, sculptors were increasingly divided over whether it was better to portray an individual "by presenting society's general notion of the subject, or by showing a significant moment, imbuing the figure with a narrative quality more akin to the painter's approach."[5] After the collapse of Napoleon's Empire, the issue was decided in favor of the new romantic view. Thereafter more sculptors sought new qualities of movement, dynamism, and vividness. Some began to depict actual people in specific situations, dressed in exact and accurate costumes; some even began to represent wild animals in action. At about the same time, romantic painters moved out of the studio in order to select and render the details of a scene while they observed it. They sought to capture the particular, kinetic event before them, and so they introduced details of light, shadow, color, and texture that had before seemed irrelevant. Their subjects were now portrait studies of simple people and views of unspoiled nature: tumbling clouds, gathering storms, rugged mountains, tangled undergrowth—details of nature untended and uncontrolled.

Before the end of the nineteenth century, in all arts the details of workers and science and industry replaced those of peasants and nature. And cameras were able to capture, record, and permanently fix in time all of the visual details exposed to their mechanical and chemical eyes. Cameras included all details without selection and without regard for meaning, mathematical formula, or emotional power: the details of a photograph were there *simply* because the details existed in real life.

In the theatre, the illusionists' careful attention to detail doubtless promoted authentication, but the inclusion of so many details that served no specific dramatic function (in the sense of furthering the action or underscoring significance) probably caused audiences to begin to demand details for their own sake and so probably caused details to lose much of their ability to signify. Furthermore, the tenacity of illusionism as a goal of production was probably obscured by the marked changes in the appearance of the stage (caused by shifts in the number, kind, and rendering of details). That is, theatrical conventions probably seemed to undergo radical changes when, in fact, they were shifting only superficially.

This age was apparently the first in which a major goal of the theatre was to produce an illusion of the real world. Early in the period, the illusion was a picture of a generalized but still recognizable scene; later it was of a specific—even an actual—location. Early, the illusion was achieved by two-dimensional scenery painted in perspective; late in the period, three-dimensional objects replaced their painted representations. Early, actors played in front of the scenery; late, they moved within the scenery. These shifts, however, were shifts in degree and technique, not intention.

The appetite for reproducing "reality" in the visual arts grew during these four hundred years so that by the twentieth century, people had grown to expect a literal, almost photographic reproduction of the real world in their pictures, statues, and plays. Not surprisingly, the development of photography and cinema affected each of the arts whose goal had been to offer an illusion of reality. After the coming of photography and cinema, for example, many painters ceased to regard the canvas as primarily a window to reality: the picture itself became more important than whatever it was to represent. Painters were no longer content to merely "photograph" their subjects; they wished instead to express their own feelings, or to study shapes and colors on canvas, or to shock viewers into a new consciousness. Many sculptors for the first time since the Middle Ages sought to free their art from its Pygmalion myth: that sculpture should always reproduce a recognizable human body. They said that "instead of art about the world (and especially *about* the human presence in the world)" they wanted to offer "an art which is *of* the world."[6] Some, therefore, began to make works about the materials that they used, about the mathematical principles involved in the work, or simply about the interpenetration of space and matter.

The theatre's response to cinema has not yet been clarified. Cinema seems to be able to offer an even greater illusion of reality than theatre. Indeed, Nicholas Vardac has argued persuasively that the age's compulsion for illusion made the invention of cinema almost inevitable: "The necessity for greater pictorial realism in the arts of theatre appears as the logical impetus to the invention of cinema." He also posed several provocative questions about the fate of an illusionistic theatre given the invention of cinema, questions that are not yet answered with certainty: "Did the cinema take over the audience of the nineteenth-century pictorial stage? Did this pictorial stage disappear? How did early twentieth-century theatrical producers combat the encroachment of the film? Was there a change in style? How do the sporadic reactionary experiments of the 'producer's' theatre in the early 1900s fit into the picture?"[7]

FIGURE 16.4

The nature of the scenery of illusionism changed from a generalized painted set before which actors played, as shown in this Terence manuscript of the sixteenth century, to a particularized, detailed, often interior setting filled with three-dimensional details, as shown in this twentieth-century production of the famous *Uncle Tom's Cabin*. [Terence manuscript courtesy of Rare Books and Manuscript Division, The New York Public Library, Astor, Lenox and Tilden Foundations. *Uncle Tom's Cabin* from *Le Théâtre*.]

Although much remains unclear, it is certain that early in the twentieth century, some theatre artists began to seek a theatre that embodied principles other than illusionism.

ENDNOTES

1. Sigfried Giedion, *Space, Time, and Architecture: The Growth of a New Tradition*, 5th ed. (Cambridge, Mass.: Harvard University Press, 1967), p. 31.
2. Giedion, p. 44.
3. George R. Kernodle, *From Art to Theatre* (Chicago: Chicago University Press, 1944), p. 179.
4. George Lukacs, "The Sociology of Modern Drama," in Bernard Dukore, *Dramatic Theory and Criticism: Greeks to Grotowski* (New York: Holt, Rinehart and Winston, 1974), p. 937.
5. Ruth Butler, *Western Sculpture: Definitions of Man* (Boston: New York Graphic Society, 1975), p. 191.
6. Chrisopher Finch, quoted in Butler, p. 282.
7. Nicholas Vardac, *Stage to Screen: Theatrical Method from Garrick to Griffith* (Cambridge, Mass.: Harvard University Press, 1949), pp. xx, xxvi.

BIBLIOGRAPHY
Part Four

Abrams, M. H. *The Mirror and the Lamp: Romantic Theory and the Critical Tradition.* New York: Oxford University Press, 1953.

Aikin-Sneath, Betsy. *Comedy in Germany in the First Half of the Eighteenth Century.* Oxford: Oxford University Press, 1936.

Allévy, Marie Antoinette. *La Mise-en-scène en France dans la Première Moitié du Dix-neuvième Siècle.* Paris: E. Droz, 1938.

Anderson, M. S. *Historians and Eighteenth-Century Europe.* Oxford: Clarendon Press, 1979.

Appleton, William W. *Madame Vestris and the London Stage.* New York: Columbia University Press, 1974.

Arvin, Neil F. *Eugène Scribe and the French Theatre, 1815–60.* Cambridge, Massachusetts: Harvard University Press, 1924.

Antoine, André. *Memories of the Théâtre-Libre,* trans. Marvin A. Carlson. Coral Gables, Fla.: University of Miami Press, 1964.

Ayling, S. E. *Nineteenth Century Gallery.* New York: Barnes and Noble, 1970.

Barlow, Graham, "The Hotel de Bourgogne According to Sir James Thornhill," *Theatre Research International* 1, 2 (February 1976): 86–98.

Baumer, Franklin L. *Modern European Thought.* New York: Macmillan, 1977.

Baur-Heinhold, Margarete. *Baroque Theatre,* trans. Mary Whittall. London: Thames and Hudson, 1967.

Belasco, David. *Theatre Through Its Stage Door.* New York: Harper's, 1919.

Bentham, Frederick. *The Art of Stage Lighting.* London: Pitman House, 1980.

Bernbaum, Ernest. *The Drama of Sensibility: A Sketch of the History of Sentimental Comedy and Dramatic Tragedy, 1696–1780.* Boston: Ginn and Co., 1915.

Besterman, Theodore. *Voltaire.* Chicago: University of Chicago Press, 1976.

Bjurstrom, Per. *Giacomo Torelli and Baroque Stage Design.* Stockholm: Nationalmuseum, 1961.

Blum, Carol. *Diderot: The Virtue of a Philosopher.* New York: Viking Press, 1974.

Boas, Frederick Samuel. *An Introduction to Eighteenth Century Drama, 1700–1780.* Oxford: Clarendon Press, 1953.

Bolgar, R. R. *The Classical Heritage and Its Beneficiaries.* Cambridge: Cambridge University Press, 1954.

Booth, Michael R. *English Melodrama.* London: H. Jenkins, 1965.

————. "A Defense of Nineteenth Century Drama." *ETJ* 26, 1 (March 1974): 5–13.

———— et al. *The Revels History of Drama in English,* Vol. 6, 1750–1880. London: n. p., 1975.

————. "Spectacle as Production Style on the Victorian Stage." *Theatre Quarterly* 8 (Winter 1979): 8–14.

————. *Victorian Spectacular Theatre: 1850–1910.* Boston: Routledge and Keegan Paul, 1981.

Boswell, Eleanor. *The Restoration Court Stage.* Cambridge, Mass.: Harvard University Press, 1932.

Bouwsma, William J. "The Renaissance and the Drama of Western History." *American Historical Review* 84, 1 (February 1979): 1–15.

Brenner, C. D. *The Théâtre Italien: Its Repertory, 1716–1793, with a Historical Introduction.* Berkeley: University of California Press, 1961.

Bright, Arthur A., Jr. *The Electric-Lamp Industry.* New York: Macmillan, 1949.

Bruford, Walter H. *Germany in the Eighteenth Century: the Social Background of the Literary Revival.* Cambridge: Cambridge University Press, 1935.

———. *Theatre, Drama and Audience in Goethe's Germany.* Reprint edition. Westport, Conn.: Greenwood Press, 1974.

Bulgakov, Mikhail. *Black Snow,* trans. Michael Glenny. New York: Simon and Schuster, 1967.

Bump, Jerome. "Manual Photography." *Texas Quarterly* 16 (Summer 1973): 90–116.

Burckhardt, Jakob C. *The Civilization of the Renaissance in Italy,* 3rd ed. New York: Phaidon Publishers, 1950.

Burnim, Kalmin. *David Garrick, Director.* Pittsburgh: University of Pittsburgh Press, 1961.

Campbell, Lily Bess. "A History of Costuming on the English Stage Between 1660 and 1823." *University of Wisconsin Studies in Language and Literature* (1918): 187–223.

———. *Scenes and Machines on the English Stage during the Renaissance.* Cambridge: Cambridge University Press, 1923.

Carlson, Marvin. *The Theatre of the French Revolution.* Ithaca, N.Y.: Cornell University Press, 1966.

———. *The French Stage in the Nineteenth Century.* Metuchen, N.J.: Scarecrow Press, 1972.

———. *The German Stage in the Nineteenth Century.* Metuchen, N.J.: Scarecrow Press, 1972.

———. *Goethe and the Weimar Theatre.* Ithaca, N.Y.: Cornell University Press, 1978.

———. *The Italian Stage from Goldoni to d'Annunzio.* London: McFarland, 1981.

Cima, G. G. "Elizabeth Robins. . . ." *Theatre Survey* 21 (November 1980): 145–63.

Clark, Dana Stone. "The Unities of Time and Place in Sixteenth-Century Theatre and Criticism." (Ph.D. diss. SUNY Binghamton, 1976).

Clement, N. M. *Romanticism in France.* New York: Modern Language Association of America, 1939.

Clough, Cecil H. "Francis I and the Courtiers of Castiglione's *Courtier.*" *European Studies Review* 8, 1 (January 1978): 23–70.

Clurman, Harold. *The Fervent Years.* New York: Hill and Wang, 1957.

Cochrane, Eric. "Science and Humanism." *American Historical Review* 81, 5 (December 1976): 1039–1057.

———. "Renaissance to Baroque in Historiography." *History and Theory: Studies in the Philosophy of History* 19, 1 (1980): 21–38.

Cook, John A. *Neoclassic Drama in Spain: Theory and Practice.* Dallas: Southern Methodist University Press, 1959.

Corrigan, Beatrice. "Italian Renaissance Drama in the Eighteenth Century." *Comparative Drama* 10, 2 (Summer 1976): 101–115.

Dannenfeld, Karl H., ed. *Problems in European Civilization: The Renaissance, Medieval or Modern?* Boston: D.C. Heath, 1959.

Darbyshire, Alfred. *The Art of the Victorian Stage.* London, 1907; rpt. New York: Benjamin Blom, 1969.

Dickens, A. G. *The Age of Humanism and Reformation: Europe in the Fourteenth, Fifteenth and Sixteenth Centuries.* Englewood Cliffs, N.J.: Prentice-Hall, 1972.

Disher, Maurice. *Blood and Thunder: Mid-Victorian Melodrama and its Origins.* London: F. Muller, 1949.

Donahue, Joseph W. *The Theatre Manager in England and America: Players of a Perilous Game.* Princeton, N.J.: Princeton University Press, 1971.

———. *Theatre in the Age of Kean.* Totowa, N.J.: Rowman and Littlefield, 1975.

Downer, Alan S. "Nature to Advantage Dressed: Eighteenth Century Acting." *PMLA* (1943): 1002–1037.

———. "Players and the Painted Stage: Nineteenth Century Acting." *PMLA* 61 (1946): 522–576.

Duchartre, Pierre Louis. *The Italian Comedy. The Improvisation, Scenarios, Lives, Attributes, Portraits and Masks of the Illustrious Characters of the Commedia dell 'Arte,* trans. Randolph T. Weaver. New York: Dover, 1966.

Dukore, Bernard. *Dramatic Theory and Criticism: Greeks to Grotowski.* New York: Holt, Rinehart and Winston, 1974.

Dunlap, William. *History of the American Theatre.* New York: J. and J. Harper, 1832.

Edwards, Christine. *The Stanislavski Heritage.* New York: New York University Press, 1965.

Ellis, John. *The Social History of the Machine Gun.* New York: Pantheon, 1975.

Ferguson, Wallace K. *The Renaissance.* New York: Henry Holt, 1945.

Garfein, Herschel, and Gordon, Mel. "The Adriani Lazzi of the Commedia dell 'Arte." *The Drama Review* 22, 1 (March 1978): 3–12.

Giedion, Sigfried. *Space, Time and Architecture: the Growth of a New Tradition,* 5th ed. Cambridge, Mass.: Harvard University Press, 1967.

Goldoni, Carlo. *Memoirs of Carlo Goldoni,* trans. John Black. London: n.p., 1928.

Gottschalk, Louis, and Lach, Donald. *Toward the French Revolution: Europe and America in the Eighteenth-Century World.* New York: Scribner's, 1973.

Gozzi, Carlo. *The Memoirs of Count Carlo Gozzi,* trans. J. A. Symonds, 2 vols. London: J. C. Nimmo, 1890.

Gregor, Joseph. *The Russian Theatre,* trans. Paul England. Philadelphia: J. B. Lippincott, 1930.

Griffith, G. Talbot. *Population Problems of the Age of Malthus.* 2nd edition. London: Frank Cass, 1967.

Grimsted, David. *Melodrama Unveiled: American Theatre and Culture, 1800–1850.* Chicago: University of Chicago Press, 1968.

Grube, Max. *The Story of the Meininger,* trans. Ann Marie Koller. Coral Gables, Fla.: University of Miami Press, 1963.

Hannaford, Stephen. "The Shape of Eighteenth-Century Drama." *Theatre Survey* 21 (November 1980): 93–103.

Hathaway, Baxter. *The Age of Criticism: The Late Renaissance in Italy.* Ithaca, N.Y.: Cornell University Press, 1962.

Hay, Denys, ed. *The Renaissance Debate.* New York: Holt, Rinehart and Winston, 1965.

Hayman, Ronald, ed. *The German Theatre/ A Symposium.* New York: Barnes and Noble, 1975.

Hedgcock, Frank A. *A Cosmopolitan Actor: David Garrick and His French Friends.* London: Stanley Paul, 1912.

Heitner, R. R. *German Tragedy in the Age of Enlightenment, 1724–1768.* Berkeley: University of California Press, 1963.

Herrick, Marvin. *Tragicomedy: Its Origin and Development in Italy, France and England.* Urbana: University of Illinois Press, 1955.

———. *Italian Comedy in the Renaissance.* Urbana: University of Illinois Press, 1960.

———. *Italian Tragedy in the Renaissance.* Urbana: University of Illinois Press, 1965.

Hewitt, Bernard, ed. *The Renaissance Stage: Documents of Serlio, Sabbattini, and Furtten-bach.* Coral Gables, Fla.: University of Miami Press, 1958.

———. *Theatre USA, 1668–1957.* New York: McGraw-Hill, 1959.

Heydenreich, Ludwig H., and Lotz, Wolfgang. *Architecture in Italy, 1400–1600,* trans. Mary Hottinger. Baltimore: Penguin, 1974.

Highfill, Philip H., Jr., and Burnim, Kalman, and Langhans, Edward. *A Biographical Dictionary of Actors, Actresses, Musicians, Dancers, Managers, and Other Stage Personnel in London, 1660–1800.* Carbondale: Southern Illinois University Press, 1973.

Hodge, Francis. *Yankee Theatre: the Image of America on the Stage, 1825–1850.* Austin: University of Texas Press, 1964.

Hotson, Leslie. *The Commonwealth and Restoration Stage.* Cambridge, Mass.: Harvard University Press, 1928.

Howard, R. "Propaganda in the Early Soviet and Contemporary Chinese Theatre." *Theatre Quarterly* 7 (August 1977): 53–60.

Houghton, Norris. *Moscow Rehearsals.* New York: Harcourt Brace, 1936.

———. *Return Engagement.* New York: Holt, Rinehart and Winston, 1962.

Hristic, Jovan. "The Problem of Realism in Modern Drama." *New Literary History* 8 (1977): 311–318.

Hughes, Allan. "Henry Irving's Artistic Use of Stage Lighting." *Theatre Notebook* 33, 3 (1979): 100–109.

Hughes, Leo. *The Drama's Patrons.* Austin: University of Texas Press, 1971.

Hume, Robert D., ed. *The London Theatre World.* Carbondale: Southern Illinois University Press, 1980.

Illardi, Vincent. "Eyeglasses and Concave Lenses in Fifteenth-Century Florence and Milan: New Documents." *Renaissance Quarterly* 29, 3 (Autumn 1976): 341–360.

Jacquot, J. *Le Lieu Théâtral à la Renaissance.* Paris: Centre National de la Recherche Scientifique, 1964.

Jammes, Andre. *William H. Fox Talbot.* New York: Macmillan, 1972.

Joseph, Bertram. *The Tragic Actor.* New York: Theatre Arts Books, 1959.

Jourdain, Eleanor F. *Dramatic Theory and Practice in France, 1690–1808.* London: Methuen, 1924.

Kaegi, Emil, Jr. *Byzantium and the Decline of Rome.* Princeton, N.J.: Princeton University Press, 1968.

Kelly, Linda. *The Kemble Era.* London: Bodley Head, 1980.

Kennard, Joseph Spencer. *The Italian Theatre from Its Beginning to the Close of the Seventeenth Century.* New York: William Edwin Rudge, 1932.

Kernodle, George R. *From Art to Theatre: Form and Convention in the Renaissance.* Chicago: University of Chicago Press, 1944.

Kolgarriff, Michael. *The Golden Age of Melodrama.* London: Wolfe, 1974.

Kingdon, Robert M. *Transition and Revolution: Problems and Issues of European Renaissance and Reformation History.* Minneapolis: Burgess, 1974.

Kistler, Mark O. *Drama of the Storm and Stress.* New York: Twayne, 1969.

Klenze, Camillo von. *From Goethe to Hauptmann: Studies in a Changing Culture.* New York: Biblo and Tannen, 1966.

Kristeller, Paul Iskar. "Between the Italian Renaissance and the French Enlightenment: Gabriel Naude as an Editor." *Renaissance Quarterly* 32, 1 (Spring 1979): 41–72.

Krutch, Joseph Wood. *Comedy and Conscience After the Restoration.* New York: Columbia University Press, 1949.

Lacey, Alexander. *Pixérécourt and the French Romantic Drama.* Toronto: University of Toronto Press, 1928.

Lancaster, Henry Carrington. *A History of French Dramatic Literature in the Seventeenth Century.* Baltimore: Johns Hopkins University Press, 1929–42.

———. *The Comédie Française, 1680–1701.* Baltimore: Johns Hopkins University Press, 1941.

———. *Sunset: A History of Parisian Drama in the Last Years of Louis XIV, 1701–1715.* Baltimore: Johns Hopkins University Press, 1945.

———. *French Tragedy in the Time of Louis XV and Voltaire, 1715–1774.* Baltimore: Johns Hopkins University Press, 1950.

———. *French Tragedy in the Reign of Louis XVI and the Early Years of the French Revolution, 1774–1792.* Baltimore: Johns Hopkins University Press, 1953.

Larson, Orville. "New Evidence on the Box Set." *Theatre Survey* 21 (1980): 79–91.

Lawrenson, T. E. *The French Stage in the XVII Century: A Study in the Advent of the Italian Order.* Manchester: Manchester University Press, 1957.

Lea, Kathleen M. *Italian Popular Comedy: A Study of the Commedia dell 'arte, 1560–1620,* 2 vols. Oxford: Clarendon Press, 1934.

Leacroft, Richard. "The Introduction of Perspective Scenery and its Effect on Theatre Forms." Part I: *Theatre Notebook* 34, 1 (1980): 21–24; Part II: *Theatre Notebook* 34, 2 (1980): 69–73.

Lee, Briant Hamor. "Origins of the Box Set in the Late 18th Century." *Theatre Survey* 18 (1977): 44–59.

Lewis, Robert. *Method—or Madness?* London: William Heineman, 1960.

Lidtke, Vernon L. "Naturalism and Socialism in Germany." *American Historical Review* 79 (February 1974): 14–37.

The London Stage, 1660–1800, 11 vols. Carbondale: Southern Illinois University Press, 1960–1968.

Lough, John. *Paris Theatre Audiences in the Seventeenth and Eighteenth Centuries.* London: Oxford University Press, 1957.

Lovejoy, Arthur O. *Essays in the History of Ideas.* New York: G. P. Putnam's Sons, 1948.

Lucaks, Georg. *Realism in Our Time,* trans. John Mander and Necke Mander. New York: Harper & Row, 1964.

Lynch, James J. *Box, Pit and Gallery: Stage and Society in Johnson's London.* Berkeley: University of California Press, 1953.

Macready, William Charles. *Macready's Reminiscences.* New York: Macmillan, 1875.

Marker, Lise-lone, and Marker, Frederick J. "Bloch, Ibsen and Nineteenth-Century Rehearsal Practice: A Note." *Theatre Survey* 16 (May 1975): 89–92.

———. "William Bloch and Naturalism in the Scandinavian Theatre." *Theatre Survey* 15 (November 1974): 85–104.

Matthews, Brander, and Hutton, Laurence. *Actors and Actresses of Great Britain and the United States from the Days of David Garrick to the Present Time,* 5 vols. New York: Cassell and Co., 1886.

Mayor, A. H. *The Bibiena Family.* New York: H. Bittner and Co., 1945.

———. *Giovanni Battista Piranesi.* New York: H. Bittner and Co., 1952.

Mazzone-Clementi, Carlo. "Commedia and the Actor." *The Drama Review* 18, 1 (March 1974): 59–64.

McClelland, I. L. *Spanish Drama of Pathos: 1750–1808,* 2 vols. Toronto: University of Toronto Press, 1970.

McDermott, Douglass. "The Development of the Theatre on the American Frontier, 1750–1890." *Theatre Survey* 19, 1 (May 1978): 63–78.

McLuhan, Herbert Marshall. *The Gutenberg Galaxy: The Making of Typographical Man.* Toronto: University of Toronto Press, 1962.

"The Meiningen Company and the London Stage." *Blackwood's Magazine* (1881).

Melcher, Edith. *Stage Realism in France Between Diderot and Antoine.* Bryn Mawr, Pa.: Bryn Mawr College Press, 1928.

Metraux, Guy S., and Crouzet, Francois, eds. *The Nineteenth Century World: Readings from the History of Mankind.* New York: New American Library, 1963.

Milhous, Judith. *Thomas Betterton and the Management of Lincoln's Inn Fields, 1695–1708.* Carbondale: Southern Illinois University Press, 1979.

Mitchell, Bonner. "Circumstance and Setting in the Earliest Italian Productions of Comedy." *Renaissance Drama*, New Series, 4 (1974): 185–197.

Mongrédien, Georges. *Dictionnaire Biographique des Comédiens Français du XVII Siècle,* Paris: Centre National de la Recherche Scientifique. 1972.

———— and Robert, Jean. Supplément (to above). Paris: Centre National de la Recherche Scientifique. 1971.

Moody, Richard. *America Takes the Stage: Romanticism in American Drama and Theatre, 1750–1900.* Bloomington: Indiana University Press, 1955.

Moore, Sonia. "Critical Response." *Theatre Journal* 33, 4 (December 1981): 527.

Moore, Will Grayburn. *Moliere,* 2nd ed. New York: Oxford University Press, 1964.

Moses, Montrose J., and Brown, John M. *The American Theatre as Seen by Its Critics, 1752–1934.* New York: W. W. Norton, 1934.

Muir, Edward. "Images of Power: Art and Pageantry in Renaissance Venice." *The American Historical Review* 84, 1 (February 1979): 16–52.

Mullin, Donald C. *The Development of the Playhouse: A Survey of Architecture from the Renaissance to the Present.* Berkeley: University of California Press, 1970.

Mullin, Donald. "Lighting on the Eighteenth-Century Stage: A Reconsideration." *Theatre Notebook* 34, 2 (1980): 73–85.

Murray, Robert H. *Science and Scientists in the Nineteenth Century.* New York: Macmillan, 1925.

Nagler, A. M. *A Source Book in Theatrical History.* New York: Dover, 1959.

————. *Theatre Festivals of the Medici, 1539–1637.* New Haven, Conn.: Yale University Press, 1964.

Nemirovich-Danchenko, Vladimir. *My Life in the Russian Theatre,* trans. John Cournos. 1936; rpt. ed. New York: Theatre Arts Books, 1968.

Newton, Stella Mary. *Renaissance Theatre Costume and the Sense of the Historic Past.* New York: Theatre Arts Books, 1975.

Nicoll, Allardyce. *A History of Early Eighteenth Century Drama, 1700–1750.* Cambridge: Cambridge University Press, 1929.

————. *History of English Drama, 1660–1900,* 6 vols. Cambridge: Cambridge University Press, 1952–1959.

————. *Stuart Masques and the Renaissance Stage.* 1937; rpt. ed. New York: Benjamin Blom, 1963.

————. *World Drama from Aeschylus to Anouilh.* New York: Harcourt Brace, 1976.

————. *The Garrick Stage.* Manchester, Eng.: Manchester University Press, 1980.

Nisbet, Robert. "The Myth of the Renaissance." *Comparative Studies in Society and History* 15, 4 (October 1973): 473–492.

Odell, G. C. D. *Shakespeare from Betterton to Irving,* 2 vols. New York: C. Scribner, 1920.

————. *Annals of the New York Stage,* 15 vols. New York: Columbia University Press, 1927–1949.

Oreglia, G. *The Commedia dell 'Arte,* trans. Lovett F. Edwards. New York: Hill and Wang, 1968.

Orgel, Stephen. *The Illusion of Power: Political Theater in the English Renaissance.* Berkeley: University of California Press, 1975.

Orrell, John. "Inigo Jones and Amerigo Salvetti: A Note on the Later Masque Designs." *Theatre Notebook* 30, 3 (1976): 109–114.

———. "Inigo Jones at the Cockpit." *Shakespeare Survey* 3 (1977): 157–168.

——— and Strong, Roy. *Inigo Jones: The Theatre of the Stuart Court,* 2 vols. Berkeley: University of California Press, 1973.

Osborne, J. "From Political to Cultural Despotism. . . ." *Theatre Quarterly* 5 (1975): 40–54.

Palmer, John. *Molière.* New York: Brewer and Warren, 1930.

Pappas, John. "Diderot in Soviet Criticism, 1917–1960." *Diderot Studies* 15 (1971): 117ff.

———, ed. *Essays on Diderot and the Enlightenment in Honor of Otis Fellows.* Geneva: Editions Droz, 1974.

Pascal, Roy. *The German Sturm und Drang.* Manchester, Eng.: Manchester University Press, 1953.

Peacock, Ronald. *Goethe's Major Plays: An Essay.* Manchester, Eng.: Manchester University Press, 1959.

Pedicord, Harry W. *The Theatrical Public in the Time of Garrick.* New York: King's Crown Press, 1954.

Peers, E. A. *A History of the Romantic Movement in Spain,* 2 vols. Cambridge: Cambridge University Press, 1940.

Penzel, Frederick. *Theatre Lighting Before Electricity.* Middletown, Conn.: Wesleyan University Press, 1978.

Phillips, Henry. "Vraisemblance and Moral Instruction in Seventeenth Century Dramatic Theory." *Modern Language Review* 73 (1978): 267–277.

Planché, J. R. *The Recollections and Reflections of James Robinson Planché,* 2 vols. London: Tinsley Bros., 1872.

Poggi, Jack. "The Stanislavsky System in Russia." *The Drama Review* 17 (March 1973): 124–133.

Pollak, Gustav. *Franz Grillparzer and the Austrian Drama.* New York: Dodd, Mead, 1907.

Price, Cecil. *Theatre in the Age of Garrick.* Totowa, N.J.: Rowman and Littlefield, 1973.

Prudhoe, John. *The Theatre of Goethe and Schiller.* Oxford: Blackwell, 1973.

Pruner, Francis, ed. *Lettres à Pauline.* Paris: Société des Belles Lettres, 1962.

——— *Les Luttes d'Antoine au Théâtre Libre.* Paris: Minard, Lettres Modernes, 1964.

Quinn, Arthur H. *A History of the American Drama from the Beginning to the Civil War,* 2nd ed. New York: F. S. Crofts, 1943.

Rankin, Hugh F. *The Theatre in Colonial America.* Chapel Hill: University of North Carolina Press, 1965.

Rees, Terence. *Theatre Lighting in the Age of Gas.* London: Society for Theatre Research, 1978.

Reynolds, L. D., and Wilson, N. G. *Scribes and Scholars: A Guide to the Transmission of Greek and Latin Literature,* 2nd ed. Oxford: Clarendon Press, 1974.

Richards, K. R., and Thomson, Peter, eds. *Essays on the Eighteenth Century English Stage.* London: Methuen, 1972.

Robertson, J. G. *The Life and Work of Goethe, 1749–1832.* London: E. P. Dutton, 1932.

———. *Lessing's Dramatic Theory.* Cambridge: Cambridge University Press, 1939; rpt. ed. New York: Benjamin Blom, 1965.

Roose-Evans, James. *Experimental Theatre.* London: Studio Vista, 1973.

Rose Anthony, S. C., Sister. *The Jeremy Collier Stage Controversy, 1698–1726:* rpt. ed. New York: Benjamin Blom, 1966.

Rosenfeld, Sybil. *Strolling Players and Drama in the Provinces, 1660–1675.* Cambridge: Cambridge University Press, 1939.

Rowell, George. *The Victorian Theatre, 1792–1914,* 2nd ed. Cambridge: Cambridge University Press, 1978.

Russell, Douglas A. *Period Style for the Theatre.* Boston: Allyn and Bacon, 1980.

Russell, Trusten Wheeler. *Voltaire, Dryden, and Heroic Tragedy.* New York: Columbia University Press, 1946.

Sabatini, Mary Hieber. "The Problem of Setting in Early Humanist Comedy in Italy: A Study of Fifteenth-Century Goliardic Theatre." (Ph.D. diss., Columbia University, 1973).

Samuels, Richard S. "Benedetto Varchi, the Accademia degli Infiammati, and the Origins of the Italian Academic Movement." *Renaissance Quarterly* 29, 4 (Winter 1976): 559–634.

Saxon, Arthur H. *Enter Foot and Horse: A History of Hippodrama in England and France.* New Haven, Conn.: Yale University Press, 1968.

Schier, Donald. "Diderot's Translation of *The Gamester.*" *Diderot Studies* 16 (1973): 229–240.

Scholz, Janos. *Baroque and Romantic Stage Design.* New York: H. Bittner, 1950.

Schrickx, Willem. "Commedia dell'Arte Players in Antwerp in 1576: Drusiano and Tristano Martinelli." *Theatre Research International* 1, 2 (February 1976): 79–85.

Schwartz, Isidore A. *The Commedia dell'Arte and Its Influence on French Comedy in the Seventeenth Century.* Paris: H. Samule, 1933.

Seilhamer, George O. *History of the American Theatre,* 3 vols. Philadelphia: Globe Printing House, 1888–1891.

Sellman, Hunton D. *Essentials of Stage Lighting.* Englewood Cliffs, N.J.: Prentice-Hall, 1972.

Shattuck, Charles H. *Shakespeare on the American Stage: From the Hallams to Edwin Booth.* Washington: Folger Shakespeare Library, 1976.

Siniavskii, Andre (Abram Tertz). *On Socialist Realism,* trans. George Dennis. New York: Pantheon Books, 1960.

Slonim, Marc. *Russian Theatre from the Empire to the Soviets.* New York: Collier Books, 1962.

Smiley, Joseph Royall. *Diderot's Relations with Grimm.* Urbana: University of Illinois Press, 1950.

Smith, Beatrice, ed. *Catalogue of Italian Plays, 1500–1700, in the Library of the University of Toronto.* Toronto: University of Toronto Press, 1961.

Smith, Bruce R. "Toward the Rediscovery of Tragedy: Productions of Seneca's Plays on the English Renaissance Stage." *Renaissance Drama,* New Series, 9 (1978): 3–10.

Smith, Winifred. *The Commedia dell'arte.* New York: New Era Printing Company, 1912.

———. *Italian Actors of the Renaissance.* New York: Coward-MaCann, 1930.

Southern, Richard. *The Victorian Theatre.* New York: Theatre Arts Books, 1970.

Speaight, Robert. *William Poel and the Elizabethan Revival.* London: Heinemann, 1954.

———. *Shakespeare on the Stage. An Illustrated History of Shakespearean Performance.* Boston: Little, Brown, 1973.

Spengler, Joseph J., ed. *Population Problems in the Victorian Age,* 2 vols. Hants, Eng.: Gregg International, 1973.

Spingarn, Joel E. *A History of Literary Criticism in the Renaissance,* 2nd ed. New York: The Columbia University Press, 1908.

Stanislavski, Konstantin. *My Life in Art,* trans. J. J. Robbins. New York: Theatre Arts Books, 1948.

————. *Building a Character,* trans. Elizabeth Reynolds Hapgood. New York: Theatre Arts Books, 1949.

————. *Creating a Role,* trans. Elizabeth Reynolds Hapgood. New York: Theatre Arts Books, 1961.

————. *An Actor Prepares,* trans. Elizabeth Reynolds Hapgood. New York: Theatre Arts Books, 1963.

Star, Leonie. "The Middle of the Yard: Calculation of Stage Sizes of Renaissance Playhouses." *Theatre Notebook* 30, 2 (1976): 65–68.

————. "Inigo Jones and the Use of Scenery at the Cockpit-in-Court." *Theatre Survey* 19, 1 (May 1978): 35–48.

Stephens, Gary. "Haunted Americana: The Endurance of American Realism." *Partisan Review* 44, 1 (1977): 71–84.

Stone, George Winchester, Jr., and Kahrl, George M. *David Garrick: A Critical Biography.* Carbondale: Southern Illinois University Press, 1979.

Summers, Montague. *The Restoration Theatre.* New York: Macmillan, 1934.

————. *The Playhouse of Pepys.* London: Kegan Paul, 1935.

Symonds, John A. *The Renaissance in Italy,* 7 vols. New York: The Modern Library, 1909–1937.

Telbin, W. "Art in the Theaters: The Question of Reform." *The Magazine of Art* (1894).

Terfloth, John. "The Pre-Meiningen Rise of the Director in Germany and Austria." *Theatre Quarterly* 6 (Spring 1976): 65–71.

Thaler, Alwin. *Shakespeare to Sheridan.* Cambridge, Mass.: Harvard University Press, 1922.

Thomson, Ian. "Some Notes on the Contents of Guarino's Library." *Renaissance Quarterly* 29, 2 (Summer 1976): 169–177.

Thomas, Richard H. *The Classical Ideal in German Literature, 1755–1805.* Cambridge, Bowes and Bowes, 1939.

Tidworth, Simon. *Theatres: An Architectural and Cultural History.* New York: Praeger, 1973.

Tollemache, Beatrix L., ed. and trans. *Diderot's Thoughts on Art and Style.* New York: Burt Franklin, 1893; rpt. ed. 1971.

Toporkov, Vasily Osipovich. *Stanislavski in Rehearsal,* trans. Christine Edwards. New York: Theatre Arts Books, 1979.

Tranter, Neil. *Population Since the Industrial Revolution.* London: Croom Helm, 1973.

Turnell, Martin. *The Classical Moment: Studies in Corneille, Moliere, and Racine.* New York: New Directions, 1948.

Vardac, A. N. *Stage to Screen: Theatrical Method from Garrick to Griffith.* Cambridge, Mass.: Harvard University Press, 1949.

Varneke, B. V. *History of the Russian Theatre: Seventeenth through Nineteenth Century,* trans. Boris Brasol, rev. and ed. by Belle Martin. New York: Macmillan, 1951.

Vasari, Giorgio. *Stories of the Italian Artists,* arr. and trans. E. L. Selley. New York: Dodd, Mead, 1925.

Vernon, Sally, "Trouble up at T'Mill." *Victorian Studies* 20, 2 (Winter 1977): 117–39.

Visser, Colin. "Killigrew Folio: Private Playhouses and the Restoration Stage." *Theatre Survey* 19 (1978): 119–138.

Waal, Carla. "William Bloch's *The Wild Duck.*" *Educational Theatre Journal* 30 (December 1978): 495–512.

Walzel, Oskar F. *German Romanticism,* trans. Alma Elise Lussky. New York: G. P. Putnam's Sons, 1932.

Watson, Ernest B. *Sheridan to Robertson: A Study of the 19th Century London Stage.* Cambridge, Mass.: Harvard University Press, 1926.

Weinberg, Bernard. *A History of Literary Criticism in the Italian Renaissance,* 2 vols. Chicago: University of Chicago Press, 1961.

Wellek, Rene. *A History of Modern Criticism: 1750–1950.* New Haven, Conn.: Yale University Press, 1955.

White, John. *The Birth and Rebirth of Pictorial Space.* New York: Thomas Yoseloff, 1958.

Wilbor, Elsie M. *The Delsarte Recitation Book,* 4th ed. New York: Werner, 1905.

Wiles, Timothy. *The Theater Event.* Chicago: University of Chicago Press, 1980.

Williams, Raymond. *Drama from Ibsen to Eliot.* London: Chatto and Windus, 1952.

Williamson, Jane. *Charles Kemble: Man of the Theatre.* Lincoln, University of Nebraska Press, 1970.

Willoughby, Leonard A. *The Classical Age of German Literature, 1748–1805.* London: Oxford University Press, 1926.

———. *The Romantic Movement in Germany.* London: Oxford University Press, 1930.

Wilson, Garff B. *A History of American Acting.* Bloomington: Indiana University Press, 1966.

———. *Three Hundred Years of American Drama and Theatre.* Englewood Cliffs: Prentice-Hall, 1973.

Wingfield, Lewis. "Realism Behind the Footlights." *Fortnightly Review,* New Series, 35 (1884).

Witkowski, Georg. *The German Drama of the Nineteenth Century,* trans. L. E. Horning, from 2nd German ed. New York: Benjamin Blom, 1968.

Wittke, Carl F. *Tambo and Bones; A History of the American Minstrel Stage.* Durham, N.C.: Duke University Press, 1930.

Wölfflin, Heinrich. *Classic Art: An Introduction to the Italian Renaissance.* New York: Phaidon, 1952.

Woodward, Llewellyn. *Prelude to Modern Europe,* 1815–1914. London: Methuen, 1972.

Wright, Richardson. *Revels in Jamaica, 1682–1838.* New York: Dodd, Mead, 1937.

Young, William C. *Documents of American Theatre History: Famous American Playhouses,* 2 vols. Chicago: American Library Association, 1973.

part five

Pluralism and Beyond

PART FIVE

Emil Pirchan's design for *The Marquis of Keith,* 1921. This stark simplicity went far beyond the simplicity of the art movement and was itself a considerable re-interpretation of the classic text. [From *Theatre Arts.*] Street theatre, 1979—an environmental, anti-nuclear play in the downtown area of a city. *Naked Lunch,* from the William Burroughs novel. Directed by Donald Sanders, set and costumes by Vanessa James. [The Chicago Project/New York, 1974.]

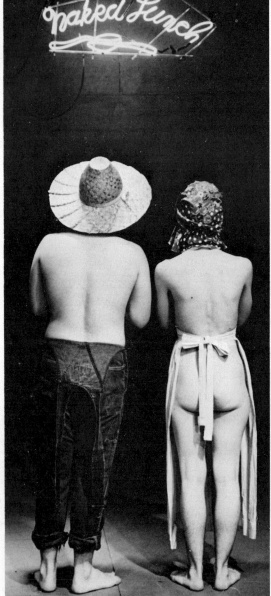

17

Theatres in Reaction, 1890–1960

Pluralism is a characteristic of the modern world, and the modern theatre has proved to be a pluralistic one. Not merely one or two, but several styles have coexisted, and even in the commercial theatre, it has been the eclectic worker who has been sought.

The coexistence of styles has not been without controversy, however. Differences have been impassioned, most of all the differences with realism.

It must be emphasized that the people to be discussed in this chapter were *in reaction*, then. They were not workers in a pure atmosphere, but in one made murky by controversy. Their predecessors and their rivals always loomed at their backs. To understand their importance, we must understand not only what they tried to do, but also what they tried to undo.

The Period

The nontheatrical framework of fact of the period is the same as that of Chapter 16. The same events had multiple effects, however. In this chapter, we look at those effects that led some people (often a social minority) away from the established pieties of the nineteenth century.

The Isolation of Art

The romantic idea of art as special and of the artist as inspired genius still was current. It alone tended to isolate art and the artist; other forces, as well, helped to push art away from the cultural center. The strong emphasis put on utility by the late nineteenth century shoved nonutilitarian art aside, while, at the same time, artists were finding themselves so offended by materialism that they often willingly let themselves be shoved. The result was that art and artists were put on the defensive, where they have remained in capitalist and Communist societies (in contrast with either "primitive" or medieval society, where art was central). Aspects of this shift included the following.

Bohemianism

The real Bohemia was part of Germany, but it had long represented the land of gypsies; it became associated with artists by a natural extension. By 1900, many cities had their own Bohemias, for example, New York's Greenwich Village and London's Chelsea. Bohemians tended to celebrate their differentness in dress, talk, and behavior to distinguish themselves from the "academic" artists favored by the establishment, who looked, lived and behaved like wealthy bourgeoisie (the Bohemians said). After World War I, would-be Bohemians flocked to Paris' Left Bank. Often, political leftism joined with the Bohemian lifestyle, and Bohemianism became a counterculture. What had begun as a separation of art became the separation of part of a generation. The division was self-perpetuating and continued through the Beat Generation of the 1950s and the flower children and

FIGURE 17.1
Time line: 1890–1960.

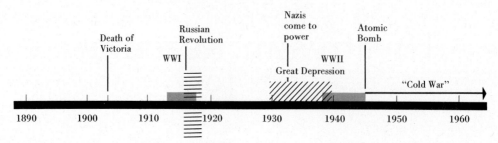

hippies of the 1960s and early 1970s. Artists were sometimes the models, although after about 1960 the communications explosion made art and the pose of being artistic almost impossible to separate. What had happened, however, was that Bohemianism had come to symbolize disaffection from the center of power to a place ("Bohemia") from which the residents had always to take the outsider's role.

Aesthetic Movements and "Art for Art's Sake"

The expression "art for art's sake" is traceable through French symbolist writing to Edgar Allan Poe. It became important to one group of artists as realism became important to another. It rejected any notion that art should be useful; rather, art should simply *be*. Perhaps the most outrageous spokesman was Oscar Wilde, whose assumptions included an elitism of sensitivity. "Art for art's sake" overlapped the "aesthetic movement," with which it shared a belief in refined artistic sensibilities. The Aesthetic Movement in England had been foreshadowed by pre-Raphaelitism and itself looked forward to the arts-and-crafts movement; all shared what one writer has called "sentimentalized archaism," the prizing of medieval art above the styles of their own day. The aesthetes spread ideas of simplicity and beauty as contrasts to what they saw as the materialism and vulgarity of Victorian art and decoration. At the turn of the twentieth century, their ideals meshed with

those of the New Arts Movement and the Art Nouveau style of France, which rejected detail, realism, and academic art.

Anti-photography

George Eastman's "Kodak" of 1888 "massified" photography. By 1900, nickelodeons were drawing the mass audience. Some visual artists were pulling away from illusionism, however—some because, they argued, photography made illusionism redundant, and some because they thought photographic realism was antiartistic. A movement began toward pure nonillusionism, marked by events like the Braque–Picasso Cubist show of 1907. There were related movements in music and dance, not all ascribable to a dislike of photography except in that it was a metaphor for the now suspect illusionism.

The Idea of an Avant-garde

With an enforced movement away from the center, art itself developed a new self-image: the avant-garde (originally, a military advance guard). Art that stayed at the center did so, it was charged, by selling off originality, courage, and indepencence. The avant-garde, on the other hand, linked itself to Bohemia; it rejected official patronage and sought to *épater le bourgeois* ("to flabbergast the bourgeoisie"). The avant-garde believed that art could be an experiment. The romantic enthusiasm for originality easily became a rage for novelty. Avant-garde art became sometimes outrageous, defining itself by the degree to which it was different from centrist art. And, its nature advertised by mass comunications, it quickly reached or created an avant-garde audience, who became as eager in the twentieth century to proclaim their awareness and sensitivity as the aesthetes had been in the nineteenth.

Reactions to Nineteenth-century Society

In addition to the displacement of art, there were nonartistic changes that were also important. New philosophies at the turn of the century rejected optimism, and new science rejected the materialistic universe and its clockwork metaphor. The new reactions included the following.

Anti-materialism
Idealism ran right through the realist period from romanticism and found new expression as a rejection of the money values of the "Gilded Age" of the late nineteenth century. In America, Upton Sinclair was attacking big business. Trustbusters were working to dismantle the great business colossi. Arms manufacturers were being called "merchants of death" and were being blamed for war itself. Underlying these movements was a belief that quantity was not enough, and that intangibles such as beauty, dignity, and the life of the spirit were necessary for human existence.

Anti-Victorianism
The European and American age to which Queen Victoria gave her name was changing before her death in 1901, but the reaction to its morality and its often stifling religiosity took time to gather. Popularization of the ideas of Sigmund Freud had enormous impact, and the reaction was strong by the 1920s. Popularized Freud turned the unconscious into a hotbed of hidden desires that everybody shared, reducing morality to mere repression (it was said). The most vigorously debated issue was sex, but others clustered around it: divorce, birth control, the work ethic, censorship, and religion. A split between generations happened at about the period of World War I. Short skirts and long, careers and marriage, cars, smoking, drinking, churchgoing—the Victorian remnant fought the battle with its children on many fronts. Victorianism was in flight by the 1930s, although many kinds of censorship remained until well after World War II, by which time a new conservatism and a new generational battle was beginning.

Anti-industrialism
It had always been clear that industrialization created human problems. Humanitarianism did not provide an answer, and some people began to want to change industrial society at its root. Work was seen as dehumanizing, the individual as being reduced to a cog in a machine. Faceless powers—"they"—were thought to rule the industrial world.

Anti-rationalism
Rationalism, science, and materialism were linked, and an attack on one drew in the others. Science—since the Renaissance, the hope of mankind—became suspect, with Faust and Doctor Frankenstein the modern images of the scientist. Rationalism became suspect when the mechanical model of nature collapsed and uncertainties appeared. Intuition was offered as a substitute. Spiritualism gained new adherents. Revealed religions attracted new members. It even became conceivable that humans were not the most intelligent creatures in the universe.

Anti-egalitarianism
The twentieth century has been one of egalitarianism and of leveling. Barriers have come down with increasing frequency, and social distinctions have been greatly blurred. The tendency has created its own reaction, however, an elitism that has often been a strengthening of old institutions. "High culture" and "popular culture" have been separated—a separation that is

FIGURE 17.2
Isadora Duncan and some pupils, 1909, barefoot, bare-armed, vaguely Greek. [From *Le Théâtre.*]

of itself, perhaps, elitist. Thus, although the major direction has been toward egalitarianism, there have been opposite tendencies toward, for example, patronage of the arts in the name of preserving them from the mass or from commerce or from both. In the same way, artists who have wanted to put themselves above business or politics have often taken elitist stances.

New Directions

In addition to these reactions, the period has also seen new attempts to establish balance.

Secular Salvation and Secular Prophets
Friedrich Nietzsche (1844–1900) had postulated a "Superman." In one form or another, the Nietzschean superman remained until World War II.

Christianity was seen by many intellectuals as dying or impotent, and new gods were being sought. George Bernard Shaw advocated a superman of intelligence; H. G. Wells envisioned superscientists; Wagnerites imagined superartists, Nazis super-Aryans. The language of religion was taken over: popular thinkers wrote of soul, spirit, and ideal in nonreligious contexts. The discrediting of Christianity became almost a parlor game, and comparative religion seemed to reduce Christianity to a cult among cults. New religions were sought: Marxism became the secular religion of many, while others turned to secular prophets in science and art. Mass communications made the world aware of its supermen, and it tried to identify and reward them by giving them prizes, of which the best advertised internationally has been the Nobel Prize, established in 1901.

Popular Action

Improved communications also allowed for the formation of movements that crossed national boundaries, for example, movements for women's suffrage, civil and human rights, and peace. Since World War II, fear of nuclear war has spurred peace drives and "ban-the-bomb" marches. Fears of pollution have caused similar action in environmental causes.

Relative Systems

Beyond Victorian absolutism lay the philosophies of relativism, in which moral systems do not derive from religious laws. Existentialism, which came to popular attention after World War II, has been the best known of these. It penetrated some aspects of theology and was sympathetic to ideas that have since entered popular jargon, like "situational ethics" and "values clarification." It is doubtful that the mass of people live by a thought-out existentialism, however; rather, this philosophy is meant to represent the relativity of the world in which many people now live.

From 1890 to World War I: Idealism

Because realism was the artistic style of materialism, materialism became a target. Polemicists conveniently ignored the fact that the first independent theatres had sponsored nonrealistic as well as realistic drama (just as the next wave of polemicists would forget that the self-styled art theatres of about 1910 also staged Ibsen, Strindberg, and other realists). In place of realism, they offered an artistic idealism that attracted some of the most formative work of the modern period. This idealism saw art as a noble end in itself and rejected art that served commerce or politics. Thus, although the idealists of the art movement were opposed to realism, they were also usually opposed to the commercial theatre and they found political causes of little interest, at best.

FIGURE 17.3

The lily dance of Loie Fuller, 1902, a significantly modern use of both body and costume. [From *Le Théâtre.*]

The idealists saw their art as self-justifying; they saw themselves as heirs of a rich past, and often as "restorers" of a lost eminence; and they were generally indifferent to using the theatre to effect change outside the theatre.

Influences on Theatre, 1890–World War I

By 1890, many of those who were turning away from realism and commercial theatre were espousing an ideal of art common to the Aesthetic Movement. Art was given as dominant a role as religion had traditionally been given, and religious language (the theatre as a temple, for example) was common. Reform of the theatre was needed because it had been debased from a temple to a shop.

The conspicuous forces in shaping new ideas of theatre were the following.

Wagnerism

Richard Wagner's influence was everywhere: in architecture, in staging (sometimes by contrast), in theory, and in language, which began to use *theme, leitmotif,* and *rhythm* almost as jargon. Important Wagnerian ideas included:

1. The high seriousness of art.
2. The elevation of the master artist to superhuman status.
3. The synthesis of theatrical elements.
4. The ideal of artistic unity.

New Directions in Dance

Modernism in dance appeared about 1890 and greatly influenced thinking about all of theatre because of the work of the following people.

Loie Fuller (1862–1928). Fuller was thirty when she came to the Follies Bergères in Paris after decades in stock, vaudeville, and burlesque in the United States. She used her body as the motive force for yards of moving silk "costume," on which colored lights and projections played. Her greatest contributions were her innovative work with electric light and her introduction of a dance art that was neither classical nor exploitative: "She dreamed of a theater of the future to be called the Temple of Light . . . a theater of metamorphosis, of shifting changeable scenery created by the ever present silk."[1]

Isadora Duncan (1877–1927). "We see Isadora Duncan every time we look at dance."[2] Raised in an "aesthetic" household in California, she went on the stage in her teens and played small roles for Augustin Daly. In the late 1890s, she and her family went to London, where she gradually made her way into the worlds of mu-

sic and art, performing her "natural" and improvisatory dances. Influenced by both the aesthetic movement and ideas of Greek art, she quickly developed the qualities that became famous: bare feet and legs, a vaguely Greek costume that revealed the body, natural (that is, nonclassical, nonballetic) movement, and the use of great music, but not music that had been intended for dance.[3] Within a few years, she was in Russia, where the great choreographer Mikhail Fokine was to say, "She was the greatest American gift to the art of dance." Her value to the theatre was threefold: a liberating influence on people like Fokine; her example of a performance art that was neither realistic nor narrative; and her demonstration that movement through space was an element of theatrical art.

Sergei Diaghilev (1872–1929) and the Ballets Russes. Diaghilev was a brilliant synthesizer. He brought together the talents of Fokine; the composers Stravinsky, Ravel, and Debussy; the dancers Anna Pavlova and Waslaw Nijinsky; and the scenographers Leon Bakst, Nicholas Roerich, and Alexander Benois (among many others) to create a special show of Russian ballet (and opera). They exploded on the European art scene with a six-week Paris season in 1909: "A contemporary compared it to a mass psychosis, to a delirium of bliss, to a paroxysm of ecstasy. What seemed extraordinary to the critics was the perfect amalgam of pictorial, musical and dramatic elements."[4] Of great importance was the nonrealistic scenery and costuming, especially that of Bakst, most of all for his daring use of color. The Ballets Russes of 1909 seemed to epitomize the new theatrical ideals, "simplicity, unity, continuity, and rhythm."[5]

Movements in Other Arts

Painting had swung away from realism well before the theatre did. The impressionists made the human sensibility, rather than material reality, the base of art. The postimpressionists sought to express what lay "beneath" so-called reality. The cubists and others were pushing the

FIGURE 17.4
Costumes by Léon Bakst, who startled Paris with the Ballets Russes in 1909. [From *Le Théâtre*.]

visual arts toward abstraction in the same years that the theatre was making its first steps away from realism.

Particularly in England, the style of illustration represented by a periodical called *The Yellow Book* was significant. It used large areas of color (often black), outline of an often Oriental kind, and what came to be called *stylization* of line. The same ideals of unity and simplicity marked both this kind of illustration and early nonrealistic theatre design.

The Art Theatre Movement (ca. 1890–World War I)

The Théâtre Libre inspired an independent theatre movement that came to be associated with realism. Hard on its heels came an *art theatre movement* that was at first associated with symbolism. Despite similarities, the independent and the art theatres came to be seen as different

by the post-1900 generation. Chief among the art theatres were the following.

The Théâtre de l'Oeuvre, Paris (1892)

Successor to the short-lived Théâtre d'Art of Paul Fort, the l'Oeuvre became a European leader in what would now be called experimental theatre. Under the guidance of Aurélien Lugné-Poë, formerly an actor with André Antoine, it was active in two directions: first, in the staging of new dramas, especially symbolist ones but including some by Ibsen, Hauptmann, and Strindberg; and second, in a search for a new visual style in the theatre—in its early years, in the work of painters.[6]

The Moscow Art Theatre (1898)

Although it is best remembered for its realistic productions, the Moscow Art Theatre early staged plays like *Prince Igor* and Hauptmann's *Sunken Bell*. Of far more importance to nonrealistic production were Maurice Maeterlinck's *Blue*

Bird (1908) and a revolutionary production of *Hamlet* in 1912. Stanislavski appears to have moved steadily away from nonrealistic acting after about 1906, but both he and Nemirovich-Danchenko had a taste for nonrealistic plays that led them in a conflicting direction. It seems doubtful that this conflict was satisfactorily resolved before the Russian Revolution.

The Irish Theatre (1899)

The poet William Butler Yeats (1865–1939) founded the Irish Literary Theatre in 1899 with the help of Lady Augusta Gregory (1852–1932) and others. Using mostly English actors, it survived until 1901; shortly thereafter, it was joined with the Irish National Dramatic Company (1902) of Frank and W. G. Fay. Licensed as the Irish National Theatre Society after 1903, it became best known as the Abbey Theatre. Yeats had seen Lugné-Poë's work, and the early Irish style was tuned to Yeats's ideas of drama and to his concentration on "the sound of the human voice."[7] The acting was static, with little gestural detail. Lines were sometimes chanted or sung. The amateur actors were trained by the Fays. London tours were successful, and an Englishwoman, Annie E.F. Horniman (1860–1937) underwrote the theatre's expenses.

The appearance of new playwrights who dealt with Irish peasant life in a realistic style, however—most notably John Millington Synge (1871–1909)—created dissension. The actors found it harder and harder to balance their jobs and their commitments to a busier theater; some of them objected violently to the earthy language and subjects of the new plays; and Yeats had squabbles with the Fays. The Fays left in 1908, and "the days of the gifted amateur were over and a new professionalism was being born."[8] In 1911, the theatre made its first tour to the United States, and, despite nationalistic demonstrations, it was a vital influence on the beginning of America's own art theatre movement.

The Abbey Theatre still exists. Many of its early actors went on to distinguished careers in films and professional theatre. After the departure of the Fays, however, it became increasingly realistic, its repertoire "effectively limited . . . to Irish peasant plays."[9]

The Studios of the Moscow Art Theatre (1905 and 1911)

An offshoot of the Moscow Art Theatre was set up for "the training of young actors" and to "try out new plays," although some historians believe that its function was to relieve pressure for nonrealistic production.[10] Leader of the Studio on Pzhanskaya Street, as the 1905 venture was called, was Vsevolod Meyerhold (1874–1940), who was to become one of the greatest of Russian directors. By 1905, he was moving away from realism. His studio productions evidently distressed Stanislavski and Nemirovich-Danchenko. The studio was ended, and Meyerhold shortly after left the Art Theatre.

The so-called First Studio of the Moscow Art Theatre was established in 1911–1912 to develop the young company. The leader who emerged from this group was Yevgeny Vakhtangov (1883–1922), a teacher of the Stanislavski system who was able to mount brilliant nonrealistic productions without cutting his ties to Stanislavski's theory.

The Munich Artists Theatre (1908)

Begun as an anticommercial, nonrealistic theatre, the Munich Artists Theatre was given a place in written history by the book *Revolution in the Theatre* (1908) by its founder, George Fuchs (1868–1949). Fuchs was a critic and a theoretician who tried to oppose what he called the "peep-show stage" of both Wagner and the realists, as well as the antiquarianism of Saxe-Meiningen.[11] He also emphasized the importance of a kinetic concept of staging and of close affinities between acting and dance. He combined forces with visual artists (mostly painters) in the productions. The theatre opened with Goethe's *Faust*, using a scenic system probably derived from the ideas of Edward Gordon Craig. Small, multipurpose units, with flexible light-

FIGURE 17.5
Seminal visual events (1899–1915).

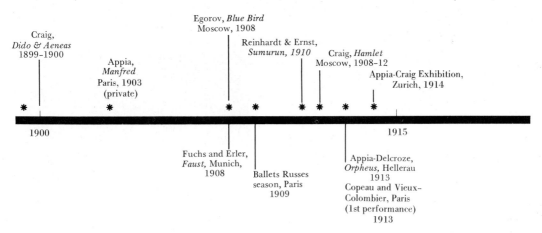

ing, destroyed realistic illusion and allowed a flow from scene to scene.

The Vieux-Colombier, Paris (1913)

Jacques Copeau (1879–1949) was a theoretician who sought to create a theatre that was both unified and simple in its spatial arrangement. He did this with his theatre, the Vieux-Colombier, by creating a permanent, simple arrangement of levels, an upper balcony, and an inner archway, which "cleared out the wings and old picture frame."[12] During part of World War I, Copeau created a version of the same theatre on the stage of New York's Garrick Theatre. His repertory relied on the traditional, although he produced French playwrights like Paul Claudel.

The Little Theatre Movement in the United States

When a British critic published a "List of Art Theatres" in 1912, there were no listings from the United States.[13] Fifteen years later, however, there were so many *little theatres,* as they came to be known, that an American could write that "they have retrieved innumerable barns, barrooms, churches, studios and other odds and ends of civilized building, all the way from Maine to California, from crowded, sophisti-

cated Greenwich Village to the open spaces of Vancouver. . . ."[14] The Irish Theatre's 1911 tour had been a powerful stimulus to the American creation of similar amateur theatres.[15] "The Chicago Little Theatre had been established in 1912. . . . The Toy Theater of Boston and the Wisconsin Dramatic Society were much talked about as pioneers."[16] More of these theatres emerged in 1915–1916, among them three that were to have a lasting influence in New York itself: the Neighborhood Playhouse, the Washington Square Players, and the Provincetown Players. The latter was particularly influential, producing the early plays of Eugene O'Neill. These amateur theatres were the conduit by which the art theatre movement came belatedly to America; from one of them came the Theatre Guild, and from the Guild, the Group Theatre.

By the early 1920s their best artists were moving into the commercial and the new educational theatre. They began to do two things that the best of the European art and independent theatres had avoided: they drew their plays from the commercial stage, and they came to depend on the box office for support. Slowly, their interest shifted from art to socializing, and they became what we now know as community theatres.

The English Repertory Movement

Analagous to the little-theatre movement, but essentially professional in character, was the English repertory movement. The idealists saw the bad effects of the commercial long-run system on actors, on audiences, and on the drama itself. An important moving force was the same Annie Horniman who had underwritten the early years of the Irish Theatre; another was the example of Harley Granville-Barker, who produced several London seasons of repertory (1904–1907). Miss Horniman began the Gaiety Theatre in Manchester in 1908; others started in Glasgow (1909) and Liverpool (1911). The Birmingham Repertory was begun in 1913 under Barry Jackson and is still in existence. The movement had an important influence both on English demands for a national theatre and on concepts of organization and repertory in England, Canada, and the United States.

Pioneers and Exemplars

As it was the taste of the age to look for giants in politics and science, so it was the taste of the age to look for them in art, as well. The Wagnerian master-artist was still sought. Messianic schemes to save art or to restore it to a former glory were conceivable, and it was possible for a few artists to proclaim a mission in art and to live their lives like zealots. The artistic and aesthetic part of the culture revered them; the practical part gave them some very hard knocks.

Two Prophets

Adolphe Appia (1862–1928) was Swiss-born, moderately well-to-do, and educated to be a musician. He became a passionate Wagnerite early in life and remained so to the end of it; however, he detested the way that Wagner's operas were being staged at Bayreuth (and everywhere else) and made it his life's mission to reform Wagnerian production: "His dreams and his thoughts . . . concentrated on a single purpose: to find the perfect solution for the staging of Wagner's great music dramas and so

FIGURE 17.6

Richard Wagner's *Die Valkyrie* (1893)—the kind of overproduction against which Adolphe Appia reacted. [From *The Picture Magazine*.]

to achieve the master's ideal of the synthesis of all the arts."[17] His reforms came to life in his drawings and in his writings; they seldom reached the stage, except through his extensive influence after about 1920. He published *La mise en scène du drame Wagnerien* (in French) in 1895; *Die Musik und die Inscenierung* (in German) in 1899, translated from his own French; and *L'Oeuvre d'Art Vivant* (in French) in 1921. (Little of his writing was translated into English until the 1950s and 1960s.) In 1903, he provided the designs for a private production in Paris of scenes from Byron's *Manfred* and the Bizet opera *Carmen;* in 1910, with Jacques Dalcroze he designed the auditorium of the Dalcroze Institute of Eurythmics at Hellerau; in 1912, he designed the music and lighting for Gluck's *Orpheus and Eurydice* in that auditorium. In the 1920s, he provided designs for Wagner's *Ring* cycle at La Scala and for a truncated production of the same work at Basel, Switzerland. His Wagnerian productions inevitably met hostility and opposition from the Wagner Societies and from Wagner's heirs.

It was not his few productions that made Appia important, however. Rather, it was his

FIGURE 17.7

A sketch, ca. 1899, for Wagner's *Parsifal* by Appia. Compare detail, mood, mass and use of light with Figure 17.6. [From Fischel.]

writing and drawings, which reveal Appia's overriding concern with light and with his sense of the importance of the actor. The drawings show plain surfaces, massive blocks as if of stone, vertical shafts and shapes without particularizing detail, and low flights of steps, the whole capable of modeling and change through the use of light.

Few people saw Appia's first book, and the people he wanted to see it (in Germany) often could not read its French text. More people read the second and saw its accompanying illustrations. His work at Hellerau was seen by "almost a Who's Who of the arts," the leaders of the new European movement in the theatre.[18] It is his influence on them and through them that makes him important.

Appia's ideas were summed up by Sheldon Cheney in 1925:

> . . . that the realistic and painted-perspective modes of stage setting are impossible artistically; that there must be unity of play, setting and action; that the actor is the factor to be emphasized within this unity—that he and not a trick of the staging must be the center of the picture; and, finally, that lighting should be largely utilized as the uniting force . . . by

providing an all-pervading spiritual atmosphere.[19]

Edward Gordon Craig (1872–1966), by contrast, was an idealist who seized or created lines of communication to those he wanted to reach. Born to the actress Ellen Terry and E. C. Godwin, an architect of romantic ideas, Craig was immersed in the theatre early and went on the stage while still a child. His "real training for life," however, began when, in 1889, he joined Henry Irving's company during Irving's famous tenure of the Lyceum Theatre in London. Irving was then England's greatest actor and an experimenter with light and with realistic staging, especially of crowds. Craig revered Irving; from him, he learned perfectionism, practical theatre work, and unending dedication to the art.

About 1894, Craig took up wood engraving, which demanded simplification and which did not yield well to detail. He became a voluble writer, as well; he bombarded newspapers with letters and articles and he began to publish periodicals of his own, the most successful being *The Mask* (1909–1929, with gaps), in which he wrote under literally scores of pseudonyms. He gave up acting and took up production (directing and design). In 1905, he published a small book, *The Art of the Theatre;* part of it was incorporated into *On the Art of the Theatre* (1911), and both books appeared in several languages and included illustrations. In this vital period of his career (1899–1914), Craig thrust himself on the consciousness of artistic Europe.

He seemed to be everywhere—producing a season of plays for his mother (1902, including a historic production of Ibsen's *The Vikings*); designing *Venice Preserved* for Otto Brahm (and getting badly burned by Brahm's realism); designing Ibsen's *Rosemersholm* for Eleonora Duse (a triumph until the sets had to be made smaller for a tour); having a long affair with Isadora Duncan, who became "a very sincere champion" but who could not give up her own idealistic art for him, as he could not for her;[20] de-

FIGURE 17.8

A Gordon Craig design, ca. 1902, for a Shakespearean tragedy. Masses of monochrome and great simplicity of line mark it; its revolutionary difference from commercial design of the period can be seen by a comparison with Figures 15.8 and 15.11. [From *Current Literature*.]

signing and directing *Hamlet* at the Moscow Art Theatre (1912); organizing exhibitions of his work; tongue-lashing those who lacked ideals; and trying to build in Germany a theatre for a "Supermarionette" that was to be "not an imitation of man, but a symbol of man."[21]

Craig's goal was the largest imaginable: to save the theatre from itself, not through destroying it, but by saving what was best in its literature and its practice, and then building on that to create a spiritual theatre that was an art not overwhelmed by literature. His production of Henry Purcell's *Dido and Aeneas* in 1899 brought "many new lighting devices and fresh ideas," including spotlighting and lighting from a bridge.[22] The Moscow *Hamlet*, however, was

the product of Craig's mature thought. Craig had invented and patented a flexible, movable screen as a basic scenic unit; a set of these was in use at Yeats's Irish Theatre, and he conceived a far more ambitious use of a more complex set at Moscow. The screens were of several widths and could fold in both directions; they could be combined to make curves, right angles, masses, corridors, and so on. Craig illuminated them (as he had *Dido and Aeneas*) with individual instruments instead of footlights and borderlights. His goal—never achieved—was a constant visual flow, uninterrupted by a curtain for scene changes, the dominant color metallic gold (the corruption of the court). "Instantaneous scene-changes of unspecified locales and characters conflated into a single golden mass, now brightly lit, now fully obscured . . . to body forth [Craig's] private vision of *Hamlet* as it unfolded in the mind's eye of the Danish prince."[23]

This production took more than three years of on-and-off preparation by Craig, who made several visits to Moscow. His ideal was not achieved; the screens did not work as hoped, and the curtain had to be used for changes. Nonetheless, it was a landmark production for both Russian modernism and European scenography. It raised scenery to the level of symbol and used color as a dazzling externalization of the inner life of the central character. It rejected antiquarianism as the mode of production for the most sacred of literary treasures, Shakespeare.

It was also about this time that Craig introduced (in *The Mask*) his idea of the *Übermarionette*, the supermarionette for which he seems even to have planned a theatre. Scholars dispute the real place of the supermarionette in Craig's vision, some contending that it was primarily a metaphor for perfection in acting—an Irving larger than life, with Irving's cool self-control and dispassion. It was *not* an invention for the removal of live actors from the theatre. Like the many model theatres that Craig built, like his drawings and his theatrical woodcuts, it was probably a necessary substitute so that, denied access to most theatres by his own idealistic standards, he could work.

To a casual eye, Craig's and Appia's drawings may look similar. However, Craig saw an important role for color; Appia did not. Craig's mind ranged across the drama and reached out for a nonliterary theatre that was all movement and mass; Appia was interested primarily in Wagner. Craig was a visionary and a polemicist, with a passionate interest in theatre history, acting, directing, and theatre training; Appia was a very quiet prophet concerned mainly with space and image. Craig saw the totality of theatre—movement, color, light, mass, and symbol—as the center of the experience; Appia saw the living actor as the center, usually of a mythic written work.

The Master Artist as Director:
Max Reinhardt (1873–1943)

Austrian by birth, Reinhardt became the great eclectic master artist for the generation of World War I, first in Germany, then in Europe and the United States. He had an astonishing reputation in the 1920s, with quantities of print devoted to him and his work, yet he had no style of his own. He was an authoritarian in the German tradition, one whose *Regiebuchs* ("promptscripts") were minutely detailed records of production. He was a master of the technology of his time because, above all, he was a master of other people's skills, especially the skills of stage designers, to whom he seemed able to give free rein.

Reinhardt started his work in Germany as an actor for Otto Brahm at the Deutsches Theater (Berlin). He began to work as a director in a cabaret and (1902) at the Kleines Theater, then at the Neues Theater (both in Berlin). He became the director of the Deutsches Theater shortly after Brahm left, and in 1905–1906 was also directing at both the Neues Theater and the Kammerspiele (Chamber Theatre). By 1910, he was the director of the Deutsches Theater and the Kammerspiele, was staging *Oedipus Rex* in Berlin's Circus Schumann (in the round), and was staging the world premier of the Richard Strauss–Hugo von Hofmannsthal opera *Der Rosenkavalier* in Vienna. In the years immediately following, he staged the *Oedipus* in Russia and England; directed productions in New York, Budapest, and German cities outside Berlin; and kept his directorship of the Deutsches Theater. Such frenetic activity was made possible by the "Reinhardt machine," the superb organization that marshaled the talents of designers, technicians, and directorial assistants, and combined them with advanced theatrical technology.

Variety was always typical of Reinhardt's work. If he directed in an intimate theatre, next he must direct in a huge one; if he worked in a proscenium theatre, he must try an arena or the outdoors or film. The range of the repertory either directed or produced by him included the Greek tragedies and works by Strindberg, Wilde, Gorki, Maeterlinck, Ibsen, Shakespeare, Schiller, Büchner, Nestroy, Schnitzler, Kleist, Molière, von Hofmannsthal, Hauptmann, Gogol, Hebbel, Grillparzer, Shaw, Goethe, Wedekind, and literally dozens of others.[24] His directorial practice was as varied as his repertory: "In 'Sumurun' he used the runway with striking effect. . . . In some comedies of Molière and Shakespeare he used curved bridges, gangways, passages, stairs to accentuate movements, utilizing all three dimensions of the space at his disposal."[25]

Two of Reinhardt's productions had particular influence in England and America. *Sumurun* (1910–1912) was a full-length pantomine of Arabian Nights exoticism. With designs by Ernst Stern, it introduced nonrealistic scenery to New York. It was Reinhardt's genius to put such a design on the commercial stage within scant years of its appearance in art theatres. Even more influential in America was *The Miracle*, another scripted but essentially wordless play first staged before the war but taken to America in 1924, now with the setting by an American,

FIGURE 17.9

A scene from *Sumurun,* design by Ernst Stern, 1910, direction by Max Reinhardt. [From *Theatre Arts.*]

Norman Bel Geddes. It gave Reinhardt superhuman status in the United States and it legitimized "serious" theatre for a new generation.

Symbolists

Symbolism was deeply antirealistic because it distrusted the world of the senses, insisting that "the exterior world has no reality except that given it by thought."[26]

The roots of French symbolism lay in the poet Charles Baudelaire's translations of Edgar Allan Poe—symbolist images of death and horror, a sense of the world as an ominous place, and the idealization of a hero who isolated himself from the world and lived in what realists would have called fantasies. The symbolist hero had a greatly heightened sensitivity to a world beyond the material that put him in touch with death. To realists, the symbolist hero was "morbid" and "decadent."

The conduit of poetic symbolism to the drama was Villiers de l'Isle Adam (1838–1889), a respected poet and novelist and "the founder of Wagnerism in France."[27] His short play *The Escape* was staged by Antoine at the Théâtre Libre in 1888. His masterwork, however, was *Axel*, which Yeats compared to a "sacred book"

and another called "the *Faust* of the later nineteenth century," but which Edmund Wilson called "a sort of long dramatic poem in prose."[28] The hero of *Axel* is pale, withdrawn, and mysterious; its setting is "the idealized image of a Germany both mystical and medieval, filled with occultism."[29] Its action involves a hidden treasure, a beautiful nun, and an intermingling of eroticism and death. The play has obvious affinities with the gothic melodrama of a century earlier, but its substance lies in its symbolism.

Although Villiers knew almost no success as a playwright, his immediate successor, Maurice Maeterlinck (1862–1949) did. Maeterlinck was Belgian and wrote in French. Of a meeting with Villiers, he wrote, "That, more than any other, had importance to my literary being."[30] Between 1899 and 1908, Maeterlinck wrote plays that made him famous and wealthy and that brought him the Nobel Prize: *Princess Maleine* (1899), which, although unproduced, was called more beautiful than Shakespeare; *The Intruder*, given one performance at the Théâtre d'Art in 1891; *The Blind*, 1891; *Pelleas and Melisande* (a single Paris performance, 1893); *Interior*, 1894; *The Blue Bird*, written in 1905–1906, but first staged in 1908 at the Moscow Art Theatre; and many others. Within a few years, they were being staged all over Europe.

Yet, when Maeterlinck's Nobel Prize came in 1911, "it came when his peak of excellence in literature was long past."[31] The last decades of his life were spent in comparative obscurity.

Maeterlinck was called "the dramatist of terror" because of the symbolist omens, fears, and shadows that filled his plays, as well as the continuing threat of death. The early plays seemed pessimistic, for they suggested that not only was the real world a sham, but the world that lay beyond it was ominous. "Behind every incident, almost behind every phrase, one is aware of a lurking universality."[32] The exciting action that enlivened romantic or realistic plays was undercut or skipped: a murder was done in near-darkness; the suffering of a mourner was

FIGURE 17.10

Maeterlinck's *Blue Bird* in Paris (1911), with Egorov's settings. The fact that the play was seen as a children's fantasy freed the designer to use a textured mass like an art nouveau surface; the central costume has the qualities of one of Loie Fuller's; the figure with the bird cage has affinities with some of Bakst's. See also Figure 3.3. [From *Le Théâtre.*]

described by a bystander, not dramatized; scenes of love were left out, and only the tormented effects of love were shown.

Maeterlinck's plays required a new kind of staging. The prosaic and highly repetitive language led to a chanting delivery. The death-haunted subjects encouraged low volume, funereally spare gesture, and limited inflection. The nonspecific medievalism of several of the plays rejected antiquarianism and encouraged geographical placelessness and timelessness. The importance of mood made lighting control important. Scrims and projections were often appropriate; the first performance of *Pelleas and Melisande*, for example, was played entirely behind a gauze. *The Blue Bird* was treated at the Moscow Art Theatre as a children's fairy tale. Thus, Maeterlinck's importance lay not only in creating a new drama, but also in giving opportunity to new theatrical styles.

Other symbolist playwrights included Yeats, Oscar Wilde (1856–1900), and Paul Claudel (1868–1955). Wilde's symbolist play was *Sa-*

FIGURE 17.11

Leading Directors of Nonrealism Before World War II

George Fuchs	1868–1949	*Faust,* 1908
Aurelien Lugné-Poë	1869–1940	*The Tidings Brought to Mary,* 1912
Edward Gordon Craig	1872–1966	*Hamlet,* 1912
Max Reinhardt	1873–1943	*The Miracle,* 1912
Vsevolod Meyerhold	1874–1940	*The Magnificent Cuckold,* 1922
Leopold Jessner	1878–1945	*The Marquis of Keith,* 1920
Jacques Copeau	1879–1949	*Twelfth Night,* 1914
Gaston Baty	1882–1952	*Crime and Punishment,* ca. 1932
Yevgeni Vakhtangov	1883–1922	*Turandot,* 1920
Georges Pitoëff	1884–1939	*Romeo and Juliet,* 1934
Charles Dullin	1885–1949	*Life is a Dream,* 1922
Alexander Tairov	1885–1950	*Romeo and Juliet,* 1920
Louis Jouvet	1887–1951	*Dr. Knock,* 1923
Erwin Piscator	1893–1966	*Flags,* 1920
Terence Gray	1895–	*Henry VIII,* 1931
Michel St.-Denis	1897–1971	*Noah,* 1935
Bertolt Brecht	1898–1956	*Mother Courage,* 1941
Tyrone Guthrie	1900–1971	*Six Characters in Search of an Author,* 1932
Antonin Artaud	1895–1948	*The Cenci,* 1935
Orson Welles	1915–	*Julius Caesar,* 1937
Jean-Louis Barrault	1910–	*Numancia,* 1937

lome (1893–1894); its blood-drenched eroticism, its exotic setting, and its fascination with death were typical. Claudel's symbolist plays were much staged in the art theatres and remain in the French repertory.

Symbolism expressed an unease with materialistic culture. It suffered after World War I from an utter lack of political relevance; it suffered in most periods from its insubstantiality. It is a drama of reference, of idea, and of language; seldom is it a drama of action.

Finally, the symbolists were elitists in a world that was becoming egalitarian. And their insistence that the real world was without substance was made untenable by the terrible reality of World War I and its aftermath.

Upheaval: From World War I to World War II

Seeds of Unrest: Futurism and Dada

Even before World War I, disgust with the existing culture created new artistic movements that, unlike the art theatre movement, turned against all art of previous ages.

Futurism was launched by Filippo Marinetti (1876–1944) in 1909 with a manifesto that asserted the need to destroy the art of the past. A new, kinetic, temporary art was required. Although more important to painting and sculpture than to the theatre, futurism influenced some directors and designers. It celebrated images of motion (machines, cyclists, industrial workers) and used the shapes of machines, heavy industry, and early aerodynamics. Futurism was strongest in Italy. It had adherents in Russia, including the playwright Vladimir Mayakovski (1893–1930). The movement's affinity for extreme politics led it toward Fascism in Italy and toward Bolshevism in Russia. It proved short-lived, however, and was effectively over by 1930; its celebration of war as the most modern and "hygienic" of activities was too much for postwar Europe to swallow.

FIGURE 17.12

Futurist costumes, Italy (ca. 1920). [From Carter, *New Spirit.*]

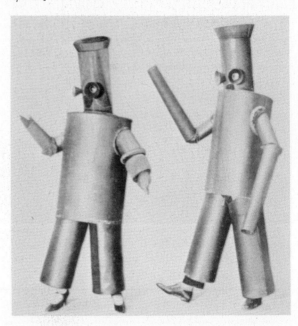

Futurism had an analogue in Germany in the *Bauhaus*, a collective of modern artists, designers, and architects of the 1920s. They, too, rejected the past and celebrated modernism, its materials and its machines. Theatre was not a main concern of the Bauhaus, but work on human engineering and mechanistic costumes influenced some avant-garde artists, especially in dance; the architect Walter Gropius designed a "total theatre" (1927) that was not built.

Dada, too, was part of the ferment of the war years. It also sought the destruction of the past and of "high" art. It did not assert much in their place, however, and the classics of dada—a fur-lined cup, a urinal as a piece of sculpture—were witty and shocking but without coherence. Dada, led by Tristan Tzara (1896–1963), tended toward anarchy; it was an important expression of the war generation's outrage, and it influenced theatre through the work of artists like Georg Grosz (1893–1959).

A precursor of dada was Alfred Jarry (1873–

1907). His remarkable play *Ubu Roi* was staged at the Théâtre de l'Oeuvre in 1896, where it was a sensation and a scandal. Scatological, anarchical, anti-past, anti-literature, anti-establishment, savage, and often uproariously funny, it went at bourgeois society with axe, scalpel, hammer, and bare hands. Somewhere at the heart of *Ubu Roi* is a parody of *Macbeth*; at its source is a schoolboy joke about one of Jarry's teachers; behind its form is the theatre of puppets. It has qualities of nightmare in its illogic and its crazy juxtaposition of events and places. It had two sequels (1900 and 1901), but the first play remains the landmark. Jarry himself died young of drug abuse, but not before he had created another foreshadowing of dada, "pataphysics," the "science of imaginary solutions."

By 1925, dada had dissipated itself into other movements. Principal among these was *surrealism*, whose manifesto was made public in 1924. Surrealism sought to create a link between the conscious and the unconscious. Many of its images and forms were derived from dreams and from Freud's work on dreams. The acknowledged leader of the surrealists was André Breton (1896–1966); its drama includes some of the work of Jean Cocteau and *The Breasts of Tiresias* (1917) by Guillaume Apollinaire (1880–1918).

The Theatrical Theatre in Russia

With the coming to power of the Bolsheviks (1917–1918), the Russian theatre erupted. "Bourgeois" theatres like the Moscow Art Theatre were deeply shaken. For over a decade, highly experimental theatres were favored by the new government, until, in the early 1930s,

FIGURE 17.13

The Breasts of Tiresias, Guillaume Apollinaire's surrealist play (1917). Both the literal illusion of realism and the careful beauty of the art movement have been rejected. [From Carter, *New Spirit.*]

the bureaucratized aesthetic of socialist realism took over.

The favored new practices were *theatricalist;* that is, they reminded the audience that they were in a theatre. The leading theatricalist artists included the following.

Yevgeni Vakhtangov

Vakhtangov's work at the First Studio of the Moscow Art Theatre (1912–1922) seemed to combine the best of both Stanislavski's acting system and the new ideas of theatre. His innovative productions included new interpretations of Chekhov, a production of Maeterlinck's *Miracle of St. Anthony,* and one of Gozzi's *Turandot;* these were done under the auspices of the Second and Third Studios, which emerged from his own circle of students in 1919–1921, when the Moscow Art Theatre was deeply troubled and divided.

Reports and photographs suggest that Vakhtangov's productions abounded in potent imagery and symbolism and that, whatever the system used with the actors, the productions themselves were very nonrealistic.

Alexander Tairov (1885–1950)

The Moscow Kamerny ("chamber") Theatre was Tairov's showplace after 1915. Tairov appears to have been an antirealistic eclectic, above all a formalist, that is, one more interested in styles for their own sake than for their aesthetic end or their potential for meaning. He appears to have been influenced by the Ballets Russes both in his concern with the modernist styles in painting (translated to the stage) and in his antirealism. One commentator of 1924 noted his "acrobatic acting and use of levels";[33] another described his productions as "Cubist."[34] It was noted that he had yet to find new plays appropriate to his style, but the truth seems to be that he had no style except a very intelligent, very knowledgeable dislike of realism. His repertory included the exotic: the Indian *Sakuntala,* Goldoni's *The Fan,* Wilde's *Salome,* Claudel's *Noel,*

FIGURE 17.14

George Bernard Shaw's *St. Joan,* directed by Tairov at the Kamerny, Moscow. The straight verticals and bleacherlike stands radically change this realistic Shavian play. [From *Theatre Arts.*]

Rostand's *Cyrano de Bergerac*, and plays by Shakespeare, Scribe, Labiche, and Racine.

Tairov staged Vishnevski's *Optimistic Tragedy* in the 1930s, but even this act of piety did not save him. He was discredited as decadent and revisionist.

Vsevolod Meyerhold (1874–1940)

After leaving the Moscow Art Theater in 1906, Meyerhold directed for some years in the St. Petersburg Theatre of Vera Kommisarzhevskaya, one of the great pre-revolutionary stars. He did a nonrealist production of Ibsen, symbolist plays, and a notorious production of Wedekind's *Spring's Awakening*. He directed opera. He studied the *commedia dell'arte* and explored its techniques, as well as circus techniques, in his school.[35] By the Russian Revolution, his sense of theatre art included: first, a strong belief in the supremacy of the director's vision; second, enthusiasm for physical, even athletic performance by the actor; and third, a commitment to revolutionary political ideas.

Meyerhold was sympathetic to futurism and to *constructivism*, a new style of painting and sculpture that emphasized structure and function, not surface decoration. Constructivism sought to strip away the "sentimentality" of the coverings that hid skeletal structure, and it "exploited the materials of mass production."[36] Like futurism, it embraced such aspects of industrial society as replication, interchangeability, and mechanical repetition.

In the decades after the revolution, Meyerhold was in the advance of the new Russian theatre. His productions, until they were suppressed, were legendary. Outstanding examples included:

1. *Mystery-Bouffe* (1918, restaged, 1921). With a text by Mayakovsky, this was a knockabout, ragtag production that featured the circus-style physical performance that Meyerhold had been exploring. Blatantly ideological, it was "an hilarious, dynamic, caricaturist rough-and-tumble, a carnival celebration of victory in the Civil War."[37]

FIGURE 17.15

Model of the setting for the second production of *Mystery-Bouffe* by Meyerhold, play by Mayakovsky. This is not strict constructivism, having elements of futurism and of what, for lack of a better -ism, a critic called cubism. [From Markov.]

2. *The Magnificent Cuckold* (1922). This was the production that most Western observers commented on when they first got to Russia after the revolution; as a result, Meyerhold has always been associated with the constructivist setting designed for it. He wanted a setting "which could be erected anywhere, without resort to conventional stage machinery,"[38] and he got the "first example of pure Constructivist setting in the history of the theatre."[39] Structure was everything—platforms, stairs, skeletal walls, a slide, a ramp; a turning windmill; a circle on which the playwright's name (the Belgian Fernand Crommelynck) minus the vowels, had been broken up into fragments, as if the playwright were an irrelevancy, and individual names, identity, and fame were fictions. Much of the acting was clownish slapstick. Gesture and costume were exaggerated. The result was extreme theatricalism, humor, and a political statement about human self-destructive indifference to politics.

3. *Woe from Wit* (1928) and *La Dame aux Camélias* (1934). In both plays, the feminine leads

were played by Meyerhold's wife, Zinaida Raikh. Both plays were classics that had elegance and even beauty (for which Meyerhold was criticized: beauty was decadent). *Woe from Wit* (Alexander Griboyedov, ca. 1825) had a now-famous dining scene where "thirty-two guests, seated bolt upright at a long table directly facing the audience, slowly relayed the false rumor of [the protagonist's] madness to the accompaniment of a tranquil nocturne . . . : with the appearance of [the protagonist], they all raised their napkins as though in self-defence, hissing menacingly like snakes at bay."[40] *La Dame aux Camélias* was staged in a delicate setting of curved lines, unusual for Meyerhold. The production was a "sensational success with the public" but was savaged by Communist Party critics as "antidemocratic" and "bourgeois."[41]

No single term has so stuck to Meyerhold's name as *biomechanics*. He used it in the early 1920s to describe the physical aspect of his acting method. The word had an older use in the study of animal and human movement (as we now use *human engineering*). An English visitor used it in the early 1920s for Russian acting in general and also used it in connection with Taylorism, an American time-and-motion method for the study of worker productivity. It was a word that came ready to Meyerhold's hand: it was of the industrial age; it had scientific overtones; it suggested efficiency; and it rejected the mysticism and emotionalism of some of the Stanislavski system. The term was not exclusively Meyerhold's, and as he meant it, it seems to have been associated with a physical tradition handed down from *commedia dell'arte*, mime, and circus acrobatics.[42]

His biomechanical exercises seem to have been used to condition the actor's body, to enhance physical skills (balance, suppleness, and strength), and to habituate neural paths. These exercises had affinities with yoga exercises and with modern dance and, in more recent times, with the work of the Polish teacher–director Jerzy Grotowski. In performance, these exercises were meant to provide patterns for action and reaction among similarly trained actors and to induce emotions, in the belief that physical action precedes feeling. The same belief underlay both Delsarte's work and Stanislavski's "method of physical actions."

Meyerhold was discredited with the charge of formalism in the mid-1930s. His theatre was closed in 1938. In 1939, he asserted his right to creative freedom in a speech that was supposed to be an apology. In 1940, he was shot to death in a Moscow prison, and Zinaida Raikh "was found assassinated in her apartment, her throat cut, her face disfigured, and knife wounds all over her body."[43]

Meyerhold presents a serious problem in historiography. Despite his "rehabilitation" after the death of Stalin, the evidence available about him remains suspect. Three quite different groups have put up screens around an understanding of his work: antirevolutionary Russians who hated his political ideas; pro-Stanislavski theatre people who saw him as a threat to Stanislavski's reputation; and the Soviet bureaucracy after 1934, which became increasingly hostile. The most often-repeated criticism—that Meyerhold dehumanized the actor—may simply be part of the Soviet rewriting of history.

In 1922, Huntley Carter called Meyerhold "the greatest living creative and interpretative producer." Recent evidence supports the likelihood that Meyerhold was one of the two most important Russian theatre figures of the century, the other being Stanislavski.

Proletcult and Blue Blouse (1918–ca. 1930)

When the Bolsheviks came to power, Lenin declared that the theatre could be a tool for the education of the people, and a number of bureaucracies were created to achieve that end. Proletcult (proletarian cultural organization) appeared under one of these to encourage theatrical production through unions and factories. It employed many theatre professionals as teachers and directors, and its prime form was

FIGURE 17.16

Schematic of lines of influence, 1899–1925. This diagram has been made intentionally complex in order to show the interlocking, multiple cross-influences of the period.

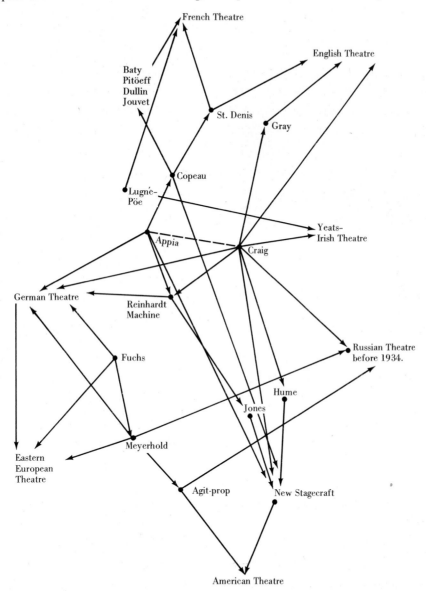

agitprop ("agitational propaganda"), including such documentary approaches as the "living newspaper"—performances centered on current news, slanted for the desired purpose.

A second kind of workers' theatre ap-

peared in the early 1920s as the Blue Blouse troupes, named after the workers' coveralls worn as basic costumes. At their most popular, there were "nearly 500 professional and about 8000 amateur Blue Blouse groups . . . with perhaps

FIGURE 17.17
A Blue Blouse troupe in performance of a skit about a message to the world (mid-'twenties). [From *Theatre Arts.*]

100,000 members."[44] Their performances consisted of a parade of performers followed by a montage of skits, acrobatics, songs, and so on.[45] They performed wherever there was space, without the trappings of formal theatre. At their height during the New Economic Policy (1922–1928), they had direction from leftist and futurist artists, published their own magazine, and received suggestions and instruction from a central office.

Both the Proletcult and the Blue Blouse show evidence of the same interest in highly physical performance that was found in Meyerhold.

An American Analogue: The Federal Theatre Project (1935–1939)

Although fundamentally different in intent, the Federal Theatre Project in the United States bore important similarities to Proletcult and Blue Blouse. The great difference was that it was not a propaganda or educational arm of the government; the most obvious similarity was that it was federally funded. Under the direction of Hallie Flanagan, it existed from 1935 until 1939 as a government effort to provide employment for theatre people in the Depression. With five

regions nationwide, it had a living newspaper, projects in new-play production, Negro theatre, children's theatre, ethnic theatre, folk theatre, theatres in conventional structures and out-of-doors, touring theatres, and innovative theatres. The project ultimately ran afoul of Congressmen who thought it was too Russian for its own good, but before being closed down it had given "63,729 performances of twelve hundred productions, featuring everything from classic and religious plays to puppetry and circus, and after playing to audiences which totaled 30,398,726."[46]

Expressionism

By the time of World War I, some artists were beginning to see themselves as victims of the industrial age and not as poetic escapees from it; they went inside themselves and their characters for a world, instead of beyond reality. The members of the new movement saw an internal truth with all the clarity of nightmare, and they presented it with hard edges, garish colors, and shocking angles. They called the new style *expressionism,* because its artistic product expressed inner states.

"Expressionistic decor exists in a theatrical context that perfectly reflects the expressionistic attitude: nostalgia for purity, struggle against the dangers of an industrial technology that threatens to stifle art, rejection of all naturalism."[47] It had precedents in productions that put a single character's consciousness at the center of a play's world—Gordon Craig's *Hamlet* of 1912, for example. Some modern historians trace its beginnings to before 1900 in the plays of Frank Wedekind (1864–1918) or to the chamber plays of Strindberg, but it appears to have risen as a movement about 1915.

"All exterior imagery [in expressionism] is the expression of interior reality. . . . The theoreticians of expressionism went as far as saying that it was necessary to close one's eyes in order to see. . . ."[48] The expressionistic protagonist from whom the scene radiated tended to be a victim and was usually a social innocent; he or she tended to be driven by irrational forces of great strength and usually saw other humans as grotesques, so that they were portrayed on the stage and in film with bulging eyes, distorted hands, and threatening gestures; he or she typically retreated and tried to escape, to no avail; and he or she was usually destroyed, at least mentally. Expressionism spoke for artists who saw the individual as being destroyed by faceless industrialism and war. Its appeal to a defeated Germany is understandable—"a Germany still anguished by the unexpected defeat and an aborted revolution, where, soon, all

FIGURE 17.18

Ernst Toller's *Man and the Masses,* Germany (1921). The bulging eyes and the rigid postures are typical of expressionism, as is the emblematic cage. [From *The Theatre* (New York).]

moral and economic value were undercut by inflation, by a doubt of all tomorrows."[49]

The outstanding playwright of German expressionism was Georg Kaiser (1878–1944). His *From Morn to Midnight* (ca. 1912) was an early expressionist success; his *Gas* trilogy (1917–1920) was produced at Reinhardt's Deutsches Theater during the war. Technology and economics are the enemy of innocence in these plays, and the relentless forces are externalized in shocking images. In *Gas One,* death from poison gas appears in a spotless industrial office in the person of The Gentleman in White, clean and impersonal. In *From Morn to Midnight,* the protagonist flees from adventure to adventure; he rests under a twisted tree in a snowstorm; the wind blows some of the snow away, revealing the pattern of a human skull in the twisted branches. He exits, manically walking backward and using his hands to cover his tracks with snow.

Elsa Lasker-Schuler's *The Wupper* was also staged at the Deutsches Theater (1919), with sets by Ernst Stern; Kaiser's *Europa* was presented at the Grosses Schauspielhaus in 1920. Other important expressionist dramas were Ernst Toller's *Man and the Masses* (1921) and, outside Germany, Eugene O'Neill's *The Hairy Ape* (1922), Karel Capek's *R.U.R.* (1923) and Mayakovski's *The Bedbug* (1929).

Especially in scenic design, the style was one that appealed to designers of advanced taste, and it was sometimes coopted for commercial production—a *Macbeth* by Robert Edmond Jones (1921), for example, that looked modern and angular. Among directors, Leopold Jessner (1878–1945) was an expressionist who often worked with the designer Emil Pirchan. Pirchan often designed settings of steps and levels for Jessner, and they became known as *Jessnertreppen,* although they derived from Appia and Craig.

The separate existence of an expressionist acting style is debated. Expressionism may have attracted actors whose personal styles included grotesque facial expression and erratic gesture. The plays themselves often challenge the exis-

FIGURE 17.19

Setting by Emil Pirchan for Leopold Jessner (1924), a fairly typical Pirchan–Jessner arrangement of levels, ramps, and stairs, or *Jessnertreppen*. [From *Theatre Arts.*]

tence of either motivation or through line, and it is questionable that the Stanislavski system was relevant to them; also, they depend so utterly on externalization of the internal that they may be said to have no subtext. German critics of the period used words like *ecstasy, intensity, violence,* and *eruption* for expressionist acting, and the German *Aufbruch* "is a favourite word of the expressionists" for the outflung arms of yearning or escape.[50] It is likely that insofar as expressionist acting was ever theorized, it was seen in terms of its effects rather than in terms of its inner impulses.

Expressionism faded by 1930. The idea of scenery as an emanation of the central character's vision is very deeply embedded in much of European scenic design, however, dating at least from Craig.

Epic Theatre

The chaotic politics and economic collapse of postwar Germany provided the climate not only for expressionism but also for a quite different form, called by its proponents *epic theatre.* The first example was Alfons Paquet's *Flags* (1920), an intentionally episodic play about an actual event in nineteenth-century Chicago. The play was produced at Berlin's Proletarian Theatre by Erwin Piscator (1893–1966). Piscator was a creative young director who "in . . . 1920 . . . published a virtual manifesto for the proletarian theatre, one that parallels in many respects the outlook of the Russian Proletcult movement. . . ."[51] With *Flags,* he embarked on a series of productions that were highly political and intensely modern; they rejected any passive, "artistic," or "aesthetic" audience attitude and tried to rouse their audience to action. Unlike the expressionists, however, Piscator sought to rouse the audience intellectually and rationally. "You cannot prove a single point . . . if your evidence is inaccurate, and it is always inaccurate when the emotions play a decisive role,"[52] Piscator contended. Emotional identification was played down, and objective understanding was encouraged through signs, unemotional technological decor, antirealism, and the breaking of narrative suspense.

In its beginnings, then, epic theatre was a political form that discouraged emotional involvement by intentionally frustrating "dramatic" development, by telling the story ahead of time, commenting on the action, and making its theatre theatrical, not realistic.

By 1927, Piscator had produced three remarkable productions at the Volksbühne: Toller's *Hurray, We Live!,* which used newsreels; Alexei Tolstoy's *Rasputin,* which used film and live action simultaneously; and *The Good Soldier Schweik,* by his "playwright's collective," with cartoon backgrounds and life-sized mannequins on treadmills by the dada artist Georg Grosz. It was at this period that Gropius designed his "total theatre" for Piscator. Piscator left Germany in 1932 and worked in Moscow, Paris, and New York until 1952. In 1962, he returned to the Volksbühne in Berlin, where he continued his career as director of political theatre until his death in 1966.

Piscator's theatre stressed political content; the acceptance of technology; the rejection of art ("Art is shit"); and an acting style that avoided emotionalism, psychology, and the actor's ego. Piscator used the word *tasks* to describe the creative steps of acting, making the actor a worker and demystifying the art. He asked that actors use social class as an important given circumstance and that they cut themselves loose from realism, especially from the realistic actor's reliance on real environment and properties.

Piscator was an influence on Bertolt Brecht, a young playwright who came to Berlin in 1924. Brecht (1898–1956) was to become the theoretician of epic theatre, and its greatest playwright. Piscator supplied original examples on which Brecht then built. Beginning as an expressionist, Brecht published plays influenced by Wedekind and Büchner; he came to Berlin to work for Reinhardt, seeming "obnoxious, smelly, but brilliant."[53] His production of *Edward the Second*—his own free rendering of the Marlowe play—was significant for two reasons: it displayed the antiartists' dismissal of the "grandeur" of traditional classics, and it showed Brecht's tendency to absorb others' works into his own.

In 1927, Brecht collaborated with the composer Kurt Weill on the music–drama *Mahagonny;* in 1928, their *Threepenny Opera* was staged in Berlin.

Didactic plays, poetry, and theoretical writings poured from Brecht. Self-exiled like Piscator and many others after 1932, he lived in Scandinavia, the United States, and Switzerland. Some of his best plays are from this difficult period, for example, *Mother Courage* (1941), *The Good Woman of Setzuan* (1943), and *Galileo* (1943). He returned to Germany in 1949, to East Berlin. An unorthodox Communist, he kept his Swiss passport. He produced his plays with his own company, the Berliner Ensemble, led by him and Helene Weigel. By the time of his death, the company was probably the most influential in postwar Europe, its tours to London and Paris giving it much of the significance of the Meininger in an earlier day.

This fully developed Brechtian style was more complex and more humane than the epic

FIGURE 17.20

Bertolt Brecht's *Mother Courage,* as performed by The Acting Company (late 1970's) with Jeffrey Hayenga, Judson Earney, Frances Conroy, and Mary Lou Rosato as Mother Courage. [Courtesy of The Acting Company. Photo by Bert Andrews.]

theatre of the 1920s and 1930s; if the goal was still epic, it was so in a subtler way, and without Piscator's obsession with technology. The style included:

1. *Nonrealism in setting,* but realism in costume and properties. This apparent contradiction was intended to keep the audience from identifying with realistic environment while allowing real objects and real clothes to give authenticity to the historical-political "lessons."

2. *Epic structure,* but without sacrifice of humane character and narrative interest. Individual scenes often had emotion, build, and climax, but the overall play did not.

3. *Brechtian acting.* Brechtian actors were neither acrobatically physical in the Meyerhold way nor inwardly emotional in the Stanislavski way. Rather, they were "rational," aiming always to show, to teach. "Not this but that" was Brecht's axiom—the actor was to show the issues of a character's decision, often ironically. Rehearsal in the third person was used. Social

matters were important given circumstances. Mere ego and mere sensation were prohibited; so, too, were mere lyricism (indulgence of voice) or mere ballet (display of body and movement). Brecht believed, however, that acting was an art to be enjoyed for its own sake, and he compared it with boxing as an objective focus for the watcher.

Brecht envisioned a new kind of audience, one that would go to the theatre to enjoy and to learn, not to watch passively or to sink into a "warm bath of comfort." It would be an audience that would think while watching. It would come away from the theatre with its consciousness sharpened, rather than with its consciousness diverted by laughter or lulled by easy tears. Essential to the theatre of this audience was *Verfremdung. Verfremdung* is usually translated as "alienation" (as in the British sense of the therapist who "alienates" the patient from his trauma), but other meanings might be "distancing," "objectification," and "focusing." *Verfremdung* is a positive concept whose goal is a clear-headed openness to the theatre. The A-effect ("Alienation-effect," the translation of *V-effekt,* or *Verfremdung-effekt*) is the goal of epic devices such as signs, songs, and narrative dramaturgy.

Antonin Artaud (1895–1948) and Cruelty

One of the most influential of theatre people of the 1920s and 1930s is something of a contradiction, for his enormous influence was felt mostly after his death. This was Antonin Artaud, who forms an important link between such early experiments as those of Jarry, dada, and surrealism, and the most recent work in nontraditional theatre.

Artaud's theatrical career was played against a backdrop of mental instability and drugs. During the 1920s and 1930s he was an actor and a writer for theatre and film, a director, a theatre manager, a poet who complained that he could not make the meanings of words hold still, and an essayist. He worked for Lugné-Poë (his first acting role), for Dullin (as a designer), for Georges Pitoëff, for Louis Jouvet, and for the surrealists. He shared the surrealists' deep interest in the role of the subconscious in art. André Breton, however, expelled Artaud from the surrealist movement, perhaps because the surrealists then viewed theatre as unworthy, decadent, and middle-class; thereafter, they pilloried Artaud in pamphlets and disrupted performances at his Théâtre Alfred Jarry, which he had founded with Roger Vitrac and Robert Arvin in 1927.

Artaud's ideas veered still more sharply away from surrealism in 1931, after he saw a troupe of Balinese dancers at the Colonial Exposition in Paris, in whom he saw the potential for a new kind of theatre based on myth, symbol, and gesture. He concluded that Occidental theatre, with its overwhelming dependence on words and psychology, was only a shadow, a "double," of Oriental theatre. Over the next several years, he wrote a series of essays on the nature of theatre, in which he exposed what he saw as the faults of Western theatre and proposed remedies that would thrust it back into its proper role as a powerful cultural element. Thirteen of these essays were collected and published as *Le théâtre et son double* (*The Theatre and Its Double*) in 1938.

Perhaps because Artaud distrusted language and rational processes, his essays abound in vivid images and shocking metaphors, through which his ideas unfold in abrupt, sometimes disconnected segments. One of these images is the plague: theatre, like a plague, can purify society by eliminating its poisonous elements: "By means of the plague a gigantic abscess, as much moral as social, has been collectively drained. . . . like the plague, the theatre has been created to drain abscesses collectively."[54] To revive Western culture, Artaud called for a "theatre of cruelty" in which "subjects and themes corresponding to the agitation and unrest characteristic of our epoch" would find expression. This cruelty was not primarily physical and in no way sadistic. He meant it in a broader sense of rigor, "implacable intention and decision, irreversible and absolute determination." He was less interested in the horrors that human beings could perpetrate on one another than in "the much more terrible and necessary cruelty which things can exercise against us. We are not free. And the sky can still fall on our heads. And the theatre has been created to teach us that first of all."

Written texts had led to the flaccid theatre that was so easily ignored. Words were inadequate and had lost their power to carry meaning. It followed, then, that a theatre that depended on a fixed text was necessarily doomed, "a theatre of idiots, madmen, inverts, grammarians, grocers, antipoets, and positivists, i.e., Occidentals."

Artaud proposed to enlarge the language of theatre until it embraced the gestures, signs, symbols, and archetypes that were shared by all people within the culture: "Words will be construed in an incantational, truly magical sense—for their shape and their sensuous emanations, not only for their meaning." This new language would assault audiences with meaning perceived "only intuitively but with enough violence to make useless any translation into logical discursive language."

Artaud put the audience rather than the artist at the center of this theatre. The collective energy of the audience would be reachable in his theatre: "The theatre is the only place in the world, the last general means we still possess of directly affecting the organism. . . ."

The spectacle was to unfold in found spaces rather than in conventional theatre buildings. Replacing settings would be sound and lights, manipulated to assault the whole being. Violent, abrupt contrasts in intensity, color, and pitch would allow light to produce "the sensations of heat, cold, anger, fear, etc." Sounds would be "noises that are unbearably piercing." Actors, dressed in neutral and ritualistic garments, would be "a kind of passive and neutral element . . . denied all personal initiative." The true creator in the theatre would no longer be the author of a text, but the controller of this complex spectacle.

After World War II, and particularly after translations into English about 1960, Artaud became the prophet of new theatre art. What had seemed madness in the 1930s became clarity in the 1960s.

The New Stagecraft in America

The European practices in design and stagecraft that were new in 1910 came to be called the *new stagecraft* when they reached America some

FIGURE 17.21

Major stylistic movements (1890–1960).

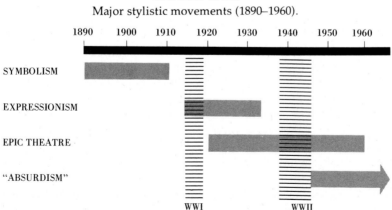

years later. As perceived by Americans, these included the search for alternatives to the proscenium stage; a rejection of narrow realism; the ideals of unity and simplicity; the use of light as a fluid, colored element; the incorporation of new artistic styles into scenery; and the idea of the theatrical designer. So foreign was the existence of the designer to American assumptions about the theatre that even the most sympathetic observers were inclined to lump all the new work in Europe under the names of the directors, overlooking the designers completely. (It is probably for this reason that Reinhardt is given such credit for visual experimentation, that Meyerhold is linked to constructivism as if he invented it, and that Jessner is tied to his *-treppen* without the work of any designer.)

The new stagecraft came to America in the same years that the little-theatre movement was getting underway. The 1912 production of *Sumurun* was a visual innovation of great importance. In the same year, the young American Sam Hume was working with Craig on the Moscow *Hamlet;* he brought Craig's ideas to America, and in 1914–1915 he organized the first American exhibition of new European design, which was seen in Boston and New York. In 1915, Robert Edmond Jones designed *The Man Who Married a Dumb Wife* for Harley Granville-Barker's New York season, and his design embodied the European innovations. Thereafter, young and energetic American designers urged the new stagecraft on little theatres and on commercial managers bold enough to experiment. Jones, Norman Bel Geddes, Lee Simonson, Cleon Throckmorton, Claude Bragdon, and then Jo Mielziner were the founders of modern American scenic design.

Sheldon Cheney, founder of *Theatre Arts Magazine,* called them prophets. Lee Simonson warned in *The Stage Is Set* that they were only theatrical designers, after all. They were a new kind of theatre artist in America, however, and they drew great attention. They had their proselytizers, Cheney and Kenneth MacGowan (*The Theatre of Tomorrow*) most of all. They had their

own lines of communication: their own books, and periodicals like *Theatre Arts, Vanity Fair,* and *Theatre Magazine;* they had their theatres, first the little theatres and then the Theatre Guild and adventurous producers like Arthur Hopkins and the scattered and equally new educational theatres, and then, finally, the commercial theatre; and by the 1920s they effectively had their own photographer in Francis Bruguière, who tried to light stage settings so that they looked the way their designers wanted them to.

By 1930, the new stagecraft led American scenography. Craig and Appia were very evident in it, most of all in the idealization of the designer, in the use of light, and in the sense of scenic symbolism. The Russians of the Ballets Russes were there, too, in the splashes of saturated color; Copeau was there in the simplified lines of the little theatres; even Reinhardt was there in the interest in new actor–audience relationships and in the rage for "sky domes"— plaster cycloramas.

Shortly after it appeared in Europe, expressionism appeared in American scenery, as well. It came, however, not from a deep commitment to the ideas behind that style, but from an aesthetic understanding of the style and its usefulness. It became evident that openness to new styles would prove both the strength and the weakness of the new stagecraft and then of American design in general. It was flexible and it made the American designer compatible with many kinds of directors; on the other hand, it had a dangerous potential for merely facile hackwork. A difference appeared between American and European (especially Eastern European) design: the new stagecraft was an aesthetic movement, not a political one, and its designs welcomed beauty but not politics. The rejection of beauty that was fundamental to some European styles (early epic theatre) did not find much sympathy among the designers of the new stagecraft. The new stagecraft showed an affection for soft edges, muted effects, and mood that made it neoromantic. It had, as well, roots in realism, despite what was said by its Amer-

FIGURE 17.22
Seminal Works in the New Stagecraft

Adolphe Appia	*The Staging of Wagnerian Music-Drama*	Fr.	1895
	Music and the Art of the Theater	Ger.	1899
Edward Gordon Craig	*The Art of the Theatre*	Eng.	1905
	On the Art of the Theatre	Eng.	1911
	Toward a New Theatre	Eng.	1919
Georg Fuchs	*Revolution in the Theatre*	Ger.	1908
Huntley Carter	*The New Spirit in Drama and Art*	Eng.	1912
Jacques Rouché	*Modern Theatrical Art*	Fr.	1911
H. K. Motherwell	*The Theatre of Today*	Eng. (Am.)	1914
Sheldon Cheney	*The Art Theatre*	Eng. (Am.)	1917
Kenneth MacGowan	*The Theatre of Tomorrow*	Eng. (Am.)	1921

ican proponents. After the dust had settled, those realistic elements showed more strongly (as in the work of Jo Mielziner, for example), and a "selective realism" became typical of American design.

The Heirs of the Art Movement

Important as politics and antiart became in Europe after World War I, the older ideals of the art theatre movement persisted—e.g., America's new stagecraft and the continuing work of Craig and Appia. They no longer had the easy appeal of novelty, and they were unacceptable to many in the avant-garde; still, they were far from dead. After 1930, political conditions in Europe sometimes worked against political theatre; in Germany, Russia, and Italy, oppressive official art gave artists in other countries a bitter reminder of some of the dangers of activism. Thus, there was a return, of sorts, to aesthetic theatre throughout some of the Depression.

Among emerging artists who were heirs of the art theatre movement or who shared its ideals were the following.

Jean Cocteau (1889–1963)

At one time a surrealist, Cocteau became a brilliant artistic jack-of-all trades and a genuine idealist of art. He was a painter, a designer, a poet, a librettist, a filmmaker, an actor, a director, and a playwright. Plays like *Orpheus* (1926) and *The Infernal Machine* (1934) were important in keeping alive an idea of mythic subject matter and serious drama. As an artist, his most important contribution may have been to film; as a theoretician, he was important for his faith in art as a spiritual experience.

Terence Gray (1895–   )

Greatly influenced by Craig, Gray was the founder and the inspiration of the Cambridge Festival Theatre in England (1926–1933). Continuing, if somewhat erratic, experiment made him an English analogue to Tairov. He worked with or provided opportunities for such subsequent luminaries as Maurice Evans, Tyrone Guthrie, and Ninette de Valois. He helped to direct the English theatre away from neoromanticism and toward stylistic eclecticism, idealism, and the revitalization of the classics.

The Followers of Copeau

In the mid-1920s, Jacques Copeau withdrew from the Vieux-Colombier and set up a theatre school and retreat in the Burgundian countryside. From that center, his influence emanated through the French and the English, and ultimately the American, theatre. His most important disciples ("les Copiaus" or "le Cartel des Quatre") included:

1. *Louis Jouvet (1887–1951)*, designer, director, and actor. Joining Copeau in 1913, he

later had his own theatre and became a director of the Comédie Française.

2. *Michel St.-Denis (1897–1971).* After years of work with Copeau, then on his own, he moved his activities to England in 1935 and became a teacher and director with great influence on the English theatre after World War II.

3. *Charles Dullin (1885–1949).* As actor and director, he had his own theatre and ran his own theatre school, ultimately joining the direction of the Comédie Française.

4. *Gaston Baty (1882–1951)* and *Georges Pitoëff (1884–1939)*, both known best as designers, although they also directed. With Jouvet and Dullin they formed the Cartel des Quatre (1927), a loose cooperative to foster quality theatre.

The Copeau influence continued for another generation, but it was these men who maintained it through World War II. The same qualities can be seen in all of them: commitment to a traditional repertory, but openness to new plays of quality (Jouvet produced the plays

FIGURE 17.23
Leading Designers in Modern Theatre (1900–1925)*

Name	Dates	Example
Transitional Figures		
Lucien Jusseaume	1851–1925	*Pelleas and Melisande,* 1902
Alfred Roller	1864–1935	*Faust, Part 2,* 1911
Joseph Urban	1872–1933	*Ziegfeld Follies,* 1910s
Vladimir Egorov	1878–?	*The Blue Bird,* 1908
Ernst Stern	1876–1954	*Sumurun,* 1910
European Innovators		
Adolphe Appia	1862–1928	*Orpheus and Eurydice,* 1912
Leon Bakst	1866–1924	*The Firebird,* 1910
Charles Ricketts	1866–1931	*Salome,* 1906
Fritz Erler	1868–1940	*Faust,* 1908
Alexander Benois	1870–1960	*Petrouchka,* 1911
Mariano Fortuny	1871–1949	Lighting system, ca. 1910
Edward Gordon Craig	1872–1966	*Hamlet,* 1912
Nicholas Roerich	1874–1947	*The Rites of Spring,* 1913
Emil Pirchan	1884–1957	*The Marquis of Keith,* 1920
Alexandra Exter	1884–1949	*Romeo and Juliet,* 1920
Liubov Popova	1889–1924	*The Magnificent Cuckold,* 1922
Oscar Schlemmer	1888–1943	Bauhaus, 1921–1930
Georg Grosz	1893–1959	*The Good Soldier Schweik,* 1927
I. Nivinski	?	*Turandot* (Vakhtangov), 1922
The New Stagecraft (America)		
Sam Hume	1885–1962	*The Tents of the Arabs,* 1913
Robert Edmond Jones	1887–1954	*The Man Who Married a Dumb Wife,* 1915
Lee Simonson	1888–1967	*The Adding Machine,* 1923
Norman Bel Geddes	1893–1958	*The Miracle,* 1924
Cleon Throckmorton	1897–1965	*The Hairy Ape,* 1922
Jo Mielziner	1901–1976	*Death of a Salesman,* 1949
Claude Bragdon	1866–1946	*Hamlet,* 1920
Mordecai Gorelik	1899–	*Men in White,* 1933
Aline Bernstein	1881–1955	*Romeo and Juliet,* 1930

*In a few cases, examples later than 1925 best typify the designer's work.

of Jean Giraudoux and Jules Romains in France; Dullin produced Luigi Pirandello); commitment to training in their own schools; and a belief in scenic simplicity and unity.

Luigi Pirandello (1867–1936)

One dramatist stands apart from the styles and schools of the period. An Italian, Luigi Pirandello cannot be closely connected with either Italian futurism or expressionism but can be seen as a response to the excessive neoromanticism of much Italian drama (that of Gabrielle d'Annunzio, for example). His form and above all his subject matter were very much his own.

A novelist until World War I, Luigi Pirandello had success with the play *Right You Are (If You Think You Are)* in 1917. Its title suggests the most important concern of his plays: the uncertain nature of human perception and of human personality. He appears to have become interested in the theatre because of its inherent perceptual question (the ambiguity of the actor–character). Pirandello's plays—*Six Characters in Search of an Author* (1921) and *Henry IV* (1922), for example—question both the fictional world of drama and the supposedly real world in which the audience sits, and they were at one time unique in questioning one of the stablest conventions in Western theatre, the integrity of the figure presented to the audience by actor and dramatist. In some Pirandellian drama, the actor pokes through the role to discuss "his" own life, except that the actor is also an invention, behind whom is another actor from the same level of reality as the audience; in other plays, fictions invented by the characters, or mistakes made by the characters, create levels of existence (fictional? real?) above that of the drama. Because he was the first to explore this subject deeply, and because he pursued it with great artistic control, Pirandello was able to create plays of disturbing but stunning theatricality. Pirandello influenced younger playwrights like Brecht and foreshadowed some of the concerns

of the existentialists. He was awarded the Nobel Prize in 1934.

Verse Drama

Prose had become the dominant language of the theatre. After about 1930, a number of playwrights tried to elevate theatre language by writing plays in verse. They did not form a coherent group, and their verse varied from regular verse to verse so free it was prosaic. Their use of poetic devices, however, (symbol, metaphor, and figuration) sometimes made them markedly nonrealistic. A number of them enjoyed success but did not restore verse to modern drama, although they provided some realists with a quasi-poetic diction that allowed them to extend the range of their language (Tennessee Williams, for example). The best of them seem to have been poets who wrote for the theatre, rather than playwrights who attempted poetry. T. S. Eliot, Archibald MacLeish, and Christopher Fry had commercial successes but have not lasted well; the Spanish Federico García Lorca is still widely respected.

T. S. Eliot (1888–1965)
Eliot was arguably the most important English-language poet of the century, perhaps after Yeats. He saw the drama as having a religious seriousness, and he believed that it made demands of the highest kind on language. His plays included *Murder in the Cathedral* (1935) and *The Cocktail Party* (1950).

Maxwell Anderson (1888–1959)
Anderson was an American who wrote an essay, "Poetry in the Theater," as well as verse plays like *Elizabeth the Queen* (1930) and *Winterset* (1935), which were successful. Time has made their value questionable.

Archibald MacLeish (1892–1982)
MacLeish, an important American poet, wrote a few early verse dramas that were probably not meant for production. After two successful verse

FIGURE 17.24
Leading Playwrights of Nonrealism

Name	Dates	Language	Example
Symbolism			
Villiers de l'Isle-Adam	1838–1889	Fr.	*Axel*, 1888
Oscar Wilde	1856–1900	Eng.	*Salome*, 1894 (in French)
Maurice Maeterlinck	1867–1949	Fr.	*Pelleas and Melisande*, 1893
William Butler Yeats	1865–1939	Eng.	*On Bailie's Strand*, 1904
Paul Claudel	1868–1955	Fr.	*The Tidings Brought to Mary*, 1912
Leonid Andreyev	1871–1919	Russ.	*He Who Gets Slapped*, 1916
Expressionism			
August Strindberg (precursor)	1849–1912	Swe.	*The Ghost Sonata*, 1907
Frank Wedekind (precursor)	1864–1918	Ger.	*Spring's Awakening*, 1909
Georg Kaiser	1878–1944	Ger.	*Gas I*, 1920
Eugene O'Neill	1888–1953	Eng. (Am.)	*The Hairy Ape*, 1922
Elmer Rice	1892–1967	Eng. (Am.)	*The Adding Machine*, 1923
Ernst Toller	1893–1939	Ger.	*Man and the Masses*, 1921
Karel Capek	1890–1938	Czech.	*R.U.R.*, 1923
Vladimir Mayakovsky	1894–1930	Russ.	*The Bedbug*, 1929
Bertolt Brecht	1898–1956	Ger.	*Baal*, 1923
Sophie Treadwell	1890–1970	Eng. (Am.)	*Machinal*, 1928
Sean O'Casey	1884–1964	Eng. (Ir.)	*The Silver Tassie*, 1928
Epic Theatre			
Alfons Paquet	1881–1944	Ger.	*Flags*, 1920
Bertolt Brecht	1898–1956	Ger.	*Mother Courage*, 1941
Collective		Ger.	*The Good Soldier Schweik*, 1927
Agit-Prop			
Vladimir Mayakovsky	1894–1930	Russ.	*Mystery-Bouffe*, 1918
Anonymous		Russ.	Blue Blouse plays, 1922–1928
Anonymous		Russ.	Proletcult "living newspapers," 1920s
Anonymous		Eng. (Am.)	*Triple-A Plowed Under*, living newspaper, 1936
"Absurdist"			
Samuel Beckett	1906–	Eng./Fr.	*Waiting for Godot*, 1952
Arthur Adamov	1908–1970	Fr.	*Ping-Pong*, 1955
Jean Genet	1910–	Fr.	*The Balcony*, 1956
Eugene Ionesco	1912–	Fr.	*The Chairs*, 1952
N. F. Simpson	1919–	Eng.	*A Resounding Tinkle*, 1959
Edward Albee	1928–	Eng. (Am.)	*The American Dream*, 1959
Harold Pinter	1930–	Eng.	*The Caretaker*, 1959
Surrealist/Dada			
Alfred Jarry (precursor)	1873–1907	Fr.	*Ubu Roi*, 1896
Guillaume Apollinaire	1880–1918	Fr.	*The Breasts of Tiresias*, 1917
Jean Cocteau	1889–1963	Fr.	*Orpheus*, 1926
Antonin Artaud	1896–1948	Fr.	*Jet of Blood*, 1926
Nonaligned			
Luigi Pirandello	1867–1936	Ital.	*Six Characters in Search of an Author*, 1921
Edouardo de Filippo	1900–	Ital.	*Filomena Maturano*, 1946
Michel de Ghelderode	1898–1962	Fr.	*Pantagleize*, 1930

FIGURE 17.24 (continued)

Jules Romains	1885–1972	Fr.	*Doctor Knock,* 1923
Friedrich Duerrenmatt	1921–	Ger.	*The Visit,* 1956
Thornton Wilder	1897–1975	Eng. (Am.)	*Our Town,* 1938
Ugo Betti	1892–1953	Ital.	*Corruption in the Palace of Justice,* 1949
Luigi Chiarelli	1884–1947	Ital.	*Mask or Face,* 1916
Verse			
T. S. Eliot	1888–1965	Eng.	*Murder in the Cathedral,* 1935
Maxwell Anderson	1888–1959	Eng. (Am.)	*Winterset,* 1935
Archibald MacLeish	1892–1982	Eng. (Am.)	*J.B.,* 1958
Federico García Lorca	1898–1936	Sp.	*Blood Wedding,* 1933
W. H. Auden	1907–1973	Eng.	*The Ascent of F-6* (with Christopher Isherwood), 1936
Christopher Fry	1907–	Eng.	*The Lady's Not for Burning,* 1948

plays for radio—*The Fall of the City* (1937) and *Air Raid* (1938)—he had a commercial success with the verse play *J.B.* (1958).

Federico García Lorca (1898–1936)

García Lorca was a Spanish poet, an amateur director, and a dramatist who was killed in the Spanish Civil War. Plays like *Blood Wedding* (1933) had a great vogue, but it is difficult to tell how much was due to the manner of his death and the politics of the day. It is said that he is now popular in some Islamic countries, perhaps because of his concern with often doomed, honor-wracked characters, many of them women, trapped in a *macho* culture.

W. H. Auden (1907–1973)

With Eliot and Yeats, Auden was one of the great English-language poets of the period. He wrote several verse plays with Christopher Isherwood (1904–   ), including *The Ascent of F-6* (1936), and he wrote a number of quasi-dramatic or readers' works alone, including the *Christmas Oratorio*.

Christopher Fry (1907–   )

Fry had a great success with *The Lady's Not for Burning* (1948).

Rebuilding and Pessimism: From World War II to 1960

Neither the theatre of Nazi Germany nor that of Stalinist Russia has proved of great interest to scholars—perhaps improperly. World War II devastated both nations and interrupted other European theatres. The result was that, at the war's end in 1945, there had been great physical damage to theatre buildings and scenic stocks; there had been losses of personnel; and the national economies of a number of nations were so shattered that they seemed unable to support an activity as costly as theatre.

What followed the war was a period of rebuilding. In England, particularly, this rebuilding was joined to a joyous sense of triumph and self-celebration. France, after years of occupation, was in a darker mood. Eastern Europe was not only devastated by the war but was also faced with the problems of what Winston Churchill would shortly call the "Iron Curtain."

There was a natural tendency to return to prewar patterns. A conservative tendency can be seen. The United States elevated realism to the dominant style; France (especially after Charles DeGaulle came to power in 1954) gave official encouragement to traditional French greatness. In most countries other than the United States, governmental funding took on new importance, and nationally funded theatres were common in most countries by 1960 or shortly thereafter, especially in East and West Germany. The Volksbühne (closed by Hitler) was restored; the Berliner Ensemble came to prominence. By 1960, Germany had hundreds of city- or state-supported theatres, and the best of its exiles (including Piscator and Brecht) had returned. In Italy, the underwritten Piccolo Teatro de Milano, opened in 1947 and led by Paolo Grassi and Giorgio Strehler was the forerunner of a resurgence of Italian civic theatres.

England: Toward a National Theatre

The British economy was in an "austerity program" until the mid-1950s, and English society was permanently shaken up by the war. Theatre flourished, however, beginning that domination of the English-language stage that Britain still enjoys. Central to this flowering were the following.

The Old Vic
The theatre building called the *Old Vic* had been built early in the nineteenth century. From about World War I onward, it had been home to productions of Shakespeare, associated with Sybil Thorndike, Tyrone Guthrie, and John Gielgud. It was damaged by bombing, but an Old Vic company emerged after the war at another location, while the old building was given over to a theatre school and a Young Vic company. In the immediate postwar years, the Old Vic Company included Gielgud, Ralph Richardson, Michael Redgrave, Laurence Olivier, Peggy Ashcroft, and Alec Guinness; its theatre school was run by Michel St. Denis and George Devine. By the early 1950s, many of this company had gone to the commercial theatre, to films, or to companies of their own, but the Old Vic continued with younger actors like Richard Burton.

It was the Old Vic group, and especially Olivier, who symbolized the excellence that justified a drive for a government-supported National Theatre. Actors like Olivier, Richard-

son, and Gielgud represented the best of the English school of acting, and it was these people and their heirs who would be the successful interpreters of still more radical drama to come in the 1960s. People like George Devine were active in new enterprises like the English Stage Company (1956 and after). When, in 1963, the National Theatre came into being, it was led by Olivier, and its first home was the refurbished Old Vic.

The Royal Shakespeare Theatre
The Memorial Theatre at Stratford-upon-Avon had been built in 1932 after a much older one had burned; Stratford thus continued as the national center of "bardolatry." After the war, this theatre successfully incorporated many of the Old Vic actors (their seasons did not conflict). It created a second company and began to do non-Shakespearean plays, and it became known as the Royal Shakespeare Theatre, with homes in both Stratford and London.

France: Gloire and Absurdity

The physical theatre of Paris had survived the war. The French sensibility was badly bruised, however. Two movements resulted, one official and rather conservative, the other avant-garde.

Renewed Tradition
The Copeau group were still active at the Comédie Française. They had been joined there in 1940 by Jean-Louis Barrault, a superb actor and director who had worked with Dullin and with the mime, Etienne Décroux. Barrault left the Comédie in 1946 with his wife, Madeleine Rénaud, to form an outstanding new French theatre. Their repertoire was weighted heavily toward Molière, Shakespeare, Marivaux, and Claudel, with a style that showed the Copeau influence, but they also staged new drama.

The other new company of importance was the Théâtre National Populaire, led by Jean Vilar (1912–1971). After early work with Dullin and ventures on his own, he founded the Théâtre

National Populaire in 1951 and directed it until 1962.

Absurdism

A new drama that had affinities with existentialism appeared during and after World War II. It has been called *absurdist* because of an early label put on it; the label has stuck, but it may prove an example of a judgment made before all the evidence was understood.

Existentialism is traceable at least to the nineteenth century and Nietzsche, but it was increasingly important in European thought after 1930. It saw human existence as defined by death and without absolutes. Existence was seen as specific to the individual. Important terms were *choice* (all actions require choice because there are no absolutes); *guilt* (most choices result in inevitable consequences that cause guilt); *boredom* (existence is repetitious); *isolation;* and *absurdity* (human beings are in the absurd po-

sition of trying to give meaning to their meaningless existence, either because it is in human nature to give meaning or because they need a form of entertainment).

Existential dramatists include Albert Camus (1913–1960), better known as a novelist; and Jean-Paul Sartre (1905–1980), a French existentialist philosopher, who wrote existentialist plays that failed to find an appropriate form.

Shortly after the war, however, three dramatists appeared who radicalized theatre by finding stylistic analogues for their new content. The three have little in common theatrically, and none of them is a coherent existentialist ideologue.

Samuel Beckett (1906–   ).   Beckett was probably the most influential dramatist of the period. Born in Ireland, and at one time an artistic familiar of James Joyce's, he came to the theatre after years of writing novels. *Waiting for Godot*

FIGURE 17.25

Beckett's *Endgame* at the University of Rochester, 1965. Directed by Kenneth Cameron.

(1952), *Endgame* (1958), and *Happy Days* (1961) are often very funny, despite their foundation of despair. Beckett's settings are stripped to essentials, as his language is stripped; every word takes on enormous meaning. Beckett was awarded the Nobel Prize in 1969.

Jean Genet (1910–   ).   Genet is a former convict who, in the late 1940s, turned from novels and essays to the theatre. *Deathwatch* (1949), *The Maids* (1947), *The Balcony* (1956), and *The Blacks* (1958) brought the theatre of Artaud to realization. Moral anarchy, eroticism, and an amused contempt for social organization mark the plays, which also show the influence of Pirandello.

Eugene Ionesco (1912–   ).   Romanian by birth, in his first play, *The Bald Soprano* (1950), Ionesco used phrases from an English textbook as its language, creating a wildly funny theatre about the failure of communication. *The Lesson* (1951) and *The Chairs* (1952) explore isolation and noncommunication. *Rhinoceros* (1959) and *Exit the King* (1962) are concerned with individualism, social organization, and aspiration. Ionesco shows clear affinities with dada and surrealism, using wit and fantasy to create surprising theatrical images.

The passage of time suggests that it may be Beckett who is the artistic prophet of the three, not because of his supposed absurdism, but because of his extreme minimalism of scene, gesture, and language, which looked forward to the minimal art that appeared in painting, sculpture, music, and dance in the late 1960s and the 1970s.

The United States: Away from Broadway

After the war, the best American theatres of the prewar period (the Group Theatre and the Mercury Theatre, an offshoot of the Federal Theatre Project) were defunct. There was no American Old Vic, no American Comédie Française.

About 1950, two new tendencies were seen.

The Regional Theatre Movement

Sometimes called *regional repertory*, the regional theatre began modestly as a scattering of small theatres, for example, in Dallas (the Margo Jones), Houston (the Alley) and Washington (the Arena Stage). Some did revivals of Broadway plays in lackluster productions, but others did new plays and had high standards. Many dispensed with the proscenium stage and performed in the round or in three-quarters staging; nonetheless, they were usually realistic and had a realistic repertory. As they gained financial stability and attracted serious critical attention, some of these theatres became alternatives to New York for serious artists. They gained great impetus from the founding of the Stratford (Canada) Festival in 1953, to which the director Tyrone Guthrie brought the experience of the Old Vic and the Cambridge Festival Theatre. When he went on to help found the theatre at Minneapolis, Minnesota (now the Guthrie Theatre), this movement may be said to have come of age.

Off- and Off-Off Broadway

There were a number of small theatres in the Greenwich Village area of New York City, some of them left from the little-theatre movement of the 1920s. After 1950, production in them came to be called *Off-Broadway*. The 1952 production of Tennessee Williams' *Summer and Smoke* at the Circle-in-the-Square (originally performed at the Margo Jones in Dallas) was the first hit. Off-Broadway producers appeared, able to mount a play for a few thousand dollars: new Off-Broadway theatres were created in a wide variety of spaces and in a variety of configurations. A repertoire of neglected classics, new American plays, and plays from the European avant-garde emerged. Off-Broadway worked out contracts with Actors Equity and the craft unions for the operation of the theatres (the contract basis being a 299-seat limit). By 1960, Off-Broadway had at least one permanent company (the Living Theatre), a number of home-grown playwrights (including Edward Albee, Jack

Richardson, and Jack Gelber), and a certifiable musical hit, *The Fantasticks.*

Ironically, Off-Broadway's success was symbolized by its increasingly expensive productions and the dissatisfaction of artists and critics who said that it had become simply a smaller Broadway. This dissatisfaction led in the late 1950s to the creation of Off-Off-Broadway, first centered in the performing cafés and coffeehouses of Greenwich Village. It seemed to take its values from either the avant-garde in other arts or simply and straightforwardly from its own needs, bypassing values that had been handed down from the art theatre movement to Off-Broadway by way of the educational theatre. Off-Off-Broadway was more truly an original, open to unusual performance spaces, new styles, and radical experimentation. Its early foci were the Café Cino and the Café La Mama. By the early 1960s, Off-Off-Broadway represented what the American theatre had lacked since the very early 1920s: a genuinely experimental wing.

ENDNOTES

1. Sally R. Sommer, "The Stage Apprenticeship of Loie Fuller," *Dance Scope* 12, 1 (Fall/Winter 1977–1978): 24.
2. Lois Draegin, "After Isadora: Her Art as Inspiration," *Dance Magazine* (July 1977): 67.
3. Ibid.
4. Marc Slonim, *Russian Theatre: From the Empire to the Soviets* (Cleveland and New York: World Publishing, 1961), p. 178.
5. Huntley Carter, *The New Spirit in Drama and Art* (London: Frank Palmer, 1912), p. 24.
6. Denis Bablet, *Esthétique Générale du Décor de Théâtre, de 1870 à 1914* (Paris: Editions du Centre National de la Recherche Scientifique, 1965), p. 157.
7. Hugh Hunt, *The Abbey, Ireland's National Theatre, 1904–1979* (Dublin: Gill and Macmillan, 1979), p. 9.
8. Ibid., p. 83.
9. James W. Flannery, "W. B. Yeats and the Abbey Theatre Company," *Educational Theatre Journal* 27, 2 (May 1975): 187.
10. Slonim, p. 182; and Denis Bablet, *Edward Gordon Craig*, trans. Daphne Woodward (London: Heinemann, 1966), pp. 134–135.
11. Georg Fuchs, *Revolution in the Theatre: Conclusions Concerning the Munich Artists' Theatre*, trans. Constance Connor Kuhn (Ithaca, N.Y.: Cornell University Press, 1959), p. 178.
12. Kenneth MacGowan, *The Theatre of Tomorrow* (New York: Boni and Liveright, 1921), p. 208.
13. Carter, p. 262.
14. Sheldon Cheney, *The Art Theater* (New York: Knopf, 1925), p. 3.
15. Richard Moody, public lecture, Columbia, South Carolina, 1982.
16. Cheney, p. 32.
17. Walter R. Volbach, *Adolphe Appia, Prophet of the Modern Theatre: a Profile* (Middletown, Conn.: Wesleyan University Press, 1968), p. 42.
18. Ibid., p. 92.
19. Cheney, p. 44.
20. George Nash, *Edward Gordon Craig, 1872–1966* (London: H. M. Stationery Office, 1967), p. 12.
21. Irène Eynat, "Gordon Craig, the Uber-Marionette, and the Dresden Theatre," *Theatre Research International* 5, 3 (Autumn 1980): 178.
22. Nash, pp. 9–10; and Bablet, *Craig*, p. 39.
23. Laurence Senelick, "Moscow and Monodrama: The Meaning of the Craig-Stanislavsky *Hamlet*," *Theatre Research International* 6, 2 (Spring 1981): 110.
24. Oliver Sayler, ed., *Max Reinhardt and His Theatre* (reprint edition, New York: Benjamin Blom, 1968, first published 1928), Appendix III.
25. Rudolf Kommer, "The Magician of Leopold-skron," in Sayler, p. 13.
26. Paul Gorceix, *Les Affinités Allemandes dans l'Oeuvre de Maurice Maeterlinck* (Paris: Presses Universitaires de France, 1975), p. 47.
27. Ibid., p. 47.
28. Edmund Wilson, *Axel's Castle* (New York: Scribner's, 1931), pp. 258–259.
29. Gorceix, p. 48.
30. Ibid., p. 47.
31. W. D. Halls, *Maurice Maeterlinck, a Study of His Life and Thought* (Oxford: Oxford University Press, 1980), p. 106.

32. Richard Hovey, "Modern Symbolism and Maurice Maeterlinck," in *Princess Maleine*, trans. Richard Hovey (New York: Dodd, Mead, 1913), p. 5.

33. Huntley Carter, *The New Theatre and Cinema of Soviet Russia* (London: Chapman and Dodd, 1924), p. 147.

34. Oliver M. Sayler, *The Russian Theatre* (rev. ed. of *The Russian Theatre Under the Revolution*, New York: Brentano's, 1922), p. 164.

35. Edward Braun, *The Theatre of Meyerhold* (London: Eyre Methuen, 1979), pp. 53 ff.

36. Nick Worrall, "Meyerhold's Production of *The Magnificent Cuckold*," *TDR* 17 (March 1973): 14–34.

37. Braun, p. 160.

38. Ibid., p. 169.

39. Worrall, p. 20.

40. Braun, p. 227.

41. Slonim, p. 328.

42. The whole question of Meyerhold's concepts of physical acting need examination. Bablet (*Craig*, pp. 111–112), for example, sees analogies between Craig's *Übermarionette* and biomechanics, and he suggests a further analogy with work at the Bauhaus; at the same time, the similarity to the "method of physical actions" cannot be ignored. Such interest in the physical side of the actor's art was to mark much of the theatre work of the 1960s in England and America, and it is not far-fetched to suggest an affinity with Artaud's concept of "gesture." The entire association of Meyerhold with biomechanics may rest on a historical error (limited information, highly selective observation by outsiders) compounded willingly by the Soviet bureaucracy after the mid-1930s.

43. Slonim, p. 330.

44. Roger Howard, "Propaganda in the Early Soviet and Contemporary Chinese Theatre," *Theatre Quarterly* 7 (August 1977): 53–60.

45. František Deák, "Blue Bouse," *TDR* 17 (March 1973): 35–46.

46. Garff Wilson, *Three Hundred Years of American Drama and Theatre* (Englewood Cliffs, N.J.: Prentice-Hall, 1973), p. 409.

47. Denis Bablet, "L'Expressionisme à la Scene," in Denis Bablet and Jean Jacquot, eds., *L'Expressionisme dans le Théâtre Européen* (Paris: Editions du Centre National de la Recherche Scientifique), p. 198.

48. Ibid.

49. Lotte H. Eisner, "Le Cinéma Expressioniste," in Bablet and Jacquot, p. 215.

50. Denis Calandra, "Georg Kaiser's 'From Morn to Midnight': The Nature of Expressionist Performance," *Theatre Quarterly* 6 (Spring 1976): 21.

51. Oscar Brockett and Robert T. Findlay, *A Century of Innovation* (Englewood Cliffs, N.J.: Prentice-Hall, 1973), p. 407.

52. Erwin Piscator, *The Political Theatre*, trans. Hugh Rorrison (New York: Avon Books, 1978; first published in German, 1929), p. 207.

53. John Fregi, *The Essential Brecht* (Los Angeles: Hennessey and Ingalls, 1972), p. 10.

54. All quotations from Artaud are from *The Theater and Its Double*, trans. Mary Caroline Richards (New York: Grove Press, 1958).

18

The Theatre in Search of
a Paradigm

We find the contemporary theatre a very difficult one to describe, both because of its seeming lack of paradigm and because of the several historiographic problems that bedevil it. There is an excess of information about some aspects of it, a sense of being too close to the picture. There is a problem of reliability of sources, for most of the available information about contemporary theatre is journalistic at best and therefore lacks rigor. There is the large problem that much of the contemporary theatre is in countries whose control of information makes objective understanding unlikely. There is the problem of language. And there is the problem of critical nationalism: each observer tends to report on his or her own theatre with more sympathy than on others; each commentator is more-or-less limited by his or her own language; and some are affected by political bias.

What follows in this chapter, therefore, is not really of the same order as the rest of this book. It is neither history nor really framework of fact; it is culled reportage that we intend as an illustration of the absence of paradigm. We hope that it illustrates the historiographic difficulty (perhaps impossibility) of presenting one's own immediate world.

The Period

As with the theatre, so with the world: since 1960, there has been an excess of information, unreliability of sources, government control of information, and too much closeness to events.

From 1960 to the present has been a quarter century seemingly packed with great events—about which we have too much information. During the period, the speed of change went on increasing, especially in technology, and the world seems a vastly different place from the world of 1900.

International Imbalances

The Cold War continued throughout the period, with a nominal "detente" in the 1970s. The Soviet Union and the United States continued as the main adversaries, although by 1980 many other nations looked on both of them as aging and stodgy contenders. Nuclear war continued to be a real threat and perhaps the single greatest shadow on human consciousness.

The emergence from colonialism of broad areas of the world, which had begun after World War II, saw the establishment of both stable and unstable regimes. Former colonies of the European powers became nations with legitimate concerns quite separate from those of Europe or the superpowers, for example, in India, Indonesia, Algeria, and Kenya. To the industrial nations, the new ones were often "undeveloped"; on the other hand, the world glut of weapons made most nations capable of sophisticated and deadly wars.

Shifting Economies

The energy crises of the 1970s brought into clear focus the economic ties that bind most of the world together. Since that time, inflation has plagued most countries, whether they are capitalist or socialist, and old solutions have often not worked. A few countries have emerged with comparatively great oil wealth. At the same time, industrial productivity seems to be shifting away from the Soviet Union and the United States to nations like Japan, changing both economic balances and national self-images. Whole industries have moved from one part of the globe to another: the world's photographic industry, for example, once centered in Germany, is now almost exclusively in Southeast Asia.

It is unclear what the deep effects of these shifts will be. A change in national identities will be one, with a resulting change in the idea of which nations are "important." Continuing inflation may undermine the stability of both political and ethical systems. Social and even religious change may result.

Technology

The "information explosion" has intensified. New industries have grown up around the reproduction of print (symbolized by the Xerox Corporation), cable television, home-generated television, electronic calculators, and computers. Computers, "massified" by the invention of the silicon chip, may create profound changes in high-technology societies because they may allow fairly large numbers of people to work at home.

Redefinition of Community

In some former colonies, there has been an impaction of enormous numbers of people in a few cities (Calcutta, India, for example); in the wealthy, industrialized nations, on the other hand, the middle class has dispersed to urban fringes. Many cities have been called unlivable, but at least the poor go on living there; in countries like the United States, "urban renewal" (which begins with gutting city centers) has become popular. "White flight" to the suburbs can

be seen in several countries. Enormous and expensive highways have made it possible to fill cities quickly in the morning and empty them as quickly at night by means of automobiles. Slums continue to fill large parts of many cities; slum residents do not leave the city at night but stay, nursing resentment, periodically erupting into riots.

Particularly in the United States, but recognizably in England, France, and other nations, "bedroom communities" lie around the cities. These communities often have no center. Automobiles are thus necessary for most activities, including shopping, which is done at "malls" that are unrelated to the political or social divisions of the communities. Lacking centrality, these communities rarely have communal institutions like theatres, museums, or art collections. Their decentralization is served well by contemporary technology, which can deliver information and entertainment into homes no matter where they are; consumers are now able to satisfy individual tastes without leaving their suburban houses.

It is believed that home computers, linked to a variety of services, will one day satisfy the needs once satisfied by public libraries, banks, bookstores, theatres, and other central institutions. The casual, social gathering places of the past—cafés, coffeehouses, bookstores, and park benches—may be replaced by the telephone. Some historians believe that the commonality of interest that created the medieval and modern city is at an end. It is unclear what, if anything, might take its place.

Philosophy

Although existentialism became faddish in the 1950s and the early 1960s, since the mid-1960s it has so entered modern thinking that it has become part of the unconscious assumptions that many people have about themselves and their world. Supporting it and agreeing with it are the contemporary threats of nuclear extinction, of pollution, and of overpopulation; undergirding it historically are the ideas of Einstein and Heisenberg, who postulated a universe in which all entities are linked into systems, and in which all systems and all parts of systems, because linked, are relative. In place of great and small are greater and lesser; in place of absolute is probable. The speck of dust pulls on the moon, and any system that accounts for the moon must include the speck of dust; the hero and the villain exist in terms of each other, linked by a system, and any form that wants to account for one must include the other.

This concept of systems has spread, in popularized form, to many other fields. Systemic philosophies suit very well with a society linked by computers and cable television, and systemic analysis works very well for a world in which pollution in Indiana affects the death rate in India. Systemic philosophy is anathema to rugged individualism, however, and acceptance of it comes hard in many cultures. Its social and moral implications have proved offensive to many people and may be partly responsible for conservative reactions in the 1980s in politics and religion.

As thought out by its founders, existentialism was a tough-minded philosophy that required courage. As it has been weakened by popular interpretation, however, it seems to have become sometimes indistinguishable from the self-indulgence of "Gather ye rosebuds while ye may." Some cultural observers have called the 1960s and 1970s the "me decades" and have noted a dominant narcissism, especially in America. They describe a culture adrift, lacking either the rigor of traditional religion or the tough-mindedness of a consistent philosophy, a culture in which large groups of people have discretionary income to spend on rather aimless, often mindless time-killing pursuits—from pop religions to drugs to all sorts of "therapies," from wind surfing to loveless sex to gadgetry—and always with television somewhere close by, droning its empty message. Such a picture is, of course, one of a culture without a paradigm.

Effects on the Theatre

Out of this complex and fast-moving quarter century, we can identify at least the following points of relevance to the theatre.

Shifting Self-image
If the theatre (like other arts) is a projection of its society's idea of itself, then the theatre in a time of changing self-understanding is a theatre in search of a self-image.

Economic Erosion
The theatre is affected whenever the potential audiences are under stress, especially economically, and most especially when they come to believe that the theatre is too expensive. This belief has become widespread in the period.

Redefinition of Commonality
Because the theatre is a social phenomenon, it needs clusters of theatrically conscious people for an audience. They must exist in sufficient numbers to pay the theatre's costs, and they must live close enough to attend under the conditions dictated by the theatre's place in the society (that is, if the performances are annual festivals, the audience can gather from a distance; if performance is daily, the audience must live within convenient traveling distance, and a transportation network must be available). The moving of large, affluent populations out of cities may have severely affected both the size and the makeup of audiences. As well, the new technology (especially television) may have had a double effect: first, it offers many rivals; and, second, it acculturates people to a different social role for the performing arts (that is, many people now seem content to watch a picture of a performance as an audience of one instead of gathering with other people to watch the performance live). As well, many people now live far from the centers where theatres still exist, and the old cities have become places mostly to flee from, associated with crime, dirt, and work.

Philosophy

The mood of the period has not been bright, and the dominant philosophy is not optimistic; we must expect to find these ideas reflected in a somewhat dour drama.

The Theatre

Many twentieth-century voices have called for an end to the traditional theatre—the futurists, the dadaists, and Antonin Artaud, for example. Despite them, however, both traditional drama and traditional theatrical practices have flourished, *sometimes in very limited situations*, in societies as diverse as those of the Soviet Union and the United States. It is one of the paradoxes of the period that both traditionalists and anti-traditionalists have strong constituencies in most countries. In the very best circumstances, the theatre of the staged play has never been healthier, and its skills have never been more highly developed. Its health depends on government subsidy in most societies, but subsidies have been common throughout the theatre's history.

The Traditional Theatre

The Great International Companies

The influence of Stanislavski in Russia and of Copeau and his followers in other nations continues. Among the great theatres are

1. Soviet Union: Moscow Art Theatre, Moscow; Maly Theatre, Moscow.
2. France: Comédie Française, Paris.
3. Great Britain: National Theatre, London; Royal Shakespeare Theatre, Statford-upon-Avon and London.
4. Canada: The Stratford, Ontario Shakespearean Festival.
5. United States: The Guthrie Theatre, Minneapolis.

The characteristics of these theatres include the following.

Preservationism. Without becoming fusty, the best traditional theatres have kept the great plays of the past in their repertoires and have recalled others from oblivion. They have also recalled lost production techniques and styles, although the present direction of most traditional production is toward a vigorous, but not revolutionary, revitalization of old texts.

Quality. From Moscow to Minneapolis, the traditional theatres represent the highest standards of acting, direction, and physical production. Although they are sometimes accused of giving roles to actors when they are past their peak (an observation made in both Moscow and Paris), it must be said that these theatres are the ones in which the great actors of the day will have their best chances to be challenged by the most demanding roles in their national theatres. Although it is true that the great traditionalist theatres emphasize artists who have established their claim on attention, it is also true that those artists then offer models for younger, less experienced artists everywhere.

Cautious Innovation. Although the traditional theatres vary in their views of new plays and new techniques, most of them have some room for both. New plays (having traditional, written texts) are sometimes presented in parallel seasons or subsidiary theatres, but they are subject to the same rigorous standards.

Nationalistic Orientation. The great traditional companies are usually showcases of their national cultures, but their repertoires are broad enough to include the best of the other cultures, as well, so that they have in common Shakespeare, Molière, Chekhov, and a few others. Max Reinhardt's "life list," with a few exceptions, would probably include most plays that the traditional theatres would do, other than new scripts.

Contractual Flexibility. Some of the national theatres are closed companies with artists on exclusive contracts; others are seasonal. Most

FIGURE 18.1

Rolf Hochhuth's *The Deputy*, directed by Erwin Piscator at the Freie Volksbühne, Berlin (1963), with Malte Jaeger, Gunther Tabor, Dieter Borsche, and Hans Nielsen. [Photo by Ilse Buhs/Jurgen Remmler.]

artists are able to work in film and television, sometimes in other theatres. In the West, there is considerable cross-seeding with commercial theatre. The English example of openness to outside, especially avant-garde influence, and of tolerance of work away from the traditional theatre, has resulted in an unusually vigorous theatre.

Selective Appeal. The great national theatres, and some of the best among their analogues in regional theatres, exert a far more powerful pull on audiences than most commercial or avant-garde theatres do. They seem to have the same social position as great museums, to be visited for their special qualities and to be talked about afterward (not "I went to the theatre," but, "I went to Stratford"). Statistical analyses suggest that attendance at such theatres goes up with educational level and that there is a rough correlation between income and attendance. Perhaps surprisingly, this correlation is about equally true in both the Soviet Union and the West.[1]

The theatres listed, and some of their analogues, are exceptions to the predicted effects of decentralization and to the rivalry of home-entertainment technology, probably because of their unique status and because of their command of information, so that their pull extends far beyond normal geographical limits. In this sense, all are "festival" theatres and their audiences show festival behavior: many audience members make special trips to attend these theatres and may stay several days to see several productions. It is hardly accidental that many of the best traditional theatres are in national capitals, where they have some of the same status as national museums and art collections. The world's great exception seems to be the United States, which has no national, traditional company. Despite repeated attempts, New York's Lincoln Center has failed as a site for such a theatre, although New York continues as the center of American commercial theatre. Washington, D.C., has the Kennedy Center, which seems to function as a tryout and road house.

The Future. In the past, traditional theatres have sometimes become cut off from their society and have grown inbred and arrogant (the Comédie Française in the late eighteenth century, for example). Some critics object to a "museum" mentality that puts certain theatres in the position of protecting a past that the culture itself seems ready to forget. However, the infusion of ideas and talent from both the commercial and the avant-garde theatres acts as a corrective force.

In England, the United States, and Canada, the great traditional theatres have become the models for many of the repertory theatres and for some of the educational theatres. (The commercial theatre is the model for most of the rest of the theatres.) The United States has seen conflict between the demands of the traditional repertory on theatre artists, especially actors, and the training systems in existence. It is likely that this problem will intensify if the prophecies of Artaud are borne out.

New Drama in the Traditional Theatre

The new plays produced in the traditional theatres (that is, those with conventional theatre spaces, specialized artists like actors and directors, and audiences drawn by theatrical attraction rather than special social or political interest) have remained rather bland. New plays from the early 1960s through the early 1970s perhaps suffered from undue attention to self-proclaimed Artaudian goals, particularly the minimization of language; a result was the widespread production (except in the Soviet Union and the Germanies) of plays more flashy than theatrically sound. A cautious evaluation of the period suggests that two important strains in new drama continued the major influences of the 1950s.

Blends of Brecht and Realism. Brecht's own plays were widely produced in the 1950s and 1960s and have become part of the repertoire of serious noncommercial theatres. His influence has been limited in many countries by his politics, yet it has been noteworthy in some cases, often in highly modified form:

1. Robert Bolt, *A Man for All Seasons* (1960). This serious play about Sir Thomas More effectively used some of Brecht's epic techniques without aiming at Brecht's (and Piscator's) political goal. The result was a highly effective play that had a successful life in the commercial theatre.

2. Arthur Kopit, *Indians* (1969). Kopit's plays have been very mixed stylistically (a modern and an American characteristic), and only *Indians* shows strong epic influence. The play was first staged in England, then at the Washington Arena Stage, then on Broadway, with changes made at each stage. It was a deeply felt examination of America's treatment of the Western Indians, made theatrically effective and often heavily ironic by presenting itself as Buffalo Bill's Wild West Show. It had expressionist elements, as well (as did some epic theatre).

3. Rolf Hochhuth, *The Deputy* (1963). A new "documentary drama" appeared in West Ger-

many in the early 1960s and provided some of the West's most controversial plays. At the Berlin Volksbühne, *The Deputy* was directed by Piscator, who found it "an epic play, epic-scientific, epic-documentary, a play for the epic, 'political' theatre for which I have fought for thirty years, a 'total' play for a 'total' theatre."[2]

4. Peter Weiss, *The Investigation* (1961) and *The Persecution and Assassination of Marat as Performed by the Inmates of Charenton Under the Direction of the Marquis de Sade* (1963). *The Investigation* was another of the documentary plays produced at the Volksbühne under Piscator and shared with them a fascination with Germany's recent history. The other Weiss play, however (shortened to the more familiar title *Marat/Sade*), is more famous in other countries for a later production style that obscured its Brechtian background (see below, "Peter Brook").

Blends of "Absurdism" and Realism.

The mature products of the influence of 1950s "absurdism" continued the verbal minimalism of Beckett, and the rhythms and sometimes even the vocabulary of Beckett sound in some of the works like palpable echoes. In the hands of many playwrights, absurdism proved to be simply a chic mannerism, but it became for some a springboard to a drama of meanings denied to realism.

Some new dramatists appear to have built on the revived realism of the 1950s (the realism of John Osborne and Arnold Wesker) to create a new style. It tends to be leftist in its political interest, lower- or working-class in its characters, and quite literal (realistically imitative) in the regional accents and the speech patterns of its characters. Its language, however, is far more concentrated—and thus individual words are far richer—than in realism. This language seems to be the product of the influence of Beckett and Harold Pinter. Its plays, like those of the "absurdists," have no commitment either to three-act structure or to the traditional two-hour running time; more important, they most often present dramatic action as self-contained and

self-justifying, qualities common to both "absurdism "and naturalism; that is, actions are often not "universalized" by overt statement, nor are they "explained" either by exposition or by a denouement that brings them to a narrative ending. As a result, these "minimalist-realist" plays are sometimes so seemingly hermetic that they have the paradoxical effect of seeming allegorical, as if their grudging refusal to yield "meaning" is a spur to a search for meaning. Such a stance is itself common to minimal art, which, believing that "meaning" lies in the observer, not the object, is so "meaningless" that it inspires a search in observers, each of whom may find a quite different "meaning"—each of which will be "correct."

British playwrights include Edward Bond (*Saved*, 1965), Trevor Griffiths (*Comedians*, 1974), and especially Harold Pinter (1930–   ).

Pinter uses a very spare language, combined with an elliptical, often mysterious action, to create serious and sometimes unsettling plays. Like Beckett's, Pinter's plays are often funny, although funny with a distinct edge because of the menace that usually underlies Pinter's character relationships. Some critics have dismissed Pinter and said that there is less to his plays than meets the eye, but he is loved by actors, by many critics, and by a good part of the audience, even of the commercial theatre.

Edward Albee (1928–   ) had an enormous success on Broadway with *Who's Afraid of Virginia Woolf?* (1962). His succeeding plays have usually been well received critically, and he has been hailed by some as the successor to Williams, Miller, and O'Neill. A mixture of symbolism and "absurdist" mannerism has made some critics impatient, however, and even the most serious of his subsequent plays (*Tiny Alice,* 1964; *All Over,* 1971) have been questioned.

Sam Shepard (*Buried Child,* 1978) has continued as a tantalizing outsider of the American theatre. Shepard (1943–   ) has some qualities in common with the English minimalist–realists, but his differences from them are probably

FIGURE 18.2

Sam Shepard's *Suicide in B-Flat,* directed by Kim Peter Kovac, Paradise Island Express and Independent Theatre Project. [Photo by Dennis Deloria.]

more significant; typically American, he seems apolitical; his language tends toward excess rather than minimalization; and his actions are mysterious and "meaningless" because they sometimes lack internal probability, not because they lack external resonance. David Mamet (*American Buffalo,* 1977) is a relentless recorder of American speech in all its rhythms, its vocabulary, and its deadening flatness and repetitiveness. The plays of Mamet are admired by realistic actors for their rich subtexts. He seems much closer to the English minimalist–realists than Shepard because the very mundanity of his actions becomes portentous.

Perhaps the significant fact that will emerge about the 1970s when they are compared with the 1960s will be the return of dramatists' concern about language. The language of these playwrights is vastly different from the language of the neoromantics and even of the realists (but it is *important* language), and these seem to be dramatists for whom the word may again be the beginning.

The Nontraditional Theatre

The term *nontraditional* covers a wider range of activities than even *traditional,* and the theatres that it identifies are nontraditional in a variety of ways. That variety is the product of directions taken by a number of arts between World War II and 1960.

New Ideas in Art

The Blurring of the Boundaries Between the Arts.

The idea of *an art* rather than several arts goes back to well before World War II and was embodied in the career of Jean Cocteau. In the 1950s, there were an increasing number of artistic events that had to be given new names, because the names derived from traditional criticism did not suffice. Many were called *happenings*, *pieces*, or *events*. They crossed supposedly established lines between, for example, sculpture and theatre, as in the activity of one of Yves Tinguely's self-destructive machines. The composer John Cage was an important force in the creation of happenings. In a number of these activities (as with the Tinguely sculpture), *time* or *duration* was added to the experience of the work of art where before it had been absent; in others, the nature of the observer of the work was redefined, from, for example, passive observer to participant. Such activity has continued, and there is now a category of criticism devoted to "performance art" that defies the traditional definition of theatre.

The Emphasis on Art as Process.

The action painting of artists like Jackson Pollock put an important emphasis on the act of painting itself, which was seen as different from either "self-expression" or "creativity." For the theatre, there were important questions raised about the relationship between performer and audience, about the nature of (and even the need for) an audience, about the difference between rehearsal and performance, and about techniques like improvisation as "action" art forms.

The Demystification of Art and the Artist.

The romantics had insisted that the artist was a special being and that art was a special kind of experience. Now, artists and critics questioned those ideas. By the mid-1960s, there were authoritative voices insisting that "everybody is an artist" and that "there is no such thing as art." These ideas fit well with theories of education, especially in the United States, and with increasing "massification," both of which were hostile to suggestions of elitism. There were important effects on artistic training, on the concept of professionalism, and on definitions of standards.

Characteristics of Nontraditional Theatres, (1960–Present)

Individual theatres displayed some, but seldom all, of the following:

1. "Guerilla" tactics—bringing the performance to people in nontheatrical places and without mediation or warning.

2. Use of "found" space, ignoring or rejecting traditional theatre architecture and the idea of an established theatre location.

3. "Environmental" theatre, whose performance space and audience space interpenetrated.

4. Redefinition of the nature and function of dramatic text, as a "pretext," a "springboard," or an irrelevance.

5. Redefinition of acting and the actor's way of life, including:

   a. Improvisation as performance.

   b. The theatre company as a community or commune.

   c. The actor as ascetic (saint) or as disciple (of a guru or a prophet).

6. Redefinition of the audience, including:

   a. Changed ideas of what is common to an audience (so that, in guerilla theatre, what became common was the accident of being in a certain place at a certain time; or, in feminist theatre, what became common was their feminism).

   b. Changed ideas of audience size; usually, these ideas rejected the commercial dependence on size as a function of income and experimented with the extremes: audiences of one or none, or audiences of a hundred thousand (as at rock concerts).

Kinds of Nontraditional Theatre (1960–Present)

These theatres can be divided into two broad categories.

FIGURE 18.3

Wendy Woodson's *Baggage and the Fates,* a dance-theatre example of the new forms called *performance art.* [Photo by Eric Poggenpohl.]

The Heirs of Artaud.   No single figure can be identified in so many aspects of theatre of the period as Artaud. Whether his influence was actually so great or whether he was a prophet of what was inevitably to come remains to be seen. His theories were widely popularized after 1960, the more so because they seemed to be borne out by events in the world (waves of assassination, riot, hijackings, and protest). Above all, Artaud's presence could be seen in:

1. The rejection of traditional drama and of the idea of text, and with that a rejection of language.
2. The search for new performance techniques and the search for a spiritual significance in performance.
3. The exploration of new actor–audience relationships, particularly the placing of the audience at the center, where it might be menaced by the performers.

These activities seemed to peak in the late 1960s and then to decline rather sharply, leav-ing a residue of persistent experimenters who were almost immediately being called dated because of their persistence. Both the quantity and the energy of avant-garde theatre seemed to decline in the 1970s, with many avant-gardists behaving as if all of the interesting experiments had already been tried. By comparison with the 1960s, the activity of the 1970s was very quiet.

Outstanding examples of Artaud's influence were the following.

Peter Brook.   In a period that abounded in British directors of the highest quality, Peter Brook (1926–   ) stood out for his enormous talent and his unpredictability. As a director of the Royal Shakespeare Company, he made great contributions to the traditional British theatre; at the same time (in the early 1960s) he formed a "theatre of cruelty" laboratory (with Charles Marowitz), from which came his production of Peter Weiss's *Marat/Sade* in a distinctly Artaudian mode. So influential was the production that the play is now associated with the style in English-speaking countries. Shocking visual and aural events, multilayered activity, overt nudity and sexuality, and convincing physical violence created a spectacular theatre work. Whether the production was "cruel" in precisely the way that Artaud meant that word is debatable; performed mostly in proscenium theatres, it did not surround its audience, and its physical threat against the audience was inhibited by centuries of custom (and became merely silly in the filmed and televised versions). Brook's *Marat/Sade,* curiously, has been hailed as a masterpiece based on a theory that proclaimed "no more masterpieces."

Brook's later productions moved still farther from the traditional: a phallic *Oedipus* (Seneca) in 1968, a dazzling white-on-white *Midsummer Night's Dream* (1970). In 1971, he set up an International Center for Theatre Research in Paris and began work on Orghast, a theatrical language to "by-pass language altogether."[3]

Kenneth Tynan has called Brook "morally neutral," by which he seems to have meant apolitical. As Tynan pointed out, Brook finds his own antecedents in Gordon Craig, as well as in Artaud,[4] and both his restlessness and his idealism have a model in Craig. So may his Orghast, which may be to Brook what the Übermarionette was to Craig.

Jerzy Grotowski and the Polish Laboratory Theatre.

The Polish director–theorist Jerzy Grotowski (1933–   ) came to American attention through the unflagging enthusiasm of *The Drama Review.* He had started his Laboratory Theatre in Wroclaw, Poland, in 1959 and continued to develop his work there into the 1970s. Grotowski may be better known and more imitated in the United States than in Europe, because of both the early *Drama Review* attention and his 1968 New York season.

Grotowski's was what he called a "poor theatre," poor in that it was stripped of such "luxuries" as lighting, properties, and scenery. The actor was the center, a lean, almost emaciated figure, an artistic athlete, the product of rigorous training that included exercises analo-

gous to those of biomechanics. The Grotowski actor was above all dedicated: art and life merged in the spiritual activity of acting. Discipline and self-denial were required for what Grotowski called the "via negativa," the denial of self and the assertion of communion with the other actors.

Until the early 1970s, Grotowski's productions were created during months of work. Although traditional plays formed the base of each work, the result was very different from the original: complex, symbolic, turned inward toward the actors instead of out toward the audience. As a result, Grotowski's theatre is often thought of as mysterious (very indebted to Eastern European Catholicism) and mythic. As in his New York appearance, Grotowski severely limited the number of people at each performance, and he tried to enforce a seriousness that was like that of the church.

In the mid-1970s, Grotowski set up a Research University and began to engage in what he called "paratheatrical" activity. He seems to have been part of the fervor of the 1960s, and his work in those years can be seen to accord very well with other innovations in acting, audience relationships, and the definition of the art.

The Living Theatre.

Julian Beck (1925–   ) and Judith Malina (1926–   ) gave a season of avant-garde plays at Greenwich Village's Cherry Lane Theatre in 1951. For the next decade, they were active in what became Off-Broadway, and their Living Theatre of 1959–1963 produced such new plays as William Carlos Williams' *Many Loves* and Jack Gelber's *The Connection*, and such older avant-garde pieces as Brecht's *In the Jungle of Cities* and Pirandello's *Tonight We Improvise*. As husband and wife, they divided the artistic tasks along traditional lines, Beck usually designing, Malina directing and often acting. Their company of these years hired actors with traditional backgrounds and was not markedly different from art theatres that had preceded it.

Beck and Malina were politically active, however, and were committed to the peace movement. When they lost their theatre in 1964, they went to Europe, and there they appear to have radicalized their art; when they returned in 1968, the company was new and both it and its works were different. Improvised and group-created, they now combined artistic idealism with an anarchical but rather benign politic. "Our intentions are to further the revolution, meaning the beautiful, non-violent, anarchistic revolution," they were quoted as saying. Their theatrical statement was made both overtly and through the very form of new pieces like *Paradise Now* and *Frankenstein*, which included gymnastic movement, "rituals," confrontations with the audience, and open violations of such taboos (and sometimes laws) as those prohibiting nudity and obscenity. They used theatrical metaphors to make their statement—beginning a performance with the actors tied to seats in the auditorium; moving through the audience whispering, "I am not allowed to take off my clothes; I am not allowed to smoke marijuana."

Many audiences of the 1960s were wildly enthusiastic and joined the company onstage in discussion and celebration. Many marched out of theatres to join them in vigils or peaceful marches near such symbols of the social order as police stations. At its most successful, the Living Theatre forged with its performance a communal bond among actors and audience and gave the audience an idealistic vision. It was perfectly in tune with the decade of protest, of communes, of "flower children," of youth. Except for Beck and Malina, its actors were untrained amateurs, and their very lack of skill was in tune with the time's rejection of elevated ideas of art and artist, of skill, elitist talent, and nonspontaneity. (Both Beck and Malina had the physiques of Grotowski actors, however, and their own training, discipline, and control were evident.)

By the mid-1970s, the personnel of the Living Theatre had changed again, except for Beck and Malina. A critic who saw them in Europe was not sympathetic and referred to them as the "radical right" of American avant-garde thea-

tre. The community of spirit that had bonded the Living Theatre of the 1960s to its audiences seemed to be missing, and the interpenetration of performance and audience seemed to have gone flat.[5]

By that time, the Living Theatre had existed for two decades at the far outpost of American theatre. It may well be that it will prove to be the most important—and perhaps historically the first—American avant-garde company.

Robert Wilson. Wilson (1941–   ) is a "performance artist" whose dreamlike, visually beautiful, resonant works have been performed in Europe, the Near East, and the United States. Trained as a painter, he creates complicated and beautiful theatrical images that develop far more slowly than traditional theatrical actions. Usually, Wilson's pieces are extremely sparing with language. In working, he uses mostly amateurs as performers and often incorporates the particularities (including physical afflictions) of the performers in the performance. His works have included *The Life and Times of Sigmund Freud* (1967), *Deafman Glance* (1970), and *Einstein on the Beach* (1976; with the minimalist composer Philip Glass). Wilson's art contains such mixed elements of painting, sculpture, theatre, and music that it defies classification. Many traditional audience members find its great length (from six hours to as many days) maddening. Its lack of "meaning" puzzles or outrages some.

Experimental Dramatists. Writers who write drama within an Artaudian context seem like a contradiction, but the recent theatre has often been contradictory. The people who follow are merely examples, and they are very different from each other. Their common quality is their unsuitability to the traditional theatre—to either its physical arrangement or its organization.

1. Dario Fo. An Italian actor–performer who creates "illegitimate theatre" for his own performance, Fo relates his work to that of *comme-*

dia dell'arte and of local performers of the Middle Ages. The works are comic, often abrasive and anticlerical.

2. Peter Handtke. Language itself is the weapon that Handtke's actors throw at each other and at the audience. Traditional critical concepts like plot and character are mostly irrelevant. *Kaspar* (1968) deals with the connection between language and identity; other Handtke pieces simply supply words to the performers without direction.

3. Richard Foreman. "The audience are watching me watch my text . . . the performance is a CONTINUATION of my writing process." Foreman creates both in anticipation of and during the performance, for he exercises control over everything: the stage is a projection of his consciousness. Plays like *Rhoda in Potato-Land (Her Fall Starts)* (1975–1976) have the quality of poems read in a foreign language, with their metaphors made visual. Plot and character usually seem impenetrable, if they exist; performances end with instructions like, "Go home. You have understood nothing."

Special-Interest Theatres. Activist theatres are not new. However, the activist theatres of this period introduced a new element: the identification of a specific audience that had to be separated from the society at large. (It could be argued that the workers' theatres of the previous century had had to work in the same way.) Moreover, these activist theatres of the 1960s and 1970s sometimes tried to create a theatrical form—and, sometimes, a theatrical organization—that was peculiar to its audience. The result was a kind of theatre that abandoned the traditional post-Renaissance idea that a theatre must somehow please and attract its audience and that substituted instead a view that the theatre should identify and raise the consciousness of its audience—with the perhaps surprising result that in that act of identification lay the reason for its existence, in many cases.

These are theatres of self-discovery and self-recognition. They often seek to educate or to persuade, but neither instruction nor delight is necessarily their aim; for some of them, simply existing with their chosen audience is sufficient. They embody a basic idea of Artaud's in that they exist to serve the audience as a communal bonding agent, putting away artistic egocentricity, "professionalism," and other concepts that are important to the outside culture.

American Black Theatre. Part of America's unrest has been racial, and a good part of that racial unrest has been violent. Underlying it is the extraordinary position in America of black men and women, who have often been "invisible," to use the novelist Ralph Ellison's word.

An aggressive black theatre emerged in the mid-1960s, in part to make blacks visible to themselves. To many whites, a black theatre seemed contradictory and self-destructive, for it seemed to run against the color blindness that many liberal whites espoused. It was, however, a realization of ideas that had been expressed in the 1920s by black leader W. E. B. DuBois: that a black theatre should exist that was about blacks, for blacks, by blacks, and located where blacks could have easy access to it. A theatre was needed that would do for blacks what traditional theatre had done for whites—give them an image of themselves.

There had long been black theatre artists, but it was not until the very end of the 1950s that a black play for and about blacks appeared on Broadway, Lorraine Hansberry's *A Raisin in the Sun* (1959). Then, it was not until the mid-1960s that black theatre found a voice powerful enough to defy both the forms and the subjects of white theatre: Imamu Amiri Baraka (LeRoi Jones), author of *Dutchman* (1964) and *Slave Ship* (1967). At the same time, theorists like Loften Mitchell, Addison Gayle, and Larry Neal were defining a "black aesthetic" that insisted that the new black theatre be judged by a criticism different from that of white theatre.

Realizing DuBois's demand that black theatres locate themselves close to black communities, theatres were created in or near urban enclaves; they included the New Lafayette and the Black Arts in New York, Spirit House in Newark, the Watts Writers Workshop (Los Angeles), and the Performing Arts Society of Los Angeles. They often attracted government or private funding. As well, many largely white theatres staged works by black writers—the American Place Theatre and the Chelsea Theatre Center in New York, for example. Most important of all to black writers, actors, and directors, however, was the Negro Ensemble Company, created by actor–playwright Douglas Turner Ward to foster a black drama and to enhance opportunities for black theatre art.

The black theatre movement slowed by the mid-1970s. It had accomplished some of its goals: there were now many places where black audiences could see black theatrical images and black theatre artists. Black actors had moved further into the mainstream, although the number of jobs for blacks in commercial theatre and television and film seems to be shrinking again in the 1980s. An impressive body of new black drama had been created, headed by Ntozake Shange's *For Colored Girls Who Have Considered Suicide/When the Rainbow Is Enuf* (1976), and including Ed Bullins's *The Electronic Nigger* (1968); Lonnie Elder's *Ceremonies in Dark Old Men* (1968); Charles Gordone's *No Place to Be Somebody* (1969); Alice Childress's *Mojo* (1970), and Douglas Turner Ward's *Day of Absence* (1967).

FIGURE 18.4

Ntozake Shange's *For Colored Girls Who Have Considered Suicide/When the Rainbow Is Enuf,* as staged by Bette Howard at the University of South Carolina (1981).

FIGURE 18.5

A Voice of My Own, directed by Amy Saltz, with Laura Hicks, Frances Conroy, Leslie Geraci, and Claudia Wilkins, The Acting Company. [Photo by Nathaniel Tileston, courtesy of The Acting Company.]

Many of the plays of the black theatre have been realistic; like the British theatre of the mid-1950s, black theatre has found expression for social anger in realism. Many of the plays were nonrealistic, however, often moving toward expressionism or surrealism. Shange's *Colored Girls* was called a *choreopoem* and mixed dance, poetry, short narrative, and song.

The black aesthetic theory suggested by black writers remains in dispute. It argued from the audience rather than from the work of art—and it stressed the need for art's immediate social usefulness. Rejected by conservative critics and antithetical to the ideas of Aristotle, the black aesthetic nonetheless demands attention for both social and aesthetic reasons.

Feminist Theatre. Feminist theatre is an international phenomenon with examples from Australia to Europe. It began to appear in the United States in 1969, and by the mid-1970s there were or had been feminist theatres all over the country. Many of them were ephemeral. Somewhat unlike black theatre, feminist theatre was a grass-roots activity not limited to urban centers and often divorced completely from theatrical professionalism.

Feminist theatre has shown some of the same characteristics as other special-interest theatres—the communal audience, for example, and a special-interest aesthetic—but it has differed in its great internal diversity. Some feminist theatres (Women's Interart in New York and the Los Angeles Feminist Theatre, for example) exist to provide opportunities for women artists and to bring them to the attention of the mainstream. Many others, however, have existed for the quite different purpose of simply existing, for by doing so they embody their consciousness and that of their audience.

Some feminist theatres have differed from traditional theatres in their organization, as well. The feminist playwright Martha Boesing has pointed out a difference apparent to her between the linear, goal-oriented, hierarchical structure set up by men and the more dispersed, collective nature of structures set up by women. She has compared women's art to quilt making: in quilting, there are no specialists, no executives, no rivals; there are only women at work on a common art project. For Boesing and many other feminist artists, the male (traditional) theatre is competitive and specialized; the nontraditional feminist theatre is cooperative and communal.

Even the creative process of some feminist theatres is cooperative. Doing away with specialists like playwright and director, some of them have formed works from their collective experience.

Most such works have had a life no longer than the few performances first given them. Nothing more was expected of them. Some feminist plays, however, have come into the theatrical mainstream and have gone the usual routes of other works: professional production, publication, and subsequent production under royalty agreements. Outstanding feminist American playwrights have included Myrna Lamb (*Scyklon Z*, 1969); Megan Terry (*Approaching Simone*, 1970); Rochelle Owen (*Futz*, 1968); Martha Boesing (*Calamity Jane*, 1979); Maria Irene Fornes (*Fefu and Her Friends*, 1977); and Shange. A stunning British work of the same period was Caryl Churchill's *Cloud Nine* (1980).

As with the disagreement over a black aesthetic, there is a dispute about the workability of a feminist aesthetic. Those who accept a view like Boesing's (of an inherently different male and female art structure) agree that a female's work for a female audience can be quite different from a male (or male-dominated) artist's work for a male (or male-dominated) audience. Traditionalists and Aristotelians (synonyms for men, feminists would say; they chuckle over such male concepts as rising action, single climax, and falling action) contend that a feminist aesthetic is a form of special pleading meant to dodge critical analysis. The matter remains to be resolved.

Other special-interest theatres have appeared (Chicano, Gay, Amerind, and others). Any definable group—or more accurately, any group seeking to define itself—may create a theatre in its own image. Recent experience suggests that the special-interest theatres may have short lives in particular cases but that the movements they represent may last. It is impossible to say at this time whether they are symptoms of the change in paradigm or whether they are examples of the new paradigm that is forming.

ENDNOTES

1. Merwyn Matthews and Mikhail Deza, "Soviet Theatre Audiences," *Slavic Review* 34 (December 1975): 723.
2. Cecil W. Davies, *Theatre for the People: The Story of the Volksbühne* (Manchester, England: Manchester University Press, 1977), p. 135.
3. Kenneth Tynan, "Director as Misanthropist: On the Moral Neutrality of Peter Brook," *Theatre Quarterly* 7, 25 (1977): 20–28.
4. Ibid.
5. R. G. Davis, "The Radical Right in the American Theatre," *Theatre Quarterly* 5, 19 (1975): 67–72.

BIBLIOGRAPHY
Part Five

Appia, Adolphe. *The Work of Living Art*, trans. H. D. Albright. Miami: University of Miami Press, 1960.

———. *Music and the Art of the Theatre*, trans. Robert W. Corrigan and Mary Douglas Dirks. Miami: University of Miami Press, 1962.

Artaud, Antonin. *The Theatre and Its Double*, trans. Mary Caroline Richards. New York: Grove Press, 1958.

Bablet, Denis. *Esthetique Générale du décor de théâtre, de 1870 à 1914*. Paris: Editions du Centre National de la Recherche Scientifique, 1965.

———. *Edward Gordon Craig*, trans. Daphne Woodward. London: Heinemann, 1966.

———, and Jacquot, Jean, eds. *L'expressionisme dans le théâtre européen*. Paris: Editions du Centre National de la Recherche Scientifique, 1971.

Braun, Edward. *The Theatre of Meyerhold*. London: Eyre Methuen, 1979.

Brecht, Bertolt. *Brecht on Theatre*, trans. John Willett. London: Methuen, 1964.

———. *The Messingkauf Dialogues*, trans. John Willett. London: Methuen, 1965.

Brockett, Oscar G., and Findlay, Robert T. *Century of Innovation: A History of European and American Theatre and Drama Since 1870*. Englewood Cliffs, N.J.: Prentice-Hall, 1973.

Byrne, Dawson. *The Story of Ireland's National Theatre: The Abbey*. 1929; rpt. ed., New York: Haskell House, 1971.

Calandra, Dennis. "Georg Kaiser's 'From Morn to Midnight': The Nature of Expressionist Performance." *Theatre Quarterly* 6 (Spring 1976): 45–54.

Carter, Huntley. *The New Spirit in Drama and Art*. London: Frank Palmer, 1912.

———. *The New Theatre and Cinema of Soviet Russia*. London: Chapman and Dodd, 1924.

Care, Richard. *Terence Gray and the Cambridge Festival Theatre*. Cambridge, Eng.: Chadwyck-Healey, 1980.

Cheney, Sheldon. *The Art Theater*. New York: Alfred Knopf, 1925.

Craig, Edward. "E. W. Godwin and the Theatre." *Theatre Notebook* 31, 2 (1977): 30–33.

Craig, Edward Gordon. *On the Art of the Theatre*. Chicago: Browne's Book Store, 1911.

———. *The Theatre—Advancing*. Boston: Little, Brown, and Company, 1919.

———. *The Mask*. (Periodical).

Croyden, Margaret. *Lunatics, Lovers and Poets: The Contemporary Experimental Theatre*. New York: McGraw-Hill, 1974.

Davies, Cecil W. *Theatre for the People: The Story of the Volksbühne*. Manchester, Eng.: Manchester University Press, 1977.

Davis, R. G. "The Radical Right in the American Theatre." *Theatre Quarterly* 5, 19 (1975): 67–72.

Deák, František. "Blue Blouse." *The Drama Review* 17 (March 1973): 35–46.

Draegin, Lois. "After Isadora: Her Art as Inspiration." *Dance Magazine* 51 (July 1977): 67–71.

Esslin, Martin. *The Theatre of the Absurd*. New York: Doubleday, 1961.

Eynat, Irène. "Gordon Craig, the Über-Marionette, and the Dresden Theatre." *Theatre Research International* 5, 3 (Autumn 1980): 171–93.

Flannery, James W. "W. B. Yeats and the Abbey Theatre Company." *Educational Theatre Journal* 27, 2 (May 1975): 179–196.

Fletcher, Ifan Kyrle, and Rood, Arnold. *Edward Gordon Craig: A Bibliography*. London: Society for Theatre Research, 1967.

Fuegi, John. *The Essential Brecht.* Los Angeles: Hennessey and Ingalls, 1972.

Fuchs, Georg. *Revolution in the Theatre: Conclusions Concerning the Munich Artists' Theatre,* trans. Constance Connor Kuhn. Ithaca, N.Y.: Cornell University Press, 1959.

Gorceix, Paul. *Les affinités allemandes dans l'oeuvre de Maurice Maeterlinck.* Paris: Presses Universitaires de France, 1975.

Gropius, Walter, ed. *The Theatre of the Bauhaus.* Middletown, Conn.: Wesleyan University Press, 1961.

Halls, W. D. *Maurice Maeterlinck, A Study of His Life and Thought.* Oxford: Oxford University Press, 1960.

Hayman, Ronald. *Artaud and After.* Oxford: Oxford University Press, 1977.

Hovey, Richard. "Modern Symbolism and Maurice Maeterlinck," introduction to his translation of *Princess Maleine.* New York: Dodd, Mead, 1913.

Hunt, Hugh. *The Abbey: Ireland's National Theatre, 1904–1979.* Dublin: Gill and Macmillan, 1979.

Kleb, William. "E. W. Godwin and the Bancrofts." *Theatre Notebook* 30, 3 (1976): 122–132.

Ley-Piscator, Maria. *The Piscator Experiment.* New York. Heinemann, 1967.

MacGowan, Kenneth. *The Theatre of Tomorrow.* New York: Boni and Liveright, 1921.

———, and Jones, Robert Edmond. *Continental Stagecraft.* New York: Harcourt Brace, 1922.

Matthews, Mervyn, and Deza, Mikhail. "Soviet Theatre Audiences." *Slavic Review* 34 (December 1975): 716–730.

Nash, George. *Edward Gordon Craig, 1872–1966.* London: H. M. Stationery Office, 1967.

Piscator, Erwin. *The Political Theatre,* trans. Hugh Rorrison. New York: Avon Books, 1978.

Rostagno, Aldo, with Julian Beck and Judith Malina. *We, the Living Theatre.* New York: Ballantine Books, 1970.

Sayler, Oliver. *The Russian Theatre,* rev. ed. of *The Russian Theatre Under the Revolution.* New York: Brentano's, 1922.

———, ed. *Max Reinhardt and His Theatre.* 1928; rpt. ed., New York: Benjamin Blom, 1968.

Schechner, Richard. *Public Domain.* Indianapolis: Bobbs-Merrill, 1969.

Schevill, James. *Breakout! In Search of New Theatrical Environments.* Chicago: Swallow Press, 1973.

Schultze-Reimpell, Werner. *Development and Structure of the Theatre in the Federal Republic of Germany,* trans. Patricia Crampton. Bonn–Bad Godesberg: Inter Nationes, 1979.

Senelick, Laurence. "Moscow and Monodrama: The Meaning of the Craig-Stanislavsky *Hamlet.*" *Theatre Research International* 6, 2 (Spring 1981): 109–124.

Simonov, Ruben. *Stanislavsky's Protege: Eugene Vakhtangov,* trans. Miriam Goldina. New York: DBS Publishing, 1969.

Slonim, Marc. *Russian Theatre: From the Empire to the Soviets.* Cleveland and New York: World Publishing, 1961.

Sommer, Sally R. "The Stage Apprenticeship of Loie Fuller." *Dance Scope* 12, 1 (Fall–Winter 1977–1978): 33–34.

Tynan, Kenneth. "Director as Misanthropist: On the Moral Neutrality of Peter Brook." *Theatre Quarterly* 7, 25 (1977): 20–28.

Volbach, Walter R. *Adolphe Appia, Prophet of the Modern Theatre: A Profile.* Middletown, Conn.: Wesleyan University Press, 1968.

Willet, John. *The Theatre of Berthold Brecht.* Norfolk, Conn.: New Directions, 1959.

Wilson, Edmund. *Axel's Castle*. New York: Scribner's, 1931.

Wilson, Garff. *Three Hundred Years of American Drama and Theatre*. Englewood Cliffs, N.J.: Prentice-Hall, 1973.

Worrall, Nick. "Meyerhold's Production of *The Magnificent Cuckold*." *The Drama Review* 17 (March 1973): 14–34.

index

Numbers in *italics* indicate a reference to be found in an illustration or a caption on the designated page; n indicates that the reference is to be found in a note.